A Guide to

Computer User Support for Help Desk & Support Specialists, Third Edition

Fred Beisse

Lane Community College

THOMSON
★
COURSE TECHNOLOGY ™

Australia • Canada • Mexico • Singapore • Spain • United Kingdom • United States

A Guide to Computer User Support for Help Desk & Support Specialists, Third Edition

by Fred Beisse

Executive Editor:
Mac Mendelsohn

Marketing Manager:
Brian Berkeley

Permissions Editor:
Abigail Reip

Developmental Editor:
Robin M. Romer

Associate Product Manager:
Mirella Misiaszek

Cover Designer:
Abby Scholz

Product Manager:
Janet Aras

Editorial Assistant:
Amanda Piantedosi

Compositor:
GEX Publishing Services

Production Editor:
Kelly Robinson

Senior Manufacturing Coordinator:
Laura Burns

Printer:
WebCom Limited

Photo credits: Figure 2-4 Courtesy of Calpine Corporation; Figure 2-5 Courtesy of Stream International, a Solectron Company; Figure 2-6 Courtesy of St. Petersburg College; Figure 2-7 Courtesy of State of Oregon Department of Administrative Services; Figures 6-4 through 6-7 Courtesy of Monarch Bay Software, Inc.; Chapter 7 CloseUp figure © Adam Crowley/PhotoDisc/Getty Images; Figures 7-4 and 7-5 Courtesy of Microsoft Corporation; Figure 7-6 Courtesy of the Information Technology Association of America; Figure 8-4 Courtesy of Honolulu Community College; Figure 10-5 Courtesy of Belkin Corporation.

BRIEF
Contents

TABLE OF

Contents

CHAPTER THIRTEEN
Computer Facilities Management   451

Preface

During the mid-1990s, Lane Community College offered a new degree program to prepare students for entry-level positions in the computer user support industry. For several years, I taught a course in the curriculum, an introduction to computer user support, without a textbook that adequately covered this field. Through this experience, I learned a great deal as I researched and developed course materials and also from my students. I wrote the first edition of this book based on what I learned.

I continue to believe that learning about user support requires exposure to trade books, vendor manuals, and Web sites, but these materials are often not designed for students or for entry-level support staff. First-time learners also need textbooks with aids to learning such as glossaries, discussion questions, exercises, and case projects that help them practice and apply their new knowledge. Since the earlier editions of this book, some aspects of user support have remained the same; however, a surprising number of changes have occurred. I was delighted when Course Technology invited me to update the book for the 21st century support environment.

In this third edition, my goal remains to address the needs of those who want to learn about the user support field and who need resources to help them learn. This edition is designed as an introduction to the wide range of topics that an entry-level user support specialist will be expected to comprehend. The responsibilities of support positions vary widely, but armed with the broad foundation of topics and activities covered in this book, specialists entering the support industry will be prepared to meet employer expectations.

The Intended Audience

This book is primarily intended for three kinds of readers:

- Readers who are considering career opportunities in computer user support and who want an introduction to the user support field. This book describes the kinds of knowledge, skills, and abilities they need to be employable in the support industry.
- Readers who were trained in another field, but find themselves in a job with growing user support responsibilities. They will be able to use this book to get additional breadth and depth in the support field. This audience includes programmers, computer operators, network administrators, customer support representatives, and computer applications specialists.
- Readers who are taking a course in a user support or a related degree program. They can use this book to tie together knowledge and skills introduced in other courses. These readers will especially benefit from the end-of-chapter activities that provide practice skills and experiences they will use on the job.

The User Support Field

Many colleges, universities, and vocational/professional schools now offer courses, certificates, and degree programs to prepare professionals to meet the demands of the user support industry. An increasing number of organizations, public and private, large and small, employ support specialists to assist other workers with their computer use. Many hardware and software vendors outsource their support operations, which creates job opportunities in support centers in almost every state and province. In most areas of the United States and Canada, small software companies develop and market software packages that require end-user documentation, training, installation, troubleshooting, and other support activities. The demand for workers in the user support field continues to be promising as the U.S. economy begins to recover during the middle part of this decade.

The Approach

A Guide to Computer User Support for Help Desk & Support Specialists, Third Edition is designed as an introduction to each of the topics covered in the chapters. I believe that a user support textbook can do little more than provide basic concepts and background information, lead the reader into the field, and point the reader toward appropriate knowledge, skills, and resource materials. To derive maximum benefit from this book, the reader must be an active participant in the learning process.

The end-of-chapter discussion questions and hands-on activities are specifically designed to develop knowledge and skills, an important percentage of which are gained through interactions with classmates or coworkers. Learning to work with others in project groups or teams is important preparation for the team-oriented work environment of the 2000s. Many of the end-of-chapter activities are designed to acquaint readers with information resources and technical tools that are essential to function effectively in support positions.

Assumed Knowledge

This book assumes that its readers have experience in the following areas, either through course work or work experience:

- Basic computer concepts or computer literacy
- Word processor, spreadsheet, and database applications
- Internet and the World Wide Web

Overview of This Book

The organization of this book is based on the knowledge, skills, and abilities commonly found in user support position descriptions and on the tasks employers expect entry-level support staff to be able to perform.

Chapter 1, Introduction to End-User Computing, explains the historical context of end-user computing, how end users increase their productivity using computer systems, the resources they need, and common problems they encounter. New to the third edition is an extended Case Project that illustrates how each chapter's material impacts one company (see Case Project 4 in each chapter).

Chapter 2, Introduction to Computer User Support, describes why end users need help, the kinds of help support centers provide, and how organizations have found ways to provide support. It also describes the knowledge, skills, and abilities a successful applicant for a support position needs. The third edition updates the outlook for user support workers following the recession in the United States in the early 2000s and the trend to outsource support jobs overseas.

Chapter 3, Customer Service Skills for User Support Agents, describes the communication and customer service skills user support staff need. It also outlines ways to develop an incident management strategy and handle difficult support situations. The third edition includes new material on basic personality types and work styles to help readers understand their influence on user and coworker behavior.

Chapter 4, Troubleshooting Computer Problems, discusses common tools and methods troubleshooters use to solve computer problems. It also describes seven problem-solving strategies that a user support specialist can apply to a troubleshooting situation. The third edition updates the troubleshooting resources that are part of a support specialist's toolkit.

Chapter 5, Common Support Problems, approaches computer problems from a practical perspective. It describes the types of common computer problems and shows how to apply problem-solving strategies to several actual problems from the experiences of working support specialists.

Chapter 6, Help Desk Operation, introduces a multi-level support model, the incident management process, and provides an overview of the features of help desk software packages. The third edition features HelpTrac software to illustrate typical features of help desk software and includes an exercise to give the reader experience with basic features of the package.

Chapter 7, User Support Management, introduces the perspectives of managers and coordinators of support operations that support workers need to understand. It describes the mission of support groups, how to staff and train them, and how to manage a support project. It also covers industry certification, professional associations, and standards of ethical conduct. The third edition features Microsoft Office Project 2003 to illustrate project management tools. An exercise in the chapter is based on a 120-day version of the software, which is included on a CD-ROM.

Chapter 8, Product Evaluation Strategies and Support Standards, describes strategies to evaluate computer products and define product standards for an organization. The third edition includes a CloseUp feature on product standards in use at Honolulu Community College.

Chapter 9, User Needs Analysis and Assessment, provides tools to help user support staff analyze and assess user needs for computer hardware, software, and network products. The third edition includes an extended case study to illustrate the steps in a typical user needs assessment project.

Chapter 10, Installing End-User Computer Systems, covers the steps to install hardware, operating systems, and applications software. The third edition updates many of the installation check lists from previous editions.

Chapter 11, Training Computer Users, explains how to plan training activities, how to prepare training materials, and how to present, evaluate, and improve training for end users. The third edition emphasizes the increasing role of Web-based training and resources.

Chapter 12, Writing for End Users, briefly examines the many types of documentation a support specialist might have to prepare, and explains how to plan, write, and evaluate end-user documents. It covers the common strategies and tools technical writers use and how to avoid common writing problems. The third edition includes increased coverage of writing for Web-based delivery.

Chapter 13, Computer Facilities Management, deals with a number of facilities management tasks support staff are likely to encounter, including security, media backups, preventive maintenance, and ergonomic issues. The third edition includes a new section on managing security problems and provides expanded information about recycling computers, peripherals and supplies, and protecting against viruses.

Appendix 1, User Support Information Resources, compiles Web site references and printed materials from each chapter and adds supplementary reading and resource suggestions for each chapter.

Appendix 2, Answers to Check Your Understanding Questions, provides answers to the end-of-chapter questions.

Features

To aid readers in understanding user support concepts, several features in this book are designed to increase its value to learners.

- **Chapter Objectives**. Each chapter begins with a list of the important concepts to be mastered within the chapter. This list provides a quick reference to the contents of the chapter, as well as a useful study aid.

- **Illustrations and Tables**. Illustrations help readers visualize common components and relationships. Tables list conceptual items and examples in a visual and readable format.

Notes. Chapters contain Notes designed to expand on the section topic, including resource references, tips, additional examples, and pointers to other information.

WWW Pointers. WWW pointers guide readers to the Internet for more information about a topic or to an example related to what was learned in the chapter, as well as to informational resources of general interest.

■ **Bulleted Figures**. Selected figures contain bullets that summarize important points. They provide an overview of upcoming discussion points and help readers review material as they skim through the chapter.

CloseUps. Most chapters contain a CloseUp, which details real-life examples that illustrate the chapter topic. Taken from actual experiences, CloseUps confirm the importance of the topic and often contribute related information to provide additional insight into real-world applications of the topics.

■ **Chapter Summaries**. Each chapter's text is followed by a summary of chapter concepts. These summaries provide a helpful way to recap and revisit the main ideas covered in each chapter.

■ **Key Terms**. Each chapter contains a listing of the terms introduced in the chapter and a short definition of each. This listing provides a convenient way to review the user support vocabulary you have learned.

■ **Check Your Understanding**. End-of-chapter assessment begins with a set of review questions that reinforce the main ideas introduced in each chapter. These questions, which are new in the third edition, gauge whether readers have mastered the concepts and also provide examples of questions readers might encounter on a quiz or exam. Answers to these questions are provided in Appendix 2.

■ **Discussion Questions**. Discussion questions, which are new in the third edition, are designed to supplement and extend chapter topics and provide an opportunity for readers to formulate positions on issues raised in the text.

Hands-On Projects. Although the theory behind the user support topics is important, no amount of theory can improve on real-world experience. To supplement conceptual explanations, each chapter provides Hands-On Projects to provide readers with experience with user support tasks. Some projects involve researching information from people in the support industry, printed resources, and the Internet. Because Hands-On Projects ask readers to go beyond the boundaries of the text itself, they provide practice in the real-world research readers will most likely perform as part of a user support position.

Case Projects. The end of each chapter includes at least four Case Projects. The cases are designed to help readers apply what they have learned to business situations. They give readers an opportunity to independently synthesize and evaluate information, examine potential solutions, and make recommendations, much as they would in an actual business situation. Re-Nu-Cartridge, a remanufacturer of printer ink and copier toner cartridges, is an ongoing scenario that appears in Case Project 4 in each chapter in the third edition.

■ **Project Management Software.** A CD-ROM included with this edition provides a 120-day version of Microsoft® Office Project Professional 2003 120 Day Trial Edition, which can be used to plan projects such as those in Chapter 7.

Instructor Support

The following supplemental materials are available when this book is used in a classroom setting. All of the supplements available with this book are provided to the instructor on a single CD-ROM.

Electronic Instructor's Manual. The Instructor's Manual that accompanies this textbook includes additional instructional material to assist in class preparation, including suggestions for lecture topics.

ExamView®. This textbook is accompanied by ExamView, a powerful testing software package that allows instructors to create and administer printed, computer (LAN-based), and Internet exams. ExamView includes hundreds of questions that correspond to the topics covered in this text, enabling students to generate detailed study guides that include page references for further review. The computer-based and Internet testing components allow students to take exams at their computers and save the instructor time by automatically grading each exam.

PowerPoint® Presentations. Microsoft PowerPoint slides are included for each chapter as a teaching aid for classroom presentations, to make available to students on a network for chapter review, or to be printed for classroom distribution. Instructors can add their own slides for additional topics they introduce in a course.

Distance Learning. Course Technology is proud to present online testing material in WebCT and Blackboard to provide the most complete and dynamic learning experience possible. For more information on how to bring distance learning to your course, contact your local Course Technology sales representative.

I also want to express my great appreciation to the professional educators who reviewed the draft manuscript and made suggestions that added significantly to the value of the book. Their experiences in both the support industry and in education contributed to the quality of the topics covered and to the content of the book as a learning tool. The reviewers are Rachelle Hall, Glendale Community College, James Harton, University of Toledo; Fred Parce, Texas State Technical College; Diane Roselli, Harrisburg Area Community College; and Harry Woloschin, Wake Technical Community College.

I am very grateful to the following industry professionals/establishments for their valuable contributions to the CloseUp sections: Dave Callaghan, Course Technology; Jonathan Vester, Hayward Community College; Kevin Kerwien, Symantec Corporation; Larry Lawson, St. Agnes Healthcare; Honolulu Community College; Mitch Geller and Kelly Hart, Nu-Design; Eric Svendsen, SCInc; Marsha E. Jones; and William Dougherty, Virginia Tech.

I want to dedicate this third edition to the memory of my parents, George H. and M. Katherine Beisse, whose emphasis on learning is a continuing inspiration and legacy to all their children.

Fred Beisse
Eugene, Oregon

Online Companion Web Site

Pointers to many sites on the World Wide Web are used throughout the book. Soo
later, these sites will change or be replaced with newer information. In some case
URLs in the book will result in a "Web address not found" message. As a means of l
ing our printed books up to date in the constantly changing Web environment, Co
Technology maintains a Web page for this book with updated Web addresses. To view
page, go to **www.course.com/helpdesk** and search by the author's last name (Beiss

The following features can also be found on the Online Companion Web site:

- Additional Web site links to supplemental topics within the chapters
- Errata for the book and Instructor Resources
- E-mail link for students and faculty to provide feedback, report broken links, and so forth

Course Technology Help Desk Scholarship Contest

Course Technology supports your pursuit of a career in the growing field of Help Desk
and Computer User Support. The winner of this scholarship will receive $1000 toward
tuition reimbursement. To be eligible, you must be currently enrolled in a Help Desk or
Computer User Support program and submit an essay on how you can contribute to the
Help Desk field. This scholarship will be awarded annually.

How do you enter? Go to **www.course.com/helpdesk** to download an application and
receive more information about the essay and deadline for this scholarship.

The contest is open to U.S. citizens who are enrolled in a U.S. public or private college or
university and are enrolled in a Help Desk course at the time of entry.

ACKNOWLEDGMENTS

I want to express my sincere thanks to the staff at Course Technology who played vital
roles on the team of people who created this book, including Janet Aras, Product Manager,
and Kelly Robinson, Production Editor. Each of them made an important contribution to
the production of this book.

I want to single out Robin M. Romer, Booktec, for special acknowledgment. Robin was
the Developmental Editor for both the second and third editions, and without her many
contributions, the book would never have taken the shape that it has. Her attention to
detail affected every aspect of the book, from its organization to the clarity of explanations,
and from the selection of figures and tables to help with the CloseUp features. Robin's
handiwork is visible throughout, and I very much appreciate her many thoughtful and professional contributions. Not to mention her patience.

1

INTRODUCTION TO
END-USER COMPUTING

In this chapter you will learn:

♦ How historical changes in computer technology have affected computer use

♦ Ways to classify end users

♦ Computing resources that end users need

♦ The major categories of end-user applications software

♦ Common problems end users may encounter

Computer use has become much more widespread during the past decade than ever before. Almost everyone who works in business offices, manufacturing facilities, educational institutions, and government agencies has a computer on their desk, near their work site, in their car, or at home. Furthermore, people interact with computers much differently than they did several decades ago. As the computer industry has grown and changed, so has the way people use computers.

This chapter provides an overview of end-user computing. You will examine some of the important trends that have influenced computer use over the last 50 years. Then, you will learn about the types of end users and the main categories of computer applications. Finally, you will look at the problems that accompany the growth of end-user computing. These problems often threaten the increases in worker productivity promised by end-user computing.

HISTORICAL CHANGES IN COMPUTER USE

End-user computing refers to the everyday use of computers for both business and personal use. At every level, many workers interact with personal computers (PCs) to accomplish their work. Many people also have computers in their homes. However, when computers were first used in business, most people did not have computers on their desks, nor did they use computers themselves—at least not directly.

The 1950s and 1960s: Early Mainframe Computers

In the 1950s and 1960s, computer systems in business and government were highly centralized. **Mainframe computers** are large, powerful computer systems that process high volumes of transactions, store databases with millions or billions of records, and often serve as the hub of a corporate network. Mainframe systems are installed in a secure central location and are operated by computer professionals. During the early days of business computer use, the professional computer staff that worked with a mainframe computer was organized into a **Data Processing (DP) department**, the division that programs and operates the organization's mainframe computer system. Only the professional DP staff had direct access to these computers and had the ability and access to write programs, enter information, perform calculations, and produce reports. Employees in other departments who wanted to process information with a computer had to request services from the DP department and then wait for the results.

1950s and 1960s vignette: Mainframe payroll processing

Juanita Hawkes, a payroll clerk, prepares a monthly payroll. At the end of each month, Juanita handwrites the hours-worked information from each employee's approved time sheet into columns on a large sheet of ledger paper. Juanita then sends the ledger sheets to the Data Processing department, where a data entry clerk keys the data into punched cards. To avoid errors, a different data entry clerk independently verifies that the correct entries were punched into the cards. When the verified punched cards are returned to Juanita, she adds some program control cards to the payroll transaction cards. These program control cards instruct the mainframe computer to run the payroll application program with the attached transaction cards. Then she walks downstairs to the DP department window and turns in the punched cards to be run on the mainframe computer.

If the mainframe software detects errors, Juanita receives the punched cards back along with a printout that lists the errors. If no errors are detected, Juanita receives a detailed payroll report and the employee paychecks that were printed on the mainframe's printer. Juanita contacts a programmer in the DP department if the payroll program terminates abnormally with an error message. Although Juanita has been a payroll clerk for several years, she once remarked that she had never actually seen the mainframe computer she relies on in her work.

Between 1950 and 1960, mainframe computers were used primarily for transaction processing and management reports. **Transaction processing** is the use of computers to input large volumes of business events or activities, process the data, and prepare printed reports. Banking computer systems that process deposits and withdrawals from customer accounts are a familiar example of transaction processing. Unlike most transaction processing today, which usually occurs as soon as a transaction occurs (sometimes called **real-time processing**), transactions in the 1950s and 1960s were often collected and stored for a day, a week, a month, or sometimes for an entire year. The collected transactions were then processed as a group, a procedure known as **batch processing**.

One goal of transaction processing using mainframe computers was to automate as much manual processing of business data as possible. Organizations commonly used transaction processing to calculate employee payroll, control inventories of raw materials and finished goods, enter product orders and shipments to customers, and perform other high-volume record keeping required to operate a business or government agency. Contrast the difference between a large organization that uses its clerical staff to record, calculate, and file payroll information manually with an organization that invests in a mainframe computer system to automate many of the manual payroll processing steps. The payroll application (software program) can input, sort, match, calculate, print, and store payroll records with little or no manual processing by clerical employees. Mainframe computers could process payroll transactions much more rapidly and with fewer errors than clerical workers. Because of their speed and accuracy, mainframe computer systems were often justified as a cost-effective productivity tool for businesses.

Another common use of mainframe systems during the 1950s and 1960s was management reporting. **Management information systems (MIS)** are computer software that automates the preparation of reports for managers and employees. Detailed data that has been previously stored on a computer disk or magnetic tape by a transaction processing system is input, summarized, and printed as reports. Management information and reporting systems dramatically reduced the manual staff hours required to summarize data and type lengthy reports. For example, a supervisor of a maintenance shop could request a weekly report that shows the number of hours worked on each repair project, which projects are over budget, or which projects require substantial employee overtime. An MIS programmer could access payroll data from the transaction processing system to prepare the necessary management reports. A computer operator would then schedule the reports to print at regular intervals to meet the supervisor's need for management information.

 To learn more about the current use of mainframe computers in large organizations, visit the IBM Web site for zSeries systems at **www-1.ibm.com/servers/solutions/zseries**. Articles on the Web site describe how IBM mainframe computers are used by organizations to gather, manage, and analyze information; provide communication tools for workers who collaborate on projects; and manage relationships with customers.

Because mainframe computers in the 1950s and 1960s were centralized, and because the technologies for computer input were very limited, data for input to a mainframe had to be delivered physically (in the form of punched cards, paper tape, or magnetic tape) to the central system location. Output (in the form of payroll checks, for example, or printed reports) had to be delivered back to the department where it was used or distributed.

Figure 1-1 summarizes how mainframe computers were used in the 1950s and 1960s.

- Located at a central site in the organization

- Programmed and operated by computer professionals in the Data Processing department

- Used primarily to automate transaction processes and to prepare management reports

Figure 1-1   Characteristics of early mainframe computer use

As you can see from this brief overview, computer use in the 1950s and 1960s was very different from computer use today. Although mainframe computers may seem cumbersome by today's standards, they met many of the objectives of that era. Early mainframes provided a substantial increase in employee productivity over manual processing methods. Although some organizations today still rely on computer processing that is similar to that of the 1950s and 1960s, other organizations took the first steps toward a different mode of computer processing and end-user computing in the 1970s.

The 1970s: The First Steps Toward Decentralized Computing

During the 1970s, computer use in many organizations gradually became decentralized as terminals became common. A **terminal** is a keyboard and a display screen that are connected to a mainframe computer by a pair of wires and used by employees to enter and access information in a mainframe system. A 1970s vintage terminal had no processor or storage capability like today's PCs. And they displayed only text output instead of the graphic output common today. They were sometimes called "dumb" terminals. However, terminals enabled clerical employees to interact directly with the mainframe computer from their own desks. Although the data was still stored and processed centrally in the mainframe computer, employees who were computer users could run programs and input and retrieve data themselves, without leaving their desks.

1970s vignette: Terminal payroll processing

Mohammed Hakkim is a clerk responsible for payroll processing for a local school district. At the end of each month, Mohammed keys the payroll information for each district employee he receives from school principals using the terminal on his desk. When the data have been entered, Mohammed enters a command at his keyboard to run the payroll processing program on the mainframe computer. If the program encounters a problem, an error message is displayed on Mohammed's terminal screen. Some problems require that Mohammed make changes to correct the data; other problems require the assistance of a programmer in the Data Processing department.

When the payroll program has completed its calculations, detailed and summary payroll reports and employee paychecks are printed on a remote printer located in the Accounting department where Mohammed works. Mohammed says that use of a terminal and remote printer to enter and correct payroll data and run the payroll program directly from his desk has significantly reduced the time it takes him to process the district payroll.

However, not every employee had access to a terminal during the 1970s. One reason was cost: the first terminals were too expensive for most organizations to provide one to each employee. In addition, some of the mainframe professionals in the DP department disliked terminals. Computer access by clerical workers and the ability to run programs whenever they want meant that the central computer staff had lost some control over the mainframe system and the information stored in it. The DP department staff often expressed the concern that errors and mistakes made by clerical workers in other departments could offset any productivity gains from terminal access to the mainframe. Furthermore, the DP department staff expressed concerns about the cost, and what they perceived as a waste of time, to provide assistance to clerical users in departments outside the DP department whenever they encountered problems.

In addition to terminals, another step toward decentralized computing was the introduction of minicomputers during the 1970s. In comparison to a mainframe, which could easily occupy much of the space in a large room, a **minicomputer** is a smaller computer, closer in size to a refrigerator or file cabinet. A minicomputer is less powerful than a mainframe, but also much less expensive. Because 1970s-era mainframe systems often cost $1 million or more, they were affordable only by large corporations and government agencies. Minicomputers, on the other hand, could be purchased for $100,000 to $500,000 and were therefore affordable by small businesses and individual departments in large organizations.

A few companies still make minicomputers. One system available for small businesses is the Sun Microsystems SunFire series. To learn more about Sun's minicomputer systems and the applications software they can run, see Sun's Web site at **www.sun.com/solutions**. IBM's current minicomputer product line is called iSeries. To learn more about the iSeries, visit **www-1.ibm.com/servers/eserver/iseries/about/why.html**.

Although minicomputers reduced the cost of computers during the 1970s for many small businesses and moved the power of computers closer to the employees who needed them, organizations that owned minicomputers often had to hire specialists (programmers and computer operators) to run them.

The 1980s and 1990s: The Growth of Decentralized Computing

It was not until the 1980s and 1990s that large numbers of employees in many companies began to use computers directly, ushering in the era of end-user computing. Several trends converged in the 1980s to make the widespread transition to decentralized, end-user computing possible. These trends are summarized in Figure 1-2.

- The backlog in requests for new mainframe applications
- An increase in the number of knowledge workers
- The availability of inexpensive microcomputers
- The availability of inexpensive productivity software
- The development of user-friendly graphical user interfaces

Figure 1-2   Major reasons for the growth of decentralized computing

Applications Backlog.   It became increasingly clear to organizations in the 1970s and 1980s that the programmers and analysts who created programs for central mainframes or minicomputers could not keep up with the demand for their services. With transaction processing systems to handle common manual processing tasks (such as payroll, inventory control, billing, and payments to suppliers), managers began to think of new ways to use computer technology. They wanted analysts and programmers to design and write computer programs that could solve a wide variety of specific business problems to make employees even more productive. For example, a marketing and sales manager might want computer analysts to create a customer contact and tracking system to help sales reps organize the large amount of customer and product information they work with every day. However, professional computer staffs could not grow fast enough to meet the increasing demands on their time. The term **applications development backlog** refers to the excess demand for new computer applications that outstripped the supply of computer professionals available to develop them. The backlog problem—widespread and well known during this period—was a source of frustration for both the professional data processing staffs and the business departments that demanded new applications. An inventory manager, for example, might develop an idea for a computer application that could potentially reduce inventory costs and staff payroll costs, only to be told that the analysts and programmers in the DP department couldn't start on any new projects for two years.

More Knowledge Workers.   A second trend that contributed to the growth of end-user computing was a dramatic increase in the number of **knowledge workers**, or employees whose primary job is to collect, prepare, process, and distribute information. The growth in the number of knowledge workers has corresponded with shifts in the U.S. economy from mechanical to electronic ways of working. Whereas factory workers need industrial equipment to do their jobs, knowledge workers need information. The most efficient way to obtain information is through computer technology, so knowledge workers need to interact directly with computers to do their jobs.

The demand for more knowledge workers continues today. An examination of the number and kinds of jobs advertised in the Help Wanted classified ads in a Sunday newspaper attests to the unmet demand for knowledge workers in many industries. To learn more about knowledge workers, read the article "The Age of Social Transformation" by Peter Drucker (who invented the term in 1959) in the *Atlantic Monthly* Web site at **www.theatlantic.com/issues/95dec/chilearn/drucker.htm**.

Declining Microcomputer Cost.   Another reason for the growth of end-user computing during the 1980s and 1990s was a dramatic drop in the cost to provide computer power to employees. As the computer costs decreased, technology capabilities (especially semiconductor power and capacity) increased exponentially. Mainframe systems were expensive to purchase and operate, even when these substantial costs were spread over a large number of employees. However, desktop microcomputers with price tags of around $2000 made computing more affordable, especially for small and mid-sized organizations and even for individual employees. A **microcomputer** is a complete computer (sometimes called a personal computer, or PC) built on a smaller scale than a mainframe or a minicomputer, with a microprocessor as the processing unit (CPU). The first microcomputers appeared in some organizations during the early 1980s. Individual employees occasionally made unauthorized purchases, despite warnings by the Data Processing department that money should not be wasted on these "toy" computers.

The cost of computer hardware is somewhat deceiving. A basic personal computer system configuration cost $2000 to $2500 in the early 1980s. Many systems still sell in that price range. If the price for a high-end system today is about the same as 25 years ago, what has changed? The amount of computing power has changed dramatically. A typical 1980s-vintage personal computer had a 1 MHz speed processor, 64 KB of RAM (that's *kilo*bytes, not megabytes—a difference factor of 1000), a 5 MB hard drive (that's *mega*bytes, not gigabytes—again a difference factor of over 1000 compared to today's hard drives), a monochrome (one-color) display screen, and a 300-baud modem. Today, a PC with a 2 GHz processor, 512 MB of RAM memory, an 80 GB hard drive, a color display, a 56 KB modem, and a readable/writeable CD drive can be purchased for about $2000. Many basic models sell for substantially less than $2000. It is not unusual for computer professionals to comment that their

$2000 desktop personal computer today is many times more powerful than the $1 million mainframe they used in their first job in the computer field. (If you are unfamiliar with any of the technical terms in this note, refer to the glossary in a computer concepts book, or consult an online glossary, such as **whatis.techtarget.com**, **www.techweb.com/encyclopedia**, or **www.webopedia.com**.)

Moore's Law is a popular rule-of-thumb in the computer industry. Gordon Moore says that the capabilities of the technology (CPU speed, for example) double every 18 to 24 months. To learn more about Moore's Law, visit the Intel Web site at **www.intel.com/research/silicon/mooreslaw.htm**.

Inexpensive Productivity Software.   The development of inexpensive applications software contributed to the rapid expansion of desktop computers in many organizations. Although mainframe computer hardware was expensive, programming applications software to run on a mainframe was even more costly. Many organizations reported that they spent more on software development than on hardware. Pre-programmed, off-the-shelf software for mainframes was relatively rare and very expensive; most software was custom developed. The availability in the early 1980s of inexpensive software packages such as Visi-Calc (spreadsheet), WordStar (word processor), Lotus 1-2-3 (spreadsheet), and dBASE (database) meant that many organizations, and sometimes even individual employees, could afford not only microcomputer hardware but also the software that would make them more productive computer users. End users were no longer dependent on the schedules and backlog of in-house program developers in the DP department. Software development vendors that specialized in mass-market productivity software for microcomputers were able to supply general-purpose programs that met user needs at a reasonable cost. In addition to inexpensive productivity software, industry-standard operating systems, such as MS-DOS, MacOS, and Windows, also contributed to the rise in end-user computing.

User-friendly Graphical User Interfaces.   Early computer systems executed commands that a user typed at a terminal to communicate with the computer's operating system. The MS-DOS operating system is an example of a text command interface. During the 1980s and 1990s, many of the programs written for personal computers incorporated menus and **graphical user interfaces (GUIs)**, or screen images that enable users to access the program features and functions intuitively, making the programs much easier to use than command-oriented mainframe software. Users no longer had to remember the correct command, and they found computers less intimidating to operate with a point-and-click mouse as a pointing device.

For more information about the development of the graphical user interface, including a timeline of development highlights, see **toastytech.com/guis/index.html**.

1

1980s and 1990s vignette: Payroll processing on a PC

Junior LeBeau is an accounting clerk for a small business of about 25 employees. At the end of each month, Junior collects payroll data from every employee and asks their supervisor to approve the time sheet information. Junior then keys the data into a payroll program on his desktop PC that is designed specifically for small businesses. The software can detect certain kinds of errors, such as an entry of 88 hours in a day that should have been 8.

When payroll transactions are entered and errors corrected, Junior selects a menu option on the PC payroll software to process the payroll transactions. Junior prints the detailed and summary payroll reports for distribution on the printer attached to his PC. However, for security reasons, Junior writes a file on a floppy disk with paycheck information, which he then sends to a payroll service bureau across town where the paychecks are actually printed.

The Late 1990s and 2000s: The Era of Distributed and Network Computing

Both centralized mainframe computing and decentralized end-user computing share a common goal: to help employees be more productive. However, the way people interact with computers, as well as the size and cost of the computers, has certainly changed. Other innovations in the way computers are used are still under way. Widespread use of computer networks (both local area and wide area networks) in small and large organizations and the phenomenal growth in the use of the Internet as a communication tool, information resource, and electronic business platform will continue to have a significant impact on business and home computer users. Figure 1-3 illustrates the transition from centralized to decentralized computing.

Although end-user computing has changed the way many people work with and obtain information, mainframe computing still plays a significant role in most large corporations and government agencies. Many enterprises own modern mainframe systems that still process transactions and management information. Corporate (or enterprise) need for centralized mainframe and minicomputer applications has not diminished and often cannot be met with desktop systems. For example, operating a large database system, such as an online airline reservation system or a transaction processing system for a multi-branch bank, would require the processing power of hundreds of the fastest microcomputers working together as a single synchronized system.

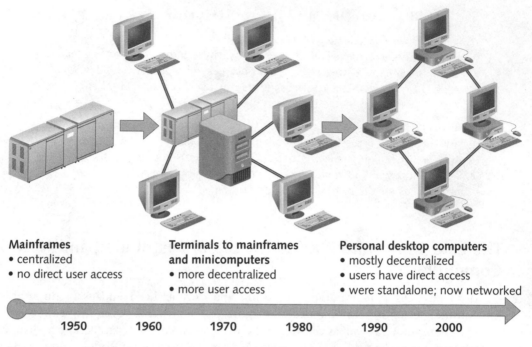

Mainframes
- centralized
- no direct user access

Terminals to mainframes and minicomputers
- more decentralized
- more user access

Personal desktop computers
- mostly decentralized
- users have direct access
- were standalone; now networked

1950   1960   1970   1980   1990   2000

Figure 1-3   Timeline of computer decentralization

Therefore, mainframe computing has not been replaced by end-user computing; rather, the two have been joined through the technology of computer networks. The term **distributed computing** describes an environment in which the needs of the organization determine the location of its computer resources. Organizations frequently require centralized mainframes, minicomputers, or network servers to perform enterprise-wide recordkeeping and transaction processing, as well as desktop tools to increase personal productivity at each employee's workspace. Distributed computing relies on network technology to link central systems and personal computers, so as to meet both corporate and individual employee needs.

The City of Orlando, Florida, uses an IBM iSeries minicomputer, along with e-mail and database software, to improve communications between city employees and customers. To learn more about how the city government uses a central minicomputer system to enhance communications, visit the Web site **www-3.ibm.com/software/success/cssdb.nsf/CS/LBHN-5FMKVY? OpenDocument&Site=software**.

2000s vignette: Payroll processing on a networked PC

Trisha Toledo is an accounting clerk for a small business of about 50 employees. During the month, employees enter payroll information into their personal desktop PC, from where it is automatically transferred into a payroll database on the company's network server. At the end of each month, Trisha sends an e-mail to remind each department supervisor to verify and authorize the data entered by employees in each department. As an additional check, Trisha runs software on her desktop to verify and validate that each piece of payroll data as submitted is within an expected range. The software alerts Trisha about any potential problems so she can correct them immediately.

When payroll transactions have been approved and verified, Trisha runs a program on the company's network server that computes the payroll, e-mails a pay stub to each employee, and then directly deposits the net pay amount into each employee account at a local credit union using electronic funds transfer over the Internet.

Yesterday's Data Processing department has been renamed **Information Systems**, **Information Services (IS)**, or **Information Technology (IT)**. The change reflects a shift in its mission and an attempt to improve the tarnished image it earned earlier due to its inability to meet the demands of the applications development backlog. The IS or IT department now operates mainframe and minicomputer systems that frequently act as hubs of corporate computer networks. Corporate networks often include mainframe, midsize, desktop, portable, and wireless systems.

Table 1-1 summarizes the main events that occurred in computer technology in the decades between the 1940s and the present.

Table 1-1   Milestones in the adoption of computer technology

Decade	Primary Types and Uses of Computer Systems
1940s	• Invention of computer processing units and mainframe peripherals
1950s	• Early use of mainframe computers in large corporations
1960s	• Widespread use of mainframes • Early use of workgroup minicomputers
1970s	• Widespread use of minicomputers in workgroups • Terminal access to mainframes and minicomputers • Early use of microcomputers
1980s	• Widespread use of home and business microcomputers • Availability of mass-market applications software and personal computer operating systems • Early use of data communications and networks to connect micro-to-micro and micro-to-mainframe
1990s	• Widespread use of data communications, local area and wide area computer networks • Distributed computing • Rapid growth of the Internet as a global network
2000s	• Increased use of the Internet for electronic business and business-to-business transactions • Availability of very low-cost PCs

A detailed timeline of events in the history of computers (with pictures) is available on the Web at **www.computer.org/computer/timeline/timeline.pdf** (requires Adobe Reader to view). Another timeline that focuses on personal computers is **www.islandnet.com/~kpolsson/comphist**. To view a slide show on the history of the Internet, go to **www.isoc.org/internet/history/ 2002_0918_Internet_History_and_Growth.ppt**.

End-User Classifications

To understand the variety of environments and situations in which organizations provide user support, it is helpful to recognize the different types of end users. Who are end users? Where are they located? How do they use computers in a business or home environment? There are many useful ways to classify end users. Figure 1-4 lists some common end-user classifications.

- **Environment:** home or personal user, corporate or organizational user
- **Skill level:** novice, unskilled, semiskilled, expert
- **Principal applications:** word processing, e-mail, accounting, and others (see "End-User Applications" in this chapter)
- **Frequency of use:** occasional, frequent, constant
- **Features used:** basic, intermediate, advanced
- **Location:** internal user, external user

Figure 1-4   Common categories of end users

Environment

For some purposes, it is helpful to distinguish between people whose primary use of computers occurs at home with non-business-related applications and those whose primary use occurs at work with business-related applications. Of course, many users fall into both groups at different times.

Skill Level

End users span the range from novice and unskilled users (who have little or no computer experience, difficulty with basic computer vocabulary, and many questions) to highly skilled users who are largely self-sufficient. Users who are highly skilled in one application program may be novices, however, in another application program or operating system.

Software Used

Users can be classified by which applications they use. For example, some home users primarily work with word-processing and e-mail programs and play computer games for entertainment. Business users often work with spreadsheet and database applications or software designed for specific business use, such as a specialized medical accounting system.

Frequency of Use

Some people use computers only occasionally; they may not use a computer every day, or even every week. Other users make frequent, possibly daily, use of a computer. A user who makes extensive use of a computer for several hours each day in an organization or home business could be classified as a constant user.

Features Used

Some users may use only basic software features. They may know only how to perform a routine set of simple tasks using common features of a program. Other users may use more features, including several that are intermediate in their power and complexity. Users who employ advanced software features have learned to use the full power of the software in order to be very productive, and are sometimes called power users.

Location

Another way to classify end users is by location, as viewed from an organization's perspective: are the users internal (in-house employees) or external (clients or customers)? Whether its users are internal or external often determines the characteristics of the support an organization offers.

Internal Users.   In-house employees at any level within an organization who use computers to do their work are called **internal users**. It is difficult to think of a department that does not use computer technology in some way. Clerical and administrative employees, whose manual tasks were the first targets of automation on early mainframe computers, continue to be a significant category of end users. Managers, professional workers, engineers, marketing representatives, and factory workers also make extensive use of computer systems to complete their work. Internal users need technical support as they use their computers to perform their daily tasks.

Even computer professionals, such as programmers and analysts, can be considered internal users. Computer professionals often use the same kinds of personal computers and software as other employees. The fact that an employee is a computer professional does not mean that he or she never requires support services. A highly skilled software programmer, for example, may know little about how to diagnose and repair a hardware or network problem. Because computer technology professionals are end users who work within a company, they are classified as internal users.

External Users.   **External users** are end users who are outside an organization, usually because they are customers or home users. Customers of hardware and software vendors are external users from the viewpoint of the vendor. Home computer users who have purchased personal computer hardware and software from a retail outlet or through the mail are external users. When external users encounter problems, they often contact the hardware or software company (the vendor) where they made their purchase.

With today's mobility, the distinction between internal and external users is sometimes blurred. A worker who telecommutes (works at home) is an internal user who shares many of the characteristics of an external user. Internal and external users both require technical support services, but the environments in which they work may affect the support services they need and the way those support services are delivered. Despite the differences among the computer users that these classifications describe, all end users need some common resources to make effective that use of computer technology.

RESOURCES END USERS NEED

People who want to use computers at home, on the job, or in school often buy their first computer on the basis of media advertising. Computer ads sometimes tout complete systems for less than $500. These are usable, but fairly basic hardware systems that may or may not include a monitor or a printer. New users often are surprised that the full cost of owning a personal computer system is more than the purchase price of the initial hardware. What kinds of costs are end users likely to encounter?

Basic Hardware

Hardware refers to the electrical and mechanical components that are part of a computer system. In addition to the system unit with a central processing unit (CPU), users need memory and storage space, a keyboard and a mouse or other pointing device, a display screen (monitor), and a printer for even a basic task such as word processing. The original cost of the hardware is only a starting point in the cost of a complete system.

Add-on Peripherals

In addition to basic hardware, end users frequently need **peripheral devices**, or hardware add-ons that plug into the computer's system unit, either externally or internally. For example, anyone who wants to connect to the Internet needs some type of dial-up or broadband modem or a connection to a local area network. Office users who want to connect to a local area network need a **network interface card (NIC)**, an adapter card located within a computer's system unit that connects their PCs to the network. The network cable plugs into the NIC, which sends and receives signals to and from a network server. Users who work with graphics and images usually purchase an image scanner or a digital camera. Anyone who wants to make convenient media backups might invest in a removable disk drive. The list of available peripheral devices is long and can add considerable expense to a basic system.

Hardware Maintenance and Upgrades

Most PCs are sold with a basic warranty and perhaps some technical assistance to cover initial installation or other operational problems. Warranties of 90 days to three years are common, during which hardware problems are repaired without charge. A few vendors also offer next-day on-site repair services. Other companies offer a warranty that specifies that the user must pay shipping to return a defective device to the manufacturer or to a repair depot. Some companies offer extended warranties on hardware components. Most extended warranties add to the expense of the hardware and are usually very expensive relative to their value, because most computer components that fail do so early, during the standard warranty period. Extended warranties may be a worthwhile expense for new users who want the assurance that help will be available during installation if it is needed, or who want to cover potential hardware problems during a fixed time period at a fixed cost. However, most computer users do not purchase additional warranty provisions. In any case, all computer purchasers should know the features of the warranty that come with a new PC and whether technical assistance is available locally or via a long-distance call.

Even after the initial purchase of a system and peripherals, additional costs may arise. During the two- to four-year life of a typical computer system, users might need to upgrade the amount of memory, the CPU speed, the size of the hard disk drive, the speed of a peripheral (such as a modem or a printer), or other system components. Some users upgrade their basic system at the time of their initial purchase, especially if they plan to run a software package that requires more than the minimum amount of memory. For example, although software vendors sometimes advertise that their products operate on a system with a minimum of 128 MB of RAM, they may perform better with 256 MB or more. As technological improvements are introduced, users may want to take advantage of new devices such as an improved sound system, a digital video disc (DVD) player, or a CD or DVD burner (to read/write CDs and DVDs). Hardware upgrades help keep systems fully functional as more complex software packages with higher memory and disk space requirements become available, and as hardware devices with more capabilities are developed.

Although the hardware components in most PCs are generally reliable over time, hardware service organizations keep busy diagnosing and repairing a multitude of malfunctions. Most organizations with a sizable investment in computer equipment need to budget for occasional hardware repairs. Although individual home users may beat the odds and never need hardware repairs, the probability is that a few users out of every one hundred will experience a burned-out power supply or a crashed hard drive, and have to pay the cost of a replacement.

Software and Software Upgrades

Most hardware packages are bundled (sold) with preconfigured operating systems. However, some users want to run one of the several alternatives to industry standard operating systems, such as Linux, instead of, or in addition to, Windows. For these users, the alternate operating system often represents an added cost.

In addition to operating system software, users can expect to spend a considerable part of their computer system budget for applications software, especially if they purchase one or more special-purpose packages. Some users require specialized packages, such as a computer aided design (CAD) program, or a software package tailored to a specific business, such as a legal billing system. Although mass-market software is often fairly inexpensive, specialized software can add thousands of dollars to the cost of a system. In the next section, you will review some common software applications.

Besides the initial purchase of the operating system and applications software, users need to budget for software upgrades. Although some software upgrades are free when downloaded from the Internet, many new software versions and upgrades must be purchased. The price can vary, depending on the extent of the upgrade and the type of software. For example, a virus protection package may have frequent, inexpensive upgrades, whereas a tax preparation program may require replacement of the product each year.

Supplies

When estimating the total cost of a computer system, end users should be sure to include consumables, such as printer paper, mailing labels, ink-jet or laser printer cartridges, cleaning supplies, media (floppy disks, removable cartridges, recordable CDs, or tape cartridges), cables, and other supplies they will need to operate their system. Laser printer cartridges and high-capacity removable disk media can be very expensive.

Data and Information

As end users communicate more with other users and get information from outside sources, they can incur costs for information services. The monthly cost of an Internet access service falls into this category, as do the costs of downloading stock market, financial, or economic data from a service such as America Online. Although many information vendors and brokers initially offer free access to their data to attract customers, over time more information providers will charge for specialized information access. Proprietary information and expert opinion, in particular, will cost more as awareness grows that information has a value to consumers.

Technical Support

As end users buy and learn new programs and discover new uses for programs they already own, they often need technical support. Support can include installation assistance, training courses, training materials, books, and magazines. Frequently, users must contact a hardware or software help desk to solve a problem. When they do, they often pay for long-distance telephone charges in addition to the cost of the support call itself. Some computer vendors sell support packages for a fixed fee. In a large organization, personal computer support is a major budget item.

Training is a good example of a technical support service that can add substantially to the cost of a computer system. Training for end users is available in a variety of formats, as described in Chapter 11. Some users try to avoid the cost of training by using a trial-and-error learning method, which would appear to be free. However, when you factor in the cost of reduced productivity and the errors made by a poorly trained user, the hidden costs of this approach to training are significant. While the purchase of a $40 tutorial, book, or online course on a software product may seem inexpensive, an employee's time must be added as a hidden cost. Commercial training courses are expensive, especially when you add in the cost of travel, lodging, and meals.

Facilities, Administration, and Overhead

Both home users and businesses should budget for the cost of facilities they will need to house and operate a computer system. Facilities include furniture, ergonomic devices (such as keyboard wrist rests and antiglare screens), electricity, air conditioning, power conditioners, space, and other workplace components that are necessary to operate a computer system.

In many organizations, overhead and supervisory costs are related to the management of end-user computing systems. These costs include acquisition assistance, purchase order processing, shipping, inventory control, insurance, security, and related costs of doing business. The cost of end-user computing must include a proportional share of overhead costs.

The list of cost categories for an end-user computing system is long. Of course, not all costs apply to each user or to every system. But what does it all cost, bottom line? The **total cost of ownership (TCO)**, or the total expenditures necessary to purchase, upgrade, and support an end user's personal computer system over its expected useful lifetime, provides this figure. The GartnerGroup, a company that researches trends in the computer industry, estimates that the total cost of ownership to an organization for a personal computer system over a five-year period is about $40,000, or approximately $8000 per year. Hardware costs account for only about 20% of the total cost of ownership, whereas software and support make up a substantial portion.

As you can see from this overview, end users need many types of resources to make their computers true productivity tools. End users who are attracted to $500 computer systems should be aware that other ownership costs must be included in the total package.

To learn more about total cost of ownership and the factors users should consider in a computer budget, see **www.jaekel.com/white3.html**.

END-USER APPLICATIONS SOFTWARE

Among the computer resources end users need, applications software is one that has a significant impact on user productivity. Tasks that formerly required considerable manual effort, such as preparing a budget report or managing a mailing list, can be done faster and more accurately with a well-designed applications software program. End users run a variety of software applications, which are grouped below into 10 primary categories—electronic mail and instant messaging, Web browser, word processing, spreadsheets, database management, graphics, planning and scheduling, desktop publishing, Web site development, and educational and entertainment software.

Figure 10-4 in Chapter 10 lists some of the popular packages in each category.

Electronic Mail and Instant Messaging

Electronic mail (e-mail) enables users to communicate privately with others. It is the most common business and personal use of computers today. E-mail is closely related to word processing because the goal is to enter, modify, format, transmit, and receive text messages and attachments (an attachment is a separate file transmitted with the e-mail message that contains a document, worksheet, graphic image, or other output from an application program). To send and receive e-mail, a computer must be connected to a network, either directly or via a modem. An e-mail client program is also required to send and receive e-mail messages from a PC.

Instant messaging is communication between two or more users who are online (connected to the Internet) at the same time. As with e-mail, it is a private communication, open only to those invited. Instant messaging software notifies a user when one or more other users from a predefined "buddy" list are online so that a "chat" session can begin. Selection of an instant messaging software package is not trivial, because there are no industry standards and competing packages cannot automatically communicate.

Web Browser

A Web browser is a primary application tool that enables end users to find and display information on the Internet. Pages of information are stored and transmitted on Internet computers in a format called Hypertext Markup Language (HTML). When an Internet user inputs the name or address of a page of interest, the Web browser retrieves the page and displays it on the user's PC. During the last 10 years, owing to the enormous popularity of the World Wide Web as an information storage and retrieval reservoir for both home and business users, Web browsers have become one of the most popular application packages.

Word Processing

Word-processing software enables users to enter, edit, format, store, and print text information as a document. Many word processors also permit users to integrate graphics, numbers, and footnotes easily into a document. Because most clerical, administrative, and managerial employees produce letters, memos, papers, reports, and other printed documents, word processors are one of the most frequently used software applications among end users. Word processors are usually part of an office "suite" of software tools, so users sometimes don't put much thought into the selection of a word processor.

Spreadsheets

Because clerical, administrative, and managerial employees frequently work with numeric information in addition to text, electronic spreadsheets are close to the top of many users' software shopping lists. Spreadsheets are used to prepare budgets, sales reports and forecasts, financial statements, and other reports in which numeric information is organized into a worksheet of rows and columns, and in which repeated calculations are necessary to produce meaningful results. Spreadsheet software is also commonly a part of an office "suite" of software tools.

Database Management

End users frequently need to track information that relates to business activities and projects. A database management program allows end users to enter, update, store, format, and print reports containing information that is stored as a series of records that share a common format in a database. Client lists, mailing lists, personnel records, office supply inventories, and class rosters are examples of common databases. Home users also use database management programs for managing personal directories, such as a club roster, or lists, such as an inventory of antique collectibles. Database software runs the gamut from easy-to-use packages that are often included in office "suites" of programs to sophisticated enterprise-wide database packages. Some sophisticated database software includes a data mart, which is a user-friendly front-end that allows employees to extract and analyze data from a database without programming skills.

Graphics

Users often need to organize and summarize information in the form of pictures, charts, or drawings. Graphics software lets a user create illustrations and charts that analyze trends, show relationships, and summarize large amounts of data. **Presentation graphics software** is used to create attractive electronic slide shows with text, pictures, charts, and diagrams for training, sales presentations, lectures, and other events where the appearance of visual information is important. Other graphics software packages are used to organize and edit digital pictures and scanned images. Although specialized graphics software packages are specifically designed to prepare graphical images on a computer, many word-processor, spreadsheet, and database packages sold today also include some graphics capabilities.

Planning and Scheduling

Office employees spend considerable time planning and scheduling their individual work as well as team projects. Software packages for planning and scheduling include **personal information managers**, which help business or home users maintain an electronic calendar, a to-do list, and an address book. For collaborative projects, some scheduling and calendar software can arrange meetings at a convenient time for all members in a group. In addition, **project management programs** allow managers to plan, schedule, and monitor the status of tasks in a group project, as you will see in Chapter 7.

Desktop Publishing

Desktop publishing software combines the features of a word processor and a graphics program. **Desktop publishing software** enables end users to design, lay out, and prepare—at a relatively low cost—high-quality brochures, newsletters, posters, computer manuals, and other printed material that would otherwise need to be designed and typeset by a printing professional. As word processing software becomes more feature-rich and powerful, the distinction between the two categories narrows. However, in general, desktop publishing packages give the user considerably more control over typographical features and have superior WYSIWYG (what-you-see-is-what-you-get) features to preview on the screen what will be printed.

Web Site Development

Web site development software is popular with employees and home users who design, develop, and maintain an organizational or personal Web site. **Web site development software** packages enable users to create, maintain, and update Web pages that include a mixture of text and graphics and incorporate features such as e-mail links, chat rooms, File Transfer Protocol (FTP), and restricted access for security. Software for Web site development ranges from features incorporated in some word processors to sophisticated packages designed for professional Web programmers.

Educational and Entertainment Software

Educational software provides learners with hands-on experience to supplement an instructor's lectures or distributed materials. Educational software can also test and provide feedback on learners' understanding of concepts or on their ability to solve problems. Tutorial software is also available to help computer users learn new software packages. Computer games are, of course, a significant portion of the entertainment industry.

Mainframe Applications

Corporations and business enterprises continue to run many of the same applications on their mainframe systems as they did decades ago: payroll, accounting, inventory and asset management, human resources, and manufacturing. Newer categories of mainframe applications software include customer relationship management (CRM) and enterprise resource planning (ERP). Although some organizations have converted their legacy (old) mainframe applications to more modern hardware platforms and applications software, some continue to run the same programs today as they did in the 1960s and 1970s. The cost to upgrade to more recent software and the cost to convert a large database of information from older mainframe systems to newer ones are often cited as reasons organizations continue to use legacy systems.

Many employees also use their personal computers as terminals to connect to company mainframes. Once connected, they can use terminal emulation software to run programs on the mainframe much as they did 25 years ago, or to download information from the mainframe to their personal computer. Transaction processing and management reports are tasks end users can now run on their personal computer systems with data extracted from a corporate mainframe. Because personal computers are much more powerful than the terminals of the 1970s, users can process some information locally on their PC's processing unit. **Client/server computing** is a form of distributed computing whereby processing tasks are shared between a mainframe system or powerful microcomputer (the server) and a local personal computer (the client). In a client/server system, some data is stored and processed on a central system; other data storage and processing occurs on a local system, such as a personal computer.

The preceding categories encompass the most common personal computer applications and include many of the primary applications employees use in business, government, education, and other organizations. New categories of applications emerge when a need develops. Whether for home or business use, almost all software applications are designed to increase users' productivity. In fact, most organizations justify their computer purchases on the basis that they help make employees more efficient. To accomplish this objective, computers should either increase the amount of output (product or service) an employee can produce based on a given amount of input (effort), or reduce the amount of input required to produce a given amount of output. In general, end-user computing has accomplished this ambitious goal, but not without problems along the way.

 To learn more about how productivity among knowledge workers is measured, read a white paper on how to measure and improve productivity at the Business Authority Web site, **www.business-authority.com/management/ time_management/productivity_management.htm**.

DOES COMPUTER TECHNOLOGY REALLY INCREASE PRODUCTIVITY?

Many employers believe that employees who use technology are more productive. But productivity for an individual worker is often difficult to measure. Is there evidence that investments in technology actually increase worker productivity?

The U.S. Department of Labor measures the productivity of all non-farm workers in the U.S. economy. First, it calculates the total dollar value of all goods and services produced each year. Then, it divides that figure by the number of hours employees worked to produce those goods and services. The result is the dollar value of worker productivity per hour worked.

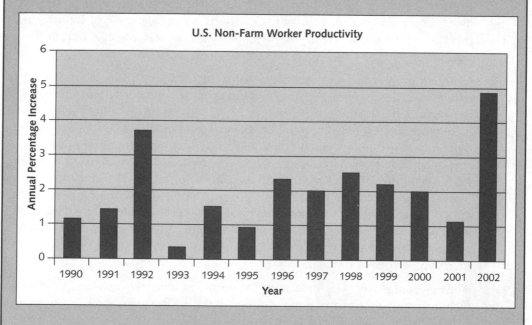

According to figures released by the Department of Labor, the value of worker productivity increased by an average of 2.5% per year between 1996 and 2002. Compare that increase with the average annual increase of 1.4% during 1973 to 1995. Economists and financial analysts think the increase in productivity is due to investments in computers, cellular phones, facsimile machines, copiers, and other technology products. Alan Greenspan, Chairman of the U.S. Federal Reserve Board, says the notable pickup in productivity is due to U.S. business investments in technology that are now paying off. Why hasn't the increase in worker productivity been more obvious until the mid-1990s? Greenspan thinks the delay occurred because it takes time for investments in technology and worker training to use new technology to result in increased productivity.

One example of increased worker productivity is occurring in the banking industry. Some banks have doubled the number of ATM machines available to customers in the last few years. The result is an increase in the number and speed of transactions for both the customer and the bank. However, automated transactions take fewer bank employees to process. The banking industry is currently working on the next big productivity gains in banking: first, banks are working to convince customers of the advantages of personal computer use and the Internet to process bank transactions, such as online bill paying; second, although its use is not yet widespread, some financial institutions are planning for the day digital money will replace paper and coin currency.

PROBLEMS WITH END-USER COMPUTING

The benefits of end-user computing are often accompanied by a new set of problems that organizations must address. Although not necessarily unique to end-user computing, the problems listed in Figure 1-5 can result from an environment in which powerful hardware and software tools are used (and can be easily misused) by a large number of employees.

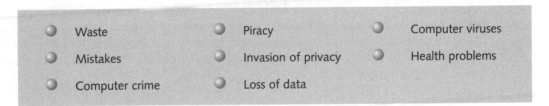

Waste	Piracy	Computer viruses
Mistakes	Invasion of privacy	Health problems
Computer crime	Loss of data	

Figure 1-5   Common problems with computer technology

There is a good chance that end users will encounter one or more of these problems in the course of their work or home computing experience.

Waste

Waste refers to the use of money, time, or other resources that do not contribute directly to increased user productivity, or may even result in lower productivity. End users who do not have the same training as computer professionals may lack the expertise and experience to make cost-effective purchase decisions about hardware, peripherals, software, and networks. For example, end users who are not knowledgeable about the relationship between hardware and software capabilities may purchase software that does not operate (or operate efficiently) on their hardware configurations. If the software an end user purchases operates inefficiently or causes the user's system to crash frequently, the result is often frustration and lower user productivity. Waste also occurs when end users purchase software that does not meet their needs as well as a competing program, or they purchase software that costs more than a similar package. Another form of waste is employee time spent viewing information on the Internet or reading and sending e-mail messages that are not directly job-related.

Mistakes

End users who are careless or not properly trained can easily make mistakes as they use sophisticated software. For example, an end user who prepares a spreadsheet to estimate a project's cost may inadvertently enter the wrong formula or data for critical calculations. The user may not understand the importance of testing even simple spreadsheet formulas for correctness, and may fall victim to a common assumption: "If the results are prepared on a computer, they *must* be correct." However, if a formula or number is entered incorrectly, then the results will be incorrect.

NOTE
A well-publicized example of a computer mistake occurred in the early days of spreadsheets when a bidder failed to get a job contract because of a spreadsheet miscalculation. The user didn't realize that adding a row to a spreadsheet in that particular program meant that he had to revise the formula to include the added row. As a consequence of one simple error, the total amount bid was unrealistically overstated. A lawsuit followed, but the spreadsheet software company won. The court ruled that the spreadsheet user was responsible for mastering documented features.

Another common mistake is a user's failure to make backups of important information. Computer mistakes can be extremely costly, especially in high-stakes business situations. All computer users need to build in safeguards and double-checks to ensure that computer errors are detected before they do significant damage.

Computer Crime

Although waste and mistakes are usually unintentional, computers are also used to commit intentional crimes. For example, an employee may have access to company information that would be potentially valuable to a competitor, and may try to profit from the sale of the information. Information theft, identity theft, fraud, sabotage, and embezzlement can be committed with the aid of a computer. These crimes are not unique to end-user computing; they emerged very early in the use of mainframe computers. However, the number of personal computer users, the lack of security measures, and the easy access to information multiply the potential for computer crimes among end users.

Piracy

Another form of computer crime is **piracy**, which is software theft that involves illegal copying, distribution, or use of computer programs or information. Because floppy disks and CDs are simple to copy, software theft is frequent. For example, employees might copy the installation disks for a software package purchased by their company, take the disks home, and install the program on a home computer. Legal or illegal? The answer depends on the software vendor's license agreement and on the employer's policies. Some organizations either do not have a specific policy about software piracy by their employees or look the other way when this kind of theft occurs. Sharing software among home users is a similar problem, and also illegal. In fact, software piracy costs software companies billions of dollars in lost sales, which in effect raises the price that software vendors must charge to cover their development and distribution costs. Because pirated software is also a source of computer viruses, the costs in lost productivity are substantially higher than the loss of sales revenue among vendors.

Invasion of Privacy

Another form of computer crime is invasion of privacy, whereby unauthorized parties exploit personal information. This problem occurs because vast amounts of information about employees, clients, patients, and students (both current and former) are stored in computer systems. Without adequate company policies and security safeguards to define who has authorized access to which pieces of information, the potential for invasion of individual privacy and identity theft is substantial.

Loss of Data

Many (perhaps most) end users do not make frequent or effective backups of important information stored on their workplace or home personal computers. Consequently, when hardware, software, or a network fails, they risk losing data. Loss of critical data can be expensive because lost data is sometimes impossible to replace. Manual reentry of destroyed data is expensive and time-consuming, and may contribute to a business failure. In contrast, restoring lost data from a backup disk or tape is an almost trivial operation.

Computer Viruses

A **computer virus** is a program created with malicious intent that can destroy information, erase or corrupt other software and data, or adversely affect the operation of a computer that is infected by the virus program. Viruses are transmitted from computer to computer via networks (including the Internet) or through exchange of media between computers (including floppy disks, CDs, DVDs, removable hard disks, and cartridge tapes). In a networked environment, such as an instructional computer lab at a school or a training department in an organization, the spread of computer viruses is a frequent problem for computer facilities managers. Virus protection software can be costly because it must be updated frequently to defend against new versions of viruses. However, the cost to an individual or an organization of virus attacks, removal, and data restoration can be many times the cost of an antivirus utility program.

Health Problems

Every tool that can be used can be misused. A common source of misuse that may not even be apparent to end users is the physical environment where a computer is operated. Without proper lighting, space, furniture, and environmental safeguards, physical injury to end users can result. Without proper operating procedures and techniques, an appropriate work environment, periodic breaks, and corrective eyewear, employees may subject themselves to a variety of physical ailments. Common ailments include headaches, nausea, eyestrain, hand or wrist pain (often the result of **carpal tunnel syndrome**, which is severe hand or wrist pain due to an inflammation of the tendons in a user's hand and wrist), and back and neck aches. In addition, stress due to the frustrations of working with technology, and possibly other longer-term health impacts due to extensive computer use, are consequences the medical profession doesn't yet fully understand or know how to treat. **Ergonomics** is a field that studies how to design a workspace that promotes employee health, safety, and productivity. Many common ailments can be avoided by paying attention to ergonomics.

NOTE

Chapter 10 discusses ergonomic concerns and workspace design in more detail.

Employees who provide technical support to end users often confront these problems. Similarly, a technical support job may include providing end users with solutions to many of these same problems.

CHAPTER SUMMARY

- Early business computer systems were primarily large, centralized corporate mainframes. They were used primarily to automate transaction processing and management reports. The first steps toward decentralized computing were the use of terminals to connect employees directly to a mainframe system, and the availability of less powerful, but less expensive minicomputers.

- The development of end-user computing was due to several industry trends during the 1970s and 1980s: (1) the backlog of requests for new mainframe applications, (2) an increase in the number of knowledge workers who work primarily with information, (3) the availability of inexpensive microcomputers, (4) the availability of inexpensive productivity software, and (5) the development of user-friendly graphical user interfaces.

◻ End users can be categorized according to skill level (novice, unskilled, semiskilled, or expert), environment (home or business), software used, frequency of use (occasional, frequent, or constant), features used (basic, intermediate, or advanced), or location (internal employee or external client).

◻ Resources that end users need to use a computer system include hardware, peripherals, hardware upgrades and maintenance, operating system and applications software, software upgrades, supplies, data and information, facilities, and technical support. These resources significantly affect the total cost of end-user computing to an individual or a company.

◻ End users run a variety of software packages on their personal computers, including electronic mail and messaging, Web browsers, word processing, spreadsheets, database management, graphics, planning and scheduling, desktop publishing, Web page development, educational and entertainment software, as well as traditional mainframe applications.

◻ A primary goal of end-user computing is to make employees more productive in their jobs. However, productivity is not without costs, because end users can misuse their personal computers. Common problems include waste, mistakes, computer crime, piracy, invasion of privacy, loss of data, computer viruses, and health problems.

KEY TERMS

applications development backlog — The excess demand for new computer applications that outstripped the supply of computer professionals available to develop them; the backlog of requests for software development was often measured in years of staff effort.

batch processing — The processing of a group of transactions that has been collected over a day, a week, a month, or a year.

carpal tunnel syndrome — Severe hand or wrist pain due to an inflammation of the tendons in a user's hand and wrist; often a result of overuse in combination with an improper and/or nonergonomic physical environment.

client/server computing — A form of distributed computing whereby processing tasks are shared between a mainframe system or powerful desktop system (the server) and a local personal computer (the client).

computer virus — A computer program created with malicious intent that can destroy information, erase or corrupt other software or data, or adversely affect the operation of a computer that is infected by the virus program.

Data Processing (DP) department — A division in an organization that programs and operates the organization's mainframe computer system; Information Technology (IT) is a more modern name for the DP department.

desktop publishing software — Software that enables end users to design, lay out, and prepare—at a relatively low cost—high-quality brochures, newsletters, posters, computer manuals, and other printed material; combines the features of a word processor and a graphics program.

distributed computing — A computing environment in which the needs of the organization determine the location of its computer resources; often includes a centralized system, such as a mainframe computer or network server, and decentralized systems, such as individual PCs on employee desks.

end-user computing — The everyday use of computer technology for both business and personal use; increases the productivity of employees, managers, students, and home users of computers.

ergonomics — The study of how to design a workspace that promotes employee health, safety, and productivity.

external user — An end user who is outside an organization, such as customers of hardware and software vendors, home workers, or personal users.

graphical user interface (GUI) — Screen images that enable users to access program features and functions intuitively, using a mouse or other input device.

Information Systems, Information Services (IS), Information Technology (IT) — The modern names of the Data Processing department; also may be responsible for network and distributed systems, such as employee PCs and user support services.

internal user — An in-house employee at any level within an organization who uses computers to do his or her work; compare with external user.

knowledge worker — An employee whose primary job function is to collect, prepare, process, and distribute information.

mainframe computer — A large, powerful computer system used by an organization to process high volumes of transactions, store databases with millions of records, and serve as the hub of a corporate network.

management information systems (MIS) — Computer software that automates the preparation of summary reports for managers and employees from detailed data.

microcomputer — A complete computer (often called a personal computer, or PC) built on a smaller scale than a mainframe or a minicomputer, with a microprocessor as the CPU.

minicomputer — A computer system that is smaller and less powerful than a mainframe, but more powerful than a microcomputer; minicomputers were used in small businesses, departments, and work groups during the 1970s and 1980s, and continue to provide a midsize option today.

network interface card (NIC) — An adapter card located within a computer's system unit that connects a PC to a computer network.

peripheral device — A hardware add-on that plugs into a computer's system unit, either externally or internally; includes input devices (keyboard, scanner), output devices (display screen, printer), input and output (modem, network interface card, touch screen display), and storage (magnetic media—tapes and disks, and optical media—CDs and DVDs).

personal information manager — A computer program that helps business or home users to maintain an electronic calendar, a to-do list, and an address book.

piracy — Software theft that involves illegal copying, distribution, or use of computer programs or information.

presentation graphics software — A computer program used to create attractive electronic slide shows with text, pictures, charts, and diagrams for training, sales presentations, lectures, and other events where the appearance of visual information is important.

project management program — A computer program that helps managers to plan, schedule, and monitor the status of tasks in a group project.

real-time processing — A form of computer processing in which each transaction or event is handled or processed as it occurs; compare to batch processing.

terminal — A keyboard and a display screen that are connected to a mainframe computer by a pair of wires; employees use terminals to enter and access information in a central system.

total cost of ownership (TCO) — The total expenditures necessary to purchase, maintain, upgrade, and support an end user's personal computer system over its expected useful lifetime; includes hardware, software, network, information, training, and technical support costs.

transaction processing — The use of computers to input large volumes of business events or activities, process the data, and prepare printed reports, usually at the time the event or activity occurs.

Web site development software — Applications software that enables users to create, maintain, and update Web pages that include a mixture of text and graphics and incorporate features such as e-mail links, chat rooms, File Transfer Protocol (FTP), and restricted access for security.

CHECK YOUR UNDERSTANDING

NOTE

Answers to the Check Your Understanding questions are in Appendix 2.

1. True or False? The goal of transaction processing on mainframe computers was to automate as much manual processing of business information as possible.

2. Large computers that process high volumes of business transactions, access organizational data, and serve as corporate network hubs are called _____ .

   a. mainframe computers

   b. minicomputers

   c. mid-range computers

   d. microcomputers

3. True or False? During the 1970s, a dumb terminal included many of the capabilities of today's personal computers.

4. A modern name for the Data Processing (DP) department is _____ .

5. Client/server computing is a form of _____ .

   a. personal computing

   b. mainframe computing

   c. centralized computing

   d. distributed computing

6. Widespread use of the Internet among business and home computer users first occurred during the _____ .

   a. 1960s

   b. 1970s

   c. 1980s

   d. 1990s

7. True or False? Economists and financial experts think the increased productivity of U.S. workers is due to low interest rates.

8. An internal user is a(n) _____ .

   a. end user

   b. employee of an organization

   c. customer of a vendor

   d. client who buys over the Internet

9. True or False? Technical support costs are generally included in the purchase price of a computer product, and are therefore free to users.

10. _____ is a field that studies how to design a work environment that promotes employee health, safety, and productivity.

11. Use of a computer for unauthorized access to information about a customer, student, or patient is _____ .

    a. waste

    b. an ergonomic problem

    c. an invasion of privacy

    d. piracy

12. A(n) _____ uses pull-down menus and screen images that are easier to use than systems that require users to memorize and type lengthy commands.

Discussion Questions

1. Why do you think so much of the software that ran on mainframe computers was custom-written by programmers, whereas today most personal computer software is purchased off-the-shelf?

2. Do you think the changes in the way computers are used since the 1950s is due primarily to advances in computer technology over the past 50 years or due primarily to demand for improvements among end users?

3. Based on your knowledge and studies of the computer industry, what other information would you add to Table 1-1 that would help someone understand important changes in computer technology? What do you think the significant new developments for the decade of the 2000s will be by the year 2010?

4. Are the end-user problems described at the end of this chapter inevitable or can they be resolved?

HANDS-ON PROJECTS

NOTE

Many of the interviews suggested as projects below could be organized as activities for an entire class or training session.

HANDS-ON PROJECTS

Project 1-1

Interview an IS employee. Talk to an employee in an Information Systems department at your organization or school, or interview a family member, friend, or acquaintance who works in an IS department. Find out the following information:

1. What is the employee's job title and responsibilities?

2. With what kind of computer equipment does the person work?

3. What purpose does the computer system(s) serve in the organization? What tasks does it perform? Who uses the output from the system(s)?

4. How has computing changed since his or her organization first used computers?

Write a one-page summary of the information you obtain.

HANDS-ON PROJECTS

Project 1-2

Interview an early computer user. Find a coworker, instructor, acquaintance, friend, or neighbor who worked with computers in the 1960s, 1970s, or 1980s. Interview the person to learn the following:

1. In what type of business did the person work?

2. With what type of computer equipment did the person work?

3. What were the principal tasks the computer performed? Who used the results?

4. What was the relationship between the computer professionals and the end users of the information?

5. Were terminals used?

6. Was the person involved with application programming? If so, did he or she experience any of the difficulties mentioned in this chapter?

7. What changes in computer use did the person experience, and over what time period?

In a one-page report, summarize the results of your interview and compare this person's experience with the information in this chapter.

Project 1-3

Predict future computing trends. Based on your knowledge of current trends in the computer industry, add more information to the decade milestones shown in Table 1-1 for the 2000s decade. What do you think the significant events and trends in this decade will be? Make predictions about computer size, cost, ease of use, and primary functions in business and home during the next decade.

Project 1-4

Interview a technical support person. Locate a technical support person at your school, your work, or a local company. Find out the following information:

1. Does the person support internal or external users?

2. With what resources does the person work (i.e., hardware, software, peripherals, networks, information)?

3. What types of applications do end users work with most frequently in their jobs?

4. Do any users or applications present difficult problems for him or her as a technical support person?

5. Which of the end-user problems described in this chapter does the person encounter most often?

6. Does the organization have a policy on software piracy, invasion of privacy, or virus protection?

Write a one-page summary of the information you collect.

Project 1-5

Discuss a privacy issue. An organization opposed to the use of supermarket identification cards maintains a Web site at **www.nocards.org/faq/index.shtml**. Find out why it thinks identification cards are an invasion of privacy. Summarize its arguments in a brief report. Do you agree or disagree with its positions? Explain why.

Project 1-6

Identify software packages. Find a mail-order computer catalog (in your computer room or library) or an Internet site that sells applications software packages of the types described in this chapter. For each category—electronic mail and instant messaging, Web browser, word processing, spreadsheets, database management, graphics, planning and scheduling, desktop publishing, Web site development, and educational and entertainment software—list the names of two or three representative packages. Include the price range for a typical package in each category.

Project 1-7

Identify computer users' health concerns. Interview three classmates or coworkers about their health concerns related to their use of computers. Make a list of their health, safety, and productivity concerns. Are there any similarities to their concerns? Did any of their concerns surprise you?

Project 1-8

Evaluate TCO. A Houston, Texas, consulting company, JDA Professional Services, provides an online worksheet for calculating the total cost of ownership (TCO) of computer technology. Read about the factors they think contribute to the total cost of ownership at its Web site **www.jdapsi.com/client/Articles/Default.php?Article=tco**. Write a one-page report that describes how the factors JDA considers significant are different from those in this chapter.

Click the **JDA's Online TCO Worksheet** link. Enter the data for the following scenario: An instructional computer lab manager wants to purchase 10 computers for a new lab at a cost of $1200 per machine. The cost of a network server and laser printer and related hardware and software is expected to be $5000. The lab will require two part-time support staff, expected to cost $15,000 each. Use the GartnerGroup's recommended percentage for hidden costs. Answer the following questions:

1. What is the total cost of ownership per machine?

2. Is this a one-time cost or an annual cost?

Project 1-9

Research computer history. Use the Web-based computer history timelines mentioned in this chapter to find answers to the following computer trivia questions.

1. Put the following familiar computer hardware manufacturers in order from oldest to newest: Apple, IBM, Hewlett-Packard

2. An error in a software program is called a "bug." How did this name originate?

3. When was a computer first used to predict the outcome of a presidential election in the United States?

4. Put these programming languages in order from oldest to newest: BASIC, C++, COBOL, Fortran. How did the C language get its name?

5. What university first organized a department of computer science?

6. The mouse and floppy disk became popular in the 1980s. When were these devices actually invented?

7. Who first noted that adding programmers to a project that is behind schedule just makes the project further behind schedule?

8. The Macintosh was not the first computer built by Apple. Name three of its predecessors.

9. A decision to store the year in computers as a two-digit code caused the Y2K crisis. When was that decision made?

10. The ARPA network, which eventually became the Internet, linked four sites. Where were they?

11. The first operating system for microcomputers wasn't DOS. What was it?

12. What computer program developed in the late 1970s convinced many people to buy their first personal computer?

13. How large was the first "portable" computer?

14. How long did it take before the first IBM PC clone was developed?

15. How old is the Windows operating system?

CASE PROJECTS

CASE PROJECTS

1. TCO of a $500 Computer

Your friend Ron has asked for your help in buying a home computer system. He is skeptical of ads for computers that cost less than $500. He intends to use the computer for word processing, e-mail, entertainment, and Internet access, and he wants your advice about how much he should budget for a home personal computer system. What is a realistic amount your friend might expect to spend, both at the time of initial purchase and over the next four years of ownership? Use catalogs, computer magazines, or the Internet to obtain current price information. Draw up a sample budget showing your recommended initial expenditure and the annual cost for the next four years. Break down the costs by the categories described in this chapter. Show the total cost of ownership over the four years that Ron plans to own the computer.

2. Technical Support for Wiley Corporation

Wiley Corporation has just relocated to a town near you and is actively seeking technical support employees. At a local job fair, you meet Cynthia, a recruiter for the company. While there, you decide to learn more about end-user computing and the technical support function. Based on what you have learned in this chapter, write a list of 10 questions you would ask Cynthia to obtain a profile of the categories of end users and the problems for which they need technical support at Wiley.

3. Tablet PC Versus Desktop PC

A new competitor to desktop PCs for some end users is a device called a tablet PC. Learn about the features of tablet PCs at the Web site **www.tabletpctalk.com**. Make a list of three important ways the tablet PC is similar to a desktop PC and three important ways it is different from a desktop PC. For what categories of end users would a tablet PC be appropriate? Some industry analysts think that tablet PCs represent a new and different form of end-user computing. Do you agree that the tablet PC is the next logical step in the development of end-user computing? Why, or why not?

4. Re-Nu-Cartridge's Network Server

NOTE

Re-Nu-Cartridge is a case study that appears at the end of each chapter in this book. You will learn more about this company and its support problems in subsequent chapters.

Re-Nu-Cartridge is a business that remanufactures and sells replacement ink-jet printer and copier cartridges. It employs a staff of about 40 workers and currently sells close to $5 million per year in remanufactured printer and copier cartridges. Re-Nu-Cartridge sells locally through a retail store located on the same site as its manufacturing plant, and it wholesales remanufactured cartridges to retail computer stores in eight nearby states. The company would eventually like to sell its products nationwide over the Internet, but does not have the technology or expertise to operate an e-business, such as an Internet store.

Fred Long, the chief executive officer (CEO) of Re-Nu-Cartridge says the company is organized into four groups:

- Cartridge remanufacturing (the largest group)
- Retail sales
- Marketing (the wholesale operation)
- Administration (including accounting, human resources, purchasing)

The cartridge remanufacturing group operates the equipment that cleans used cartridges, mixes ink chemicals to original manufacturer specifications, refills the cartridges, and packages and ships cartridges to both retail and wholesale customers. The retail sales group operates a retail store that sells cartridges and printer supplies direct to local customers. The marketing group consists of outside sales representatives who call on retail computer stores that carry the Re-Nu-Cartridge brand of remanufactured cartridges in the region.

Fred reports that the company currently has about 25 desktop computers, mostly in the Administration department, although there are a few in each of the other departments. Most of the computers are standalone PCs that the company has purchased over the last 12 years, although several of the PCs can connect to the Internet via a dial-up capability.

Several of Fred's employees who use computers have suggested that the company could increase employee productivity if they made better use of e-mail communications. And, they point out, Re-Nu-Cartridge could move toward operation of a Web-based e-business if they had a company-wide network. Fred has an appointment next week with a local vendor that provides network computer solutions for small businesses. He is very concerned about the cost of a company network, and wants to be prepared to ask the network vendor about all the cost factors he should budget for as the company considers a network.

1. Prepare a list for Fred of the cost categories he should ask the network vendor about.

2. Which of the cost categories you listed are initial, start-up costs, and which are ongoing, operational costs?

3. What other issues should the Re-Nu-Cartridge company be concerned about when it considers the problems of installing and operating a network server in its business?

Write a memo to Fred that responds to these questions.

2

INTRODUCTION TO
COMPUTER USER SUPPORT

In this chapter you will learn:

♦ What the job market demand is for user support employees

♦ Common ways that organizations provide a user support function

♦ Services that user support groups provide

♦ Typical position descriptions for user support staff members

♦ The knowledge, skills, and abilities needed to qualify for an entry-level user support position

♦ Career paths for user support workers

As you learned in Chapter 1, the widespread use of computer technology by employees and home users has created a new industry called end-user computing. End users are usually not computer professionals, yet they need to use computers to get their work done. In the course of their work, they frequently encounter situations in which they require help or information. They often look for someone to turn to when they have a question or problem, need advice or information, want training, or are just plain frustrated because they cannot accomplish what they want or need to get done.

Many organizations recognize the need for a user support function for their employees or their clients who use a computer at work or home. To fill this need, organizations have formal or informal ways to provide user support. Although user support may bring to mind an employee of a software vendor at the other end of a telephone line or a problem solver at a help desk at school, user support often includes a wide variety of tasks. In this chapter, you will learn about many of these tasks. Then you will look at sample job descriptions for the kinds of jobs in user support.

INCREASED NEED FOR USER SUPPORT EMPLOYEES

A manufacturing, service, or consulting organization may provide computers for its knowledge workers to help them be more productive. But the organization's role usually does not end there. Most organizations must also provide some form of ongoing assistance to their workers so that the computers become tools that increase employee productivity instead of stumbling blocks and sources of frustration. Similarly, a hardware or software vendor provides products to its clients who, in spite of rigorous product testing and extensive documentation, inevitably encounter problems that the vendor must help them solve.

Organizations have recognized an increasing need for the user support function, and therefore for user support workers, in the past decade. With the growth of end-user computing in offices and homes, along with the growth of the Internet as a way to obtain information, organizations often find themselves unable to meet the need for user support and support workers. The demand for user support positions grew significantly during the 1990s while the economy grew and the unemployment rate in the United States declined from around 7.5% in the early 1990s to about 4% in 2000, according to the U.S. Bureau of Labor Statistics.

During the early years of the first decade of the 21st century, three important trends have influenced the demand for user support employees in organizations.

First, the economic recession that began in March 2001 caused a gradual increase in the unemployment rate to about 6%. As a result, hiring in all information technology fields, including user support, decreased from the levels of the 1990s.

Second, U.S. companies are increasingly moving technical support jobs overseas (especially to India and Asian countries), where well-trained workers are available and wages are comparably lower. This has reduced the demand for IT and technical support workers in the United States.

Third, some organizations that need technical support workers now contract with temporary employment agencies for the workers they need. Some of these temporary work opportunities evolve into permanent positions over time, so that the temporary assignment is effectively a trial period for both the employee and the employer.

 To learn about temporary employment agencies in your area that seek computer professionals, see the Web site of the American Staffing Association at **www.staffingtoday.net**.

The Information Technology Association of America (ITAA) periodically reports on the need for workers in all information technology fields. In 2003, it reported a total of 10.3 million workers in information technology, of which about 1.9 million, or 18.5%, were in technical support fields and another half million (5%) were technical writers. Thus, about one-fourth of the workers in information technology are in some user support capacity.

ITAA forecasts that about a half million positions in IT will be filled during 2003, down from a peak of over 1.5 million in 2000. It concludes that hiring in IT fields continues, but at a much slower pace than during the 1990s.

 To learn more about the ITAA survey of the current need for workers in the information technology fields, visit its Web site at **www.itaa.org**.

The Office of Employment Projections in the U.S. Bureau of Labor Statistics reports that about one-half million workers were employed in the job category *Computer Support Specialist* in 2000. It forecasts an increase in employment in that job category of almost 100% by the year 2010. By comparison, over 200,000 were employed in the job category *Network and Computer System Administrators* in 2000, with growth in this category by 2010 forecast at 80%. However, these forecasts were made prior to the U.S. recession that began in 2001, and before large numbers of user support jobs began to be outsourced to India and Asian countries.

Robert Half, a consulting company that specializes in jobs in the IT industry, publishes an annual salary survey of technology professionals. Robert Half also publishes its forecast of employment trends in technology and frequently lists computer networking and help desk/end-user support as two of the fields in IT where the demand for workers will continue to be strong during the next year.

 You can order a free copy of Robert Half's current *Salary Guide* and read recent press releases with information about employment trends in the IT industry at **www.rhic.com**.

Some organizations have formed partnerships with community colleges or vocational/technical schools and have developed training programs to prepare both new and current employees to meet the need for well-trained workers in support services.

How Organizations Provide a User Support Function

Computer user support (or simply user support) provides information and services to employees or clients to help them use computers more productively in their jobs or at home. Computer user support includes a broad spectrum of services provided to computer users to help them resolve problems that arise and to help them be more productive when they use computer technology. **Technical support** is a level of user support that focuses on high-level troubleshooting and problem solving. In some organizations, user support is called technical support, especially if the support staff consists of workers who are technicians or who have high-level technical skills. In other situations, user support may be called technical support for marketing or public relations purposes. Despite different naming conventions, what is important are the tasks user support performs in an organization.

NOTE The user support function is known by a variety of informal names and formal titles in various organizations. Common names for user support include:

User Support	Help Desk
Client Services	Client Support Services
Technical Support	Computer Assistance
Computer Help Hotline	Call Center
Hardware/Software/Network Support	Information Center
Support Services	Computer User Services

Organizations provide support to their employees or clients in a variety of ways. Figure 2-1 lists the most common methods of organizing the user support function, which are described in more detail in the following sections.

- Informal peer support

- User support combined with other responsibilities

- User support as a separate position or group

- Help desk support

- User support center operation

- User support as an Information Services (IS) responsibility

- User support outsourced to a vendor

Figure 2-1   Common ways that organizations provide a user support function

The strategy that an organization chooses to provide user support often depends on the organization's size, type, location, financial situation, and goals for computer support services, as well as the skill level and the support needs of employees and clients. In fact, an organization may use different support strategies at different times as the needs of its employees and clients change, and it may use more than one strategy at the same time.

INFORMAL PEER SUPPORT

Many small organizations and sometimes departments in larger organizations provide support for computer users informally. One or more employees, whose job titles usually have little to do directly with computers (for example, they are office managers, administrative specialists, or Accounting department heads), are generally recognized as *the* person to turn to when a computer user has a question. This form of support is called **peer support** because workers look to their colleagues, or peers, when they need computer assistance. For

2

example, a sales representative with a special interest in computer technology may become the "guru" for computer problems that arise in the Marketing department.

Employees who provide peer support may have little special training or preparation for their computer support role. They accept the responsibility perhaps because they have greater interest in or more experience with computers than other employees do, because they enjoy using their skills and having their expertise recognized, or simply because no one else is willing or able to provide help when it is needed.

 Microsoft has extended the strategy of peer support to the Web in the form of virtual user groups of peers who share common interests. To learn more about Microsoft user groups, go to **www.microsoft.com/communities/usergroups/ default.mspx**. Click the **Find a Community** link to see a list of peer user groups.

An informal network of peers who provide user support to their colleagues often precedes the formation of a more formal organizational structure. Informal peer support also occurs in schools and colleges, where students quickly learn who among their classmates is a good source of information and assistance. You may have provided informal peer support in a computer or training lab when the person next to you asked for your help in solving a hardware or software problem.

Because peer support is informal, communication with end users in this situation is often informal, as well. Information about computer technology is often exchanged during coffee breaks or in ad hoc meetings where interested parties discuss technology problems and issues of mutual concern.

User Support Combined with Other Responsibilities

The first step an organization often takes toward a formal computer support function may occur when some user support responsibilities are written into an existing employee's position description. This step may formalize a responsibility that existed informally for some time. The combination of user support with other responsibilities is a good way for very small organizations to meet the need for computer support when they cannot justify the cost of a full-time support employee. Employees who are assigned user support responsibilities in conjunction with other duties often see the designation as a positive career step because their expertise is recognized formally and perhaps rewarded financially. On the downside, these workers can become overloaded and stressed because computer support tasks can make significant demands on their time and can interrupt or compete with other assigned tasks. As the number of computers and users increases, or as an organization installs new software that may increase the number of problems to solve, employees for whom computer support is only a part-time responsibility may find it difficult to complete both their computer support tasks and their other responsibilities successfully.

Small organizations that sell computer hardware or software often provide informal client support during the early stages of product development and sales. When the volume of sales is small, client support may be assigned to a product development engineer or a programmer along with other duties. As sales increase, the need to provide client support becomes greater. At that point, the support function usually becomes more formal, in the form of full-time support positions or a user support group.

User Support as a Separate Position or Group

When organizations find that part-time, peer staff can no longer handle the volume or variety of requests for computer support, or that the hidden costs of peer support are growing, they have several options. One alternative is to devote a full-time position to provide support. Some organizations recognize that they have reached this point when a number of employees are engaged in informal peer support roles or when several employees have computer support as one of their official responsibilities. Organizations that devote a full-time position to provide user support seek the expertise of a support employee who has a greater breadth and depth of technical skills or improved communications skills.

A second alternative is to organize the part-time support employees into a **user support group**, a formal workgroup that is organized to provide computer support services. Depending on the needs of the organization, a user support group can consist of employees who provide support in addition to other job responsibilities. The advantage of using part-time support employees is their familiarity with the day-to-day operation of the organization. A user support group can also combine full- and part-time staff whose primary job function is to provide user support. The group may provide support either internally to employees or, in the case of a hardware or software vendor, to external clients. Although a dedicated computer support staff may provide a higher level of technical expertise, these specialists are usually less familiar with the organization's daily operation and the tasks that end users perform.

A third alternative open to companies that experience a growing demand for computer support is to outsource their support needs, a strategy that is discussed below.

Help Desk Support

When individual employees need assistance, they may turn to the staff of a user support group or they may contact a help desk facility. A **help desk** is organized to provide a single point of contact for users in need of technical support, whether they are internal employees or external clients. A help desk manages client problems and provides solutions-oriented support services. A help desk may be part of a larger user support group, or it may stand alone as the primary source of user support. In a large organization with many internal users, a help desk may be one of many support services offered. In a computer products vendor organization, a help desk may be the only support service provided to customers.

A help desk facility often includes one or more of these options:

- A physical location where internal employees or external clients can go when they have a question or problem, or want to request an office visit or a field service call

- A telephone number (sometimes called a **hotline**) that external clients or internal employees can call for assistance with a hardware or software product

- An e-mail address, Web site, or online **chat session** that employees or clients can contact for technical assistance

Regardless of its location or method of contact, the help desk staff attempts to resolve problems as soon as possible. If they cannot, they will ensure that someone else to whom they refer the problem resolves it. For example, the help desk may serve as an interface between an internal user with a problem and an external vendor who can solve the problem.

NOTE

The operation of a help desk is described in greater detail in Chapter 6. User support provided through a hotline or telephone help desk is actually part of a much larger industry. The call center industry includes incoming, outbound, and blended telephone centers. A user support hotline or telephone help desk is technically an incoming call center. Telemarketing and political surveys are examples of activities in outbound call centers. Blended call centers combine both incoming and outbound telephone operations.

User Support Center Operation

Another organizational model for support services is a user support center. A **user support center** (also called an **information center**) provides a wide range of services to an organization's computer users who are primarily internal users. These services can include consultation on computer purchases (it may even sell computer products to employees); a training center or training program to provide learning experiences, manuals, and other documentation on supported hardware and software products; and a help desk for information, troubleshooting, and assistance. The user support center in some organizations often provides facilities management and hardware repair services as well.

User Support as an IS Responsibility

Although some organizations view computer user support as a separate function, other organizations place this responsibility with the Information Services (IS) department. In this arrangement, either the technical staff in the IS department provides user support services directly or a specialized group within IS provides them.

Making technical support part of the IS department has advantages and disadvantages. On the one hand, because the IS department's primary responsibility is usually to design and develop application programs and operate the organization's mainframe systems and telecommunications networks, some organizations have found that the IS department is not a good location for the end-user support function. The IS staff is often busy working on its own priorities, and may have little time to devote to end-user problems. On the other hand, some organizations believe that all corporate computing activities should be centralized under one umbrella (the IS department) in order to provide a single point of contact for all mainframe, network, and personal computer users. Whether end-user support is organized separately or combined with other computer activities in an IS department depends on an organization's history, its experience with computer support, its organizational culture, and its users' needs. Either structure can be successful, and, similarly, either structure can fail to meet user expectations.

Ed Engelking, in a TechRepublic article at **techrepublic.com.com/5100-6269-5028769.html** (registration required), relates some perspectives from TechRepublic members on the issue of whether a help desk operation should be part of the Information Technology (IT) department, or separate from it.

User Support Outsourced to a Vendor

Outsourcing is another alternative for organizations that need to provide support services to their employees and clients. To **outsource** its user support services, an organization contracts with a vendor that specializes in user support functions to handle support incidents. Organizations can outsource support services for both internal and external users. For example, employees may contact a support provider via a dedicated telephone line or e-mail. Alternately, an organization's internal help desk operation may handle some incidents itself and refer difficult technical problems to an external support provider.

Outsourcing can be an attractive option for an organization that wants to control its costs or take advantage of expertise it does not have among its existing support staff.

To learn more about the advantages of outsourcing help desk and user support services, visit the Web site of EDO Technical Services Operations, a company that provides outsourced support for other organizations and vendors, at **www.compusupport.com**.

Several disadvantages of outsourcing computer user support include:

1. Outsourced support usually occurs by telephone or e-mail because on-site assistance can be prohibitively expensive and is rarely included in an outsourcing agreement.

2. Outsourced support costs are predictable, but not necessarily lower than internal support.

3. When an organization outsources support, it relies on a vendor's staff for an important organizational function. It does not develop its own in-house technical support expertise. As a result, little transfer of knowledge occurs from the support provider to internal staff about computer use issues.

4. When support is outsourced, the support staff rarely develops a personal relationship with an organization's end users. A personal relationship between end users and support staff often encourages users to report problems and request help.

Client Outsource is an example of a technical support vendor that reflects the trend for support providers to locate in India and Asian countries. Visit their Web site at **www.clientoutsource.com**.

2

No single correct organizational structure for end-user support works well in every situation. More often than not, an organization's approach to user support evolves over time, depending on its goals, resources, expertise, and needs.

USER SUPPORT SERVICES

User support centers in organizations provide a variety of services. The range of services provided depends on the goals of the organization, the specific needs of the employees or clients, and the resources the organization decides to devote to the support function. Figure 2-2 lists some common user support services.

- Staff a help desk, hotline, or chat session to provide information
- Provide technical troubleshooting assistance for hardware, software, and network problems
- Locate information to assist users
- Evaluate hardware, software, and network products
- Coordinate organization-wide support standards
- Perform needs assessment and provide purchase assistance for users
- Provide system installation assistance
- Provide training on computer systems and procedures
- Prepare documentation on computer use
- Perform computer facilities management tasks
- Assist users with software development projects

Figure 2-2   Common user support services

Figure 2-3 illustrates the variety of support services users need. User support, as a field within information technology, includes all of these functions. Not every organization provides all these services to its employees or clients, but organizations that provide user support offer at least some of these services to respond to employee or client needs.

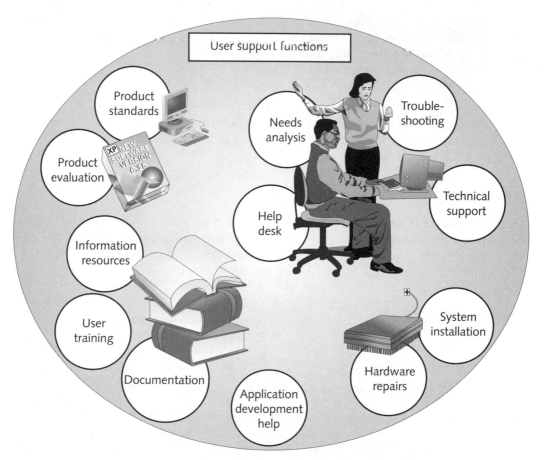

Figure 2-3   Common user support functions in organizations

Staff a Help Desk, Hotline, or Chat Session to Provide Information

Users who encounter problems with their computer system need a place to turn for information. A help desk, hotline, or chat session often meets this need for information. Providing information is one of the most common types of service provided by a user support organization. A help desk, hotline, or chat session can provide a variety of information services, such as:

- Respond to requests for product information
- Market and sell products and services
- Provide solutions to common problems
- Receive and log user complaints about product features
- Handle warranties and authorize product returns or exchanges

Chapter 3 describes the client service and communication skills that support staff need in a help desk environment. Chapter 6 describes the operation of a help desk from the perspective of a support center staff.

NOTE

2

Provide Technical Troubleshooting Assistance

Although a help desk, hotline, or chat session can handle common user problems and questions, some problems fall outside the help desk's boundaries. Most organizations recognize the need for a level of technical troubleshooting that has the expertise to resolve intractable problems that occur. These problems can include hardware diagnosis, repairs, or upgrades, fixes or workarounds for difficult applications software problems, and trouble-shooting network crashes or poor performance. Solutions to technical problems often require a level of support staff expertise that exceeds what a help desk or hotline can provide.

Chapter 4 describes some strategies for troubleshooting difficult technical problems. Chapter 5 provides examples of common user support problems.

NOTE

Locate Information to Assist Users

A challenge that continually confronts user support staff is the need to locate information to resolve a user's question or problem. Although organizations provide their employees with computers and software, they often do not supply manuals or other useful materials. In other cases, manuals get misplaced, lost, or thrown away by end users, or become obsolete. Users can use online help, which is sometimes excellent in commercial software products. But online help is often neither in-depth nor technical enough to help users solve every problem, especially difficult ones. And sometimes vendor documentation is just not very good. For their information needs, users often turn to the support staff. Therefore, the ability to access, search for, locate, and work with information is a critical skill for user support staff members. Information can exist in a variety of locations: printed manuals from vendors, trade and text books, online help, CD-ROM databases, Internet Web sites, interactive fax services, and automated telephone voice-response units. User support workers need to understand the characteristics of each of these information resources and be able to use them effectively. For example, the ability to ask the right question is an important skill needed to locate information quickly.

Several chapters in this text contain pointers to information resources that user support staff have found helpful. Appendix 1 suggests other information you may want to have in your support toolkit.

NOTE

Evaluate Hardware, Software, and Network Products

Most organizations are constantly on the lookout for new technologies that will help their employees enhance productivity. Consequently, the user support center must continually research, compare, and evaluate new technology products and services, including hardware, software, and network products, against existing products. The user support staff must find answers to such questions as:

- Will a new product make employees more productive?
- Will a specific product meet employee needs better than another product?
- Should some or all users upgrade from software version 2000 to version 2003? Or wait until version 2005 or later?
- What features are important to evaluate in the purchase of a new computer?
- Will a particular system or software package be cost-effective?

Individual employees do not always have the information and expertise they need to make these decisions wisely. When employees make individual purchasing decisions, organizations can encounter compatibility, cost, usability, and productivity issues that can be difficult to resolve. For example, employees in the Accounting department of a small manufacturing organization may use the latest version of QuickBooks to prepare company financial statements. The Production department in the same company may use an older version of the QuattroPro spreadsheet to prepare and monitor its budgets. Consequently, the Production department cannot use the Accounting department's data files unless Accounting personnel remember to save QuickBooks files in a format that is compatible with the older version of QuattroPro. This kind of software compatibility problem can cause wasted time, possibly require manual reentry of data, and affect employee productivity. The evaluation of new hardware and software products is an important, challenging, and ongoing task for user support staffs.

Chapter 8 describes some tools to help support staffs with product evaluation tasks.

NOTE

Coordinate Organization-wide Support Standards

A task closely related to product evaluation is the establishment of support standards. **Support standards** are lists of computer products that an organization allows its employees to use and that it will support. Support standards limit the hardware, software, and network products that a support staff must be able to support. Therefore, standards reduce support costs. Support standards are important because it is impossible for an organization to support every hardware configuration marketed by all hardware vendors or all software packages. To arrive at a set of standards, the user support center evaluates competing products and often consults with users and management.

2

Chapter 8 describes the role of support standards in organizations.

Perform Needs Assessment and Provide Purchase Assistance for Users

In addition to evaluating computer products and establishing support standards, the support center staff tries to match supported products with the needs of each user. Occasionally the match between a user's needs and specific products is obvious. In other cases, support staff may perform a user **needs analysis** (or needs assessment), which is an investigation to determine the features and configuration of hardware and software (from among those supported) that will best match a user's specific needs. Based on the needs analysis, the support staff then can recommend the purchase or upgrade of a system to improve the user's productivity. Most support centers that offer this service also assist users with the paperwork required to purchase a system, such as justifying the purchase, placing an order, and processing the paperwork to pay for the system.

Chapter 9 describes how to perform a needs analysis for an end user.

Provide System Installation Assistance

Once an organization or individual user has purchased a system or upgrade, the support center may offer to unpack, set up, install, and configure the system for an end user. The purpose of this service is efficiency: the support center staff has the tools and expertise to make sure the installation is done correctly and can identify and solve many common installation problems that might frustrate an inexperienced user. Where applicable, the support staff can ensure that the appropriate network software is installed and configured to connect a computer to the organization's network. They can also install peripheral devices, such as printers and scanners, and install and configure driver software for these devices. Some end users might be able to perform these tasks, but user support staff members can often get the work done faster and with fewer errors because they tend to have more experience with system installations than end users do.

Chapter 10 describes the system installation process.

Provide Training on Computer Systems and Procedures

Users who have new hardware or software, or new job responsibilities, may require training to use their new or upgraded system effectively, or to use their existing system more efficiently. With proper training, users can become productive more rapidly than if they learn by trial and error. User support centers in many organizations provide end-user training. The support center may have periodic group training sessions, provide one-on-one training, or suggest ways to learn a new system that match a user's personal learning needs and style. Training programs can include basic, introductory classes to help users get started quickly with a new system or with new software. Training can also provide experienced users with the knowledge and skills they need to use advanced features of hardware and software.

Chapter 11 provides guidelines on how to prepare effective user training materials and conduct training sessions.

Prepare Documentation on Computer Use

Although end-user training is a necessary and often efficient way to teach computer users how to use a computer system, documentation is equally important. Whereas a training session is generally a one-time event, documentation is always available to answer questions or to remind users how to perform a task they may perform only occasionally.

Documentation includes introductory "getting started" manuals for new users, explanations of organizational computer use procedures and guidelines, as well as "how to" tutorials and reference manuals on specific software products. It also includes online documentation in the form of help files, answers to frequently asked questions (FAQs), and e-mail responses to remote users.

Chapter 12 provides pointers on how to write documentation and other materials targeted to end users.

Perform Computer Facilities Management Tasks

Large, mainframe computer installations often employ a professional staff of computer operators; hardware, software and network maintenance engineers; and facilities managers who ensure that the computer systems run on a daily basis. In a distributed PC environment, the need to keep the computers operational is just as great. To accomplish this goal, user support centers often perform **computer facilities management** tasks such as network security, media backups, virus detection and prevention, ergonomic analyses, supplies management, preventive maintenance and repairs on hardware and peripherals, and other related tasks.

Chapter 13 describes some facilities management challenges, resources, and tools in an end-user environment.

2

Assist Users with Software Development Projects

Most user support centers do not provide software development or programming as part of their regular services to users. However, in some organizations, the support center staff may *help* users develop software applications to solve specific problems or meet specialized requirements for information. For example, support staff may advise users on the most effective way to program a difficult task in a spreadsheet.

Software development has long been considered the domain of the IS department. However, with today's powerful application development tools, such as scripting languages, spreadsheets, database management packages, and Web-page development tools, end users often can develop applications independent of the IS department. But when end users encounter problems during the development process, they frequently turn to the support staff for assistance.

Supporting users by developing applications software can be a potential source of conflict between the IS department staff and the support center staff. User-developed applications may not include compatibility features, design standards, documentation, security, and other capabilities and controls that the IS department feels are necessary in a well-designed application. While software development is probably the least common service provided by user support centers, it is a service some support centers provide.

Because software development is an extensive topic, no chapter in this book is devoted specifically to software development tasks for support staffs. Interested readers should consult books dedicated to this topic, such as:

- Baldwin and Paradice, *Applications Development in Access 2000*, Course Technology, 2000.

- Rob and Semaan, *Databases: Design, Development & Deployment Using Microsoft Access, 2nd edition*, Irwin McGraw-Hill, 2002.

- Birnbaum, *Microsoft Excel VBA Professional Projects*, Course Technology, 2003.

Although the missions of user support centers differ considerably, the tasks they perform define their service profile in an organization. Whereas most support centers provide help desk services and troubleshooting assistance, a smaller percentage provide documentation or product training. Few provide applications development assistance. A job applicant for a position in a support center should ask about the amount of emphasis placed on various user support tasks to obtain an accurate picture of the user support role in a particular organization.

DAVE CALLAGHAN
ASSOCIATE VICE PRESIDENT FOR INFORMATION TECHNOLOGY
COURSE TECHNOLOGY (PUBLISHER)
BOSTON, MASSACHUSETTS
WWW.COURSE.COM

The internal support function at Course Technology (CT) is part of the IT department, and since the company's creation in 1989 has evolved from a technical support focus to a customer support focus. We now think of CT employees as clients, and we act as consultants to them. Our goal is to produce 100% client satisfaction.

Organization. We have three workstation support specialists and a manager, who support 260 employees. In the past, employees experiencing hardware or software problems would call one of these specialists for help. This worked in many cases, but not all. If a specialist was away from his or her desk, on the phone, or on vacation, the client didn't know when the problem would be solved. We now use a help desk at our corporate parent's facility to take calls, enter them in our call tracking system, and provide first line support. Only those problems that cannot be handled are passed off, via problem queues, to the CT help desk. The help desk manager constantly monitors the problem queue and assigns the tasks to the individual technicians based on expertise and availability. This allows individual technicians uninterrupted time to work on big projects or to improve their knowledge base through study.

Tasks. PC purchases are done in bulk with a yearly standard model for all employees. Our support specialists prepare master "ghost" images of a standard hard drive configuration that are heavily tested. They spend a significant amount of time upgrading users to new machines and preparing machines for "new hires." They also help clients troubleshoot and solve problems, and train users on things like e-mail, the network, and dial-in access. Specialists sometimes prepare documentation. For example, if there is a new virus going around the office, a specialist will write instructions on how to identify and get rid of it, and will circulate the instructions to our clients. Their facilities management responsibilities include managing user accounts on servers, as well as file backup and recovery tasks. For a while, one support specialist held regular office hours to supplement on-call support by offering one-on-one help with standard applications or other issues.

We also have three business analysts who help individuals and departments with specialized software needs. Most applications they develop are custom database solutions. They also do group training.

Standards. We have company standards for hardware and software products, and we aim to maintain them. But having strict policies can sometimes conflict with getting the job done. Sometimes we find we have to be flexible in order to meet client requirements.

POSITION DESCRIPTIONS FOR USER SUPPORT STAFF MEMBERS

2

Positions in the user support industry often include some combination of the tasks outlined in the previous section. Position descriptions reflect how an organization structures its user support function. For example, an organization with a full-fledged support center is more likely to include in a user support position description the ability to analyze employee computer needs and recommend hardware and software purchases. On the other hand, an organization that relies primarily on part-time support positions is much less likely to expect applicants to assess user needs or to be able to train end users. Similarly, an organization that provides a hotline service to external clients often does not expect its staff members to be able to provide facilities management or a wide variety of other support services to clients.

To understand more about the specific job of a user support center staff member, let's look in detail at three position descriptions of actual support positions. The first position description, shown in Figure 2-4, describes the duties and responsibilities of an end user support analyst at Calpine Corporation, an electric utility in California. The position is part of an Information Services group at Calpine, called Management Information Systems (MIS). The description provides a good picture of the wide range of activities you might encounter in user support positions in today's job market. If you are a prospective user support center employee, you should know that managers would probably look for these kinds of capabilities.

The second user support position description, shown in Figure 2-5, is from Stream International, a national support services vendor that provides a range of information services to other organizations, including contract end-user support. Organizations that outsource their support function would consider a vendor like Stream International. For example, when Microsoft unveils a new software product and expects a large volume of support calls, it may contract with Stream to augment its own support staff. The position description describes a support services representative. Employees in these positions primarily provide telephone support to client organizations that have purchased Stream's help desk support services. Compare the responsibilities in this position, which is primarily a telephone support position, with those listed in the Calpine position, which primarily provides on-site support to internal employees.

The third position description represents a recent trend in the user support industry: a position that combines network support with user support. The position description, shown in Figure 2-6, is for a network technical support specialist at St. Petersburg Junior College.

Although many of the job duties in the network technical support specialist position description are similar to those of other user support positions, some of the duties are more like those you would expect to find in a position description for a network administrator. This example emphasizes the wide variety of tasks that user support specialists may be expected to perform, depending on the specific needs of the organization in which the support position is located.

Calpine Corporation
Job Description

Position: Desktop Support Technician

Position Summary: Provide technical support and service to include computing tools, installations, upgrades, support, maintenance, and issue resolution for Calpine's end-user community, which encompasses a complex, multi-platform, 7x24 environment; and establish and maintain lines of communication with end users to ensure continuity of their computer systems and peripheral devices.

Essential Duties and Responsibilities:

1. Under direct supervision, provide level one and two workstation technical support to company's end users, including computer tools, installations, upgrades, maintenance, and issue resolution; and ensure that users have appropriate PC hardware, software and network connectivity; includes service to executives, senior management, and other critical divisions.

2. Work closely with the help desk to improve the level of support and expertise within that group through feedback and documentation; document standard software installation and configuration procedures; troubleshoot and repair workstation and peripheral hardware within service levels; maintain and track computer asset information; and perform computer device moves, adds, and change (MACs) service order requests.

3. Establish and maintain effective lines of communication with end-user community to ensure continuity of company's computer systems.

4. Collaborate with and inform management of critical issues and status of ongoing projects, and work effectively towards team and corporate goals.

5. Provide highly responsive service, and stay current with appropriate technologies, support processes, new releases, and upgrades; assist with server, network, and voice issues at the direction of the IS teams directly responsible for support, especially at remote locations.

6. Assist in establishing "best practices" policies and procedures ensuring efficient and highly responsive service and issues resolution; and assist in identifying, diagnosing, recording, dispatching, coordinating, resolving, and escalating issues in accordance with service level agreements.

7. Assist in researching, recommending and implementing new technologies, solutions, and features to improve performance and reliability of services and systems.

8. Assist in computer asset refreshes and in the disposal process of retired equipment.

Figure 2-4   Position description for desktop support analyst at Calpine Corporation

Knowledge, Skills, and Abilities

One way to better understand the requirements for a specific position is to analyze them in terms of **KSAs**, the knowledge, skills, and abilities needed to perform the job. Human Resources personnel often analyze a position description and prepare a check list of KSAs to screen applicants.

Knowledge.   Each position includes a description of what an employee needs to know in order to do the job. The knowledge component may be stated in terms of a specific number of years of education, a degree in a specified field, or a list of topics an employee is expected to know.

2

Position: *Support Services Representative*

- Spend most of your day on the phone helping customers solve a wide variety of technical problems and/or filling orders for products and offering suggestions that provide a more complete solution to their needs—some routine and straightforward, some complex and challenging.
- Work as part of a highly trained team of technical professionals--interesting people from diverse backgrounds as unique as you are.
- Regularly access a state-of-the-art knowledge management database to research technical problems, offer advice to customers, and help sell new products.
- Work in a friendly, fast-paced environment where personal initiative is rewarded.
- Be on the phone 7 hours a day and typically handle between 10 and 40 calls per day, depending on the products you support and the type of solutions you provide.
- Have access to a technical specialist who can help you work through especially difficult problems, or sales trainers who can help you match products to solutions.
- Need to be at work on time, all the time, so that you're available when our customers call for help or products.
- Have to be well-organized and thorough in order to manage important details such as inputting customer data or completing sales orders.
- Be expected to meet high performance standards every day.
- Become an expert in the product that you support, learn valuable technical knowledge, problem-solving skills, and state-of-the-art contact center tools.
- Always be expected to provide world class customer service quickly and efficiently.

Figure 2-5   Position description for support services representative at Stream International

St. Petersburg College

POSITION DESCRIPTION

POSITION TITLE: **Network Technical Support Specialist**

DEPARTMENT: **Academic Computer Support**

BASIC FUNCTION:

Provides technical network expertise for the instructional labs, office computers, printers, network electronics, and other network devices. Cooperates with other technical staff in installing, maintaining, and troubleshooting technical equipment. The position is primarily assigned to work at one or two of the operating sites of the college.

RESPONSIBILITIES:

- Provides the first line of on-site network technical support to resolve network-layer issues related to passive and active network hardware, servers, IP address problems, network connection problems, and network-centered system configuration issues.
- Works as the direct information conduit and liaison between the end users and the Administrative Information Systems managers responsible for centrally managed network-centric services like e-mail, student registration and course management systems, the finance system, Web-based systems, the college-wide area network, and other information management systems.
- Works in cooperation with the site computer support specialist to install, maintain, and troubleshoot end-user computers, printers, scanners, and other network devices.
- Assists in the design of network systems.
- Performs preventative maintenance on network systems.
- Researches network-related solutions to technical and business process problems.
- Performs related duties as required.

Figure 2-6   Position description for network technical support specialist at St. Petersburg College

Examples of knowledge required for the end user support analyst position listed in Figure 2-4 include:

- Knowledge of basic computer operation
- Knowledge of applications software

Skills. Each position requires specific job skills or tasks that a support specialist must be able to perform well. User support positions may require advanced skills in one or more areas. In general, a skill is a task that a support specialist can perform better (at a higher level of effectiveness or efficiency) with practice and experience.

Examples of skills required for the end user support analyst position shown in Figure 2-4 include:

- Skill in troubleshooting hardware and software problems
- Skill in configuring desktop computers to optimize performance

Abilities. Each position requires special tasks that a support specialist must be able to perform. Abilities are functions that an applicant can either do or not do. For example, some positions may specify abilities such as being able to lift 50-pound boxes or communicate in Spanish. Other abilities are based on combinations of knowledge and skills that help a support specialist perform a specific task.

Examples of abilities required for the end user support analyst position shown in Figure 2-4 include:

- Ability to work as a member of a team
- Ability to write documentation

If you have difficulty with the precise difference between skills and abilities, don't worry. People often use the terms interchangeably.

If you want to learn more about the KSAs required for entry-level positions for computer support specialists, visit America's Career InfoNet Web site at **www.acinet.org/acinet/ksas1.asp?soccode=151041&stfips=41**. The Web site includes a short video on help desk technicians (requires RealOne Player to view, which is a free download). You can also get information on the employment outlook and typical wages for computer support specialists for your state at this site.

How does one person ever learn to do all the tasks described in these position descriptions? Few employees in an entry-level position start on day one with all the knowledge, skills, and abilities they need to perform every task listed in the job description. Most user support positions include a training program before a support employee ever answers an actual telephone call or installs and configures a piece of network hardware. Most user support positions also include a significant amount of continuing education or on-the-job learning. So don't get discouraged if you can't do everything in these job descriptions today.

To assess some of your skills with software tools, you can try a simple assessment activity at the ACE Training Web site, **www.ace.co.nz/tools/ skills/index.asp** (registration is required, but the skill assessment is a free service).

If you compare the services offered by user support centers and the job duties in the position descriptions with the table of contents, you will find that this book is organized around these job duties—many of the primary tasks of a support staff member are described in this book. Chapters are devoted to each of the major topics to expose you to the many and varied responsibilities that are required of user support staff in today's job market.

ALTERNATIVE CAREER PATHS FOR USER SUPPORT WORKERS

Many user support workers select this field as an entry into other, more advanced positions. Into which careers can an entry-level position in user support lead?

Programmer/Developer

Some user support workers who are technically oriented want to work toward a position as a computer programmer or Web applications developer. Workers in these positions write code (instructions) in a computer language such as C++, Java, or Visual Basic, or in a scripting language such as JavaScript, VBScript, Perl, or PHP. Advancement into a programmer/developer position usually requires coursework in programming languages and a four-year degree.

Network Technician

Another career path for user support workers is into network technical positions. These positions often involve tasks such as installing and configuring network servers and client systems, network cabling and troubleshooting, performance analysis and configuration, facilities management, and related tasks. Although many user support workers perform simple network administration and monitoring tasks, a career as a network technical support worker usually requires a two- or four-year degree that specializes in advanced network topics.

Web Site Maintainer

A Web site maintainer is a worker who uses software packages, such as Dreamweaver, FrontPage, GoLive, or CityMax, to build and maintain Web sites. These positions are less technically demanding than Web applications developers described above, but require someone who has a good eye for visually pleasing layouts and understands Web navigational tools to make Web sites usable. A Web site maintainer can take coursework or read self-teaching books on site design and on the software tools required to perform these tasks.

Support Management

End-user support workers who enjoy the challenge of user support can aspire to a lead worker or supervisory position in a support group. These workers often plan and schedule the work of other support employees as well as prepare budgets, hire and evaluate support staff, and work with user departments or groups to better understand their support needs. Many colleges and vocational/technical schools offer courses aimed at workers who want to become supervisors or managers. Courses that are designed for beginning supervisors or managers of technical and professional employees are especially useful for those who aspire to a support management position.

Project Management

A career path that many entry-level support workers do not consider, but perhaps should, is project management. Information Technology projects in both business and government often require leaders who can successfully manage other workers, as well as budgets, schedules, and deadlines.

NOTE Chapter 7 describes some project management tools you should learn about if you have an interest in project management as a career. Some schools and colleges offer coursework on project management and how to use project management software tools.

Trainer and Technical Writer

Many entry-level support positions include some percentage of time devoted to end-user training and technical writing, which are described in detail in Chapters 11 and 12. Support employees who enjoy these tasks may want to specialize in either of these areas. A full-time trainer designs, prepares, presents, and evaluates training materials not only for computer users, but also for other employees. Common training topics include company orientations for new employees, introductory supervisory training, time and project management, stress management, conflict resolution, and other subjects. A full-time technical writer designs, writes, and edits a variety of technical documentation, such as brochures, newsletters, user's guides, management reports, Web-based materials, and other printed and online documents. A support employee who is interested in training as a career should take some "train-the-trainer" courses or courses in education. Those who aspire to technical writing careers can take additional preparatory coursework in a college or vocational/technical school.

Security Specialist

A growing job category after the attacks on the United States on September 11, 2001 is computer security specialist. Workers in these positions develop and implement plans to protect computer systems and networks from various sources of threat that could result in destroyed, lost, or stolen information. These positions generally require additional study and specialization beyond a basic user support degree.

To learn more about the job duties, knowledge, skills, and abilities associated with the jobs described in this chapter, visit the Occupational Information Network (O*NET) Web page at **online.onetcenter.org/gen_search_page**. Enter a keyword from the list below:

Job Category	O*NET Keyword
User support specialist	Computer support specialist
Network support specialist	Network administrator
Computer security specialist	Computer security specialist
Computer programmer	Computer programmer
Trainer	Training specialist
Technical writer	Technical writer
Project manager	Information system manager
Network technical support specialist	Network analyst

CHAPTER SUMMARY

- End users who are not computer professionals often need help when they encounter problems with their computer system. Help can be organized in several ways, including peer support from a colleague, support from a user support group, a help desk/hotline/ chat session operation, a user support center, directly from the technical staff in the Information Services department, or from a vendor who contracts to provide support services.

- Users need a variety of support services, depending on how they use their computers and their level of expertise. User support centers frequently provide help that includes: operating a help desk, hotline, or chat session; troubleshooting difficult problems; locating information; evaluating new hardware, software, and network products; establishing organization-wide product support standards; analyzing and assessing user needs; installing systems; training users; writing user documentation; managing computer facilities; and assisting with software development projects.

- The job descriptions for support staff members reflect the variety of services a support center offers. Many jobs require a combination of knowledge, skills, and abilities in hardware (microcomputers and mainframes), operating systems, applications software, networks, interpersonal communications, problem solving and analysis, and supervision or leadership.

Key Terms

chat session — A Web-based interactive service that allows two or more users who are both online to communicate by alternately typing and viewing messages; also called instant messaging.

computer facilities management — Support services to help users with information and questions about security, media backups, viruses, ergonomics, purchase of supplies, preventive maintenance, and other tasks required to keep a computer system operational.

computer user support — A job function or department in an organization that provides information and services to employees or clients to help them use computers more productively in their jobs or at home.

help desk — A single point of contact for users in need of technical support, whether employees or external clients; may provide information and problem-solving services face-to-face, by telephone, by e-mail, or in an online chat session.

hotline — A telephone number that an internal or external user can call to reach a help desk service.

information center — An older name for a user support center.

KSAs — The knowledge, skills, and abilities required to perform a job.

needs analysis — An investigation to determine the features and configuration of hardware and software that will best match a user's specific needs; also called needs assessment.

outsource — An arrangement or agreement in which an organization contracts with a vendor that specializes in user support functions to handle support incidents for internal and external users.

peer support — An informal level of user support whereby colleagues in an organization or department exchange information and provide assistance about computer use and problems encountered.

support standards — A list of computer products that an organization allows its employees to use and that it will support; product support standards limit the hardware, software, and network components that a staff supports in order to reduce support costs.

technical support — A level of user support that focuses on high-level troubleshooting and problem solving; whereas computer user support deals with a broad spectrum of support issues, technical support deals with the more complex and difficult problems that users encounter.

user support center — A group or department in an organization that provides a wide range of services to an organization's computer users who are primarily internal; services may include a help desk, consulting on product purchases, training, documentation, and facilities management.

user support group — A formal workgroup that is organized to provide computer user support services.

CHECK YOUR UNDERSTANDING

1. True or False? Small companies often meet their need for computer support by combining user support with another position.

2. True or False? A help desk provides a single point of contact for computer users in need of support.

3. Help desk services can be provided by _____ .

   a. a physical location where users can get help

   b. a telephone hotline number users can call for help

   c. an e-mail address where users can send a message for help

   d. any of the above

4. Which of the following statements is an advantage to outsourcing as a way to provide user support?

   a. Outsourcing is a low-cost support method.

   b. Outsourcing develops in-house support expertise.

   c. Outsourcing takes advantage of expertise a company may not have.

   d. Outsourcing provides on-site assistance

5. True or False? The purpose of product standards is to limit the hardware and software configurations a support staff must support and therefore reduce support costs.

6. The process of matching a user's needs with supported computer products is called a(n) _____ .

7. In order to make effective use of a new or upgraded computer system, a user may require _____ .

   a. user training

   b. programming

   c. facilities management

   d. a computer operator

8. _____ are lists of approved and recommended computer products that an organization is committed to support.

9. True or False? End users do not encounter the same kinds of security, media backup, preventive maintenance, and ergonomic problems that are common in mainframe computer facilities.

10. Which of the following responsibilities would you least expect to find in a position description for a user support specialist?

   a. troubleshoots problems

   b. recommends product standards

   c. operates a mainframe computer

   d. installs hardware and software

11. Printed or online tutorial or reference materials for computer users is called _____ .

12. True or False? The ability to search for, locate, access, and work with information is an important job skill for user support staff members.

13. What you need to know or be able to do to perform in a job is called _____ .

14. A Web-based communication between two Internet users who are online at the same time and alternately type and view messages is called _____ .

   a. peer support

   b. e-mail

   c. hotline

   d. chat session

Discussion Questions

1. Do you agree or disagree with the following statement: "Facilities management is more of a concern with large mainframe computer systems than in an end-user computing environment." Explain your position.

2. Which is more important to a user support staff member, the ability to solve difficult technical problems or the ability to communicate with a difficult user? Why?

3. How do you think the knowledge, skills, and abilities needed for telephone support are different from the KSAs needed to provide e-mail or chat session support? Compare these to the KSAs needed for face-to-face support.

Hands-On Projects

Project 2-1

Explore an organization's user support services. Find the user support function at the organization where you work, the school you attend, or another organization. Learn how its user support is organized and where the support function is located within the larger organization, and get a list of the services it provides. If possible, ask two computer users whether they feel the user support function is responsive to their needs. Write a summary of your findings.

Project 2-2

Evaluate user support position descriptions in your organization. Locate one or more position descriptions for user support staff members at your organization or your school. How do the duties and responsibilities compare with those described in this chapter? What are some similarities? What are some differences?

Project 2-3

Evaluate user support position descriptions in government and national databases. Use the Internet to locate position descriptions for user support jobs in government and other organizations. ind information for positions in your state government or local employment area. Some Internet sites you could visit are listed in Table 2-1. How do the duties and responsibilities you found compare with those described in this chapter? What are some similarities? What are some differences?

Table 2-1   Internet sites with information about user support positions

URL	Description
hr.dop.wa.gov/lib/hrdr/specs/00000/03271.htm	State of Washington job description for an information technology systems specialist
www.ci.des-moines.ia.us/departments/HR/Job%20Descriptions/ User%20Support%20Technician.htm	City of Des Moines, Iowa, job description for a user support technician
www.computerjobs.com Click the link for a region in which you are interested, and then click the **Help Desk** link.	IT employment Web site
www.JustHelpDeskJobs.com Select the geographic area in which you are interested.	Site specializes in user support positions
jobsearch.monster.com Click a location and/or job category to narrow the search, and/or type a phrase such as "help desk" in the Enter Key Words text box; then click the **Get Results** button. You'll need to create an account to access the site.	Global online network for careers
www.dice.com Click in the Quick Job Search box, enter a keyword, such as "help desk" or "computer support," then click the **Search** button.	Job search Web site for computer professionals

Project 2-4

Evaluate user support positions. Select a position description for a user support staff in this chapter or one you have found. Answer the following questions:

1. Would you classify the job described in the position description as primarily a technical position or a people-oriented position? Why?

2. Do you think the position description requires a person who is a specialist (one with depth of knowledge) or a generalist (one with breadth of knowledge)? Why?

3. What personal qualities do you think would be necessary for someone to be successful in the position?

If you are a member of a project group, meet with the other members and discuss your answers to these questions. Write a one-page summary of your conclusions.

Project 2-5

Maximize power users. Sometimes people use the term "power user" to describe users who have extensive experience, excellent breadth and depth of knowledge, and well-developed skills. Assemble a team of at least three classmates or coworkers, and discuss the following questions:

1. What are some characteristics of a power user? Be as specific as possible.

2. Are you a power user? Is anyone in your group?

3. Is it necessary to be a power user, according to you or your group's consensus definition, in order to be a user support agent?

4. How can an organization make maximum use of a power user to assist with support functions within a department?

Write a one-page summary of your conclusions.

Project 2-6

Compare your KSAs to a user support position. The position description in Figure 2-7 is an example of a user support position in a government agency. List the knowledge, skills, and abilities (KSAs) you would need to perform the duties in the position description. Don't worry too much about the differences between skills and abilities. Compare your list of KSAs with three classmates or coworkers. Where do you agree and disagree? How do the KSAs you listed correspond to courses you are taking now or have taken in the past? Which additional courses could you take to satisfy some of the KSAs on your list?

2

State of Oregon
DEPARTMENT OF ADMINISTRATIVE SERVICES
Human Resource Services Division

INFORMATION SYSTEMS SPECIALIST 1

The ISS 1 provides support in operating, maintaining and installing systems and helps staff use the systems.

This is an entry-level position.

The ISS 1 has daily contact with system users to answer questions, solve problems and clarify instructions and with other Information Systems support staff for assistance with solving problems and to ensure conformity of methods and practices.

The ISS 1 works within well-defined guidelines and receives supervision from a supervisor or team leader. Work is spot-checked for accuracy and completed assignments reviewed for conformance with timelines, production standards and policies and procedures.

Processing standards and procedure manuals provide guidelines to ensure conformity of operations. Technical manuals are used for references and assistance is readily available from other IS staff or vendors for solving non-routine problems and clarifying instructions on new procedures or assignments.

1. Customer Assistance (help, use and fix)
Answers common user questions from internal employees about Software, Hardware, Communications or Data. Identifies problem by asking established questions and using basic diagnostics. Provides operational assistance. Follows established processes to fix problems or coordinates solutions with other staff resources. Tracks and reports problems. May test new features. Provides one-on-one operational training to users.

2. Operations (day-to-day)
Tasks in this function relate to keeping the computer operations going on a day-to-day basis. This includes installation, performance monitoring, access, security, backups, scheduling, inventory management and processing orders.

Uses precedents and basic troubleshooting techniques and does installations following established instructions. Examples of typical installations at this level include installing established software with limited impact to other software or simple hardware memory upgrades. Monitors daily performance of communications system, software or database and identifies and reports performance problems and issues.

Figure 2-7 Position description for information systems specialist in Oregon

To compare your personal skills with those in some basic job categories, visit the Occupational Information Network (O*NET) Web site at **online. onetcenter.org/gen_skills_page**. Check the skills you have or are working to build in the list of skills and learn which job categories best match your skills. Is Computer Support Specialist on your list? Click the 'Skills Matched' column to learn why or why not.

Project 2-7

List KSAs for advertised positions. Find two ads in the Help Wanted section of a city newspaper (the Sunday edition usually carries the most Help Wanted ads) or on a Web site such as **www.monster.com**, **www.dice.com**, or **www.computerjobs.com**. Locate one for a position that supports internal users in an organization and one for a position that supports clients of a hardware or software vendor. For each ad, list the knowledge, skills, and abilities (KSAs) the position requires. At the end of your lists, discuss whether the KSAs for an internal and external support position are different, and if so, how.

Project 2-8

Interview a user support staff member. Find an organization that has a user support or help desk staff (such as one at your workplace or school), and interview a member of the staff. Ask the staff member if he or she will share the position description for his or her position with you. Find out the answers to the following questions:

1. How does his or her position description and job duties compare with those in this chapter?

2. Does he or she actually perform tasks that are not listed in the official position description?

3. What percentage of his or her time is spent on each job duty in the position description?

4. How has his or her job duties changed in the last couple of years?

Write a one-page summary of what you learned from the interview.

Case Projects

1. Training Facility Problems at Cascade University

Mary Ann Lacy is the coordinator of Cascade University's computer training facility. The facility offers courses in computer applications software to Cascade's regular students and faculty, and local organizations that send their employees to Cascade's Continuing Education Division to upgrade their computer skills.

The computer training facility consists of two rooms: a training facility where scheduled classes are conducted and an open lab facility where students can work on assignments outside of class time. The entire training facility is open from 8 A.M. to 5 P.M., Monday through Friday. Each room is equipped with 24 Pentium 4 computer systems. Mary Ann operates a Windows 2003 server so that students can access software on the network, store data files on the server, and access e-mail and the Internet. She also teaches some of the continuing education classes in the training facility. Cascade University's computer faculty members teach in the training facility when it is not in use for continuing education classes.

2

Mary Ann recently conducted a user satisfaction survey to learn how Cascade students, faculty, and continuing education students rated the entire training facility. She was pleased that users were very satisfied with the equipment because she tries to keep the systems properly maintained and gets units repaired as soon as a problem arises. The Electronics Shop at Cascade maintains the hardware. The users also expressed satisfaction with the operation of the network server and with the selection of software that is available to them. However, Mary Ann was less pleased about some of the comments users wrote on their survey forms. Here is a sample of some comments she was willing to share:

"I am an advanced user of the open lab. Some of the inexperienced students have discovered that I know quite a bit about the hardware and the network. They ask me a lot of questions. I don't mind answering them, but when I have a class assignment due, I can't take time out to help everyone who has a question. After a while, some of the questions get pretty repetitious."

"The open lab runs smoothly when the coordinator is in the room. But when she is next door teaching a class in the training facility, there is no one to ask for help. I feel badly when students have to interrupt her training session to report a problem like a server crash or even to get a new ink cartridge put in the printer."

"The software manuals are in a locked cabinet. When I need one, I have to track down Mary Ann to get the key. Why can't the documentation cabinet be left unlocked?"

"Last year, there was seldom a wait to get a computer in the open lab. This year, with more classes in the training facility, the wait is longer. It would be nice if the lab were open more than 8 to 5. Some evening and weekend hours would be great."

Mary Ann has decided to ask a small group of training facility users, consisting of students, faculty, and continuing education students, to meet to discuss the responses to her survey. If you were a member of the group, what advice would you give Mary Ann that would address the concerns described about the operation of the training facility? What support issues have users raised? What are some other ways Mary Ann could address these issues? Are some alternatives more expensive than others?

2. Employment Trends in the User Support Field

CASE PROJECTS

Research the current employment trends in the user support and help desk industry. Look for both current employment statistics and forecasts of the future need for workers with the job titles described in this chapter. Also, see if you can locate employment statistics and outlook for your local area, region or state. Write a report on your findings.

Here are a few Web resources that contain current information as of the publication date of this book. Can you find more up-to-date information?

- **www.microsoft.com/traincert/training/careers/trends.asp**
- **www.itaa.org/workforce/studies/03execsumm.pdf** (requires Acrobat Reader)
- **www.dol.gov/wb/factsheets/hitech02.htm**
- **www.computerworld.com/careertopics/careers/labor**
- **biz.yahoo.com/prnews/030827/sfw014_1.html**

CASE PROJECTS

3. Computer User Satisfaction at Indiana University Bloomington

Indiana University Bloomington (IUB) is a public university in Bloomington, Indiana. University Information Technology Services (UITS) conducts a survey of its students, staff, and faculty to measure their satisfaction with computer use on campus. A summary of the results of their survey for 2003 is available at **about.uits.iu.edu/~uitssur/2003/iub/ summary03.html**. Most questions are answered on a scale of 1 to 5, where 5 is very favorable. Analyze the results of the survey and respond to the following:

1. Use responses to questions 3 through 6 to write a description of a typical (average) computer user at IUB.

2. Based on the responses to question 5a, which kinds of computers should be supported by UITS staff? Which should not be supported?

3. Based on responses to question 8, which e-mail software should be supported by UITS staff? Which should not be supported?

4. Describe and explain any differences you see between students, staff, and faculty in the kind of e-mail software used.

5. Based on the responses to question 12, if you were on the computer support staff in UITS, what services would you target for improvement over the next year?

6. Are users at IUB satisfied with the computer services they receive? Explain your answer.

CASE PROJECTS

4. Productivity at Re-Nu-Cartridge

NOTE

For background information about Re-Nu-Cartridge, see Case 4 in Chapter 1.

Re-Nu-Cartridge currently has about 25 desktop computers. These machines range from 386s to the latest Pentiums and run a variety of software. Most employees use Microsoft Word for word processing (but there are several versions in use including 2.0, 6.0, 97, and 2000), and even one user who uses AmiPro. AmiPro is used by Joleen, the executive secretary at Re-Nu-Cartridge. Joleen learned AmiPro more than ten years ago, and says that

2

she is used to the program, that it meets her needs very well, and that she doesn't want to learn to use a new word processor. She has told CEO Fred Long that she would rather retire than learn a different word processor.

Fred says he is aware of a growing frustration among his employees. During the last six months, he has talked with several of them about the computer situation at Re-Nu-Cartridge. The employees are particularly concerned about how hard it is to get help with computer problems when they need it. Several said they feel that they are on their own whenever they run into problems with their computers.

Fred says that most of the four departments (manufacturing, retail sales, marketing, and administration) have a person whom everyone recognizes as the computer "expert." For example, the head bookkeeper, Patricia, is very knowledgeable and willing to help people in the administrative office when they have problems with Lotus 1-2-3 or with the accounting program that Re-Nu-Cartridge purchased to prepare financial reports. However, employees in the administrative office point out that she is not always available when they need help.

Examples of some of the complaints Fred hears from employees include:

- They can't find the manuals when they want to look up something.

- Department computer "experts" are frequently busy, so employees have to wait for help with a problem.

- Employees occasionally lose data because of hardware or software problems and lose time when they have to reenter the data.

When employees at Re-Nu-Cartridge need new hardware or software, they usually talk to one or more of the computer experts or other employees who have computers to learn how they like their systems and what they would recommend for purchase. This procedure seems to have worked well in the past, although some employees report that they are sometimes confused when they get conflicting recommendations, depending on whom they talk with.

Fred has approached you for advice about dealing with the frustrations he hears from his employees. He is concerned about what appears to be both a productivity and a morale problem among his employees. Either by yourself or working with a team of coworkers or classmates, answer these questions:

1. What problems do you see at Re-Nu-Cartridge based on Fred's description of the situation. (List as many problems as you can.)

2. Which of these problems are technical and which ones are organizational?

3. What recommendations would you make to Fred about solutions he should consider to address the problems you listed? (Don't worry too much at first about whether your recommendations are feasible or not; list as many possible recommendations as you can.)

4. Which solutions are more feasible than others? Why?

Write a report that summarizes your analysis.

3

CUSTOMER SERVICE SKILLS FOR USER SUPPORT AGENTS

In this chapter you will learn:

- The importance of communications skills and customer service relationships
- Reasons for careful listening and reading
- How to build and communicate understanding
- Three important aspects of effective speaking in a support interaction
- How to develop an incident management strategy
- How to understand different personality types and work styles
- Strategies for handling difficult clients
- Guidelines for client-friendly support Web sites
- Other components of excellent customer service

As you learned in Chapter 2, communications and interpersonal skills are very important for help desk and user support agents. Whether they supply help to end users face to face, via telephone, by fax, in e-mail messages, through a Web site, or in a chat session, all successful support staff must be able to listen, understand, communicate with, and work effectively with users to solve end-user problems.

Excellent communications and interpersonal skills are often more challenging for new user support workers to learn than technical skills or business skills. These skills are also more difficult to measure and evaluate. It takes practice to learn how to use communications skills effectively. But experienced user support agents and their managers know that client satisfaction is directly related to how well agents listen to, understand, and communicate with users. Support agents who concentrate solely on finding the correct technical answer may be frustrated and surprised to learn that clients are less than satisfied with their support interactions.

In this chapter, you'll learn some practical listening, understanding, speaking, and client-relationship skills. User support staff can apply these skills to almost any support situation to help solve user problems and achieve two goals of every support request: client satisfaction and excellent customer service. Although many of the skills discussed in this chapter apply directly to telephone support, these skills also apply to written communication. In fact, written communication is often trickier than oral communication because the tone and voice intonations are missing. The point is that strong communication and interpersonal skills are essential in any support environment.

COMMUNICATION AND CUSTOMER-SERVICE SKILLS

Communication skills are essential to provide high-quality customer service. Communication is a process that involves both listening and responding. Some communications, notably face to face, telephone, e-mail, and chat sessions, are two-way interactions between a support agent and an end user. Other communications, including a support Web site, are primarily one-way. To listen effectively, user support agents must be able to hear or read and understand a user's problem or question, and then reflect their understanding of the problem or question by their spoken or written response. Listening, understanding, and responding are essential to solving user problems. A support organization that can solve user problems effectively and efficiently, and does so using good interpersonal skills, creates client satisfaction and demonstrates that the support organization provides excellent client services.

Help desks and user support organizations frequently incorporate a customer-service ethic into their mission statements. A **customer-service ethic** is an organization-wide philosophy—shared by everyone from top management to operational staff—that client relationships and client satisfaction are the most important aspect of a business. Many organizations aim for a target of 100% client satisfaction 100% of the time. This ethic means that the user support staff aims to satisfy every client in every support incident.

NOTE

Chapter 7 discusses mission statements in detail.

NOTE

How important are customer services to organizations? In an article in *Harvard Business Review* (*HBR*), Thomas O. Jones and W. Earl Sasser, Jr. discuss "Why Satisfied Customers Defect" (*HBR*, Nov–Dec, 1995). They describe a study of Xerox company customers in which totally satisfied customers were six times more likely to purchase other Xerox products than customers who were just "satisfied." The authors conclude: "Merely satisfying customers who have the freedom to make choices is not enough to keep them loyal. The only truly loyal customers are totally satisfied customers." Another author, Frederick Reichheld, writes in a March 1996 *HBR* article, "Learning from Customer Defections," that "On average, the CEOs of U.S. corporations lose half of their customers every five years."

Today, support organizations place a greater emphasis on customer-service excellence than they did in the past. Why? First, satisfied clients are likely to be repeat clients. A frequent reason that clients leave a hardware or software vender for another is the poor service they receive. In fact, excellent service may be more important to clients than product features, price, convenience, or any other aspect of a business transaction. Second, it usually takes more support resources to handle incidents from dissatisfied clients than from satisfied ones. A dissatisfied client is more likely to generate:

- Lengthy incidents

- Repeated callbacks or help desk contacts

- Complaints and ill-will among clients (which can translate into poor public relations and lost sales)

- Incidents that need to be rerouted to a higher-level support agent or a user support manager

- Product returns for a refund

Because dissatisfied clients consume more support resources, any of these results reduce support staff productivity and may lead to a reputation for poor support service.

Jeff Davis shares tips on the importance of communications skills for support professionals in his article "Improve Your Communication Skills with these Techniques" at **www.techrepublic.com/article.jhtml?id= r00320030107jed01.htm&src=hr**

What are the characteristics of a support organization that is devoted to a customer-service ethic? A customer-service ethic means that, in the pursuit of customer service excellence, support staff members:

- Provide clients with the information, service, or solutions they need, if there is any reasonable way to do so.

- Explain to clients what they *can* do for them if the clients' problem cannot be resolved.

- Treat clients and potential clients with respect.

- Communicate to clients how long they are likely to be on hold, how long it will be before they receive a return call or e-mail, and provide time estimates of how long it may take to provide information or solve a problem.

- Return phone calls or e-mails when promised, even if just to report that no progress has yet been made.

Think of each user as a valued client. Always remember that user support is essentially a customer service business and that the goal is to create satisfied clients. If users are not treated as valued clients, they may not remain clients for long. If clients have a choice of vendors, where will they choose to shop? Usually, they will go where customer service is taken seriously. Even in telephone support, users measure your attitude and react to the way you communicate and handle an incident. Support agents inevitably communicate by their voice or written responses whether they consider an incident interesting or boring and whether they value the user or view the incident as an intrusion on their time.

Treat each incident as an opportunity to build client satisfaction. To create client satisfaction and help attain an organization's customer service goals, support agents must master the essential communications skills: listening, understanding, and responding.

LISTEN CAREFULLY

In any support conversation, learn to listen before you speak. Listen initially to a caller's description of the question or problem to develop a thorough understanding of it. Interrupting a caller is one indication that you are not listening carefully. In any written communication, read all the text and try to understand the user's problem before you jump to a response.

In Chapter 4, you'll learn about a technique called active listening, which is a way to restate and clarify what you heard to reach a common understanding of a user's problem.

During the problem description, carefully evaluate two other features of the user's communication.

1. Listen to or observe the *language* the user uses to describe the problem. A user's language frequently provides important clues as to whether the user is a novice or an experienced user. Support agents can target their language level slightly below the user's to avoid language that is too complex or too technical for the user to understand.

2. Listen to *how* the user describes the problem, which can provide further insight into the problem and the user. What tone of voice does the user use? Does the user sound angry or frustrated? Does he hesitate or struggle with technical terms? Does she sound distracted or in a hurry? Subtle cues like these can provide valuable information about how to handle an incident.

Although detecting a user's "tone of voice" is more difficult in written communications, support agents can look for statements that indicate frustration. For example, a user who writes, "This is my third chat session to try to resolve this problem," is undoubtedly making more than a simple factual statement.

A short online article by Lillian D. Bjorseth, "Shhh! Listen, Don't Just Hear," offers some useful strategies for becoming a better listener. Read the article at **www.selfgrowth.com/articles/bjorseth4.html**.

To build listening skills, look for courses in small group or interpersonal communications, which often place equal weight on listening and speaking skills. Many vocational-technical training programs and professional development seminars on customer service skills also include opportunities to work on listening and speaking skills. To develop skills with written communications from users, look for opportunities to study e-mail messages from friends or colleagues. Practice analyzing messages to examine the language used and to look for clues about how the sender feels. Ask yourself whether you can accurately restate their message.

BUILD UNDERSTANDING

Once you have listened to and heard or read a user's problem description, try to develop an understanding of the user's situation. Ideally, you will develop some level of empathy with the user. **Empathy** is an understanding of and identification with another person's situation, thoughts, and feelings. Support agents who can empathize with a user understand the problem or question from the user's point of view. One measure of empathy is whether you can express a user's problem in your own words. Another measure of empathy is whether a user agrees with your expression of the problem; in other words, have the two of you reached consensus? Empathy does not mean that you should take complete ownership of and responsibility for a problem, but that you understand and can relate effectively to the user, who does own the problem. Try to understand, for example, why the problem is important to a user, why a user might want to know a piece of information, or why a user is frustrated, upset, or angry. The following are examples of empathetic responses:

> "Clearly, we need to get this system running again so you can create the report. Here's where we'll start . . ."
>
> "It sounds like you've had a very frustrating morning, but I think I can help you with this . . ."
>
> "To help you close your accounting month on time, I can give you a workaround for this problem. Then, when that's finished, we can diagnose the problem you're having, so it doesn't happen again."

To view an article on empathy and trust in customer relations, visit the Web site **www.businessballs.com/empathy.htm**.

WWW

As you develop an understanding of the user and the problem, communicate to the user that you view him or her as a person, rather than as a support incident. One technique that experienced support agents use is to visualize the user. Even if you don't know the user personally, think of someone in your own experience who sounds like or is similar to the user and then communicate with that image rather than with a voice at the other end of the phone line or a chat message on your monitor. A second technique is to use inclusive language, such as "we" rather than "I" and "you." A telephone technique you can use effectively is to smile while you are talking with a user. Even though a conversation is audial and not visual, many users can tell if you are smiling.

RESPOND EFFECTIVELY

In a support interaction, all aspects of your speech or writing communicate your understanding of a situation, lead to successful incident resolution, and influence the user's level of satisfaction with the incident. Three important aspects are your greeting, how you use scripts, and your tone and style.

Use a Sincere Greeting

If every journey begins with a single step, all support communications begin with a **greeting**, which can affect the course of the entire interaction with the user. The greeting is the icebreaker. Users form their first impressions of the support staff person, the support service, and ultimately the entire organization that provides support based on the greeting. The greeting also sets the tone for the remainder of the incident. A sincere, positive greeting can be the first step toward calming a frustrated user and channeling an incident in a fruitful direction. Most support organizations train their staff members to use a standard greeting, which often includes the agent's first name and the name of the organization or other identification. A common greeting is:

> phone: "This is Joel in Computer Support. Thank you very much for your call. How can I help you?"
>
> e-mail: "I'm Leticia at the Help Desk. Thanks very much for contacting us with the problem you encountered. Here is how I understand the problem . . ."

Practice using a sincere greeting with a tone that communicates interest and enthusiasm and avoids sounding stiff, overly rehearsed, faked, or bored. A sound recorder or colleague can help provide feedback on your telephone greeting style. By the way, the immediate "thank you" in these examples communicates to the user that you appreciate and value the contact. Also, a sincere "thank you" contributes to a positive first impression, even if the user is upset or frustrated. If a user gives his or her name after your telephone greeting, write it down so you can use it during the incident. Many support organizations prefer the use of Mr. or Ms. and a user's last name in preference to a first name, unless the user specifically invites first name use.

Use Scripts Appropriately

Many support organizations supply their agents with a script to help handle routine aspects of an incident. A **script** is a prepared sequence of questions and statements that covers the important parts of an incident. A script can include branches and decision points so that a support agent follows a path through the script that matches a user's answers. Scripts can be useful training aids for new support agents as well as tools to handle complex technical problems and difficult users. However, a user should never suspect that you are simply reading a script or any other information unless you make it clear beforehand that you are reading a piece of technical information to ensure accuracy. Furthermore, experienced support agents recognize situations in which they should deviate from the script, such as when the user demonstrates expert knowledge of the problem situation. Scripts are also useful if an incident evolves into an argument or other inappropriate communication. Reverting to a script can help you get an interaction back on track and make sure that the incident is handled according to organizational policy.

Some help desks maintain a database of frequently asked questions (FAQs) and prepared responses to them. When using prepared responses, use them like scripts. Don't read lengthy responses, unless you make it clear that is what you are doing. Instead, restate the responses in your own words.

 As part of a training program, a support agent may be asked to learn or develop model answers to questions. Experienced support staff and supervisors are useful sources of information about what constitutes a "good" response to an FAQ. For an example of an online FAQ database, see the Microsoft Office FAQ at **www.microsoft.com/office/faq.htm**.

Use Tone and Style Effectively

How you communicate with a user is often more important than the content of the communication. Your tone and style have a direct impact on a user's satisfaction with a support incident. Which of these user statements best illustrates the desired outcome of a support incident?

> "The support agent provided me with adequate information, but I felt through the whole conversation that I was intruding on his time. He spoke rapidly and curtly, and wasn't very pleasant. I felt like he had 'been there, done that', and wasn't interested in my problem."
>
> "The support agent couldn't tell me what I needed to know, but explained why the information wasn't available yet, when it would be, and invited me to call back. I felt like a valued client and that my call was important to her."

Note that the first user received the information he sought, but was dissatisfied with the interaction; whereas the second user was fully satisfied even though her question was not answered.

Often, as part of help desk or user support training, support organizations describe in detail the type of communications style they want their agents to use—whether formal or informal, casual or professional, or somewhere in between. They realize that style is important because it communicates the organization's image. In reality, support staff members often modify the organization's desired standard somewhat, depending on their experience, on user feedback, and on their own personalities.

NOTE Researcher Albert Mehrabian reports that the specific words people use to communicate account for only 7% of the information other people receive in a communication, as shown in Figure 3-1. Tone, voice inflection, voice pitch, and other aspects of language style account for about 38% of the information received. Nonverbal communication, sometimes called body language, actually accounts for more than half. In telephone, e-mail, and chat session communications, where nonverbal cues are missing, language style takes on even greater significance.

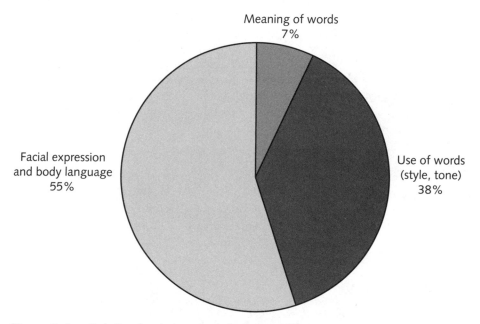

Meaning of words
7%

Facial expression
and body language
55%

Use of words
(style, tone)
38%

Figure 3-1   Relative importance of elements of communication

Use clear, succinct speech and match your speed to the user's proficiency level. Many inexperienced support agents have a tendency to speak too fast, which is often a natural reaction to pressure to be productive and job stress. Practice speaking slowly, but not so slowly as to sound condescending. Remember, too, that shorter sentences are easier for a user to follow than long ones. Avoid a rising inflection at the end of sentences, which sounds like you are asking a question or are unsure.

Many of the suggestions about writing for end users in Chapter 12 also apply to verbal user support communications style, including the use of gender-neutral language and avoiding wordiness, long words, overly technical terms, acronyms, and jargon.

NOTE

3

Avoid using empty phrases in support incidents. Inexperienced support agents, in particular, sometimes continue to talk just to fill the pauses. Avoid empty phrases, such as "Now let me see . . . ," "I think I've seen that problem before . . . ," or "I'm sure I must have that information somewhere here . . . ." These phrases do not convey useful information and do not instill confidence that the agent is on top of the problem, although it appears that communication is occurring. Instead of empty phrases, learn to be comfortable with pauses.

Phrase communications with end users positively, rather than negatively. For example, instead of saying or writing, "The problem with your file occurred because you didn't follow the procedure described in Chapter 2 of the manual," use a positive statement, such as "I think the procedure on file handling in Chapter 2 describes a way to avoid the problem you experienced with the file. Let me find the page for you . . . ."

Although technically correct solutions to user problems are critical, they will not by themselves guarantee satisfied clients. Successful support agents use greetings, scripts, and their tone and style to communicate their willingness to help, their regard for the client's value, and their organization's concern for the client's satisfaction. They also use effective listening, reading, speaking, and writing skills as part of an incident management strategy.

An organization that offers Web-based training courses in call center (help desk) customer service and communications skills is SkillSoft. Learn about its courses at **www.skillsoft.com/corporate/curicula/bus_cs.htm**. Click the **Front Line Call Center Skills (0110)** link, for example, to see course topics, including Call Center Communication Skills (CUST 0112). Another organization that offers online courses in communications and listening skills aimed at customer support workers is LearnCustomerServiceOnline.com. View a list of available courses at **www.learncustomerserviceonline.com/CustServiceModules.htm**.

WWW

To increase your skills with telephone communications, try the tutorials and exercises in the book by Jeannie Davis, *Beyond "Hello": A Practical Guide for Excellent Telephone Communication and Quality Customer Service*, Now Hear This, Inc., 2000.

NOTE

JONATHAN VESTER
NETWORK/COMPUTER SUPPORT TECHNICIAN
HAYWOOD COMMUNITY COLLEGE
CLYDE, NORTH CAROLINA
WWW.HAYWOOD.EDU

The technical support office at Haywood Community College consists of three full-time employees (a network administrator and two network/computer support technicians). My responsibilities range from user support to managing the content and virus filter for the college network. My duties change from day to day and no two days are ever the same.

I have found that to be successful in my position, I have to be patient and have good communications skills. Listening is by far the most essential skill for this position. My job requires active listening and strong note-taking skills so that I have all the information I need to solve an employee's problem. When a staff or faculty member calls me with a computer problem, I listen closely to the problem description. If possible, I have them walk through a procedure from the beginning to make sure that they are going through every step correctly. I also have them read any error messages they see. If I don't know the solution to a particular problem, I refer the user to someone who does, or explain that I will need to call him or her back with a solution. I always strive to maintain the client's confidence that I will solve the problem quickly or have another technician work with the user when it is outside my skill area.

Over the past few years, I have helped implement an online support request system at the college that enables our department to track requests by the users. I have found that this system helps to keep up with the requests of the hundreds of employees. The online request system is also beneficial because it requires our users to verbalize the problem, which helps them better understand what is happening. Writing about a problem is also an advantage of e-mail messages, which is another major communications channel in technical support. Although most of us are very comfortable with writing messages to our friends in the traditional, informal e-mail style, when you communicate with users via any medium, you should always keep the tone professional and courteous.

There are times when I have to handle difficult users. Older employees occasionally have negative attitudes about problems with computer technology but respond eagerly when they understand how easy it is to fix a problem. As a technical support employee, it is always important for me to remember that there was a time when I knew less than the people I am trying to help now. Remaining calm and logical will help the user better than matching their frustration with hostility. Let clients know you are there to help them and that you enjoy solving problems. If they feel you don't have time or don't want to bother with them, they will not ask for help again.

DEVELOP AN INCIDENT MANAGEMENT STRATEGY

Support agents who provide telephone, e-mail, or chat session support often have many incidents waiting in their queue. At the same time that they provide correct technical answers and excellent customer service, they must also handle incidents efficiently. An **incident management strategy** is a collection of tools, techniques, and strategies that successful support agents use to move through an incident effectively and efficiently, from the initial greeting to the end of the incident. The four goals of incident management are to:

1. Provide the user with the information he or she needs.

2. Manage stress levels for both the user and the support agent.

3. Ensure that the incident progresses from start to finish in an effective and efficient way.

4. Make the user more self-reliant.

All support agents develop and refine their own incident management strategy. However, you do not have to invent an incident management strategy from scratch. Resources you can build on and incorporate in your personal strategy include:

- Organizational policies on incident management philosophy and expectations

- Incident management strategies covered in support agent training programs

- Observation and imitation of respected senior support agents

- Your personal communications experience and style

- Feedback from users, peers, and supervisors on your incident management strengths and areas for improvement

An incident management strategy begins with knowledge of the support organization's philosophy and policies, an understanding of the operation of automated help desk and user support tools such as the telephone and e-mail systems and help desk software package (described in Chapter 6), and guidelines that experienced support agents have found useful. Figure 3-2 lists some examples of incident management guidelines.

Ask Goal-Directed Diagnostic Questions. Each diagnostic question should be designed to move an incident toward a successful resolution. Diagnostic questions can be embedded in a script or they can be based on a support agent's experience. Chapter 4 suggests several critical questions to ask in a troubleshooting situation.

Be Honest. It is better to be honest and forthcoming with users about product features, limitations, known bugs, and future product releases than to try to hide or cover up product problems and limitations. However, you must also abide by organizational policy on what information you are authorized to provide to users. For example, some vendors, as a matter of organizational policy, will not disclose future product features or availability dates. So you may encounter situations in which you have the information a user requests, but cannot

- Ask goal-directed diagnostic questions
- Be honest
- Say "I don't know" when you don't
- Apologize
- Say "Thank you"
- Use incident management, not user management
- Teach self-reliance

Figure 3-2   Incident management guidelines

divulge it yet because your employer asks you not to. Many organizations also have a policy that discourages communicating negative comments about a competitor's products, even though you may have an honest opinion about them.

Say "I Don't Know" When You Don't.   It is often more productive to admit that you don't know an answer than to waste both your time and the user's time trying to suggest possibilities you aren't sure of. A user rarely expects a support agent to know everything. However, never use a tone that conveys, "I don't know, and therefore your question is stupid," "I don't know, and I don't think anybody else does," or "I don't know, and I don't care." If you honestly don't know an answer, refer the user to another person or information source where she or he can get the needed information. You can also promise to research the question and get back to the user with the needed information.

Apologize.   An apology to a user who feels that they have been done an injustice is never a sign of weakness. One way to defuse a potentially difficult situation is to empathize with a user's situation and offer a sincere apology for the perceived injustice, whether a user has spent a long time on hold, been the victim of a runaround (however unintentional), or purchased a product ill-suited for his or her needs.

Say Thank You.   Thank the user for contacting the user support group at both the beginning and end of the support incident. "Thanks for contacting the Support Center" is a simple but effective way to communicate that the user and the contact are important. A "thank you" ends the incident on a positive note, even if the problem has been a difficult one.

Use Incident Management, Not User Management.   Be sure to distinguish between *incident* management and *user* management: manage the incident, not the user. Do not attempt to manipulate users by judging how well they communicate their needs, how they organize their files, or how well they use their computers. The relationship between a support agent and a user is not a boss-to-worker relationship, and should not be based on different levels of power. Although you can recommend that a user read a particular chapter in a manual or reorganize the files on his or her hard disk, you should not make it a condition for helping the user. Do not communicate that you are upset or be defensive if a user chooses not to take your advice. Users who feel that a support agent is trying to manage them or their work habits will rightfully feel resentful or manipulated and are more likely to be dissatisfied with a support incident.

Teach Self-Reliance. An immediate goal of each support incident is to provide information or to solve a user's problem. A secondary, longer-term goal is to make each user more self-reliant. To create **self-reliance**, support agents explain solutions so that a user understands the reasons they encountered a problem and how to fix it. Agents also help create self-reliance when they refer to relevant printed or online documentation where users can locate additional information about problems or questions. User support has a built-in contradiction: the support staff would like every user to call back (because their jobs depend on support incidents), but the staff hopes to resolve each user's problem so that he or she does not have to call back.

In reality, users will never become completely self-reliant. As computer use becomes even more widespread and systems become increasingly complex, both new and experienced users will continue to need an increased array of support services. Even power users and computer gurus occasionally need assistance. In addition, some users don't want to become self-reliant; they feel that it is the support staff's job to solve their problems. Recognize that you cannot force users to change their behavior. However, assume that a user is interested in understanding a problem and your solution to it until the user indicates clearly that they are not interested. Though complete user self-reliance may never be achieved, it is an important long-term goal for a support staff.

Successful incident management is rarely a skill or ability that comes easily to support agents. It takes practice to develop your own incident management strategy, and even then, some incidents still go awry. As you will see in the next section, even the best incident management approach can sometimes be derailed by the personalities or work styles of the participants.

CUSTOMER SERVICE AND PERSONALITY TYPES

A personality test commonly used in business and industry is the Myers-Briggs Type Indicator (MBTI). The test results determine where a test taker falls on four basic personality dimensions. The four dimensions of personality measured by the MBTI are:

- **Where do you direct your energy? Introversion (I) versus Extroversion (E)**
  This dimension measures whether you direct your energy to the external world of activity and words (Extroversion) or to the inner world of thoughts and emotions (Introversion). An Extrovert is more social and expressive, whereas an Introvert is more private and quiet.

- **How do you process information? Sensing (S) versus Intuition (N)**
  Sensing (S) people work more with facts and experiences they obtain through their senses, whereas Intuitive (N) people tend to emphasize personal insight and the future. A Sensing person tends to prefer direct communication, while an Intuitive person seeks creative or novel ways to communicate with others.

- **How do you make decisions? Thinking (T) versus Feeling (F)**
  Thinking (T) people base decisions on logic, analysis, principles, and objective factors, whereas Feeling (F) people base decisions on personal values and subjective factors.

- **How do you organize your life? Judging (J) versus Perceiving (P)**
  Judging (J) people prefer a structured lifestyle in which they are well-organized and make structured decisions. Perceiving (P) people prefer to be open, flexible, and explore their options. Judging people like to be in control, whereas Perceiving people like spontaneity.

Each person is not a pure type of any of these, but falls on a continuum of the four dimensions. Furthermore, these basic personality types can be combined into any of 16 combinations. For example, one personality type is an ISTJ, while another is an ENFP. There is obviously no one, correct personality type. Most people are a mixture of these types.

One use of the Myers-Briggs personality types is to help people understand how users and coworkers—either as individuals or in workgroups—view the work world differently. This understanding can help work groups avoid conflicts and help support agents understand different approaches taken by end users.

WWW
For a thumbnail sketch of any of these types, visit **www.knowyourtype.com** and click one of the 16 types listed at the bottom of the page. To learn more about the MBTI personality test and the 16 personality types it measures, consult one of these resources:

- Jean M. Kummerow, Nancy J. Barger, and Linda K. Kirby, *Worktypes.* New York: Warner Books, 1997.

- Otto Kroeger and Janet M. Thuesen, *Type Talk at Work.* New York: Delacourt Press, 1993.

- The Team Technology Web site at **www.teamtechnology.co.uk/tt/t-articl/mb-simpl.htm**.

Some communication difficulties that arise between a support agent and an end user may be traced to differences in basic personality type. For example, imagine the differences in communication style that may arise when a support agent, George, works on a problem with an end user, Hamida.

George, a support agent, is an ISTJ personality type on the MBTI scale. He is a very quiet, private person who prefers to work on problems independently by collecting data, and he often bases decisions on evidence he has carefully evaluated and analyzed. George prefers e-mail communications with users so that he has a written record of each incident.

Hamida, an internal end user, is an EHFP personality type. She is a warm, outgoing person who enjoys a collaborative, teamwork approach to problems. Hamida prefers to work on problems face to face so she can see a help desk agent's facial expression and read his or her body language. She likes the challenge of problem solving by trial and error and is often willing to make guesses and take risks to try to find a solution.

George thinks Hamida is overly aggressive and disorganized. Her approach to problems seems illogical. He finds working on a problem using her hit-and-miss approach to be stressful and a waste of time. Hamida thinks George fits the stereotype of a typical computer nerd who can't see over his pencil protector. She is frustrated that he seems unwilling to engage in give-and-take about a problem. She doesn't understand why he isn't willing to work on a problem together, but instead prefers short meetings and then quickly returns to his office to work.

As a support professional, George works hard to accommodate Hamida's work style. He understands that personality type differences can help *explain* communication problems between himself and Hamida, but are not an *excuse* for a lack of cooperation or communications that aren't civil.

Although George and Hamida are very different personality types based on the Myers-Briggs classification scheme, even small differences in basic personality can affect work and communication styles. Apart from differences in basic personality types, other barriers to effective communication between user support and end users occur because of difficult situations with which support agents must learn to deal.

STRATEGIES FOR DIFFICULT CLIENTS AND INCIDENTS

Although most users are rational and polite when they contact a support service, support agents may encounter several kinds of difficult users. A **difficult client** is one who requires special handling strategies because the user is angry, not communicative, rude, or exhibits a variety of other hard-to-handle attitudes or behaviors. The challenge for a support agent is to transform a difficult situation into a successful one. You will never be able to change a user's personality. Instead, focus on the specific problem, on getting the user the needed information, on providing excellent customer service in a respectful manner, and on moving to the next incident. To deal with difficult situations that might interfere with these goals, consider the strategies that experienced agents use.

Users Who Complain

Instead of simply describing a problem, some users want to complain about an organization's products or services. Complaint handling and management is often an important function of a help desk staff. Give users ample opportunity to voice their complaints or concerns. Don't switch into problem-solving mode too early in an incident when a user wants to complain. Instead, use empathy:

> "I understand why someone who has experienced this problem would be upset . . ."

Many support organizations treat complaints as a valuable source of feedback and suggestions for future product and service offerings. Try to understand that most complaints are not directed at you personally, and learn (it takes practice) not to be defensive about complaints.

Contacts by "Power Users"

In this context, **power users** are those who are technically very knowledgeable (or think they are) or who believe they warrant special attention or treatment because they have personal connections with significant people in an organization. These users often describe their powerful position early in an incident in an attempt to establish how important they are and occasionally to mask their actual lack of knowledge about their computer system. They may, for example, try to impress a support agent to direct attention away from what they don't know. One strategy for handling these users is to use inclusive language that makes them feel like a member of a team. Use pronouns like "we" to refer to the problem-solving process, such as:

> "I think we can solve this problem if we work on it together. . ."

Use an authoritative tone or speaking style because important, knowledgeable users like to communicate with important, knowledgeable agents. Remember that your role is not to diminish their sense of self-importance but to solve the problem they contacted you about.

Incidents That Get Off Track

Occasionally in the course of resolving an incident it becomes apparent that the process has taken a wrong turn and needs to get back on track. For example, a user might make a statement that contradicts an earlier statement. Or perhaps repeated attempts to isolate a problem have not succeeded. An incident during which a user becomes confused or that results in some unfruitful approaches indicates the process is off track. When this happens, try to refocus the process. Apologize to the user for the lack of a prompt resolution, summarize the basic incident information, and offer to continue to work toward a solution. Express confidence that, together, you will find a solution to the problem if you continue to work on it and that perhaps a different approach will achieve the results you both want.

Users Who Are Upset or Angry

Angry users are the most common kind of difficult incident. Angry users may be upset because of the way they have been treated. They may have been on hold too long, sent or received too many e-mails, worked with too many support agents, or explained the problem too many times. Or, they may be upset because of real or perceived inadequacies in a product. They may also be angry due to circumstances that are totally unrelated to the problem at hand, such as a negative encounter with a coworker or family member.

The first principle for handling angry users is to let them vent their anger. Say little during this period, and especially don't offer an explanation or switch to problem solving too early. Explanations to an angry person sound like an invitation to argue. The second principle is to reassure angry users that the problem is an important one, and that you are willing to work with them resolve it. The third principle to remember is that angry users may continue to vent several times before they work through their anger. A polite question that refocuses the angry user may be effective, such as:

> "What would you like me to do to help at this point?"
>
> "How can we resolve this situation to your satisfaction?"

Remember to avoid defensiveness and don't sound patronizing. An angry user is rarely upset with you personally. As with all incidents, continue to follow up on promises made to an angry user to build trust and confidence.

Users Who Are Abusive

Abusive users are rude, use inappropriate language, or make personal attacks on a support agent. A support agent's first goal is to transform an incident with an abusive user into an incident with a user who is just angry, and ultimately into an incident with a satisfied user.

This goal is not always achievable. Some support centers have support staff who have special training and skills to handle abusive users; these workers pride themselves on their ability to defuse difficult situations. In general, handle abusive users according to the support organization's policies and procedures for this type of user. For example, some support organizations instruct their agents to terminate an incident when abusive language is used. In other organizations, the support agents are trained to invite the user to use more appropriate and professional language:

> "We would like to work with you on this problem. But we need to communicate about it in an appropriate and professional way. Is that agreeable with you?"

Users Who Are Reluctant to Respond

Users who will not answer questions or are reluctant to provide information are often confused, lack confidence, or don't understand the questions. They may be inexperienced computer users. To obtain the information you need from these users, use very simple language and avoid technical jargon. Try different kinds of questions. For example, if open-ended questions fail to initiate a fruitful conversation, switch to questions that can be answered with yes or no, and begin with very simple questions, such as "Is there a Start button in the lower-left corner of the screen?" Or, switch to discussing the problem-solving process, such as "I'll ask you some questions about what you see on the screen and you answer them if you can. Any information you can give me will help us solve the problem." Also give positive feedback when a reluctant user does provide useful information, such as "I think that information will be helpful." Finally, if a user continues to be reluctant to respond, suggest exchanging information in another mode (e-mail, chat session, telephone, or face to face) as a way to facilitate the problem-solving process.

Users Who Won't Stop Responding

Some users have a hard time letting go of a problem. Even after a problem is solved, they may continue to explain how bad it was or how similar it was to another problem they encountered. To deal with excessive communicators, use behavior that indicates the contact is over. For example, briefly summarize the incident and describe the conclusion. Thank the user for contacting the support group. Express your conviction that the problem is solved. Use very short answers that don't provide the user with lead-ins to additional responses.

You can find some tips from Kate Nasser on handling difficult users that she gave at a conference at the University of Florida in September, 2000 at **www.health.ufl.edu/itcenter/cs/frontlines2.shtml**. Jeff Dray, a help desk professional with over 15 years of experience, has published suggestions for dealing with abusive users at the TechRepublic Web site, **www. techrepublic.com/article.jhtml?id=r00320000726det02.htm** (requires free membership). Another useful resource is a paper written by Leslie Barden, who works in Customer Support for the National Institutes of Health. His paper, "Dealing with Difficult Customers— The Most Fun You Can Have at Work," is available to download at **www.awcncc.org/2001/Barden_article.rtf**.

Handling difficult users is never an easy task, but over time you can improve your skills with practice and patience. Inexperienced help desk and support staff can learn a great deal about difficult users from experienced support agents. Veteran agents are a good resource for organization-approved and time-tested techniques for dealing with difficult situations. Training sessions for new help desk and support agents often cover organizational guidelines for dealing with these situations.

CLIENT-FRIENDLY WEB SITES

Unlike face-to-face contacts, telephone calls, e-mail, and chat sessions, which are interactive, two-way forms of communication between clients and support agents, a **support Web site** is primarily a one-way method of communication. User support Web sites are a cost-effective way to communicate with end users, whether internal or external. Users like support Web sites because they can get answers to common questions quickly, at any time, and from anywhere there is Internet access. Because support Web sites are cost-effective and popular with end users, these sites are increasingly used to augment other modes of user support. However, customer service concerns and a customer-service ethic also apply to the design and construction of support Web sites. You have probably visited Web sites that were well-organized and simple-to-use with information you could find easily. And you've probably visited some that failed the ease-of-use test. If an organization is going to spend the resources to build a support Web site, it should build a client-friendly one. An organization's support Web site is as much an extension of the business or agency as the other forms of contact with clients.

Simple support Web sites can be built and maintained with popular word processors as well as with more powerful Web Page development tools such as Microsoft FrontPage, Macromedia Contribute, or Adobe GoLive. Although knowledge of Hypertext Markup Language (HTML) is useful, it is not a require ment with today's Web development tools.

Because a support Web site is usually limited to one-way communication, a user support specialist who has a responsibility to maintain a support site needs a heightened awareness of customer service concerns, and additional job skills to implement a successful site. The first issue in support Web site design is the purpose of the site. Common purposes of support Web sites include:

- Provide product information
- Take sale orders
- Contact technical support
- Provide software updates and downloads
- Communicate with end users

Four general criteria apply to written communications with end users, including Web site design. These four criteria are content, organization, format, and mechanics. A support Web site implementer uses these criteria as tools to evaluate how a Web site measures up to the customer-service ethic.

Content

Keep the product, support, and contact information accurate and up-to-date. Present a smaller amount of information that can be maintained and kept current rather than a larger amount of information that is out-of-date. Make the content relevant to what users need to know.

Organization

The design of a support home page is critical. An effective home page is eye appealing and well-organized, but avoids information overload and too many special graphic effects. Extensive graphics can affect download time for users with slower Internet connections. Some sites offer a text-only option to accommodate users with slow connections. The best support Web sites have menus, icons, and information "teasers" (summaries) on the home page, with links to more detailed information if a user desires.

Support Web sites can be organized by product, by function, or in other ways. Sites organized by product should include search capabilities in case a user cannot find a specific product by model number. Sites organized by function may include separate pages for product features and information, an FAQ knowledge base, software downloads, a shopping cart, support contact information, a site map, and a site feedback mechanism.

Format

Information should be formatted into small units. A document that takes more than two or three PgUp or PgDn keystrokes to access it can be broken into multiple pages or easy-to-find sections.

Navigation aids expand the usability of a Web site. A well-formatted Web site includes multiple ways of accessing information, including navigation aids (to return to the top of a long page, to jump to the next or the previous page, or to return to the home page), a search engine to help locate specific information, and menu icons to access main topics. The pages, navigation aids, and menu bars should be consistent across the site. Fonts and format features should maintain a consistent style and feel.

Mechanics

Check spelling and grammar on all Web documents as well as FAQ databases. Use a briefer writing style with a fairly low readability index for most Web site information.

Chapter 12 discusses these four criteria—content, organization, format, and mechanics—in more detail.

NOTE

A good example of a Web site that illustrates many of these design elements is Dell Computer's site at **support.dell.com**. Another good example is Gateway's site at **support.gateway.com**. What Web sites have you discovered that you think are easy to use and contain support information useful to you?

WWW

A Web site devoted to user support is useless unless users know about and visit it. A support site can be registered with popular search engines so that Web surfers who enter relevant keywords will locate the site. A support Web site can be prominently displayed in user manuals and in online documentation (for example, a link on the toolbar of a software product). The Web site reference can be included in product literature, organizational newsletters and brochures, as well as business cards. Pointers to a support Web site can also be included in support phone calls, e-mails, and chat sessions.

To learn more about the features of Web sites that increase their usability for clients, visit **www.usabilityfirst.com/index.txl**.

WWW

Many colleges and professional-technical schools offer coursework in Web site design, implementation, and maintenance. These courses are a good way to add value to a user support resume.

COMPREHENSIVE CLIENT SERVICES

Whether client services are two-way (as in face-to-face contacts, telephone calls, e-mail, or chat sessions) or one-way (as in a support Web site), communication and interpersonal skills are essential to provide excellent client services. Yet a comprehensive approach to excellent client service is also based on specific organizational values, attitudes, and actions.

First, client services start when each employee, from high-level managers to the newest support agent, recognizes that its clients are the primary reason for the organization's existence. Each employee's job depends directly on client satisfaction. Most support organizations' mission statements express the commitment that each end user's enhanced productivity is a primary objective of the support staff. In a user support environment, client productivity and satisfaction are directly related to the extent to which each user is treated as a valued client at all levels.

Second, customer service excellence is based on whether a support staff is willing to take extra steps to make sure clients are satisfied. For example, an excellent support organization keeps its clients apprised of the progress or lack of progress toward a problem solution. It actively promotes win–win outcomes for each incident. It seeks agreement that problems have been adequately addressed, and then conducts follow-up client surveys to measure the extent of client satisfaction and identify areas where client relationships can be improved.

Third, excellent customer service depends on adequate support resources. Customer service excellence rarely happens by accident, but is based on advanced planning, adequate staffing, and a sufficient budget for help desk tools and information resources that encourage excellence. A sufficient support budget is not always easy to achieve because support expenses are sometimes difficult to justify, as you will learn in Chapter 7.

NOTE   Excellent customer service does not necessarily mean that the client is always right. Sometimes requests by even the most valued clients cannot be met for a variety of sound business reasons. In those situations, stress what you *can* do for a user, and look for alternate ways to meet user needs.

A comprehensive client service orientation among a support staff must apply not only to every staff member in an organization, but also to every mode of communication with users. Although most of this book covers technical problem solving and operational details associated with the day-to-day operation of a help desk or support center, this chapter on communication and customer service is the most important one in the book. Why? Because you can perform all the technical and operational duties of a support job adequately and still fail if you don't provide excellent service to your clients.

CHAPTER SUMMARY

❏ Communication and interpersonal relationships are the foundations of excellent customer services, which is a goal expressed in many support organizations' mission statements. Communication is a process that involves listening and reading, understanding, and speaking and writing skills.

❏ The most important communications skill for help desk and user support staff is the ability to listen to or read information provided by clients. In addition to a description of a user's problem, help desk staff need to evaluate a user's language level so the staff can pitch their responses to a similar level. Help desk staff need to listen or read for cues that indicate whether a user is frustrated, confused, or angry.

❑ Understanding a client involves being able to restate a problem, but it also means an ability to empathize with the user's situation and feelings and to understand why the problem is an important one for the client.

❑ The ability to respond effectively includes skill with a greeting, the use of scripts as aids, and the ability to use a tone and style that helps rather than hinders. An appropriate tone is often more important than the content of a communication with a user.

❑ Support agents should develop a personal incident management strategy. Goal-directed diagnostic questions, honesty, as well as an ability to say "I don't know," to apologize, to create user self-reliance, and to thank a user for contacting a support group are all components of a personal incident management strategy.

❑ Some barriers in communication between a user support agent and an end user may be related to differences in basic personality types and work styles based on the Myers-Briggs classification scheme.

❑ Difficult support incidents include user complaints, incidents with power users, incidents that get off track, incidents from angry or abusive users, and incidents from users who are either reluctant to respond or who won't stop responding. Skilled support agents develop specific strategies to channel difficult users into satisfied ones.

❑ A user support Web site is a cost-effective way to communicate with users. Web site developers need additional skills to manage information content, site organization, a client-friendly format, and writing mechanics to build a support Web site that meets the goals of a customer service ethic.

❑ A comprehensive approach to client services includes not only communications skills but also an organization-wide recognition of the importance of each client, a willingness to take extra measures to satisfy users, and adequate support resources to provide client satisfaction. Comprehensive customer service applies equally to telephone, face-to-face, and written interactions with users.

KEY TERMS

customer-service ethic — An organization-wide philosophy—shared by everyone from top management to operational staff—that client relations and client satisfaction are the most important aspects of a business.

difficult client — A user who requires special handling strategies because he or she is angry, not communicative, rude, or exhibits other hard-to-handle behaviors. The challenge for a support agent is to transform a difficult client into a satisfied one.

empathy — An understanding of and identification with a user's problem situation, thoughts, and feelings; a support agent who can empathize with a user understands the problem or question from the client's perspective and why it is important to the client.

greeting — The first few sentences in a support incident that introduce the agent, form the basis for the first impression of the support service by the user, and get the incident started with a positive approach.

incident management strategy — A collection of tools, techniques, and strategies that support agents use during an incident to move effectively and efficiently from the initial greeting to the conclusion of the incident.

power user — A user who is technically knowledgeable (or believes that he or she is), or who may have a relationship with an organization that he or she feels warrants special attention to his or her incident.

script — A prepared sequence of questions and statements that support agents can use to handle parts of an incident; may include decision points and branches to handle different situations.

self-reliance — A goal of support service providers that seeks to increase user self-sufficiency and reduce a user's dependence on support services.

support Web site — A Web site devoted to provide clients with product information, software downloads, support staff contacts, and a sales channel; support Web sites are a cost-effective method to communicate with users, but should be designed to be client-friendly.

Check Your Understanding

1. True or False? Communications skills are often more difficult for a new help desk agent to learn than technical skills or business skills.

2. A(n) _____ is a choice each support agent makes about how professional or casual, how respectful or condescending, how formal or informal, or how terse or verbose they will be in their interactions with users.

3. A user's first impression of a support agent usually comes from the _____ .

   a. incident greeting

   b. solution to the problem

   c. incident script used

   d. agent's tone and style

4. True or False? Empathy means a user support agent takes ownership and responsibility for a user's problem.

5. A support agent should make liberal use of the word _____ .

   a. I

   b. you

   c. we

   d. they

6. One measure of whether a support agent understands a user's problem is that they can express the problem in _____ .

   a. the user's actual words

b. the support agent's own words

c. industry standard vocabulary

d. the wording of the script for the problem

7. About _____ percent of the meaning in a communication is based on the actual words used.

8. True or False? Of the three essential communications skills, listening or reading comes before understanding and responding.

9. True or False? Scripts designed to guide a user support agent through an incident should be memorized or read verbatim to a user to be effective.

10. True or False? One of the goals of incident management is to help users be more self-reliant.

11. Which of the following is not a primary strategy for a support organization that aims for customer service excellence?

a. Treat clients with respect.

b. Explain to clients what you can do for them.

c. Agree to any demand a client makes.

d. Return calls to clients when promised.

12. Which of the following is not a recommended incident management strategy for support agents?

a. Ask goal-directed diagnostic questions.

b. Say thanks.

c. Teach the user self-reliance.

d. Never admit that you don't know.

13. True or False? A customer-service ethic is an organization-wide philosophy that the client is always right.

14. A support Web site implementer uses four tools to evaluate a client-friendly site: content, _____ , _____ , and mechanics.

DISCUSSION QUESTIONS

1. Why are communications skills often more challenging for inexperienced support agents to learn than technical or business skills?

2. Should a support agent ever just hang up on a caller who is rude or uses abusive language? Describe some pros and cons to this approach, and explain your position.

3. Are providing excellent user support and teaching user self-reliance contradictory strategies? Explain why or why not.

4. Will different work styles and communication differences among workers who have different MBTI personality types inevitably lead to conflict? Explain your position.

HANDS-ON PROJECTS

Project 3-1

Update a mission statement. A mission statement is a list of guiding principles that communicates support goals and objectives to staff, users, and management. Modify the following mission statement to include a greater emphasis on excellent communication and customer service. (For more information on mission statements, see Chapter 7.)

> ### User Support Group Mission Statement
>
> The mission of the user support group is to: (1) maximize operational efficiency among users in an organization by providing timely resolution to technology use questions, and (2) effectively manage problems to continuously improve the:
>
> - Quality of support services provided to users
> - Usability of information systems
> - Effectiveness of documentation and training
> - Users' satisfaction with support services

Project 3-2

Differentiate difficult users. This chapter described several kinds of difficult users, including two that are not always easy to differentiate: users who complain and users who are angry. Sometimes few differences exist between the two. Assemble a team of three classmates or coworkers and compare your personal experiences with users who want to complain and those who are angry. List at least three characteristics of complainers and at least three characteristics of angry users that would help support agents distinguish between the two user types.

Project 3-3

Develop an incident management strategy. Based on the ideas in this chapter and on your personal experience (or on the experiences of a team of your classmates or coworkers), write a list of at least eight incident management do's and don'ts that could be covered in a training session for inexperienced help desk agents.

Project 3-4

Interview a support agent about difficult users. Invite a help desk agent in your school or company to talk with you and your classmates. Ask the agent to describe any experiences with difficult users and the techniques he or she uses to handle them. In addition to those described in this chapter, what kinds of incidents does the support agent find difficult to handle? What is the most common kind of difficult incident in his or her experience? Write a brief report that summarizes the main points of the interview.

Project 3-5

Explore ways to improve client service. Read an article about customer service available on the Internet at **techupdate.zdnet.com/techupdate/stories/main/ 0,14179,2804648,00.html** ("Improve Customer Service—And Cut Costs" by George Lawton). Write a short abstract of the article that lists the title, author, and source of the article (URL), and then answers the following questions:

1. Who should read this article (intended audience)?

2. What recent trends in customer service does the author describe?

3. What will readers of this article learn (list the main points)?

Project 3-6

Encourage client self-reliance. Voiceboard Corporation is an organization that develops and sells hardware and software products for PCs, including network and processor components, boards, and software drivers. The Voiceboard Web site, at **www.voiceboard. com/support1.htm**, includes several guidelines for its clients on the company's support policies and procedures. First, read Voiceboard's support guidelines. Then prepare a list of at least three ways that Voiceboard tries to make its clients more self-reliant.

Project 3-7

Evaluate a help desk phone incident. Read a report of an actual help desk phone incident online at **www.bizjournals.com/sacramento/stories/2000/01/24/smallb4. html** (Jeffrey Gitomer, "Help Desks Could Use Help with Customer-service Skills," *Sacramento Business Journal*, week of January 24, 2000). Then do the following:

1. List the three worst mistakes that were made in the incident described in the report.

2. For each mistake you listed, describe the customer service principles and guidelines in this chapter that were violated.

3. Write a recommendation from you to the help desk manager that summarizes how she or he should deal with future incidents like the one described in the report.

Project 3-8

Read an article on effective Web site design elements by Jennifer Stewart on her Write101.com Web site at: **www.write101.com/101web.htm**. Make a list of five suggestions for support Web site developers that are different from those described in the chapter.

CASE PROJECTS

CASE PROJECTS

1. An E-mail Reply for Bug-Free Software Limited

You are a support agent for Bug-Free Software Limited, which develops customized software for businesses on a contract basis. You receive the following e-mail message from a large client:

> We received the custom Visual Basic programs from your new programmer and installed them on our system last week. It was obvious from the first time we ran the programs that the programmer was new to your organization. It was not clear if the programmer had much prior experience with programming or with Visual Basic. The new programs we received converted the information from our old COBOL programs to our report formatter fairly well, according to the specifications we provided her. But we discovered that she built the specific data conversion instructions into the Visual Basic programs. The programs lack the flexibility we need to handle all of the different data formats we have to convert. The programs should have been written with the conversion information in tables that are easily modified. The way they were written means we have to modify the programs every time we run them.

Write a reply to this e-mail that shows empathy for the problem and a good customer-service ethic.

CASE PROJECTS

2. A Script for Scott Shipping Corporation

You have been working as an internal user support agent at Scott Shipping for six months and have been chosen by your manager to help coach a new user support employee, Gene Rosso. Like many organizations, Scott Shipping records selected support conversations for training purposes. To give you some training and mentoring experience, your manager has asked you to examine this transcript of one of Gene's support interactions and write Gene a memo with suggestions about how he can improve his communications skills and demonstrate an improved customer service orientation. Suggest alternate responses for Gene that improve the quality of the customer service interaction.

Gene:	This is the problem hotline. What's your problem please?
User:	This is Wes in Accounting.
Gene:	Oh, yes, I remember you. I've talked with you several times before. What's the problem now?
User:	I'm having trouble printing a report this morning.
Gene:	What kind of trouble?
User:	I've clicked on Print three times and gone down the hall to get the printout, but each time there is just a stack of about 50 sheets in the printer with a line or two of junk characters on each one. But my report is not there.

3

Gene:	Oh, we've been hoping whoever was wasting those reams of paper would call.
User:	I'm sorry, but I've never had this problem before. What am I doing wrong?
Gene:	What are you trying to print?
User:	The report is in a file named REPORT2004.EXE.
Gene:	Didn't the training course you took cover printing .EXE files? .EXE files are programs, not reports. You can't print an .EXE file, you can only run them.
User:	Oh, I see. I guess I forgot about that. I feel like an idiot.
Gene:	Yes, well, see if you can find a file on your hard drive named REPORT2004 with a different extension and call me back.

**CASE
PROJECTS**

3. User Support Personality Types

Based on your understanding of the 16 personality types in the Myers-Briggs classification and on your knowledge of help desk communications and customer service skills described in this chapter, work with a team of three classmates or coworkers to identify which of the 16 MBTI types you think is best suited to provide a strong customer service orientation. Would more than one of the 16 types be effective?

If you have never taken the Myers-Briggs test or have not taken it recently, you may be able to take the test at your school's Counseling department or at your organization's Human Resources Office. If you would like to take a shorter, online version, go to The Keirsey Temperament Sorter II Web site at **www.advisorteam.com/user/kts.asp**.

If the results indicate that your personality type is not as well suited for help desk or user support work as other personality types, understand that the 16 MBTI personality types are not absolutes. Each person is actually a mixture of the eight pure categories in the test. The MBTI test simply measures tendencies. Most people are more adaptive than the test often indicates.

Write a summary of your research into the MBTI personality types and customer service orientation among help desk staff.

4. A Complaint Handling Script for Re-Nu-Cartridge

For background information about Re-Nu-Cartridge, see Case 4 in previous chapters.

NOTE

Molly Jeavsey, who works in the administrative group at Re-Nu-Cartridge, is the person to whom complaints about company products are directed. Molly has kept a tally of which products generate the most complaints. She periodically passes the complaint tallies to the product design engineers in the manufacturing division as feedback on problems end users or retail stores encounter with Re-Nu's cartridges.

Recently the engineers became aware of a large volume of complaints about a particular cartridge for a new model of printer. They have asked Molly to collect more information from users and retailers about the problems with the new cartridges. One engineer suggested that Molly collect more information from complaints about any Re-Nu cartridge than a simple count.

Help Molly by writing a draft of a script she could use to collect basic information about the problems users and retailers are encountering with Re-Nu's cartridges. The script you write should respond to two goals: (1) to collect basic product information that would be useful to Re-Nu-Cartridge's engineers, and (2) to exhibit a diplomatic way of asking for information that reflects an excellent customer-service ethic.

Compare your script with that of others in your class or workgroup to look for ideas on how to improve your script.

TROUBLESHOOTING COMPUTER PROBLEMS

In this chapter you will learn:

♦ The troubleshooting process and the thinking skills required for successful troubleshooting

♦ Communication skills for troubleshooting

♦ Information resources to help solve computer problems

♦ Which tools are used to troubleshoot computer problems

♦ Strategies for troubleshooters

♦ How to develop a personal problem-solving strategy

Solving computer problems is one of the most critical and frequent tasks user support agents perform. Computer problems that end users encounter cover a wide range, including requests for information, questions about how to perform a task, complaints about a product or feature, or a problem that prevents an end user from operating hardware or software. Many problems are relatively easy for support agents to solve quickly. The problem may be a common one; they may have seen the problem before and already know the solution, or they can find the solution quickly in a database of problem solutions.

Some problems are more difficult to solve. These include problems that support agents have never encountered or those whose solutions are not obvious. Despite attempts to find a quick solution, the problem-solving effort may not succeed at first. On occasion, a seemingly innocent problem report may turn out to be the first in what will become a long series of separate incidents about a significant problem with a new or recently modified product.

This chapter describes the tools, methods, and strategies that support agents use to work on user problems, especially difficult ones. After examining these strategies, you will be encouraged to use these tools to develop a personal problem-solving strategy.

WHAT IS TROUBLESHOOTING?

Troubleshooting is the process of defining, diagnosing, and solving computer problems. Some people think the process of solving computer problems is a fixed sequence of steps that can be followed to diagnose and repair a malfunction with computer hardware, software, or networks. The ability to follow a sequence of steps, such as one would encounter during a software package installation, is an important job skill for support agents. However, any single sequence of steps is unlikely to diagnose every computer problem. Troubleshooting computer problems is often more complex than that.

Troubleshooting is usually an **iterative process**, a process that involves several paths or approaches to problem solving. This means that a troubleshooter follows one sequence of steps for a while, then loops back and performs perhaps similar steps, but down a different path. The process can include many false starts and temporary pauses, as a troubleshooter pursues an approach, hits a dead end, switches to an alternate approach, makes some progress, only to hit a snag, and starts down another path. Figure 4-1 graphically compares a sequential process with an iterative process.

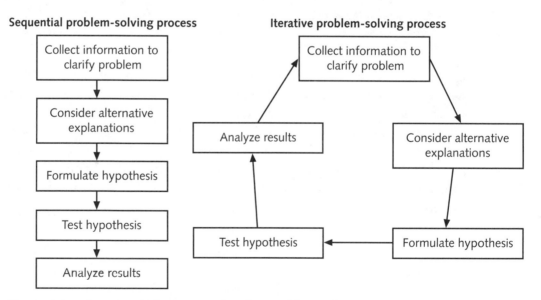

Figure 4-1   A sequential versus an iterative problem-solving process

An iterative process may seem repetitious, and in a way it is. Troubleshooting is not always a neat, linear, and orderly process. It is often both a structured and a creative process that requires flexibility and thinking skills and patience that will eventually lead to a satisfactory solution. It is partly a scientific process that follows rules of logic and partly an artistic process that relies on insight and creativity.

The perspective on troubleshooting advocated in this chapter differs from two alternate approaches: The first treats troubleshooting as a fixed sequence of steps to follow (1, 2, 3, etc.) until a problem is solved. Sometimes a predefined sequence of steps moves troubleshooters toward resolution, and sometimes it doesn't. A second alternative might be described as a hit-or-miss or trial-and-error approach to troubleshooting. It consists of randomly trying various things in hopes of eventually hitting on something that works. "I'll poke around and see what I can find" is a common way to describe the hit-or-miss approach. Occasionally, hit-or-miss stumbles across the solution and resolves a problem, but often it doesn't. And sometimes troubleshooters using the hit-or-miss approach try things that actually make matters worse.

Like woodworkers, troubleshooters use a variety of tools and skills in their work as they try to solve a difficult problem. They may pick up one tool, work on an aspect of a problem, set that tool aside for a while, and pick up another tool, only to turn back to a tool or skill used previously. The tools user support agents employ in troubleshooting can be physical tools, such as a diagnostic program or a database of information, or they can be thinking skills, such as problem solving, critical thinking, and decision making.

Problem-Solving Skills

The term **problem solving** is often used in business and mathematics to describe a process of moving from a current state of events X (the problem state) to a future desired state of events Y, sometimes called the **goal state**. Figure 4-2 illustrates this problem-solving model applied to a malfunctioning printer.

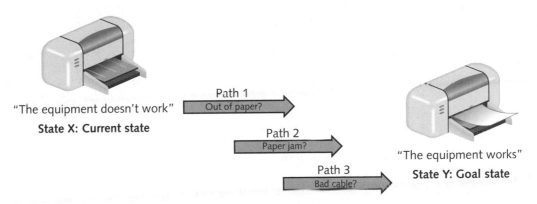

"The equipment doesn't work"

State X: Current state

Path 1
Out of paper?

Path 2
Paper jam?

Path 3
Bad cable?

"The equipment works"

State Y: Goal state

Figure 4-2   Problem-solving model

In computer problem solving, troubleshooters want to move from the problem state (the equipment doesn't work) to the goal state (the equipment works again). The problem solvers are looking for a path from the problem state to the goal state that locates the correct answer. Good problem solvers are skilled in getting from problem to goal quickly, accurately, effectively, and efficiently.

Problem solvers use a variety of thinking skills. For example, a problem solver may analyze a problem on the basis of:

- **Analogies.** Ways in which the current problem is similar to other problems that have been solved; for example, "This problem with fonts in Excel is very similar to a problem with fonts I've seen in Word."

- **Contradictions.** Situations in which two facts cannot be true at the same time; for example, "If this network card doesn't operate in one computer, but works in another one, the problem is unlikely a defective network card."

Analogies and contradictions may lead problem solvers to a possible problem solution.

Critical-Thinking Skills

Critical thinking describes the cognitive skills a problem solver uses to analyze a situation, search for the underlying logic or rationale for it, and strive for alternate ways to explain it. To think critically is to use personal experience, the power of logical thinking, "mental models" of how things work, and various analytic tools to understand and explain a situation. Computer problem solvers rely on critical-thinking skills in many situations to try to understand the possible causes for the observed behavior (or misbehavior) of a computer system.

Critical-thinking skills include:

- **Creativity.** The ability to find a novel or innovative solution to a problem. Creative troubleshooters have the ability to see a problem from new or different perspectives. For example, a computer problem solver may discover a unique solution to a problem he or she has never seen before by thinking about how a similar piece of hardware or software operates. Some troubleshooters refer to the search for a novel approach as "thinking outside the box."

- **Hypothesis testing.** The ability to formulate a **hypothesis**—a guess or prediction based on experience—about the cause of a problem and then to design a test that will prove or disprove the hypothesis. Troubleshooters usually formulate a hypothesis based on their prior experience with other problems they have encountered or read about. For example, a problem solver may make an initial guess that garbage characters output on a printer are due to a faulty signal cable from the computer to the printer, and then use critical-thinking skills to devise a series of tests to determine whether the signal cable is indeed the cause of the problem. For example, a critical thinker may look for an operational printer cable nearby to use in place of the original signal cable as a test.

- **Metacognition.** The ability to think about thinking. Good troubleshooters have the ability to step back from a problem-solving situation and analyze their thought process. Using metacognition, for example, a troubleshooter may realize that he or she is assuming that a problem is hardware-related, when, in fact, it may be software-related. Metacognition is a critical-thinking skill that can help good troubleshooters become better ones, because it involves self-analysis.

NOTE

Examples of metacognitive questions troubleshooters can ask themselves include:

- What assumptions did I make that led me in the wrong direction?
- Where did I go wrong solving this problem?
- Why did one problem-solving approach work well when another one didn't?
- How could I have solved this problem more effectively or efficiently?

Decision-Making Skills

Decision making is the ability to select one alternative from among a number of alternatives, based on some evaluation criteria. For example, business decisions can be based on criteria such as cost, output volume, profit margin, quality, customer service, or employee morale. Good decision makers often define several effective alternatives, weigh the pros and cons of each alternative against some predefined criteria, and reach a decision.

Decision making in computer problem solving is important when support agents are confronted with several explanations for a problem. For example, when a number of diagnostic tests can be run to gather information, a problem solver must decide which test is most likely to produce useful and informative results. To select the wrong test could delay progress toward the correct solution and reduce the efficiency of the problem-solving process.

Troubleshooters routinely use skills such as problem solving, critical thinking, and decision making in their work, whether they are computer support agents, auto mechanics, clock repairers, or medical doctors. Several of the problem-solving scenarios in this and the next chapter illustrate problem-solving methods that use these thinking skills.

TOOLS TROUBLESHOOTERS USE

Most successful troubleshooters use tools that fall into one of five broad categories, which are listed in Figure 4-3. Think about the tools you have used to work on computer problems in your own experience and try to determine how the tools fit into one of these categories.

Communication Skills

Communication and interpersonal skills are important troubleshooting tools, because most computer problem situations require at least some interaction with an end user, and sometimes with a vendor. Troubleshooters use communication skills to get a basic description of a problem, to learn the user's perspectives on the problem, and to probe for additional information. After a problem has been solved, troubleshooters also need to communicate the solution effectively to the user. The five principal types of communication skills used to troubleshoot computer problems are basic listening skills, active listening, probes, critical

- Communication skills
- Information resources
- Diagnostic and repair tools
- Problem-solving strategies
- Personal characteristics

Figure 4-3   Categories of problem-solving tools

questions, and explanation and verification skills. Successful support agents are adept at using these skills in almost every user support situation.

Basic Listening Skills.   To get a troubleshooting opportunity started on the right foot, support agents try to obtain as accurate a description of the problem as possible from the user's perspective. Therefore, the foremost communication skills every troubleshooter needs are listening skills.

Listen to the words the end user chooses to describe a problem. The danger of support agents not listening carefully, or of not giving the user enough time to explain the problem, is that the agent may jump ahead of the user and begin to work on the solution to a problem before really understanding the problem. When troubleshooters turn their attention away from what a user is saying to focus on the solution to a problem, they can miss important pieces of information. The result is a troubleshooting process that is less efficient and perhaps frustrating for the end user, who feels that he or she has to repeat information unnecessarily.

Listen to the user describe the problem symptoms. Some support agents take notes about the symptoms. Listen for causal If...Then statements of the form, "If I do X, then the result is Y." For example, "If I try to adjust the monitor, then the screen goes blank" or, "When I click Cancel, my system freezes." User reports of computer behavior in this If...Then form often provide clues that lead to a possible path toward a solution more quickly than simple statements such as, "My monitor doesn't work."

Active Listening.   If basic listening skills are the most important communication skill, active listening skills rate a close second place. In **active listening**, the listener is as engaged in the communication process as the speaker, rather than being a passive receiver of information. An active listening skill that is often extremely helpful to user support agents is **paraphrasing**—restating in your own words what you heard the user say. The user can then verify that you understood him or her. Paraphrasing is especially helpful to clarify a problem description and leads to resolving misunderstandings. In describing a problem, a user might include unclear, unnecessary, or even contradictory information. As a troubleshooter paraphrases a problem statement, the user may correct the words to clarify the meaning. The following examples show how paraphrasing can help clarify the problem definition.

4

End-user description:	I don't know what happened, but the program doesn't work. I wonder if it is a defective program or if I am doing something wrong.
Support agent paraphrase:	Let me make sure I understand. The program used to work, but now it doesn't?
End-user description:	No, I just got the program installed, and it doesn't start up right. You would think they wouldn't sell this stuff until it operates correctly.
Support agent paraphrase:	So you installed the program following the instructions in the manual, and when you double-click the program icon, the program doesn't run at all?
End-user description:	Well, the box on the screen asks me for a file to open, but there are no files listed. Can't the program find its own files?
Support agent paraphrase:	The program opens a window and starts to run, but when the Open Files dialog box appears, the file list is empty?

Probes.   Follow-up questions intended to elicit more information from a user about a problem are called **probes**. Good troubleshooters learn to ask effective follow-up questions. Consider the following situation, where examples of probes appear in italics.

User:	When I am in the middle of working on a spreadsheet or word processing a document my computer frequently starts running another program automatically. Something just pops up in the middle of the screen and takes over my computer. Is there something wrong with the CPU or a short in the memory?
Troubleshooter:	Maybe, but maybe not. When a program pops up in the middle of the screen, is it always the same program, or different ones each time?
User:	Usually it is my e-mail program.
Troubleshooter:	*Does it ever automatically run any program other than e-mail that you can remember?*
User:	No, I guess not. Do I need to reinstall my e-mail program?
Troubleshooter:	How often does this problem happen?
User:	Every once in a while.
Troubleshooter:	*Like, once a week, once a day, or more often?*
User:	It seems like several times a day.
Troubleshooter:	*Does the e-mail program seem to pop up on a regular basis or at random times?*
User:	Now that you mention it, it is about every half hour.
Troubleshooter:	OK. Most e-mail programs have a feature to automatically check to see if you have any new e-mail messages. That feature may be turned on in your e-mail program. You can check to see if it is on, and if it is, either turn it off or set the time interval to a longer period, like an hour.

Notice the importance of the italicized probes as follow-ups in this exchange. Through a series of probing questions and careful listening, the troubleshooter was able to determine that what the user thought was a hardware problem probably wasn't, and to suggest a course of action to try to solve the problem for the user.

Critical Questions.   Another helpful troubleshooting tool is a list of **critical questions**, questions designed to elicit important information from a user. These questions also serve to challenge assumptions support agents may make (sometimes incorrectly) about a problem situation. Five examples of critical questions are:

1. Has the problem system, component, or feature *ever* worked?

2. Have you ever had this problem before? When?

3. Is the problem repeatable (can it be replicated)?

4. What were you doing on your computer just before you first noticed the problem?

5. Have you made any recent hardware or software changes to your system?

In their responses to critical questions, users often reveal information they wouldn't have thought to give to a support agent. Consider several examples: A user might forget to say that her failure to print from Corel Draw is because she has *never* been able to print from Corel Draw. Another user may neglect to say that he had the same problem formatting removable hard disks the last time he bought a particular brand of inexpensive disks. Or another user may omit the information that his network logon problem occurs in only one computer lab on campus and not in any other lab. Or a user doesn't mention that a power outage occurred immediately before she noticed a problem with her color monitor. Finally, a user may not tell a troubleshooter that the sluggish speed of a system corresponded with the installation of Office XP software.

In each of these examples, responses to one of the five sample critical questions could provide important additional information, or force support agents to challenge some assumptions they may have made intentionally or unintentionally about a problem situation. Critical questions often enable support agents to move beyond a situation in which a problem investigation has reached a dead end.

All successful support agents have a check list of favorite critical questions. These questions are especially useful to break new ground after an agent has asked every other question or probe possible, but still hasn't arrived at a solution, and is momentarily stuck.

Explanation and Verification.   Communication skills are also important at the end of a troubleshooting session. Effective troubleshooters explain a problem's solution to the end user. **Explanation** is a communication skill whereby a support agent describes the solution to a problem so the user understands why the problem occurred and what steps are required to resolve it. If the solution is one the user can implement immediately, the user can confirm that the solution did solve the problem.

For many users, a word of explanation is helpful and is more satisfying than a mere suggestion, such as "Click the Cancel button to fix the problem." One way help desks and support groups can reduce repeated callbacks is to explain a problem solution at a level the user can understand. The user will then have some insight into the cause of the problem and into how the given solution fixes that problem. Otherwise, the user in the example above may incorrectly assume that the solution to every problem is to click the Cancel button. Communication at the end of a troubleshooting process also provides important closure to the process. It permits troubleshooters to verify their perception that a problem is fixed with the user's perception (called **verification**). Sometimes the user and troubleshooter's perspectives are different, and verification can help resolve the differences.

Information Resources

Support agents can't possibly have had prior experience with every troubleshooting situation they will encounter, so they must have access to information resources to consult when they need to research solutions for new (to them) problems. Because new products and versions are released every day, support agents' prior experience and the information they can immediately recall instantly are less important than their ability to use information resources effectively to locate what they need to know.

Technical information about how computer systems work—and an understanding of some reasons they don't—are invaluable for support agents to bring to a troubleshooting situation. The more information support agents know from experience, the more likely they will be able to find a quick solution to a problem. However, all troubleshooters encounter problems they have never seen or problems with hardware or software they have never worked with. Examples of information resources include personal experience, scripts and check lists, knowledge bases, professional contacts and coworkers, support vendors and contractors, and escalation and team problem solving.

Personal Experience.   Most support agents have a personal store of knowledge, based on their education, career background, and previous experiences that they bring to each problem-solving event. One of the first steps in any troubleshooting situation is to search your personal knowledge for information about the problem or related problems: "Have I seen this problem before?" "How is this problem similar to or different from the problem I worked on last week?" "What did I do last time the printer beeped three times and quit printing?" This type of personal knowledge search happens almost automatically.

Successful troubleshooters often make notes after they have solved a problem. Notes can be informally organized in a loose-leaf binder or formally entered in a problem solution database. Written troubleshooting notes can help avoid a situation in which troubleshooters too often find themselves: "I know I've seen this problem before, but I don't remember what we did to fix it." Notebooks with reminders of past problems solved become an important personal resource for troubleshooters and can be used even if a help desk or support center doesn't have a formal problem record keeping procedure. A troubleshooting notebook can be organized by symptoms, equipment or software category, or date, or in any other logical way that makes the information easy to find.

Scripts and Check Lists.   Organizations that provide computer support on a contract basis or that provide telephone help desk support often develop scripts and check lists to aid in the troubleshooting process. Among other benefits, these tools assure a uniform response to user questions. A **script** is a document that lists questions to ask and, depending on the user's response to each question, follow-up probes. Often organized in the form of a flowchart or a decision tree, scripts are arranged in a logical sequence and cover many of the possible (known) paths to solve a problem. Although scripts tend to be oriented toward common problems, they can also contain valuable pointers to unusual problems, such as problems that occur very infrequently or only in a few relatively rare configurations. Figure 4-4 shows an example of a script to diagnose problems with a hypothetical printer model based on the control panel LED lights.

WWW

For more information about the use of scripts in a call center environment, visit the Digisoft Web site at **www.digisoft.com/solutions/telescript/ts-scripting.htm**. Digisoft is a vendor for Telescript, a call center script development tool. For examples of scripts implemented as a flowchart or a decision tree, see **www.extremetech.com/article2/0,3973,16621,00.asp**   or   **support. mfm.com/support/troubleshooting/copyprot.html**.

NOTE

Figure 9-7 in Chapter 9 shows an example of a flowchart.

4

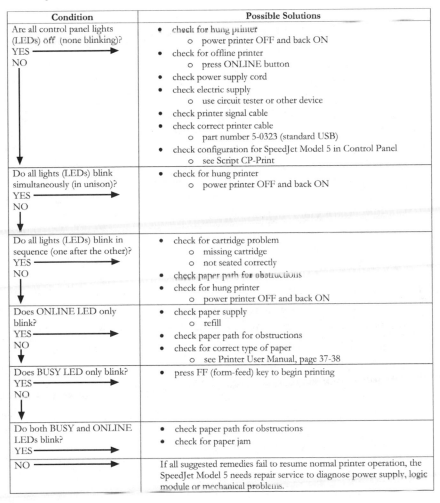

SpeedJet Model 5 Printer Diagnostics Script (revision March 8, 2004)

A SpeedJet Model 5 printer has several LEDs on its control panel that indicate its status: 1) ONLINE, 2) BUSY and 3) OTHER LEDs. When a printer problem occurs, the behavior of the LEDs often provides important diagnostic information. Use the script below when a user calls about a problem with the SpeedJet Model 5 printer.

Condition	Possible Solutions
Are all control panel lights (LEDs) off (none blinking)? YES ⟶ NO	• check for hung printer 　o power printer OFF and back ON • check for offline printer 　o press ONLINE button • check power supply cord • check electric supply 　o use circuit tester or other device • check printer signal cable • check correct printer cable 　o part number 5-0323 (standard USB) • check configuration for SpeedJet Model 5 in Control Panel 　o see Script CP-Print
Do all lights (LEDs) blink simultaneously (in unison)? YES ⟶ NO	• check for hung printer 　o power printer OFF and back ON
Do all lights (LEDs) blink in sequence (one after the other)? YES ⟶ NO	• check for cartridge problem 　o missing cartridge 　o not seated correctly • check paper path for obstructions • check for hung printer 　o power printer OFF and back ON
Does ONLINE LED only blink? YES ⟶ NO	• check paper supply 　o refill • check paper path for obstructions • check for correct type of paper 　o see Printer User Manual, page 37-38
Does BUSY LED only blink? YES ⟶ NO	• press FF (form-feed) key to begin printing
Do both BUSY and ONLINE LEDs blink? YES ⟶	• check paper path for obstructions • check for paper jam
NO ⟶	If all suggested remedies fail to resume normal printer operation, the SpeedJet Model 5 needs repair service to diagnose power supply, logic module or mechanical problems.

Figure 4-4   Example script to diagnose printer problems

Knowledge Bases.   Good troubleshooters have at their fingertips a variety of information resources to augment their personal experience. A **knowledge base** is an organized collection of information, articles, procedures, tips, and solutions to existing problems that can serve as a resource in problem-solving situations. In effect, a personal troubleshooting notebook of previous problems and their solutions that a support agent maintains is a simple knowledge base. Knowledge bases come in a variety of other forms from several sources.

- **Vendor manuals.** Most hardware and software products come with tutorial or reference manuals, sometimes in print, but frequently in a machine-readable format. Support agents who provide technical support for specific products need easy access to the vendor manuals for the products for which they are responsible. Vendor manuals often contain chapters on troubleshooting and frequently asked questions.

- **Trade books.** Because some vendor manuals are poorly written, a thriving trade book industry has developed to fill the vacuum for well-written information about popular hardware and software products. Internet booksellers such as **www.amazon.com**, **www.barnesandnoble.com**, and Jim's Computer Books at **jimsbooks.vstorecomputers.com** have search capabilities to help users locate trade books for a specific hardware or software product. Computer trade books are also available at most general bookstores and large computer stores, where you can browse the books to find one that is suitable. Over time, most successful troubleshooters build a small personal or professional library that is a convenient source of information about problems with products they support. Microsoft Press publishes an excellent series of books on troubleshooting for several popular Microsoft products. To see a list of the titles in the troubleshooting series, see **www.microsoft.com/mspress/troubleshooting/default.asp**. Note that examples from several of the books are available free as links on the Web page.

- **Online help.** Most software products, and some hardware products, have an online help feature. Sometimes the online help is no more than a convenient way to access the same information covered in the vendor manual. However, some online help systems include interactive troubleshooting wizards that provide useful insights into problem situations. Wizards are a form of online script or flowchart that guide a user or support agent through a series of steps to diagnose a problem. Windows 2000 and Windows XP incorporate several online troubleshooters into the operating system. To access them, press **F1** and search Help for the keyword *Troubleshooting*.

- **Web sites.** Web sites maintained by product and service vendors are popular and widely available support information resources. Most sites provide product information and problem-solving suggestions; some include interactive troubleshooting assistance. Microsoft offers an extensive Web knowledge base for its products at **support.microsoft.com/default.aspx**. Microsoft's knowledge base contains articles, problem reports, and other support resources. Figure 4-5 shows part of the Microsoft knowledge base that many support agents turn to when troubleshooting.

■ **Search engines.** When looking for information resources on a specific problem, don't forget to try a general purpose search engine, such as **www.google.com** or **www.dogpile.com**. These search engines are likely to turn up reports and suggestions from other users who have encountered a similar problem to the one you're researching.

Figure 4-5 Search of Microsoft Support Knowledge Base for information on macro virus problems in the Office 2000 Suite

Professional Contacts and Coworkers. Access to other computer professionals is an important resource for problem solving. The term "professional contacts" means work colleagues, but also can refer to computer experts in the industry. Access to these experts is often through ListServs and newsgroups via the Internet. Several Web sites also provide access to industry professionals and experts. Examples of Web sites that provide access to industry professionals and experts are:

- TechRepublic at **www.TechRepublic.com** (click the **TechnicalQ&A** link, registration required).

- About.com at **www.about.com** (click the **Computing & Technology** link, select a topic from the menu, and then click the **Forums** or **Chat** link).

- Cyber Tech Help at **www.cybertechhelp.com/forums/index.php**.

NOTE   Some support agents report that informal relationships with other user support students or trainees have served them well later in their careers. It is never too early to begin to develop professional relationships and networking.

Coworkers are also an important resource for many troubleshooters. When troubleshooters experience a "block" trying to solve a problem, a different perspective or "another set of eyes" can often help break through the block. On occasion, just the process of describing a problem to a colleague may trigger new insights into the problem. When a problem is especially complex or of high priority, a meeting of the team members in a support group may be convened to address the problem. Although a team approach to problem solving may be expensive, it is sometimes the only way to solve really difficult problems because team members often bring different personal experiences and creative energies to finding a solution.

A **ListServ** is an automated e-mail service that distributes all (or selected) e-mail messages posted on the ListServ to every subscribed member. Some computer vendors operate ListServs to provide their distributors with information and a communications channel for technical problems. An active ListServ can be an excellent information resource but can also result in a high volume of mail in your inbox.

WWW   A list of ListServs can be found on the Internet at **www.lsoft.com**. Click the **CataList** link, click the **Search** link in the List information section, and then enter keywords to describe a topic that interests you. For example, to find ListServs that address topics of interest to Macintosh computer owners, enter *Macintosh* as a keyword. Support agents interested in adaptive technology can join a ListServ that discusses accommodations for various disabilities.

Many ListServs maintain archives of past e-mail messages distributed to their membership. ListServ archives can be used by a prospective member to get a feeling for the kinds of topics discussed on a ListServ prior to joining. And you can often search the archives for answers for specific problems that were previously posted.

Newsgroups are Internet discussion groups in which participants with common interests in a topic post messages. They are like an electronic bulletin board. Participation is open to anyone who has an interest in the topic, and access is through a newsreader, which is built into most Web browsers or search engines, such as Google. Many support agents find newsgroups an effective way to ask questions and to obtain and provide information. Most newsgroups provide new participants with an FAQ archive that can be a valuable resource for troubleshooters.

Most Web browsers maintain lists of current newsgroups. For example, in Google (**www.google.com**), just click **Groups**. Tens of thousands of active newsgroups are in operation. Some are very general; others are highly specialized. For example, support agents who work extensively with spreadsheet users may be interested in the newsgroup **comp.apps.spreadsheet**. Support agents interested in a general site for hardware problems can find others with similar interests in **comp.hardware**, which is a popular question and answer site. Professionals with interests in a specific field are often regular contributors to newsgroups.

Support Vendors and Contractors.   Product vendors are often an extremely useful information resource. A vendor may have seen a baffling problem before and be able to offer suggestions to resolve it. Some vendors provide e-mail access to their technical support staff or open access to their proprietary troubleshooting knowledge bases.

An alternative troubleshooting resource is companies that provide outsourcing of support services. As you learned in Chapter 2, outsourcing companies provide problem-solving assistance for a fee. They can provide a useful resource to augment the internal support services in an organization. For example, an organization could contract with a support service provider to handle incidents for products that are beyond the expertise of its help desk staff or to provide backup to the internal help desk when the volume of problem reports is greater than the support staff can handle.

Stream International is an example of an external technical support provider. You can learn more about the company's services at its Web site: **www.stream.com/Stream.nsf**.

Escalation and Team Problem Solving.   When all other problem-solving attempts fail, a problem referral to a higher support level, called **escalation**, is often an option. Escalation usually involves referring a problem from a level 1 or level 2 support agent to a higher level of technical support. However, some organizations deemphasize support levels and organize their support agents into teams where mutual assistance and group problem solving is encouraged; in these organizations, the whole team is responsible for solving problems, not just individual staff members.

Diagnostic and Repair Tools

Support agents often use a variety of diagnostic tools to detect and repair hardware, software, and network problems. Many of these tools correspond to the carpenter's hammer and saw, the auto mechanic's wrench and test equipment, and the physician's x-ray machine. Hardware repair and network technicians and engineers use hardware diagnostic tools, such as circuit testers, signal loop back tools, and network protocol analyzers. The purpose of diagnostic software tools, sometimes called utility software, is to provide troubleshooters with information, problem diagnosis, and even repairs for common computer problems.

General-Purpose and Remote Diagnostic Tools.   These tools include software utilities that aid troubleshooters with the diagnosis of computer problems, including those that permit support agents to control the operation of a user's computer remotely over a network or telephone connection. Remote access tools are an economical way to provide support for users in distant locations, because a support agent does not have to be in the same physical location as the user. Examples of remote control software include Expertcity's GoToAssist product (see **www.gotoassist.com**; use the Quick Tour demo to see how this technology works), LapLink Gold from LapLink.com (see **laplink.com**), and pcAnywhere from Symantec (see **www.symantec.com/pcanywhere/Consumer**).

To learn more about remote control software and another product, NetOp Remote Control, read the NetOp white paper at **www.crossteccorp.com/ support/resources/NetOpWP.pdf** (requires Adobe Reader to view).

Hardware Problem Diagnosis.   These tools include software utilities that help diagnose common hardware problems. Many desktop and laptop systems are sold with hardware diagnostic utilities. Diagnostic software can detect some defective hardware components, identify performance enhancements, recover some kinds of lost data and fix other problems with media, document hardware configuration information and common configuration problems, and monitor the operation of a system. Examples of hardware diagnosis utilities include Norton SystemWorks that contains Norton Utilities from Symantec (see **www.symantec.com/sabu/sysworks/basic**), PC Certify (see **www.pccertify.com**), and WinCheckIt from TouchStone Software (see **www.touchstonesoftware.com**).

Software Problem Diagnosis.   These tools include software utilities that can identify the configurations of desktops, laptops, and servers, as well as identify and repair various kinds of software installation and configuration problems. They can detect authorized and unauthorized software installations, identify incorrect or incompatible software versions, and repair some kinds of problems with the Windows registry. Both experienced troubleshooters and novice support agents who need assistance with basic problem identification can use diagnostic software tools. Examples of problem diagnosis software include Triage eSupport products from MetaQuest (see **www.metaquest.com** and click the **Demo** button) and Dean Software Design's PC Surgeon (see **www.winutils.com/pcsurg.htm**).

Network Problem Diagnosis.   These tools include network monitoring software and remote management. Network monitoring software runs in the background on a local area network to search for network connectivity problems, configuration problems, unauthorized access, and performance problems. Remote management software can help manage the distribution and configuration of software to a few or hundreds of networked PCs, as well as restore software and configurations on PCs that have failed for a variety of reasons. Examples of network diagnostic tools include Norton Ghost from Symantec (see **www.symantec.com/sabu/ghost/ghost_personal**), InCharge products from SMARTS (see **www.smarts.com/products**), and SolarWinds.NET, network management tools (see **www.solarwinds.net/Tools/Standard/index.htm**).

Successful troubleshooters keep several of their favorite diagnostic utilities at their fingertips to aid in solving hardware, software, and network problems.

Problem-Solving Strategies

Troubleshooters often apply one or more common strategies to solve problems. Figure 4-6 summarizes seven commonly used logical approaches to problem solving that are often effective in a variety of troubleshooting situations, even difficult ones.

- Look for an obvious fix.
- Try to replicate the problem.
- Examine the configuration.
- View the system as a group of subsystems.
- Use a module replacement strategy.
- Try a hypothesis-testing approach.
- Restore a basic configuration.

Figure 4-6 Seven common problem-solving strategies

Look For an Obvious Fix. Because most computer problems are not difficult to solve, the first problem-solving strategy in any situation should probably be to look for an obvious solution. For example, if a monitor does not work, and you've tried to adjust it without success, consider the possibility that it may have become unplugged. But remember that there are four possible ways for a monitor to become unplugged, as shown in Table 4-1.

Table 4-1 Ways for a monitor to become unplugged

	At the Monitor	At the Other End
Power cord	Is the power cord plugged into the back of the monitor?	Is the power cord plugged into the wall outlet? Is the wall outlet working?
Signal cable	Is the signal cable plugged into the back of the monitor?	Is the signal cable plugged into the video card on the back of the system unit?

Experienced troubleshooters sometimes find it amazing how often a nonoperational system is due to a custodian who accidentally unplugged equipment while moving furniture to clean the floor. The table illustrates that even a simple problem-solving incident requires some logical thinking skills. The example also illustrates another simple problem-solving tool: a diagram or check list of possible alternatives, which reduces the chance that a potential source of the problem will be overlooked.

Another "old standard" in every support person's toolkit is, "If every other obvious fix fails, try rebooting the system." This advice falls into the category of looking for an obvious fix, because rebooting a system can eliminate a number of stubborn problems (low memory resources, device conflicts, or inoperative peripheral devices, for example). However, sometimes old standbys, such as rebooting a system to clear a problem, actually mask the real cause of the problem and will eventually result in a callback when the problem reoccurs.

Try to Replicate the Problem.   **Replication** is the process of trying to repeat a problem in a different situation or environment. A user may report that a problem occurs every time she performs a specific activity or series of steps. Although most users do not intentionally try to mislead a support agent, their problem description may omit an important piece of information. First, support agents should try to replicate the problem on the user's computer if possible. Second, they should try to perform the same task or reproduce the same situation on another system or on their own support system. If they can't get the problem to reoccur on the user's system, it may be traceable to a mistake the user is making. If the problem won't reoccur on another system, a difference in the configuration of the two systems may account for the problem. Then a troubleshooter can begin to look at differences between the two systems (hardware and operating system configuration differences, different software versions, and so on) to get to the root of the problem.

Examine the Configuration.   Some problems with computer systems occur because a particular combination of hardware, operating system, and applications software doesn't work well together. In technical jargon, they don't interoperate well. Examining the ways hardware and software are configured may lead to an understanding of the problem or a solution. For example, failure of an applications software package to work with a user's modem may be traceable to one of the following:

1. The operating system may not have been configured to work with the modem.

2. At the time the applications software package was installed, it may not have been configured to work with that particular brand of modem.

3. The modem may be a different one than was originally installed, or the settings in the modem may have been changed.

4. The configuration of the modem, operating system, and applications software may have changed since the last time the modem operated correctly.

5. Software or hardware has recently been installed that conflicts with the modem or its software.

The documentation for most hardware and software packages includes a description of the configuration requirements (for example, amount of memory, type of processor, disk space, video card requirements) needed to operate correctly. A comparison of the configuration requirements with the actual installation configuration can often resolve incompatibilities.

View the System as a Group of Subsystems. A computer system is actually a group of subsystems linked together to form a complete system. One problem-solving strategy is to consider the subsystems as a sequence of linked components, some hardware and some software. For example, consider the problem of a user who wants to print a memo in Courier font. However, when printed, the memo is in Arial font. Where does the problem lie? Several subsystems are involved in the process of printing the memo in the correct font. These include:

- The applications software module that prepares the output
- The printer driver in the operating system that adds printer control codes
- The operating system software that transmits the output to the hardware
- The BIOS operating system component that sends data to the printer
- The parallel or USB port where the printer is connected
- The cable from the port to the printer
- The software in the printer that translates data received from the computer into formatted characters
- The hardware in the printer, including the print head, that transfers the formatted characters onto the paper

Some of these subsystems, such as the printer cable and the print head, may be less likely culprits in this situation. However, a short in one of the signal lines in the printer cable may turn out to be at fault. There is not enough evidence yet to eliminate this possibility.

One strategy in this situation is to interrupt the sequence in the chain of subsystems at some point (the midpoint is often a good place to start), and see on which side of the midpoint the problem occurs. In this example, you might select the point at which the printer cable connects to the parallel or USB port as the midpoint. A support agent could observe, perhaps with a different printer, whether the font problem is on the printer side or the system unit side of the midpoint. Another strategy is to start at one end of the sequence of subsystems and trace the problem either forward or backward. Used with the module replacement strategy described next, treating a system as a group of subsystems can serve as a strategy to help isolate a problem.

Use a Module Replacement Strategy. Hardware technicians frequently use module replacement as a tool to diagnose computer hardware problems. **Module replacement** is a problem-solving strategy that replaces a hardware or software component whose operational status is unknown with one that is known to be operational. For example, if a DVD drive fails to work correctly, the problem may be the DVD drive itself or a piece of hardware or software related to its operation. One way to determine whether the problem really is the DVD drive is to disconnect it from the computer where it malfunctions and connect it to a second system. If the DVD drive works correctly in the second system, then the problem is not with the drive itself, and the technician can consider other options, such as the DVD driver software or signal cables that connect the drive. Many organizations troubleshoot only to a field replaceable unit (FRU) level, such as an expansion card, a circuit board, the motherboard, the power supply, a disk drive, and so forth, and replace the entire FRU because it may not be cost effective to go further to identify a smaller defective component.

The module replacement strategy also works for software. In the case of malfunctioning software that used to work, the equivalent of rebooting a computer is to reinstall the software package. Occasionally, the image of a software package stored on a hard disk becomes corrupted when some of the bits in the instructions are accidentally overwritten. The faulty software image loads into memory when the program runs, but the software fails to perform as it did previously. Reinstalling the software package replaces the copy of the program (module) on the disk with a fresh image. Some software packages also include a "repair" option. Instead of reinstalling the entire program image, only a smaller module that is defective is reinstalled.

NOTE Experienced troubleshooters take several steps as a precaution before they do a module replacement. For example, hardware technicians routinely draw a sketch and label cable connections before they unplug any hardware components. (Chapter 10 describes some do's and don'ts for working safely around computer hardware.) Furthermore, support agents routinely back up any software prior to reinstallation in case a problem arises during the installation process. Finally, prior to reinstalling a software package, support agents uninstall the package to avoid any possible contamination between the inoperable image and the fresh installation.

Try a Hypothesis-Testing Approach.   In hypothesis testing, the troubleshooter formulates a hypothesis about the cause of a problem. Then the troubleshooter carries out an experiment to determine whether the hypothesis is true or false. For example, a user may report that he is unable to log on to a network server:

> **User:**   I type my username and password, just as I usually do. The system gives me an error message that the username and password are invalid.

The troubleshooter listens to the problem description and may formulate some hypotheses that would explain the problem:

4

Troubleshooter (to herself):	This problem may be a hardware, software, or network problem. Where should I start? It is unlikely a hardware problem, so I'll assume (hypothesis) that it is a network problem. If it is, then the user should not be able to log on from any other workstation on the network. So I'll try an experiment to see if the problem is specific to a particular workstation.

In this case, suppose the user can, in fact, log on from another workstation.

Troubleshooter:	Ah, ha! If it is a network problem, it must not be on the server side. So I'll look at (hypothesis) the client side. If there is a problem with the client software, then no one else should be able to log on from the user's workstation. Let me try (experiment) to log on to my own account from the user's workstation.

In this scenario, suppose the troubleshooter was indeed able to log on to the server from the user's workstation using her own username and password.

Troubleshooter:	Interesting! We've apparently eliminated the network as a culprit. Maybe (hypothesis) the user is the culprit. Maybe he's forgotten his password (not likely). Let me try (experiment) to log on to the user's account from his workstation.

In this case, the troubleshooter's attempted logon was unsuccessful, too. She was able to replicate the user's problem.

Troubleshooter:	OK! What now? Perhaps (hypothesis) the username and password are not in the user access database of valid usernames and passwords.

A call to the network administrator determines that the user access database does include the correct username and password entries for this user.

Troubleshooter:	Hmmm! I assumed (hypothesis) that the problem was unlikely to be hardware. Maybe I should reconsider that assumption. Suppose I plug a different keyboard (experiment) into the user's system and try again. Ah, ha! Success. The problem is a defective key on the keyboard, and it is a key that happened to be in the user's password.

Although this scenario is oversimplified, it illustrates the hypothesis-testing and experiment method that is at the heart of many problem-solving efforts. The ability to formulate hypotheses and carry out experiments to test them is a valuable skill for any troubleshooter to build. This skill is based in large part on a troubleshooter's experience with a number of different problem situations, the ability to devise a successful experiment to test a hypothesis, and the ability to think clearly and carefully about a problem situation. An important component of hypothesis testing is critical thinking. The hypothesis-testing strategy works best when a support agent can think of several alternate explanations for a situation. Sometimes it helps to brainstorm alternatives with other support agents in a team environment.

Restore a Basic Configuration.   Some problems occur when hardware or software interacts with other parts of a system. If a problem cannot be traced to a configuration problem, another problem-solving strategy is to remove components (hardware or software) to "pare back" a system to a basic configuration. This approach is suggested last intentionally, because modifying a configuration can have side effects that are unpredictable and cause other problems. This strategy eliminates **variables**, or factors in a problem-solving situation that can change or be changed to make a problem too complex to solve easily. For example, if a piece of hardware such as a CD-RW drive will not operate correctly when added to a system, a support technician may try removing one or more other components to see if the new hardware component will operate correctly in a stripped-down system. If a technician finds that the CD-RW drive works fine when another component is removed, but fails when it is connected, then incompatibility between the two devices can be researched.

In another common scenario, a software package may fail to run when installed on a computer system connected to a network. One approach is to disconnect the computer from the network and observe whether the program runs on the standalone system. This situation removes a variable (the network connection) to see whether that factor makes a difference. If the software runs on a standalone PC but not on a networked system, then the technician can examine the network configuration requirements for the software.

The problem-solving strategies described above are critical tools in a troubleshooter's repertoire. They involve logical, organized, and critical-thinking skills that should, eventually, lead to a satisfactory solution. Problem solving is a skill that can be learned, but practice and experience really build problem-solving expertise. Other factors that contribute to successful problem solving include several personal characteristics.

KEVIN KERWIEN
PRODUCT SUPPORT ANALYST
SYMANTEC CORPORATION
SPRINGFIELD, OREGON
WWW.SYMANTEC.COM

4

Kevin Kerwien works in the Enterprise Support group at Symantec. He supports primarily corporate users of Symantec's AntiVirus and mail server filtering products. He spends about 6.5 hours per 8 hour day on the phone working with customers and takes 15 to 20 calls on an average day. Kevin says that supporting a product is more than just answering the phone, because it involves working on documentation for Symantec's knowledge base, testing products, and researching problems for customers.

What are some key pieces of information you listen for when talking with an end user about a problem they've encountered?

When I listen to a problem description, I focus on two areas: diagnosis of the user and diagnosis of the problem. Obviously diagnosis of the problem is the main goal. I find it very helpful to let users complete their entire description of a problem without interrupting with a lot of clarifying questions. Not only does their description tell you about the logic that the user is using to approach the situation, it also can reveal relevant details that you wouldn't have thought to ask for. Once their problem description is complete, if I feel that I have a good picture of the user and how they are approaching the problem, then I start to ask technical questions about the problem itself. If I am not totally certain why the user did some of the steps that they did, then I ask clarifying questions to understand their mental approach to the situation. Oftentimes a problem isn't really a problem but is just perceived to be one by the user. As a result, the only way to effectively address the problem is to approach the user's understanding of the issue. A really great question to use is, "How did you determine that?" If you trust the user's technical ability, then maybe you can just take them at their word. However in my experience, asking about how the user discovered the information they are basing their assumptions on can help reveal the solution to the problem.

How do you diagnose a user?

To diagnose the user, I listen to their explanation of the problem for technical terms to quickly assess their level of technical expertise. I listen to how they confirm information to see if they are working from assumptions or confirmed fact. And I listen to the user's confidence level to help me better gauge how to interact with the user. There can be very different communication styles for different users. If the user indicates that they do not have a high level of technical knowledge, then I use more explanations and simpler terms to describe the situation. However, an expert user can see that as condescending, so it is important to adapt to the user.

What problem-solving strategy do you find most useful when confronted with a new and unfamiliar problem?

A strategy I use frequently is deductive reasoning. Also known as "Holmesian Logic" after the famous Sherlock Holmes, the idea is that if you eliminate all the impossible explanations, then the remaining answer will be true. Technical problems can be very complex and have potentially hundreds of possible explanations. Sorting through all those possible explanations can be a daunting task. As a result, it is helpful to me to begin by ruling out possible causes before attempting to guess at what the cause may be. I start simple and rule out the things that clearly cannot be the cause. Then I turn my attention to the things that are unlikely to be the cause and rule them out. Finally, I evaluate the factors that are the likely causes to see if any of them fit the facts better than others. Approaching a technical issue in this manner helps me avoid the hit-and-miss approach of just guessing one possible cause after another.

Do you see differences in communication or interpersonal skills you use when you help internal users versus external clients?

Communication with external clients often places me in the role of ambassador for the company. I have to be able to listen to customer issues, switch gears quickly to respond to new questions, and filter information to provide the appropriate and most relevant information for the customer. Being able to relate to a customer's situation is paramount. Customers sincerely appreciate it when you consider their specific situation as opposed to giving them a general rule of thumb. Sometimes I get placed in a difficult position where I can't explain all of the reasons behind something because the information is internal in nature and can't be shared with the customer. Focusing on the information that you can provide to the customer is always more positive than telling them that there are certain things that you can't tell them.

4

How about internal users?

Internal customers are of a different nature altogether. Internal customers give me the allowance to be more casual in my communication style. However, the importance of building strong relationships with people in other departments should never be overlooked. Even if you don't see the immediate advantage in helping someone else do his or her job, try to recognize that there is a value to fostering the relationship even if you personally have nothing to gain from the immediate situation.

Personal Characteristics of Successful Troubleshooters

Personal characteristics play an important role in the troubleshooting process. Some personal characteristics can contribute directly to one's success as a troubleshooter. These are listed in Figure 4-7.

- They are patient and persistent.
- They enjoy the problem-solving process.
- They enjoy working with people.
- They enjoy continuous learning.

Figure 4-7   Characteristics of successful troubleshooters

To some degree, these characteristics are part of a support agent's basic personality. However, personal experience, feedback from users, and coaching by other support staff can affect the degree to which a support agent makes effective use of these characteristics.

Patience and Persistence.   Problem solving is often difficult work. It is sometimes frustrating to follow a strategy, reach a dead end, admit you've hit a wall, and have to try a different approach. A certain amount of frustration over an especially difficult problem is inevitable, but successful troubleshooters find ways to deal with frustration. One useful strategy to regain patience and perspective is to take a break from a problem. Go for a walk or perform a task where some progress is possible, and then return to the problem where progress seemed impossible. When you return, you can take a fresh look at the problem and can perhaps see other alternative solutions you overlooked earlier.

These characteristics are important in two respects. Troubleshooters not only need to be patient and persistent with themselves, but they also need to be patient and persistent with users. Successful support agents are able to shield users from their own frustrations. Expressing impatience with a client or a problem only impairs communication with the client, a situation that will not help resolve the problem. Users may also lack persistence. They may be too willing to give up on a difficult problem and may need to be reassured that a problem is not insurmountable—that all possible approaches and resources have not yet been exhausted.

Enjoy the Problem-Solving Process.

Successful support agents get enjoyment from the problem-solving process. Where users may see the computer world as a never-ending sequence of technical problems and frustrations, support agents tend to see challenges and opportunities. They enjoy finding the sometimes obscure relationship between a problem and its cause. Like physicians, who often see only sick people, user support staff members are hired to solve problems for end users. If you don't enjoy the challenge of solving problems and the satisfaction when an apparently difficult problem gets solved, you should perhaps consider a career in a field other than user support.

Enjoy Working with People.

The ability to work with all types of people is critical in the user support industry. User support agents don't have to like every user they encounter, and they don't have to treat each user as a personal friend in order to solve problems successfully. But they do need to communicate with users and to interact with them in a professional manner. If you don't enjoy working at a professional level with users, user support is not a field you'll likely enjoy for very long.

Enjoy Continuous Learning.

Change is one of the constant features of the computer industry and the user support field. The hardware or software package you learned in school is not the one you will likely get assigned to support on the job. Last year's products you knew inside and out will become obsolete. Anyone with a serious commitment to the user support field must enjoy learning about new products.

Continual learning is an important job skill in a support position, whether it is written into a formal position description or not. Most user support agents subscribe to one or more computer industry periodicals to keep up to date with changes in the computer applications field and with industry trends. Support agents regularly attend training sessions or must teach themselves new software packages. They look for opportunities to learn from other support agents. Some support organizations sponsor formal professional development opportunities, such as training sessions and informal sessions over lunch to encourage support staff to exchange information about products and the computer industry.

Trade publications that offer a broad perspective on trends in the computer industry include:

Computer Industry Periodical	Web Address
ComputerWorld	www.computerworld.com
InformationWeek	www.informationweek.com
InfoWorld	www.infoworld.com

DEVELOPING A PERSONAL PROBLEM-SOLVING PHILOSOPHY

The problem-solving approach in this chapter treats troubleshooting computer problems as a process, but not a process with a fixed sequence of steps that are guaranteed to work every time. You have learned about several problem-solving tools that you can apply to many troubleshooting situations. Like a carpenter or auto mechanic, support agents reach into a tool bag, grab a tool, use it, then pick up another tool, use it, and so on. Either the trouble gets resolved, or the troubleshooter recognizes that they don't have the tools they need to solve the problem and look for other resources.

All support agents are eventually confronted with problems they cannot solve easily. At these times, they need a personal approach to problem solving. A personal problem-solving philosophy includes an understanding of the strengths a support agent brings to each problem. It is based on the experience that selected tools and skills have been successful in solving past problems. It relies on information resources that have proved useful in past situations. It is improved by the metacognition process described in this chapter, whereby problem solvers carefully examine their own thought processes. Without a personal problem-solving approach, support agents are more likely to use a random, hit-or-miss, trial-and-error strategy instead of a logical, well-organized problem-solving approach. They are more likely to get frustrated by difficult problems or overly reliant on others when they encounter a dead end. Successful troubleshooters recognize a dead end not as a stopping point but as an opportunity to get a fresh start, question assumptions, and try another alternative with perhaps a different tool.

How do you develop a problem-solving philosophy?

1. Use your own experience, knowledge, skills, thought processes, access to information, and communication skills as the basis for your personal strategy.

2. Improve your troubleshooting skills and learn to use the problem-solving tools described in this chapter.

3. Analyze your troubleshooting approach. Recognize your strengths and weaknesses. For example, some support agents develop extremely good skills at finding information about a problem on the Internet. They learn to use search engines effectively and bookmark Web sites on their browser's favorites list that have been useful in the past. They pride themselves on their ability to find information quickly. Other support agents develop a network of colleagues with whom they regularly exchange e-mail or phone calls about difficult problems. They are proud of the fact that if they don't know an answer, they know someone who does.

Of course, no one support agent is equally adept at all the strategies in this chapter. But successful troubleshooters develop a sense of what works for them (a plan of attack), and what doesn't, and they try to take maximum advantage of their strengths. A problem-solving philosophy is not necessarily something a support agent writes down. However, a personal philosophy about problem solving is something a support agent thinks about a lot and works to improve.

Chapter 5 provides some common support problems you can use to help develop your own problem-solving philosophy.

NOTE

CHAPTER SUMMARY

- Most computer problems are not difficult to handle. They are requests for information, complaints, or problems with which a support staff member has experience.

- Troubleshooting is the process of solving more difficult computer problems. Rather than a series of sequential steps, troubleshooting is an iterative process—a creative process in which support agents try an approach, and if it doesn't work, they try another.

- Troubleshooters use an assortment of thinking skills in their work, including problem solving, critical thinking, and decision making. They also use several kinds of trouble-shooting tools, including communication skills, information resources, problem-solving strategies, and personal characteristics. Troubleshooters apply these tools, skills, and resources to various aspects of a problem.

- Communication skills include listening to a user's description of problem symptoms, active listening (or paraphrasing) to verify understanding of a problem, using critical questions to obtain information from a user, and challenging a support agent's own assumptions that may block the path to a solution. Helpful communication skills also include the ability to ask probing questions and explain a problem resolution to a user.

- Information resources include a troubleshooter's personal experience with similar or related problems, prepared scripts and check lists that follow a logical path to a solution, and various knowledge bases. Vendor manuals, trade books, online help, ListServs, news-groups, Web sites, and search engines are rich sources of information about problems. Coworkers, industry professionals, friends, and vendors are other information resources that may lead toward a problem resolution.

- Problem-solving strategies include seven logical thinking processes that are often useful to troubleshooters: (1) look for an obvious fix; (2) try to replicate the problem; (3) examine the configuration; (4) view the system as a group of subsystems; (5) use a module replacement strategy; (6) try a hypothesis-testing approach; and (7) restore a basic configuration.

- Personal characteristics that aid successful troubleshooters include patience and persistence, enjoyment of the problem-solving process, satisfaction in working with people, and the desire to continually learn new materials.

- All support agents need to develop their problem-solving skills, to think about the problem-solving process, and to develop their own problem-solving philosophy. The philosophy should include an awareness of their strengths and weaknesses when working with the problem-solving tools and resources described in this chapter.

KEY TERMS

active listening — A communication skill in which a listener is as involved and engaged in the communication process as the speaker; paraphrasing is an example of an active listening skill.

analogy — A way in which a current problem is similar to other problems that have been solved; an analogy between similar problems may suggest a possible problem solution.

contradiction — A situation in which two facts cannot be true at the same time; investigating a contradiction may suggest a possible solution.

creativity — The critical-thinking ability to find a novel or innovative solution to a problem; the ability to see a problem from new and different perspectives.

critical question — A question designed to elicit important information from a user that may force a support agent to challenge some basic assumptions about the problem.

critical thinking — Cognitive skills a problem solver uses to analyze a problem, search for the underlying logic or rationale, or strive for alternate ways to explain an event or situation.

decision making — The ability to select one alternative from among a number of alternatives, based on some evaluation criteria; an important skill for troubleshooters.

escalation — A problem-solving tool whereby a difficult or complex problem is referred to a higher-level support person or team for resolution.

explanation — A communication skill whereby a support agent describes the solution to a problem so the user understands *why* the problem occurred and the steps required to resolve it.

goal state — A desired outcome or objective; in troubleshooting, a common goal state is to diagnose or repair a computer subsystem to return it to a normal operational state.

hypothesis — An initial guess, hunch, or prediction based on experience.

hypothesis testing — The ability to formulate a hypothesis about the cause of a problem and design an experiment that will prove or disprove the hypothesis.

iterative process — A process that involves several paths or approaches to problem solving; steps are repeated in a loop until a fruitful path is found; troubleshooting is an iterative process in that it uses and reuses a variety of tools and skills.

knowledge base — An organized collection of information, articles, procedures, tips, and solutions to existing problems that can serve as a resource in a problem-solving situation.

ListServ — An automated e-mail service that distributes all (or selected) e-mail messages posted to the ListServ to every subscribed member and is organized around a topic of special interest to its members.

metacognition — The ability to think about thinking; the ability of a troubleshooter to step back from a problem-solving situation and analyze his or her thought processes.

module replacement — A problem-solving strategy that replaces a hardware or software component whose operational status is unknown with one that is known to be operational.

newsgroup — An Internet discussion group in which participants with common interests in a topic post messages; similar to an electronic bulletin board.

paraphrasing — A communication skill whereby you restate in your own words what you think you heard the speaker say.

probe — A follow-up question designed to elicit additional information from a user about a problem; a sequence of probes often clarifies a problem situation.

problem solving — A process of moving from a current state of events X (the problem state) to a future desired state of events Y; the objective of problem solving is to get from X to Y quickly, accurately, effectively, and efficiently.

replication — The process of trying to repeat a problem in a different situation or environment.

script — A document that lists questions to ask and, depending on the user's response, follow-up probes; often organized as a check list, flowchart, or decision tree that shows many of the possible (known) paths to a problem solution.

troubleshooting — The process of defining, diagnosing, and solving computer problems; involves the use of several thinking and communication skills, information resources, strategies, and methods.

variable — A factor or aspect in a problem-solving situation that can change or be changed; eliminating variables simplifies a complex problem so it is manageable and can be solved.

verification — A communication skill whereby a support agent can confirm his or her perception that a problem is fixed with the user's perception; if the perceptions are different, verification can help resolve the differences.

CHECK YOUR UNDERSTANDING

1. Which of the following is not an example of a difficult support problem?

   a. a problem a support specialist has never seen before

   b. a problem where the solution is not obvious

   c. a problem where the caller is angry or upset

   d. all of these are difficult support problems

2. True or False? Troubleshooting computer problems is a fixed sequence of steps a support agent follows from the initial problem description to the resolved problem.

3. True or False? Problem solving, critical thinking, and decision making are different names for the same skill.

4. The idea that a listener is an equal participant with the speaker in a communication is called _____.

   a. probing

   b. active listening

   c. paraphrasing

   d. replicating

4

5. A mental model to help a computer troubleshooter understand and explain a problem situation is based on _____.

    a. metacognition

    b. critical thinking

    c. decision making

    d. problem solving

6. The troubleshooting process that involves selecting one alternative from among a number of possible alternatives based on some evaluation criteria is called _____.

7. True or False? To restate a problem description using the user's exact words is called paraphrasing.

8. _____ is a problem-solving tool whereby a difficult or complex problem is referred to a higher-level support person for resolution.

9. The ability to step back from a troubleshooting situation and analyze one's own thinking process is called _____ .

10. A follow-up question a troubleshooter asks to get additional information about a problem situation is called a(n) _____ .

11. An organized collection of information, articles, procedures, tips, and problem solutions is called a _____.

    a. script

    b. flowchart

    c. knowledge base

    d. newsgroup

12. True or False? A troubleshooting strategy that swaps a hardware or software component whose status is unknown with one that is known to be operational is called module replacement.

13. Rebooting a system in an attempt to fix a problem is an example of which of the following problem-solving strategies?

    a. Look for an obvious fix.

    b. Try to replicate the problem.

    c. Use a module replacement strategy.

    d. View a system as a group of subsystems.

14. A successful troubleshooter recognizes a dead end (or block in progress) as

    _____.

    a. a frustration

    b. the end of the troubleshooting process

    c. an opportunity to look at other alternatives

    d. a stopping point

15. Show that you understand the concept of paraphrasing by writing a paraphrase for the follow problem statement: "The screen on my PC is blank."

DISCUSSION QUESTIONS

1. Suggest some additional critical questions that you would add to the list of five described in the chapter to help a support agent and a user who have reached a roadblock in their search for a problem solution.

2. Which of the personal characteristics in this chapter is the most important for a successful troubleshooter to possess? Describe some other attributes of successful troubleshooters that were not discussed in the chapter.

3. Which is more important to a successful computer troubleshooter: good technical skills or good people skills?

4. If you worked as a help desk specialist to support internal users, what tool or information resource would you want to have available to you if you could pick only one?

HANDS-ON PROJECTS

HANDS-ON PROJECTS

Project 4-1

Listen actively. Team up with another student or coworker and practice listening and paraphrasing skills. One person takes the role of the user, the other takes the role of a support person. The user describes a common problem with a computer system to the support person, who then paraphrases the problem description back to the user.

The user's role is important because he or she needs to listen for important parts of the problem that the support person omitted, that didn't exist in the original problem description, or that the support person modified. Continue the paraphrasing activity until the person in the support role can correctly paraphrase the original problem description. Then change roles and repeat the process. (Note that the purpose of this activity is to practice paraphrasing, not problem solving.)

Project 4-2

Ask questions. Study the following problem description. Then determine what additional information you, as a support agent, would want from this user. Design several questions you could ask to obtain the information you would need to resolve this problem.

> My computer is hung up. I don't know what I did wrong. The screen is frozen. Nothing I try does any good. I press keys on the keyboard, and nothing happens. The mouse pointer won't move.

4

Project 4-3

Provide explanations. Write an explanation to a user who wants to know why the Office XP software package will not operate on a PC he purchased in 1995. The user has a 486 system with 8 MB of memory that runs the Windows 95 operating system.

Project 4-4

Examine the configuration. A software package runs correctly on computer A, but the same package does not operate correctly on computer B. Make a list of basic computer system configuration information you would like to know to diagnose this problem further.

Project 4-5

Consider the subsystems. The chapter states that a computer system can be viewed as a group of subsystems. List several of the major subsystems that comprise a complete computer system, and briefly describe the role each one plays in a computer system.

Project 4-6

Ask the wizard. Experience a troubleshooting wizard for Windows 98 printer problems on Microsoft's Web site at **support.microsoft.com/default.aspx?scid=/support/windows/tshoot/printing98/default.asp**. Select the first problem, "My document was not printed." Make a brief list of the questions the troubleshooter asks to help a user diagnose a printer problem.

Project 4-7

Evaluate a troubleshooting event. Think about the most difficult troubleshooting problem you've encountered in your recent experience—one where the solution was not straightforward and where the problem was not a simple request for information. The problem you pick might be one you experienced personally, one you encountered at work or while serving as a lab helper, or one you encountered while helping a friend. Write a description of the troubleshooting event that answers the following questions:

1. What troubleshooting tools, methods, and strategies did you use? Describe them using the concepts in this chapter.

2. What subsystems were involved in the problem?

3. What communications tools, information resources, and problem analysis/diagnosis tools did you use?

4. Were the troubleshooting methods you used effective? Why or why not?

5. How could you have improved the effectiveness of your troubleshooting strategy?

Project 4-8

Learn about Windows system utilities. The Windows operating system includes several diagnostic utility programs that are of use to troubleshooters. Use the Windows Help system to learn the purpose of each of these utilities:

- System Information
- System Monitor
- System File Checker
- Disk Cleanup
- Disk Defragmenter

Write a brief description of the purpose of each of these utilities. Include in your description in what situation a troubleshooter might need to use each. Finally, briefly explain the difference between Disk Cleanup and Disk Defragmenter.

Project 4-9

Create and solve a practice problem. Based on your personal experience, write up a problem statement similar to the examples in Case Project 1. Then, exchange problem statements with another student or coworker and see if you can solve the problem he or she described. Try to make your problem a common one you've encountered, and don't make the problem you write too difficult. Remember, they are writing a problem for you to work on, too!

CASE PROJECTS

1. Problem Solving: Your Turn

See how many of these problems you can solve working by yourself. Use books, manuals, online help, and other resources, as necessary. Some of these problems are easier than others, so don't work too long on a problem that seems difficult; ask your instructor for help. As you work on these tasks, make some brief notes that describe your experience. Do some metacognition about your problem-solving approach.

1. A user with a Hewlett-Packard (H-P) model DeskJet 960cxi printer reports that she frequently gets a General Protection Fault error when attempting to print from Windows Me. What information about the recommended ways to deal with this problem can you provide her?

2. A user gets an error message: "Error Loading Kernel. You must reinstall Windows." What is the likely cause of this message? Do you really have to reinstall Windows to fix the problem?

3. A Microsoft Excel user often selects the Shrink-to-Fit feature in Microsoft Word to force a memo that is a little too long to fit on a single page. He wants to know if a similar feature is available in Excel to force a worksheet to fit on a single page without overlapping to a second page. Is there a Shrink-to-Fit feature in Excel?

4. Unplug the keyboard from your computer while it is turned off. Then power up your system. During the POST boot up diagnostic tests, one of the devices tested is the keyboard. What message appears to alert the user to the keyboard problem? If you plug the keyboard back in, will the system recover without rebooting? If necessary, plug your keyboard back in and reboot.

5. Use the operating system utilities on your computer to answer the following questions about your system. For each question, indicate what utility tool you used to find the information.

    a. What model of processor is in your system?

    b. What type of bus architecture is used?

    c. How much total memory does your system have?

    d. Is the subdirectory C:\NET in the search path?

    e. How is the environment variable TEMP defined?

    f. For the mouse on your system, what are the IRQ, COM port, and port memory addresses?

    g. What is the size of the hard drive? How much free space is available on it?

6. Run the utility ScanDisk on your hard drive. What problems, if any, did ScanDisk find? If problems exist, what is the procedure you would follow to eliminate them? What precautions should a user take before running ScanDisk to eliminate lost clusters? (On Windows 2000 or XP systems, use Help and search for "disk errors" to learn to run a comparable utility program.)

7. A user received a floppy disk from a friend in another organization, but can't read it on her system. The user says she has never had this problem before and doesn't understand why she can't read the disk. Make a list of the questions you would ask the user to help determine the solution to this problem.

8. A user reports that she has a program named ERU.EXE on her hard disk. She doesn't know its purpose and doesn't want to try running it for fear it will damage her system, and doesn't want to erase it for fear it is necessary for Windows to operate correctly. What can you tell her about the function of ERU and who should run it?

9. A user in engineering says he has a very old program on a floppy disk that he used to run 25 years ago to perform a special analysis on steel structures. He now has a client for whom he needs to run the program. It ran on an operating system named CP/M. The program could be rewritten to run on a modern system, but the rewrite would take several weeks. Is there any way to run a CP/M program on today's computers?

10. An accounting user received a program from the corporate office. The program is in a file named AUDIT.ZIP. The instruction manual is in a file named AUDIT.PDF. The user is puzzled because she does not have any software on her system that can run the program or read the documentation file. Can you help her?

11. A user reports that when he runs a program on his hard drive, he always gets an error message about a missing VBRUN400.DLL file. He has searched the hard drive and cannot find the missing file. How can he get a copy of the missing VBRUN400.DLL? He mentions that his computer does have a file named VBRUN300.DLL. Can he use it instead? If so, how?

12. A user who has recently changed departments from manufacturing to product design says that all the e-mail messages he sends have two lines appended automatically to the end of each message:

    GRIGORY VLADNIK

    MANUFACTURING DEPT, XT 555

    He wants to change the department name to PRODUCT DESIGN, but does not know how the automatic lines get there because he doesn't type them. How can he make the change in his e-mail program? (Use Microsoft Outlook or another e-mail program with which you are familiar to answer this question.)

1. A Microsoft Excel user noticed that another user in her department has more than four files listed in the recently used files list in the Files pull-down menu. How can she increase the number of files listed on her computer?

2. A user who has just installed a new computer notes that it has a peripheral plug-in labeled USB 2.0. She wants to install a printer from her old system that used USB 1.1 technology. Will her old USB 1.1 printer work on the USB 2.0 port?

3. A panicked user writes the following e-mail: "I just accidentally deleted a Microsoft Project .mpp file from my hard drive, and I really need to get it back. My job may depend on it. Can you help me get the deleted file back?" Describe the strategies you would use to help the user.

2. A Friendlier Send To Command for The D'Amico Company

Jane D'Amico owns The D'Amico Company, which provides curriculum development consulting services to education boards across the midwestern United States. The consultants who work for D'Amico are former teachers, and although they use computers in their work, they are not always confident in their technical abilities. Jane likes to find ways to make it easier for the consultants to interact with their computers.

As you know, it is sometimes not easy to move or copy a file in Windows from one folder to another. For example, to use the drag-and-drop method, you need simultaneously to display both the file you want to copy and the folder to which you want to copy it. The Send To command is useful if you want to copy a file to a floppy disk. However, Jane feels the Send To command would be more useful if a user could use it to copy or move a file to any folder, even if it was not visible on the screen.

Research a utility program called OtherFolder that extends the capability of the Send To command. The utility is available on the Internet from **www.annoyances.org/exec/ software/anyfoldr**. Click the **OtherFolder** link. Install OtherFolder on a system to which you have access.

Test the capabilities of OtherFolder to solve the problem described above. Write a brief description of the problem and how OtherFolder solves it. Describe any problems you encountered with the installation and use of the OtherFolder utility.

3. Dale Andrew's Macintosh Disk

Dale Andrews, a hardware repair technician, walked into the support center late one afternoon after a busy day repairing PCs. He called out to anyone who was listening, "Help!" Dale explained to the support agents who were in the office that he has a machine-readable copy of the manual for a hardware component on a floppy disk that he couldn't read on the PC in his shop. He said, "The box says the manual on the floppy is in Word format, but I suspect the disk was created on a Macintosh because that manufacturer used to do a lot of work with Macs. I am stuck until I can find a way to read the manual on this disk. I don't think there is a Mac in the entire organization! I would ask the manufacturer for a manual in PC format, but the manufacturer doesn't support this product anymore." One of the support staff jokingly said, "Go out and buy a Mac!"

List as many alternate ways you can think of that the support center staff could help Dale solve this problem. Describe each alternative you listed in terms of its cost and speed. Are some of the alternatives more feasible than others, given that Dale needs the manual now and doesn't want to spend a lot of money to get it? What approach would you recommend to Dale?

4. Diagnostic Software for Re-Nu-Cartridge

For additional background on Re-Nu-Cartridge, see Case 4 in previous chapters.

NOTE

Tamara Harold received the e-mail message shown below from Fred Long, president of Re-Nu-Cartridge.

> To: TamaraHarold@ReNuCart.net
>
> From: FredLong@ReNuCart.net
>
> I would like to help computer users at Re-Nu-Cartridge become more self-reliant when they encounter problems.
>
> Because you are one of the most knowledgeable computer users at Re-Nu, I wonder if you would look into whether a diagnostic utility program would be useful. I am especially interested in the kinds of problems this software can detect and whether the software would make our employees more productive when they have problems. Could you pull together some information about the capabilities a diagnostic program might offer us so that we can make a decision about whether to purchase one for our workers' use?
>
> I will very much appreciate your advice on this one.

Tamara is busy working on a project, and asks you to help with this assignment. Download a demonstration or evaluation copy of a diagnostic software utility, such as PC Certify, WinCheckIt, PC Doctor, Norton Utilities, or another similar package with which you are familiar, and try it out. Write a short description of the capabilities of the program that Tamara can send to Fred.

COMMON SUPPORT PROBLEMS

In this chapter you will learn:

♦ The types of common end-user computer problems

♦ How problem-solving processes are applied to several typical support problems

As you learned in Chapter 4, many problems that a user support agent handles are not particularly difficult or complex. You also learned about the problem-solving and troubleshooting process and some tools support agents use to solve problems that are more difficult. In this chapter, you'll examine some actual problem-solving situations and how user support agents solved them.

This chapter is not a comprehensive catalog of every kind of problem a user support agent might encounter; that would be an impossible task. However, experienced support agents frequently see some common problem types. You will look at several problem examples to see how the end user described the problem, what problem-solving strategies the user support agent employed to resolve the problem, as well as the user support agent's conclusions about the process. All of the examples are based on actual support situations.

COMMON END-USER PROBLEMS

Although computer problems come in a variety of forms, most problems fall into one of six categories. Figure 5-1 lists these common problem categories. The following sections discuss each category in more detail.

●	Hardware problems	●	Documentation problems
●	Software problems	●	Vendor problems
●	User problems	●	Facilities problems

Figure 5-1   Six common problem categories

NOTE In each section below, example problems are described to illustrate the kind of problems support specialists may encounter. You may have had personal experience with some of these problems or similar problems, or you may not have encountered anything like them before. The details about specific problems are less important than the categories they illustrate.

Hardware Problems

Many hardware problems stem from one or more of three sources: installation and compatibility, configuration, and malfunctions.

Hardware Installation and Compatibility Problems.   End users encounter a large percentage of hardware problems when they first purchase a new hardware product or upgrade an old one and attempt to use it. The product may be incompatible with existing hardware, or the end user may not have installed it correctly. **Incompatible** computer components are those that cannot operate together in the same system. The following example illustrates the discovery of hardware incompatibility during installation and the user support agent's solution.

Problem: A user purchased a scanner for a computer system. The scanner was designed to plug into a parallel port. However, the user already had a printer connected to the system's parallel port. Fortunately, the scanner included a printer bypass option so the printer could be connected to the scanner, which in turn could be connected directly to the parallel port. Although the printer worked fine when it was plugged directly into the parallel port, it did not operate when it was attached to the scanner according to the instructions in the scanner documentation.

Solution: A telephone call to the scanner vendor's support help desk revealed that the printer bypass feature does not work reliably with all brands of printers. The scanner vendor recommended that the user purchase a second I/O adapter card with an additional parallel port so that each device (the scanner and the printer) could be plugged directly into its own port.

Information about many hardware compatibility problems can be found in vendor manuals, in README files on distribution media, and on vendor Web sites. For example, see a list of hard drive compatibility problems on Monarch Computer Systems' Web site at **www.monarchcomputer.com/Merchant2/ merchant.mv?Screen=CTGY&Store_Code=M&Category_Code=HDFAQ**.   An alternative approach to hardware compatibility is to plan in advance for upgrades and installation. Some vendors provide information about compatible hardware devices. For example, Microsoft provides a Windows Catalog that lists devices   certified   to   be   compatible   with   Windows   XP   at   **www. microsoft.com/windows/catalog/default.aspx?subid=22&xslt=hardware**.

Hardware Configuration Problems.   **Configuration problems** are difficulties that occur when hardware (or software) options are set incorrectly for the computer environment in which a component must operate. Hardware settings may be changed in several ways, including with small jumper pins, by DIP switches, or by a software utility program that selects among various hardware configuration options. In some cases, the computer startup files have to be modified by installing a vendor's software driver to get its hardware components to operate. For example, a serial port on a communications adapter card can be addressed as COM1, COM2, COM3, or COM4, depending on how the jumper pins are set.

To learn more about the role jumper pins and DIP switches play in hardware configurations and to see a diagram of each, read definitions of these terms in the Webopedia at **webopedia.internet.com/TERM/j/jumper.html** and **webopedia.internet.com/TERM/D/DIP_switch.html**.

Hardware configuration problems were much more common before the widespread adoption of **Plug and Play standards**, which are industry-wide agreements among hardware and operating system vendors about hardware installation and configuration options. These standards specify the communication methods and rules that an operating system uses to recognize and incorporate hardware components into an operational system. With Plug and Play, an operating system can often recognize the existence of a new hardware component and select configuration options that permit the component to communicate successfully with the operating system.

To learn more about Plug and Play standards, visit the Web site of the UPnP Forum that describes industry initiatives to reduce configuration problems at **xml.coverpages.org/upnp.html**.

Although Plug and Play standards have reduced the frequency of hardware configuration problems, these problems have not disappeared, as shown in the following example.

Problem: A user purchased a new video graphics adapter card to increase the resolution of the display screen from 800 × 600 pixels to 1024 × 768 pixels. The card installed easily, and the Windows operating system recognized on startup that a new piece of hardware had been added to the system. The Windows Add New Hardware Wizard went through the process of installing an updated software driver to support the new video card. However, when the user restarted the computer after installation, the video image was the same resolution as before.

Solution: A PC repair technician suggested that the new video graphics adapter card actually supported several different display screen resolutions, including the older 800 × 600 and the newer 1024 × 768 settings. The technician pointed out that the default resolution set in the operating system was probably still 800 × 600. The technician then suggested that the user open the Display Properties in the Control Panel and change the default settings for the display to 1024 × 768. Once the user changed the operating system's settings to match the new video card's capabilities, the screen image appeared at the higher resolution.

Although Plug and Play can help an end user load the appropriate drivers, it does not always automatically adjust software settings to take maximum advantage of the new hardware's capabilities.

Hardware Malfunctions. A small percentage of hardware problems result from components that have either never worked or no longer work. To avoid future hardware problems, the user support staff may "burn in" a new system before installing it at an end user site. **Burn-in** is a 48- to 72-hour period during which a new computer or component is operated nonstop in an attempt to discover obvious operational problems and to identify any marginal or temperature-sensitive components. The burn-in period gives the support staff the opportunity to identify hardware malfunctions before they become a source of frustration to an end user. The burn-in strategy is effective because a defective component often fails during its first few hours of operation. After the burn-in, the probability that a component will eventually fail is much lower.

Electromechanical devices that have moving parts (such as hard and floppy disk drives, CD and DVD drives, and printers) are much more likely to develop hardware problems than components that are entirely electronic (such as CPUs, memory, bus slots, and expansion cards).

Vendors that sell hardware components often include a diagnostic utility to help users and support agents detect possible problem components. Vendors also sell diagnostic software, such as Symantec's Norton SystemWorks, that are hardware diagnostic tools to help user support agents detect common hardware malfunctions, such as a device that is not getting power, a device that is not communicating correctly with other hardware devices, or a device that has a defective logic circuit on its controller card. Although some hardware components that malfunction can be repaired after a problem is identified, the hourly charge for electronic shop labor often makes it more cost-effective to replace rather than repair faulty devices. Support specialists who work with a large population of computers may keep a small supply of spare parts on hand when a device needs to be replaced. Others rely on overnight shipping from hardware vendors when a replacement part is needed quickly.

5

Problem:	A user reported a problem with his PC's keyboard to a help desk. The problem appeared to be an inoperative S key. The user asked if the S keycap was somehow broken and could it be replaced, and whether he could bring the keyboard in to the service department to get it repaired. He also asked about the cost to repair the S key.
Solution:	The user support agent at the help desk said that physical damage to a keycap is rare and that, more frequently, the contacts located underneath the keycap wear out or get sticky. The support agent explained that hardware technicians rarely try to repair a keyboard malfunction. The support agent also noted that the cost of a replacement keyboard is usually much less than a technician's time to diagnose and repair a broken keyboard.

To solve hardware problems, user support agents should be sure to do the following:

1. Look in the Control Panel for possible interaction problems between hardware devices and software drivers. (For information on Control Panel troubleshooting options in Windows, click Help on the Start menu, click the Contents tab, click Troubleshooting, and then click the appropriate troubleshooter; the Hardware Conflict troubleshooter is a useful tool, as are several of the other troubleshooters.)

2. Examine any applicable README files on the distribution media that accompanies the hardware component for updated compatibility information.

3. Check vendor Web sites for updated drivers and software patches.

These resources often lead to solutions to hardware installation and incompatibility problems. Chapter 4 described several diagnostic utility programs that provide useful tools for diagnosing common hardware problems.

Software Problems

Many software problems stem from one of four common sources: installation and compatibility, configuration, bugs, and performance.

Software Installation and Compatibility Problems.   Installation of new software products or upgrades to existing products is generally easier today than it was in the past. And problems are more common during the installation process than after software is operational. During the 1970s and 80s, a user would manually create a subdirectory (or folder) for the new software, copy files from the distribution media to a system's hard drive, and then configure software drivers and system startup files to set software options to match the hardware configuration. Because command strings were lengthy and the probability of a typing error was great, the potential for mistakes during this manual procedure was substantial. Today, the software installation process is usually automated, and users who install software can avoid common problems that once plagued both users and support agents. **Installation software** is special-purpose utility software that aids in the installation of other software packages. An installation utility can automatically create folders with correct path names, examine the hardware configuration to determine whether the software and hardware are compatible, and set configuration options in the software and the operating system to match the hardware.

A popular installation utility is Install Shield (see **www.installshield. com/default.asp**); however, shareware vendors sell alternatives at a much lower cost.

Information about many software compatibility problems can be found in vendor manuals, in README files on distribution media, and on vendor Web sites. For example, see Microsoft's Web site that addresses application software compatibility problems with Windows and offers diagnostic tools at **www.microsoft.com/windows/appcompatibility/default.mspx**.

In spite of installation programs that know about common hardware and software configurations, user support agents still deal with installation problems. Not all software installs automatically. In addition, user support agents are occasionally asked to install older software, as in the following example.

Problem: A support agent installed a software package that was designed to run in an MS-DOS environment on a Windows PC. The support agent investigated how to run a DOS application in a Windows environment using a feature called DOS-compatibility mode. Unfortunately, the DOS program did not operate correctly in this mode because the program bypassed some of the Windows operating system features and performed its own input and output operations. The program appeared to be incompatible with Windows, even in DOS-compatibility mode.

Solution: The user support agent called the software vendor and learned that, to run the older program on a Windows PC successfully, he had to set up the computer as a dual-boot system so that it could run both MS-DOS 6.2 and Windows. In a dual-boot environment, the user chooses which operating system to use at boot up time. The dual-boot solution meant the user could continue to run a valuable DOS application on a Windows PC. Although the dual-boot option is not a solution in every case of incompatibility because dual-boot systems can also *create* problems, in this case it solved the problem without undesirable side effects.

A popular utility to implement a dual-boot system is VCOM's System Commander. To learn more about its capabilities, visit **www.v-com.com/product/ sc7_ind.html**.

Shareware software downloaded from the Internet can be another source of compatibility problems. **Shareware** is commercial software that users can try out with the vendor's permission during an evaluation period (usually 10 to 45 days—30 is common) prior to making a purchase decision. Although many shareware programs are written to industry programming standards and are designed to be compatible with operating systems and other applications, some shareware programs may produce conflicts with hardware or other software. A **conflict** is a situation in which a computer component uses systems resources (CPU, memory, or peripheral devices) in a way that is incompatible with another component. Conflicts often make systems inoperable or prevent them from operating normally (for example, performance may be slow).

Another category of software that can sometimes cause compatibility problems is **freeware**, which, as the name implies, is distributed without cost or a licensing fee. Although a donation is sometimes solicited, users are free to use, but not sell, the software. Some freeware can run trouble-free, but users are advised to take precautions, such as making a backup copy of the system Registry (described below), prior to the installation of freeware programs. Those who write and distribute freeware do not intend to provide software that is incompatible. However, some shareware and freeware may not be tested for compatibility to the same extent that commercial software is.

Distributors of shareware programs include **www.tucows.com**, **www.jumbo. com**, **www.shareware.com**, and **download.com.com**.

Software Configuration Problems. Some software problems are related to the way the software is configured to run on a system. Configuration problems result when software options are not set correctly for the specific operating environment or hardware. These problems may occur when end users install or upgrade new hardware or software or attempt to use a software feature for the first time, as in the following example.

Problem: A Windows user installed a new software application that uses a utility program called WordViewer. After the installation, the end user could not open any Microsoft Word document by double-clicking it. When the user double-clicked a .DOC file, WordViewer opened the document rather than Word itself. However, the user reported that if he started Word and used the File menu's Open command, he could successfully open a document in Word. For convenience, he would like to be able to double-click a .DOC file and have it open in Word.

> **Solution:** A support agent researched the problem on the Internet and found that WordViewer is a free Microsoft utility. It is designed to let a user who does not have the Word program view, but not modify, any Word .DOC file. The support agent suggested that perhaps when the new application was installed, it erroneously configured WordViewer as the default application for all .DOC files. The support agent suggested that the end user should perform the following steps: Click any Word .DOC file to select it, then press and hold down the SHIFT key and right-click the highlighted file. Next, click the Open With command. Select the WINWORD application from the Open With dialog box, and click the check box so a check mark appears in the Always use this program to open this type of file check box. (In some versions of Windows, the Open With command includes a Choose Program option from which the WINWORD application is selected.)

Another source of problems related to software compatibility and configuration in the Windows operating system, starting with Windows 95, is the system Registry. The Registry is an improvement over previous methods of storing configuration information, because much of the information that the operating system needs about hardware and software components is collected in one large Registry file. During normal system operation, the Registry is frequently read from and written to by applications and system software. The Registry file can also be edited with a software utility, REGEDIT.EXE or REGEDIT32.EXE (depending on operating system version). However, end users and support agents who are unfamiliar with the Registry, its entries, and how to modify configuration information, should avoid making or modifying entries in the Registry. Improper Registry information can result in an inoperable system. Due to the frequency of Registry problems, new versions of Windows include a feature to restore a prior version of the Registry on a computer that fails to operate because of invalid changes to Registry information. Support agents who need to learn about the role of the Registry should consult one of the many trade books that describe its use and proper procedures for modification.

Warning! No modification of the Windows system Registry should ever be attempted by anyone who is not entirely familiar with its organization, use, backup, and restore procedures and modification. A damaged Registry can cause serious problems. To take a tutorial on Registry basics, visit: **www.winguides.com/article.php?id=1&guide=registry**. A list of utility tools to modify and repair a Registry can be found at **www.winsite.com/tech/reg**. Any tool that works with the Registry should be used with care and appropriate precautions.

NOTE To guard against an inoperable system due to Registry corruption or other problems, many support specialists advise users to make a set of boot up and emergency system recovery floppy disks or CDs for each system, and learn to use automated Registry recovery utilities when an operating system offers these tools. For more information, use an operating system's help feature to search for detailed procedures.

Software Bugs.   **Bugs** are errors in a computer program that occur when a programmer writes incorrectly coded instructions during program development. Bugs occur more often in custom-written and shareware programs than they do in mass-market programs. In all software, bugs are encountered for the most part in infrequently used features of a program. Many bugs are eliminated during the testing period that occurs before a software product is released for sale. However, even the most popular software products have known bugs several years after their initial release.

In order to fix bugs and provide new features, software vendors often distribute new versions, upgrades, new releases, updates, patches, and service packs for existing versions, or even distribute new products.

- A new **version** of a software package contains significant new features and is usually the result of a substantially rewritten program.

- An **upgrade** is a new version of an existing program that is sold at a reduced cost to owners of a previous version of the program.

- A new **release** of a program is a distribution that contains some new features not found in the original program.

- An **update** is a bug-fix distribution that repairs known problems in a previous version or release of a software package; some vendors now include an **automatic update** feature that periodically checks the vendor's Web site for updates that are recommended to solve specific problems.

- A **patch** is a replacement for one or a few modules in a software package to fix one or more known bugs.

- A **service pack** (or service release) contains both updates and patches to fix documented problems with a version of a program.

NOTE

Although no industry standards dictate how vendors should number software releases, some software vendors use the version number to indicate the release type. For example, version 2.0 is the first distribution of a new version, version 2.1 is an update with new features, and version 2.11 (or 2.1.1) is a bug-fix release or an update of version 2.1 but does not necessarily include major new features. Other vendors add a service pack/release letter to a version number. For example, version 2.5A is the first (A-level) patch of release 2.5. Some software vendors now use the year of release to number their software versions. For example, Windows 2000 is the release of the Windows operating system issued in the year 2000. Although there is usually no direct correspondence between competing vendors' version numbering schemes, for marketing purposes vendors may intentionally skip a version number in order to maintain parity with the version number of a competitor's product.

The following example illustrates how one end user obtained a patch.

Problem: An end user experienced a formatting problem that appeared in only very large dollar amounts in an accounting program.

Solution: When the end user contacted the software vendor's help desk, the user learned that the problem was a known bug, that it had been repaired, and that a patch could be downloaded from the vendor's Web site or requested on CD-ROM. The vendor's help desk staff provided the end user with instructions on how to download the patch and explained that it would self-install when the user double-clicked the downloaded file.

Before a user or support agent installs any patch, he or she should verify that the patch is for the software version that is actually installed on the user's system. A cautious user or support agent may choose to back up the original copy of a program before updates are installed. In addition, any software upgrades, new releases, or patches that are installed on a computer should be documented in the site installation notebook, as described in Chapter 10. Whenever a patch is installed, it must be reinstalled if it should become necessary to reinstall the original software from the distribution media. Therefore, support agents should maintain a record of all updates and patches installed on a system as a reinstallation reminder. In general, new software releases or versions incorporate all bug fixes that have been reported and fixed prior to the new release. For example, software version 3.1 contains all patches released for version 3.0. However, the documentation for some patches may include a note that patch 3.4A must be installed before patch 3.4B can be installed.

In cases where no patch exists for a software bug, a support agent or software vendor may be able to suggest a workaround for a problem. A **workaround** is a procedure or feature that accomplishes the same result as a feature that does not work due to a bug or other malfunction. For example, a command in a GUI environment can be entered in several ways: keyboard commands, menu commands, toolbar icons, and shortcut keys. If a menu option does not work correctly, a keyboard shortcut may offer a successful workaround.

Software Performance Problems. **Performance problems** occur when a computer is operational, but does not operate as efficiently as it can or should. Performance problems often result from a combination of hardware and software problems. For example, a user may report that a PC's hard disk drive light comes on more frequently now and stays on longer than it used to and that the system seems sluggish. The response time from when the Save command is selected to the completion of the Save task has become increasingly longer. The user may suspect that the problem is due to hardware—perhaps the hard disk drive is beginning to fail. However, performance problems are usually related to how the software, the operating system in this case, is managing the hardware. A support agent might investigate alternate explanations, such as those in the following list, before concluding that a hard drive failure is the likely problem.

- The hard disk drive may be nearly full; the operating system may not have adequate unused space to write temporary files to the hard drive during its file management tasks. The user may need to back up and delete infrequently used programs and data files, or add a second, inexpensive hard drive to the system.

- The hard disk may be fragmented; files written on the disk in small chunks may take longer to read and write than files in contiguous sectors on the disk. A defrag utility can often fix this problem.

- The hard drive may contain wasted space because links to free space are lost. ScanDisk or another Windows utility program can often locate and reclaim lost space resulting from improperly linked allocation units on a disk.

- The system may not have enough RAM memory to run the software and may be using the hard disk as an extension of RAM (called swap file space) to accommodate large amounts of data. The swap file space may need to be enlarged, or the computer may need more internal memory to run the software efficiently. Hardware experts often emphasize that the most effective way to improve software performance is to add RAM memory.

Closely related to software problems is a user's ability to operate the software.

User Problems

Users unintentionally cause many support problems. Although most users try to be well informed and do their best to use hardware and software correctly, even the best-intentioned users can introduce problems.

Mistakes. All end users, including computer professionals, make mistakes. During the initial design of a program, systems analysts may not adequately understand all the detailed aspects of a business process and may design a software solution incorrectly. Programmers may make mistakes in the code they write and introduce software bugs. A professionally trained and experienced data entry operator may type an erroneous keystroke every few thousand characters. Even user support agents make an occasional error. What can be done about user mistakes? Well-designed computer systems anticipate many potential user mistakes, alert the user, and provide corrective action. For example, an accounting program may be able to perform a validity check on input data and detect input errors. A common example is a range check on the number of hours each employee worked in a week to identify input that exceeds some programmed maximum.

Despite the best efforts of software developers, users occasionally press a wrong key or click the mouse in an unintended situation and end up in a part of a program where they didn't want to be. Users can easily press one key sequence or click a sequence of mouse operations when they didn't mean to. Some inadvertent user choices are invalid, and have no consequence other than a beep. Other errors can have more drastic consequences. For example, in some word processors, if a passage is selected (highlighted) and the user presses a key, the character representing the pressed key replaces the entire selected passage. If a user doesn't know how to recover from this situation, the user can easily lose some work and not understand why.

Although end user mistakes account for a significant percentage of common problems, support agents need to consider carefully how to handle these problems from a client service perspective; some users do not like to be told that they made a mistake. Chapter 3 suggested strategies for handling difficult interactions with users.

NOTE   User mistakes sometimes provide an occasion for a support agent to tactfully point a user toward a training opportunity, whether an in-house session, a trade book, or a computer-based tutorial.

Misunderstandings.   Other end-user problems stem from misunderstandings about product features or limitations. Users may expect a product or service to be able to perform tasks for which it was not intended, as shown in the following example.

> **Problem:** Most Internet service providers now advertise nationwide access via a toll-free telephone number. These vendors provide several local access numbers for larger towns and cities in the United States, but tell users to use the toll-free number when no local access number is available in the area where a user is located. However, a user who travels and wants to take advantage of nationwide access is often surprised to find an extra charge on the Internet service provider's bill.
>
> **Solution:** On investigation, the user learns that, although the nationwide access number is a toll-free number, the Internet service provider actually charges an extra fee for every connected minute whenever the user configures the software to dial the vendor's toll-free number.

Wrong Products.   Users occasionally purchase the wrong product to accomplish a task. They may purchase a software package or hardware peripheral that is incompatible with their existing system. A common problem occurs when users of older model PC systems hear about a new software product they want to use. They may not understand that the software requires a later model processor or more memory than their computer has. Users with Windows computers may inadvertently purchase the Macintosh version of a software package because they have not read the packaging carefully.

Users may also purchase software without understanding its capabilities and limitations or without knowledge of alternatives, as in the following example.

5

Problem: A Macintosh user who wanted to create a newsletter bought a collection of clip art on a CD-ROM from an office supply store because the packaging included an illustration of clip art embedded in a newsletter. The user assumed that the software was capable of producing a newsletter like the one illustrated on the package. When the user installed the clip art on his system, he called the support number in the documentation to complain that the software did not produce the newsletter form he wanted.

Solution: The software vendor's customer support agent provided the user with a Return Merchandise Authorization (RMA) number and suggested that the user return to the store to look for a desktop publishing program with a newsletter template.

A similar problem can arise with the purchase of new hardware. For example, an end user purchased an external hard drive to back up data on a computer's internal hard drive. However, the new external drive was equipped to connect to a computer's USB port. Unfortunately the user's computer was an older model that wasn't equipped with a USB port. Because the user didn't understand where to plug the drive into his computer, he stored the drive in his closet, awaiting an opportunity to ask for assistance. It is still in his closet today. He was unaware that external hard drives that connect to parallel ports are readily available, or that a USB port expansion card could easily be added to his system.

Inadequate Training. Many computer problems arise because users are inadequately trained or do not read the documentation that comes with the hardware or software. A high percentage of calls to support centers can be answered by referring to a user manual, a tutorial, or online help, but users often do not know where to find the information they need, or they don't want to take the time to search for information. Users who have not been adequately trained or who do not recall information from a training session pose a challenge to help desk staff. Ideally, training sessions should not only provide users with the information they need, but also include pointers to where they can locate the information later, without help desk assistance. **Quick start behavior** is a tendency among computer users to skip the installation manual and attempt to get new hardware or software installed and operational as rapidly as possible. Many vendors now include a very brief quick start guide, or "Getting Started with . . ." manual, in an attempt to get users at least to read something before they begin to use a new product.

Lack of adequate training ultimately translates into waste and lost user productivity. For example, the Macintosh user described earlier who wanted to produce a newsletter did not realize that his word processor included most of the features he would need to produce a reasonably complex newsletter. He actually had the software he needed, but did not realize it; appropriate training could help him learn how to use an existing program to produce newsletters.

User problems that result from inadequate training and documentation provide both a challenge and an opportunity for support specialists who enjoy training and writing, as you will learn in Chapters 11 and 12.

Forgotten Information.   At times, users just plain forget how to perform a task or don't remember how to find the information they need. For example, local area network administrators report that the single most common contact they experience is from users who have forgotten the password to their accounts. Web sites that register users receive volumes of phone calls and e-mails from users who cannot remember the PIN (personal identification number) they need to log on to the site. Many Web sites have automated the password recall process via an e-mail reminder so that no support staff time is required to respond to the volume of requests for passwords.

Support agents should caution users against writing their passwords on paper. One of the biggest security problems in many organizations is end users who write their password on a Post-It note and attach the reminder to their display screen. For users who are forgetful or who infrequently need a password, one strategy is to keep a written note in an obscure location that does not contain their actual password, but contains a word or phrase that will remind them of their password. Some operating systems and application programs now include a feature to store and automatically retrieve passwords for users or ask a prompting question to help refresh a user's recollection of a password. These features should be used with caution in an office or school environment where others may have access to a system.

Users who make infrequent use of their computers are especially likely to forget information. Reference sheets (formal or informal notes) and scripts or check lists are an effective aid to help users recall how to perform infrequent tasks that are difficult to remember.

Documentation Problems

Another source of end user support problems can be traced to documentation problems. The readability of computer vendor documentation has generally improved in recent years. However, documentation that is poorly organized, inaccurate, and omits important points is still the direct cause of much misunderstanding and contributes to user frustration and the volume of calls a help desk receives.

The best user documentation includes a quick start guide, a tutorial that walks a user step by step through the major features of a software package, a reference manual that contains information organized by topic, a troubleshooting guide, and online help. Online help should include information that users can search by keyword and troubleshooting wizards to assist users with common problems. Support staff who prepare user documentation should follow the suggestions offered in Chapter 12 on end-user documentation.

Well-written user documentation takes time to develop. Support staff who write documents, whether in print or online, should make good use of graphic information, because users learn faster and retain information longer when graphics are used to supplement narrative explanations. Support staff should also consider user quick start behavior when they design and develop documentation. Finally, support staff should ask several coworkers and end users to serve as testers to try out drafts of documents before publication and help identify points that need clarification before publication.

Vendor Problems

Calls to a help desk or hotline are often related to vendor performance. Some vendors consistently oversell their products; they promise features that may not be delivered as part of the final product. Vendors may also release a beta software version for widespread use that contains known bugs that can put user data at risk. Some vendors are also notorious for late deliveries of new products, long after they were promised.

NOTE

Rebates on hardware and software purchases account for a significant percentage of end-user frustration with vendor performance. Vendors offer rebates to encourage sales because a price with a rebate subtracted is often attractively low. And a rebate is effectively a no-cost loan from the consumer to the vendor for the two- to three-month period that it takes to process the rebate. Furthermore, a sizeable percentage of consumers fail to send in the rebate request, or send it in after the deadline. Failure to produce a rebate during the time period promised in an advertisement is a client service issue, and can be as important as product features or other aspects of vendor performance when a user forms an impression of a vendor. Some vendors are very conscientious about rebate deadlines and provide telephone numbers or Web sites where consumers can check on the status of a rebate. But in other cases, rebate fulfillment centers are understaffed and struggle to keep up with the volume of calls and e-mails related to expected rebates.

Vaporware refers to hardware or software products that appear in ads or press releases but that are not yet available for sale. A vendor may announce a product that doesn't yet exist in order to study market reaction or to confuse its competitors. A help desk that handles incidents for external users should establish a policy for its support staff on how to handle disgruntled clients who are upset about vendor product performance. Chapter 4 described some client service and communications skills that are useful in handling these incidents.

Facilities Problems

A relatively small percentage of support calls involve facilities problems. Support calls related to viruses, backup media, security, and ergonomic issues fall into this category. Chapter 10 discusses solutions to several ergonomic problems, and Chapter 13 deals with common tools and strategies for other facilities management problems that user support agents may have to solve.

Most support problems can be grouped into the six categories described above—problems with hardware, software, users, documentation, vendors, and facilities. Networks are a frequent source of problems that user support agents encounter. However, because network problems are often traceable to hardware (including hubs, routers, bridges, switches, and gateways), software, operating systems, or other categories of problems discussed earlier, networks are not necessarily a unique problem category. However, network problems are often among those that are most difficult for a support staff to handle because they frequently involve the interaction of hardware, software, and other components. Furthermore, an increasing number of end users connect to a network via the Internet, a company intranet, a dial-up modem, or a local area network that supports client/server applications. Although network problems account for a large percentage of all support calls, most turn out to be related directly to hardware, software, or some combination of the problem categories described above.

ONLINE RESOURCES FOR USER SUPPORT

Many sites on the World Wide Web provide helpful information for user support staff who are working on specific problems or want to know more about the troubleshooting and problem-solving process. Examples of these sites are described in the table.

Support Area	URL	Description
General	pcsupport.about.com/cs/pctroubleshooting/index.htm	This About.com site contains a wealth of information on PCs and troubleshooting.
	www.askdrtech.com/default.asp	Ask Dr Tech is a fee-based site that provides 24/7 support services via phone or Web.
	www.computerarchitect.com/ask_find/askus2.cfm	ComputerArchitect's Web site offers to answer computer questions free via e-mail.

5

Support Area	URL	Description
Hardware	www.pcguide.com/ts/index.htm	The PC Guide is one of the largest Web sites dedicated to information on PC hardware and troubleshooting.
	www.pcmech.com/guides.htm	PC Mechanic's Web site includes troubleshooting guides for several kinds of hardware components.
	www.tomshardware.com	Tom's Hardware Guide contains a database of searchable articles on common hardware components.
	www.macintoshos.com/troubleshooting/troubleshooting.html	MacintoshOS.com's Web site provides a troubleshooting guide for MacOS systems.
Software	www.windows-help.net/index.shtml	InfiniSource's Windows trouble-shooting tips links to articles on a variety of common problems (select the version of Windows in the left pane).
	support.microsoft.com	This is Microsoft's product support center for operating system and applications software.
	www.all-windows.com/index.html	This Web site contains articles on problems with Windows operating system and applications software.
Other resources	www.google.com	The Google Internet search engine can locate Web sites for specific problems; hardware and software names, as well as version and model searches.
	www.ask.com	The Ask Jeeves search engine accepts questions in an informal question and answer format.
	www.zdnet.com	ZDnet is an extensive Web site with product and troubleshooting information and tips. The home page includes a keyword search feature.
	www.about.com/compute	About.com is a collection of moderated Web sites with information on a variety of topics. The home page includes an extensive menu and keyword search feature.

THE PROBLEM-SOLVING PROCESS APPLIED TO TYPICAL END-USER PROBLEMS

As user support staff solve the kinds of computer problems described earlier in this chapter, the solutions become common knowledge among members of the staff. They use this ever-expanding bank of knowledge to solve new problems. In fact, the greater the variety of problems user support agents learn about, the better the knowledge and experience they will have at their command to tackle new problems. User support agents employ the problem-solving processes described in Chapter 4 to find appropriate solutions, as shown in the following accounts from support agents about how they resolved some typical support problems.

Problem 1: Sounds Like Trouble

Problem: A user in a remote branch office sent me an e-mail message that she had lost the sound in her system. I started the troubleshooting process by asking about her basic configuration and some critical questions, such as "Has this problem ever happened before?" and "What programs were you running when you noticed the sound was lost?" She wrote back that the system is a Pentium III running Windows 98, that the sound had been working fine, and that she couldn't remember exactly which program she was running when she first noticed the sound no longer worked. She also mentioned that two other employees had access to her system.

Problem-solving strategy: My first reaction was to try some obvious fixes. I suggested that she:

- Reset the sound card in the expansion slot
- Try the sound card in a different expansion slot
- Check all the connections and cables to the sound card
- Check the Windows 98 device manager to see if there were any IRQ conflicts between the sound card and other devices

The user responded that she checked these items, but that the sound still didn't work. I discussed the problem with some support colleagues, describing what we had already tried. They came up with a few other suggestions:

- Make sure that the volume is turned up on the speakers.
- Make sure that the volume is turned up in the Windows 98 media player.
- Check that the speakers are connected correctly.
- If the speakers require electrical current, make sure they're plugged in.

The user checked all these possibilities and reported that there was still no sound. I asked her if there were any changes made to her system recently. She wrote back that apparently one of her work colleagues had downloaded a shareware version of an antivirus program from the Internet about the time the sound problem first occurred. The colleague said that, after several attempts, he couldn't get the antivirus program to work correctly on the system, so he uninstalled it. The fact that new software had recently been installed on her system got me thinking in a different direction. I looked on the Internet and found a Web site for her brand of sound card. They listed about 20 different models of cards, one of which was hers. So I e-mailed back the Web address where she could download the latest version of the software driver for her particular card. Later that day, I received a message that she had downloaded the sound card driver, installed it in Windows 98, and her sound worked again.

Conclusion: I'm not certain of the diagnosis, but I think the shareware program may have affected the driver software her sound card used. Once she reinstalled the driver, the problem was fixed.

I was pleased that I solved the problem. I used communication skills to get information from the end user, which was not easy using e-mail. I also used critical questions that opened up a different avenue of investigation. I used several information resources, including my support colleagues and the vendor's Web site on the Internet. I used some troubleshooting strategies, including looking for an obvious fix, some hypothesis testing, and module replacement. *(Based on an incident described by Billie Brendlinger.)*

Problem 2: The Problem with Modems

Problem: I was at a client's site to troubleshoot an Internet setup on their Macintosh computer. I had previously installed Internet access software and configured the client's machine for Internet access. I had also trained the user to log on and run the software to access the Internet. After the installation, everything appeared to be in working order.

The user called our help desk about a week later, saying that she had an occasional problem with Internet access from her Mac. The modem usually dialed the Internet server's computer successfully, but occasionally it would report than it couldn't get a dial tone.

Problem-solving strategy: On my follow-up visit, I asked a series of questions about her telephone service, including whether she had any features added to her basic phone service, such as caller ID, call waiting, or other services. The end user assured me that her telephone was a standard line with no frills. I checked the modem with the terminal emulation software, and the diagnostic check indicated that the modem was correctly connected. Because the setup had worked after the original installation, I suspected the modem connection was OK, but I was glad to get the confirmation.

Then I decided to unplug the modem and connect the telephone handset directly to the phone line. My hypothesis was that there was something wrong with the telephone service that was affecting the modem. When I picked up the handset, I heard a blip-blip-blip-blip sound, then a long pause, and finally a dial tone. The blips did not sound abnormal, but my own phone doesn't make that sound. Then I recalled that I had heard the blip sounds before at a friend's house. I realized that it is the sound that the telephone company's voice mail system makes when the client has a message waiting. My friend used to check her voice mail messages first, clear them, and then dial out with the modem. If there were no voice mail messages waiting, there were no blip sounds.

Conclusion: I advised the user always to check for voice mail messages before dialing the Internet phone number. I also found a setting in the Internet access software that controls the amount of time the software listens for a dial tone before it gives up. I set the time to 20 seconds in case the user forgot to check for voice mail messages.

The problem was an interesting one, and I was glad I was able to solve it. I learned that users don't always know the answers to the questions I ask. In this case, the user's answers threw me off track. I also used my personal experience to identify the source of the voice mail tones on the phone line. The rest of the process was eliminating variables (when I replaced the modem with the telephone handset) and hypothesis testing. *(Based on an incident reported by Jaime Chamoulos.)*

Problem 3: Give Credit Where It Is Due

Problem: I am a support person in an online ticket sales company. A computer operator is responsible for running an electronic data interchange (EDI) software package to process credit card transactions. The program uses a modem to send batches of credit card transactions to a credit card processor. The credit card processor then authenticates each transaction and processes it with the financial institution that issued the credit card.

The computer operator was frustrated and unhappy with the EDI software because the program would not process batches of transactions correctly, so she had to call in each transaction individually. She had contacted the EDI software vendor about the problem. The vendor said the problem was likely on the credit card processor's end. When the operator called the credit card processor, they pointed the finger back at the EDI software package. I was assigned the task of finding the cause of the problem.

Problem-solving strategy: Before I contacted the software company myself, I wanted to make sure I understood how the procedure was supposed to work and that I understood what the real problem was. I put together a list of the subsystems in the procedure.

1. Computer operator batches together credit card transactions.

2. EDI software transmits via modem the batch of transactions to credit card processor.

3. Credit card processor posts transactions to customer accounts.

4. Credit card processor returns via modem a confirmation report of processed transactions to computer operator.

5. Computer operator verifies the status of processed transactions.

I considered that the problem could be with the EDI software program, the credit card processor, or the computer operator's procedures. I started at the top of the list and assumed that the problem was with the EDI software. I decided to install it on my own computer, read through the manual, and use the computer operator's notes to learn how to process batches of transactions. Although the software documentation was skimpy, I eventually pieced together enough information so that I understood how the program worked. I put together a few sample transactions to test the system. The test cases that I constructed seemed to work fine. I decided to write up some better documentation for the computer operator based on the software manual, her notes, and a couple of calls I made to the EDI software company to clarify some points in the batch-processing procedure.

Then the computer operator and I went through the process of building a batch of transactions with some actual data. We used my expanded documentation as a guide and a check list. The batch file we sent seemed to process okay, but we did not receive an expected confirmation that the transactions were received or accepted. According to the software manual, the credit card processor should have returned a report file to us to indicate a normal termination of the batch process along with the status of each transaction. The next day, I called the credit card processor to see if they could verify that the transactions we sent had indeed been received and approved. They had been, so I was fairly confident that the expanded procedure documentation I wrote was accurate. We could transmit batches of transactions that were received and processed by the credit card processor.

However, we now had a new problem: Why didn't we receive the confirming report file from the credit card processor? I tried to display the report file from within the EDI software, but nothing happened. It appeared the report file was missing. I looked around on the hard drive on the system and eventually found the report file. It was there after all. I used a file diagnosis utility to examine the report file. My examination revealed that the report file actually did contain all the information indicating that successful batches of transactions had been sent and received, including the ones we had sent the previous day. But somehow the EDI program could not display the report file. Then I noticed some corrupted data at the beginning of the report file that was in a different format than the remainder of the file. I made a backup copy of the report file as a precaution and then deleted the original report file. The next day, we ran a batch of about 200 transactions. The credit card processor received the transactions, processed them, and returned the report file successfully.

Conclusion: I figure the corrupted data in the report file may have been due to an error the computer operator made because she didn't really understand all the steps necessary to transmit batches. When the confirmation for each day's transactions was added to a corrupted file, it could not be displayed. Once I removed the corrupted data, the confirmation report displayed correctly.

I used a list of subsystems and a lot of hypothesis testing on this problem. I also tried to replicate on my own system the problem the operator had experienced. To this day, I'm not sure I understand the exact error the computer operator made. She was very frustrated and obviously needed better documentation. Based on the documentation I prepared, she has been able to process transactions correctly ever since I worked on this problem. *(Based on an incident described by Mark Gauthier.)*

Problem 4: The Worst Hard Drive Crash Ever

Problem: A user called the technical support desk early one morning and reported that he turned on his Windows computer as usual, but the screen displayed the error message

"Non-system disk or disk error." The user was very concerned that his system had been hit by a virus attack or that his hard drive had crashed. He was very concerned because he said it had been several weeks since he'd backed up his hard drive, and the implications of the problem for lost and unrecoverable data were enormous.

Problem-solving strategy: I thought about the most common explanations for this error message, and asked if he had a diskette in his floppy disk drive. He checked the drive and replied that there wasn't one. I then suggested that he try to reboot his computer again to see if the problem was a one-time event. The second reboot try produced the same result. I began to suspect at this point that the problem was not a simple one.

I asked the user whether he had ever made a reboot floppy or rescue disk for his system. He said he thought he had when the system was new, and would look for it. He called back in a few minutes to report that he couldn't find a boot floppy for his system, and wondered how much trouble he was in. We discussed several options, which included some simple problems all the way up to and including a damaged hard disk drive. The user immediately wanted to know whether I could get data off a damaged hard drive for him. I responded that some utility software includes data recovery features, and that I knew a few commercial vendors provide data recovery services, but that I thought they would probably be expensive and take a lot of time. I suggested that we not jump ahead to data recovery strategies just yet.

I made arrangements with my support desk colleagues to leave the technical support center and go up to the end user's office area. I have rarely seen an end user as distraught as this user. He said that in all his years of using an office computer, he had never had an experience like this one. I explained that we would eliminate some other possible causes before we concluded that the worst had happened to his hard drive. I thought that it was possible the problem might be a bad disk controller card, and wanted to eliminate that option before going further. I rebooted his system and pressed the Del key, as instructed on the screen, to go into the CMOS setup utility program. I first checked to make sure the hard disk drive was defined in the setup (it was), and that the boot sequence was C: first, then A:. Then I rebooted his system with an MS-DOS boot floppy that we keep in the support center for these situations. His system booted onto the A: drive without any trouble. The first success of the morning! Although the floppy boot success was not conclusive, I felt it was unlikely that the problem was the disk controller card. However, the user was upset at this result, too, because we were getting closer to a damaged hard disk drive as the real problem.

I used some DOS utilities on the boot floppy, including ATTRIB to look at the system files COMMAND.COM, IO.SYS. MSDOS.SYS, AUTOEXEC.BAT, and CONFIG.SYS on the user's hard drive. Nothing appeared to be unusual. Then I noticed that the MSDOS.SYS file was listed in the root directory as 0 bytes in size. It appeared that, perhaps among other problems, at least the MSDOS.SYS file, which is crucial during the boot process, had been corrupted. At that point, I considered several options, including reinstalling Windows. Before proceeding, I made a call back to the technical support center to ask their advice. One of my support colleagues suggested that before we spent the time to reinstall all of Windows, we should first see if there was a comparable system in the office we could use, either to get a copy of the correct version of the MSDOS.SYS file or to make a Windows startup disk. The end user said that most of the computers in his office had been replaced at the same time and were similar configurations to his. So we booted another system and used a floppy disk to get a copy of the MSDOS.SYS file. Then I transferred the file onto the user's system to replace the corrupted one. We both held our breath as I attempted to boot his system from his hard drive. We were both relieved and felt very lucky when the Windows boot up logo appeared. The user spent several minutes checking the files on his hard drive. I also insisted that we reboot again, just to be certain everything was normal.

Conclusion: I used a variety of troubleshooting strategies in this incident. I started by looking for an obvious fix. I used both my knowledge of MS-DOS and the boot process and information from my support colleagues to arrive at a final strategy. I used a process of elimination to rule out CMOS settings and the disk controller card as potential problems. I also used the DOS recovery disk as a diagnostic tool. I was pleased that I didn't "lose" the user, but explained each step and alternative as we worked on his machine. Before I left the user's office that day, we made a boot disk tailored for his specific machine. I am also certain that the user learned a valuable lesson from the "near miss" and will make more frequent backups of important data files.

Problem 5: The Path Not Taken

Problem: The phone call came into the support center late one afternoon. A user said that one of his PC systems could no longer access my company's vertical market software. The rest of our support staff was in a training seminar for the afternoon, so I had to solve the problem on my own. As a new member of the support staff, I was a little nervous. The user on the phone said that he had been able to run the software successfully earlier in the day, but he had lost the desktop icon to run our software package.

Problem-solving strategy: After asking a few questions and paraphrasing some of his statements, I clarified that the icon for our software was actually still on the desktop but that double-clicking it produced no results. I asked several other questions, including the critical question, "What were you doing on the system when the icon stopped working?" The user responded that he had been deleting some unwanted files.

My first thought was that perhaps the user had accidentally deleted the .EXE file associated with the icon. I led him through the steps to see if the .EXE program file was still in the correct folder, and it was. My next thought was that perhaps the shortcut path from the icon to the .EXE file had been destroyed. After checking the shortcut properties, we confirmed that the path was in place. Then I wondered whether the user had somehow deleted the path to some of the files the program needs to operate. I wasn't sure how to check that, but I knew that some of the files were on a server and that each client machine defines the drive mappings to the network drives when it boots up. I explained my reasoning to the user and suggested that he quit all applications and shut down his system, just as if it were the end of the day. We waited a few seconds and then rebooted his system. After the reboot, everything worked fine. Apparently, he had accidentally erased the drive mappings during his system housekeeping.

Conclusion: I was pleased to be able to handle the call, which was one of my first as a user support agent. I used several troubleshooting strategies, including communication skills to listen to the user's definition of the problem, paraphrasing, and asking critical questions to give me the information I needed to formulate a hypothesis. I also used a mental image of the sequence from the icon to the disk files to troubleshoot the problem. *(Based on an incident reported by Andra Heath.)*

Problem 6: The Nonresponsive Network

Problem: I am the network support assistant for an economic research think tank. One afternoon I received a call from a staff member who reported that something was wrong with his workstation. He said it was very sluggish. I walked down the hall and looked at his workstation, which was running Excel. The user was in the process of saving a worksheet on the file server, but Excel had not yet responded to the save command.

Problem-solving strategy: I canceled the save operation. Before I investigated the problem further, as a precaution, I tried to save the user's worksheet on the local hard drive instead of on the file server. This time the save operation worked fine, so I thought it was unlikely the user's PC was the problem. My attention immediately turned to the network server.

I went to the computer room where the server is located and found that the display screen was blank. I noticed, however, that the power lamp indicators were lit on both the server and the display, so I eliminated the likelihood of a power supply problem. I used a workstation we keep in the computer room to monitor network activity to try to log on to the server, but the attempt failed. Then I tried to reboot the server. It did not appear to boot, but I couldn't tell much because the display screen was still blank. I thought that perhaps there was a problem with the monitor, but I wasn't sure. However, I felt that I needed to determine first whether any problem existed with the monitor, so that I could diagnose the situation with the server. I disconnected the monitor from the server and borrowed a monitor and cable from the nearby workstation. After I plugged in a different monitor, the server still didn't appear to boot and the display screen was still blank. So the monitor was probably not related to the problem.

Because I was focused on the blank monitor screen, my next thought was to replace the video card in the server. So I pulled the video card from the nearby workstation and replaced the one in the server with one I knew was operational. When I rebooted the server, the result was the same blank monitor screen. At this point, I stopped to think about the subsystems that were involved in the display screen problem. I sketched on a notepad the monitor, the cable, the video card, the motherboard, and the power supply. Because the power supply lamp was lit, and because I had replaced everything else, I looked at the motherboard. I could not see any visible problems with it. I decided to set up a substitute server. First I returned the borrowed video card and monitor to the workstation. I then removed the hard drive from the inoperable server and installed it in the workstation. Finally, I crossed my fingers and rebooted the substitute server. It came up OK. The motherboard apparently was the problem.

Conclusion: I received a call from the repair shop the next day that confirmed my suspicion that the server motherboard was damaged. It had several burned-out components and needed to be replaced. I relied heavily in this situation on a module replacement strategy and on my knowledge of how the subsystems in a computer are linked together. The incident confirmed for me that users are not always capable of diagnosing the problem, which turned out to be with the server and not with the user's workstation.

 Only authorized network support personnel should reboot a server.

NOTE

Problem 7: Out of Time

Problem: I recently had a conversation with a user in the Accounts Receivable department when she happened to mention that her Dell desktop computer loses time. She also stated that it is important for the postings she does in the accounting program to be recorded with an accurate time stamp, and besides, it just plain bothers her that an expensive computer can't keep time. She said it wasn't a major problem because she knew how to right-click on the time display on her desktop and adjust the time based on the wall clock. But she admitted she frequently forgets to check it, and the time gets way off the mark.

Problem-solving strategy: I explained to the user that the hardware clock in her computer's BIOS keeps track of the time when her computer is off, and that the operating system keeps the time up-to-date when her computer is turned on. I asked if she was aware whether her machine lost time when it was on, off, or both. She replied that she hadn't paid that much attention, so I suggested that we try an experiment. I asked her to update the time on her machine now, and then keep track of the time loss for a few days to see if she could help pinpoint when the time loss occurred.

My reasoning was that if the BIOS battery was weak, that might explain why time-loss occurs when the computer is turned off. However, if the slippage occurs during the time the computer is turned on, then we had to search for a different solution. While she kept a time log for her machine, I researched possible explanations for time-loss on Dell computers. I found an extensive article on the topic at **support.ap.dell.com/ap/en/kb/document. asp?DN=HO1016518#har**.

About a week later, the user called to report that so far the time-loss problem seemed to be worst when the computer was turned on for long periods. I told her that we had probably eliminated the BIOS battery as the culprit. She immediately wanted to know about problems with the clock in the operating system. I explained to her that the software clock can be affected by things like the temperature in her office, how much she uses her machine (how frequently interrupts are generated), and how long she leaves the machine on. I suggested that she might like to install a utility program that would update her computer's clock automatically based on the time on the Internet. I told her about NISTIME, a utility she could download, that would periodically get the correct time from the Internet and automatically update her computer's clock. I gave her the Web address **www.boulder. nist.gov/timefreq/service/its.htm**, where she could download the NISTIME utility. I also mentioned that she should have a current backup of her Registry and other important files prior to installing any new software.

Conclusion: She called later that week to say that she had been able to install NISTIME and put it in her system tray so that the program would run in the background and keep her clock up to date. She thanked me and said she was delighted with the tech support. My experience with PCs helped me to understand the types and possible sources of clock problems. Then, we designed an experiment to help narrow the possible alternative hypotheses that would account for the problem. I also used Web resources to look for the possibility of a hardware problem with her brand of machine, and to confirm the approach we took. Finally, I had recently read about the NISTIME utility program to synchronize PC and Internet time in a computer trade magazine.

Chapter Summary

- ☐ Although computer problems vary widely, a few categories of problems account for most end user contacts with help desks, hotlines, and support centers. The common categories include problems with hardware, software, users, documentation, vendors, and facilities. Network problems are often a combination of these categories.

- ☐ Common hardware problems include difficulties with the installation of hardware components, compatibility of new or upgraded components with other hardware in a system, hardware configuration problems, and actual malfunctions that require repair or replacement of components.

- ☐ Common software problems include difficulties with installation (although these problems are less common today than they were with earlier generations of software), incompatibilities with other software packages or with hardware, or configuration problems that prevent the software from operating correctly. Other software problems may be due to bugs or performance problems.

- ☐ User problems are caused by mistakes (which all users make), misunderstandings about how a system operates to perform a task, the purchase of the wrong product, inadequate training, failure to read product documentation, and forgotten procedures or passwords.

- ☐ Other problems include difficulties with documentation (such as poor organization, and incorrect or incomplete information), vendor problems (such as a tendency of some vendors to oversell their products, misrepresent product features, deliver software with known bugs, or deliver products later than they were promised), and facilities problems (such as problems with security, viruses, backups, and ergonomic issues).

❑ The greater the variety of problems and solutions user support agents learn about, the better the knowledge and experience they will have at their command when they tackle new problems.

KEY TERMS

automatic update — A feature of operating systems and applications software that periodically checks a vendor's Web site for updates that the vendor recommends be downloaded and installed to bring the version of the software up to current specifications.

bug — An error in a computer program that occurs when a programmer writes incorrectly coded instructions during program development.

burn-in — A 48- to 72-hour period during which a new computer or component is operated nonstop in an attempt to discover obvious problems and identify any marginal or temperature-sensitive components.

configuration problem — A difficulty that occurs when hardware or software options are set incorrectly for the computer environment in which a component must operate.

conflict — A state in which a computer component uses systems resources (CPU, memory, or peripheral devices) in a way that is incompatible with another component.

freeware — Computer software for which no purchase price or licensing fee is charged. Compare to shareware.

incompatible — Describes computer components that cannot operate together successfully in the same system. See also conflict.

installation software — Special-purpose utility software that aids in the installation of other software packages; often able to detect and correctly configure software for most operating environments.

patch — A replacement for one or a few modules in a software package to fix one or more known bugs.

performance problem — A category of computer problems where a system is operational, but does not operate as efficiently as it can or should; often results from poor interaction between hardware and software.

Plug and Play standards — Computer industry-wide agreements among hardware and operating system vendors about how an operating system will recognize, install, and configure hardware components with little manual effort required.

quick start behavior — A tendency among computer users to skip reading an installation manual and attempt to get new hardware or software installed and operational as rapidly as possible.

release — A distribution of a software program that contains some new features not found in the original program.

service pack (or service release) — A software revision that contains both updates and patches to fix documented problems with a version of a program.

shareware — Commercial software that users can try out with a vendor's permission during an evaluation period (usually 30 days) prior to making a purchase decision.

5

update — A bug-fix distribution that repairs known problems in a previous version or release of a software package.

upgrade — A new version of an existing program that is sold at a reduced cost to owners of a previous version of the program.

vaporware — Hardware or software products that appear in ads or press releases but are not yet available for sale.

version — A software package that contains significant new features and is usually the result of a substantially rewritten program.

workaround — A procedure or feature that accomplishes the same result as a feature that does not work due to a bug or other malfunction.

CHECK YOUR UNDERSTANDING

1. True or False? Most hardware component problems are the result of failures due to incorrect voltages in a computer system.

2. During _____ , a computer system is operated nonstop for a 48- to 72-hour period to give marginal components a chance to fail.

3. When do most hardware problems occur?

   a. at the time a component is purchased and installed

   b. during the warranty period for new hardware

   c. after the warranty period has expired

   d. none of these

4. True or False? Plug and Play–compatible hardware guarantees that users will not experience installation problems with new or upgraded hardware.

5. Which of the following hardware devices is more likely to fail during the operation of a computer system?

   a. CPU

   b. memory

   c. hard disk drive

   d. peripheral adapter card

6. A mismatch between the type of printer connected to a system and the software printer driver installed is an example of a _____ .

   a. design problem

   b. conflict

   c. bug

   d. configuration problem

7. A(n) _____ is a situation where two software packages use system resources in different and incompatible ways.

8. True or False? By the time a software package has gone through extensive testing and quality assurance, all the bugs have generally been eliminated.

9. A substantially rewritten software package that contains major new features is called a(n) _____ .

   a. update

   b. patch

   c. new release

   d. new version

10. A procedure or method to accomplish the same result as a feature that does not work due to a bug or other malfunction is called a(n) _____ .

11. True or False? A computer system that operates at some level, but not as efficiently as it should, is called vaporware.

12. True or False? One difference between end users and computer professionals is that the latter do not make mistakes while using a computer.

13. Performance problems in a computer system are usually due to _____ .

    a. hardware problems

    b. software problems

    c. both hardware and software problems

    d. neither hardware nor software problems

14. True or False? Freeware and shareware may cause compatibility problems when installed because they may not be tested as extensively as commercial software.

15. _____ is a tendency among users to want to get a new hardware or software product operational without reading the installation documentation.

16. List three strategies for dealing with users who forget important information.

DISCUSSION QUESTIONS

1. Why do support staff members rarely know in advance whether a specific problem is hardware-related or software-related?

2. Do you agree or disagree with the statement: "Network problems are not really a unique category of computer problems; all network problems are basically either hardware or software problems"? Explain your reasoning.

3. Why are so many computer problems traceable to user mistakes? Describe a recent mistake you made as a computer user. Do you think it is a common mistake or a rare one? What could be done in the future, if anything, to prevent the kind of mistake that was made?

4. Is freeware or shareware easier or more difficult to support and troubleshoot than commercial software? Explain your answer.

HANDS-ON PROJECTS

The Hands-on Projects in this chapter provide an opportunity to gain additional experience with troubleshooting and problem solving. The projects vary in difficulty from easy to challenging. They require a variety of problem-solving skills and information resources to find the answers. Use them as practice to build your troubleshooting and problem-solving skills. Do not spend too long on any one project. If you run into a roadblock and can't find the answer, ask your instructor or colleagues for assistance.

Project 5-1

Find Excel's Data Analysis Tools. A user wants to use the advanced statistical functions and features in the Excel spreadsheet program because she does a lot of statistical work in her job. She has a book that explains how to use these features. She clicked the Tools menu in Excel but did not find the Data Analysis menu item that the book had described. She also tried to use some of the built-in statistical functions that are supposed to be included in Excel according to the book, but she got an error message, #NAME?, wherever she entered one of the function names. Describe the steps the user would need to take to be able to use the statistical functions.

Project 5-2

Explore the MSInfo program. Find out if there is a utility program on a Windows 95/98/2000 system named MSInfo32.exe. If you can find it, where is it located? Use the MSInfo32 help system to learn about the features of the program. Write a brief description of its purpose and indicate for whom it would be useful.

Project 5-3

Evaluate hard drive symptoms. A frantic user called a help desk to report that his hard disk drive does not appear to work. He related that the drive produced neither noise nor any indication of obvious activity. In fact, the drive light on the PC case does not light up. The user fears the worst: a hard disk drive failure. List any other alternative causes you can think of for the behavior he describes.

Project 5-4

Troubleshoot a bug in Excel. An e-mail message from a user says, "I am just beginning to use Excel spreadsheets after using Lotus 1-2-3 spreadsheets for several years. Whenever I enter a number in a cell, Excel adds a decimal point, even if the number format I use doesn't include a decimal point. It just doesn't look right to have an integer number like 5280 displayed as 5280. (with the decimal point). Is this a bug in Excel? How can I fix the problem?" Research the problem and write an e-mail response to the user with the information you found.

5

Project 5-5

Link Notepad to .RPT files A user asks your advice about how to load an ASCII text file into Notepad automatically. He says that he knows Windows automatically recognizes certain file extensions. For example, Windows knows that a .TXT extension is a text file, and when the user double-clicks the file, Windows will automatically open it with Notepad. An .XLS extension indicates an Excel worksheet, and Windows will automatically open it in Excel. The user says he regularly receives ASCII text files from an information clearinghouse with an .RPT extension. He would like to be able to double-click the file and open it automatically with Notepad. Describe the procedure that will let the user tell Windows to open any file with an .RPT extension with Notepad.

Project 5-6

Restore photos in Web browser. A user complains that she sees only blank rectangles where she should be able to see photos and pictures on some Web pages. She wants to know whether this is an Internet problem or if something is wrong with her browser settings. Use either Internet Explorer or Netscape Navigator and respond to her question.

Project 5-7

Use disks interchangeably. A user has an Iomega Zip disk drive in his PC system. It can write up to 100 MB of data on a removable disk. The user purchased some Iomega brand disks, but the packaging indicates the disks are 1 GB Jaz disks. The user wants to know if he can use the Jaz disks in his Zip drive, and whether his system will write 1 GB of data on the Jaz disks. Are these disks interchangeable? What about capacity differences? Write a short explanation to the user that provides the information he needs.

Project 5-8

Set up an automatic time log. A user who is away from her office for much of the day wants to keep a simple log of contacts and short notes about client meetings she has throughout the day. She wants to include the current date and time for each entry in the log. She says a work colleague has an icon on her laptop that automatically opens Notepad and inserts an entry in the file that contains the current date and time. Then, a short note about a meeting with a client is easy to write. She wants you to set up her laptop with a similar feature. Write a documentation sheet listing the steps she should take to accomplish this task.

Project 5-9

Recover Word's Normal.dot file. A trainer who instructs classes in Microsoft Word reports that one of her students, Heather, accidentally saved a document as Normal.dot. Each time a student at that computer in the training center opens a new Word document, Heather's document appears instead of a new, blank document. She says she has tried to fix the problem, but hasn't hit on a solution yet. What would you suggest to the trainer? Is there more than one solution to this problem?

Project 5-10

Decipher an Internet error message. An e-mail from a user says: "I have been searching for information on the Internet with Google.com and received a message, 'Error 403: Forbidden', when I attempt to access a Web site that interests me. What does this message mean, and how can I view the page?" Research the problem and write a response to the e-mail.

CASE PROJECTS

1. Document Internet Error Messages

Find out the most common error messages users are likely to encounter on the Internet. Learn what the messages mean, and what users should do to work around each type of error. Then write a brief document intended for end users that lists the common Internet error messages, provides end users with information about each message, and explains how to work around it, if possible.

2. Media Critic for the Library

Your town's public library sponsors several lecture series on topics of interest to residents. One series is for computer users. They have asked you to participate in a presentation on resources for computer users. They would like you to critique locally available radio, TV, and newspaper computer problem-solving resources.

Many local radio stations carry programs aimed at computer users. Some feature local experts; others are nationally syndicated programs. They invite listeners to phone or e-mail the program about problems they are having with their computer systems. Similarly, local newspapers frequently publish advice columns specifically for computer users. They often offer advice to users who write or e-mail their problems.

Consult your local newspaper to identify radio and TV programs or newspaper columns intended for computer user audiences. Your instructor may be able to help you identify programs or columns in your local area. Listen to a couple of computer-oriented programs or read several newspaper columns that answer questions for computer users. Using the categories of common problems described in this chapter, analyze the kinds of questions users ask. Are some categories more common than others? Do you agree or disagree with the answers provided? How could the answers be improved? Evaluate their technical accuracy, communication style, and alternative explanations or solutions. Write a short paper that analyzes the categories of questions, the answers provided, and your evaluation of the program or column.

CASE PROJECTS

3. Computer Upgrade for Evelyn Tonolo

Evelyn Tonolo is a teacher in the English department at Willagansett Community College. She teaches courses in literature, including a very popular course in films as literature. As a help desk staff member at the college, you received the following e-mail from Evelyn:

> To: helpdesk@wcc3.edu
>
> From: etonolo@wcc1.edu
>
> Date: 1-Mar-06
>
> Re: Computer Upgrade
>
> I've read in one of the academic journals to which I subscribe that an increasing number of classic films are now available on a digital video disc (DVD). I would like to be able to obtain and view films distributed in this format. If possible, I want to upgrade the PC in my office to be able to play the DVD films. Otherwise, I need to ask my department chair for a new computer.
>
> My current system is a 133 MHz Pentium with 16 MB RAM, a 1-GB hard drive, and a 12X CD-ROM drive. I currently run Windows 95 but could upgrade to Windows 98 if that would be desirable. Could you please tell me whether my PC can be upgraded to play DVDs? What is involved in the upgrade and approximately what would it cost?
>
> Thanks very much for your advice!
>
> Evelyn

Investigate digital video disc drives and the PC configuration necessary to support them. Collect the information you need to answer her questions, and then respond to Evelyn's e-mail.

4. Disk Space Management at Re-Nu-Cartridge

For additional background information on Re-Nu-Cartridge, see Case Project 4 in previous chapters.

NOTE

The user support group at Re-Nu-Cartridge has analyzed the log of support calls it received in the past month to identify the 10 most common calls. As part of a project to write model answers for end users' frequently asked questions, the support staff wants you to research and write a short document on disk space management that can be sent to users. Specifically, the support staff finds that many callers with disk space complaints say that they have run out of space on their hard drives. Most of these calls come from active e-mail users and users who frequently download information from the Internet. Other calls come from users who have older PCs that were purchased with smaller hard drives than those available today. In each of these cases, the hard drives on their Windows PCs are now full, and they would very much appreciate a solution that doesn't require replacing the hard drive.

Investigate common ways that the space on a hard drive gets filled up. As one resource, you may want to compare your ideas, experiences, and findings with those of your coworkers or classmates. Then write a document for support staff to provide to end users that briefly describes the reasons that hard drives become full and the procedures you recommend to free up disk space. Organize your document as a check list, but include any explanations and precautions you feel are necessary before a user embarks on a procedure to reclaim disk space on a hard drive.

6

HELP DESK OPERATION

Recall that an organization can choose to provide support to its employees and clients in several ways. Some organizations opt for informal peer support for their computer-using employees. Others choose a more formal structure, such as a user support group or an information center, or they delegate computer support to an Information Technology department. Some organizations outsource all, or a part, of the computer support function. Although the specific structure may differ, many companies organize their user support function internally as a help desk because: (1) the help desk is easily identifiable to employees or clients, and (2) it provides a single point of contact for users who need technical support. To reach this point of contact, users might visit a physical location, telephone a hotline, send an e-mail message, or go to a Web site. In each case, users interact with a help desk agent to ask questions or request help with problems.

A help desk operation, like other support methods, can be costly. Therefore, organizations that have a substantial investment in end-user computer systems or many external users continually search for cost-effective ways to provide technical support. This chapter describes a number of strategies and tools that help desks employ to support end users in an effective and efficient way.

WHAT IS A HELP DESK?

A help desk is an organization that provides a single point of contact for users in need of technical support, whether they are internal employees or external clients. Why is a single point of contact important? In a user support center that has multiple points of contact, the support agent who responds to an incident might not have the expertise to answer a particular question. The agent may have to refer the user to a different support agent, or even a different department, for an answer. But the next agent may not have the answer either. In extreme cases, multiple points of contact may disagree about the source of a problem or the strategy to resolve it. To avoid situations like these, many companies have consolidated their user support function into a help desk operation.

 TriActive sells products and services designed to help companies manage their computer resources. They have published two white papers on best practices and industry trends in help desk support with suggestions on how to optimize services to users. See **www.triactive.com/demo/ whitepapers/pdfs/BP_HelpDesk_Staffing.pdf** and **www.triactive.com/demo/ whitepapers/pdfs/optimizing_help_desk.pdf**.

Although the specifics of the support provided in telephone, face-to-face, e-mail, and Web contacts differ somewhat, there are also similarities in the way help desks organize, provide support, and in the kinds of skills they require. Some help desks provide a wide range of support services, like those you learned about in Chapter 2. Others focus on limited services. For example, a telephone support hotline for a popular software package may limit its services to questions about the specific product. The help desk in a large medical center, in contrast, may provide a more extensive array of computer support services to its employees. Whether a help desk includes a hotline, information center, lab assistance, support consultant, or any number of other services, its purpose is the same: to provide end users with a single point of contact for computer problems to help keep them productive.

Organizations structure their help desks differently, depending on whether their users are internal or external, the number of users and products they support, and the organization's goals and objectives for computer support. Organizations frequently structure their help desks into several levels (or tiers) of support, sometimes called a **multi-level support model** or frontline/backline model, shown in Figure 6-1.

In this model, each level is staffed by a person with different skills. The level 1 incident screener (also called an incident dispatcher or receptionist) is usually an entry-level employee. Higher levels of support staff require greater knowledge and experience. The level 2 product specialist is usually a more experienced help desk employee; the level 3 technical support position is often staffed by a programmer, product designer, or engineer; and level 4 support is staffed by a supervisor or manager.

Some multi-level help desks and support groups have more or fewer levels than those described in Figure 6-1. In general, help desks try to handle as many incidents at the lowest

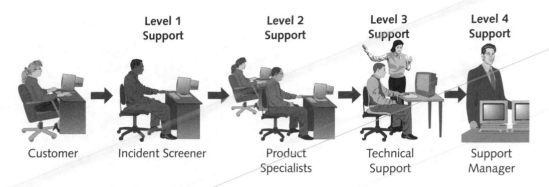

Figure 6-1   Multi-level support model

possible level in the support hierarchy. They want to save their higher-level, more experienced staff resources for situations in which their skills are necessary. Lower-level help desk staff members usually have higher-level, more experienced staff members to whom they can refer complex problems and even difficult callers.

Regardless of the help desk structure, all help desks have the same goal: to promote client satisfaction by effectively and efficiently resolving problems and questions. To accomplish this goal, help desk staff use well-defined processes, tools, and strategies.

THE INCIDENT MANAGEMENT PROCESS

Incident management is a well-defined, formal procedure that help desk staff follow to handle problem incidents, get the information users need or solve their problems, and close the incident. Because it refers to telephone, face-to-face, e-mail, and Web-based forms of support, incident management is a more general term than call management. **Call management** describes the steps in handling primarily telephone contacts between end users and support agents. Figure 6-2 shows the major steps in the incident management process. Each of these steps is described below.

1. **Receive the incident.** Whether an incident is received in person, by telephone call, in an e-mail message, or via a Web-based contact, the first step is to establish a relationship with the end user. Some support groups have a specific script that recommends actual language to use when contact with a user begins. The script can be in the form of a recommended greeting in a phone conversation or a predefined introductory paragraph that is inserted in a reply to an e-mail message. For example, in a telephone support call, the level 1 help desk agent may confirm the name of the support organization and provide his or her own first name. The agent may then ask the name of the caller. Other common early incident management tasks include providing a warning that the incident may be monitored (this is a legal requirement in most states) and an apology for any wait time. If a callback is likely, the support staff may request the caller's phone

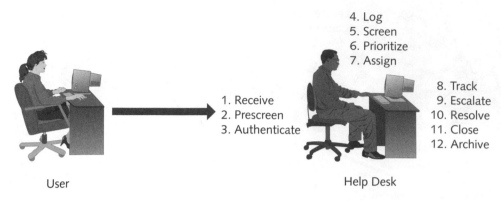

1. Receive
2. Prescreen
3. Authenticate

4. Log
5. Screen
6. Prioritize
7. Assign

8. Track
9. Escalate
10. Resolve
11. Close
12. Archive

User

Help Desk

Figure 6-2   Incident management process

number or e-mail address. As you'll learn later in this chapter, some of these tasks can be automated. In all incident-handling situations, the guidelines on client service, communications, and interpersonal skills described in Chapter 3 apply to each step in the incident management process.

NOTE

The incident management process described here applies primarily to telephone calls; however, many of the same steps also apply directly to face-to-face, e-mail, and Web-based contacts with a help desk. Although the specific steps and tools differ somewhat for written and verbal communications between a user and help desk staff member, the general flow and communications guidelines described here apply to each.

2. **Prescreen the incident. Prescreening** is essentially a filtering process to try to identify and respond to simple requests for information quickly, sometimes without even initiating an official incident. Not all help desks prescreen incidents. If their incident management procedures include prescreening, a level 1 employee asks questions to determine if the incident is a simple request for information that the incident screener can provide. Many help desk incidents fall into this category. For example, a user may want to know when the next version of a software package will be released and whether a known problem will be fixed in the new release. The user may want to receive product information or find out where to buy the product. Frequently, information request calls can be handled quickly and easily at support level 1 and then closed without proceeding to the steps below.

3. **Authenticate the user.** If an incident is more than a simple request for information, many help desks or hotline services have an **authentication procedure** designed to answer the question, "Is the help desk authorized to handle this incident or to provide information or services to this user?" Authentication (also called an entitlement verification) may involve asking a user for a product ID number, product serial number, model number, or software license number. In other situations, the screener may ask for the user's name (and

perhaps, department or e-mail address), and query a database to learn whether the user is a registered owner of a product or which level of help desk support services the user has purchased. If the user is a client on a pay-per-call basis, the staff member may have to obtain billing information from the user (usually a credit card number). Like prescreening, authentication is a filtering process. The help desk staff member determines whether the user has a legitimate claim to support services, and if so, at what service level. Once a staff member has authenticated a user, the incident-handling process can begin.

4. **Log the incident.** The goal of incident **logging** is to begin to document the incident and its related problem. The help desk agent may make an initial entry on a problem log, on a trouble report form, or in an incident tracking database. If user information already exists in a product registration database or user support knowledge base, logging an incident may be a simple matter of clicking a button that opens a new incident record that is linked to the client's user record. Some incident management software packages automatically fill in the user contact information. Figure 6-3 shows an example of a help desk incident log.

5. **Screen the incident.** During incident **screening**, the help desk agent asks a series of questions to categorize and describe the incident. Incidents are often categorized according to whether they are a:

- Request for information that could not be handled earlier during prescreening ("Will the latest release fix my font problem?")

- Question ("How do I get rid of commas in the numbers on my spreadsheet?")

- Problem ("My printer works with every known software package in the world except yours.")

- Complaint ("Your software is so full of bugs it locks up my computer every time I run it.")

- Work order ("Will you please upgrade the operating system software on my machine so I can use the latest version of Internet Explorer as a browser?")

In addition to the incident category, the support agent enters a brief written description of the request, question, problem, complaint, or work order into the problem log or into the incident tracking database. An experienced help desk staff agent learns to capture the essential facts of a problem report in a few key words or phrases. Lengthy verbatim details of the problem description are usually not necessary, although the support agent should include relevant facts that might be useful later to solve a problem. The following is an example of a problem description:

> Outlook Express icon missing from Windows XP desktop after reboot this a.m.

Incident Tracking # ☐

Incident Tracking Log

User: _____   Dept: _____   Phone: _____

E-mail address: _____

Date opened: ☐ / / ☐   Time opened: ☐   Taken by: ☐

Problem Category:
☐ Request for info   ☐ Question   ☐ Complaint
☐ Hardware   ☐ Software   ☐ LAN   ☐ Internet

Priority Code: ☐

Problem Description:

Incident assigned to: _____

Action Taken:

Incident escalated to: _____   Incident escalated to: _____

Incident Resolution:

Incident closed by: _____ Date closed: ☐ / / ☐ Time closed: ☐

Figure 6-3   Incident tracking log

When an incident is contained in an e-mail message or received via a Web-based contact, the user's entire correspondence may be captured in a database or included in the problem log.

1. **Prioritize the incident.** Based on the category and the nature of the problem or request, the support agent assigns the incident a priority code. A **priority code** indicates how serious the problem is, how many users are affected, and perhaps the consequence of not addressing the problem immediately. Help desk staff may determine that a problem affects only one user and is therefore a lower priority than an incident, for example, in which a malfunction in a network affects an entire department. An example of priority codes used in some support organizations is shown below.

> 1 — Urgent
>
> 2 — High priority
>
> 3 — Medium priority
>
> 4 — Low priority

During their orientation and training, help desk staff usually receive guidelines to help them prioritize incidents. In other situations, an incident management software package may automatically assign a priority code to a problem report. The priority code is frequently based on the type of call, its severity, the number of users affected, and the help desk's policy for handling that type of incident. For users who have purchased a service level agreement, the user's service level may also affect the priority. Instead of assigning priority codes, some help desks simply distribute incidents to support staff on a first-in, first-out (FIFO) basis.

When working with an internal user, a support agent may ask the user to help set an incident's priority, or to agree to a priority level. Consensus about an incident's priority ensures that those involved have the same expectations for help desk performance. Some support organizations defer to a user's priority assessment if a user and an agent disagree on the priority level. Furthermore, a priority level may change during the life of an incident. For example, a problem may be defined initially as a Priority 1 problem because a network is down. If a quick workaround can be implemented and the network becomes operational, the problem that caused the downtime may be re-prioritized to a Priority 2 or Priority 3.

The type of incident and its priority often determine the queue into which an incident will then be placed. A **queue** is a waiting line, like the line at the cash registers in a grocery store. Just as a grocery store may have separate lines or queues for regular and express checkout, a help desk may have queues for different types and priorities of incidents. The incident queues in a help desk may be defined by product, by priority code, or on any other basis that the help desk uses to allocate and assign incidents to support staff.

1. **Assign the incident.** When the level 1 help desk staff cannot respond to an incident directly, they may assign the incident to another help desk agent who has the technical expertise to provide the information, respond to the request, or solve the problem quickly and effectively. Help desks often maintain a list of staff members who specialize in specific products or types of problems. In some automated incident management systems, the process of assigning the incident simply moves it from one queue to another.

   New help desk employees sometimes find it difficult to learn the best place to refer an incident they cannot resolve. However, they learn quickly who among the experienced technical support staff have good problem-solving skills, give quick and correct answers for a specific type of problem, and can help deal with incidents effectively so that user contacts can be handled at the lowest possible support level in a multi-level structure.

2. **Track the incident.** Whenever the essential facts associated with an incident change, such as by receiving additional problem information, assigning a new priority code, or assigning the incident to a different staff member, the help desk staff update the incident information record. Incident **tracking** refers to the process of updating the incident record with information about a problem as it progresses. An automated help desk system often records the date and time of each incident tracking entry into a database to provide a complete record of what happened and when. Incident tracking provides an important history of the problem and how it was handled. A record of how an incident was handled can be useful information to help desk staff when they encounter a similar problem. Incident tracking information is also important input to measure the quality of incident management, evaluate the performance of help desk employees, and identify support staff training needs.

3. **Escalate the incident.** If initial attempts to resolve a problem are unsuccessful, most support groups have policies and procedures to escalate an incident. Incident **escalation** is a normal process in which a problem is transferred to a higher level of support that has a greater ability or resources to handle more difficult problems, as was shown in Figure 6-1.

   In some automated incident management systems, the escalation process is automatic. For example, help desk software can often be programmed to escalate an incident to the next level automatically if a support agent cannot resolve it within a specified period of time. If a problem has been active, but unresolved, for more than a specified amount of time (usually a few hours), an incident management system may automatically display it on a support manager's screen, where he or she can monitor it closely to make sure that staff members are progressing toward a solution.

4. **Resolve the incident.** At some point in the incident management process, a help desk staff member resolves the user's problem or question. Incident

6

resolution means that the user's problem has been solved or a complaint has either been noted or referred to product designers as a suggestion for the next product revision cycle. Alternately, incident resolution may involve giving the client authorization to return a product for replacement or a refund. Incident resolution doesn't necessarily mean the user or client is completely satisfied, however.

A small percentage of all calls, usually those that involve complaints about product bugs or features, cannot be satisfactorily resolved during the incident management process. Obviously, one of the goals of a help desk is to minimize the percentage of problems that cannot be resolved satisfactorily, but the percentage is rarely zero. The help desk goal, however, is a win-win situation in which users receive the information or problem resolution they need and feel that the problem has been resolved to their satisfaction.

5. **Close the incident.** In incident **closing**, the support agent may review the steps the help desk took to solve the problem. The agent may also get feedback from the user about her or his satisfaction level. The help desk agent usually terminates the incident by thanking the user for calling or sending e-mail and inviting the user to recontact the help desk if further problems arise or if the recommended solution to the problem doesn't work. In reality, the help desk hopes the user won't need to call back or e-mail again, but extends the invitation, anyway. Closing an incident may also involve additional entries on a problem log or in a database to indicate the disposition of the problem and how it was resolved.

NOTE

Incident closing can be a challenge, especially in a telephone support environment. Some users either can't accept that their problem cannot be resolved in a reasonable way, or don't want to hang up because they enjoy talking about technology with help desk staff. These cases fall in the category of difficult calls, which you learned about in Chapter 3.

6. **Archive the incident.** Closed incidents are often retained in an incident management system for some predefined period in case the user calls back or sends a follow-up e-mail. The help desk's policies usually specify how long a closed incident is retained before it is archived. An incident **archive** maintains a copy of resolved incidents in a database of completed incidents. The system then deletes archived incidents from the active incident management system. In a manual system that uses written problem logs or trouble reports, the resolved incident archive process may simply involve moving a folder of resolved incidents from one file drawer to another.

Incident archives provide data that can be incorporated into a help desk knowledge base. Recall from Chapter 4 that a knowledge base is an organized collection of information, articles, procedures, tips, and previous problems with known solutions that can serve as a resource in a problem-solving situation. An activity associated with closing an incident may be to enter it into a help desk knowledge base. Support staff members can then search the knowledge base in future problem-solving situations to find past problems with the same or similar characteristics as an active incident. Incident archives may be analyzed to produce statistical reports of the frequency of various categories of incidents. These reports are useful to help desk managers to make staffing decisions and observe help desk performance trends over time, as you'll learn in Chapter 7.

The incident management steps described here are examples of the kinds of activities that occur during incident processing. Each organization's support policies and procedures may dictate a somewhat different sequence of incident processing events, based on unique business requirements, user expectations, help desk policies, and an organization's resources. Training for entry-level help desk employees usually includes an orientation and hands-on practice with the specific steps the staff is expected to follow.

Mary Baldwin College describes its user support incident management procedures for faculty and staff and how priorities for problem resolution are set at its Web site at **academic.mbc.edu/cis/policy/Acceptable_Use_Policy_Nov2001.html#5.0%20Computer%20and%20Telephone%20User%20Support**. The University of Connecticut School of Law provides information about its help desk policies and procedures at **www.law.uconn.edu/infosys/sla.htm**.

PHYSICAL LAYOUT OF HELP DESK WORK AREAS

In most large-scale help desk operations, each support agent works in a cubicle that is enclosed on three sides by carpeted wall panels. The wall panels are between four to six feet high; the height depends on whether visual contact with coworkers is deemed desirable, and on the need to reduce background and equipment noise. A typical cubicle is eight to ten feet long by six to eight feet wide.

In the cubicles, support agents sit at a desk that includes space for one or more computer systems. All support agents have their own system on which they run incident (call) management software as well as the specific packages they support. Support agents may have other computer systems in their cubicle that run different hardware and operating system platforms, which they can use to replicate, or reproduce, a user's problem. In some situations, problem replication systems may be located in a separate computer room where they can be shared among support staff. Mainframe access (where necessary) may be available through a terminal emulator on the support person's desktop, or through a separate terminal located in the cubicle. The work cubicle usually contains a reference library of manuals and information on the specific products that the agent supports.

To answer or initiate telephone calls, most support agents prefer a headset instead of a standard telephone handset. The headset permits considerable freedom of motion, helps prevent neck and shoulder problems, and can easily be unplugged when necessary to confer with a coworker or supervisor about a problem. Some headsets are wireless, which increases portability and flexibility in the physical support environment.

To view a tutorial by Jim Hanks on how telephone headsets can affect call center productivity, visit **telecom.hellodirect.com/docs/Tutorials/Productivity.1.080701.asp**.

Workplace ergonomic issues, important for end users in general, are even more critical for help desk staff who provide telephone support. Chapters 10 and 13 discuss ergonomic and facilities management concerns that apply to the design of workstations for end users as well as help desk staff.

Job stress is a common complaint of help desk employees. The physical environment of the help desk work areas can either contribute to job stress or diminish it. The work areas should be designed to reduce distractions from excessive noise, motion, and other interruptions as much as possible. Frequent and scheduled breaks are useful stress reduction tools. Some support groups provide employee lounges, cafeterias, and break rooms with refreshments, televisions, pool tables, computer games, and other diversions.

A comprehensive Web site about job-related stress is **results.about.com/stress/#1**.

HELP DESK TECHNOLOGY AND TOOLS

Automation has significantly impacted the help desk industry in recent years. These effects include help desk software packages, computer telephony, and Web support.

Help Desk Software

The incident management process described above often collects, processes, and stores a large volume of transactions. Some help desks organize these transactions in a database, where tables contain information about clients, products, computer configurations, help desk staff, and perhaps an archive of solved problems. Transactions occur when links in the database are established between a client and a product (such as a product registration), or between a client, a computer, and a help desk staff member (such as a problem incident report).

A large-scale help desk operation may receive and process hundreds (or even thousands) of incidents every day. A small-scale help desk may handle only a few incidents each day. Commercial software packages are available to help both large- and small-scale help desks manage the volume and processing of support transactions. These packages have features and capabilities, described below, that are useful to support both internal and external clients.

Log and Track Incidents.   Most help desk software packages include features to log and track incidents. They often work in conjunction with a telephone or e-mail system to manage incident queues, set incident priorities, assign incidents to agents, and escalate incidents when necessary. An incident tracking system is useful even in a very small support center staffed by one or a few people. No user who needs technical support likes to "get lost in the system." Automated incident management capabilities help support staff keep track of the call volume, their priorities and status, and clients who need attention. As the size of the help desk staff increases and manual systems become cumbersome, an automated incident management system is almost a requirement.

Contact Information.   Support incidents invariably involve contacts with people. Many help desk packages include capabilities to store, edit, and recall contact and location information about internal clients, external clients, help desk and information systems staff, and vendors. These packages often include a contact database with names, job titles, phone numbers, e-mail addresses, Web site URLs, fax numbers, and other information.

Product Information.   Many help desk users request either information about products sold by an organization or about other manufacturers' products. A help desk package that contains information about hardware, software, networks, and services enables support staff to respond to many common questions about product features, limitations, new versions, configuration constraints, known bugs, product availability, and related information. An organization's Web site may provide users with links to product information in order to reduce the volume of support contacts required to answer requests for information.

Configuration Information.   Help desk software often includes the ability to document hardware, software, and network information about client systems. Although configuration information about external client systems is useful, it is difficult to collect and keep up to date, unless a service or facilities management contract covers the users' systems. But configuration information is critical to help desk staff who support internal clients. Much of the configuration check list information you will learn about in Chapter 10 can be stored in a database. That way, support agents who must troubleshoot or upgrade a system for an in-house client can easily access basic information about the user's system.

Diagnostic Utilities.   Some help desk software packages include diagnostic utility software to assist a support agent with a specific system problem. **Diagnostic software** is useful to analyze the performance of a remote system and to look for potential problem areas. As you learned in Chapter 4, some diagnostic utilities permit support agents to attach directly to a client's system, which can facilitate the problem diagnosis and repair process. Using remote access software, support agents can open a window on their system that shows the remote user's PC desktop. When support agents work in the remote access window, their keystrokes and mouse clicks are performed on the user's system.

Problem Solution Knowledge Base.   Knowledge bases (sometimes called "smart data-bases") used as a support tool can contain information about common problems and their solutions. Some knowledge bases are built as user problems are solved and archived. Other knowledge bases with a store of common problems and their solutions can be purchased ready-made. Because a knowledge base of support problems and solutions can be huge and grows daily, the ability to locate relevant information is critical to their effective use. Training for help desk staff often includes practice problems that require locating the information in a support knowledge base.

NOTE   The "smart" part of a knowledge base is a set of search tools to help locate past problem situations that are similar to a current problem. Some help desk products incorporate search strategies based on artificial intelligence tools. Expert systems (sequences of IF-THEN rules), neural networks (automated learning systems), case-based reasoning (pattern-matching strategies), and natural language processing (the ability to formulate questions in English) are often incorporated into help desk knowledge bases to help support staff quickly locate the specific information they need to solve a problem.

Product Order Entry.   Marketing is often an important help desk function because a user's request for information about a product can lead directly to an order for it. Therefore, many help desk software packages include an order-entry capability that permits a user or a support agent to enter an order online. Product order entry in a help desk system may be integrated directly with other business systems, such as shipping and invoicing. In this way, a help desk subsystem can be integrated with other enterprise-wide applications.

Client Feedback.   Help desks can collect at least two types of user feedback that is useful to an organization. **Client feedback** information includes the level of user satisfaction with an organization's products or services, as well as with help desk support.

Measures of satisfaction with products and services can range from complaints about features that don't work as advertised to suggestions for new features. The help desk staff needs a way to capture user feedback and route the information to product designers and engineers. This feedback is often a source of useful ideas for the next round of product feature planning.

Measures of satisfaction with help desk support can include feedback about the handling of a specific incident, the problem resolution process, or the help desk support in general. Some help desk software packages provide an ability to collect, analyze, and report information from surveys that measure user satisfaction with help desk support services. These surveys are an important form of feedback that assist managers and staff to identify strengths and areas for improvement in help desk support services.

Asset Management.   Some support groups are responsible for technology asset management. They keep track of an organization's inventory of computer hardware, peripherals, software package licenses, network components, spare parts, and related equipment. Many help desk packages include asset and inventory control features. This capability is designed to help the support staff manage an organization's fixed assets. Computer equipment is often tagged with an asset ID number and recorded in an asset management database, which may be part of the help desk package, or linked to it. The asset management system may also store information about software licenses owned by a company as well as to which employees

6

each software package is assigned. Because support staff are often involved in the purchase and installation of computer systems, an automated help desk system is a convenient place to record computer installation information. And because support staff can be involved in moving equipment from one office to another, they can update the asset database at the time of the equipment transfer.

Service Management.   Organizations often outsource hardware and peripheral mainte-nance and repairs to outside vendors. In addition to configuration and asset information, some help desk packages include features to manage hardware service contracts and agreements. These capabilities can include warranty information and a service history for each product, as well as reminders of when the next preventive maintenance or service is scheduled to be performed and by whom.

Telephone System Interface.   Another useful help desk software feature is an ability to interface with a telephone system. Because many help desk support groups deal with a large volume of incoming and outgoing calls, integrated access to an organization's telephone system is important. Automated telephone systems are discussed in the next section.

Communications and Information Resource Links.   Most help desk software packages recognize that connections to communication and information resources are critical for both end users and support agents. These packages often include external connections to e-mail and Internet resources as well as internal connections to online help files, product documentation, and problem archives.

Statistical Reports.   Help desk software includes built-in statistical reports to meet the information needs of help desk staff and management. Reports such as the abandonment rate (callers who hang up), the number of unresolved incidents by hour and day, the average length of time telephone callers spend on hold, the average length of incident processing (from receipt to closure), the productivity of staff members (incident closure rate), inventory control reports, and frequently asked questions are examples of predefined reports that are commonly available in help desk software packages.

You'll learn more about statistical reports that are helpful to help desk managers in Chapter 7.

NOTE

Customizable Interface and Reports.   Some help desk software includes features that let a help desk group modify the user interface, toolbars, menus, and data-entry forms the support staff uses. Customization may also allow a help desk to add or modify fields in the database tables to meet special needs, and often include a report generator that prepares custom reports of database information. Custom reports enable the help desk staff to augment built-in reports with ones designed to address specific staff and management information needs. Some help desk packages include a programming language that staff can use to write macros or code to support extensions of the basic package.

This list of help desk software features and capabilities is not in any order of importance, because their importance depends on each help desk group's needs. And although no single help desk package necessarily offers all of these features and capabilities, many packages offer several of them. Selecting a help desk software package from among those on the market (and there are many) is often one of the most important product evaluation decisions a help desk staff makes.

6

The list of companies that sell help desk software packages is long. Some of the most popular packages for large-scale help desk operations are:

- Remedy Help Desk
  www.remedy.com/solutions/servicemgmt/help_desk.htm
- Peregrine ServiceCenter
  www.peregrine.com/us/Products/ServiceManagement/ServiceCenter/default.htm
- Magic Solutions Service Desk
  www.networkassociates.com/us/products/magic/magic_service_desk.htm
- Clientele for Help Desks
  www.coastalsoftware.com/products/clientele/helpdesks/index.htm
- HEAT Service & Support
  www.frontrange.com/heat

Packages aimed primarily at small or mid-scale help desks include:

- HelpTrac
  www.helptrac.com
- Track-It!
  www.itsolutions.intuit.com/default.asp
- Manage-IT!
  www.baronsoftware.com
- Soffront Customer Helpdesk
  www.soffront.com/crm/Products/CustomerHelpdesk.asp
- BridgeTrak
  www.helpdesksoftware.com/default.htm

Several of these packages offer downloadable evaluation versions. Other help desk packages are listed at **dir.yahoo.com/Business_and_Economy/Business_to_Business/Corporate_Services/Customer_Service/Software/Help_Desk**

eHelpDesk offers several white papers on evaluating and selecting help desk software packages on its Web site at **www.help-desk-software.net/library.html**. TechRepublic offers a call tracking software evaluation toolkit as a download at **techrepublic.com.com/5129-6249-10219695.html** (registration required).

The next four figures illustrate typical help desk software with a package named HelpTrac, which is sold by Monarch Bay Software (**www.helptrac.com**). The HelpTrac package is a commercial help desk program that includes several of the features you just learned about. Like many help desk software packages, HelpTrac is customizable for specific help desk situations. Users can add, delete, or modify fields in the HelpTrac database. Figure 6-4 shows a sample HelpTrac screen with contact information for a user, Kevin Barnes, a production supervisor at TBSI Corporation. Several kinds of information can be displayed in this window. For example, a support person can find information about how to contact Kevin, a profile of Kevin as a computer user, what his equipment configuration is, which hardware and software products Kevin uses, and even billing information, if relevant. Information about Kevin's past history of problem incidents and equipment maintenance history can also be displayed.

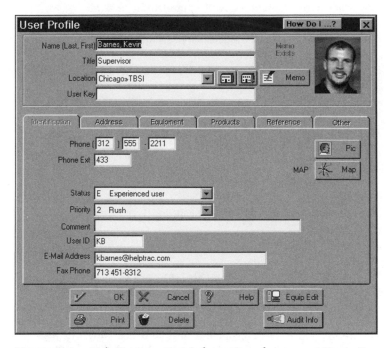

Figure 6-4   HelpTrac contact information for a user, Kevin Barnes, complete with a picture and a map of Kevin's location in case a help desk agent needs to go on-site

You can download a demonstration copy of the latest version of HelpTrac at **www.helptrac.com**. Install and run the demo version to get experience with the features of a help desk software package. For sample exercises, see Case Project 2 at the end of the chapter.

Figure 6-5 shows an example of a problem ticket that a support agent, Bill Miles, took from Kevin Barnes one afternoon. Much of the information on this problem report, such as Kevin's contact information and the incident's date and time, are filled in automatically.

When support agent Bill Miles receives the problem report from Kevin, he categorizes the call. Kevin is having a problem printing e-mail messages. Bill selected the general category *Network Software* from among the relevant categories, and the product category *Email*. From the list of possible symptoms, Bill selects *Unable to print*. These categories were custom-designed by the help desk for which Bill Miles works; the specific categories vary from one help desk to another, and Bill can add categories as needed to describe a problem.

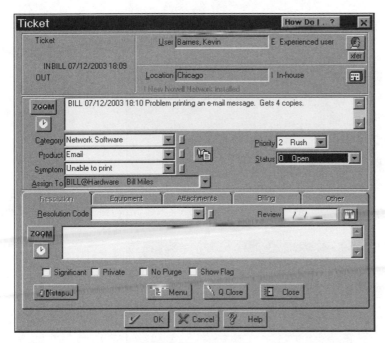

Figure 6-5   HelpTrac problem ticket from Kevin Barnes that reports a problem printing from e-mail

One of the buttons in the incident ticket next to the problem categories in Figure 6-5 is a Solution Tree. The Solution Tree in HelpTrac is like a database organized as a decision tree. Bill uses the database to search past problem tickets in the Solution Tree for other problem reports for *Network Software, Email, Unable to print*. In this case, Bill finds an earlier entry, shown in Figure 6-6, by one of his help desk colleagues, Ken Wilson. Ken had solved an e-mail printing problem that a user, Al Thomas, had encountered that sounds very similar to the problem Kevin Barnes has contacted Bill about. Bill is able to ask Kevin follow-up questions to see if his is the same or a different problem, and Bill can see how Ken dealt with the problem.

Figure 6-7 is an example of a management report that is predefined in HelpTrac. This report shows the number of incidents the help desk received during a week for each of the problem priority codes the help desk uses. These codes can also be customized. The report shows that, for the week of the report, most of the problem tickets (17) were normal priority (code 3),

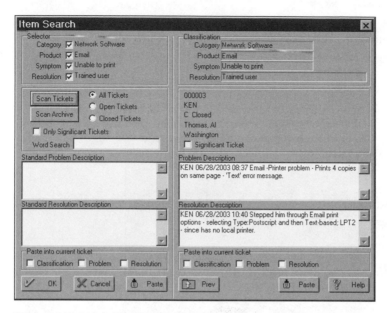

Figure 6-6   HelpTrac Solution Tree database record of a previous problem ticket that reports an incident similar to the one Kevin Barnes has reported

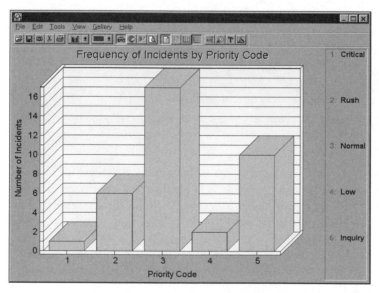

Figure 6-7   HelpTrac management report of calls received for each priority code

and 10 of the tickets were inquiries. The help desk staff can use a report generator named Crystal Reports to prepare custom reports to supplement those built into the software. Week-to-week comparisons can help managers spot trends in the types of incidents reported by users.

Other commercial help desk software packages have similar features and capabilities to those in the HelpTrac package. Many help desk packages can be integrated with telephone systems to provide a powerful suite of tools for help desk staff.

NOTE   To learn more about software packages and tools targeted at the user support industry, consult *A Guide to Help Desk Technology, Tools & Techniques* by Dione McBride, Course Technology, 2000, ISBN 0-7600-7151-9.

Computer Telephony Systems

6

Computer telephony is the name used to describe products that incorporate telephone and computer technology into an integrated package. Computer telephony is popular among support organizations that make heavy use of both technologies to provide help desk services. Whereas many small support centers rely on a help desk receptionist or a call dispatcher to respond to incoming telephone calls, an increasing number of help desk facilities invest in automated telephone systems.

Automated call distributors (ACD) are telephone systems that can answer calls, greet callers, provide menus to indicate the type of call, and route the call to a specific support agent or to a call queue. When integrated with a help desk software package, an ACD system can take incident management a step further. When an appropriate support agent becomes available, an ACD system can match the support agent with the highest priority caller, signal the support agent on his or her computer screen, and display information about the caller and the problem on the agent's monitor. The ACD then routes the call to the agent's telephone.

WWW   To learn more about the features of an ACD system and its role in a user support environment, visit the Nortel Networks Web site at **www. nortelnetworks.com/ products/01/norstar/call_centers/minuet.html**. Another ACD product, Database Systems' Pacer, is described at **www.databasesystemscorp.com/ psacd.htm**. An online article by Lee Hollman, "Supplying Satisfying Solutions," at **www.callcentermagazine.com/article/CCM20000727S0006** describes how several support organizations use ACD and other technologies to meet clients' changing expectations for support service.

ACD systems can also collect information about the performance of the help desk operation, such as the average length of phone calls, the length of hold queues, the average amount of time on hold, and the average length of calls for each support agent. They can also monitor calls by recording them for training and employee evaluation purposes. The major benefit of an ACD system is that it reduces the amount of employee time needed to manually respond to calls and route them to support staff. Because ACD systems increase the efficiency of help desk staff, they are help desk productivity tools.

Although computer telephony systems are designed to make efficient use of scarce support staff resources, many of these systems have a (richly deserved) poor reputation among users. Lengthy hold times, long and complex menu options, repetitious requests for information, and dropped calls are common complaints of users who must navigate ACD systems. The recent emphasis on client relationship management in the support industry may eventually provide users with some relief from poorly designed computer telephony systems.

Another computer telephony product with applications in user support is an interactive voice response system. An **interactive voice response (IVR)** system allows a user to interact with a database of information by pressing keys on a telephone handset or speaking simple words into the telephone. The IVR unit retrieves information from the database and plays the response for the user. IVRs can be programmed with decision tree logic to ask questions to narrow a search for the information the user needs.

To learn more about interactive voice response technology, visit the International Engineering Consortium's Web site at **www.iec.org/online/tutorials/speech_enabled/index.html**.

Web-Based Support

As support organizations and their clients search for more efficient and cost-effective ways to provide support to end users, the role of the Internet and the World Wide Web has increased dramatically since the mid-1990s. Virtually every large hardware component manufacturer, system integrator, software developer, network services supplier, and computer support provider operates a Web site. Vendor Web sites offer a variety of support services to users, including:

- Product information, specifications, updates, pricing, and licensing
- Product order initiation and order fulfillment status reports
- Product rebate status
- Automated requests for literature, newsletters, and special e-mail notifications
- Online manuals and documentation
- Software downloads of drivers, patches, updates, diagnostic tools, templates, product tutorials, and demonstration versions of software
- Troubleshooting wizards
- Knowledge base access to frequently asked questions (FAQs), articles, problem reports, white papers, and technical information
- A search engine to locate information and problem solutions

- Bulletin boards and chat rooms to connect knowledgeable users with other users
- E-mail access to technical support staff
- Problem report submission
- Contact information for support staff
- Feedback on client satisfaction with products and support services
- Links to other sites with information about related products and services

Although few vendor Web sites offer all of these services, increasing numbers of vendors now see the Web as an ideal supplement to telephone, face-to-face, and e-mail support services. One of the reasons Web support has become popular, even for small support organizations, is that the cost to provide Web support is often less than other methods. Users find that they can frequently locate the information they need on a Web site without a phone conversation or an e-mail exchange with a support agent. Anytime a support organization can respond to a user's needs without directly involving a support staff member, it saves money and sometimes reduces errors due to misinformation. And anytime a user can quickly locate information on a Web site, the user's time is better spent than in a telephone queue waiting for the next available support agent. Web-based support is another tool employed by the support center to meet its objective of making users more self-reliant.

HelpDesk Expert for IT Support is an incident management system designed for Web-based support. A video demonstration of its features is available at **www.helpdesk-expert-it-support.com/demo.html**. Take the Quick Tour at Step 2. Viewing the video requires Macromedia's Flash Player (a free download).

To get experience with an example of a Web-based support site, visit IBM's Web support site at **www.ibm.com/support/us**. While you are there, make a list of the services IBM provides users at its support site.

Even when an e-mail exchange between a user and a support staff member is required, e-mail is less costly than telephone support. First, e-mail is **asynchronous**, which means that the communications between a user and support staff do not have to occur at the same time. A support agent does not have to respond to a user's e-mail request immediately, and does not have to be available to communicate on the client's schedule, as is the case with a telephone call. Also, e-mail support makes more efficient use of support staff resources than telephone support does. Second, e-mail responses to frequently asked questions can be composed in advance, checked for accuracy, stored, and then easily pasted into a response to a user. When appropriate, use of "canned" responses to e-mail requests is a cost-effective use of support staff time.

NOTE   As with automated telephone systems, the potential to abuse the client relationship with canned e-mail responses is enormous. Users who submit a specific question to a support Web site sometimes receive several pages of canned response. On occasion, when a user asks a follow-up question on the same subject, the same, lengthy canned response is e-mailed back. This problem occurs because support staff do not always read an inquiry carefully, or because support organizations that receive huge volumes of e-mail automatically scan the e-mail and send canned responses to users based on keywords in the user's message. Neither of these practices is likely to improve the client relationship.

Increased use of the Web as a user support tool means that some knowledge, skills, and abilities that were important for a support staff member are now less important, whereas other skills are becoming more important. Telephone support emphasizes verbal skills, pleasant voice quality, an ability to recall information quickly, and patience with clients; Web-based and e-mail support require staff members who are skilled in written and graphical communications. The ability to recall information quickly is less important in an online environment than the ability to locate information in a knowledge base. The ability to speak is less important than the ability to write clearly. The ability to listen is less important than the ability to read and understand. However, the ability to ask probing questions and use good client service skills are important in every support environment.

Web-based and e-mail support is also an attractive option for small organizations and organizations that provide primarily internal support. Many organizations now use an intranet to deliver information and user support services to their employees. An **intranet** is a network modeled after the Internet, with information organized into Web pages, but accessible primarily or exclusively by employees within an organization. An intranet provides a way to support internal users with tools they already know, such as their Web browser, but also provides security from access by unauthorized external users. At small organizations and departments in large ones, help desk staff may need skills in Web site design and usability as well as Web applications software and programming languages to build support pages that provide clients and employees with Web-based user support services.

NOTE   To learn more about intranets and their benefits to an organization, visit the Intranet Road Map at the OpenConsult Web site, **www.intranetroadmap. com/default.cfm**. The site includes a short tutorial on intranets.

LARRY LAWSON
DIRECTOR, TECHNICAL SERVICES
ST. AGNES HEALTHCARE
BALTIMORE, MARYLAND

St. Agnes HealthCare is a full-service community teaching hospital located in Baltimore. It services metropolitan Baltimore and the surrounding region with a staff of approximately 2900 employees, and is well-known for its comprehensive cardiology services to patients.

Larry Lawson is the Director of Technical Services for St. Agnes. Among other services, he is responsible for computer support for 2000 users with a support staff of seven employees. The 2000 users include physicians, nurses, lab workers, hospital service workers, and administrative staff. Users range from very computer literate to new users. The help desk operation keeps in contact with hospital users via phone, face-to-face interactions, e-mail, the Web, remote control, instant messages, and text messages.

The computer support staff at St. Agnes has used the HelpTrac software described in this chapter since the mid-1990s to automate user support tasks. Many users at St. Agnes now contact the support staff by filling out a trouble ticket on the Web. Users are also able to search the solution tree knowledge base in HelpTrac and are sometimes able to resolve their own problems. When they can find their own answers, it reduces the number of problems Larry's support staff must handle directly and makes the staff more productive. Larry says, "We use the solution tree with religious fervor. It saves us so much time and is a valuable teaching aide for some of our less experienced help desk personnel. We especially like the hierarchical features in HelpTrac, where support staff can drill down on a problem that resembles one we have seen before and where the solution may be similar."

Larry also makes extensive use of the reporting features in HelpTrac. "It is easy to learn from the reports when during the day or week the staff is busy, the causes of common problems, and trends in problem types. The reports help us pinpoint with accuracy the users that may need additional training. We also use the reports to help schedule our staff, to plan training programs, and to track metrics that document the performance of the support staff and justify the expenditures on the support operation."

St. Agnes' use of HelpTrac doesn't end with support for computer systems. For example, when a patient is admitted and is not yet in the clinical information system, a nurse calls the same number as for computer support. The nurse enters the patient's name, room number, bed number, and dietary needs into HelpTrac. A Nutrition Aide, who carries a text pager, receives a page for a special meal, which can be delivered in five minutes or less. The facilities maintenance team is also on the same central telephone number.

When a patient room needs any maintenance or repair services, an entry is made into HelpTrac. The maintenance supervisor pulls each request from a HelpTrac queue and assigns it to a facilities mechanic via a text message to a pager. The maintenance supervisor uses HelpTrac as a tool to set priorities and dole out work assignments to a mechanic who is already in the area where help is needed. The result is less time wasted by mechanics. As these examples illustrate, the Technical Services group at St. Agnes continues to search for innovative ways to use technology such as HelpTrac to increase staff productivity and improve services to its patients.

TRENDS IN HELP DESK OPERATIONS

Help desk operations is a field that is changing rapidly. As you learned in Chapter 2, a recent trend is to outsource some help desk jobs to Asia, especially India, because relative wages are significantly less than in North America. This trend will reduce the need for workers in the United States to answer help desk telephone calls, respond to e-mails from users, and operate self-help Web sites. In other words, outsourcing will primarily impact help desk operations that serve external clients. Outsourcing help desk operations overseas raises several issues that are unresolved, including the long-range impact on the U.S. workforce, whether quality support standards can be maintained, and the role of help desks in building and maintaining customer relationships. On a practical level, outsourcing help desk operations overseas means relatively fewer jobs available for help desk agents in the United States. On the other hand, relatively more entry-level positions will be available in North America for support workers who serve internal clients. This trend will impact academic and training programs for future help desk workers. Less emphasis on telephone help desk operations will give way to a greater emphasis on more comprehensive training to prepare workers for the broader spectrum of knowledge, skills, and abilities required to support internal users.

 To learn more about outsourcing and its impact on U.S. employment, read a *Business Week* article, "The New Global Job Shift," at **www.businessweek. com/magazine/content/03_05/b3818001.htm**, or a ComputerWorld article, "Exporting IT Jobs," at **www.computerworld.com/managementtopics/ outsourcing/story/0,10801,80661,00.html**.

Automation will continue to impact help desk operations. Whereas many help desks in the past were based on walk-in, on-site, or telephone support, future help desks will undoubtedly rely to an increasing extent on e-mail, the Internet, self-help, and remote diagnosis to provide help desk services. **Remote diagnosis** is the use of a computer system at a help desk site to connect to a client's system, and then test various components of the user's hardware, examine the user's software configuration, and replicate a problem scenario. Furthermore, help desk technology in the future will likely incorporate advances in voice recognition and response in products aimed at the user support industry. The key to the successful help desk of the future is to reduce users' reliance on help desk staff by helping them be more self-sufficient, and to increase the productivity (often by decreasing the effort expended) of help desk staff when users cannot be self-sufficient for whatever reason.

Help desks of the future will likely be more proactive and less reactive than current help desks They will be better able to anticipate user needs and changes in user support requirements. For example, the ability to store end-user configuration information in a help desk database means that support agents can contact a user about potential problems even before the user encounters them. Help desks will be in a better position to distribute and install software via a network connection to meet a user's needs or solve a problem a user reports.

Help desks of the future will be seen as the front-end of a **client relationship management (CRM)** program. Client relationship management is a relatively new name for an old objective: to meet the needs of a client by providing excellent client service. CRM views each client as the reason an organization exists. It recognizes that the cost to an organization to replace a client is much greater than the cost of managing a successful relationship with an existing client.

As help desks make increasing use of the Web as a delivery vehicle for support services, the specific skills required of support workers in many support organizations will change, as described earlier in this chapter. Another computer industry trend that will have an impact on help desk staffing is the certification process. Not only will future help desk staff in some organizations be expected to pass certification tests for the products they support, but associations for help desk professionals are beginning to offer certification programs for help desk agent skills.

Chapter 7 describes the certification process in greater detail.

Finally, as more help desk functions become automated, help desk management will need access to high-quality reports and statistical information that will alert managers and staff to trends in the volume of incidents, the kinds of questions users ask, the need for help desk staff with particular skills, and the kinds of future problems users are likely to encounter.

CHAPTER SUMMARY

- ◻ Simply stated, the goal of most help desk operations is to provide clients with a single point of contact for information requests and problem resolution.

- ◻ Most help desk processes and procedures involve the effective management of problem incidents. Incident management addresses the details of how problem incidents are received, prescreened, authenticated to determine the user's right to various types and levels of service, logged for record keeping purposes, and screened to determine importance. They are then prioritized, assigned to an appropriate staff person, tracked as they move toward satisfactory resolution, escalated if necessary, resolved, closed, and archived in a database.

❑ The physical environment of a help desk facility includes the workspace, furniture, equipment, and computer systems help desk agents use in their work. Headsets that permit flexibility of movement are an important tool. The physical layout of a workspace also impacts agents' job stress.

❑ Several tools are available to assist in managing problem incidents. These include help desk software packages with features designed to automate many incident management tasks and procedures, computer telephony systems (including automated call distributors and interactive voice response units) that automate call routing and task assignment, and the Web as a support delivery tool.

❑ Help desks of the future will undoubtedly continue to evolve. Outsourcing of help desk services overseas will impact industry employment trends as well as training programs. Increased automation of help desk functions and attempts to be more proactive by anticipating user problems will improve the productivity of help desk staff and operations. In an increasing number of organizations, help desks will be viewed as an important component in client relationship management.

KEY TERMS

archive — A special database designed to store and retain copies of closed calls; in a manual incident management system, the archive may be a file of closed calls.

asynchronous — A method of communication in which the communicators do not have to participate at the same time; e-mail and Web-based communication are examples.

authentication procedure — An incident management step that determines whether help desk staff are authorized to handle a call; usually includes checking product registrations or support services contracts.

automated call distributor (ACD) — A computer telephony system that automates many of the first steps in incident management, such as a greeting, menu options, caller authentication, call holding, queue management, and staff notification.

call management — A well-defined, formal procedure that help desk staff follow to handle primarily telephone contacts between end users and support staff; compare to incident management.

client feedback — Information collected from help desk users about their level of satisfaction with a product or service, a specific help desk incident, the problem resolution, or help desk services in general.

client relationship management (CRM) — A process that aims to meet the needs of clients by providing excellent client service; CRM is based on findings that the cost to an organization to replace a client is much greater than the cost of managing the relationship with an existing client.

closing — An incident management step that leads toward the conclusion of an incident; may include a review of the solution, mutual agreement that a solution has been reached, an invitation to call back, and final entries in an incident management database.

computer telephony — Integration of computer technology and telephone technology into tools designed to increase help desk staff productivity by providing a seamless interface between the two.

diagnostic software — Computer programs designed to help support agents collect information and analyze problems with a computer system.

escalation — An incident management step in which a problem is transferred to a higher level of support that has a greater ability or resources to handle more difficult problems.

incident management — A well-defined, formal procedure that help desk staff follow to handle face-to-face, telephone, e-mail, or Web-based problem incidents, get the information users need or solve their problems, and close the incident; compare to call management.

interactive voice response (IVR) — A computer telephony system that allows a user to interact with a database of information by pressing keys on a telephone handset or speaking simple words into the telephone.

intranet — A network modeled after the Internet, with information organized into Web pages, but accessible primarily or exclusively by employees within an organization.

logging — An incident management step that begins an official document or record of a problem incident.

multi-level support model — A help desk structure that organizes support staff and services into several levels, or tiers, of support; sometimes called a frontline/backline model, the goal is to handle calls at the lowest possible support level.

prescreening — An incident management step that tries to identify and respond to simple requests for information without initiating an official incident; essentially a filtering process.

priority code — A designation assigned to an incident that indicates how serious the problem is for users, how many users are affected, and perhaps the consequence of not addressing the problem immediately.

queue — A waiting line or list into which incoming calls or incidents are placed when they cannot be addressed immediately; queues are often established for different types and priorities of incidents or specific products, clients, or levels of support.

remote diagnosis — The use of a computer system at a help desk site to connect to a client's system, and then test various components of the user's hardware, examine the user's software configuration, and replicate a problem scenario.

resolution — An incident management step in which a user's problem has been solved, a complaint has either been noted or referred to product designers, or authorization has been given to return a product for replacement or a refund.

screening — An incident management step in which a help desk staff member asks questions to categorize and describe the incident; incidents are categorized as a request for information, a question, a problem, a complaint, or a work order.

tracking — An incident management step that updates the incident record with information about a problem as it progresses.

CHECK YOUR UNDERSTANDING

1. A telephone help desk may also be called a(n) _____ .
   a. hotline
   b. information center
   c. support consultant
   d. any of these

2. True or False? In a help desk that uses the multi-level support model, the goal is to handle as many calls at the lowest possible support level.

3. In a help desk patterned on the multi-level support model, what is the common title of employees at each level?
   a. level 1 assistant; level 2 product specialist; level 3 programmer; level 4 support manager
   b. level 1 incident dispatcher; level 2 technical support; level 3 product specialist; level 4 support supervisor
   c. level 1 incident screener; level 2 product specialist; level 3 technical support; level 4 support manager
   d. level 1 incident screener; level 2 product specialist; level 3 support manager; level 4 programmer

4. _____ is a well-defined, formal procedure that help desk staff follow to solve user problems.

5. True or False? Every help desk incident, no matter what kind, goes through the 12 steps of the incident management process described in the chapter, even if some of the steps don't apply.

6. Look at the following sequences and choose the correct order of the steps, shown below in the incident management process: (a) authenticate the incident; (b) archive the incident; (c) log the incident; (d) prioritize the problem
   a. d – c – a – b
   b. c – a – b – d
   c. a – c – d – b
   d. a – b – c – d

7. True or False? The percentage of incidents that cannot be resolved during the incident management process is frequently zero.

8. In which category of help desk incident does the following question fall? "My computer runs slowly when I attach to the Internet with a modem in the evenings."

   a. a question

   b. a problem

   c. a complaint

   d. a work order

9. A common strategy for assigning a priority to help desk calls is _____ .

   a. first in, first out (FIFO)

   b. last in, first out (LIFO)

   c. calls are answered in random order

   d. calls are answered in the order the help desk agent prefers

10. An incident management step in which an incident is transferred to a support staff member who has greater experience or resources to handle difficult questions is _____ .

    a. incident assignment

    b. incident screening

    c. incident tracking

    d. incident escalation

11. A(n) _____ is a waiting line or list into which incoming calls are placed when they cannot be answered immediately.

12. True or False? An automated incident tracking system is primarily useful in a large help desk operation, but is of limited use in a small help desk operation.

13. True or False? Knowledge bases that have special search tools and other help desk software features, such as HelpTrac's Solution Tree, are sometimes called smart databases.

14. True or False? The purpose of client feedback features in a help desk software package is to terminate support agents with poor customer service skills.

15. A telephone system that can answer calls, greet callers, provide menus, and route calls is a(n) _____ .

    a. incident dispatcher

    b. computer telephony system

    c. hotline

    d. automated call distributor

Discussion Questions

1. Should a help desk organization hire additional agents in order to satisfy 100% of its users 100% of the time? Explain why or why not.

2. Based on your experiences with checkout lines in grocery stores or fast-food restaurants, discuss whether the number of queues makes a difference in the level of service. For example, if five clerks are available, is it better to have one long queue, where the next client in the queue gets served next, or five separate queues, one for each clerk, where a client has to decide which queue to select. Does either arrangement really make any difference? If so, to whom? Relate your discussion to help desk incident management.

3. Which of the help desk industry trends discussed in this chapter do you think will have the greatest impact on the work of future help desk agents? Explain your answer.

4. Is job stress among agents in a help desk operation inevitable? Explain your viewpoint. What factors in a help desk operation increase or reduce job stress?

Hands-On Projects

Project 6-1

Interview a help desk support agent. Find a support agent at your organization or school, or one employed in a local business. Interview the agent to find out how his or her help desk is organized and what services it provides. Ask about this person's career path; if possible, obtain his or her current position description. Write a summary of the interview highlights.

Project 6-2

Visit a local telephone help desk. Arrange a visit to an organization that provides primarily telephone help desk support. Study how the physical workspace for help desk employees is organized to facilitate their work. Find out if the organization has a written incident management process, if it uses a help desk software package, and if it uses a computer telephony system. Write a summary of your findings, including the pros and cons of working in the facility you visited. Draw a sketch of the physical layout of the help desk operation you observed.

Project 6-3

Assign priority codes to help desk problems. Use the priority code system shown below to assign codes to various types of situations.

Code	Meaning
U	Urgent
H	High priority
M	Medium priority
L	Low priority

6

When assigning a priority code to the following situation, consider these criteria: (1) the severity of the problem, (2) the number of users affected, (3) the availability of a reasonable workaround, and (4) your own judgment.

1. A user calls with a question about how to format a chart in Excel.

2. The administrative assistant in the manufacturing division calls to report that the server in his building is down.

3. A user e-mails to report a suspected bug in the way a toolbar works in a software package, but she says the equivalent pull-down menu does work.

4. The president of the organization calls to request the latest performance data on the help desk operation.

5. A bug is reported in the beta release of a software package; the production version is scheduled to ship next week.

6. Several calls are received from irate users complaining that the accounting software package they purchased 12 months ago does not handle end-of-year processing correctly and the reports prepared are erroneous.

7. A user calls to report that a diagnostic hardware utility has detected an error in her CD-ROM controller card.

Discuss your priority code assignments with one or two classmates or coworkers. Explore any problem incidents where you differ by more than one priority code. Write a summary of your conclusions, and explain how much difference of opinion you found assigning priority codes.

Project 6-4

Define information in an incident management database. List the important pieces of information about a typical problem incident that you would expect to find in an incident logging/tracking system. Use a word processor or database form feature to design a data-entry form that captures the information you identified to track incidents.

Project 6-5

Evaluate a telephone system user interface. Based on your experience as a user with a help desk or other telephone service that uses an ACD telephone system, write an evaluation of the user interface. Describe the first level of menus and at least one other menu level. Evaluate the menus and menu navigation from a user's perspective. Write at least three suggestions on how the ACD interface could be improved.

Assemble a team of at least three classmates or coworkers, and compare your suggestions with those of the members in your group. What are some common design principles the members in your group agree on for an ACD system?

Project 6-6

Investigate diagnostic utility software. Find information about a PC diagnostic utility program that is advertised in a trade publication or on the Internet and that offers a demonstration copy. Obtain a copy of the program and try out its features. Make a list of the software features that you think would be especially useful to support staff to help them diagnose hardware problems.

Project 6-7

Investigate a support Web site. Visit the product support site for IBM at **www.ibm.com/support/us**. Explore the features on the Web site that provide self-help information, troubleshooting, and support services to clients. Use the list of services described in this chapter to evaluate the support services provided by IBM for its clients.

Write an e-mail message you could send to the site Webmaster that describes what you like about the site and what could be improved. What services would you recommend be added to the site?

Project 6-8

Identify help desk job stressors. Based on your understanding of help desk operations and job stress in this chapter, make a list of 10 or more different factors in a help desk environment that can increase or decrease the job stress experienced by agents. Use the Internet resources listed in the chapter as resources if you need ideas. Then put the stressors into a few categories. Compare your list with those developed by your classmates or coworkers. Do you have the same or different categories?

CASE PROJECTS

1. A Support Web Site for a Training Facility

You've been hired to design a support Web site for a training facility for end users. Look at examples of existing support Web sites for ideas. Suggested support sites to visit include:

- Gateway Computers support Web site at **support.gateway.com/support/default.asp**
- Adobe software (vendor of Adobe Acrobat) support site at **www.adobe.com/support/main.html**
- Symantec Web support site at **www.symantec.com/techsupp/index.html**
- Alamo Community College District's support Web site at **www.accd.edu/is2/support/**

You could also visit other product and services support Web sites with which you are familiar. Analyze what you like and what could improve in the sites you visit. Use a word processor or other tool to lay out your basic ideas for the home page and perhaps other important pages for the site you design. Your design layout does not have to include the information on the site, but should describe the kind of information you would include on each page. Give special attention to:

- The information users would expect to find on the Web site
- The selection of support features to incorporate in the Web site
- How the support features are organized and presented to users
- The navigation between pages

When you have finished your design, meet with three classmates or coworkers and compare your designs. How did your designs differ? How were they similar? What features of Web site design did you learn from them?

2. Features of the HelpTrac Software Package

Download a demonstration copy of the latest version of HelpTrac at **www.helptrac.com**. Install the demo version to get experience with the features of a help desk software package, following the steps listed below.

1. **Slide Show.** After you have installed the demo version of HelpTrac on a computer, view the slide show, which is an overview of the features of the product. To start the slide show, find and click the file *ht7Slide.exe* in the folder *ht7demo*. Use the slide show to compare HelpTrac's features with those described in the chapter.

2. **Enter transactions.** As you enter information into HelpTrac, your instructor or trainer may ask you to print various profiles and other information from the activities described below.

a. Use the Profiles menu or appropriate toolbar button to add a location for Re-Nu-Cartridge, 123 Main Street, Kalispell, MT 59901; phone 406-555-1234.

b. Use the Profiles menu or appropriate toolbar button to add a user—Rachel Mock, Sr Accountant at Re-Nu-Cartridge, e-mail. RMock@ReNuCart.com. She is an experienced user whose default priority for problems is *Rush*. What information from the location profile for Re-Nu-Cartridge gets copied to Rachel's user profile?

c. Use the Profiles menu to add Rachel's PC to the equipment database: an H-P Pentium IV class desktop PC, serial number 54321, with 256 MB of RAM memory and a 40-GB hard disk drive. Make sure the PC is assigned to Rachel Mock.

d. Find the toll-free number for the vendor Hewlett-Packard.

e. Use the HelpTrac help system to find out how to add a category of problems that users report with a modem. (*Hint:* Search help for *add category*.) Or, open a problem ticket for Rachel Mock, and then click *How do I . . .?* at the top of the ticket window.

f. Open a problem ticket for Rachel Mock, using the Ticket menu or toolbar. Rachel called to report that her 3Com modem, which worked yesterday, doesn't dial today. Note that no category currently exists for modem problems. Add one. (*Hint:* Use the small button next to the Category text box on the trouble ticket; don't forget to click OK when finished to add the new category to the database.) Note that no product category for 3Com modems already exists. Add one. Also add a symptom to describe Rachel's problem with her modem. Finally, assign the problem ticket to Technician Bill Miles.

g. No Solution Tree entry for modem problems currently exists. Explain why not. In this case, the wire from the telephone jack was damaged and shorted out. Make an entry in the problem ticket resolution tab that replacing the telephone wire solved the problem. To add this problem to the Solution Tree, click the Solution Tree to the right of the problem category text box.

h. In the problem ticket equipment tab, link this problem report to Rachel's H-P desktop computer (see Step c above).

i. Use the Reference menu and select the Solution Tree. Find the Solution Tree entry for modem problems.

j. Use the HelpTrac help system to learn how to change the status of Rachel's problem ticket from open to closed. Change the ticket status to closed.

3. **Investigate other HelpTrac features.**

   a. Research the QuickFind feature in HelpTrac. What is its purpose?

   b. What is a QuickTicket? Explain its purpose and how it impacts support agent productivity.

   c. Explore other HelpTrac demonstrations listed in the table on the next page.

Features	Run this program in the *ht7demo* folder
To see a demonstration of the program the help desk supervisor uses to customize HelpTrac for a specific situation, such as to add a new support agent	supdem32.exe
To see examples of the management reports built into HelpTrac	DemoRept.exe
To see examples of the graphic reports built into HelpTrac	DemGraph.exe
To see a demonstration of the support agent calendaring program	DemoSched.exe
To see a demonstration of the billing program that accompanies HelpTrac and is used by help desks that charge for their support services	HTBillDemo.exe

d. HelpTrac has an optional Web site support facility. You can see sample support Web pages at **www.monarchbay.com/htweb/HelpTrac.dll**. Log on as Kevin Barnes. Leave the password field blank.

3. An Incident Management Script for Re-Nu-Cartridge

NOTE

For background information about Re-Nu-Cartridge, see Case Project 4 in previous chapters.

The help desk staff at Re-Nu Cartridge is small, but growing in its responsibilities in the company. It provides support primarily for internal users who work in multiple offices and some employees who are traveling sales representatives. The current help desk procedures rely primarily on informal communication between staff members, such as scribbled notes and phone messages about requests for support assistance that get posted on a bulletin board in the help desk center, a clipboard that lists pending calls that need resolution, and the wastebasket as a closed incident archive. The help desk staff wants to transform its current method for handling support problem incidents into a more structured incident management procedure.

Based on what you learned about incident management in this chapter, write a first draft of a sample script that could be used to train new agents in the help desk at Re-Nu-Cartridge. Your script should cover the basic tasks in incident management that you learned about in this chapter. Your script should also cover how to close an incident. Incorporate your own ideas in your script on effective handling of incidents and help desk client relationships.

4. A Help Desk Tool for Re-Nu-Cartridge

NOTE

For background information about Re-Nu-Cartridge, see Case Project 4 in previous chapters.

Use your experience with a spreadsheet, database package, or programming language to design and develop a prototype for a software tool that could be used by a small help desk, such as the one at Re-Nu-Cartridge. A prototype is not necessarily a complete system with every possible useful feature, but one that contains basic functions that could be enhanced and expanded later. The primary purpose of the help desk tool you develop for Re-Nu-Cartridge is to keep track of problem incidents. A user of the help desk tool should be able to enter, store, retrieve, update, and close problem reports received from internal users. The system should also include the ability to print one or more reports from the stored data that enable the help desk supervisor at Re-Nu-Cartridge to obtain summary information on problem status and to analyze the kinds of problems that arise, including hardware, operating system, applications software, network, user, and other common problem categories.

Assemble a team of three classmates or coworkers and develop design specifications, such as:

❑ What are the possible features and capabilities of a simple problem tracking system?

❑ What information (data elements) needs to be input and stored to meet the primary objectives?

❑ How will the user interface to the help desk tool be designed to facilitate efficient use by staff?

❑ How will the data entry screens appear to a help desk agent?

❑ What query capabilities should the help desk system provide a staff member?

❑ What reports should be predefined to provide problem tracking summary and status information?

❑ What are the highest priority features for development in the first version (prototype) of the help desk tool you are designing?

This project can be a large one. Whether you work alone or with a team, remember to keep the design simple, and make decisions about what you can reasonably accomplish in the limited time you have to devote to this project. Remember that additional features can be added later.

7

USER SUPPORT MANAGEMENT

In this chapter you will learn:

◆ The mission of a support group and the parts of a mission statement

◆ The steps in staffing a support position

◆ The contents of a training program for support staff

◆ How to manage a user support project

◆ Which software tools help with project management tasks

◆ The industry certifications that are available to support professionals

◆ About professional help desk and user support associations

◆ Ethical principles that guide the professional behavior of support workers

Some workers in the user support field aspire to become user support or help desk managers; others do not. Whether or not their career plans include a future management position, it is important for user support workers to have a basic understanding of the managerial perspective. When applicants interview for a user support position, the interviewer will likely be a user support manager or supervisor. If hired as a user support worker in a very small company, an employee may be expected to perform some tasks that require management, supervisory, lead worker, or project coordinator skills.

User support management encompasses a variety of positions. In many organizations, a help desk or user support manager directly manages the user support staff. The managers of large support groups may oversee one or more supervisors or lead workers who in turn supervise a team of support agents. For example, an organization that provides several levels of support, as described in Chapter 6, may have a level 1 team (call screening) supervisor, a level 2 team (product specialist) supervisor, and a level 3 team (technical support) supervisor. Even small support groups may assign some project leader or coordinator responsibilities to user support workers. A user support staff member may be assigned a project to learn the details about a new software or hardware product and then disseminate information about it (documentation, training, and anticipated user problems) to other support staff.

NOTE

When searching for additional information on user support management, be aware that some organizations and authors use alternate terms, such as help desk management, client support management, call center management, and customer support management. These terms are usually interchangeable.

Although most of this book focuses on the knowledge, skills, and abilities required to be an effective user support staff member, this chapter examines some of the tasks, skills, issues, and concerns that confront user support and help desk managers. These tasks include developing a mission statement, evaluating a user support operation, staffing, and training. This chapter also describes project management in user support. It concludes with information about two emerging help desk industry trends that confront both workers and managers: certification and professionalism.

MANAGERIAL CONCERNS: MISSION, PERFORMANCE, STAFFING, AND TRAINING

From the moment you decide that you want to pursue a help desk or user support position, you should be aware of the support management's perspectives. Every decision a help desk manager makes affects the people who work there. Conversely, the more support staff members know about their manager's concerns and priorities, the better equipped they will be to understand the need for certain task assignments and to focus their efforts on completing them. Knowing the big picture enables support staff to improve client satisfaction and help the support team succeed. A managerial perspective also helps prepare entry-level staff to advance into positions with more responsibilities and higher salaries.

NOTE

For more detailed information about the job of a user support or help desk manager, refer to several books on the topic. *Running an Effective Help Desk, 2nd edition* by Barbara Czegel (John Wiley, 1998) is one of the most popular books on help desk management. It describes planning, organizing, staffing, and marketing a help desk; procedures that make a help desk more efficient and effective; and tools to automate a help desk and measure its performance. An alternate resource is Bob Wooten's book, *Building & Managing a World Class IT Help Desk*, Osborne, 2001. Francoise Tourniaire and Richard Farrell's *The Art of Software Support,* Prentice Hall, 1998, is aimed at managers of user support in organizations that sell and support software products.

Four areas of user support management directly affect the support staff's job: the support mission, performance measures, staffing, and training.

User Support Mission

Support groups often develop a **mission statement**, which is a list of guiding principles that communicate support goals and objectives to staff, users, and management. It says, in effect, "Here is what we think is most important to our support group." Support groups also use mission statements as a yardstick against which to measure whether they have met their goals. Figure 7-1 shows an example of a user support mission statement. The example addresses primarily support for internal employees, but it could be modified to apply to external clients or customers. The italicized terms highlight important concepts.

USER SUPPORT GROUP MISSION STATEMENT

The mission of the user support group is to: (a) maximize *operational efficiency* among users in an organization by providing timely resolution to *technology use questions*, and (b) effectively *manage problems* to continuously improve the:
- *quality* of support services to users
- *usability* of information systems
- *effectiveness* of documentation and training
- *users' satisfaction* with support services

Figure 7-1   Sample user support group mission statement

Several points in the sample mission statement in Figure 7-1 directly address end users' productivity. Increased employee (or client) productivity is usually a primary goal, because every support group or help desk must justify its existence in the organization by the services it provides to other employees or to clients. It must prove to the parent organization that its benefits outweigh its costs. Other mission statements may include goals such as user self-sufficiency, ethical professional conduct of staff members, increased company profitability, and career path development for user support workers. However, mission statements that include a laundry list of goals are sometimes less effective than shorter, more focused, guidelines.

User Support Performance and Justification

Performance statistics and measures of client satisfaction are one way to document and justify the value of user support services. **Performance statistics** are objective summary information about the user support or help desk operation. Performance statistics are often directly related to the user support mission statement. For example, if a help desk's mission statement sets a goal of responding to 90% of telephone calls received within 60 seconds, then a statistic that the help desk actually responded to 88% of the calls last week in 60 seconds or less is a direct measure of how successful the help desk, as a team, has met its objective.

Performance statistics can help a user support group measure how effectively and efficiently it responds to incidents. Examples of common help desk performance measures include:

- Average time to respond to incidents (sometimes called **wait time**)

- Percentage of incidents that were abandoned (user hung up or gave up before the support staff responded); also called **abandonment rate**

- Average resolution time for incidents that require problem solving

- Percentage of problems that could not be resolved

- Percentage of closed incidents that had to be reopened

- Number of incidents currently in an unresolved status (perhaps counted for each priority code)

These performance statistics can be reported for one point in time, but are more useful when they are compared across various times of the day, days of the week, or months. Information about changes in performance statistics over time is more useful to support workers and managers than data collected at a single point in time, because trends in performance are more meaningful than isolated measurements. Performance statistics can be reported for an entire support group working as a team or for individual workers. These statistics are often used to answer the question, "Is the help desk operation more (or less) productive or responsive over time?" or "How does the productivity or accuracy of agent Emily compare with other help desk workers?" Many automated call distributor systems (ACDs) collect the raw data from which reports on these and other support performance statistics can be prepared.

In addition to objective, statistical measures of user support performance, support groups may collect subjective information from end users. An internal support group, for example, may periodically conduct a user satisfaction survey. A **user satisfaction survey** is a questionnaire that attempts to measure how satisfied users are with the support services they have experienced. Questions, such as the following example, are often used to prepare a report card for the user support group.

> On a scale from 1 (very satisfied) to 5 (very dissatisfied), how would you evaluate the user support services you get as an employee in this organization?

User satisfaction surveys may also ask end users to identify a support staff member who has been especially helpful to them. A help desk that provides external support may ask similar questions of a selected sample of clients. Data from external clients is often collected in a follow-up phone call or via a mail or e-mail questionnaire. Organizations that provide Web-based support may include a feedback mechanism to help evaluate the quality of information and client services their Web site and support team provides. For example, information on a Web page may be accompanied by a question such as, "Did you find this information useful? Click YES or NO."

Some support groups treat user support as a cost center or an administrative overhead cost in their budgets. In this situation, the cost of support is an expense to the organization without a corresponding revenue source. In other words, user support is treated as an expense center instead of an income center. These organizations often find it difficult to justify support expenses solely on the basis of performance statistics or client satisfaction, because there is no revenue stream to offset the costs. One reason many hardware and software manufacturers now charge clients for help desk services is the need to relate the support services they provide to the costs associated with providing the services. Product vendors may offer several levels of user support services, including a free level, a standard (fee-for-service) level, and a premium level for clients who want and need immediate service. Although the premium level may be more responsive to users than the free service or standard service, it also costs more to provide.

Support workers at all levels, even in entry-level positions, need to understand the importance of performance measurements and the justification for support services. Performance statistics impact user support management decisions that directly affect support workers. A support group or worker who ignores performance and the need to justify support services may end up without a job. To justify user support operations, managers often perform cost-benefit analyses, a tool you will learn about in Chapter 9.

As one of its services to the help desk industry, The Help Desk Institute (HDI) provides an assessment to support centers that want to do an in-depth evaluation of their support organization. Although HDI charges a fee for its assessment, you can learn about the criteria it uses to evaluate the performance of a support group. Download an HDI white paper that describes 67 criteria HDI uses as part of an on-site evaluation at **www.thinkhdi.com/files/pdfs/ SupportCenterCert.pdf**.

Staffing the Help Desk

A challenge for many user support and help desk managers is to determine how many support agents are needed to meet the service levels that are expected of the support group. Obviously, support managers want to employ and schedule sufficient staff to meet the performance expectations described in the help desk's mission statement. On the other hand, support managers do not want to hire extra staff beyond what they need to be responsive to end users. A support group that employs staff who are idle incurs expenses that do not generate support services or revenues. Its performance statistics when compared to staff expenses suffer, because costs are higher than they would be if idle time could be used productively or if extra staff could be reduced or rescheduled to a time when they are needed. So what is the right number of support staff? This problem is similar to determining the number of cashiers a grocery store needs to keep checkout lines from getting too long (which frustrates customers) or too short (which leaves cashiers idle). A calculation tool called an Erlang is often used in these situations. An **Erlang** is a unit of traffic (*user calls* in the case of support groups) processed in a given period of time. The Erlang calculation is used in a variety of situations in which there are queues (such as support calls on hold, or clients waiting for grocery store cashiers or bank tellers). Managers may also use trial and error, previous experience, or a sophisticated calculator to assist in help desk staffing decisions.

Westbay Engineers provides an online Erlang calculator to estimate support center staffing needs. See its Web site at **www.erlang.com**, click **Free Calculators**, and then click **Call Centre Calculator**.

An applicant for a help desk or user support position should be aware of the support manager's staffing concerns. Staffing a user support operation begins with support group's mission statement. Based on the mission statement, a user support manager writes one or more position descriptions: one if the user support operation is new or small; several for a help desk operation that has a large staff or a multi-level structure. The position descriptions (like those you read in Chapter 2) are also based on an analysis of the knowledge and skills that user support staff members need. The mission statement, position descriptions, and the specific knowledge, skills, and abilities (KSAs) for a user support operation are important tools for managers who must staff a help desk or support group.

Most user support positions require a combination of technical skills, business skills, and communications skills. A KSA analysis begins with a written list of technical, business, and communications qualifications for a position. These qualifications spell out the level of proficiency required with:

- Hardware, operating systems, and applications software
- Technical skills
- Network experience and skills
- Internet and Web skills
- Troubleshooting and problem-solving skills
- Communications, listening, writing, and telephone skills
- Working in a project team
- Understanding business information systems and business perspectives

Support managers use categories like these as a check list to develop detailed job-related requirements for specific positions. For example, an open support position may require a person with KSAs to work with Intel-compatible hardware platforms in an office local area network (LAN) environment, Windows 98/Me/2000/XP operating system experience, a working knowledge of Microsoft Office applications software, and so on. An entry-level position in a help desk that provides primarily telephone support might emphasize communications skills and interpersonal relationships. A position that provides more advanced technical support would probably place greater emphasis on technical knowledge and troubleshooting skills.

After a support manager has developed a specific list of KSAs, the next step is to develop a position description. The position description contains a clear explanation of the staff member's duties and responsibilities, like those in Chapter 2. A support manager then uses the position description and KSA check list to prepare a classified ad (for a newspaper) or position order (for an employment or temporary worker agency). But the position description and classified ad are really a wish list. The support manager may or may not find applicants who match 100% of the characteristics and skills in the position description and KSA check list.

An increasing number of user support positions are now advertised on the Internet (see Chapter 2 for a list of sites). However, only a fraction of help desk and user support job openings are advertised publicly in any medium. Many job seekers learn about open support positions through informal channels, such as a current employee in an organization or an instructor in a vocational/technical school or community college who has contacts with support employers.

The search for a new staff member continues when the support manager receives applications. The next step often involves a team who represent the current support staff, user support management, Information Services department (if applicable), and Human Resources department. This group screens resumes and applications to narrow the list of applicants. Applicants whose personal KSAs most closely match the position requirements advance to the next stage in screening—the interview. Some support groups check applicants' employment and academic references prior to an interview; others check these references after the interview.

During an interview, managers use selection tools that may include a knowledge and skills test as well as several kinds of interview questions. A **knowledge and skills test** is a test that measures a prospective worker's knowledge and problem-solving abilities. These tests may include written, verbal, and/or hands-on components. The tests may be supplied from a vendor that provides testing materials, or they may be developed by a support group specifically for applicants for its open positions.

An example of a vendor that sells help desk aptitude and skills tests is Keith Geddes and Associates. Its products and services are described at **www.pcskillstests.com/Testing/techsupport.html**. Another vendor is Walden Personnel Testing and Consulting, at **www.waldentesting.com/tests/tests.htm**.

Employment interviews often include general questions about applicants' educational and work background and experience.

To view some sample interview questions designed by Adrian Rose, Manager of the Enterprise Response Centre at Rogers Shared Services-IT in Toronto, download the PDF files at **www.ksasystems.com/cgi-local/prolink2.cgi?link=iq990701** (requires Adobe Reader).

In addition to general questions, applicants should be prepared for scenario questions, which help to identify candidates' strengths and weaknesses. A **scenario question** gives applicants a specific problem (or set of problems) representative of the kinds of problems that user support agents actually encounter. A scenario can be a written exercise (sometimes provided as a supplemental questionnaire when an applicant first applies) or a problem-solving exercise during an interview. Interviews for a telephone support position often include an activity that requires an applicant to answer questions in a simulated telephone environment so the applicant's telephone skills can be evaluated. Scenario questions often provide insights into an applicant's problem-solving skills, conflict-resolution and communications skills, and ability to perform in stressful work situations. When combined with traditional interview questions, the scenario approach is often more effective than traditional interview questions by themselves to identify staff who can work well under pressure. Here is an example scenario:

> Suppose a user in the manufacturing division approaches you and wants to bend your ear about the endless network problems that affect the productivity of manufacturing workers. The user relates that manufacturing workers have experienced an increasing volume of network crashes on the department's server in recent weeks. The user says that it takes forever to get the network restarted when it crashes, and the downtime affects the workers' productivity. The user also mentions that other manufacturing workers feel that they would be better off scrapping the network and working with the manual system they used to have.
>
> As a new user support staff member, how would you respond?

Scenario questions can often be answered from a number of perspectives. Some applicants might treat the above scenario as an opportunity to display their technical knowledge about networks. Others might discuss the problem-solving and communications process they would use to address the problem within the organization.

User Support Staff Training

One of the most important aspects of user support operations is the training needs of the support staff. Support **staff training** includes both new employee orientation and ongoing training for staff to keep their knowledge and skills current. The challenge in support staff training is often to schedule training time for staff members who are in constant demand. Managers sometimes assume that support staff will simply pick up information about new products in the course of their everyday work. Sometimes that happens; most of the time, it does not. To leave support staff members time for training, special projects, and paperwork, many managers schedule agents for only a fraction of their total work shift (for example, six hours of an eight hour shift).

NOTE Many of the end-user training methods and strategies you will learn in Chapter 11 are also effective for user support staff. Eric Svendsen shares his perspectives on training support staff in the Chapter 11 CloseUp.

If one goal of a support group mission is to provide high-quality service to its users, support staff members also need time to learn how to be productive with new technology. Successful user support operations, which recruit and retain staff members, invest in new employee training and continual on-the-job training to keep the staff's support job skills up to date.

Training for new support employees often includes:

- Orientation to the organization
- Payroll and employee benefit information

- Specific job skill training
- Use of help desk tools, including phone system and incident management software
- Support group policies and procedures
- Performance appraisal criteria and procedures
- Professional development and career path opportunities

Of these training topics, information about the support group policies and procedures is especially important. New employees must know specific job skills to function effectively, and they also need to learn where to find answers to questions such as, "What is the company's policy if a client insists on a refund?" or "What is the recommended procedure if a client demands to speak to a supervisor or the company president?" Although it is not possible to learn about every organizational policy or procedure during orientation, it is important that training sessions cover basic information about the organization's general user support philosophy.

WWW

TechRepublic's Web site frequently carries articles on the training needs of help desk workers. For example, read Jeff Davis' article *Training Tips Can Jump-Start Your Help Desk Team* at **www.techrepublic. com/article.jhtml?id=r00320010612jed01.htm**, or Jeff Dray, *Create Structured Training for Help Desk Staffers* at **www.techrepublic.com/article.jhtml? id=r00320030415dra01.htm**.

Training programs for user support workers should help keep support staff current with changes in computer technology and how the changes affect their client base. However, keeping staff knowledge and skills current is a joint obligation. Company training programs for support staff are only half of the solution; personal professional growth is an equal responsibility. User support workers are computer professionals who are expected to invest in their own continuing education. They should expect to attend conferences, training sessions, and workshops, read widely in trade publications and books, own a home computer, and make an investment in their professional growth commensurate with their employer's investment.

Support managers should also communicate with support workers about when and how job performance is evaluated. A **performance appraisal** is a process to evaluate a user support worker according to established criteria. The performance appraisal criteria should be related to the support group's mission, to the worker's position description, and to the worker's personal growth objectives. If performance statistics like those described above are used as part of the performance appraisal process, how they are collected, interpreted, and used should be communicated to support workers. Support managers often use recordings of monitored support calls to help workers identify areas where performance improvement is needed. In many support groups, results of a performance appraisal provide input to support employee training needs.

MANAGING A USER SUPPORT PROJECT

User support work can be divided into routine operational tasks (such as staffing a help desk) and special projects. When staff members respond to calls for assistance, they often rely on well-established procedures or scripts or their previous experience. Much of the work a support group provides falls into this category of routine tasks or activities. A **special project**, on the other hand, is a user support task that does not happen regularly. A special project may be based on less well-defined steps and procedures, usually takes longer than a few minutes or even a few hours to accomplish, and is often more complex than routine user support work. Factors that contribute to a special project's increased complexity often include the involvement of several staff members (and perhaps external vendors or consultants), a time commitment of several days, weeks, or even months, and expenditures that include substantial costs in staff time, equipment, software, supplies, and other resources.

In a user support environment, staff members may be assigned special projects to:

- Develop or update computer product standards or support policies in an organization

- Select and install a new network server or enterprise-wide application software package

- Plan and implement a new training facility

- Upgrade organizational PCs (may include hardware, applications software, operating system software, and network enhancements)

- Select and implement an automated help desk management system

- Develop end-user documentation or a user training session for a new software package

These examples of special projects are not routine tasks that occur every day, although some support groups may tackle more special projects than others. As organizations rely more and more on teams rather than individual workers to accomplish tasks, the abilities to manage and work on a project team have become increasingly important skills.

Project Management Steps

Support specialists who are assigned a special project, like those listed above, should know the basics of project management. **Project management** is a step-by-step work plan and process designed to reach a specific goal. It usually involves five distinct steps, listed in Figure 7-2.

Step 1. Project Definition.   **Project definition** includes early work on a project to define the scope of a project, including its goal(s), a tentative project calendar (beginning and ending dates, important due dates), a project budget, and the project participants, including users, support staff, technical staff, management, and a project manager, lead, or coordinator (the specific title varies). A **project goal** is a specific, measurable result that is the ultimate

Step 1. Project definition

Step 2. Project planning

Step 3. Project implementation

Step 4. Project monitoring

Step 5. Project termination

Figure 7-2   Steps in project management

target or outcome of a project. It is important that the project goal be specific and measurable, even if the calendar and budget are rough estimates at this step. Compare these two goals:

- Improve user satisfaction with help desk services.

- Evaluate, select, install, and implement a help desk management software package.

The first goal is neither specific nor measurable. It does not specify how user satisfaction will be improved or even measured. Ask yourself, "How will I know I have achieved this goal?" For the first goal, the answer is not obvious. The second goal is more specific. It describes the scope of the project (evaluation, selection, installation, implementation), and specifies a measurable result. A successful project will result in an operational help desk management package. Although the second goal is more specific, it could be further improved by specifying a timeline, budget limit, staff participation, and other project specifics.

Step 2. Project Planning.   After a project's scope is defined, the bulk of the project planning activities include dividing a project into specific tasks (or objectives), estimating a time (or duration) for each task, identifying available resources and the cost of each, and assigning resources to tasks. Typical project resources are staff time, budget, space, equipment, supplies, support services, overhead, and management support. During the planning step, the project manager defines each project task. A **project task** is a specific action or objective (outcome) that must be performed to meet the project goal. Examples of tasks include assigning a support staff member to write a handout on a specific topic for a training session, evaluating three help desk software packages for possible purchase, and installing a DSL modem in four office computers. A **project plan** pulls together all project tasks into a document that answers the questions:

- What tasks will be accomplished?

- Who will perform each task?

- How long will each task take?

- What resource costs does each task require?

During the project-planning step, the project schedule (calendar) and costs become more definite. Earlier, during project definition, the project manager may receive information from organizational management or users such as, "It would be really great if this training session was ready by the second week of next month," or "Our drop-dead date for installation of Office 2003 in all offices is the end of the year." However, until each project task has been identified in detail, assigned to a staff member, and given a time and cost estimate, the project manager cannot make commitments. As a result of project planning, a project manager wants to be able to make statements such as, "If the staff and budget resources we have identified in the project plan are available, we estimate the project can be completed by the second week of next month." Detailed project planning hones the preliminary estimates of schedule, resources, and costs prepared during the project definition step.

When developing time and cost estimates, experienced project managers know that several things can and usually do throw a project off its planned schedule. A project's **risk factors** are an analysis and assessment of the problems that can arise during the life of a project. Risk factors include poor initial estimates of schedule, costs, or resources and incidents that may occur during the project. Incidents that are common risk factors are: a sick employee, a task that takes longer to complete than estimated, a hardware component that is unavailable when needed or costs more than expected, and a conflict between two employees over the best way to accomplish a task. Do these risk factors mean that it is useless to try to manage a project, or that it is better to "wing it" without a project plan? No. Experienced project managers anticipate risks like these and try to estimate their impact on the project results. They set preliminary time estimates to complete a task to reflect a time somewhere between the minimum, best-case scenario and the maximum, worst-case scenario. They factor in time for unexpected incidents that conspire to throw a project off its plan. Likewise, they prepare project budgets with a contingency factor for poor initial estimates.

Step 3. Project Implementation.   The implementation phase of a project is where the real work gets done. During **project implementation** support staff members perform the work on each task or objective according to the schedule in the project plan. The project manager's responsibility shifts from project planning to task coordination. When tasks are interrelated, the project manager spends time resolving conflicts between staff members over how resources are allocated, and solving problems that will surely arise during any moderately complex project. During implementation, project managers must also be able to answer questions such as, "Will the project get completed on time?" and "Will the cost of the project exceed its budget?" So an additional task for project managers is monitoring the project's progress and status.

Step 4. Project Monitoring.   Parallel to the implementation step is another important project management task: project monitoring (or tracking). **Project monitoring** involves assessing the status of all project tasks to learn whether they are on target as compared with the time and budget estimates. Ideally, if each project task came in on time and under budget, monitoring would not be necessary. Because that seldom happens, project managers need to evaluate each project task regularly to determine:

- How much work has been completed?
- What remains to be done?
- How should staff or other resources be adjusted or reassigned?
- What impact will changes in tasks have on the completion date?

Project managers need to be able to quickly answer questions such as, "Will this project task, which is behind schedule, benefit from adding additional staff for some time period?" and "How will adding resources affect the project's completion date?"

Another management responsibility during project monitoring reflects a reality that experienced project managers understand: projects often change during their implementation to meet new or unexpected demands. (In other words, the project's goals or objectives are adjusted.) Modifications during a project's implementation are another project risk that must be managed. **Scope creep** is the tendency for a project to grow or change in unexpected ways that increase the time frame, resources, and cost to complete the project. During project monitoring, managers analyze and approve "change orders" and communicate with stakeholders (managers, users, support staff, and vendors) about the impact on schedule and costs. Project managers may periodically prepare project reports to communicate the results of project monitoring and tracking.

Step 5. Project Termination.   The final stage in a project, **project termination**, may include communicating the project's completion to stakeholders, preparing a final project report, and analyzing and evaluating the performance of the project and its participants. The project termination activities help project managers to learn from the mistakes of past projects and use their knowledge to improve performance on future projects.

Figure 7-3 illustrates a sample plan for a project. Some projects, because of their complexity, implementation time frame, resources, staff coordination, and budget, require more project management effort than others. For example, the preparation of a new training session for a software product, such as Outlook Express, by a trainer is a relatively straightforward project. Its project plan may be as simple as the one shown in Figure 7-3.

The beta testers described in Figure 7-3 are support staff or end users who are often skilled users of the target of the training (Outlook Express, in this example) and help the trainer evaluate the accuracy and usefulness of the training materials. They participate in a dry run of the training activity to help shake out any bugs. Based on the time estimates in Figure 7-3, a support manager or training supervisor can quickly determine that about a week and a half of trainer time is required for this project. If the project begins on a Monday, it will conclude by Tuesday or Wednesday of the following week, assuming that the project calendar is compatible with the trainer's schedule and other responsibilities, the schedule of the beta testers, and the schedule of the trainees. If the cost of a trainer's time is billed at $35 per hour (including salary, benefits, and overhead costs), then the estimated total cost of the

Step	Task	Time Estimate
	*Project: Outlook Express Training Session*	
1	Plan training session • analyze position descriptions for job skills required • interview supervisor and two trainees to learn backgrounds • document skill needs of trainees • define learning and performance objectives (scope) of training	8 hours
2	Prepare training materials • develop outline of topics covered • schedule trainees and training facility • locate or develop Outlook Express demonstration examples • develop hands-on activities • develop cheat sheet of Outlook Express features	30 hours
3	Prepare evaluation materials • develop hands-on performance test • prepare training session feedback form	4 hours
4	Beta test training materials • present training to two support colleagues (2 hrs each) • analyze results and revise as needed	12 hours
5	Present Outlook Express training session • present a two-hour session • evaluate and revise as needed	4 hours
	Total:	**58 hours**

Resources Required
Software:
• Outlook Express (available)
• PowerPoint (available) Facilities:
• Training Room (schedule 2 hrs)
Materials:
• position descriptions of trainees (from Human Resources)
Personnel:
• access to supervisor and two trainees for interviews
• two beta testers (2 hours each)
Miscellaneous supplies (available)

Figure 7-3   Project plan for Outlook Express training session

training session is \$35 per hour x 58 hours = \$2030, which covers the cost of preparing and presenting one training session. This project is not complex, although even a simple project like this one makes some assumptions about the availability of resources, such as the training facility and personnel besides the trainer. Even a simple project may have risk factors that a project manager needs to evaluate. The project manager may also want to include a contingency factor of, say, 10% (\$200) to account for the fact that the completion times in the plan are estimates. In general, the more experience with a project its manager has, the more confident in time estimates he or she can be, and the lower the contingency factor can be.

Project Management Tools

As projects become increasingly complex because they involve additional staff members (and therefore greater coordination), more resources, a bigger budget, a larger time frame, and additional risk factors, a one- or two-page project plan is not sufficient. Fortunately for managers of large user support projects (or several smaller ones) software tools are available to assist them with the project management tasks described above. For example, project managers who want to automate some project management tasks can use one of several kinds of tools. Two are listed below:

- Microsoft Office Project Professional 2003 is a project management tool, compatible with the Microsoft Office suite (**www.microsoft.com/office/project/prodinfo/default.mspx**)

- Milestones Simplicity 2002 is a project scheduling tool, one of several sold by Kidasa Software (**www.kidasa.com/Simplicity/index.html**)

Project management software tools, however, are no substitute for careful project planning, including good time estimates, accurate budget and resource forecasts, thorough analysis of project risks, and other human inputs to the project planning process.

Figure 7-4 shows a Microsoft Project 2003 diagram of the steps to complete the Outlook Express Training Session project described above. A **Gantt Chart**, in the right pane in Figure 7-4, is a common project planning tool that shows the basic information about each task in a project as a horizontal bar on a graph. It identifies each task, its relationship to other tasks, the expected calendar for task and project completion, and task assignments to project participants. The left pane, in spreadsheet format, shows the input information that produced the Gantt Chart. The two leftmost columns list the steps (Task Name) and estimated times (Duration) for each activity that was listed in Figure 7-3. The Resource Names column lists four types of participants: TRN1 is the trainer, USR denotes users, SVR is the supervisor of the trainees, and TST represents the beta testers. Although the project is estimated to take 58 hours total, 4 of the 58 are hours spent by the two Training Session Beta Testers; so the Gantt Chart shows that the total elapsed time to complete the project is 54 hours. The Gantt Chart reflects the time spent by user support staff on this project, but it does not reflect the time spent by trainees or their supervisor.

Suppose the support group examined the draft Gantt Chart in Figure 7-4 and asked some what-if questions, such as, "What if additional support staff are added to this training project?" In other words, "Could we shorten the project if we identified some tasks that other support staff members could accomplish by working simultaneously with the one trainer planned?" "What if . . . ?" questions are often easier to answer with a project management or scheduling software tool. Figure 7-5 shows a modified Microsoft Project 2003 draft plan. First, the five original steps in the training plan are divided into more detailed tasks. Second, some tasks are listed as predecessor tasks for other tasks (see the new Pred (Predecessor Tasks) column in the spreadsheet). A **predecessor task** is an activity that must be completed before another task can begin. For example, Step 1 is a predecessor task to Step 2 because the training session must be planned before the training materials can be

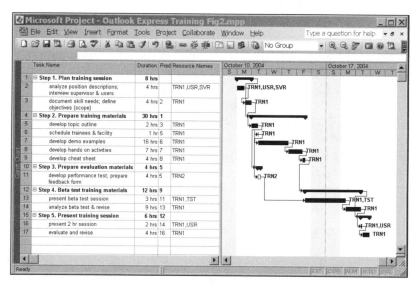

Figure 7-4   Steps in the Outlook Express Training Session project in Microsoft Project 2003

prepared. In other words, Step 2 cannot begin until Step 1 is completed. Third, arrows have been added to the Gantt Chart to show the predecessor tasks on the diagram. Fourth, instead of assigning one trainer (TRN1) to the entire project, as in the first draft plan, a second trainer (TRN2) is assigned to help with a task (the original Step 3) that can be accomplished at the same time that TRN1 is working on Step 2 tasks. By adding a second trainer to work on tasks that can be performed at the same time as another task, the project completion is moved up from Wednesday morning to Tuesday afternoon.

Figure 7-5   A revised Outlook Express training project showing the critical path

As Figure 7-5 shows, the tasks assigned to TRN1 must be completed on time if the project is to be finished on time. However, the task assigned to TRN2 has a flexible completion time. For example, TRN2 can complete Step 3 (prepare evaluation materials), which is estimated to take 4 hours, any time during the 30 hours that TRN1 is working on Step 2 tasks. The dark bars in Figure 7-5 show this project's critical path. A **critical path** is the sequence of project tasks that must be completed on time to meet the project's completion time. The critical path establishes important milestones in a project's calendar. Steps 1, 2, 4, and 5 are critical path steps that are important milestones. If any one of these milestones is missed, the project completion is in jeopardy. However, the task for TRN2 in Step 3 in Figure 7-5 is not on the critical path. If the expected completion time for Step 3 slips, the completion of the project will not necessarily be affected.

The critical path is important in another way. Suppose a support staff member asks another "What if . . . ?" question: "What if we added a third trainer to this project? Could we speed up its completion time even more?" Whether more resources speed up any project depends on the tasks to which additional staff resources are assigned. One obvious place to look is the large, 30 hour block in Step 2 that is assigned to TRN1. It may be possible to assign some parts in Step 2 to TRN2, or to a third trainer. For example, perhaps TRN2 could develop a quick reference of Outlook Express features while TRN1 is working on other training materials. Because Step 2 is on this project's critical path, assignment of additional resources to Step 2 may speed up the project's delivery time, but would not reduce the total number of hours (30) estimated for Step 2. In fact, as additional resources are added to a project, project managers often spend additional time to coordinate activities among staff members, which tends to add hours and lengthen the project timeline. Furthermore, adding resources to steps that are not on a project's critical path will not speed up its completion. For example, assigning a third trainer to Step 3 to work on the performance test and feedback form would not shorten the timeline because Step 3 is not on the project's critical path.

These examples illustrate project tasks, task time duration, assignments to staff members, what-if analyses, the critical path, and estimated completion time, but they barely scratch the surface of project management tools. Project management software can complete other important project management tasks by using features to:

- Monitor partial completion of project tasks and periodically update the Gantt Chart to produce a progress report

- Identify project tasks that are behind schedule for which additional resources could be used effectively

- Assign personnel, facilities, equipment, supplies, and overhead costs to prepare a project budget

- Define report formats that are alternatives to Gantt Charts, including project calendars, budget and variance reports, PERT diagrams (also called network diagrams), e-mails to staff members with their project assignments, and other project management output options

Many project management software packages now incorporate features that permit project workgroup members to view not only the overall project plans, but also detailed project task information, each group member's individual assignments, an updated project calendar, and a revised budget. In addition, the software packages enable workgroup members to communicate online via e-mail or project Web pages about project details, such as task progress reports.

NOTE A 120-day trial version of Microsoft Office Project Professional 2003 is included on the CD that accompanies this book. To learn more about project management skills, see Kathy Schwalbe, *Information Technology Project Management*, 3rd edition, Course Technology, 2003.

WWW To locate additional information about project management, visit the Web site of the Project Management Institute (PMI), a professional organization of project managers, at **www.pmi.org**. PMI offers a certification program for professional project managers.

USER SUPPORT CERTIFICATION

A significant trend in education, training, and employment in the computer field in recent years is certification. **Certification** is an assessment process to measure and document employee knowledge and skills in a specialized segment of the information technology field. Several kinds of certification are popular today:

- Formal education that results in a certificate, diploma, or degree

- Vendor-specific product knowledge and skill certification

- Industry-standard knowledge and skill certification in a specific area, such as hardware, networking, or support

- Certification that measures the fitness of a support group against industry-standard criteria

Community colleges and vocational/technical schools have been in the certification business for many years. After a student has successfully completed a well-defined program of study of required (and perhaps elective) courses, the student graduates with a certificate, diploma, or degree. However, certification based on formal education or training from a degree or certificate-granting educational institution frequently signifies only general knowledge and skills. Employers are often also interested in a job applicant's specific expertise. For example, a degree in computer user support, or a related field, does not necessarily guarantee that a graduate (job applicant) has specialized expertise in, say, Windows XP, although many user support degree programs today include coursework in that subject. Similarly, coursework in *operating systems* does not guarantee that a graduate can apply what he or she has learned specifically to the Linux operating system.

Partly in reaction to the industry-wide need to certify product-specific knowledge and skills, several vendors in the computer industry offer a variety of certificates that assess knowledge and skills in a specialized product area. One of the first vendor-specific certifications was Novell's Certified NetWare Engineer (CNE) in the early 1990s. The CNE certification process resulted in thousands of network specialists who were certified as specialists on Novell network products. Because the CNE was vendor-specific, however, it did not indicate that a certificate holder necessarily knew anything about other vendors' network products, such as Microsoft's or Cisco's network infrastructure products. As a result, other network vendors began to offer separate certification in their specific product lines. Furthermore, some job applicants who excelled at studying a body of material and passing a test discovered that they could study a CNE preparatory book, take and pass the certification exam, and advertise that they were qualified CNEs. They had the paper to certify their expertise, but no real expertise (other than the ability to pass a test). Employers coined the term "paper CNE" to describe a person who had passed the CNE test, but did not have any practical knowledge or hands-on experience with network operation.

Today, certification is available for many vendor-specific products. Some examples are described in Table 7-1.

7

Table 7-1   Examples of vendor-specific certifications

Vendor	URL	Certificate/Area of Expertise
Microsoft	www.microsoft.com/traincert/mcp/default.asp	Microsoft Office Specialist (MOS) in applications such as Word, Excel, Access, and PowerPoint; for most products, Microsoft offers two proficiency levels: core and expert (formerly MOUS certificate)
		Microsoft Office Specialist Master Instructor, a certified teacher or trainer of Microsoft Office Suite products
		Microsoft Certified Professional (MCP), professional certification in the implementation of a Microsoft Product, such as Windows XP
		Microsoft Certified System Administrator (MCSA), professional certification for the skills to manage and troubleshoot system environments
		Microsoft Certified Systems Engineer (MCSE) in advanced networking, including the implementation of Microsoft desktop, server, or networking products
Cisco	www.cisco.com/en/US/learning/index.html	Cisco Certified Network Associate (CCNA) in network administration
Novell	www.novell.com/training/certinfo/cna/index.html	Certified Novell Administrator (CNA) in basic networking
	www.novell.com/training/certinfo/cne/index.html	Certified Novell Engineer (CNE) in advanced Novell networking projects
Oracle	www.oracle.com/education/certification	Oracle Database Administrator certified in database development and administration
Sun	developers.sun.com/dev/certification	Certifications in Java Programming, Solaris operating system, and Sun servers

To see a more complete list of hardware, software, and networking product vendors' certification Web sites, visit **certification.about.com/cs/vendorsites**.

An alternate kind of certification is not vendor-specific, but aims to measure industry-standard knowledge and skills. Because it is not tied to a specific vendor or product line, this kind of certification is more general or generic, and is vendor-neutral. Examples of certification targeted at a general, industry-wide audience of employers and employees are listed in Table 7-2.

Table 7-2   Examples of general, industry-wide certification programs

Organization	URL	Certificate/Area of Expertise
Computer Technology Industry Association (CompTIA)	www.comptia.org	A+ certification; covers hardware and operating systems, including basic knowledge of configuring, installing, diagnosing, repairing, upgrading, and maintaining micro-computers
		Network+; covers network architecture, and operating systems, including installing, configuring, and troubleshooting a network client
		Security+; certifies professionals with skills in organizational security including access controls, authentication, infrastructure, and operational security
		Project+; certifies project management skills
Chauncey Group (ETS)	www.chauncey.com/Services/ATS.htm	Associate Technology Specialist; covers core IT skills, plus specialties in database, digital media, enterprise systems, networking, programming, technical support, technical writing, and Web development
Institute for Certification of Computing Professionals (ICCP)	www.iccp.org/iccpnew/acp.html	Associate Computer Professional (ASP); certifies knowledge and skills earned primarily in academic or vocational degree programs
Linux Professional Institute	www.lpi.org	Linux Professional Institute Certification (LPIC); certifies workers who administer the Linux operating system at three levels

Table 7-2 Examples of general, industry-wide certification programs (continued)

Organization	URL	Certificate/Area of Expertise
Society of Internet Professionals	www.sipgroup.org/certification.html	Certified Member of SIP (CMSIP); covers Web site design, management, and e-business skills
Help Desk Institute	www.thinkhdi.com/certification/individualCertification/	Customer Support Specialist (CSS); covers customer support skills
		Help Desk Analyst (HDA); includes entry-level help desk agent skills
		Help Desk Senior Analyst (HDSA); certifies advanced support professionals, team leaders, and supervisors
		Help Desk Manager (HDM); includes management skills described in this chapter
Help Desk 2000	www.stiknowledge.com/certification_advisory/courses.asp	Certified Help Desk Professional (CHDP); includes entry-level help desk skills
		Certified Field Support Technician (CFST); includes skills for support specialists who call on external clients
		Certified Help Desk Manager (CHDM); includes management skills described in this chapter

7

As the entries in Table 7-2 indicate, in addition to certification in a technical specialty, user support specialists and help desk staff can also get their support skills certified. The Chauncey Group, Help Desk Institute, and Help Desk 2000 professional organizations have developed certifications for support professionals. These certificates vary in the topics covered in the exam. Visit their Web sites, listed in the table, for current details on certifications available, topics covered, how to prepare, and costs.

Finally, some certifications are aimed at organizations, rather than individuals. For example, the Help Desk Institute and Help Desk 2000 offer programs to certify entire help desk groups as part of the professional services they provide to their members. Some of these certification programs include consulting services on support industry best practices. **Best practices** are support industry procedures, tools, and methods that very successful support groups employ; these practices often set apart very successful support operations from mediocre ones.

For help desk and user support specialists, some of the benefits of certification include:

- A recognized benchmark of minimum-level job skills and expertise in the area covered by certification

- A justification for receiving higher pay, as a new or experienced worker

- An opportunity for promotion and career advancement because of documented knowledge and skills

- A way to document for an employer efforts to keep up to date in the computer field

- A feeling of pride of accomplishment and increased job satisfaction upon passing a certification milestone

Is certification a requirement for a support position? Some employers specify in job announcements and ads for support positions that they expect applicants to be certified, perhaps in addition to their formal education. The most common certification expected for user support and help desk positions is either MOS or A+ certification. The MOS Core level certification documents that a job applicant meets a minimum level of expertise in popular Microsoft applications software packages. The MOS Expert level documents advanced proficiency. Although the emphasis in A+ certification is on hardware, the exam also covers operating systems and troubleshooting strategies. However, many employers do not expect or require applicants to be certified. Even these employers, however, may treat certification as additional evidence of qualification for a support position. Organizations that expect prospective support employees to be certified as a help desk professional are rare, because these certification exams are relatively new and not yet widely recognized.

Individuals interested in gaining certification can do the following:

1. Acquire the knowledge and skills covered by the certification exam.

2. Evaluate certification skills by taking a pretest assessment exam; based on results, repeat Step 1 or proceed to Step 3.

3. Take the certification exam, for which there may be a substantial fee, especially if accompanied by a preparatory course or boot camp.

4. Retake any part of the certification test that was not passed.

Many college and vocational/technical schools now match the curriculum in their courses with certification in the area covered by the course. For example, an introductory spreadsheet course may be targeted to students who wish to prepare for the MOS Excel Core exam. An advanced spreadsheet course may be advertised as preparatory for the MOS Excel Expert exam. An advantage of a preparatory course in a college or vocational/technical school is that assistance is usually available when a student encounters problems with the course material. Other common ways to prepare for a certification exam include crash courses, online tutorials, and self-study courses. **Crash courses**, sometimes called boot camps, are intensive classes designed to prepare participants in a short time (a few days or a couple of weeks) to take a certification exam. Crash courses are expensive, and a student usually must travel to the site where the course is offered. However, for professionals who have previous background in a subject area, crash courses are a quick way to prepare to get certified. Several training vendors now offer **online tutorial courses** targeted at certification exams in either computer-based training (CBT) or Web-based training (WBT) formats. CBT and WBT preparatory courses usually cost substantially less than crash courses, but frequently do not include assistance if a student needs help with course materials. Finally, **self-study courses** are preparatory materials usually in book format that readers complete at their own pace. The books are often 1000 or more pages. Some are packaged with CBT tutorials and with practice exam questions. Although generally less costly, self-study courses rarely provide student assistance. The market for certification preparatory courses is large, and both product vendors and third-party training vendors offer materials and services to meet the growing interest in industry certification.

WWW

Organizations that offer courses in a variety of formats designed to prepare workers to meet certification exam requirements or assess a test taker's readiness to take a certification exam include MindLeaders at **link.mindleaders.com/e-learn/courseprice.jsp?**, Netwind Learning Center at **www.netwind.com/index.html**, InfoSource at **www.infosourcetraining.com**, Specialized Solutions at **www.quickcert.com/ittraininglibrary.htm**, Aaron's Computer Training at **www.aarons-computer-training.com/index.htm**, and Learnthat.com at **www.learnthat.com/courses**. Many of these training vendors offer a free sample lesson on their Web sites. For other training and certification vendors, see an online list at **dmoz.org/Computers/ Education/Certification**.

Most certification exams are administered on a computer workstation. Some are traditional tests that ask test takers a fixed-length sequence of questions, similar to the final exam in a college course. In the traditional format, each test taker answers the same set of questions. However, certification exams often use a newer type of test, called an adaptive test. An **adaptive test** asks questions selected from a test database to try to estimate the test taker's ability quickly. The test database in an adaptive test consists of questions that are graded from easy to moderate to difficult. The first question asked in an adaptive test session is of moderate difficulty. As the test taker answers each question, an adaptive test uses a mathematical formula to estimate the test taker's level of ability. Subsequent questions asked are either easier or more difficult, based on the pattern of previous right and wrong answers. An adaptive test continually selects questions from the test database and revises its estimate of the test taker's ability until it is relatively certain that it has an accurate measure. Sometimes the estimation process requires as few as 15 questions. Thus, some test takers may answer more questions than others; some may respond to easier questions, others may respond to more difficult ones, as an adaptive test hones in on the test taker's ability. One advantage of adaptive testing is efficiency: it saves time because fewer questions are asked, reduces boredom from too many easy or repetitive questions, reduces intimidation from very difficult questions, and tries to make the testing process shorter and less stressful.

WWW

To learn detailed information about various certification tests, see InformIT's Exam Cram 2 Web site at: **www.informit.com/examcram2**. For a detailed article on computer adaptive testing (CAT), visit **www.winnetmag.com/Articles/Index.cfm?ArticleID=5694**. To take a free certification exam for a Computer Technical Support agent, visit the Brainbench.com Web site at **www.brainbench.com/xml/bb/common/testcenter/taketest.xml?testId=68**. An organization that specializes in pretest assessment exams is Transcender at **www.transcender.com**.

Some certification tests also include scenario questions that require the test taker to answer questions using a simulated version of a product. Certification exams frequently include a hands-on component to eliminate the "paper CNE" phenomenon described earlier.

MICROSOFT CERTIFIED DESKTOP SUPPORT TECHNICIAN
MICROSOFT CORPORATION
REDMOND, WASHINGTON
WWW.MICROSOFT.COM

Beginning in 2004, Microsoft announced the availability of a new certification program designed for user support workers. The Microsoft Certified Desktop Support Technician (MCDST) certification can be earned by studying for and passing two exams. Because of the popularity and widespread industry recognition of the Microsoft Office Specialist (MOS) certification, the MCDST certificate will undoubtedly become recognized as a useful credential in organizations that have adopted Microsoft operating systems and application software as product standards.

The MCDST certification program was introduced in October 2003 in a Webcast by John Norby, the Product Manager of Microsoft Learning. The entire 80-minute TechNet Webcast announcing the details of the MCDST is available for replay online at **www.microsoft.com/usa/webcasts/ondemand/2378.asp**. The Webcast requires registration and a download of InterWise Participant software, both of which are free.

Who is the target audience for the MCDST certificate?

The MCDST is aimed at new entrants into the user/technical support field and existing support staff. Microsoft expects the certificate to be attractive to help desk technicians, customer support representatives, PC support specialists, and technical support representatives as well as employers who hire these job titles.

Which exams must be passed for the MCDST?

Two exams are required. One covers Windows operating systems; the other covers Microsoft applications software.

Supporting Users and Troubleshooting a Microsoft Windows XP Operating System covers topics such as:

- Windows XP installation, upgrades, and migrating users to a new PC
- File and directory management in a network environment
- Hardware and device driver configuration and troubleshooting
- The Windows user environment, account administration, security, and system performance
- Network client configuration and troubleshooting

Supporting Users and Troubleshooting Desktop Applications on a Microsoft Windows XP Operating System covers topics such as:

- Microsoft Office, Internet Explorer, and Outlook Express configuration and troubleshooting
- Office application usability and customization
- Application configuration and security issues in a network environment

How much hands-on experience is required for the MCDST?

The certification is targeted at those with six months of hands-on experience; however, Microsoft does not indicate whether hands-on experience is a requirement, or how the experience will be verified.

Does the MCDST exam cover all of the skills that might be expected of a user support worker, such as soft skills, hardware repair, or help desk operation?

No. In fact, John Norby mentions in the Webcast that the MCDST certification is designed to complement other certification programs offered by The Help Desk Institute, CompTIA, and Microsoft's MOS certification that covers features of applications software.

In conjunction with the MCDST certification program, Microsoft announced the availability in 2004 of training courses and materials targeted to the MCDST exams. To learn more about the Microsoft Certified Desktop Support Technician certification, visit the Microsoft Web site at **www.microsoft.com/traincert/mcp/mcdst**. Information on the MCDST is based on preliminary announcements and is subject to change.

USER SUPPORT AS A PROFESSION

The number of user support and help desk positions in the United States and worldwide increased significantly in the 1990s. However, the recession in the United States in 2001 through 2003 has reduced employment in the user support industry, as has the trend to outsource some low-level support positions overseas. The Information Technology Association of America (ITAA) estimates that of the more than 10 million U.S. workers in Information Technology in 2003, nearly 2 million were employed in technical support positions and another half million were employed as technical writers. However, estimates of the need for new technical support workers (open positions) in the late 1990s of more than 600,000 have dropped to 150,000 in 2003.

 To learn more about the ITAA study of the demand for technology workers, download its *2003 Workforce Study* at **www.itaa.org/workforce/studies/ 03execsumm.pdf** (requires Adobe Reader).

As a result of the total size of the user support field, several groups have been organized in recent years to provide a professional association for these workers. A **professional association** is a formal organization that represents the interests of a group of professionals and provides services to its membership. These groups are similar to professional associations in other employment fields, such as the American Medical Association (AMA), which represents physicians, and the National Education Association (NEA), which represents educators. Professional associations that are targeted to user support and help desk staff are listed in Table 7-3.

Table 7-3   User support and help desk professional associations

Association	URL
Help Desk Institute	www.thinkhdi.com
Help Desk 2000	www.stiknowledge.com/helpdesk2000/index.asp
Association of Support Professionals	www.asponline.com
Information Technology Association of America	www.itaa.org
Service and Support Professionals Association	www.supportgate.com
Network and Systems Professionals Association	www.naspa.com

Professional associations perform a number of functions for their membership. They often publish journals or magazines with articles of interest to the support profession.

These associations encourage their members to grow professionally by offering books, seminars, conferences, and other professional growth and development activities. Some associations offer certification programs for their membership. All associations maintain Web sites with links to other sites of interest to support professionals. Some offer chat rooms, newsgroups, local chapters, and e-mail services with industry news, and encourage interactions among members in other ways.

One function that a professional association can provide is to publish a code of ethical principles or conduct standards to guide its members' professional behavior. An example of a code of ethics for the information technology industry is published by the Information Technology Association of America (ITAA). The ITAA code of ethical standards includes six basic principles, which are listed in Figure 7-6.

7

CODE OF ETHICS
Information Technology Association of America (ITAA)

1. Exercise independent judgment and objectivity
2. Communicate in a manner that facilitates clarity and understanding
3. Provide clients with quality service and results
4. Demonstrate dedication to the support profession
5. Assist in maintaining the integrity of the information technology industry
6. Conduct business in a manner that results in respect and acceptance for the profession and industry

Figure 7-6   Information Technology Association of America's code of ethics

For detailed information about the six principles in the ITAA code of ethical standards, see its Web site at **www.itaa.org/itserv/ethics.htm**. Compare the ITAA code of ethics with the code of ethics and standards of conduct published by the Association of Information Technology Professionals (AITP) at its Web site, **www.aitp.org/organization/about/conduct/conduct.jsp**.

The purpose of this chapter has not been to provide a comprehensive primer on user support management, but to discuss selected aspects of management with an emphasis on information that is likely to be of interest and useful to support job applicants and entry-level user support or help desk workers. If you are interested in career advancement into a user support management position, consider taking a community college or vocational/technical school course on business management for a comprehensive look at the activities that challenge managers.

Examples of two "hot topic" issues in the support industry that are not included in this chapter are support salaries and employee retention. Each October, *ComputerWorld* conducts an annual salary survey of the information technology field. The survey includes job titles such as help desk/technical support specialist. The survey for 2003 is available online at **www.computerworld.com/careertopics/careers/salarysurvey2003/home**. The survey is nationwide, but includes some breakdowns to reflect regional differences in support salaries; however, it is a useful data point for support managers concerned about typical salaries. For another perspective on salaries, consult **www.salary.com**, select **IT - Computers**, **Software** from the Select a job category list, select a help desk position from the job title list, and then click the Create Basic Salary Report button. Support managers concerned with employee retention should consult a TechRepublic article, "Strategies to Boost Morale and Retention in Call Center Environments," at **techrepublic.com.com/5100-6269-5088913.html** (free registration required).

Chapter Summary

❏ People in user support and help desk management positions include those who work as supervisors, lead workers, and project coordinators. Many support groups develop a mission statement to describe their guiding principles and objectives against which each group can evaluate its performance.

❏ Performance statistics are used to measure the extent to which a support group and its staff members meet the objectives described in its mission statement. Support groups also use satisfaction surveys to collect data on individual and group performance. Performance measures are often used as part of a periodic performance appraisal of support workers.

❏ Support managers with an open position analyze the knowledge, skills, and abilities (KSAs) needed for that position and prepare a position description to describe job qualifications required of applicants. The interview process for support positions usually includes both general and scenario questions to gauge an applicant's ability to think under pressure and solve problems.

❏ Training programs for support staff include both new employee orientation and ongoing professional development.

❏ In addition to routine support tasks, some support workers are assigned special projects. Project management activities include project definition, planning, implementation, monitoring, and termination. Project managers plan project tasks, allocate staff, define timelines, develop a budget, and allocate resources, such as equipment and facilities, to accomplish a project's goal.

❏ Automated project management tools, such as Microsoft Project 2003, help project managers with the details of a specific project, including the preparation of a Gantt Chart to help project participants understand a project's critical path, their individual task assignments, and what is expected of them.

- Certification in the information technology industry includes college degrees, vendor-specific certification, and industry-standard certification programs. Support professionals can earn certification in specialized products as well as certification of their support skills. Adaptive tests are often used in the certification exam process.

- In addition to the industry trend toward certification of skills, associations of support professionals are evolving to meet the needs of workers in the support field. Some professional associations publish codes of ethics and standards of conduct to guide their members.

KEY TERMS

7

abandonment rate — The percentage of calls in which the user hung up before support staff responded.

adaptive test — A method used in certification exams that asks questions from a test database that are graded in difficulty from easy to moderate to difficult to try to estimate a test taker's ability quickly.

best practices — Support industry procedures, tools, and methods that very successful support groups employ; these strategies often distinguish very successful support operations from mediocre ones.

certification — An assessment process to measure and document employee knowledge and skills in a specialized segment of the information technology field.

crash course — An intensive class designed to prepare participants to take a certification exam in a few days or a couple of weeks; sometimes called a boot camp.

critical path — The sequence of project tasks that must be completed on time to meet the project's completion date; establishes important milestones in a project's calendar.

Erlang — A unit of traffic (*user calls* in the case of support groups) processed in a given period of time; used to estimate the number of support staff required to respond to an expected volume of calls in a given time period.

Gantt Chart — A common project planning tool that shows the basic information about each task in a project as a horizontal bar on a graph; it identifies each task, its relationship to other tasks, the expected calendar for task and project completion, and task assignments to project participants.

knowledge and skills test — A test that measures a job applicant's knowledge and problem-solving abilities.

mission statement — A list of guiding principles that communicate the goals and objectives of a support group to its staff, users, and management.

online tutorial course — Computer-based training (CBT) or Web-based training (WBT) format targeted at preparing participants for certification exams.

performance appraisal — A process to evaluate a user support worker according to established criteria; criteria should be related to the support group's mission, to the worker's position description, and to the worker's personal growth objectives.

performance statistics — Objective summary information about a user support or help desk operation; often directly related to the user support mission statement; usually expressed as important percentages, such as the percentage of support calls answered in two minutes or less.

predecessor task — An activity in a project that must be completed before another project task can begin.

professional association — A formal organization that represents the interests of a group of professionals and provides services to its membership.

project definition — A project management step to define the scope of a project, including its goals, a calendar, a budget, the participants, and coordination.

project goal — A specific, measurable result that is the ultimate target or outcome of a project.

project implementation — A project management step during which the work on each task is accomplished by participants.

project management — A step-by-step work plan and process designed to reach a specific goal; includes project definition, planning, implementation, monitoring, and termination steps.

project monitoring — An assessment of the status of all project tasks to learn whether they are on target when compared with the time and budget estimates.

project plan — A document that pulls together all project tasks and answers the questions: What tasks will be accomplished? Who will perform each task? How long will each task take? What will each task cost?

project task — A specific action or objective that must be performed to meet the project goal.

project termination — The final step in managing a project during which the project results are communicated and evaluated; a final report is often prepared to summarize the project.

risk factors — An analysis and assessment of the problems that can arise during the life of a project that would affect the project's successful, on-time completion.

scenario question — An interview method that gives a job applicant a specific problem (or set of problems) representative of the kinds of situations user support staff actually encounter; used to measure the applicant's problem-solving skills and ability to work under pressure.

scope creep — The tendency for a project to grow or change in unexpected ways that increase the time frame, resources, and cost to complete a project.

self-study course — Preparatory materials, usually in book format, that readers complete at their own pace prior to taking a certification exam.

special project — A user support activity that happens only occasionally, in contrast to routine activities; these projects require more time, more staff members, and a larger budget, and are more complex and less well-defined than routine support activities.

staff training — Training designed to orient new support employees to their jobs, and ongoing training to update the skills and encourage professional growth among experienced support staff.

user satisfaction survey — A questionnaire that attempts to measure how satisfied users are with the support services they have experienced.

wait time — The average time it takes a help desk to respond to calls.

CHECK YOUR UNDERSTANDING

1. True or False? The employee selection process for a help desk position can be described as an attempt to find applicants with the knowledge, skills, and abilities that most closely match the position's requirements.

2. True or False? Unlike a question in a skills test, there is only one correct answer to a scenario question in a job interview.

3. What is the primary purpose of help desk performance statistics?

   a. respond to computer auditors' information requirements

   b. justify the value and expense of help desk services

   c. report to company stockholders

   d. respond to complaints from angry users

4. True or False? Organizations that treat user support as an income center may have difficulty justifying the cost of support services.

5. Which of the following aspects of help desk operation would you least expect to be covered in a help desk mission statement?

   a. operational efficiency of users

   b. help desk fees for services

   c. customer satisfaction

   d. effectiveness of help desk services

6. A(n) _____ is a process to evaluate a help desk or support employee according to established criteria.

7. A measure of the number of support calls that can be processed in a given time period, often used to determine staffing levels in a help desk operation, is _____ .

   a. a Gantt unit

   b. scope creep

   c. the critical path

   d. an Erlang

8. True or False? Support managers often use recordings of monitored support calls to help employees identify areas where performance improvement is needed.

9. Which of the following characteristics does not describe the work performed on a special project?

  a. is based on less well-defined steps and procedures

  b. usually takes longer to perform than routine work

  c. occurs on an irregular schedule

  d. includes simpler tasks than operational work

10. Which sequence of letters below shows the correct order of steps for managing a support project? (a) monitor (b) plan (c) terminate (d) define (e) implement

  a. b – d – a – e – c

  b. a – b – d – c – e

  c. d – b – e – a – c

  d. b – a – e – d – c

11. True or False? The risk factors associated with a special project mean that experienced project managers avoid making commitments about a project's budget, timelines, and resource needs.

12. True or False? A Gantt Chart allows a project manager to ask "what-if" questions about how changes in resources impact the timeline of a project.

13. A(n) _____ is a project activity that must be completed before another task can begin.

14. True or False? Although industry certification is relatively new, it is now essentially a requirement for any user support position.

15. Which of the following testing methods is often used in industry certification exams?

  a. adaptive test

  b. boot camp

  c. traditional fixed-length test

  d. best practices

DISCUSSION QUESTIONS

1. Is it ethical for a company that operates a telephone help desk to monitor its agents? Under what circumstances should this practice be permitted? Under what circumstances should this practice not be permitted?

2. Will industry certification ever become a minimum job requirement for employment in the user support field? Why, or why not?

3. Is a code of professional ethics, like the one from ITAA in the chapter, useful for a field as diverse as user support in which there are so many different kinds of jobs? How would you make the ethical principles more specific?

HANDS-ON PROJECTS

Project 7-1

Evaluate a user support mission statement. Locate the mission statement for the help desk or user support group at your school or organization. Compare the mission statement with the sample in this chapter. List the similarities and differences you find. Choose one of the mission statements and write three measurable criteria that a manager could use to evaluate the performance of the support group based on the mission statement.

Project 7-2

Develop a professional growth plan. Write a one-page personal professional development growth plan for yourself. Base your plan on your personal assessment of your strengths and areas where you would like to improve, either as a student and future job applicant, or as a current worker. In your development plan, describe the kinds of training, courses, seminars, or other experiences that would make you a more attractive job applicant or more valuable employee. Then compare your plan with ones developed by three classmates or coworkers. What useful ideas did you get from them?

Project 7-3

Write a classified ad for a user support position. Study classified ads in your local paper or on the Internet for information technology (IT) and user support positions. (These ads are usually located under *computers* or *technology* headings.) Note what is included in a typical help wanted ad in the IT field and the format of the ad. Select one of the user support position descriptions in Chapter 2, and write a classified ad that could be used to attract job applicants for that position.

Project 7-4

Write a scenario question for an interview. Develop a scenario question for a user support or help desk position that would measure whether a job applicant is a good problem solver. Start by brainstorming some ideas with three classmates or coworkers, then select a scenario that is feasible for an interview, and finally refine the scenario question. Exchange your scenario question with another team and write a model response to its question.

7

Project 7-5

Online training course evaluation. Use the Web-based resources described in this chapter to locate an online training course you can try out at low or no cost. Complete the course, and then answer the following questions:

- ❏ Did you finish the course? Why or why not?

- ❏ Did you find the course materials easy to use? List examples of any problems you encountered.

- ❏ Is an online learning environment effective for your personal learning style? How could the course you took be improved?

- ❏ How could the online training course you took be used as part of a training program for end users or support specialists?

Project 7-6

Take a certification exam. Visit the Brainbench Web site at **www.brainbench.com**, and then click the **Individuals** link. Learn about the advantages of online certification. Pick one of the exam areas Brainbench offers and take the exam. Do not worry if you don't pass the exam. The Brainbench tests are not easy, and the passing rate is low for some exams. The purpose of the exercise is to give you experience with a typical certification exam. Was the exam in a traditional format or was it an adaptive test? Write a summary of your experience, and explain how you could improve your performance on the next certification exam you take.

Project 7-7

Evaluate associations for support professionals. Pick two of the associations for support professionals listed in this chapter. Visit their Web sites to find out about their missions and the services they provide to their members. Compare the two associations and describe the kinds of support professionals they target for membership. If you had a choice, which would you choose to join? Explain what factors influenced your choice.

CASE PROJECTS

1. Help Desk Performance at Virtual-Soft

Beth Goldman, supervisor of Virtual-Soft's Help Desk service, gets weekly data from a help desk software package on her support specialists' performance. She wants to use the data to measure her staff members' productivity. Use a spreadsheet program to enter the data for Beth's staff from last week shown in the table below.

Support Specialist	Calls Handled per Week	Available Hours per Week	Average Minutes per Call
Susan	112	31.5	14.2
Jose	127	31.0	11.3
Sue	0	0.0	0.0
Barbara	87	25.1	15.9
Ekaterina	151	30.0	9.2
Shere-Kahn	63	24.2	13.6
Dennis	77	29.6	11.9
Kristen	63	27.1	10.6

7

Beth thinks that productivity should be measured as *amount of work accomplished* divided by *effort expended*. Use your spreadsheet to calculate a measure of productivity you think would be appropriate for these workers. Who is the most productive agent on Beth's staff? Is there more than one right way to approach this problem? Print your spreadsheet and explain your results.

2. Develop a Simple Project Management Plan

Suppose a friend asked for your help in selecting a home computer to purchase. Even though this is potentially a very small project, apply what you learned in this chapter about project management to the goal of analyzing your friend's needs and selecting a computer to purchase. List the project tasks you would follow in a home computer selection project. Can some of the tasks be broken down into subtasks? Use paper and pencil or a spreadsheet program to design a simple Gantt Chart that illustrates the project tasks. Could some of the project subtasks be performed simultaneously by one or more persons? List four examples of risk factors and scope creep that could affect the project's timeline. Finally, describe how you would monitor the progress on this project.

3. Help Desk Staffing at Game Shack Software

Game Shack Software develops and sells computer games and related products. Ronald Liew has recently been hired to manage Game Shack's help desk operation. The management at Game Shack is concerned about the best way to schedule agents in the help desk operation. They want to employ enough help desk agents to respond to the calls they receive from users, but they cannot afford to have an excess of agents scheduled to work when there are relatively few calls.

Ronald wants your advice about the size of the help desk that Game Shack needs, and the best way to schedule agents during the day. Ron has collected data for a couple of weeks on the number of calls the Game Shack help desk receives. The busiest time of the day is from 9 AM to 4 PM, during which the help desk receives an average of 155 calls. The calls average about 12 minutes, and it takes an agent an average of two additional minutes to finish a database entry and close the call. The current help desk guidelines at Game Shack are that

85% of the calls should be answered in 30 seconds or less. (No more than 1% of the calls should be lost because of insufficient phone lines available.)

The 155 calls each day are distributed approximately, as shown in the table below.

Hour	Calls
9 AM	10
10 AM	25
11 AM	25
12 PM	35
1 PM	20
2 PM	15
3 PM	15
4 PM	10

Use the Call Center Erlang calculator on the Web at **www.erlang.com** to advise Ronald about the following problems:

1. How many agents does Game Shack need to handle the volume of calls listed above?

2. How many telephone lines are required to meet Game Shack's objectives?

3. When is the peak call volume? How long will an average caller wait during the peak hour?

4. Describe the impact on staffing and number of lines Game Shack needs if the policy guideline on the percentage of calls answered in 30 seconds or less is increased to 95%.

4. LAN Selection for Re-Nu-Cartridge

Bridgette Petrang, a support supervisor at Re-Nu-Cartridge, has asked you to learn to develop a project plan with Microsoft Project 2003. To learn the basic features of project management software, you'll input the tasks from a current project at Re-Nu-Cartridge, shown in the table below. The goal of the project is to select a new local area network (LAN) for the company.

	Project Plan: Re-Nu-Cartridge's LAN (local area network) Selection	
Step	**Task**	**Time Estimate**
1	Conduct a user needs analysis among Re-Nu-Cartridge's managers and employees for a new LAN system.	8 days
2	Develop a specification of the features required in the LAN system.	4 days
3	Define the selection criteria based on mandatory and desirable features, vendor support, costs, compatibility with existing equipment, and other factors; decide on a weight for each criterion.	2 days
4	Write a Request For Proposal (RFP) document for vendors to describe LAN requirements, bidding procedures, and decision criteria.	4 days

	Project Plan: Re-Nu-Cartridge's LAN (local area network) Selection	
5	Send RFP document to LAN vendors.	1 day
6	Vendors prepare written responses to RFP.	14 days
7	Analyze responses to RFP and evaluate bids.	5 days
8	Select a vendor and award the contract for the LAN.	1 day

Install the 120-day trial version of Microsoft Office Project 2003 from the CD that accompanies this book. Start **Microsoft Office Project 2003**. By default, a Project Guide opens in the left pane of the Project window that will help you set up a basic project plan. Find the **Open** menu in the Getting Started pane on the left of the Project screen, and then click the **Create a new project** icon. In the New Project pane on the left of the screen, click **Blank Project**. The Tasks pane on the left lists the steps to set up a simple project plan. For the Re-Nu-Cartridge LAN project, you will need to enter the following Tasks:

- **Define the project:** enter the start date (use the first business day of next month as the start date for the project)

- **Define general working times:** use the default definition of a work week, but enter any holidays your school or company recognizes

- **List the tasks in the project:** enter the task descriptions and durations listed in the table

- **Organize the tasks into phases:** an optional step

- **Schedule tasks:** use this tool to establish links between project steps (or use the Predecessors column in the Project worksheet)

- The remaining tasks in the Tasks Pane are optional for the Re-Nu-Cartridge project

- To display the Gantt Chart in less space, you can change the time scale displayed on the chart from days to weeks. Right-click the time scale column headings at the top of the Gantt Chart and modify the time scale settings.

You can get additional information about any task by clicking the **Hint** and **More Information** icons on each task screen, or by using the Help system. Remember that Project 2003 is part of the Microsoft Office suite. Many commands and icons in Project have the same functions as in other Office programs.

Your task is to learn enough about Microsoft Project 2003 to prepare a Gantt Chart similar to the ones illustrated in the chapter for the project described in the table. Experiment with the features of Project 2003 if you would like, but keep focused on the objective to prepare a project plan so the management at Re-Nu-Cartridge can understand the project timeline.

CHAPTER 8

PRODUCT EVALUATION STRATEGIES AND SUPPORT STANDARDS

In this chapter you will learn:

♦ How product and support standards emerged

♦ Common tools and methods support specialists use to evaluate and select computer products

♦ How organizations develop and implement support standards

In addition to help desk support tasks described in earlier chapters, user support workers often evaluate computer products and services as well as help set product standards for end users in their organization. These tasks are more common for support groups that provide services to internal users; however, some support workers occasionally consult on product evaluation and standards for external users. User support groups spend time and resources on product evaluations and standards for several reasons. First, support workers often have the expertise to evaluate competing products and set organizational standards that end users do not have. However, just because support specialists may have greater expertise does not mean that end users should not be involved in the process. On the contrary, end-user involvement is critical, as you'll learn in this chapter. Second, assigning support staff the responsibility for product review and evaluation can eliminate duplication of effort. If each end user continually researches and evaluates products of special interest to him or her, the result can be wasted time and a lack of product standards. Third, support groups are often able to play a role as a liaison between end users and the Information Technology staff to ensure that all viewpoints are represented when computer products are evaluated and selected.

In this chapter, you'll learn about several commonly used methods and strategies that support specialists use to evaluate computer products and services, and how product evaluations contribute to the definition of support standards. Support standards within an organization are important for a variety of reasons, not the least of which is to reduce the burden on the support staff. When support staff resources are limited, supporting a reduced number of standard products is preferable to supporting any product an end user might choose to use. At the end of the chapter, you'll examine one organization's product support standards.

How Product Standards Emerged

When the era of end-user computing first began, few product standards existed. **Product standards** are lists of hardware, operating system, network, and applications software products that have been selected to meet the needs of users in an organization. In the early 1980s, it was not unusual for users within the same department to use several hardware platforms. Some of the first PC hardware manufacturers included Apple, KayPro, IBM, RadioShack, Commodore, Osborne, AlphaMicro, and Atari, each of whom claimed a significant share of the PC market. Each PC manufacturer touted the advantages of its system for users in specific application areas where its hardware had competitive strengths. Because manufacturers believed that significant differences between competing products represented a marketing advantage, they felt little pressure to move toward an industry standard in PC hardware. For example, Atari hardware was designed to emphasize graphic displays and computer games; it appealed primarily to the home entertainment market. Meanwhile, KayPro built one of the first portable computers and aimed it at students and business people for whom portability was important. These two hardware platforms were incompatible in virtually all respects; neither became an industry standard, except perhaps in their niche markets.

As widespread as the problem of incompatible and competing hardware platforms was, the problem was worse in the software market. Owners of identical hardware models of IBM PCs, for example, could choose a word processor from a long list that included WordStar, Microsoft Word, DisplayWrite, WordPerfect, PerfectWrite, and PFS Write. Because word processing was the leading application in businesses, many products competed for market share. The list of competing spreadsheet and database software was shorter, but several popular choices competed in those software categories, as well.

 To learn more about computer industry standards, read an article by Jack Schofield on *Computer Industry Standards*, at **www.tiscali.co.uk/reference/dictionaries/computers/data/f0000190.html**. The History of Computing Project (THOCP) presents information about many early hardware and software vendors on its Web site, **www.thocp.net**.

It might appear that product incompatibility and competition simply reflected a healthy, competitive market environment. However, from the perspective of an organization that purchased hardware and software products in the 1980s, the lack of product standards caused several problems, which are summarized in Figure 8-1.

- Limited opportunities to transfer and share information between users

- Large inventories of PC hardware parts required to repair computers

- Increased difficulty to train and equip hardware service technicians to repair different hardware platforms

- User skills difficult to transfer from one system to another

- Increased costs as support groups struggled to assist users with so many different types of PCs and software

Figure 8-1   Problems caused by product incompatibility

8

Limited Data Transfer.   Incompatible hardware and software products meant that two employees might have difficulty sharing data, because the primary method of exchanging information was by transfer on a floppy disk. And a floppy disk written on one manufacturer's computer frequently could not be read or modified on another manufacturer's hardware. Even different models of hardware products from the same manufacturer were occasionally incompatible.

Excessive Parts Inventories.   Organizations often repaired their own hardware during the 1980s. However, there were few industry standard power supplies, disk drives, or motherboards, and each hardware manufacturer made its own central processor and memory chips. For example, memory chips for a RadioShack computer could not be used in another manufacturer's system and vice versa. Consequently, to repair all its computers, an organization needed to maintain a large inventory of different and incompatible components. Hardware incompatibility substantially increased the cost to make even simple component repairs.

Hardware Repair Problems.   In addition to large inventories of incompatible parts, it was difficult to train and equip hardware technicians to understand, diagnose, and repair all the different kinds of computers on the market. The architecture of each platform was different. For example, some floppy disk drives included the disk controller as an integral part of the drive, whereas other disk controllers were separate from the drive. Furthermore, each type of floppy disk drive required a read/write head alignment procedure that was often unique to each drive.

Lack of Skills Transfer.   Employees could operate their own desktop systems, but often knew little about the systems on their colleagues' desks. The lack of a standard operating system and applications software meant that employees often had difficulty filling in for an absent coworker, which reduced overall employee productivity. Furthermore, the cost to train employees to use several software packages was substantial. For example, an employee who transferred from a department that used the Quattro Pro spreadsheet to another that used Lotus 1-2-3 represented an additional cost to the organization for applications software retraining.

Increased Support Costs.   Finally, and perhaps most importantly, incompatible computer systems dramatically increased user support costs. In the late 1970s and early 1980s, information centers in large organizations were confronted with the need to provide training, documentation, troubleshooting assistance, hardware problem diagnosis, and software support and upgrades for a very large number of incompatible hardware and software products. A user who called a help desk or support group might reach someone who was a specialist on Microsoft Word on the Macintosh, but knew little about WordPerfect on an IBM PC. If training sessions were offered, they were often targeted at a small group of employees who used a particular configuration of hardware and software, but were less useful to other employees who worked on different hardware platforms, operating systems, or application packages.

During the 1980s, organizations with large investments in computer hardware and software began to realize that a policy (or lack of one) that permitted employees to purchase the computer systems of their choice imposed significant additional costs on the organization. Incompatible systems clearly resulted in computer technology and related support costs that were more expensive than necessary. To help control and reduce costs, organizations began to develop product standards. Companies enforced product standards in an attempt to reduce the cost of acquiring and supporting computer systems. First, they standardized on a small number of hardware platforms and configurations selected to meet their users' needs. Second, they adopted standard operating systems and, in the 1990s, network operating systems. Third, they limited the choice of applications software to one or at most a few standard application packages in each software category.

NOTE   Are industry standard computer products really a good thing? During 2000, the U.S. Department of Justice successfully filed suit against Microsoft Corporation for illegal trade practices and stifling competition in the operating system market with its Windows products. Although the case was complicated, many computer users who remember the lack of industry standards in the 1980s feel that Microsoft did the computer industry and users a favor by developing what has become an industry standard operating system. The Department of Justice, on the other hand, argued that Microsoft used its dominant position in the operating system market to give other Microsoft products an unfair advantage over competitors' products. The suit was partially resolved in late 2001 when Microsoft agreed to cease some anti-competitive practices and give other vendors access to the code for the Windows operating system, and the federal government agreed not to pursue breaking up Microsoft into smaller, competing companies. However, several individual states and foreign governments continue to pursue legal action against Microsoft Corporation.

You'll learn more about product standards later in this chapter. But first you'll learn how organizations evaluate products so they can set effective standards.

METHODS FOR EVALUATING AND SELECTING COMPUTER PRODUCTS

The ultimate responsibility for setting organization-wide support standards varies. In some organizations, the head of the IT department, sometimes called the chief information officer (CIO), is responsible. The CIO may delegate the responsibility to a committee composed of users, support staff, and technical IT staff. In many organizations, the responsibility to establish and/or enforce computer product standards falls on the user support staff. To establish standards, the staff evaluates competing products. During **product evaluation**, the support staff researches and analyzes computer product features, capabilities, and suitability to meet specific user needs. In the evaluation process, they collect product information, conduct performance tests, compare competing products, make decisions or recommendations, and communicate the results of their work throughout the organization. Recommendations and decisions about which specific products to support are often made with input from end users, the user support staff, technical staff, and the organization's management.

The user support staff, with access to information resources and input from end users and others, continually evaluates new hardware and software products and upgrades of existing products. When the support staff considers a new product, they are guided by questions such as:

1. Does the product or upgrade work as advertised by the vendor?

2. Is a competing product significantly better than one currently being used?

3. Is a new product or upgrade compatible with existing hardware, network, and operating system configurations the organization has in place?

4. Is the product cost-effective to acquire and support, and will it help increase user productivity?

5. Will the product help reduce the total cost of ownership to the organization?

6. Is the product likely to become an industry standard?

7. Is it better to upgrade now or to wait for a future release?

8. Is the product stable enough (has few bugs) that it will solve more problems than it creates?

Members of the user support staff who know about end-user needs, computer products, and industry trends can research these and related questions. They can interview and observe end users, collect relevant product information, conduct product tests, and ask critical questions to identify the advantages and disadvantages of competing products. Product tests often take place under controlled conditions. It would not be cost-effective for each end user in an organization to perform product tests, because thousands of new computer products and upgrades are introduced to the market every year. End users who attempt to become knowledgeable about even a few new products could lose focus on their primary jobs and would duplicate the efforts of others.

The user support staff has several tools and information resources at its disposal to help evaluate computer products. These resources include:

- Vendor literature, marketing information, Web sites, and user manuals

- Demonstration and evaluation versions of products

- Product reviews and comparison articles in computer periodicals and on the Web

- Opinions of industry experts available in trade publications and Internet newsgroups

- Opinions of employees in their organization who may have experience with the product

Examples of some of these resources are shown in Figure 8-2. Although all are useful information resources, independent tests and reviews that provide side-by-side comparisons of several competing products are often among the most useful to evaluators.

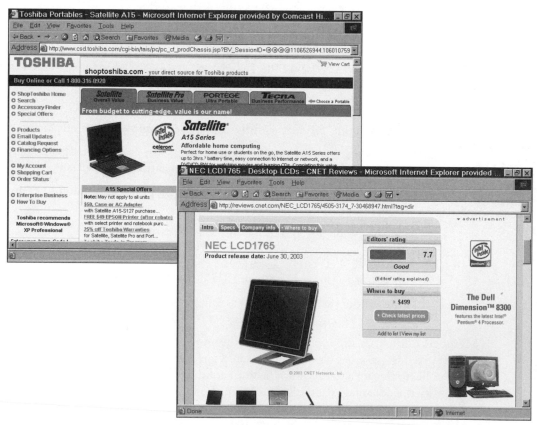

Figure 8-2   Sources of product information include vendor Web sites, product comparisons, buyer's guides, and trade publication ads

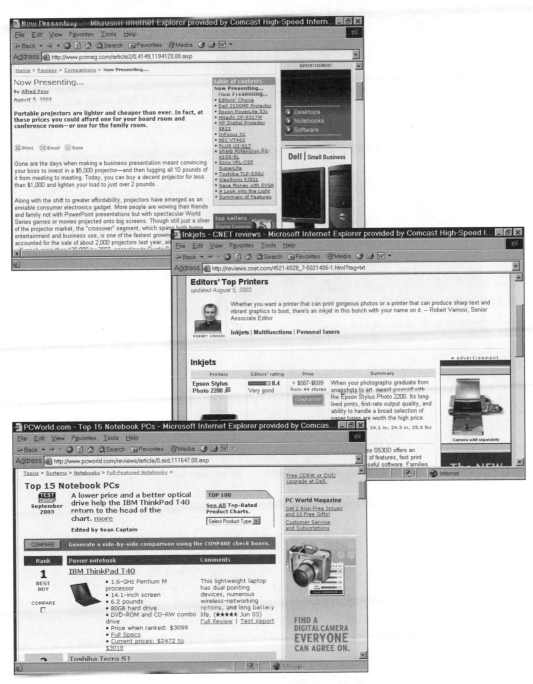

Figure 8-2   Sources of product information include vendor Web sites, product comparisons, buyer's guides and trade publication ads (continued)

Figure 8-2   Sources of product information include vendor Web sites, product comparisons, buyer's guides and trade publication ads (continued)

Several industry trade publications provide comprehensive, up-to-date product comparisons, both in print and **e-zine** (electronic magazine) format on the Web, including those listed in Table 8-1.

 For a list of popular computer trade publications, see the Open Directory Project Web site at: **dmoz.org/Business/Retail_Trade/News_and_Media**; see also **directory.google.com/Top/Business/Resources/News_and_Media/ Magazines**. For a list of e-zines targeted at the computer field, visit **www.ezine-dir.com/Computers**.

The product information examples in Table 8-1 are resources primarily within the computer industry. Alternately, many trade publications that are targeted to a specific applications area, such as accounting, manufacturing, transportation logistics, office administration, marketing, medicine, finance, law, and education, also publish articles that evaluate hardware and software products in their industries. Product comparisons in industry-specific publications are especially useful because they often address issues and concerns that are unique to each application area.

Table 8-1   Computer industry periodicals and Web sites that publish product reviews and comparisons

Publication	URL for Product Information and Reviews
Computing Review	www.computingreview.com/reviewscrx.aspx
InfoWorld	www.infoworld.com/testcenter/tst_rev_hom.html
Macworld	www.macworld.com/reviews
MaximumPC	www.maximumpc.com/ranking/rankings2.html
Network Computing	www.networkcomputing.com/departments/buyersguides.html
PC Magazine	www.pcmag.com/category2/0,4148,13,00.asp
PC World	www.pcworld.com/reviews/index/0,00.asp
Smart Computing	www.smartcomputing.com/editorial/productreview.asp?guid=xidt4kg0
Tom's Hardware Guide	www.tomshardware.com
ZDNet	reviews-zdnet.com.com

The following are examples of articles and Web pages that compare and evaluate computer products. For each, note the evaluation criteria used, compare how competing products are rated against the criteria, and look for ways the evaluators highlight the pros and cons of each product. Some articles provide numerical evaluation scores or "best buy" designations for products the evaluators prefer.

- "Top 10 CD-RW Drives" by Melissa Perenson, June 2003, rates the best CD-RW drives on PC World.com's Web site at **www.pcworld.com/reviews/article/0,aid,110332,00.asp**.

- "Top 17- to 18-inch LCD" rates the best flat panel displays on ZDNet's Web site at **reviews-zdnet.com.com/4521-6529_16-1008543-4.html?tag=txt**.

- "Notebook Buying Guide" rates notebook computers on CNET.com's Web site at **reviews.cnet.com/4520-3121_7-1016082-1.html?tag=cal**.

- "Search Engine Features Chart" is a Web page sponsored by Search Engine Showdown that compares the features of several popular Internet search engines; view this site at **www.searchengineshowdown.com/features**.

- "PDFing Cheap" by Ben Z. Gottesman rates some alternatives to Adobe Acrobat for writing files in PDF format in *PC Magazine*, August 2003; view this article at **www.pcmag.com/article2/0,4149,1190639,00.asp**.

- "Least Taxing Software?" by Mike Hogan, rates tax preparation software for 2002 federal returns in the February 2003 edition of *PC World* magazine; view this article online at **www.pcworld.com/reviews/article/0,aid,108208,00.asp**.

In addition to studying reviews in periodicals of new and competing products, support staff can frequently request or download demonstration or evaluation copies of software products. A **software evaluation copy** permits support staff to try out a product's features independently and assess its ability to meet an organization's needs. Evaluation copies are frequently advertised through the mail or on vendor Web sites, and may be available on a CD-ROM ordered via a toll free telephone number, or downloaded from a vendor's Web site if the size of the demo version is not prohibitive. Evaluation copies may have fewer features than the full commercial version, or they may operate only for a limited trial period (often 30 or 60 days), or for a limited number of launches or file-save operations.

 Another way to try out commercial software prior to purchase is to use a service that provides evaluation and demonstrations of packages that users can run on a Web server. Visit the Runaware Web site at **www.runaware.com/ list_alpha.jsp** to learn more about this approach.

Although demonstration and evaluation copies of software packages are common and freely distributed, vendors usually do not offer hardware products for evaluation. However, some vendors will provide evaluation components, or even complete systems, if a potential sale to an organization has a substantial dollar value. In these cases, support groups routinely and successfully request an evaluation copy of a hardware product they are seriously considering.

When decision makers need to decide which of several products they will select to purchase and support, they can use several tools, methods, and strategies as decision aids. These decision tools are listed in Figure 8-3 and are described in the next sections.

- Industry standard or bestselling products

- Products used by competitors

- Benchmarks

- Weighted point evaluation method

- Request for proposal (RFP)

- Acknowledged subjective criteria

Figure 8-3   Product evaluation and decision-making tools

Industry Standard or Bestselling Products

When user support staff need to choose administrative and office automation applications, they often select and recommend **industry standard products**, hardware, software, and accessories that are market leaders in sales. Many so-called standards in the computer industry are not really standards in the traditional sense. No industry-wide group has necessarily participated in and agreed to their design. Often products become standards based on sales leadership and market share. Few organizations spend very much staff time evaluating popular word processors or spreadsheets, for example, because the bestselling products usually have competitive features and perform the most frequently needed tasks. However, when an organization has specialized needs, such as software to prepare a significant volume of legal documents or software to process medical insurance claims, product evaluators often look beyond mass-market leaders. In these cases, evaluators research features available in lesser-known products that are targeted at users with specialized needs. Mass-market products often lack industry-specific features that some organizations need.

Similarly, the way that accounting software is evaluated depends on the size and scope of an organization. The evaluation process may be a simple task for a small business, because one of the mass-market accounting systems targeted at small businesses will probably meet its needs. Medium- to large-scale businesses often undertake a more extensive evaluation of accounting packages because off-the-shelf products vary considerably in how they handle situations such as multiple divisions, different geographical locations, global operations, and tax issues that smaller businesses do not encounter. Most very large businesses develop their own accounting systems or modify a commercial package to obtain the level of customization they need to meet their unique circumstances.

NOTE

In addition to applications software product evaluations, even many small businesses consider the option of outsourcing some applications. Payroll processing is a common example. The complexity and frequent changes in payroll laws and accounting standards means that small businesses may find it difficult to hire the expertise to operate and maintain an up-to-date payroll system. Service providers such as PayChex (**www.paychex.com**) offer outsource services to provide payroll processing.

Selecting industry standard hardware and software products can reduce an organization's support costs. Popular software products are more likely to be featured in trade books, third-party training courses and materials, and support service vendors. However, market-leading products do not necessarily always match the specific and perhaps unique requirements of end users. Furthermore, market leadership changes over time. A product that appears to be a safe purchase and supported decision today may become obsolete, and therefore a poor choice, within a short period. For example, during the late 1980s, WordPerfect was an obvious pick as a word processor, Lotus 1-2-3 was the leading spreadsheet package, and dBASE IV was often the database software of choice. None of these packages is the bestseller in its category today.

Before selecting applications software to recommend for organization-wide purchase and support, a support group should always get user input. Product evaluators should find out which products end users have experience with, the advantages and disadvantages of competing products for specific tasks, and whether users have preferences among products. Support groups that fail to seek user input during the selection process can make an expensive mistake if the software they select is not a good match with user needs or is too difficult to learn and use.

Products Used by Competitors

In addition to industry standard and bestselling products, support specialists who do product research and evaluation should consider products used by an organization's competitors, especially within a niche or vertical market. A **niche** or **vertical market** is one that is highly specialized, such as the automobile insurance industry, beauty salons, or beer distributors. An organization's competitors often have thoroughly researched the market and identified strategic reasons for adopting the computer products they use, even if those products are not market leaders. If the information can be obtained legally, a product evaluator should attempt to learn which products are used by competing organizations. Then the support staff can evaluate the strengths and weaknesses of computer products the competitors use. Evaluators who consider products used by the competition are not simply "copy cats"; they know that organizations in the same industry often have very similar technology needs.

Benchmarks

A **benchmark** is an objective test or measurement that is used to evaluate the speed, capacity, capabilities, or productivity of rival products. Evaluators use benchmarks to compare two or more competing products. Benchmarks are a popular way to compare hardware products, and they are also useful for software packages or even entire systems. When using the benchmark method to compare products, an evaluator begins by defining one or more criteria that are critical factors in the product selection. Examples of common benchmark criteria include system speed, storage capacity, software performance, and user productivity. Benchmarks are based on **objective evaluation criteria**, or factors used in a product selection procedure that are relatively unbiased. A neutral evaluator should be able to use objective criteria to reach the same conclusion as another evaluator, because the criteria and measurement methods are not influenced by personal opinions. The evaluator uses a controlled test environment to measure competing products on the same objective criteria, such as transaction processing speed. In the test, the evaluator attempts to control all extraneous variables that do not relate to the product being evaluated. For example, in an evaluation of software performance, the same user operates two or more competing software products on identical hardware, in identical operating environments. **Extraneous variables**, those that could bias the results of a benchmark test in one direction or the other, have been eliminated. Therefore, observed differences in test performance are most likely due to real differences in product capabilities.

An evaluator who wants to use benchmarks to compare the speed of competing printers, for example, defines a constant unit of work, such as printing 100 pages. The pages are selected to represent different examples (text and graphics, color and black-and-white, heavy and light coverage) from among those that users frequently print. Then, the evaluator runs a series of tests, using competing vendors' printers that should run at the same speed, in which the sample of 100 pages is printed. (Due to product design, performance differences are possible, even among printers that have the same print speed specifications.) As part of the test, the evaluator attempts to eliminate other variables that could affect the benchmark results. The evaluator uses the same computer system, the same operating environment, the same application software, and the same network environment. The only variable that changes from one trial to the next is the printer itself. In this controlled test environment, an evaluator can determine whether one brand of printer has a significantly faster print speed than competing printers.

An evaluator can also use benchmarks to evaluate software. As with hardware benchmarks, the evaluator defines a constant unit of work, for example, the time it takes a data entry clerk to enter and process 100 typical accounting transactions. Then the evaluator measures the amount of time a data entry operator takes to enter the same 100 transactions using competing accounting packages. Finally, the evaluator compares the benchmarked times for each package.

Benchmarks are often used to help evaluate computer products, but they are seldom the only factor considered. In the selection of a printer, accounting software, or any other product, factors other than speed should also be considered, as you'll see in the next section.

In addition to evaluator-defined benchmarks in product evaluations, vendors and users can use several common industry standard benchmarks to evaluate their products against the competition. To learn more about benchmarks, see an article on the Byte.com Web site at **www.byte.com/bmark/bmark.htm**.

Companies that provide hardware and software benchmarks include:

- Business Applications Performance Corporation (BAPCO) at **www.bapco.com** (click **Products**)

- PassMark Software at **www.passmark.com**

- Standard Performance Evaluation Corporation (SPEC) at **www.specbench.org**

- VeriTest at **www.etestinglabs.com/benchmarks/bwinstone/ bwinstone.asp**

Benchmark comparisons are popular because they are designed to use objective criteria and because they try to eliminate vendor or user bias in the evaluation of a hardware or software product.

Weighted Point Evaluation Method

Articles in computer periodicals sometimes use a weighted point evaluation method, a strategy that support staff can use in their own evaluation projects. The **weighted point evaluation method** is a product comparison method that uses several evaluation criteria of predetermined importance to grade competing products and arrive at a numerical score as a basis for selection. This method is also called the Kepner-Tregoe method, after two authors who described some rational methods that managers can use to help make decisions. As with benchmarks, the goal of the weighted point method is to make the evaluation and selection process as objective as possible. It attempts to treat competing products equally, to eliminate possible favoritism or bias among evaluators, and to force evaluators to specify in advance the important factors in the evaluation of competing products. Because weighted point evaluation is an objective procedure that requires the use of well-defined criteria, public agencies are often required to use this method or a variant of it.

 For more information about this method and an example of a weighted point evaluation of software options, see the article "Guide to Selecting a Software and Services Partner" at Software Magazine's Web site, **www.softwaremag. com/L.cfm?Doc=archive/2000aug/Selecting-a-Partner.html**.

Next, you will learn the mechanics of the weighted point evaluation process. You can apply this method equally well to selecting a 1000-user computer network or to selecting a home personal computer. To perform a weighted point evaluation, evaluators follow these steps:

1. Decide on the evaluation criteria.

2. Determine the importance of each criterion.

3. Rate each competing product against all the evaluation criteria.

4. If more than one evaluator rates products, compute the average rating for each product for each criterion.

5. Weight the product ratings for each criterion by the importance of the criterion.

6. Compute the total rating for each product.

7. Compare product ratings.

The evaluation criteria selected in the weighted point method are based on several important factors, including:

- The specific type of hardware or software product to be evaluated

- The needs of end users

- Support issues

- Cost

Evaluation articles in periodicals are an excellent source of ideas for criteria to use to evaluate specific products. Table 8-2 provides some examples of criteria in several categories.

Table 8-2   Examples of criteria used in the weighted point evaluation method

Category	Examples of Criteria
Hardware or software	• Processing or access speed • Storage capacity • Capabilities and features • Transaction volumes • Compatibility with existing systems • Upgradeability (scalability)

Table 8-2 Examples of criteria used in the weighted point evaluation method (continued)

Category	Examples of Criteria
End-user needs	• Ease of learning • Ease of use • Mandatory features (must have) • Desirable features (nice to have)
Support availability	• Technical support services • Installation assistance • Training • Documentation • Troubleshooting • Maintenance and repair
Cost	• Total cost of ownership (see Chapter 1)

8

 To learn about the extensive evaluation criteria used by the Information Technology Planning Board at UCLA, visit **www.itpb.ucla.edu/Documents/ 2001/Jan/Matrix-ComputerPrinterSrvcsRFP.htm**.

Consider the following example of a simple weighted point evaluation method. Suppose an organization wants three evaluators in the user support group to rate two computer systems for purchase. The evaluators first decide on the comparison criteria to use, as illustrated in Table 8-3. They also agree on the relative importance of each criterion. The relative importance of each criterion is usually based on its significance to the organization, the end users, and the support group. For example, a relatively unimportant criterion might receive a weight of 5–10%. The sum of the criteria weights should total 100%.

Table 8-3 Criteria and weights for evaluating two computers

Criterion	Criterion's Importance (Weight)	System X Evaluation	System Y Evaluation
Hardware configuration	25%		
Software bundled	35%		
Vendor reputation	10%		
Vendor support	30%		
TOTALS	**100%**		

The evaluators then rate the capabilities of the proposed products and assign points, usually between 1 and 100, to each product on each criterion. For example, an evaluator could learn from a survey of a vendor's current clients that the vendor is very well regarded and might assign the vendor a score of 95 out of 100 on the *vendor reputation* criterion. The evaluators work independently to rate each system.

Next, the three evaluators consolidate their results. They could average the points earned for each criterion. Or, the evaluators might discuss their preliminary ratings to identify and negotiate any large discrepancies and arrive at a consensus rating. For example, if one evaluator rated the System X *hardware configuration* at 60 and the other evaluators rated it at 100, the three evaluators should discuss the discrepancy to determine why there was such a significant difference and to arrive at a mutually acceptable rating of perhaps 80 out of 100. Small discrepancies of a few points are ignored. In this example, after discussion, the evaluators agreed that the *hardware configuration* for System X was worth 90 points (out of 100), and the competing System Y was worth only 70, as shown in Table 8-4.

Table 8-4   Weighted point evaluation method with points assigned to criteria

Criterion	Criterion's Importance (Weight)	System X Evaluation	System Y Evaluation
Hardware configuration	25%	90	70
Software bundled	35%	70	70
Vendor reputation	10%	50	95
Vendor support	30%	60	90
TOTALS	100%		

In the next step, the number of points the evaluators assigned to each system is multiplied by the weight of each selection criterion. The resulting points for each system are then summed to arrive at a total number of points, as Table 8-5 shows. The system with the larger number of total points is the preferable system.

Table 8-5   Weighted point method example with evaluation points

Criterion	Criterion's Importance (Weight)	System X Evaluation	System Y Evaluation
Hardware configuration	25%	90 x 25% = 22.5	70 x 25% = 17.5
Software bundled	35%	70 x 35% = 24.5	70 x 35% = 24.5
Vender reputation	10%	50 x 10% = 5.0	95 x 10% = 9.5
Vendor support	30%	60 x 30% = 18.0	90 x 30% = 27.0
TOTALS	100%	70.0/100	78.5/100

In this example, System Y's higher scores on *vendor reputation* and *vendor support* offset its lower score on *hardware configuration*. The weighted point method can be used to evaluate more than two products, and it can accommodate as many criteria as evaluators think are important. For simple product evaluations, a product evaluation worksheet can be prepared using a spreadsheet program.

Sky Hunter Partners distribute DecideRight, a software package that implements the weighted point evaluation system. To download a demonstration version of the package, visit PC World's Web site at **www.pcworld.com/downloads/file_description/0,fid,3971,00.asp**.

An advantage of the weighted point evaluation method is that it forces evaluators to address two important questions early in the evaluation process: (1) What criteria are important to us in the product purchase decision or recommendation? (2) How important to us is each criterion relative to other criteria? Some argue that this method applies numeric values to criteria where the points have little meaning. However, the weighted point method forces evaluators to ask important questions when they might be tempted to use more subjective criteria. It relies on measurable criteria in place of subjective beliefs. Sometimes the objective results of a weighted point method conflict with an evaluator's subjective feelings. If a product evaluator finishes the process and receives the "wrong" result according to his or her "gut" feelings, the evaluator may be able to reexamine the criteria and the weights and ask why he or she got those results. Sometimes it's the "gut" that is wrong.

Request for Proposal (RFP)

A **request for proposal (RFP)** is a product selection tool or competitive bidding procedure that uses objective criteria to choose among products proposed by competing vendors. By law, many public agencies are required to use an objective evaluation process, such as a bidding process or a request for proposal procedure. Because the RFP process is objective, many businesses also use RFPs or a similar procedure to aid in making purchase decisions. For example, an organization may issue an RFP that invites competing vendors to submit product and price proposals for a particular computer system. Employees must then select products from vendors who win the bidding competition or who submit the most competitive response to the RFP. As a result of an RFP process, an organization may designate the successful bidder as the sole authorized vendor for computer products covered in the RFP.

To complete the RFP process, an organization follows these eight primary steps:

1. Conduct a user needs analysis (discussed in Chapter 9).

2. Develop a purchase specification for the equipment or software, based on the needs analysis, to describe the technical characteristics and features of the hardware or software it wants to acquire.

3. Define the decision criteria and the importance of each criterion. Many criteria are based on mandatory or desirable product features; other criteria include technical support, vendor stability, product costs, and compatibility with existing systems.

4. Write the RFP document, which describes the user requirements, bidding procedure, and decision criteria.

5. Send the RFP document to prospective vendors (some organizations maintain a list of vendors who are prescreened to meet acceptable financial stability criteria).

6. Receive written proposals from interested vendors that address how their products meet or exceed the user requirements and include a bid price at which each vendor can supply the products or services.

7. Analyze the responses to the RFP and have the user support staff evaluate them, often using weighted point evaluation methods.

8. Select a vendor and award the purchase contract.

To learn more about the RFP process, see the RFP Handbook for North Carolina State University at **www.fis.ncsu.edu/materialsmgmt/purchasing/ proposal.htm**. St. Charles County in Missouri is an example of a government agency that uses an RFP for personal computer equipment for county employee use; read the county's bid specifications at **www.win.org/ county/bids/misequip.htm**. Or, read an RFP to design and develop a Web site for the city of Shoreline, Washington, at **www.mrsc.org/RFPs/S55WebRFP. pdf** (requires Adobe Reader). Note the evaluation criteria and weights the city of Shoreline uses to select the successful vendor.

The RFP process is a common and objective decision-making tool. Because RFPs are an involved process that includes several lengthy steps and considerable staff time, they are used primarily for purchases of significant dollar value, rather than for purchases of off-the-shelf products.

Acknowledged Subjective Criteria

The evaluation tools and methods just described are based primarily on objective criteria, where a neutral observer should be able to reach the same conclusion as an evaluator. Either a product performs as well on a benchmark comparison as another product or it doesn't. Although product evaluators base many hardware and software purchase decisions on objective criteria, they sometimes use criteria that are known to be subjective. **Subjective evaluation criteria** are factors used in a product selection procedure that are not directly related to the fit between a product's features and a user's needs. Subjective factors include personal relationships with vendors, convenience, personal preferences, and reliance on traditional or historical purchasing channels. (A comment such as, "We've always bought network equipment from this vendor" is a good indicator that subjective criteria are in use.) Subjective criteria are neither measurable nor repeatable from one evaluator to another, and two evaluators may well disagree on the result.

There may be legitimate reasons to base a purchase decision on a personal relationship between an organization and a vendor: An organization and its supplier may have a lengthy business or personal relationship or a partnership agreement that overrides all other evaluation criteria. Occasionally an organization may refuse to consider a product from a particular vendor because its staff has a low regard for the vendor's product reputation, business ethics, or client service standards. When an organization has a special relationship with a vendor based on prior experience, reputation, location, or a personal contact, other factors, including price, are often irrelevant.

Large organizations, both public and privately held, often use an objective evaluation or selection procedure for computer products; smaller organizations often use more subjective criteria. Support specialists who evaluate and select computer products use objective or subjective methods, depending on their employer's guidelines. However, the purpose of all product evaluation and selection strategies is to arrive at the best product choice for each user. Once an organization has researched and selected products and vendors, the next step often is to develop product support standards.

Product Support Standards

As you learned in the first part of this chapter, organizations often control support costs by establishing computer product standards to limit the number of hardware and software options users can choose. Although the decision to adopt product support standards may sound like a "one-size-fits-all" approach, it doesn't have to be. Within the standards adopted by an organization, options and alternatives are often permitted. Most organizations try to strike a reasonable balance between the two extremes of "Select only this product" and "Select anything you want."

Honolulu Community College in Honolulu, Hawaii, is a comprehensive community college that has adopted computer product standards and support policies to minimize the drain on college resources for providing user support to its faculty, staff, and students. Figure 8-4 contains several excerpts from the college's policy that describes the limits it places on hardware and software acquisitions. This policy illustrates a need many organizations recognize: the need to adopt product support standards.

Honolulu Community College's list of supported products includes both PCs and Macintosh computers. The list of approved products specifies selected software packages in several categories. Honolulu Community College's lists of recommended and supported hardware and software products are described in this chapter's CloseUp.

Not every organization spends the time to research and evaluate products and develop standards as described in this chapter. However, larger organizations with a substantial investment in computer technology tend to expend the staff resources to evaluate products and set purchase standards because the potential for waste is large. Based on the results of product research and evaluation, user support specialists can prepare lists of approved and supported computer products. Armed with a list of approved products, they can more easily answer questions such as, "What kind of computer should an employee buy?" and "Is this printer model compatible with the organization's computer systems?"

Honolulu Community College (HCC)
Policy on Desktop Computer Technology

The intention of this policy is to provide a standard base-line hardware and software configuration for all HCC campus desktop computers. The Supported Products List will include Workstations, Operating Systems and Application Software for use by faculty, staff, classrooms, and student labs. The current Supported Products List will include hardware and software specifications for both PC/Intel based computers and Macintosh computers.

The Supported Products List will serve to set standards for the campus community for desktop hardware and software as well as server hardware and network operating systems. Members of the campus community will then follow the published standards or understand that they may not receive support from HCC Technical Desktop Support to solve problems they encounter using non-standard hardware and/or software.

All new purchases of computers and desktop workstations must conform to the current Supported Products List. Specifications will be for minimum hardware configuration.

The benefits of this policy are:
- Simplify the hardware acquisition and upgrade process
- Provide a network safe software image for all computer users
- Improve support services by promoting migration to selected technologies and concentrating on these limited products in greater depth
- Plan effectively for introducing new products and phasing out older products
- Develop precise goals and objectives for the Technical Desktop Support office to optimize staff training and development in order to offer reliable, high quality services
- Encourage a more consistent environment through the use of a standard suite of appropriate technologies

If a product is on the HCC Supported Products List, faculty and staff can get assistance with problems related to the use of those products. If a product is not on the list, those who need assistance will receive consultation as resources allow.

The Desktop support policy is accompanied by the following list of responsibilities:

Technical Desktop Support (TDS) Responsibilities with Regards to Providing Support for Supported Products
Maintain expertise for supported products
- Provide or facilitate support
- Work with the Information Technology Center to coordinate support, training and documentation for the supported product
- When appropriate and cost effective, recommend site or volume licensing for supported products

TDS Responsibilities in Providing Assistance with Unsupported Products
- Limited support is available

Figure 8-4   Computer product support policies at Honolulu Community College

Honolulu Community College
Information Technology Center (ITC)
Excerpts from Honolulu Community College's
Product Support List (for current version, see
www.hcc.hawaii.edu/itc/recommend)

**ITC Microcomputer Recommendation:
June–September 2003**

The following recommendations will meet the needs of Honolulu Community College's faculty and staff for email, wordprocessing, spreadsheet and database functions. The systems listed are ITC minimum level recommendations. ITC recommends purchasing the systems listed below or systems that exceed these specifications.

IBM Compatible

Dell OptiPlex™ GX260, Small Mini-Tower
- Intel Pentium 4 Processor 1.80 GHz
- 256 MB RAM
- 40 GB Hard Drive
- CD-ROM drive
- 10/100 Mbps Ethernet Connection
- Windows 2000 Professional
- 3-year On-site Warranty
- Surge Protector

Macintosh OS X Systems

Power Mac G4
- GHz G4 processor
- 256 MB RAM
- 40 GB hard drive
- CD-ROM drive
- 10/100 Mbps Ethernet Connection
- Mac OS 10.2
- Applecare (3-year warranty)
- Surge Protector

Printing

ITC recommends the internal JetDirect Ethernet adapter cards with the Hewlett Packard LaserJet series printers with Adobe PostScript. Administrative applications requiring printing have also been tested by UH with the HP 4000N printer with an emulated PostScript. Since the same PostScript is used in HP's other laser printers, we

8

can recommend the HP 2100TN, 4050N, 5000N, and 8000N or equivalent printers for administrative use as well. Make sure an "N" is in the printer model number. Anyone purchasing other printers must take full responsibility for testing all applications for themselves and resolving any incompatibilities with the vendor on their own behalf.

Recommended Software List

Microcomputer Operating Systems and Applications

	Macintosh Computers		MS Windows Based Computers	
Category	Product	Versions Supported	Product	Versions Supported
Operating System	Mac OS	8.x, 9.x, 10.2.x*	Windows	9X, 2000 Pro, XP Pro*
Word Processing	Word	98, 2001, X/10*	Word	97, 2000, XP
Spreadsheets	Excel	98, 2001, X/10*	Excel	97, 2000, XP
Presentation Packages	PowerPoint	98, 2001, X/10*	PowerPoint	97, 2000, XP
Database Management			Access	97, 2000, XP
Virus Protection	McAfee Virex	6.x, 7.x*	McAfee VirusScan	4.5
Web Browser	Internet Explorer, Mozilla, Netscape Navigator	5.x, 1.3, 4.7x	Internet Explorer, Mozilla, Netscape Navigator	5.x, 1.34.7x
FTP Client	MacSFTP	1.x	SSH Secure File Transfer Client	3.x
E-Mail Client	Mozilla Mail, Netscape Messenger	1.3, 4.7	Mozilla Mail, Netscape Messenger	1.3, 4.7
Disk Utilities	Norton Utilities		ScanDisk	
Document Browser	Acrobat Reader	5.x	Acrobat Reader	5.x

How Organizations Develop Computer Product and Support Standards

An organization's computer product and support standards can arise from a variety of sources. In some organizations, product standards evolve over time as a "computer culture" develops. For example, because the early adopters of technology in an organization may have been predominantly Macintosh users, the organization might adopt a standard that primarily

Macintosh systems are supported. Alternately, organizations that adopted WordPerfect as their preferred word processor during the 1980s may be reluctant to change to a different one, even though WordPerfect is no longer the most popular word-processing product sold today.

Whereas organizational culture and traditions are one source of product standards, some organizations assign the task of developing and maintaining standards to the user support group or to a product standards committee. A **product standards committee** is a group of support specialists, end users, technical support staff, and managers whose task is to define the current product support standards, maintain the list, and coordinate their use in the organization. Once established, standards must be effective; that is, they must help users get their work done. They must be evenly administered and enforced. If users have to work around the standards to get the equipment, software, and services they need to do their jobs, that indicates the organization's computer standards are ineffective. Some organizations recognize that a "one-size-fits-all" standard is counterproductive in special situations. The standards are generally enforced, but a caveat may be added: "Standard products will be purchased and supported, *unless a compelling business reason requires an exception to the standard.*"

NOTE   Product and support standards committees usually define software standards before they recommend hardware standards. If a standards committee defines a hardware standard first, it may discover later that one or more software packages it wants to select as standard will not run on the hardware standard it defined earlier. Software products determine the minimum hardware requirements in most cases, not vice versa.

A change in standards for supported computer products is often an emotional time for workers who are comfortable with the old standards. Worker resistance to changes in standards frequently occurs in statements such as: "This technology has worked fine for many years, why change it now?" Whenever changes in standards are contemplated, new products should be thoroughly tested. The need for a change in standards should be discussed with workers and their feedback should be sought on how new hardware and software products meet, or fail to meet, worker needs. Changes in product standards tend to be smoother when workers are consulted and included in the decision process.

The same committee that sets standards for supported computer products, or a different committee, may also address organizational standards in another area: acceptable computer use guidelines. **Acceptable use guidelines** are often adopted by an organization and publicized among employees to communicate policies about what end users are permitted and not permitted to do with their computer systems at school or at work. These use guidelines often describe how end users are permitted to use their computers, what users are not allowed to do, and the consequences or penalties for unauthorized or illegal use. The guidelines may describe both activities that are illegal according to federal or state law (such as accessing confidential information) or violations of licenses and agreements (such as copying commercial software), and activities that are prohibited by organizational policy (such as use of organizational e-mail for personal messages).

For an example of "Acceptable Use of Computing Resources" guidelines at the University of Oregon in Eugene, see the school's Web page at **cc.uoregon.edu/policy/index.html**.

How Organizations Implement Product and Support Standards

In many organizations, two forces often influence the adoption and implementation of computer product and support standards. One influence is an organization's existing inventory of hardware and software products. Unless it is very small or has a very large computer budget, an organization could not discard its entire investment in computer systems and adopt a new standard overnight. When they define support standards, product support groups often take into account the predominant hardware, software, and network architectures that currently exist in the organization. Support for obsolete computer products may be phased out over time, with ample notice to users, to minimize inconvenience. To deviate substantially from what employees currently use can result in a large, one-time expense to an organization as employees convert to equipment or software that meets a new standard.

A second force that drives changes in product and service standards is the continual introduction of new products, services, and product upgrades. An important task of the user support group is to learn about and evaluate new products that have the potential to replace existing product standards. The decision to modify and update existing product support standards is usually based on criteria such as the following:

- New products offer technical improvements over current products.

- New products have features with the potential to improve employee productivity.

- Employee preferences in products have changed over time.

- New products and services are available at a lower cost than existing products, which makes them more attractive financially.

- New products may be compatible with changes in industry standards, unlike older products.

- New products have become more popular than the products they replace.

However, the decision to replace an existing product or service standard is often difficult to make because organizations often have a sizable investment in the existing standard. Similarly, employees may have invested the time to learn how to use existing products and may be reluctant to change because the conversion means retraining and usually reduced productivity until they learn the new product. For these reasons, organizations that want to move to new standards may decide to phase in the new product standards over time. A transition period occurs when both old and new products are permitted and supported under the standards policy. Of course, transition periods strain the support staff, because they must provide support for both old and new products. During the transition period, increased support costs are often incurred, as support and maintenance of existing hardware, software, and network products continue for some users, while other users convert to and are trained in the use of new products.

For example, when the Windows XP operating system first became widely available in 2001, many organizations were reluctant to convert from Windows 98/Me/2000 to Windows XP. They were not convinced that the advantages of the new Windows XP operating system were worth the conversion costs, and they had a substantial existing investment in earlier Windows software and peripherals. Consequently, some organizations have stayed with the Windows 98/Me/2000 operating system standard. Other organizations included both earlier Windows versions and Windows XP as standards during an extended transition period, because they had an inventory of applications software, computers, and peripheral hardware that ran on earlier versions. Many users found their existing hardware and software inventory would not operate correctly under Windows XP, or required upgraded drivers and new software versions. However, as versions of new software applications that specifically require Windows XP come on the market, more organizations will feel pressure from their employees to convert to it, and to purchase new hardware and software when necessary. Reluctance to convert to new industry standards explains why some organizations are still running MS-DOS and Windows 3.1 applications.

 To test a PC for Windows XP readiness, use PC Pitstop's readiness evaluator at **www.pcpitstop.com/xpready/xptests.asp**, or use Microsoft's compatibility checker at **www.microsoft.com/windowsxp/home/howtobuy/upgrading/ checkcompat.asp**.

Product and support standards will continue to change in the future. In the mid–2000s, organizations face decisions about when to adopt, convert to, and support new peripheral devices based on the Universal Serial Bus (USB), rewritable CDs and digital video discs (DVDs), and voice recognition input technology. Users with networks are evaluating whether to adopt a wireless (Wi-Fi) network standard. Every decision to modify an existing technology standard or adopt a new one requires analysis and evaluation of products and services by the user support group. It also triggers potential support cost increases for installation, upgrades, training, documentation, troubleshooting, and help desk services.

CHAPTER SUMMARY

❑ During the 1980s, organizations with a substantial investment in desktop computer technology recognized the need to evaluate computer products and set purchase and support standards. Because few widely recognized industry standards existed, incompatible hardware and software increased the cost of computer technology and reduced productivity among users. Today, organizations lower their support services costs by restricting purchases to a limited list of approved products.

❑ User support employees spend time evaluating computer products and services so they can recommend to users and departments in an organization what purchases will and will not meet their needs. Support employees often help an organization set standards for computer hardware and software products. Standard products help increase the compatibility among various hardware and software components and help to reduce the resources (costs) required to support end-user computer systems.

❑ Support staff members use a variety of information resources to evaluate hardware and software products, including vendor literature, Web sites and user manuals, product demonstration and evaluation versions of software, product reviews and comparison articles in computer periodicals, and opinions of organization or industry experts.

❑ Several decision aids can help support specialists make selection decisions among competing products and services. These aids include industry standard or bestselling products, analysis of products used by competitors, product benchmarks, the weighted point evaluation method, the request for proposal (RFP) procedure, and acknowledged subjective criteria.

❑ Many organizations adopt industry standard and bestselling products. These products are in widespread use and make the selection decision look easy. However, simply because a product is a bestseller does not mean that it is the best fit with a user's unique needs. A less popular product may have features not found in the bestsellers that are actually a better match with a particular user's needs.

❑ Benchmarks are an objective way to compare two or more products by observing them perform a standard, predefined task or workload. The weighted point evaluation method forces a product evaluator to make a list of important criteria and assign a weight to each criterion that reflects its importance. Competing products are evaluated against the criteria, and the product that best matches the criteria is selected. Common criteria include product features, ease of learning, ease of use, compatibility with existing products, availability of technical support, and total cost of ownership.

❑ Hardware and software standards are important to organizations because standards help control user support costs. Whereas some support standards are based on organizational culture and tradition, many standards are the result of systematic analysis and evaluation of new products. The decision to adopt or modify a standard is often made by a group or committee with representatives from end users, user support, technical support, and management. Implementation of new standards is often influenced by the investment in existing hardware and software and the potential loss of employee productivity during the conversion to the new products.

❑ Organizations also define standard, acceptable use guidelines for their users, which describe activities end users are permitted and not permitted to do with computer systems in an educational or business environment.

KEY TERMS

acceptable use guidelines — Standards adopted by an organization and publicized among employees to communicate policies about activities that end users are permitted and not permitted to do with their computer systems.

benchmark — An objective test or measurement used to evaluate the speed, capacity, capabilities, or productivity of rival products.

extraneous variables — Factors that could bias the results of an objective benchmark test; product evaluators try to eliminate these factors to isolate and measure the performance of the product under evaluation.

e-zine — An electronic magazine organized like a print publication, but distributed via a Web site or e-mail; e-zines (or Webzines) aimed at the computer industry often display product reviews and comparisons.

industry standard products — Hardware, software, and accessories that are market leaders in sales; standards in the computer industry often are not standards in the traditional sense (no industry-wide group participated in their design); standards are frequently based on sales and market share.

niche (vertical) market — A market for applications software that is highly specialized for a specific industry (such as the automobile insurance industry); niche software contains features that would not necessarily be useful in other industries; compare to mass market software.

objective evaluation criteria — Factors used in a product selection procedure that are relatively unbiased; a neutral observer should be able to use objective criteria to reach the same conclusion as an evaluator.

product evaluation — A process of researching and analyzing computer product features, capabilities, and suitability to meet specific user needs.

product standards — Lists of hardware, operating system, network, and applications software products that have been selected to meet the needs of users in an organization; standards are often enforced to reduce the cost of acquiring and supporting computer systems.

product standards committee — A group of user support specialists, end users, technical support staff, and managers who develop and maintain a list of organization-wide standard products and services; these products are then recommended for purchase by employees and are supported by the user support staff.

request for proposal (RFP) — A product selection or competitive bidding procedure that uses objective criteria to choose among products proposed by competing vendors; often used as the basis for awarding a contract to provide computer products.

software evaluation copy — Limited, trial copies of software products that permit users and support staff to try out features independently and assess a product's ability to meet user needs.

subjective evaluation criteria — Factors used in a product selection procedure that are not directly related to the fit between a product's features and a user's needs; subjective factors include personal relationships with vendors, convenience, personal preferences, and reliance on traditional or historical purchasing channels.

weighted point evaluation method — A product comparison method that uses several evaluation criteria of predetermined importance to rate competing products and arrive at a numerical score as a basis for selection; also called the Kepner-Tregoe method.

8

CHECK YOUR UNDERSTANDING

1. True or False? By the early 1980s, hardware and software for personal computers were standardized in most organizations.

2. True or False? The larger the number of incompatible software packages an organization owns, the greater the cost to train and retrain employees.

3. _____ are an attempt to strike a reasonable balance between "select only this product" and "buy anything you want."

4. True or False? In order to avoid bias, product evaluation and selection decisions are usually made by user support staff working independently of other employees.

5. _____ adopted by an organization often describe how end users are permitted to use their computers, what users are not allowed to do, and the consequences or penalties for unauthorized or illegal use.

6. _____ copies of new software packages may have limited features or operate for a limited trial period, and are used to evaluate products.

7. True or False? Industry standard computer products are those selected by a panel of industry experts for use in most organizations.

8. True or False? As a general rule, dominance in the software industry does not change over time; the bestselling products in the early 1980s are still the bestselling products today.

9. A(n) _____ is an objective test or measurement used to evaluate the speed, capacity, capabilities, or productivity of competing computer products.

10. Which of the following product evaluation methods uses several criteria of predefined importance to arrive at a numerical score for each competing product?

    a. industry standard method

    b. benchmark method

    c. subjective criteria method

    d. weighted point method

11. A(n) _____ is a purchasing procedure that invites competing product vendors to submit product and price proposals for a system a user needs.

12. When support staff select general office productivity software such as word processors or spreadsheets, they often use which of the following decision strategies?

    a. weighted point evaluations

    b. industry standard products

    c. request for proposals

    d. benchmarks

13. Which of the following letter sequences represents the order of steps in the request for proposal process: (a) send RFP to vendors, (b) develop product specifications, (c) evaluate RFP responses against criteria, (d) define selection criteria

    a. a – b – c – d

    b. b – d – a – c

    c. d – a – c – b

    d. a – d – b – c

14. When selecting among competing computer products, _____ are selection criteria that are neither measurable nor repeatable.

15. True or False? A benchmark test of competing products is designed to use objective evaluation criteria instead of an evaluator's personal opinions.

16. Computer product standards are often defined by which of the following?

    a. an organization's computer culture

    b. early adopters of technology

    c. a product standards committee

    d. any of these

8

DISCUSSION QUESTIONS

1. Describe a product standard issue or concern you think will confront organizations (perhaps one where you work or attend school) during the next 12 months. How will the issue impact end users? How will the issue impact user support staff?

2. Based on your personal experience, what is your position on monopolies in the software industry and their impact on end users? Is it preferable to have one vendor who has a substantial monopoly in a specific software product, or is it preferable to have several competing, incompatible products? Why?

3. How would you design a benchmark test to evaluate competing brands of modems?

4. What is the role of end users when an organization selects new hardware and software products and updates its list of supported products? Describe some strategies for overcoming user resistance to changes in standards.

HANDS-ON PROJECTS

Project 8-1

Investigate product comparison information. Locate a magazine or Web site that contains one or more articles that present a side-by-side comparison of two or more products. Evaluate the product comparison by considering the questions listed below. Write a summary of your findings.

- ❑ What criteria are used to compare the products?
- ❑ What additional criteria could have been used?
- ❑ What evaluation method was used to do the product comparisons?
- ❑ Did the method(s) produce an objective or subjective result?
- ❑ Do you agree with the result? Why or why not?

Project 8-2

Compare computer product support standards. Locate the computer product support standards for your workplace or school, or use the Internet to locate computer product support standards for an organization. Write a short comparison between those you find and those in effect at Honolulu Community College described in this chapter.

Project 8-3

Try a benchmark utility program. Several benchmark utility programs are available on the Internet, including the ones listed below. Download one of these utilities and run it on one or more different systems to which you have access. Compare your results with those obtained by others. Write a brief summary of your findings.

- ❑ BYTEmark at **www.byte.com/bmark/bmark.htm**
  BYTEmark, developed by Byte Magazine, is a series of 10 tests that evaluate the speed of a computer system. Documentation at the Web site describes the tests.

- ❑ System Analyser at **www.sysanalyser.com**
  System Analyser, developed by Hans Niekus, is a DOS system information utility similar to the MSD utility distributed as part of DOS, but it measures the speed of a system's CPU, hard drive, and other components.

- ❑ Dacris XMark 7.0 at **www.dacris.com/bmarknet**
  XMark, developed by Dacris Software, is an extensive test and evaluation utility. The download version is limited to a 14-day trial.

Project 8-4

Identify industry standard products. Choose a category of computer products from among the following: hardware, peripherals, operating systems, applications software, and local area networks. Make a list of at least two computer products you think fit the description "industry standard" in the category you selected. Compare your list with the list of a team of three classmates or coworkers. Do your team members agree or disagree about the industry standards? Write a short paper that lists the agreed-on standards, products over which there are disagreements, and your explanation of the reasons for any disagreements.

Project 8-5

Compare evaluation criteria for Internet browsers. Find two Internet users, one who uses Netscape Navigator as a Web browser and the other who uses Microsoft Internet Explorer. Ask them why they prefer their browser choice in comparison with the other. What criteria do they use? Are they subjective or objective criteria? How do their evaluations compare with your own choice? Write a summary of your findings.

8

Project 8-6

Plan a product standards committee meeting. Suppose that you are the leader of a product standards committee whose assignment is to develop a product standard for your organization. Write an agenda for the first committee meeting that lists the highest priority tasks the committee should undertake. (*Hint:* Think about the information the committee will need, the decisions it will need to make, and what the end result will look like.)

Project 8-7

Develop a weighted point evaluation worksheet model. Use spreadsheet software to develop a worksheet that product evaluators can use for the weighted point evaluation method. Set up columns and formulas that will make the worksheet easy to use. To test your worksheet, enter the data from the example in this chapter. Design your worksheet to be as general as possible to make it simple to add more products or more evaluation criteria. Save and print your worksheet.

Project 8-8

Interview a product standards committee participant. Interview a support specialist or other member of a product standards committee in your school or work organization. Learn about the process the committee uses to set and maintain product and service standards. How does the committee ensure that it gets end-user input? Also ask about difficult decisions to include or exclude products that the committee had to address the last time it updated the product standards. Write a short summary of what you learned from the interview.

Project 8-9

Evaluate an acceptable use policy. Find out whether the organization where you attend school or work has an acceptable computer use policy for employees or students. Summarize the activities that are permitted and those that are not permitted. Note which activities are illegal and which are not permitted according to organizational policy. Compare your organization's computer use policy with the one in effect at the University of Oregon referenced in the chapter. Describe the similarities and differences.

CASE PROJECTS

1. File Splitter Utility Evaluation at Les Deux Vaches

You are a user support specialist at Les Deux Vaches, an organization that publishes a trade publication for the dairy industry. Several employees have approached you about a problem with which they want help. Each of the employees has a home computer with a modem connection to the Internet. They occasionally need to download Internet files on their home system, but find that the download speeds, even with a 56K modem, are very slow, especially for large files. Because Les Deux Vaches has a fast T1 link to the Internet, file download speeds are much faster on the computers at work. The company has a policy that permits the use of the company's Internet connection for personal file downloads, as long as they are done on the employee's time after work or during lunch or a break. The problem is that downloaded files are often too large to fit on a 3.5″ floppy disk. So after a file is downloaded at work, how does an employee get it transferred onto his or her home computer? The employees want to know if a utility program is available that would permit them to split a large file, such as a 4 MB file, into three pieces that could then be copied onto 1.4 MB 3.5″ floppy disks that they could take home and install on their home computer.

Investigate some file splitter utility programs that are available and make a recommendation to the employees about which program to use. Complete the following tasks:

1. Develop evaluation criteria for a file splitter utility.

2. Select two or three of the utilities you locate with a search engine or from the list of file splitter utilities on the Moochers Web site at **www.moochers.com/index. html?w95split.html**. Download and install the utilities on a computer to which you have access.

3. Read the documentation and try the features of each program you downloaded.

4. Create an evaluation criteria check list for a file splitter utility. Develop as complete a list of criteria as you can, but keep in mind the problem the employees want you to help them solve. You can also consider any software support or other issues you think are relevant.

5. Evaluate each of the programs you downloaded in terms of the criteria you established.

6. Write a summary report about the file splitter utilities you evaluated and your recommendation about which utility you would suggest the employees at Les Deux Vaches use.

2. Evaluate Online User Satisfaction Survey Web Services

The supervisor of the help desk where you work has asked for your help with a small user satisfaction survey project. The supervisor wants to get some experience with online user satisfaction surveys as a way to measure client satisfaction with help desk services. Your task is to evaluate the following two Web services that facilitate collecting survey information:

❑ SurveyMonkey at **www.surveymonkey.com**

❑ CreateSurvey at **www.createsurvey.com**

Each site requires a valid e-mail address to register, but offers a free service as an alternate to its fee-based services. Limit your evaluation to the free services.

1. Develop some evaluation criteria for an online user satisfaction survey. (You may want to brainstorm some criteria with colleagues.)

2. Read the documentation and view the demo survey to get experience with the features each service offers.

3. Create an evaluation criteria check list for an online survey tool. Develop as complete a list of criteria as you can, but keep in mind the problem your supervisor wants you to help solve. You can also add to your check list any technical support or other issues you think are relevant.

4. Evaluate the two services in terms of the criteria you established.

5. Write a summary report about the survey tools you evaluated. Include your recommendation about which service you would recommend to your supervisor.

3. Invoicing Software for Columbia Sand & Gravel

Mark Allen, owner and operator of Columbia Sand & Gravel, needs some computer advice and hires you as a consultant. Due to several large construction projects and subdivision developments, Columbia has grown dramatically in recent years, and needs to replace its soon-to-be-obsolete computer billing system. The existing software runs on an IBM PC system and was purchased more than 12 years ago. Although Mark is still very pleased with the features of the current billing system, the hardware and software no longer have the capacity and speed to process invoices and record payments for Columbia's client base. Unfortunately, the company that sold the software to Mark is no longer in business, so an upgrade of the existing system is not an option.

8

Mark is aware of two software companies that sell invoicing applications specifically tailored for use in the sand and gravel industry. Both Digital Rock and Extractasoft claim to have the bestselling software available for sand and gravel invoice applications. Mark wants you to evaluate these two competing products and make a recommendation on which software invoicing package Columbia should adopt as its new standard.

Mark is also aware that his company will have to purchase new hardware to run whichever software is selected. In recent years, Columbia Sand & Gravel has developed a good working relationship with Modular PC, a local company that sells and services computer hardware products. The owner of Modular PC is a close personal friend of Mark's, but does not sell invoicing software as specialized as Mark needs. Although Mark has already decided to purchase the computer hardware from Modular PC, and is preparing a purchase order for the new system, he wants you to evaluate the software products.

Based on this information from Mark and on what you learned in this chapter, write a letter to Mark in which you:

1. Describe any concerns you have about the product evaluation approach and methods at Columbia Sand & Gravel.

2. List any changes or suggestions you would make in Columbia's approach to select a replacement invoicing system to use in its business.

3. Discuss your concerns and suggestions.

CASE PROJECTS

4. An RFP Check List for Re-Nu-Cartridge

NOTE

For background information about Re-Nu-Cartridge, see Case Project 4 in previous chapters.

Fred Long, CEO of Re-Nu-Cartridge, wants to develop a Web site to sell the company's ink-jet printer and copier toner cartridges directly to Internet users in the United States and Canada. He wants your help with the preparation of a Request for Proposal (RFP) to local vendors who design and develop commercial Web sites.

Fred wants you to start researching the contents of an RFP and to make an outline of topics the Web site development RFP should cover. You do not need to write the RFP, but Fred will use your outline of topics and questions that the RFP should cover to make assignments for various staff members to pull together the information needed to produce a written RFP.

Begin by doing some research on the content of an RFP. One place you might look is at Web sites that contain guidelines on RFP preparation. These sites often include lists of topics or information that should be included in an RFP. Some sites you might consult are:

- *How to Write a Request for Proposal for a Web Project* by Bruce Morris at **www.webdevelopersjournal.com/columns/writerfp.html**

- *How to Write a Request for Proposal (RFP)* by Instructional Designs at **www.internetraining.com/6art2.htm**

- *The Three Cs of RFPs* by James E. Powell at **www.esj.com/features/article. asp?EditorialsID=122**

Here are pointers to a couple of examples of Web site design RFPs you could study:

- *RFP for Web Page Design Services* by the Academy of Human Resource Development at **www.ahrd.org/docs03/siteRFP.pdf** (requires Adobe reader)

- *Clark County RFP: County Web Site Design, Clark County, Washington* at **www.mrsc.org/rfps/C52rfpweb.pdf** (requires Adobe reader)

Or, you may be able to find a book on RFPs, such as:

- *Request for Proposal: A Guide to Effective RFP Development*, by Porter-Roth and Young, Addison Wesley, 2001.

Fred asks you to submit a check list of topics or questions that should be included in the written Web site RFP.

5. Select a Spell Checker for Re-Nu-Cartridge

For background information about Re-Nu-Cartridge, see Case Project 4 in this and previous chapters.

Re-Nu-Cartridge plans to purchase an inexpensive, laptop computer for each of its outside sales representatives so they can prepare narrative notes and summaries of their sales calls. Because the sales representatives are not skilled computer users, one goal is to make the computers as easy as possible to use. Another goal is to keep the cost of the laptops as low as possible.

The sales manager does not want the reps to spend time learning a full-featured word processor. So Re-Nu-Cartridge plans to teach all the sales reps to use a simple text editor, such as Notepad or WordPad, to prepare their sales summaries. None of these Windows accessories, however, includes a spell checker. As a computer user support specialist at Re-Nu-Cartridge, you are assigned to help the Marketing department research and recommend a spell checker that can be used in the Windows environment.

First, develop evaluation criteria for a Windows spell checker program. As resources for an evaluation check list, use your personal knowledge and experience with spell checkers in popular word-processing programs, product evaluation articles in trade periodicals, and discussions you have with your classmates. Then, create your own criteria check list for a spell checker. Develop as complete a list of criteria as you can, but limit your criteria to spell checker features you think the sales reps at Re-Nu-Cartridge would be likely to use; do not include infrequently used features. Also consider any software support issues you think are relevant.

If your computer location allows you to download shareware, and with the help of your instructor if necessary, obtain two Windows shareware spell checkers you can evaluate against the criteria you developed. Install and test each one. Then evaluate each program in terms of the criteria you established. If you add other criteria based on your test of the spell checkers, identify the additional criteria you used in your evaluation.

Finally, write a summary of your evaluation of the two spell checker packages and your recommendation to the Marketing department at Re-Nu-Cartridge.

9

USER NEEDS
ANALYSIS AND ASSESSMENT

In this chapter you will learn:

♦ Basic strategies to perform user needs analysis and assessment

♦ Major steps analysts undertake to analyze and assess a user's needs

♦ Common tools that aid support specialists in a user needs analysis project

U ser support specialists are often asked to help users select computer products and services. Sometimes they must select from among a limited group of products and services, especially when an organization maintains lists of standard, supported products, which you learned about in Chapter 8. This chapter describes how to analyze and assess user needs and help users decide among competing products and services. The chapter applies primarily to user support specialists who work with internal users; it does not apply directly to support specialists who work primarily on help desks or provide telephone support to external users. Support specialists who work with internal users in small organizations are more likely to help assess end-user needs and recommend products for purchase. Where the scale of an assessment project is larger, it may be conducted by a team that includes a senior support staff member or a supervisor and one or more junior-level support staff who assist. In very large organizations, professional staff in an Information Services department are likely to have primary responsibility for needs assessment projects.

If you have taken previous coursework in computer systems analysis and design or information systems, you will probably recognize some of the issues, resources, and tools described in this chapter. In some academic programs, students study systems analysis or information systems before they take courses in end-user computing support. Experience in systems analysis and design provides a good background for this chapter and for user needs assessment, because the role a support specialist plays in user needs assessment is very similar to the role of a systems analyst in an IT department. However, the tools that support specialists use are not always the same as the ones used by systems analysts, whose primary concern is often to design an application program for a programmer to code. This chapter focuses on analysis and assessment tools that support specialists use to match a user's needs to available products and services.

OVERVIEW OF USER NEEDS ANALYSIS AND ASSESSMENT

The support staff often analyzes and assesses user needs to determine which hardware and software products or computer services will best meet an end user's requirements. These tasks may be performed by any member of the support staff or by a staff member who has special skills and possibly the title of support analyst. Once a support analyst understands a user's environment and work situation, the analyst can investigate various products and services to meet the user's needs. The analyst can then help decide on a solution to meet the user's needs and determine whether to purchase or build the solution.

A user needs analysis and assessment project can take many forms. An assessment project can result in selection of a product, such as a new computer system or a new application software package. It may select a service, such as a training program or a hardware repair vendor. An assessment project can be informal, such as a friend or colleague who asks for help with the purchase of computer hardware or software for home or work use. A project can also be formal, such as when a supervisor assigns a user support specialist or a support group the task of working with users in a department to select a new Internet service provider (ISP), a new printer, or even a new office network. Whether informal or formal, or for the purpose of selecting a product or service, most needs assessment projects follow the same sequence of steps, which are summarized in Figure 9-1.

Support analysts don't always perform every step listed in Figure 9-1, and not all steps are always of equal importance. But analysts must start with a list of activities such as those in Figure 9-1 to guide a needs analysis project to a satisfactory solution. To leave out one or more of these steps is to risk basing a decision on incomplete or inaccurate information. Similarly, an experienced support analyst knows that user needs analysis and assessment is not a perfect process or a science that results in obviously right and wrong answers. End users are rarely certain of their exact needs and may not know how to state their requirements in words. End users may also have unrealistic expectations about the capabilities of computer technology at an affordable price. However, a support specialist should begin with the right list of questions—even if the answers are sometimes inexact.

I. Preparation Activities

    1. Understand the personal or organizational goals.

    2. Understand the decision criteria and constraints.

    3. Define the problem clearly.

    4. Identify the roles of stakeholders.

    5. Identify sources of information.

II. Investigation Activities

    6. Develop an understanding of the existing situation.

    7. Investigate alternatives to the existing situation.

III. Decision Activities

    8. Develop a model of the proposed solution.

    9. Make a build-versus-buy decision.

Figure 9-1   Steps in the needs analysis and assessment process

USER NEEDS ANALYSIS STEPS AND TASKS

Each step in a user needs analysis project can be grouped into one of three phases: preparation, investigation, or decision. In the **preparation phase**, analysts try to understand the personal or organizational goals as well as the decision criteria and constraints; they try to define the problem, identify the roles of stakeholders, and identify sources of information. In the **investigation phase**, analysts try to understand the present situation and alternatives to it. Finally, in the **decision phase**, analysts develop a model of the proposed solution and decide whether to build or buy it. Within each phase, analysts take specific steps that allow them to obtain information and propose a solution in an orderly fashion. By performing certain tasks for each step, analysts ensure that they have considered relevant sources of information in order to arrive at an appropriate solution for each unique situation. The following sections describe the major tasks of each step of the analysis and assessment process.

Case Study:
Re-Nu-Cartridge Production Reports

The case study in this chapter illustrates all the steps in a typical needs analysis project. The case is based on Re-Nu-Cartridge, a company you've worked with in previous chapters' Case Projects. Re-Nu-Cartridge is a local company that manufactures and sells inkjet and toner cartridges for computer printers. The Manufacturing department of Re-Nu-Cartridge prepares and distributes production reports to management on the quantities of each type of cartridge it remanufactures and fills with ink. These reports are important because they are the basis of production planning and decision making in the company.

As Re-Nu-Cartridge has grown, additional production reports have been required. Each new report is designed and developed with either a spreadsheet or a database program by a team that includes Glen, the manufacturing supervisor; Leroy, a manufacturing employee who collects the data; and Rachel, an accountant who helps develop the reports for the Manufacturing department. Fred Long, the CEO at Re-Nu-Cartridge, has recently asked Glen to reduce the time lag between when a new or revised report is requested and the time that the team begins to produce it. Once a new report is designed and implemented, it can be produced in a timely way. However, several weeks or months can elapse between when a new report is requested and when it is ready to be produced for the first time. Glen talked with the team members about why the time lag to develop new production reports is so long. Part of the problem, they agreed, is that the design and development of new production reports is not a very high priority for any of them, and thus the reports do not get completed on time. The team members asked Margaret, a new user support specialist at Re-Nu-Cartridge, to attend their next meeting. Although new to the company, Margaret had user needs analysis experience in a previous job at a governmental agency.

Step 1: Understand the Personal or Organizational Goals

Before support analysts can recommend new computer products and services, they must get an overall perspective of either the organization's goals or an individual purchaser's objectives, or both. Many medium- to large-size organizations maintain a written strategic business plan or a mission statement that describes the goals and objectives of the organization. Some organizations have specialized business plans devoted specifically to information technology. If these documents are not available, support analysts can usually interview managers or supervisors, and/or individual purchasers, to learn about their vision, goals, and future plans.

Regardless of whether support analysts obtain the information through written documents or interviews, they should learn the answers to the following questions:

1. What are the goals of the organization, department, or individual purchaser that will affect the need for computer products or services?

2. Is the organization for-profit or not-for-profit?

3. What plans does the organization have to grow or expand?

4. What is the organization's attitude (or culture) about technology?

5. What is the organization's budget for computer systems and services?

6. Does the organization's staff or the individual purchaser have the experience and expertise to operate, maintain, and support a computer system?

The purpose of these questions is to learn the big picture—the environment and culture into which the future system or service will fit. Growth or expansion plans are especially important to consider during the assessment process. The solution an analyst might recommend to an organization that is growing 5 to 10% per year would probably be very different from the solution he or she would recommend to an organization that expects to grow 25 to 50% per year. Similarly, a smaller organization or an individual purchaser may not be able to operate, maintain, or support a sophisticated system with a lot of features and flexibility; a more straightforward package might be a better choice.

9

Case Study:
Re-Nu-Cartridge Production Reports

Because Margaret, the user support specialist, is relatively new to Re-Nu-Cartridge, the manufacturing reports team briefed her on the role their department plays in the company. They took Margaret on a tour of the Manufacturing department, and showed her where used cartridges are disassembled, cleaned, repaired, reassembled, filled with ink, and then repackaged. They also showed her the PC system, spreadsheet software, and database software that Leroy currently uses to input the data and prepare the daily, weekly, and monthly inkjet and toner cartridge production reports. They indicated that a computer has been used to prepare the manufacturing reports for several years; however, in the early days of Re-Nu-Cartridge, production reports were prepared manually. With the recent growth of Re-Nu-Cartridge, Fred Long and other managers have requested new production reports or revisions to existing reports almost every month during the past year. Although Leroy can collect the report data, enter it, and produce the reports as part of his job, the Manufacturing department does not have employees on its staff with the cost accounting and software expertise to design and develop its own reports, which is why Rachel, the accountant, is an important member of the team. The team concluded by brainstorming some ideas for reducing the time between the point when a new report is requested and when Leroy can begin to prepare and submit the report. Their ideas included hiring an additional staff member to develop the reports, hiring a consultant to make a recommendation about how to produce more timely reports, purchasing a report generator software package and training Leroy to use it, and improving the management of development projects to design and implement new or revised reports.

Step 2: Understand the Decision Criteria and Constraints

Another question support analysts need to ask early is the criteria the organization will use to make a decision. Analysts usually recommend solutions to users or managers rather than decide on a solution themselves. However, the more support analysts understand about the decision criteria, the more they can focus on realistic alternatives.

Support analysts need to clarify what is feasible, or possible, in terms of time, money, or technology. **Feasibility** is an investigation into the economic, operational, technical, and timeline constraints that apply during a user needs analysis and assessment project. Analysts often consider several kinds of feasibility:

- **Economic feasibility.** What budget constraints will influence the final decision on the project?

- **Operational feasibility.** With what other systems or procedures does this system need to interact? What personnel will be required to operate this system? Do the personnel have the knowledge, skills, and abilities they need?

- **Technological feasibility.** What limitations or constraints does the state of existing technology impose on possible solutions?

- **Timeline feasibility.** Do time constraints rule out some possible alternatives?

Support analysts also need to understand the factors that will influence the final decision. For example, is the organization extremely sensitive to cost so that only low-cost solutions should be considered? Does the organization pride itself on doing business with well-known, established, and reputable vendors, so that systems from established vendors should be considered more seriously than those offered by relatively smaller, unknown vendors? Does the organization try to stay on the leading edge of technology, or does it take a relatively conservative view of new, and perhaps untried, products? Are the users and managers comfortable with the introduction of new technology? What priority does the organization place on vendor support? For example, some organizations rely on their own support staff and don't need extensive vendor support. The answers to all these questions help define criteria and constraints that support analysts must consider in order to recommend an appropriate solution.

Geary Rummler has developed a project feasibility guide that lists several kinds of questions an analyst can ask about the feasibility of a project. View this guide at **www.performancexpress.org/0304/images/Project_Feasibility_Guide.pdf** (Adobe Reader required).

Case Study:
Re-Nu-Cartridge Production Reports

The user support specialist, Margaret, asked about the budget for a solution to the production report development problem. Glen said that no budget had been defined. However, he noted that the management at Re-Nu-Cartridge used the production reports to make plans and decisions about production goals, staffing levels in the Manufacturing department, purchases of raw materials, and marketing campaigns. Because the requests for new reports were important to the profitability of the company, he believed that the management at Re-Nu-Cartridge would approve expenses the team felt were likely to reduce the time lag for the development of new reports.

Margaret asked whether hiring a programmer for the Manufacturing department was feasible. Glen said that he thought the cost of a programmer would be difficult to sell to management, and that the volume of requests for new reports, currently about one per month, probably did not warrant a full-time programmer. He said that hiring a part-time programmer or contracting with a software development company might be more feasible, but would still be expensive, and might still take several months to achieve the results they wanted.

Margaret also asked whether the group had considered packaged software, such as a report writer, as a possible solution. Rachel replied that they had talked about a report writer briefly, but felt that existing spreadsheet and database software had the features they needed to prepare the reports. Leroy added that he didn't have time to learn a new software package.

Step 3: Define the Problem Clearly

Problems come in a variety of shapes and sizes. Some are well formulated; others are not. Support analysts who work on user needs assessment projects must clearly define the root or underlying problem they are trying to solve. Furthermore, not all problems are technical; some "computer" problems actually turn out to be organizational, personnel, workflow, user training, office politics, management, or resource problems. Experienced analysts look beyond the symptoms of a problem to search for its root causes, which may or may not be a technical problem.

"Do I really understand the problem I'm trying to solve for this user?" is a question that should guide a needs analysis from beginning to end. For example, a user may complain that the accounting application does not work correctly and that replacement with one that is more robust—that doesn't hang up his computer like the current one does—is desirable. If the real problem is the accounting program, the user may have correctly deduced that he needs new software. However, the problem may actually be related to the way the existing program is configured to operate on the user's computer system or in a network environment. To recommend replacing expensive hardware or software when the real problem is something else can be a costly mistake. Therefore, clearly defining the root or underlying problem is critical to any user needs analysis.

Furthermore, support analysts should not assume at the outset that the user has correctly analyzed the problem. A user may not understand the real problem, or a user may know *what* is wrong, but not understand the array of possible causes or the variety of options available to fix the problem. Support analysts need to ask many questions, observe as the user operates the existing system, and consider solutions other than the obvious ones.

> ## Case Study:
> ## Re-Nu-Cartridge Production Reports
>
> Margaret asked the production report development team if they thought the time lag problem was actually due to a lack of staff to design and develop the new production reports. Rachel, the accountant who developed the reports in the past, said that most of the reports were not difficult to produce, once the report's purpose, the data needed for input, and the report format were understood. Rachel said part of the problem was that she had other responsibilities in accounting that had a higher priority than the production reports, and that when she needed to talk with Glen or Leroy about the details of a new report, they were often working on other manufacturing tasks and could not respond to her questions in a timely manner. Rachel suggested that the real problem was that the report development project was not assigned a high enough priority to get it done in a timely way. Glen and Leroy agreed that the way the team had organized the development of new production reports in the past could be improved, but expressed doubt that they had the resources to improve the process.

Step 4: Identify the Roles of Stakeholders

Stakeholders are the participants in a user needs analysis and assessment project who might gain or lose from its success or failure. Stakeholders include end users, managers, technical support staff, and the needs assessment analyst. Some stakeholders participate in the entire assessment project. Others may contribute their expertise and support in only one or a few of the project steps and then leave the project, perhaps to rejoin it at a later step. Four kinds of stakeholders are important in a needs analysis project—users, managers, support analysts, and information technology or technical support staff.

Users. Support analysts should learn who the ultimate end user is, or who the users are if there are several. What are their job responsibilities? What computer experience do they have? What training have they received? What is their background? How long have they worked for the organization? In addition to information about the users' backgrounds, a support analyst should learn about the role users will play in an assessment project, including their participation levels and how their feedback will be obtained and used.

Managers. After identifying the end users and their roles, support analysts should identify the manager who will be involved in any final decision to purchase a computer system or service, or implement another solution. The support analysts should determine the following: Who will make the final decision? How knowledgeable about the application are the managers who will participate in the decision? What organizational and computer experience do they bring to the process? Sometimes the final decision makers lack technical expertise, and a support analyst needs to spend project time to educate them so that they can make an intelligent decision.

The management perspective is important input to any assessment project. Managers provide important information about the background of the problem, insights into possible solutions to the problem, an indication of the priority a problem has, support and sponsorship for a project, and financial and decision-making expertise. In some cases, the owner of a small organization provides the management perspective. In other situations, a department manager, supervisor, or project leader may provide the management perspective. Experienced support analysts know that one of the biggest mistakes they can make in a needs assessment project is to ignore the management perspective.

Support Analysts.   Support analysts who coordinate and conduct needs analysis projects are obviously key participants in the process. As important as it is to understand the roles of other participants, analysts also need to clarify their own role in the needs assessment process. Is the analysts' role to assist existing company staff with the needs assessment, to perform the analysis and describe the pros and cons of various alternatives, to make a recommendation, or to make the final decision? How much time and resources has the organization allocated to the project, and how do these affect the analysts' work on this and other projects?

Information Technology or Technical Support Staff.   If an organization has an existing IT or technical support staff, these stakeholders are often important participants in a needs assessment project. IT staff members may be ultimately responsible to install, configure, maintain, and troubleshoot the system an analyst recommends. They may have important perspectives on possible alternate solutions and on technical feasibility. To ignore the input and advice of these professionals can be a mistake.

NOTE   In some needs assessment projects, one or more vendor representatives may be key project participants. Vendor representatives can play a role at various stages in a project if they have perspectives on the problem or will provide part of the eventual solution. Obviously vendors' roles may be limited by a bias toward their own products or services.

Support analysts who work on a large project that involves several users, managers, and IT or technical support staff may want to develop a profile that summarizes information about each participant in a project. A profile can include contact information such as phone numbers and e-mail addresses, position title and description (if appropriate), background, primary job functions, and notes on their interests in the outcome of the project.

Case Study:
Re-Nu-Cartridge Production Reports

By this point in the discussion, Margaret had a fairly good understanding of Glen's role as manufacturing supervisor. She noted that he was ultimately responsible for seeing that new reports were designed, developed, and prepared for delivery to the management at Re-Nu-Cartridge. The end user in this situation was Leroy, who collected the data and printed each production report. Margaret also understood the role of Rachel, the accountant, who knew how to program a spreadsheet or database program to produce the new reports. Based on Glen's statements, Margaret felt that the management of Re-Nu-Cartridge was committed to a solution to the problem, although she had not yet interviewed any managers other than Glen.

Margaret told the team that she felt there was one key stakeholder they hadn't discussed yet and who wasn't involved: Naseem, Rachel's supervisor in Accounting. Because Rachel felt that there were possible problems with getting a higher priority for new reports, Margaret said it would be important to include Naseem in whatever approaches or decisions were made. Rachel agreed.

Margaret concluded by asking what role the report production team wanted her to play. Glen said that the team would like Margaret to learn enough about the new report development process to recommend to the team how to reduce the time lag from initial request to implementation.

Step 5: Identify Sources of Information

Closely related to understanding the roles of various participants in a project is the need to learn about sources of information that are necessary during the project. Support analysts should arrange to obtain some common sources of information, such as:

- Interviews with end users and managers
- Surveys or questionnaires sent to end users who will be affected
- Procedural manuals that detail how to operate the current system, if one exists
- Direct observation of the existing system or situation
- Forms used for input into the existing system
- Reports that are output from the existing system
- Problem reports or help desk logs for the existing system
- Reports and recommendations from consultants or auditors who have studied the existing system

Analysts often start with a check list of resources, like the one above, to help them gather information about the system or situation they have been asked to analyze. This list seems like a lot of information to consider, and the list may expand, contract, or change, depending on the details of a specific project. Obviously the amount of time that analysts spend on various information resources depends on the size of the project, its budget, and its timelines.

These information resources are not all equally useful in every project.

Case Study:
Re-Nu-Cartridge Production Reports

Margaret said she would like some time to think about the report development problem and possible alternatives. On the way back to her desk, she began to compile a list of additional information she would need to make a recommendation to the report development team.

1. Interview Fred or another top manager in the company to gauge his or her commitment to solving the problem.

2. Interview Naseem, the accounting supervisor, to discuss Rachel's role in the development process and get Naseem's perspective on the time lag problem.

3. Observe the development of the next new production report that was requested to learn more about the development process and identify the problems that the team encountered.

Margaret sent an e-mail to the team members that outlined the information she needed. She asked to be a participant in the next report development project, and asked that the team keep a simple time log of when each step (key meetings, decisions, and problems) occurred.

Step 6: Develop an Understanding of the Existing Situation

During the investigation phase, support analysts must learn as much as possible about the existing system or situation, whether it is manual or computer-based. In this step, analysts collect and examine important pieces of paper (examples of forms, reports, and documentation), interview key participants (end users, managers, and technical support staff), observe the operation of the existing system, and develop a clear understanding of what the existing system does and how it works.

Analysts should organize the information they collect so they can easily locate what they need. Analysts often use a project notebook or a set of file folders to keep records of various forms, reports, meetings, and interviews. One way to organize information is according to the steps in the analysis process described in this chapter. Some analysts organize project information according to its function: input, processing, storage, and output.

The primary objective of this step is to build a model that describes the existing system. A **model** is a narrative or graphic diagram, or both, that represents a business activity in an organization (such as paper workflow), a computer system, or a network. A model can be a written description or a diagram, such as a flowchart or an organization chart. Analysts can also create a model by using analytic and planning tools, such as software designed specifically for systems analysts.

A popular tool support analysts use to diagram a model of an existing business system is Microsoft's Visio. To learn more about Visio and take a tour of the product, visit the Visio home page at **office.microsoft.com/home/office. aspx?assetid=FX01085798**. A shareware product that has similar capabilities is Chartist by Novagraph; visit its Web site at **www.novagraph.com**, where you can download a trial copy.

After constructing a model, analysts can show it to other project participants to make sure the model accurately represents the current system. Sharing a model with users, managers, and other staff often uncovers misunderstandings about the capabilities or features of the existing system.

Support analysts should be able to answer *yes* to the following questions at the end of Step 6:

1. Do I understand the existing system well enough to explain how it operates to other participants?

2. Do I understand which features of the existing system users like?

3. Do I understand what users think is wrong with the existing system?

Without an understanding of each of these aspects of the existing system or situation, analysts may be unprepared to consider alternatives with which to replace or repair it.

Case Study:
Re-Nu-Cartridge Production Reports

During the next week, Margaret interviewed both Fred, the company president, and Naseem, the accounting supervisor, to get a managerial perspective on the importance of the production report development process. She learned from Fred that management considers the reports vital to the profitability and future growth of the company, but was probably reluctant to approve the expense of hiring a programmer. She also learned that Naseem was unaware that Rachel encountered conflicts in priorities between accounting tasks and the development of new reports for manufacturing. Naseem also expressed reluctance to devote any more of Rachel's time to developing reports. Naseem said that the Manufacturing department should take responsibility for the reports, and that to some extent, she felt manufacturing was taking unfair advantage of Rachel's expertise.

During the week, Margaret had an opportunity to observe the development team work on a new production report. She concluded that the PC and software were appropriate for the reporting tasks, that Rachel had good knowledge of the software tools used to develop reports, and that it took Rachel only a few hours to develop a new report once she understood the specifications and resolved questions with Glen and Leroy. Margaret was able to confirm from her observations and the logs the team kept that conflicting priorities and lack of coordination among team members accounted for much of the time lag in implementing a new report.

The model that Margaret developed, based on her research and analysis, showed that the report development time lag was not primarily a technology problem. Her analysis was that the spreadsheet and database software were simple tools but up to the task, that the existing staff could develop new and revised reports effectively (but not efficiently), and that it was important to Re-Nu Cartridge to fix the report development time lag problem. The more she learned about the problem, the more she felt that the likely solution would involve changes in work roles and relationships among personnel in the manufacturing report team. She shared her perspectives with the team at its next meeting.

Step 7: Investigate Alternatives to the Existing Situation

In previous steps, the analysts' goal was to understand as much as possible about the existing system: its purpose, features, users, advantages, disadvantages, problems, and other important characteristics. In this step, analysts' attention shifts to ways to fix the problems with the current system or situation. They consider several kinds of alternatives:

- **Additional resources.** To operate effectively or efficiently, the existing system may need additional resources, such as personnel, new equipment, larger budget, greater time commitment, or increased priority. Some additional resources are technical solutions; others are organizational.

- **Changes to resources.** The existing system or situation may continue to meet the needs of the organization if changes are made to it. For example, the configuration of a software package may be the cause of low user productivity and dissatisfaction with a system. If the software is reinstalled or reconfigured, the software may continue to meet the organization's needs. Another common problem is that users may require additional training to use the features of a system effectively.

- **Upgrades.** The organization may need to upgrade hardware or software components to resolve the documented problems. Upgrades may improve processing speed, storage capacity, or compatibility, or offer new features that address identified problems.

- **New hardware.** New hardware may be necessary to address capacity constraints, run software efficiently, or operate new software with features that solve users' problems.

- **New software.** New software may be necessary to address issues the analyst identified in the needs assessment project. Software alternatives include packaged, off-the-shelf software, and custom-developed software that can be designed to meet specific, and perhaps unique, user requirements. Another solution might be an off-the-shelf software package that can be modified to meet specific user requirements.

When developing alternatives to consider, analysts often investigate the tools used by users who perform similar tasks in other organizations. Before they recommend replacing an entire system to meet users' needs, analysts should investigate the solutions others have implemented successfully in similar situations. These solutions may not solve all the identified problems, but an analyst should inquire rather than risk spending scarce resources to reinvent a solution someone else has already devised.

As you learned in Chapter 8, trade magazines targeted at a specific industry are a good source of ideas and products that address specific needs. Articles in trade magazines often report on successful computer system implementations in similar organizations. Some trade magazines publish articles that evaluate and compare technology options. Finally, advertisements in trade periodicals often identify vendors who supply hardware and software products and services aimed at a specialized market niche. The Internet is yet another resource for locating products and service solutions for an organization. For example, a support analyst looking for software tailored to a video rental store or a veterinarian clinic could find leads with a search engine on the World Wide Web. Examples of project management software that Margaret researched for Re-Nu-Cartridge are shown in Figure 9-2.

Case Study:
Re-Nu-Cartridge Production Reports

Margaret reported to the development team her conclusion that the time lag problem was not primarily a hardware, software, or staffing problem, but one that could be addressed by a combination of better project management procedures, staff training, and perhaps project management software. She recommended that the team focus on better ways to manage and coordinate projects. Glen said that he had hoped the problem was, in part, hardware-related, because he wanted to purchase a more powerful PC for the Manufacturing department. However, the team members agreed that the current informal method used to develop new reports was not as well organized and managed as it could be, and asked Margaret for suggestions.

Margaret said that, as the number of new report projects increased, the development team would need to implement a project management strategy. She recommended that the group consider a project management software package to help plan the steps in each development project, the staff resources required (both team members and other Re-Nu-Cartridge employees), the timelines that needed to be met, the points of coordination between Rachel, Leroy, Glen, and others, and the critical tasks that, if delayed, meant that a new report would be held up. She felt that the timelines and staff resource plans that would result from the use of project management software could help the development team to understand the priorities better, and also help the team communicate priorities and resource needs to Re-Nu-Cartridge management, including Rachel's supervisor, Naseem. Margaret mentioned that a side benefit of the project management software would be that Glen could monitor each report development project and provide Fred and other managers with regular status reports.

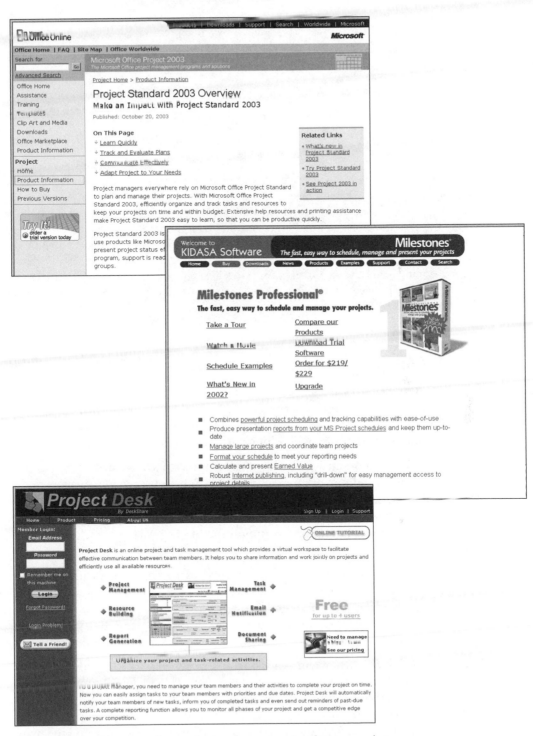

Figure 9-2   Web pages for project management software packages

Margaret handed out a summary of alternate ways to improve report project management:

1. Purchase a project management software package to run on the Manufacturing department's existing PC, if possible.

2. Send one or more team members to an industry seminar on project management.

3. Contract with a seminar vendor to present an in-house workshop on project management.

4. Ask a support specialist at Re-Nu-Cartridge to lead a project management workshop using an industry trade book on the topic.

The team asked Margaret to investigate the cost of each alternative. In conclusion, she cautioned the team not to go overboard on project management, because the report development projects were relatively simple. She pointed out that too much project management overhead would only contribute to the time lag problem, not solve it. But she thought that the team could improve its project coordination efforts and reduce the development time lag by using a project scheduling approach tailored to their specific situation. The team members expressed some concern about whether project management would add to a project's overhead and lengthen the time to develop a new report even further. However, they said they would like to know more about the effects a project management strategy could have on their projects.

Step 8: Develop a Model of the Proposed Solution

Once analysts have completed the preparation and investigation phases, they reach the decision phase. With a clear description of the problem, an understanding of the current system or situation, and a list of possible alternatives to the present system, analysts can develop a model of the proposed solution to recommend to users and management.

The model that support analysts build often includes a narrative description of the proposed system or solution and one or more graphic aids to help users and managers understand the proposal. The narrative should include a description of the alternatives the analysts considered, as well as the pros and cons of each alternative. The model should answer the question, "Why is the proposed solution an improvement over the present system and the best available alternative?"

The decision on which of the various alternatives to recommend may be obvious. One solution may be clearly the most feasible, or the advantages of a solution may clearly outweigh its disadvantages. Frequently cost is a major issue: the best solution may be the most expensive. In this case, the analyst may recommend a **satisficing solution**, one that solves the problem in a reasonable way, but is not necessarily an optimal solution.

When the solution to a problem is not obvious, or when legally required, analysts may do a cost–benefit analysis of several options to help them choose from among the alternatives. A **cost–benefit analysis** compares the expenses a project will incur to the project's payoffs. A cost–benefit analysis often looks like a balance sheet (a sheet of paper divided into two columns) with the costs of a proposed system or solution on one side and the benefits on the other. Later in this chapter, you will look more closely at the factors to consider in a cost-benefit analysis.

Experienced support analysts recognize that performing a cost-benefit analysis is not an exact science. For a cost-benefit analysis to be most useful, alternatives in the same general category and with the same features should be compared. For most small projects, a detailed cost-benefit analysis is not necessary, but even an informal cost-benefit analysis can increase the likelihood that analysts have considered the significant advantages and disadvantages of each alternative.

When a needs assessment project results in a decision to purchase a new computer system, the users' needs drive the specifications for the new system. End users frequently believe hardware is the most crucial component of a system and often focus on the hardware specifications to the exclusion of more important components. What can be more important than hardware? When users' needs determine the specifications, software solutions should be considered first. The software requirements should then drive the hardware selection. Only when software is specified for an existing hardware platform should the software selection depend on the hardware configuration.

9

Case Study:
Re-Nu-Cartridge Production Reports

Margaret prepared for the next meeting of the report development team by printing examples of screens and reports from a project management software package. She used as an example the Microsoft Project 2003 package described in Chapter 7, but noted that other project management software products might also serve Re-Nu-Cartridge's needs, including some free Web-based products (see Figure 9-2 for examples). She presented project management tools as a model solution to the time lag problem and walked the team members through some common uses of project management software.

Margaret also presented some cost estimates that she developed for the various alternatives she had suggested:

1. Project management software ($500)

2. Industry project management seminar ($1000 registration plus $2500 travel per participant)

3. In-house workshop on project management ($7500)

4. Support analyst-led workshop ($750 staff time to develop plus $50 per book for each participant)

The development team spent the remainder of the meeting discussing the pros and cons of each approach, including the cost of each alternative, how long each would take to implement, and the staff time required both in house and at a training seminar. Glenn expressed the view that the group needed to try something soon because Fred, the CEO, was very frustrated about the current report development process. Margaret concluded the meeting by responding to Glen's earlier comment about his desire for new computer hardware in manufacturing. She suggested that, although project management software would probably run on manufacturing's existing PC, the system requirements of the software should be the factor that dictated whether new hardware was required.

Step 9: Make a Build-Versus-Buy Decision

A significant decision for many organizations is the **build-versus-buy decision**: whether to build a custom solution or purchase one off the shelf. The build-versus-buy decision can apply to building computer hardware, developing software, and providing services. For example, many organizations have employees who have the skills to assemble a PC from components. Would an employee-assembled system be cost-effective and who would maintain an assembled system are important issues. In most cases, however, the build-versus-buy decision applies primarily to software and services. Although many needs assessment projects result in a decision to purchase off-the-shelf software, custom-developed software can be designed to suit the user's exact needs. For other organizations, buying a turnkey system is more appropriate. A **turnkey system** includes an integrated package of hardware, software, and support services purchased from a single vendor. Table 9-1 summarizes some of the advantages and disadvantages of building versus buying a system.

Table 9-1   Advantages and disadvantages of building versus buying a solution

	Building a Custom Solution	Buying an Off-the-Shelf Solution
Advantages	• System can be designed to meet special and specific needs • System may provide strategic advantages over competition	• Lower acquisition cost due to market competition • Faster implementation • Better documentation • Standard user interfaces and components • Fewer bugs due to more exhaustive testing • Ongoing technical support may be available
Disadvantages	• Higher development or acquisition costs • Longer timeline to develop and get operational • Bugs are more likely in custom-developed hardware or software • Diverts organizational resources (such as programmers) from other projects • Higher maintenance costs	• Fewer opportunities to customize to meet special needs • One-size-fits-all approach to capabilities and features • Upgrades may not contain needed features

Developing a complete custom system or solution may be prohibitively expensive for many organizations, especially those that do not have an in-house programming staff. Even for organizations with staff members who have programming expertise, the costs of custom software development generally outweigh the benefits when reasonable preprogrammed (off-the-shelf) alternatives are available.

Each needs assessment project is a unique situation, which means that the steps in this chapter need to be tailored to the specific situation. In some instances, budget constraints may limit the possible options that can be considered. In other situations, political issues, such as a long-term relationship with a vendor, may outweigh other factors and make a cost-benefit analysis of little use.

Needs analysis and assessment projects can be used for purposes other than selecting hardware, software, or network systems. As you learned in the Re-Nu-Cartridge case study in this chapter, assessment projects often investigate problems that have organizational, rather than technological, solutions. A Web site devoted to assessing the need for end user training, **adulted.about.com/ cs/trngneedsasst**, provides several papers that offer more detail and examples of needs assessment projects. The site focuses on measuring the need for user training projects, a topic covered in Chapter 11.

For more information about needs assessments and conducting an assessment project, consult a book by Laura Connelly, *Needs Assessment and Project Planning*, Pearson Custom Publishing, 2000.

Case Study:
Re-Nu-Cartridge Production Reports

After all the alternatives were considered, including the advantages, disadvantages, and costs of each, the report development team decided to purchase a project management and scheduling software package (alternative 1) and ask one of the support specialists at Re-Nu-Cartridge to lead a workshop for the development team on project management (alternative 4). The team chose the in-house workshop option in part because, when other departments in Re-Nu-Cartridge learned about the possibility of a workshop on project management, they asked to be included. The cost of the support specialist's time to develop a project management workshop could be shared with several departments, and the support specialist could also use relevant examples from Re-Nu-Cartridge in the workshop. The report development team felt that these two alternatives were the most cost-effective solutions to address the report development time lag problem. They thanked Margaret for her assistance in their needs assessment project.

The Re-Nu-Cartridge needs assessment you followed in this chapter illustrates that user needs assessment and analysis projects do not need to be time-consuming, large-scale, and costly. In fact, many are of a smaller scale variety, like the Re-Nu-Cartridge production reports time lag problem. Many needs assessment projects do not proceed as smoothly as this example due to office politics, differences in basic personalities and work styles, employees who feel threatened by change, and lack of consensus on the definition of the problem and possible solutions. The role of Fred Long, CEO of Re-Nu-Cartridge, and other managers illustrates the importance of management participation and influence in a project.

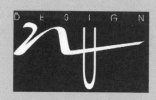

MITCH GELLER AND KELLY HART
PARTNERS: ARTISTS AND PROGRAMMERS
NU-DESIGN (A FULL-SERVICE MULTIMEDIA AND WEB
    DEVELOPMENT COMPANY)
ARLINGTON, TEXAS
WWW.NU-DESIGN.COM

Nu-Design is a multimedia and Web development company that integrates creative art with technical know-how and innovation. Partners Mitch Geller and Kelly Hart provide solutions for clients ranging from medium-sized companies to large international corporations. They deliver solutions for all types of multimedia, Web, and computer needs (including design, acquisition, and support of computer systems and networks). This CloseUp describes how Nu-Design worked with one client to completely redesign the company's use of computers.

Problem Identification. Nu-Design produces digital images of a client's products and creates and maintains an online shopping cart for its Web site. While finalizing the shopping cart design for its Web site, one of the client company staff members said, "Working with computers is the worst part of my job." Further investigation revealed that the client company's non-networked computers were becoming increasingly unreliable and that its dial-up Web connections were often difficult to access. Nu-Design agreed to help investigate the reliability problem.

Assessment. For Nu-Design, the process of analyzing needs and implementing computer solutions parallels the process of assessing and planning the construction of a Web site. They approached this assessment phase seriously, paying specific attention to improving reliability, decreasing costs, and eliminating redundancy. While working with the client on Web projects, Nu-Design staff had noticed some specific problems. They tested the client's systems and followed up on problems they identified. Rather than relying entirely on their observations, however, Nu-Design staff made sure to talk with the client's workers and in some cases to have them demonstrate how they accomplish some of their usual tasks. These conversations were the best indicators of which problems were the most urgent. Some consultants look only at the technical factors, but Nu-Design placed additional focus on the human factors, finding that improved technical efficiency often goes hand in hand with improved ergonomics and convenience.

Proposal. Nu-Design recommended several major changes and a series of minor ones that would drastically improve the reliability and effectiveness of the client's current system. Their analysis showed that the cost savings would pay for the increased expenditures during the first fiscal year after implementation. Knowing that their proposal would be evaluated by the non-technical officers of the client company, Nu-Design explained its recommendations in plain language, clearly indicated the benefits, costs, and savings, and included a realistic plan for implementation.

Nu-Design's proposal included the following changes:

- Eliminate dial-up service and dedicated phone lines (nearly a $500/month savings).
- Add system monitoring, maintenance, backup, and virus protection software.
- Add high-speed DSL with Web hosting as a package (nearly an 80% savings).
- Add peer-to-peer networking to facilitate sharing the Web connection and peripheral resources.
- Reinstall and/or upgrade operating systems and software as needed.
- Replace three worn or malfunctioning monitors with newer models with improved resolution and power saving features.
- Redesign users' severely confined work areas to increase workspace and user comfort:
  - Replace 14-inch standard monitor with 15-inch flat screen monitor.
  - Move PC to a remote location and extend connections to the user's desk
  - Adjust desk, keyboard, and chair heights for appropriate viewing and typing angle.

Implementation. Careful planning was necessary to coordinate the installation while minimizing disruption to the client's workflow. Nu-Design staff overlapped the new Web connection and hosting services with the operation of the existing PC system so that they could be thoroughly tested before the company relied on them. In addition, workstations that required a full-system reinstallation to ensure reliability were worked on over the weekend so that they would be ready for regular Monday morning office hours.

Support. After implementation, Nu-Design staff conducted a brief orientation and retraining of users to help ease the transition. During this time, several minor enhancements and adjustments (such as adding software or peripherals) were made to optimize the system for the unique needs of specific users. Nu-Design scheduled regular service visits and ongoing telephone support to keep the new system in top working condition.

Results. With careful planning, Nu-Design was able to stabilize the client company's existing hardware, upgrade where needed, and replace slow dial-up connections with always-on broadband, while significantly decreasing monthly expenditures. Worker frustration has decreased as the new system has become a more reliable asset. Productivity continues to improve as workers begin to take advantage of file sharing and networked peripherals. And working with computers is much less frustrating; in fact, some employees now describe it as fun.

NEEDS ANALYSIS AND ASSESSMENT TOOLS

The needs analysis steps mentioned several tools that analysts often use as aids in the assessment process. The latter part of this chapter describes in more detail some of these tools, which are listed in Figure 9-3.

- Project charter
- Cost-benefit analysis
- Data collection instruments
- Charts and diagrams
- Prototyping software
- Other tools

Figure 9-3 Needs assessment tools

Some of these tools are relatively easy for analysts to write or create, whereas others require more extensive work and, in some cases, special software. To be effective, these tools require the cooperation of users, managers, and support staff, as well as an extended timeline.

Project Charter

In needs analysis and assessment projects that involve more than a few participants, all stakeholders should understand basic information about a project. One way to ensure a common understanding is to develop a project charter. A **project charter** is a short narrative that answers basic questions, such as:

1. What are the objectives of the assessment project? What will be achieved if the project is successful?

2. What is the scope of the needs analysis project? What is included in the project and, sometimes more important, what is excluded?

3. What methods will be used to achieve the project's goals? What tools and resources will be used?

4. Who are the key project participants (stakeholders)? What are their roles?

5. What are the project deliverables? (A **deliverable** is the end result of an analysis project, such as a written report or a recommendation to purchase, modify, upgrade, or build a system, or acquire a service.)

6. What are the major steps in the needs assessment project?

7. What is the project timeline? What are the significant project milestones that indicate whether the project is ahead of or behind schedule?

8. How will the project's success be measured?

The form shown in Figure 9-4 is an example of a project charter template that you can use directly or modify. Although some are longer, this project charter is only a page long. A charter need not be not a detailed document, but rather a high-level overview of the project. Some organizations use a project request form (more like a work order) instead of a charter, but its contents are similar to a charter, and it serves a similar purpose.

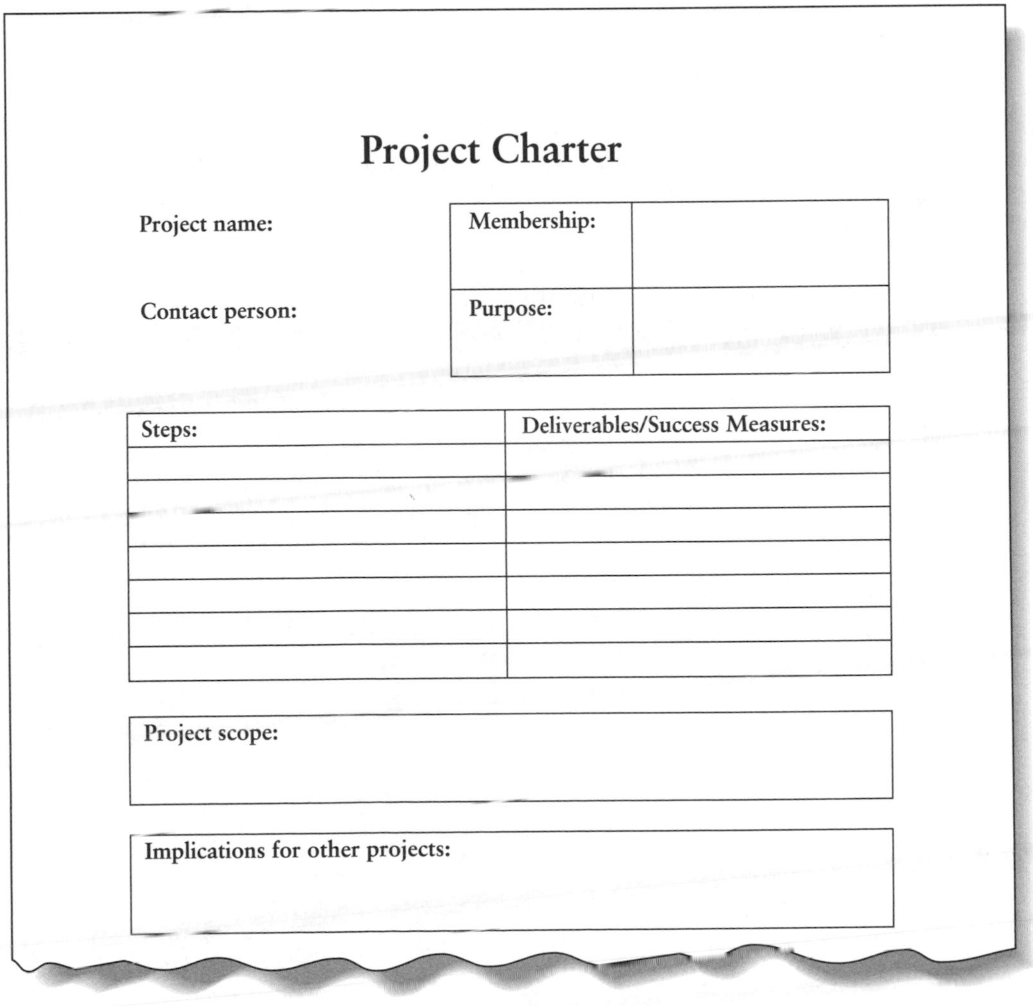

Project Charter

Project name:	Membership:	
Contact person:	Purpose:	

Steps:	Deliverables/Success Measures:

Project scope:

Implications for other projects:

Figure 9-4   Project charter

To learn more about the contents of project charters and view examples, visit the University of Minnesota's Extension Division Web site on project charters at **www.extension.umn.edu/projects/mentor/plan/plan2.asp**. To review an alternate project charter template, see **www.ce.umn.edu/~smith/MOT8221/ charterform.pdf** (requires Adobe Reader).

Cost-Benefit Analysis

As you learned earlier in this chapter, a cost-benefit analysis is a tool to help identify the costs and the corresponding benefits of a proposed solution. A cost-benefit analysis is often in the form of a side-by-side comparison, or balance sheet, that lists costs on one side of the sheet and benefits on the other.

Table 9-2 lists items that might appear in a cost-benefit balance sheet. It shows that costs can be categorized as acquisition costs (whether built or purchased) and operating costs (ongoing costs). Benefits can include reduced expenses, increased revenue opportunities, and intangible benefits.

Table 9-2   Cost-benefit balance sheet

Costs of Alternative	Benefits of Alternative
Acquisition costs • Purchase computer equipment • Purchase software packages or licenses • Software development costs (programming) • Purchase computer services • Purchase supplies and materials • Time to implement alternative • Administrative costs • Unanticipated costs	**Reduced expenses** • Less expensive hardware and software • Fewer personnel required to operate system • Lower manufacturing or inventory costs • More efficient use of staff time or equipment (productivity) • Faster response to client needs
Operating costs • Equipment lease or rental • Personnel (salaries and benefits) • Computer supplies and materials • Hardware and software maintenance • User training	**Increased revenue opportunities** • New products or services for clients • Expanded markets (new clients) • Increased volume of business transactions • Ability to raise prices due to higher quality products or services
	Intangible benefits • Ability to take advantage of new technology • Improved image of the organization • Improved service to clients • System easier to learn and use • Higher employee morale

The goal of a cost-benefit analysis is to weigh the benefits of each alternative against the costs of each alternative. However, cost-benefit analyses are not always easy to do because some benefits may be difficult to quantify. **Intangible benefits** are expected results from a project that are difficult to measure, quantify, or calculate. Although increased user productivity may be measurable (tangible), increased employee morale is not (intangible). A project may be expected to "improve the image of the organization," but what is the dollar value of a more progressive image? How many new or repeat clients will an enhanced image of the organization produce? Analysts should always try to produce a best guess estimate of intangible benefits of various alternatives, if possible. However, experienced analysts recognize that if most of the benefits of a proposed alternative are intangible, and if few quantifiable benefits will reduce expenses, improve productivity, or increase revenue, then they should seriously consider other alternatives.

 For a more in-depth understanding of cost-benefit analyses, read an article about this tool at the Mind Tools Web site, **www.mindtools.com/pages/article/ newTED_08.htm**.

Data Collection Instruments

Several steps in the needs analysis process depend on analysts' abilities to collect relevant information. When analysts gather information, they often use the sources summarized in Figure 9-5. The sections that follow contain a brief overview of each data collection instrument.

- Input forms
- Output forms
- Procedure documentation
- Operating or problem logs
- Interviews and questionnaires
- Direct observation

Figure 9-5   Data collection instruments

Input Forms.   An **input form** is a paper document or display screen image used to collect information about a business transaction. Because business transaction processing is the purpose of many computer systems, input forms are obviously an important source of information about an organization's business activities. Information on a paper input form is usually designed to be entered into an organization's computer system. A paper input form and the corresponding data entry screen often look as similar as possible to reduce confusion and data entry errors. Input forms are sometimes called **source documents**. For example, a copy shop might use a form like the sample in Figure 9-6 to collect information about a copy order for a client.

ORDER   Date _____   the print works

1473 Main St.

Sold to _____   Stamford, CT 06902

PHONE 555-2697

Paid By   ☐ Cash   ☐ Check # _____   FAX 555-2698

FAX Send _____ pgs Receive _____ pgs	
Photocopies	
Taken By: TOTAL	

Figure 9-6   Sample input form for a copy shop

The form in Figure 9-6 contains spaces for the basic order information the copy shop collects. If a needs assessment project for the copy shop includes automating the order form, a support analyst should understand how employees use the form. Who fills out the form and when? Does the form serve as a receipt for the client? Is the client's address or phone number ever included? What problems arise with the use of the existing form? For example, does the form not work well for some types of copy shop orders?

Output Forms.   **Output forms** contain the results of a business transaction or process. Examples include a sales receipt from a grocery store or restaurant, a paycheck stub, and a report card at the end of a school term. In Figure 9-6, once a copy shop employee fills in the input form and records the prices of each item, the form also serves as an output form, or receipt for the client.

Procedure Documentation. Written instructions about how to perform a business transaction or handle a routine operational procedure are called **procedure documentation**. Procedure documentation is written for an organization's employees. In the copy shop example, procedure documentation might describe the steps to fill out the order form for various kinds of copy orders, how to price each item on the form, what to do with the form after it is filled out, and where to file the form when the transaction is completed. Procedure documentation is often used to train new employees or to answer questions about business procedures that arise infrequently.

Good procedure documentation is rare, because procedures are often communicated verbally instead of in writing. Business procedures also change frequently, and the documentation that describes them may not be up to date. However, even out-of-date or handwritten documentation can be useful information to help analysts understand an organization's transactions and how they are processed.

Operating or Problem Logs. A **log** is a list of events or activities recorded in the sequence that the events occur. Logs can be used to record routine, periodic information about events that occur regularly, such as a media backup of a computer system (including when, by whom, what was backed up, the location of the backup, how long the backup should be retained, and so on). Logs can also be used to capture unusual events, errors, problems, shortages, or complaints. Analysts can make use of logs as a supplement to direct observation to collect information as input to a needs assessment project.

Interviews and Questionnaires. Analysts often use interviews and questionnaires to collect relevant information from users about the work they do, the problems they encounter, and how an existing or proposed computer system might affect their work. The advantage of face-to-face interviews is that interviewers can ask probing questions, where appropriate, to learn the details of issues that are of special interest. The ability to probe is especially useful because it is frequently difficult to anticipate every possible question one might like to ask on a printed questionnaire. However, interviews take more time than a questionnaire, and when analysts need to obtain information from many users, they often use a questionnaire to save time. When many users are affected, a combination of face-to-face interviews with a few users and a questionnaire for the remainder can be a good compromise. Another alternative when many users are potentially impacted is a **focus group**, which is a small representative group of selected users. A focus group often generates ideas that may not occur in a one-on-one interview, as focus group members interact with each other. A focus group also allows different opinions and options to be discussed by representatives of various stakeholders.

Interviews and questionnaires need to be structured to extract the appropriate information. Two basic kinds of questions an analyst can ask in either an interview or a questionnaire format are forced-choice and open-ended. In a **forced-choice question** (also called a close-ended question), a user chooses from among several predetermined responses. An example of a forced-choice question is shown in the shaded box that follows.

9

> How many copying orders do you process in a typical day?
> - ▫ none
> - ▫ 1–5
> - ▫ 6–10
> - ▫ 11–15
> - ▫ more than 15

In an **open-ended question**, users choose their own words, instead of predetermined responses, to answer the question. The answer can be any response the user thinks is appropriate. For example, to the question, "How many copying orders do you process in a typical day?", one employee could respond, "an average of 10," another might reply, "anywhere from 5 to 15," and yet another could say, "more than 5."

Both open-ended and forced-choice questions are appropriate in various situations. Analysts need to consider at least three issues when they design a question. First, what information do I want to get? Second, how am I going to analyze the information when I get it? Third, how can the question be asked so it makes sense to users and helps them respond accurately?

Both the forced-choice and open-ended question examples above elicit information on the number of orders processed. However, the open-ended question may require analysts to take the additional step of grouping (or coding) the responses into meaningful categories for analysis.

Forced-choice responses are usually easier to tabulate. Analysts can simply count the number of responses in each category. However, some users do not like to be forced to fit their answer into fixed response categories, or don't think their answer fits a single category, and they may refuse to answer. Additionally, forced-choice answer categories must relate to each user's experiences or the choices will be meaningless. For example, consider the following question:

> How many hours per day do you spend on e-mail messages?
> - ▫ none
> - ▫ 1 hour
> - ▫ 2 hours
> - ▫ 3 hours
> - ▫ more than 3 hours

Which box does a user check if he spends an hour and a half per day on e-mail messages? This question may be improved if the response categories are changed to ranges that accommodate partial hours.

How many hours per day do you spend on e-mail messages?

☐ less than 1 hour

☐ 1–2 hours

☐ 2–3 hours

☐ more than 3 hours

Although the ranges handle responses in factions of hours satisfactorily, there is a new problem: Which box does a user check if she spends exactly 2 hours on e-mail? Consider this revision:

How many hours per day do you spend on e-mail messages?

☐ less than 1 hour

☐ 1 hour or more, but less than 2 hours

☐ 2 hours or more, but less than 3 hours

☐ more than 3 hours

9

The response ranges in this example may be better defined, but the question now takes more space and time to read. From these few examples, you can see that construction of effective forced-choice questionnaire items is challenging and takes practice.

Open-ended responses have the advantage that they do not force a user to pick a category; however, they often take longer to complete because the user or interviewer must write out the answer, rather than check a box. Also, open-ended responses are often more difficult to tabulate than forced-choice responses because an analyst must read through the responses and make decisions about into which category each response fits. As a compromise, some analysts use a combination of forced-choice and open-ended questions to allow ease-of-tabulation with flexibility in responses.

Questionnaires and interviews are very useful tools to acquire information from users during a needs assessment project. However, they require care to design so that they extract information that is clear and unambiguous, and so that they elicit information the analyst can use. Most textbooks on systems analysis and design contain a chapter on interview and questionnaire methods that provides suggestions on and examples for interview and questionnaire design.

To ensure that they have high-quality questions, analysts who participate in a project with many users—where more formal interviews or questionnaires are used—often ask other analysts to help with question design. Questions designed by a team are often better than those written by one analyst. Another strategy to produce better questions is to field-test them on a small group of users who can give feedback on which questions were difficult to answer.

To learn more about interview and questionnaire methods for user surveys, visit a Web site that describes in greater detail how to design questionnaires and interview questions, such as **www.cc.gatech.edu/classes/cs6751_97_winter/ Topics/quest-design**.

Direct Observation.   Support analysts can often gain critical insights into user needs by simply watching users work. Direct observation can be a powerful method of data collection in situations where procedure documentation, questionnaires, interviews, and other forms of data collection aren't possible, or as a supplement to other methods. One key to successful direct observation is to plan sufficient time for the activity with the users. Take notes on what the users do, when they do it (the sequence of tasks), what tools and strategies they use, with whom they interact, and where they store information.

Data collection instruments help analysts collect useful, relevant information about an existing system that they can then use not only to evaluate how the system functions, but also to determine its strengths and weaknesses.

Charts and Diagrams

A chart or diagram can illustrate the flow of information in an organization, relationships between employees, or the parts of an information processing system. Or it can describe an entire system, the relevant parts of a system, or the details of a workflow. Because they are visual, charts and diagrams are often easier for users to read and understand than lengthy narratives written in technical language.

Analysts create charts and diagrams either manually or with a variety of graphic design tools. Some of these tools are highly specialized and take considerable training; books on systems analysis describe these tools in detail. Other graphic design tools are more accessible and allow analysts with a minimum of experience to create charts and diagrams. Analysts can use relatively simple tools to create two common types of charts: flowcharts and I-P-O charts.

Flowcharts.   A **flowchart** is a schematic diagram that uses symbols to represent the parts of a computer system or the steps in a procedure. Figure 9-7 shows a flowchart of the procedures in a computer repair shop.

In a flowchart, rectangular boxes often represent departments in an organization, nodes on a network, or processing steps that an employee performs. Diamond-shaped symbols usually represent decision points or questions that need to be answered. Lines connect various symbols in a flowchart to illustrate how the parts of the diagram are related or the sequence of processing steps.

To view example flowcharts and take a tutorial on flowcharting, visit the Flowcharting Center at **www.smartdraw.com/resources/centers/flowcharts**, where you can also download a trial version of the SmartDraw flowcharting tool.

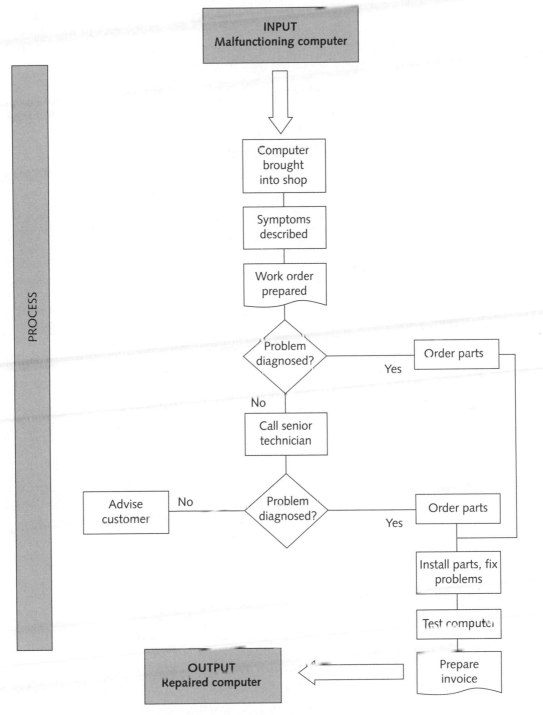

Figure 9-7 Flowchart showing a PC repair process

I-P-O Charts.   Most manual procedures or computer processing tasks can be described as some combination of input, processing, and output steps. An **I-P-O chart** represents the input, processing, and output steps required to perform a task. An I-P-O chart answers three fundamental questions about a procedure that a user or computer performs:

- **Input.** Where do I get the information with which to work?
- **Processing.** What tasks do I perform to process or transform the information?
- **Output.** What happens to the information when I'm done?

Figure 9-8 shows a simple I-P-O chart that describes a procedure in a brokerage firm to prepare a stock portfolio report for a client. A related chart is a H-I-P-O chart, which can be used to describe more complex processes. The *H* in H-I-P-O stands for hierarchical. It represents the idea that a complex task may be made up of a hierarchy of input, processing, and output steps, where each level in the hierarchy shows a different level of detail. Flowcharting software can often be used to draw H-I-P-O charts.

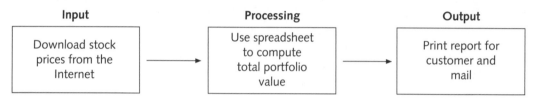

Figure 9-8   I-P-O chart to prepare a stock portfolio report

L. Murray Smith, a CPA, describes several graphic diagramming tools, including H-I-P-O charts, at **acct.tamu.edu/smith/system_tools/systools.htm**. Click the Exhibit 9 link at the bottom of the page to see an example of a H-I-P-O chart.

Analysts use a variety of analytic and design tools as aids in a needs analysis. Dataflow diagrams, entity-relationship diagrams, and CASE tools are used (see Smith's Web site above for examples), in addition to those previously mentioned. However, these more complex tools are probably of less use to support analysts than to systems analysts who design custom computer software applications. A textbook for a course on systems analysis and design describes these and other tools in considerable detail.

Prototyping Software

A **prototype** is a working model that support analysts build to let users experience and evaluate how the finished product of an analysis project will actually work. The purpose of a prototype is to provide an easy, quick, low-cost way for end users to view the characteristics an operational system will have when one is built.

When an application design project involves software development, prototyping tools can be used to build a working model. For example, programming and database languages such as

Microsoft Access, Microsoft Excel, Visual Basic, and Tcl/Tk can be used to build a working prototype of the menus, data input screens, processing steps, output forms and reports, and user interface for a system. Figure 9-9 shows a data entry form for a database of help desk problems created with Visual Basic for Applications in Microsoft Access. Once a model is built, end users can try out the prototype, evaluate whether it meets their needs, and provide useful feedback to the developer.

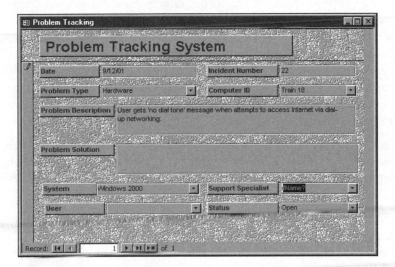

Figure 9-9   Data entry form for a database of help desk problems

 A group of faculty and students at the University of California, Berkeley has developed a prototyping tool for Web page layouts. Learn about their work and download a beta test version of their prototyping tool, DENIM, at **guir.berkeley.edu/projects/denim**.

Prototyping has become an increasingly popular tool for support analysts. A prototype is much faster and less expensive to develop in a database language than to write a program in a production language such as C++, COBOL, Java, or Fortran. For small processing systems, the prototype may actually become the production system after users are satisfied that it meets their needs. For larger processing systems, once users have accepted the prototype, the model is usually translated into a production programming language. Although prototype systems can give users a realistic preview of how a new system might operate, prototypes usually operate slowly or have limited capacity for data storage. These limitations can be reduced or eliminated when a programmer converts a working prototype into a production system written in a programming language for efficient operation.

Other Needs Assessment Tools

Two tools you learned about in Chapter 8 are also useful to support analysts: benchmarks and weighted point comparisons. These are especially useful when analysts need a decision aid to compare two or more products, services, or approaches to solving a user problem.

As you learned in the case study for Re-Nu-Cartridge in this chapter, and earlier in Chapter 7, many user support projects can make effective use of project management software such as Microsoft Project 2003. **Project management software** can help project leaders and workers organize the steps in a large project, set priorities, establish and monitor project costs, and schedule staff and activities. Figure 7-5 in Chapter 7 is a Microsoft Project 2003 screen that shows the steps involved in a project and how the relationship of the steps affects the staff, time, and resources needed to complete the project. Project management software is most appropriate for large-scale needs assessment and development projects that will involve a number of users, analysts, and steps.

The needs analysis tools described in this chapter are among those that support analysts find helpful when they undertake needs assessment projects. However, the tools described here just scratch the surface of the information resources and tools available. New tools, especially automated ones, become available every year.

Not every needs assessment project requires all the steps and the use of every resource or tool described in this chapter. In an actual project, support analysts choose from among the approaches described here to make the resources and tools fit the task. Support analysts who spend a significant amount of time on user needs assessment projects may benefit from a course on systems analysis and design such as those offered in many two- and four-year schools. The most important fact to remember is that user needs analysis and assessment is a process, and the process and tools analysts choose to solve one problem will likely be different from the process and tools for another.

CHAPTER SUMMARY

❑ User support specialists (also called support analysts) who undertake a needs assessment for end users follow a sequence of steps designed to obtain relevant information and help end users make an informed decision. In the needs assessment process, support analysts use several tools and information resources to aid them in their task.

❑ Steps in a user needs assessment follow three distinct phases and include:

Preparation phase—Before the detailed work on an assessment project begins, analysts should learn about the project.

1. Understand the personal or organizational goals
2. Understand the decision criteria and constraints
3. Define the problem clearly

4. Identify the roles of participants

5. Identify sources of information

Investigation phase—Analysts examine the current system or situation and evaluate possible alternatives for changes that will improve it.

6. Develop an understanding of the existing system or situation

7. Investigate alternatives to the existing system

Decision phase—Analysts create a model of what the proposed system will look like and decide how the new system will be obtained.

8. Develop a model of the proposed system

9. Make a build-versus-buy decision

Decision and documentation tools are available to support analysts who work on needs assessment projects. Popular tools include a project charter, cost-benefit analysis to weigh the costs of a proposed alternative against its payoffs; several data collection instruments (including input and output forms, procedure documentation, interviews and questionnaires, and direct observation); graphic design tools to draw flowcharts, I-P-O charts, and related schematic representations of systems; and prototyping tools to model the operation of software systems. Large assessment projects often require use of a project management software package.

KEY TERMS

build-versus-buy decision — The decision an organization makes about whether to build a custom solution or purchase one off the shelf; can apply to hardware, software, or complete systems, but most often involves software.

cost-benefit analysis — A comparison of the expenses a project will incur and a project's payoffs; organizations are reluctant to spend resources on projects for which the costs outweigh the benefits.

decision phase — The third phase of a user needs analysis and assessment project, in which analysts develop a model of the proposed solution and decide whether to build or buy it.

deliverable — The end result of a needs analysis project, such as a written analysis of alternatives, a feasibility report, a recommendation, or a decision to build, buy, or upgrade a system.

feasibility — An investigation into the economic, operational, technical, and timeline constraints during a user needs analysis and assessment project.

flowchart — A schematic diagram that uses symbols to represent the parts of a computer system or the steps in a procedure.

focus group — A small group of selected users who represent a larger group of users in a needs assessment project; a focus group participates in an interview when including every user is impractical.

forced-choice question — A question on a questionnaire or in an interview with predetermined response categories; a multiple-choice test question is forced-choice; also called a closed-ended question.

input form — A paper document or display screen image used to collect information about a transaction; also called a *source document*.

intangible benefit — An expected result from a project that is difficult to measure, quantify, or calculate; increased user productivity may be measurable (tangible), whereas increased employee morale is difficult to measure (intangible).

investigation phase — The second phase of a user needs analysis and assessment project, in which analysts try to understand the present system or situation and alternatives to it.

I-P-O chart — A diagram that represents the input, processing, and output steps required to perform a task.

log — A list of events or activities recorded in the sequence that the events occur; used to record information about routine, periodic events or unusual events, such as errors or problems.

model — A narrative or graphic diagram that represents a business activity in an organization (such as paper workflow), a computer system, or a network.

open-ended question — A question on a questionnaire or in an interview in which users choose their own words, instead of predetermined responses, to answer a question; a short-answer test question is open-ended.

output form — A document that contains the results of a business transaction or process.

preparation phase — The first phase of a user needs analysis and assessment project, in which analysts try to understand the personal or organizational goals, decision criteria, and constraints; define the problem; identify the roles of stakeholders; and identify sources of information.

procedure documentation — Written instructions about how to perform a business transaction or handle a routine operational procedure.

project charter — A short narrative statement that describes the objectives, scope, methods, participants, deliverables, steps, timeline, and measures of success for a needs assessment project.

project management software — An applications software tool to help project leaders and workers organize the steps in a project, set priorities, establish and monitor project tasks and costs, and schedule staff and activities.

prototype — A working model that support analysts build to let users experience and evaluate how the finished product of an analysis project will actually work; contains enough features of an actual system that users can operate the model to evaluate its ability to meet their needs.

satisficing solution — An alternate solution that solves a problem in a reasonable way, but is not necessarily the optimal solution; satisficing solutions are often adopted when an optimal solution is too expensive.

source document — Any form used to collect information about a business transaction for input into an organization or computer system; examples include payroll timecards, a problem log, a membership application, and an expense account record.

stakeholder — A participant in a user needs analysis and assessment project who might gain or lose from its success or failure; includes end users, managers, technical support staff, and the support analyst.

turnkey system — An integrated, packaged solution that provides hardware, software, and support services purchased from a single vendor.

CHECK YOUR UNDERSTANDING

1. True or False? The goals and objectives of an organization are usually long-term and do not usually impact decisions about a user's immediate needs for computer systems and services.

2. Which of the following is not a primary step in the needs analysis and assessment process?

   a. preparation

   b. investigation

   c. decision

   d. purchase

3. True or False? A payroll clerk is a reliable source to determine whether a new payroll software package is needed.

4. In a user needs assessment project, the fact that an organization is uncomfortable with risks due to reliance on a new, untested software package would be considered as part of _____ .

   a. economic feasibility

   b. operational feasibility

   c. technological feasibility

   d. timeline feasibility

5. True or False? Some problems user support analysts study turn out to be organizational problems instead of technology problems.

6. Which sequence of letters represents the correct order of the following four steps in the user needs analysis process? (a) investigate alternatives to the current system (b) make a build-versus-buy decision (c) identify sources of information (d) understand the organization's goals

   a. a – b – c – d

   b. d – c – b – a

   c. c – a – d – b

   d. d – c – a – b

7. True or False? The criteria an organization uses to make a decision about a new computer system or service is often based on the feasibility of time, staffing, money, and technology.

8. True or False? In a user needs assessment project, software requirements should generally be considered first, followed by hardware needs.

9. A(n) _____ considers whether to purchase a system off-the-shelf or construct one from scratch.

10. A narrative or diagram that explains the structure and operation of a new or existing computer system is called a _____ .

    a. prototype

    b. layout

    c. model

    d. report

11. A(n) _____ is the end result of an analysis project that recommends purchase, modification, upgrade, or construction of a system.

12. True or False? A turnkey system is a package that includes hardware, software, and support services from a single vendor.

13. True or False? The build-versus-buy decision in a needs analysis project applies primarily to computer hardware.

14. True or False? A cost-benefit analysis is often in the form of a side-by-side comparison of the expenses associated with a project and its advantages to the organization.

15. In a cost-benefit analysis, the development or purchase of software is generally considered a(n) _____ .

    a. acquisition cost

    b. operating cost

    c. reduction of expenses

    d. intangible cost

16. A(n) _____ is a written narrative that describes the objectives, scope, methods, participants, deliverables, and timeline for a needs assessment project.

17. A(n) _____ is a schematic diagram that uses symbols to represent the parts of a computer system.

18. True or False? Open-ended questions are generally preferable to forced-choice questions because they take less analyst time to tabulate the results.

Discussion Questions

1. Do you agree or disagree with the following statement: "Because a small dollar amount is involved, a needs assessment to purchase a $600 PC for an employee is overkill?" Explain your answer.

2. Why is it important for a support analyst to learn who will make the final decision on a needs assessment project and what decision criteria will be used?

3. In a cost-benefit analysis, which are more difficult to measure, costs or benefits? Explain why.

4. In order to save time and money in a user needs analysis project, you could choose to omit one of the steps described in the chapter. Which step would you omit, and why?

Hands-On Projects

Project 9-1

Assess the need for a personal computer. Think about how you would modify the steps described in this chapter if you were asked to recommend a personal computer system to a friend for home use. Which steps would you omit? Which steps would be most important? Write a two-paragraph summary of your conclusions.

Project 9 2

Avoid needs assessment problems. Some support analysts have expressed the view that the steps in a needs assessment project really should be described as:

1. Unbridled euphoria

2. Questions about the feasibility of the project

3. Growing concern about the project results

4. Unmitigated disaster

5. Search for the guilty

6. Punishment of the innocent

7. Promotion of the uninvolved

Behind each piece of humor may be some grain of truth. Write a two page report that discusses ways a support analyst can prevent the steps in a needs assessment project from turning into the seven described above.

Project 9-3

Design an input form. Design an input form that could be used to record information about a computer system problem in an instructional lab or a training facility. Include spaces on the form to record information such as:

- □ System identification
- □ Date and time the problem was reported
- □ Who reported the problem
- □ Description of the problem
- □ Who was assigned to work on the problem
- □ Problem resolution (how the problem was fixed)
- □ Date and time the problem was fixed

Project 9-4

Analyze costs and benefits for a home computer. Study the categories included in a cost–benefit analysis in Table 9-2. Think about how these categories apply to the purchase of a home computer system. Are there categories of costs or benefits you would add to Table 9-2 for a home computer? Which cost categories do you think are most important in the purchase of a PC for home use? Are the benefit categories you listed tangible or intangible benefits? Explain why.

Project 9-5

Develop a project charter. Think about the last time you purchased a PC, stereo, or other electronic equipment, or helped a friend or relative purchase one. Write a project charter that describes the purchase process you followed. Use the project charter form in the book as an example to create a project charter form of your own.

Project 9-6

Develop an I-P-O chart and a flowchart. Select a common sales transaction, such as an automobile gasoline purchase or a grocery store purchase. Analyze the transaction and make a list of the items of information that are input, the processing that takes place as part of the transaction, and the resulting output. Record your analysis in the form of an I-P-O chart, as shown in this chapter. Then sketch a flowchart of the transaction. Compare the information communicated in the I-P-O and flow diagrams. Which do you prefer? Explain why.

Project 9 7

Perform a cost-benefit analysis for CD burners. Research the relative advantages and disadvantages of internal and external CD burners using the Internet or library resources. Although internal CD burners are generally less expensive, are there reasons why a user would want to pay more for an external CD burner? Using the format in Table 9-2, develop a simple cost-benefit analysis for internal and external CD burners.

CASE PROJECTS

1. Feasibility Analysis of a Computer Facility Problem

Based on your personal experience or on conversations with classmates or coworkers, select a current problem in a computer facility at work, in a lab at school, or in a training facility. Meet with a group of your classmates or coworkers to perform the first several steps in a needs analysis aimed at solving the problem. First, make sure your group has a clear definition of the root problem. Then identify the stakeholders and sources of information available to you. Brainstorm alternative solutions to the problem. Finally, analyze the feasibility of each alternative.

- Are some alternatives more feasible than others? Explain why.
- What additional information resources would you need to complete the analysis?
- Did your group reach consensus on a recommendation it could make to management?

Write your conclusions in the form of a feasibility report.

2. Needs Assessment for Video and Beyond

Kathleen Marsh is a recent community college graduate who plans to open a video rental store in the next couple of months. Kathleen majored in small business management, but also took a number of computer courses as electives in her community college degree program, including:

- Introduction to Business Information Systems
- PC Operating Systems
- Spreadsheets (Excel)
- Database Management (Access)
- Introductory and Advanced Visual Basic
- Systems Analysis
- Introduction to Computer Networks

Kathleen did well in these courses and feels very comfortable with computer technology, but she wants an independent perspective on the feasibility of a computer system for her video rental company. That's why she has asked for your advice.

Although this is her first real venture as an entrepreneur, Kathleen has had considerable part-time work experience in video rental stores during high school and college.

Kathleen's video rental store, Video and Beyond, will be in a new shopping center. Kathleen chose the location because a sizable bedroom community is nearby, and because no major competition is located in the area, which is about 15 miles from the nearest large town. She has arranged to rent 1500 square feet of space in the shopping center.

Kathleen has located a video distributor who can supply her with a start-up inventory of 3000 to 3500 current releases and popular classic videos, DVDs, and games. The distributor can also serve as a one-stop supplier for new videos, DVDs, and games as they are released to the video rental market.

Kathleen has identified her major expenses, both start-up and ongoing, which are listed in Table 9-3.

Table 9-3   Video and Beyond's expenses

Start-up Expenses	Ongoing Expenses
Furniture	Rent & utilities
• Counters	Payroll & taxes
• Video and game racks	New video, DVD, and game releases
Popcorn machine	Advertising
Initial inventory of videos, DVDs, and games	
Computer system (?)	

Kathleen's initial thinking about a computer system is that she probably cannot afford one in her start-up budget. Instead, she had worked out a simple manual system for keeping track of videos and client rentals. In her system, each video, DVD, or game will have an ID number recorded on the plastic case, and on a card she would keep in a *Video* card box on top of the counter. In a separate box on the counter, she would keep a card for each *Client*. The client cards would be filed by telephone number, which she would use as a client ID number. When a client rented one or more videos, she would clip the video card(s) to the client card, and put them together in a third box labeled *Rentals*, which is organized by the due date. When a rental is returned, Kathleen would unclip the video and client cards and return them to their respective card files. At 6 PM each day, if there were cards in the rental box for rentals that were past due, Kathleen would contact the client and assess a late charge.

Kathleen thinks this simple manual system would work until her business volume grew and she could afford a computer system. But she wonders whether a computer system would be feasible immediately, when she opens the doors in a couple of months. She even thought perhaps she could buy a PC and write a simple program in Access, Visual Basic, or Excel to replace the manual card system. Kathleen would appreciate your advice.

1. Prepare a list of interview questions you would like to ask Kathleen that would help you make a recommendation to her.

2. After you have a list of potential questions to ask in an interview, compare your questions with those of three classmates or coworkers. Merge your questions into a single list from your group. Try to arrange the questions into categories with other similar questions.

3. When you have completed the list of interview questions, your instructor will provide you with Kathleen's responses to several of the questions from an interview with her. Based on her responses, answer these questions:

    a. If Video and Beyond decides to purchase a computer system, what major decisions will the owner need to make?

    b. Would you recommend that Kathleen Marsh build her own software system or purchase one? Why?

    c. Make a list of the software Video and Beyond will need to meet the needs Kathleen described in the interview.

    d. In order to build or buy a transaction processing program to handle rentals and returns, Video and Beyond would probably need a database of videos and a database of clients. Select either the Client or Video table and list the fields you think Video and Beyond will need.

    e. A word processor or a database language such as Access can be used as a tool to build a prototype (model) of a report. Use one of these tools to design a prototype of the video rental agreement that would be printed for clients to sign each time they rent a video.

    f. Given what you know of Video and Beyond's business plan and needs and its financial situation, do you think a computer system is feasible? Why, or why not?

CASE PROJECTS

3. Computer Recommendation for Amy Lee

Amy Lee was recently hired as a personnel assistant in the Human Resources department where you work. Because you are the user support specialist, she has contacted you for some help with a computer she will use in her job in employee benefits administration. You want to make sure that she gets the computer tools she will need to be productive.

Amy says that she will need an office suite and that her boss gave her a choice of Microsoft Office 2003 or WordPerfect Office 11. Because she has previous work experience with the WordPerfect word processor, which is part of WordPerfect suite, she would like to use it. The WordPerfect suite includes most of the tools Amy needs, so her other software requirements are minimal. In addition to WordPerfect Office, Amy needs the Windows XP operating system. She also needs a Web browser to access the Internet, because an increasing amount of information about benefits and employee compensation is available on the Web.

Where she needs your help is with hardware. Amy's boss said that she has very little money left in this year's Human Resources equipment budget for hardware. So she suggested that

Amy try to find a basic starter system, but one that could be upgraded next year when there will be more equipment money available. Amy wants you to recommend a hardware configuration that meets her immediate needs, is reasonably priced, and can be upgraded next year. It needs to be able to run the software Amy has selected. Whatever hardware she buys must also be compatible with the local area network in Human Resources. It operates from a Windows 2003 server. The network server can provide Amy with access to one of two laser printers, so the hardware system she buys need not include a printer. However, Amy wants to be able to scan documents into her system, and no scanner is available on the network.

Analyze Amy's situation and recommend a specific hardware configuration that will meet her immediate needs. In addition, find equipment for sale in a trade magazine, advertised in a local newspaper, or for sale on the Internet that you believe is the appropriate configuration for Amy. When you are finished, prepare a recommended list of hardware specifications (and prices, if available) that Amy could take to her boss.

CASE PROJECTS

4. Cost-Benefit Analysis for Re-Nu-Cartridge

NOTE

For background information on Re-Nu-Cartridge, see Case Project 4 in previous chapters.

The outside sales representatives at Re-Nu-Cartridge currently create their orders and sales reports in the field as they call on clients. Although the sales orders and reports are often quite lengthy, some reps prepare these documents manually, and a few use portable typewriters they carry for that purpose. When the orders and sales reports are completed, and if the sales reps plan to return to Re-Nu-Cartridge's office in the next two or three days, they just bring the orders and sales reports back with them. If they will be on the road for more than three days, the sales reps usually mail them to the office. Consequently, there can be about a week lag between the time the orders are taken from a client and the time Re-Nu-Cartridge staff at the office can process the information about the order.

This lag means the sales staff, including other sales reps, do not have up-to-date information on sales volumes, commitments of existing inventory to clients, and changes in the popularity of various models of inkjet and toner cartridges. Furthermore, a lag occurs between the time the Sales department receives information about the order and the time that information is transmitted to the manufacturing division where cartridges are remanufactured and filled with ink.

In addition to the time lag, the manual processing of sales orders and reports by the sales reps introduces errors. On one occasion, ten cases of Canon black ink cartridges were shipped to a client when the client actually ordered colored ink cartridges. The problem was traced to an error on a handwritten sales order.

As a result, Fred, the CEO at Re-Nu-Cartridge, is considering buying the six outside sales reps laptop computers to address these specific problems that the reps encounter. He asks you for your advice.

1. List the factors you would consider in a cost-benefit analysis for the laptop computers for Re-Nu-Cartridge's outside sales representatives.

2. Describe some of the major costs that Re-Nu-Cartridge would encounter and some of the major benefits that might accrue to Re-Nu-Cartridge if it purchases the laptop systems. Provide some dollar estimates where you can.

3. Do you think the benefits to Re-Nu-Cartridge will outweigh the costs? Explain your answer.

Write a one- to two-page report to Fred that summarizes your findings.

9

CHAPTER 10

INSTALLING END-USER COMPUTER SYSTEMS

In this chapter you will learn:

- Major site preparation steps for computer installations
- Important tasks to prepare an installation site
- The purpose and contents of a site management notebook
- Tools needed to install hardware
- Steps to install and configure hardware
- Steps to install and configure an operating system and network connection
- Steps to install and configure applications software packages
- Wrap-up tasks that installers often perform

After you have evaluated computer products (Chapter 8), conducted a needs assessment (Chapter 9), and perhaps even helped justify and purchase an end-user system, the next step is to install the system. Installation can include hardware, peripherals, operating systems, utility software, and applications software—either packaged together as a turnkey system or sold individually. During the installation process, you may also need to deal with user training, user documentation, and site management issues; you will learn more about these activities in Chapters 11, 12, and 13.

The system installation process can easily intimidate end users, especially new users. Support specialists are often able to set up and get a system running in a fraction of the time it would take an end user to figure out the procedure and work around the pitfalls. This chapter describes some typical tasks for many personal and office computer installations, although every installation poses different challenges. You will learn about site preparation tasks as well as the tools and steps necessary to install hardware, operating systems, network connections, and applications software.

SYSTEM INSTALLATION OVERVIEW

User support specialists are often responsible for installing end-user systems. With adequate preparation, the proper tools, and a well thought-out procedure to track important details, system installation should run smoothly and efficiently so that end users' computers can be up and running with a minimum of interruption to their work. This chapter emphasizes the importance of installation check lists and system documentation. Whether the installation is for a single home computer, a small office system, or hundreds of networked systems, experienced system installers know that important details are easy to forget—whether at the time they install a system or later when the system needs to be repaired or upgraded.

The major installation steps are summarized in Figure 10-1 and discussed in detail throughout the chapter.

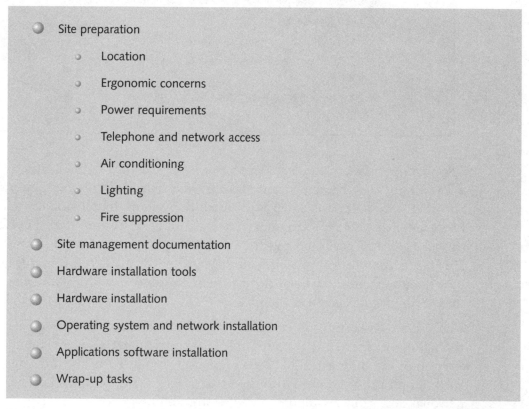

- Site preparation
  - Location
  - Ergonomic concerns
  - Power requirements
  - Telephone and network access
  - Air conditioning
  - Lighting
  - Fire suppression
- Site management documentation
- Hardware installation tools
- Hardware installation
- Operating system and network installation
- Applications software installation
- Wrap-up tasks

Figure 10-1   Overview of system installation steps

Support specialists may not be involved in all the system installation steps listed in Figure 10-1. For example, they might not need to install or configure an operating system if one is preinstalled. Or a specialized network technician may be responsible for connecting the computer system to a network. The check lists in this chapter are generic; you should consider them a starting point and modify them to fit specific situations. In some cases, you may need to add steps; in other cases, some steps may not directly apply to your situation. For example, if a new or upgraded software package needs to be installed on an end-user system, the check lists for hardware, operating system, and network connections don't apply.

SITE PREPARATION

Before installing a complete system, support specialists often visit the end user's location for a preinstallation inspection. The purpose of the site visit is to anticipate problems that may arise so the installer can address them before the installation. Many installers use a written check list to make sure that they address certain critical questions during the visit. A typical site installation check list would contain the following queries:

1. What are the space requirements for the computer system or workstation?
2. What materials need to be stored near the computer?
3. What space constraints are potential problems at the user's site?
4. What ergonomic issues need to be addressed?
5. Do special ADA (Americans with Disabilities Act) or OSHA (Occupational Safety and Health Administration) issues or accommodations apply to this installation?
6. Is the power supply accessible and adequate for the system?
7. Is power conditioning required?
8. Where is the nearest telephone and/or network access?
9. Is air conditioning required?
10. What lighting problems may need to be addressed?
11. Is a fire suppression system installed and operational?

Experienced installers need not carry an actual check list. Observation of the site may be sufficient to determine what problems exist, if any. However, if they have several installations to perform at numerous sites, a check list for each site can help them keep track of the conditions and special requirements at each location.

Location

When user support specialists install a complete computer system, they must determine the best location for the system unit, display screen, printer, keyboard, mouse, and other peripherals and accessories. A system that has properly located components will be easy and efficient to use, will not cause discomfort for the user, and will ensure the physical safety of both the user and the system itself. Each installation site presents unique challenges, and support specialists try to adapt the installation to the space and layout constraints of each site.

10

System Unit Location.   The system unit is usually located within four to five feet of the user's work area, a distance dictated by the length of signal cables between the system unit and the keyboard, mouse, and other peripherals. If the system unit is a desktop model, the table or desk surface is often the most convenient location for it, especially for users who frequently access the peripherals inside the system unit case (such as the floppy disk drive, removable hard drive, DVD drive, or CD drive). However, the **footprint** of a desktop case, which is the number of square inches (length × width) of usable space the computer case occupies, is relatively large, and reduces the work area on a desk. Minitower cases, which are popular because they have a smaller footprint, can be located on the work surface, a bookshelf, or even the floor.

Although installation on a floor reduces the desk space a system occupies, floor installations are not without problems. First, most floors are dusty areas, and internal fans may pull dust into the case. If possible, arrange for the case to be installed six inches above floor level. Second, system unit cases located on the floor should be placed where they cannot be accidentally kicked or obstruct foot traffic. For some users, frequent bending to reach a floor unit can cause back strain. Wherever possible, disk and tape drive peripherals should be located within arm's reach of an end user in a normal working position.

 If a system unit must be located some distance from a user's work area, extender cables for the keyboard, mouse, and display screen can be purchased to accommodate a longer distance.

NOTE

Keyboard and Mouse Location.   Ideally, a computer system should be installed in a work area where the table or desktop surface is 26 to 28 inches from the floor, which is a comfortable keyboard and mouse height for most users. A typical office desk surface is 30 inches from the floor; a keyboard or mouse used on a regular office desk or table at 30 inches can cause users discomfort because the angle of their wrists at the keyboard is unnatural. To prevent wrist and finger pain, make sure that when a user's hands rest on the keyboard or mouse, they extend in a relatively straight line, making them flat or tilted slightly downward, from the forearms. If a 30-inch office desk or table is the only possible keyboard location, it may be possible to make one of the following adaptations:

- Shorten the desk or table legs to get the keyboard to a comfortable height.
- Adjust the chair height so the user's wrists are in a comfortable position.
- Add an adjustable keyboard shelf to the underside of the desk or table.

The solution to one problem can cause another. In a situation where a chair seat is adjusted high enough to enable wrist comfort, the user's feet may not rest comfortably on the floor, and leg problems can result. An adjustable footrest may help in this situation.

NOTE As laptop computer models increase in popularity, support specialists need to be aware of the special ergonomic challenges they present. Because laptops are often transported from one location to another and may be used with docking stations or port replicators, the height of a laptop keyboard will vary according to the location and environment where it is used. A laptop should ideally be used on a surface that is at the lower end of the 26- to 28-inch recommended height range, because the thickness of the laptop itself can add one to two inches to the keyboard height. A laptop used on a standard office desk may result in a keyboard that is 32 inches off the floor—too high for comfortable, long-term use.

Display Screen Location.   Position the display screen so the user can look straight ahead or slightly downward at it. The most comfortable display screen position is often the same as where a user would hold a book to read at the workspace. The user should not have to look up at the display screen. Tilt the display so the user can view it with a natural head position, without neck strain.

Printer Location.   A printer does not have to be placed on the user's desktop but can instead be located on a work table or bookshelf or, where available, on a printer stand. A printer should be in a convenient location where users have easy access to load paper and ribbons or cartridges and where the case can be opened to remove paper jams. Expander or extension signal cables from the system unit to the printer can be purchased to provide additional flexibility in printer location, but some printer models have distance limits that must be considered when expander cables are purchased. The location of networked printers that will be shared among several users in an office is a critical decision. Printers located some distance from frequent users can result in productivity losses.

Supplies.   Users frequently want various supplies located conveniently near their computer equipment. These supplies include printer paper, mailing labels, ribbons or ink or toner cartridges, media (floppy disks, cartridge tapes, removable hard disks, and blank CDs and DVDs), computer manuals and books, cleaning supplies, tools, and other accessories. Supplies can be stored in an office file drawer, bookcase, or closet. Some supplies need to be stored in a special location to avoid certain problems. For example, paper should not be stored where it can draw excessive moisture. Magnetic media should not be stored near motors, generators, or electrical or telephone equipment that can generate a magnetic field.

Furniture Issues.   A user's chair probably has more impact on comfort, health, and safety than any other piece of office furniture, workspace layout, computer system design, or other ergonomic factors. Adjustability is the key criterion in an office chair: adjustable seat height, seat swivel and tilt, backrest, and arm rests. The seat height should be adjusted so the user's feet rest comfortably on the floor. Seat swivel and tilt features permit a user to vary the position with respect to the computer system and work area. This avoids the monotony of sitting in a single position for long periods. The seat backrest should be adjusted so it fits and supports the user's lower back. The arm rests should be adjusted so the user's elbows rest comfortably on the tops of the rests when the user is sitting in the chair with a comfortable posture. Most ergonomic chairs now have a "waterfall" front edge designed to reduce the pressure on the back of a user's legs. Other chair selection features include a five-leg base (rather than a less stable four-leg base) on rollers, and padding that is supportive and comfortable. When possible, a user should have an opportunity to try out an ergonomic chair. Low-cost chairs often do not hold up well over several years of use, and even very expensive chairs may still be uncomfortable and/or lack features a user desires.

Space Constraint Solutions.   Where space permits, a separate computer worktable or an extension to the user's office desk (that is the recommended 26- to 28-inch height) can be used in addition to or in place of a user's desk. For office desks that do not have much available space, or in a situation where a user wants to maximize the desk space, a flat panel (LCD or plasma) display screen takes much less desk space than a traditional CRT-type monitor, but is also more expensive. To accommodate CRT monitors, a monitor arm can often be attached to the tabletop or to the wall. A monitor arm holds the display screen three to four inches off the desktop, but not every model works with every type of desk design. Some monitor arms have a storage area for the keyboard when it is not in use, which frees up additional desk space.

Both system units and CRT monitors produce heat when they operate. The vent holes in the cases of these units should not be blocked by office or bookcase walls or by shelves. Air should be able to circulate around the cases of all computer peripherals.

Many ergonomic desks have keyboard shelves built in under the work surface. These shelves can usually be added to standard office desks and worktables. Keyboard shelves are often adjustable. In addition to saving desk space, adjustable keyboard shelves enable a user to position the keyboard at a comfortable height. They are especially useful when multiple users share a work area, such as at a shared desk or in a computer lab or training facility.

With careful planning, desk space can be freed by locating the system unit, display screen, printer, and other peripherals close to the user's desk area but not actually on it. Several vendors manufacture furniture specially designed for computer equipment that can save desktop space.

In some offices, end users want systems installed on furniture that was never intended for computers, such as older or antique furniture or on a credenza. In these cases, furniture may need to be significantly adapted to avoid ergonomic problems later. Monitor arms and keyboard shelves can help with these difficult situations. Be sure adequate knee room is available, especially if the user is tall.

Many office supply and computer vendors carry furniture and other products designed to address the issues discussed in this section. To see examples of products described here, visit the Web site of K-Log and check its online catalog at **www.k-log.com**.

Ergonomics

Ergonomics is the study of how to design computer systems (hardware and software) and lay out workspaces to minimize health problems and maximize employee safety, productivity, comfort, and job satisfaction. Some large organizations employ a safety engineer whose job responsibilities include office and factory floor ergonomics. In small organizations, user support specialists are often the primary resource of advice about ergonomic issues in an organization.

A well-planned computer installation can help users avoid several common ergonomic problems, described below.

Back or Neck Muscle Pain. Pain in the back or neck muscles can have more than one source. A user may be straining neck muscles to see a display screen that is placed too high. When a user's chair is too low, it can force the user to look up to view the screen. The user's chair may not be well designed for computer use. Poorly designed chairs can cut off circulation in legs or force the user to use back and neck muscles that should be relaxed. The keyboard may be too high so that the user's arms are angled in an unnatural position. A user, despite a correctly designed workspace, may work too long at a keyboard and display screen without adequate breaks or without changing body position.

Solutions to back or neck muscle pain can include keyboard height adjustments, a chair with both back and seat adjustment levers, and sufficient back support and adequate cushioning. Some users find that a pillow in the curve of their backs helps them sit more comfortably in their chairs. Users should be reminded to take "stretch" breaks at least once an hour. Frequent finger, hand, wrist, and neck stretches during breaks can be effective to prevent and sometimes cure pain, as can isometric exercises.

Leg Pain. Leg pain can result from an office chair that is too high for the user's feet to touch the floor or that is improperly designed and impairs leg circulation. Leg pain can also result from a work area with too little knee room, or one that forces a user to sit in an uncomfortable position for extended periods.

Solutions to leg pain include ergonomically designed office chairs with back and seat adjustment levers, sufficient back support and adequate cushioning, and a "waterfall" seat design that takes pressure off the backs of a user's legs and promotes better circulation. A footrest placed at a 15-degree angle may be necessary to support the user's legs and reduce strain.

Eyestrain and Headaches. Eyestrain and headaches can result from screen glare. A user's display screen may reflect sunlight or room lights, which is one of the primary causes of eyestrain. (Also see the "Lighting" section later in this chapter.) Users' glasses or contact lenses may not be appropriate for the distance they are sitting from the computer screen.

Solutions to eyestrain and headaches include changing the orientation of the computer to the light source, or using window shades to reduce glare. The level of lighting in the computer area may need to be reduced. Antiglare screen filters are available from office and computer supply stores. Users can ensure that eyeglass prescriptions are correct for extended computer use, and that they take breaks at least once an hour. Users should also look away from the display screen at distant objects periodically to minimize eyestrain.

Wrist and Finger Pain.   Wrist and finger pain is usually the result of a keyboard that is too high or too low. Hand and wrist muscles and tendons should not be tense or strained at the keyboard; a user's arm should be angled downward slightly, and the wrist should have support. Physical problems called **repetitive strain injuries** result from continuous use of joints in a limited range of motion. The symptoms of repetitive strain injuries include swelling, numbness, tingling, and stiffness in joints. The most common form of repetitive strain injury is **carpal tunnel syndrome**, which affects wrists and fingers.

Solutions to help avoid repetitive strain injuries include placing the keyboard at the optimal 26 to 28 inches from the floor, using an adjustable keyboard shelf, a keyboard wrist rest, a chair with arms, and stretch breaks at least once an hour. A product that may help reduce strain is an ergonomic (or natural) keyboard, which splits the right and left hand keys in an inverted V shape so that the user's hands, wrists, and forearms are in a more natural and comfortable position. These keyboards take some time to acclimate to, but those who use a keyboard extensively and have tried them generally do not want to return to a conventional keyboard.

Figure 10-2 illustrates some of the important dimensions that will ensure user comfort and avoid many of the potential ergonomic problems that can arise. These ergonomic problems and possible solutions are summarized in Table 10-1.

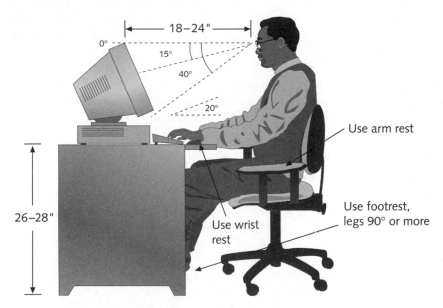

Figure 10-2   Workstation ergonomics

Table 10-1   Ergonomic problems and solutions

Ergonomic Problem	Possible Solutions
Back or neck muscle pain or numbness	• Replace office chair with one that can be adjusted. • Adjust keyboard height. • Install adjustable keyboard shelves. • Encourage frequent breaks and exercises to reduce stress.
Leg pain or numbness	• Replace office chair. • Place footrest on floor.
Eyestrain Headaches	• Reorient computer to reduce display screen glare. • Adjust office lighting. • Install display screen antiglare filter. • Check for proper eyeglasses and prescription. • Replace display screen with larger size and better resolution. • Encourage frequent breaks and exercises to reduce stress.
Wrist and finger pain or numbness Carpal tunnel syndrome	• Adjust keyboard height. • Install adjustable keyboard shelf. • Use keyboard wrist rest. • Encourage frequent breaks and exercises to reduce stress.

10

With the amount of attention repetitive strain injuries and other ergonomic problems have received in recent years, it is no surprise that a number of devices now marketed are designed to avoid or reduce the impact of extended computer use on end users. These devices include:

- Adjustable tables and work surfaces
- Adjustable chairs
- Footrests
- Keyboard shelves
- Alternative (natural/ergonomic) keyboards
- Alternative pointing devices (trackballs and touchpads)
- Wrist rests
- Mouse support rests
- Document holders
- Monitor arms
- Task lighting

- Antiglare screens
- Assistive devices

NOTE

Assistive devices are computer peripherals and software that adapt a computer system to permit end users with various physical limitations to be more productive. For example, users with visual impairments may be able to use special software that displays extra-large type fonts on a display screen. Users who cannot see a display screen may be able to use hardware and software devices that "read" the contents of a screen to a user. Users who do not have the motor skills to type can use a keyboard alternative such as a stylus pointer or voice recognition software that inputs spoken commands.

WWW

Before support specialists recommend the purchase of ergonomic devices, both the support staff and the end users should understand the advantages and disadvantages of these devices. A Web site that explains the pros and cons of several types of ergonomic devices is **www.office-ergo.com/pros&.htm**. Or, read an excerpt from *Your Guide to Office Ergonomic Furniture and Accessories*, by Alison Heller, at **www.worksiteinternational.com/downloads/excerpt.PDF** (requires Adobe Reader). *BusinessWeek* published an article by John M. Williams in its December 29, 1999 issue about the future of assistive devices, which is available online at **www.businessweek.com/bwdaily/dnflash/dec1999/nf91229c.htm**.

Support specialists should treat end–user ergonomic concerns seriously. Many computer users have experienced painful repetitive strain injuries that require medical treatment. Some repetitive strain injuries can disable a user for an extended period, or even permanently; some users require a job change to compensate for injuries resulting from ergonomic problems that were not addressed promptly or properly. Employers that ignore state and federal (OSHA) rules and regulations that cover worksite ergonomics have been the target of legal action by workers.

WWW

Several Web sites contain useful information about ergonomics, including the latest research findings, specialized products, and treatment options. For example, see the Ergoteam site at **www.ergoteam.net/ergoinfo** or the Cornell University Ergonomics Web site at **ergo.human.cornell.edu**. Each of these resources includes pointers to a number of articles and links to specialized Web sites on ergonomic issues.

Ergonomics is an area in which user support specialists can develop special expertise that adds value to their employment. It takes extra effort to keep up with the latest research and products in ergonomics, but support specialists who devote the time can become recognized as the company experts on office ergonomics.

Power Requirements

Many small computer systems do not require special electrical power. They plug into standard three-prong outlets; however, before installing a computer, several electrical power situations should be checked.

1. **Outlets.** If an installation is in an old building with two-pronged outlets (that is, those without the third ground prong), special wiring may be necessary. Avoid "cheater" plug adapters, which convert two-pronged plugs to three-prong, because they defeat the ground feature that protects electronic circuits.

2. **Outlet wiring.** Test three-prong outlets to make sure the hot, neutral, and ground prongs were correctly wired when the outlet was installed. Incorrect wiring is uncommon, but it can cause problems if a computer system is plugged into an outlet that was improperly wired. A simple, inexpensive tester with LED lamps to check each outlet is available from most electrical suppliers.

3. **Circuit amperage.** If a system is installed in an environment with a significant number of peripheral devices or other office equipment (copiers, typewriters, coffeepots, radios, refrigerators, fax machines, or calculators), add up the amperage currently drawing on the circuit to determine whether it can handle an additional load. Most appliances, including computers, display screens, and printers, display the number of amps of current they draw on an information plate. If the circuit breaker at the electrical distribution box is 15 amps, and the total amperage of devices on the circuit is even close to 15, then use a separate electrical circuit. Note also that during startup, some appliances draw more amps than their rating.

4. **Shared circuits.** A computer system should not be installed on an electrical circuit that services devices with heavy motors, generators, or air conditioners. These devices can, at times, draw large quantities of power, which may reduce the available amps on a circuit to less than that required for the proper operation of computer devices. For example, hard disk drives rely on electrical current for timing during read and write operations. Inadequate power during one of these operations could cause loss of data on the media in a drive.

5. **Power stability.** In some local areas, the quality of the electric supply varies considerably, even during normal operation. When installing computer equipment in areas with unstable power, consult with the local electric company to determine whether special equipment is recommended to protect computer hardware. The electric company may recommend a power conditioner for a circuit where the computer equipment will be installed. A **power conditioner** is an electrical device installed between a computer and its power source that regulates the electrical power to ensure it is within acceptable limits. It inputs electrical power, makes sure that the frequency, voltage, and waveform are within acceptable specifications, and then outputs clean power to the computer system. Power conditioner prices vary; purchase a unit that has the capacity to condition power for the total load it must service. For example, the load on a circuit may

10

include the system unit, display screen, printer, scanner, other computer peripherals, and perhaps other office equipment. Electrical contractors or electricians can usually advise about the need for a power conditioner. They can connect a special metering device to a circuit to monitor it for 24 to 48 hours. Metering devices print out a statistical summary of electrical quality and the number of spikes, surges, or brownouts that occurred during the test period.

6. **Multiple computers.** In any location where multiple computer systems will be installed, such as an office, training room, or computer lab facility, the total electric power requirements need to be planned in advance and an electrical contractor consulted to verify that the power is adequate and well conditioned. The need to get specialized help with electrical power also applies to the installation of minicomputers and high-end workstations, whose power requirements may be unusual.

In a standard computer installation, electrical power strips are convenient because the user has only one switch to turn on an entire system. The system unit, display screen, printer, and other peripheral devices can be plugged into the power strip. However, power strips should not be used as electrical extension cords. Each power strip should be plugged into an electrical outlet and not into another power strip. This requirement is part of the electrical code in many areas and makes good sense where it is not. The best power strips, called surge suppressors or protectors, include protective circuits that help prevent damage to computer equipment due to power surges and spikes. Surge suppressors may also include filters that protect against radio frequency interference. Uninterruptible power supplies that permit a computer to be operated for a limited time during a power outage are discussed in Chapter 13.

Not all surge suppressors provide adequate protection from power surges and spikes. Inexpensive models do not have the circuitry to protect against extremely powerful surges, such as a lightning strike. Electric utilities generally recommend a surge suppressor with the following specifications: UL 1449 (second edition) listed; 40,000 amps or more peak protection; 330 volts or less clamping voltage level; 1 nanosecond or less clamping response time; 750 joules or more energy rating; and diagnostic LED status lamps. For more information about surge suppressors, visit the CherryLand Electric Web site at **www.cherrylandelectric.com/memberprograms/surgeqa.cfm**.

Some surge suppressor manufacturers offer a specific warranty that pays a user if computer equipment is damaged while plugged into a surge suppressor and operated according to their recommendations.

Electrical power and peripheral signal cables should be installed so they cannot be damaged or stressed during regular use. When computer wires are installed in an existing building, surface-mounted cable conduits (or runways) can be installed along an office or computer lab wall. These conduits provide access to the cables if they need to be upgraded or repaired, but they protect the cables from potential problems due to shorted or broken cables. Avoid running power cables or signal cables over a tile office floor or under a carpet. If power or signal cables must run over or under any kind of flooring, purchase protective rubber conduits to protect cables from the wear and tear of traffic. Plastic cable ties can be used to bundle cables and secure them to furniture to get them off the floor or out of the way, and to avoid stress on the cable runs.

Telephone and Network Access

Few computer systems today are standalone installations. Many systems require access to a telephone line for modem connections with other computers. Telephone companies offer DSL (digital subscriber line) or ISDN (Integrated Services Digital Network) services in some service areas that provide very fast data and voice connections over the same line. Cable television companies frequently offer broadband cable modem service to meet customer needs for fast Internet connections. Most office computer systems today require connection to a local area network in an office or computer lab. Determine the location of the nearest telephone and network access points before installation, in case telephone or network extension lines are necessary to reach the installation site.

10

Air Conditioning

Just as many computer installations do not require special electrical work, most do not require air conditioning beyond what is necessary for employee or user comfort. However, in locations where a large number of computer systems will be installed in close proximity, such as in a small office, training room, or computer lab facility, additional air conditioning may be required. An engineer or consultant who specializes in heating, ventilating, and air conditioning (HVAC) can help determine the requirements. HVAC specialists use a formula that considers the total wattage of electrical devices and the heat generated by people to compute the number of BTUs (British thermal units) of air conditioning capacity required to maintain the temperature within a predetermined range.

Minicomputer and high-end workstations are more likely to require air conditioning than small office computer systems. However, the total wattage within a space determines air conditioning requirements. Even a few computers in a small office can create a need for air conditioning, especially during summer months.

Lighting

Incorrect office lighting can cause significant ergonomic problems. The lighting can be too intense, directed from the wrong source, or just the wrong type altogether. The result can be lower employee productivity due to eyestrain or headaches.

Light Intensity.   Many offices were initially designed primarily for paper-and-pencil activities and are over lit for computer use. Too much light on a user's work surface can cause glare on a display screen. One solution is to turn off some light fixtures to reduce the amount of glare. In cases where four florescent bulbs are housed in a fixture, for example, an electrician may be able to remove two of the four bulbs by making a simple modification to the fixture. Where adjusting the amount of light is not possible, consider an antiglare filter that covers the entire display screen area and reduces or eliminates glare from light sources.

Light Source.   In addition to the amount of light, the source of light may cause problems. For example, in an office or training room with windows, position users' display screens so they are at a 90-degree angle (perpendicular) to the light source. This position is preferable to a light source that hits the screen directly, which will happen when the screen is positioned directly opposite the light source. Users generally should not face a light source, because direct light can cause discomfort.

Light Type.   Finally, the type of lighting can cause problems for the monitor and ultimately the user. Some florescent bulbs flicker at the same frequency as the refresh rate on a CRT-type monitor. The result is a noticeable flicker or visible moving horizontal scan line on the computer display screen. In these situations, an electrician or lighting consultant may be able to recommend a florescent bulb with less flicker or one that flickers at a different rate than the monitor. Screen flicker is not a problem with LCD flat panel displays.

Fire Suppression

Fortunately, computer systems rarely burst into flames. However, computer equipment is electrical and mechanical, and electromechanical equipment can cause fires, primarily due to problems with power supplies. Devices that have moving parts, such as disk drives or printers, can also cause fires, although fires from these sources are unusual. Although forecasting when a fire may occur is impossible, it is possible to be prepared for a fire. If an office does not have an existing fire suppression system, place portable fire extinguishers near the equipment. Choose a fire extinguisher that is rated for electrical fires, because an extinguisher that is designed for wood or paper fires contains a dry chemical that can further damage computer equipment.

The most effective fire extinguishers for use on and around computer equipment contain Halon gas. However, the Environmental Protection Agency (EPA) has made the manufacture of new Halon systems illegal because it depletes ozone gas in the atmosphere. Existing Halon systems can continue to be used, and a few used systems are still available for purchase. Manufacturers have invented substitute fire extinguisher gases that are effective, such as INERGEN and FM-200.

For additional information about Halon, see the EPA Web site at **www.epa. gov/Ozone/snap/fire/qa.html**. For information about alternatives to Halon, see the HARC (Halon Alternatives Research Corporation) list of approved alternatives on its Web site at **www.harc.org/index.html**.

Figure 10-3 is a check list of questions to resolve during the installation planning stages.

Site Preparation Check List

❏ Perform preinstallation site inspection
    ❏ Electrical power access
    ❏ Telephone and network access
    ❏ Space for system unit, keyboard, mouse, monitor, printer, other peripherals
        ❏ requires keyboard shelf
        ❏ requires monitor arm
        ❏ requires minitower case
        ❏ requires printer stand
    ❏ Check cable lengths to peripherals, such as printers
    ❏ Ergonomic issues:
        ❏ height of work surface and keyboard location
        ❏ location and viewing angle of monitor
        ❏ lighting source and problems
        ❏ adjustable seating
        ❏ footrest
        ❏ wrist rest
    ❏ Ventilation and air circulation
    ❏ Location of nearest fire extinguisher rated for electrical equipment
    ❏ Location of electrical supply cutoff
    ❏ Special site problems (moisture, dust, static electricity, humidity, temperature, accommodations for physical disabilities)
    ❏ Storage space for manuals, supplies, site management notebook
❏ Arrange time for system installation

Figure 10-3   Site preparation check list

SITE MANAGEMENT DOCUMENTATION

The primary goal of any installation is, of course, to achieve an operational system. However, support specialists may want to accomplish other goals during a system installation. One of these is to build a **site management notebook**, a binder that consolidates important information about the system's hardware, operating system, network, and applications software configurations, as well as facilities management information, in one location. An installation management notebook contains much of the information a support specialist might need in the future to operate, diagnose, troubleshoot, reconfigure, upgrade, and repair the system and its components. A site management notebook is also a useful guide when a support specialist installs several systems that have very similar configurations.

The site management notebook documents important details about the system, including a sheet or a section for.

- Hardware configuration
- Operating system configuration
- Network configuration
- Software licenses
- Applications software configuration
- Special operating procedures
- Warranty and repair information
- Problem log
- Backup media log

A site management notebook may be overkill for a simple installation of a home or small office computer; however, one is often a necessity for systems installed in any volume in offices, training facilities, and computer labs. Even home or personal computer users have sometimes found a site management notebook a useful tool and worth the time it takes to develop and maintain the information. A site management notebook is especially critical in locations where a large number of computers are installed, systems are configured differently, and multiple support staff members are likely to work on various parts of the systems from time to time. The notebook acts as a one-stop source of information to answer questions support specialists may have, such as:

- What software is legally licensed to be installed on this system?
- What kind of bus architecture does this system contain?
- What is the speed of the internal modem?
- Who should the user contact when the display screen doesn't work?
- Where are the media backup disks and when were they created?
- Has the printer problem we're seeing today happened before?

Figure 10-4 contains examples of the kinds of information that is often included in a site management notebook, including hardware and software configuration sheets and configuration details. Other sheets that may be included in a site management notebook include software licenses, operating procedures, a list of contacts (phone numbers and e-mail addresses) for problems, warranties on components, a problem log to record prior problems with this system, and a backup media log. Operating system utility software, such as MSCONFIG, WinCheckIt, PC-Check, MSD, HWINFO, or MSINFO (hardware vendors may also supply system information utility software), often print a report that includes some of the information in the sample pages shown in Figure 10-4.

PC Hardware Configuration Sheet

SYSTEM: _____ Serial # _____

1. **System unit**
    ❑ Desktop   ❑ Laptop/Notebook
    Manufacturer _____   Power supply (watts) _____

2. **CPU**
    ❑ Intel _____   ❑ AMD _____
    ❑ 386   ❑ 486   ❑ Pentium   ❑ II   ❑ III   ❑ 4
    Clock speed _____   Chipset _____
    Bus: ❑ ISA   ❑ MCA-IBM   ❑ EISA   ❑ VESA   ❑ PCI
    BIOS: Manufacturer _____   Version _____

3. **Internal memory**
    RAM _____ ❑ MB ❑ GB   Type: _____
    Memory access speed _____ NS   Parity: ❑ Odd   ❑ Even   ❑ None
    Modules: Pins _____   ❑ SIMM   ❑ DIMM   ❑ RIMM
    Cache memory: L1 _____ KB   L2 _____ KB   L3 _____ KB

4. **Storage**
    Controller card   ❑ IDE   ❑ EIDE   ❑ SCSI
    Hard drive _____ GB   Second hard drive _____ GB
    ❑ 5.25" floppy drive
    ❑ 3.5" floppy drive
    ❑ CD-ROM _____ X   ❑ CD-RW _____ X   ❑ DVD _____ X   ❑ DVD-RW _____ X
    ❑ Removable hard drive: _____ ❑ MB capacity   ❑ GB capacity

5. **Input**
    ❑ Keyboard: ❑ Standard   ❑ Ergonomic
    ❑ Mouse: ❑ Bus   ❑ PS/2   ❑ Serial   ❑ USB   ❑ Wireless
    ❑ Trackball   ❑ Keyboard pointer   ❑ Touchpad pointer
    ❑ Scanner: Manufacturer _____ Model _____ Resolution _____ DPI

6. **Output**
    ❑ Graphics adapter: ❑ VGA   ❑ XVGA   ❑ XGA   ❑ SXGA   ❑ UXGA
    ❑ Video memory: _____ MB   ❑ AGP port
    Display screen size: _____ inches diagonal
    Resolution: ❑ 640x480   ❑ 800x600   ❑ 1024x768   ❑ 1280x1024   ❑ 1600x1200
    ❑ CRT monitor: dot pitch _____   Colors: _____
    ❑ LCD flat panel: ❑ dual scan ❑ active matrix   Colors: _____

    Printer: Manufacturer _____   Model _____
    ❑ Ribbon dot matrix: _____ cps Ribbon #: _____
    ❑ Inkjet: ❑ B/W: _____ pages/min (ppm) _____ DPI   Cartridge #: _____
    ❑ Color: _____ pages/min (ppm) _____ DPI   Cartridge #: _____
    ❑ Laser printer: _____ pages/min (ppm) _____ DPI   Cartridge #: _____

7. **Communications**
    ❑ Modem: Manufacturer _____ Model _____ Speed _____
    ❑ NIC cards: Manufacturer _____ ❑ 10-Mbps   ❑ 100-Mbps

8. **Expansion**
    Ports: ❑ Serial _____   ❑ Parallel _____   ❑ Mouse _____   ❑ Game _____
    ❑ USB 1.1 _____   ❑ 2.0 _____
    Slots: ❑ 8-bit _____   ❑ 16-bit _____   ❑ 32-bit _____
    PC-card (PCMCIA) slots: ❑ I _____   ❑ II _____   ❑ III _____

10

Figure 10-4   Sample pages from a site management notebook

Software Configuration Sheet

SYSTEM: _____ Serial # _____

1. **Applications needs analysis**
   - ❑ Accounting
   - ❑ CAD/CAM
   - ❑ Database management
   - ❑ Decision support
   - ❑ Desktop publishing
   - ❑ e-mail

   - ❑ Financial
   - ❑ Forecasting
   - ❑ Graphics
     - ❑ analytic
     - ❑ presentation
     - ❑ draw/paint
   - ❑ Groupware

   - ❑ Internet access
   - ❑ Multimedia
   - ❑ Project management
   - ❑ Spreadsheets
   - ❑ Statistics
   - ❑ Word processing

   ❑ _____   ❑ _____   ❑ _____

2. **Operating systems and networks**   **VERSION**
   - ❑ MS-DOS
   - ❑ Windows   ❑ 3.1   ❑ 95   ❑ 98   ❑ Me   ❑ 2000   ❑ XP   _____
   - ❑ Linux   ❑ UNIX   _____
   - ❑ Mac OS   ❑ Mac OS X   _____
                                                                             _____

3. **Tools and utilities**   **VERSION**
   Programming languages: ❑ Visual BASIC   ❑ C/C++   ❑ Java   _____
                            ❑ Fortran   ❑ COBOL   ❑ Pascal   _____
   Utilities: ❑ Norton Utilities   _____
   - ❑ Antivirus: _____   _____
   - ❑ Adobe Reader   _____
   - ❑ Backup: _____   _____
   - ❑ Winzip   _____
   - ❑ _____   _____
   - ❑ _____   _____

4. **Applications software**   **VERSION**
   Office suite: _____   _____
   Word processing: _____   _____
   Spreadsheet: _____   _____
   Database: _____   _____
   Presentation: _____   _____
   Accounting: _____   _____
   Financial: _____   _____
   Personal info mgr: _____   _____
   Draw/Paint: _____   _____
   Desktop publishing: _____   _____
   Web development: _____   _____
   Communications: _____   _____
      remote access: _____   _____
      e-mail client: _____   _____
      browser: _____   _____
      FTP: _____   _____
   Internet service provider: _____   _____

Furniture/Supplies/Accessories

- ❑ desk (26–28" height)
- ❑ printer stand
- ❑ LCD projector
- ❑ diskettes/removable media
- ❑ power strip
- ❑ books and manuals
- ❑ wrist rest
- ❑ antiglare screen
- ❑ security devices
- ❑ cleaning supplies: ❑ compressed air   ❑ vacuum

- ❑ chair (ergonomic)
- ❑ printer paper
- ❑ headset
- ❑ media case
- ❑ surge suppressor
- ❑ bookshelf/rack
- ❑ mouse pad
- ❑ footrest
- ❑ toolkit

- ❑ printer forms
- ❑ microphone
- ❑ camera
- ❑ extender cables

- ❑ antistatic mat

❑ wipes   ❑ alcohol

Figure 10-4   Sample pages from a site management notebook (continued)

Configuration Details

SYSTEM: _____ Serial # _____

CMOS settings: CMOS setup key _____ Password _____
Date battery last replaced: ____ / ____ / ____
HDD type # _____ HDD: Cyl _____ Head _____ Sector _____ Size _____
HDD: Other settings: _____
Floppy drives: _____ Boot sequence: _____
Display type: _____ Display settings: _____
Notes on CMOS settings: _____
Power management notes: <u>Device</u>   <u>Time delay</u>

IRQ use (note changes from defaults)

IRQ	Address	Typical Use	Notes
0	____ : ____	system timer	
1	____ : ____	keyboard	
2	____ : ____	access to IRQs 8-15	
3	____ : ____	serial port COM2 and COM4	
4	____ : ____	serial port COM1 and COM3	
5	____ : ____	sound card	
6	____ : ____	floppy disk controller	
7	____ : ____	parallel port LPT1	
8	____ : ____	real-time clock	
9	____ : ____	available	
10	____ : ____	available	
11	____ : ____	SCSI or available	
12	____ : ____	PS/2 mouse or network card	
13	____ : ____	math coprocessor	
14	____ : ____	IDE hard drive controller	
15	____ : ____	secondary hard drive or available	

❏ Attach printout of AUTOEXEC.BAT
❏ Attach printout of CONFIG.SYS
❏ Attach printout of SYSTEM.INI
❏ Attach printout of WIN.INI
❏ Attach printout from MEM/C

Port use: LPT1: _____ LPT2: _____
           COM1: _____ COM2: _____
           COM3: _____ COM4: _____
           USB: _____

Figure 10-4   Sample pages from a site management notebook (continued)

10

NOTE

For additional details and information on the terms used in the PC Hardware Configuration Sheet in Figure 10-4, see the Webopedia Web site at **webopedia. internet.com/Hardware** or The PC Guide Web site at **www.pcguide.com**. Follow links on these Web sites to learn more about each hardware option. These sites also include pointers to additional hardware articles, product reviews, and information on the Web.

HARDWARE INSTALLATION TOOLS

User support specialists who work frequently with hardware may purchase or assemble a toolkit with the basic tools needed to perform simple tasks with computer equipment. Computer, electronic supply, and mail order vendors sell toolkits, which start at about $10 for a few basic tools. Figure 10-5 shows a typical toolkit you can obtain from an electronics supplier.

Tools for use around computer equipment should be nonmagnetic. Most basic kits contain the following:

- **Screwdriver set.** Used to remove and insert screws. Should include both slotted blade and Phillips heads; heads should be smaller than general-use screwdrivers, because computer screws are often small. Some hardware repairers prefer a socketed screwdriver with interchangeable heads.

- **Nut driver.** Used to remove the case from a system, because the screws are often six-sided nuts. (Nut drivers come in several sizes; get one designed for computer equipment.) Note that some socketed screwdrivers are the correct size for a nut driver when the screwdriver heads are removed.

- **Pliers.** Used to hold and clamp parts. Should include both regular pliers and needle-nose pliers for working with small parts.

- **IC chip extractor/inserter.** A useful tool if you work with older types of memory or ROM BIOS chips.

- **Parts-picker.** Used to pick up small screws, nuts, and bolts in tight work spaces; some kits contain tweezers and a magnetic parts grabber for small parts.

In addition to these common tools, support specialists who work frequently on hardware installations or end-user problems may want to augment a basic toolkit with one or more of the following:

- **Pocketknife.** Used for tasks when perhaps no other tool will do the job. (Victorinox now makes a version of the Swiss Army Knife, called the CyberTool, that is specifically designed for work with computer hardware.)

- **Small parts container.** Used for keeping track of screws, nuts, washers, and other small parts while working on a computer system. An empty plastic film canister makes a good parts container.

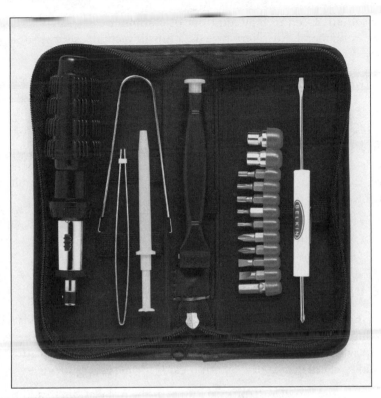

Figure 10-5   A typical hardware installation toolkit

- **Mirror.** Used to view in tight spaces and behind components that are difficult to move.

- **Small flashlight.** Used to illuminate hard-to-see places.

- **PC Pocket Reference.** Used as a source of information about PC hardware in a compact form (for more information, see **www.sisweb.com/books/ pcrefer.htm**).

- **Isopropyl alcohol.** Used to clean electrical components, display screens, keyboards, and mouse parts. (Isopropyl alcohol should be handled with care, like any chemical; it should not be consumed or inhaled under any circumstances.)

- **Lint-free cloth or foam-tipped brush.** Used to apply isopropyl alcohol for cleaning; antistatic wipes are also recommended.

- **Antistatic wrist strap.** Used to ground a technician to the computer power supply or case whenever a need arises to handle components inside a computer case. A strap reduces the risk of damaging a component with an accidental static charge. Inexpensive antistatic wrist straps sell for $6 to $10.

- **Electrician's tape.** Used for simple repairs or in lieu of tie-wraps.

10

- **Compressed air.** Used to blow dust out of computer cases, keyboards, printers, and other equipment. An alternative is a small vacuum cleaner designed for electronic equipment, available in many parts supply catalogs.

- **Circuit tester.** Used to determine whether an electric outlet has been properly wired (tests hot, neutral, and ground); inexpensive models are simple plug-in devices.

- **Multimeter.** Used to determine whether an electric circuit is active, whether a cable has a short, or whether a battery still has a charge; sometimes called a VOM (volt–ohm–meter). For many tasks, inexpensive analog multimeters can be purchased for $10 to $15; for work on motherboards, a digital multimeter is recommended.

Once you have inspected the installation site and are sure you have the proper equipment and tools, you can proceed with installing the hardware components.

COMMON HARDWARE INSTALLATION STEPS

Installing computer hardware for most users in homes and organizations today includes unpacking, connecting, and testing the basic components. Basic components usually consist of a system unit, display screen, keyboard, mouse, and perhaps a printer. Installation can also include installing additional memory or expansion cards for peripheral devices.

An important first step in the installation process is to plan the installation. In addition to the preinstallation site check list and steps described earlier in this chapter, planning also includes a review to make sure you have all the components and tools you will need. An installation time that is convenient for the user should also be arranged. Technicians who install a large volume of systems usually build a check list to use on-site to make sure they perform all the steps required and bring all the necessary components with them. The check list later becomes a form of documentation that they did so. Figure 10-6 shows a typical hardware installation check list. The purpose of this check list, and the others in this chapter, is to provide a starting point for support specialists who want to develop their own check lists and procedures that are specific to each organization and situation.

Support specialists who install systems don't necessarily perform all the steps shown in Figure 10-6 at every installation. To make the check list more useful, installers can delete steps they never perform or insert additional steps they do perform.

NOTE

The check list in Figure 10-6 assumes that the support specialist is installing a preassembled system. In some hardware installations, the installer assembles a system from basic components, which include a case with power supply, CPU, memory, disk drives, and adapter cards. Trade books on installing or upgrading a computer system describe in detail the steps to assemble a system at the individual component level.

Hardware Installation Check List

BEFORE INSTALLATION

- ❏ Review safety check list (see Figure 10-7)
- ❏ Get toolkit and spare parts container
- ❏ Unpack hardware components and note any missing or damaged parts
- ❏ Save boxes and packing in case components need to be returned

BASIC INSTALLATION

- ❏ Connect basic components, connect power and signal cables, and test basic system operation
- ❏ Remove case and inspect components for proper installation
- ❏ Fill out hardware configuration sheet in site management notebook
    - ❏ Record serial numbers in site management notebook
    - ❏ File warranty information

OPTIONAL INSTALLATION

- ❏ Install any memory upgrade and expansion cards:
    - ❏ Multifunction I/O
    - ❏ Graphics adapter
    - ❏ Internal modem
    - ❏ Sound card
    - ❏ Network interface
    - ❏ Other: _____

COMPLETE INSTALLATION

- ❏ Connect peripherals (monitor, keyboard, mouse, printer, external modem, telephone, removeable hard drive, speakers, scanner, microphone)
- ❏ Connect power and signal cables
- ❏ Install power strip, surge suppressor, or UPS power unit, and connect power cables
- ❏ Power up system and adjust display screen
- ❏ Run diagnostic tests on hardware devices
- ❏ Install ergonomic devices (screen glare filter, copy holder, wrist rest)
- ❏ Attach network cable to NIC card
- ❏ Check cables for excess tension and install tie-wraps to bundle cables
- ❏ Attach security cables for theft prevention
- ❏ Record vendor contact numbers and e-mail addresses in site management notebook

10

Figure 10-6   Hardware installation check list

Whenever installers remove the case from a computer system, they should follow the basic safety precautions described in Figure 10-7.

Guidelines for Work Inside the System Unit

Before you begin . . .

❑ 1. Understand what tasks you are going to do and how you are going to do them (what are your goals?).
❑ 2. Get documentation on how to do the tasks you are going to do.
❑ 3. Clear an adequate workspace. Remove food and beverages from the work area.
❑ 4. Get the hardware components, tools, and software you will need to do the tasks. (include paper and pencil for notes).
❑ 5. Get a collector container for small parts, such as screws.

Before you remove the case . . .

❑ 6. Turn off the power switch (is there more than one power switch?).
❑ 7. Unplug the power cord (is there more than one power cord?).
❑ 8. If in doubt, check for electric current with a tester or turn off the power at the breaker box.
❑ 9. Work with at least one other person in the vicinity of where you are working.
❑ 10. Remember: YOU should not take off the case from a power supply or a CRT monitor, or try to repair those devices.
❑ 11. Avoid loose clothing while working around mechanical parts, such as printers.

After the case is removed . . .

❑ 12. Observe proper handling procedures and warnings for chemicals, such as isopropyl alcohol and printer ink.
❑ 13. Before you begin work, attach an antistatic wrist strap, especially if you are working on memory components, IC chips, the motherboard, or adapter cards.
❑ 14. Before you unplug any components, make notes or a diagram of how it is mounted and how cables are connected to it.

Before you restore power to test a component or system . . .

❑ 15. Double-check signal cable connections and especially power connections to make sure they are secure.
❑ 16. Before you test the system, check inside the system case and around the work area to make sure you can account for all components and tools.
❑ 17. Before you complete installation or troubleshooting, thoroughly test both the components you worked on, and other system components.

After you have tested a component or system . . .

❑ 18. If you restored power to the system to test the components, turn off the power switch and unplug the power cord before you resume work inside the case.

After you are finished . . .

❑ 19. Put away your tools.
❑ 20. Document any changes you made to the system or its components in the site installation notebook.

Figure 10-7   Hardware installation safety precautions

COMMON OPERATING SYSTEM AND NETWORK INSTALLATION STEPS

Support specialists do not always install an operating system. Most preassembled computer systems have an operating system preinstalled on the hard drive. In situations that do require support specialists to install an operating system, most are supplied on a CD. Others provide operating system updates, patches, and special drivers that users can download from a Web site. In cases where support specialists install identical operating system configurations on a large number of machines, an image of the system can be written on a removable hard drive or CD-RW media. Alternately, updates to an existing operating system on computers that are connected to a network can usually be installed on a large number of machines from the network server.

The installation process is usually not complicated, but can take an hour from beginning to end. The steps to install operating system software can include partitioning the hard disk if necessary, installing the operating system software and any device drivers required, and installing the network operating system. After the operating system and network operating system have been configured for hardware peripherals and meet site-specific standards, support specialists install other necessary software, including virus checkers, screen savers, and security and utility software.

Many computer systems use a version of Windows as an operating system, which lessens the need to install device drivers, because recent versions of Windows automatically recognize devices that conform to Plug and Play standards. In these cases, Windows installs a default driver for devices it recognizes during the boot process. However, Windows may not recognize peripheral devices manufactured prior to 1995 and some manufactured after that date; device drivers may need to be installed manually in those cases. The vendor Web site should also be checked to see if an updated device driver is available for download, because bugs may have been discovered in earlier versions. Installers of Macintosh systems usually have an easier task, because Mac OS automatically recognizes many peripheral devices, but some peripheral devices are sold with specialized device drivers for Mac OS, as well.

NOTE

Experienced installers know that incompatibility between hardware, operating systems, and device drivers can cause many hours of lost time during installations. These installers check system requirements and vendor Web sites prior to installation to reduce the probability that incompatible components will waste their time.

WWW

Microsoft provides tools to test the compatibility of hardware devices with its operating system products. Visit the Microsoft Web site at **www.microsoft.com/whdc/hwtest/default.mspx**. A list of hardware devices that are certified compatible with Microsoft operating systems is published at **www.microsoft.com/whdc/hcl/search.mspx**.

10

Vendor manuals are a good source of specific information about how to install an operating system. However, the process has been highly automated in recent releases, so little printed documentation may be available. User manuals may be included on distribution CDs or on a vendor Web site. Trade publications also cover how to install and configure popular operating systems.

Network connectivity is implemented with a combination of hardware, software, and operating procedures. The role of a support specialist in network installation is primarily concerned with the client or user workstation components. A support specialist may perform tasks such as:

- Install client software
- Configure network connectivity
- Perform network administrative tasks:
  - Administer user accounts (login IDs and passwords)
  - Grant rights to access network resources such as applications software, disk space, peripheral devices, and shared printers
  - Perform periodic server media backups
  - Monitor network performance
  - Monitor network security
  - Report problems to the network support staff

In situations where the support staff has primary network installation and configuration responsibility, such as in a small organization, a network vendor or consultant often provides assistance with network server installation and configuration details. Figure 10-8 is a check list installers can use when installing an operating system and network connection.

The steps to install and configure network software are specific to each type of network and specific user needs. For installation of a standalone system, the steps related to network connectivity can be skipped. A typical network installation involves many of the steps described in Figure 10-8. A network administrator often builds a disk or CD that contains preconfigured network client software so it can be copied to a computer easily during installation. Vendor manuals and trade books are available that describe the details of network client software installation.

Operating System and Network Installation Check List

PRELIMINARY STEPS (as necessary)
- ❏ Make backup copy of existing operating system (if applicable)
- ❏ Make backup copy of any user data files (if applicable)
- ❏ Run FDISK to partition hard drive (if necessary)

BASIC INSTALLATION
- ❏ Install operating system software
- ❏ Install special device drivers required by peripherals
- ❏ Configure operating system and startup files (consistent with organization standards)
- ❏ Modify startup and configuration files

OPTIONAL INSTALLATION
- ❏ Install and configure antivirus, media backup, utilities, security software, and screen savers

DIAL-UP NETWORK INSTALLATION
- ❏ Verify that modem hardware is operational
- ❏ Configure dial-up networking client and communication protocols
- ❏ Test dial-up network connectivity

LAN NETWORK INSTALLATION
- ❏ Verify that network hardware connection is operational
- ❏ Install client software on workstation
- ❏ Modify startup files to connect to network
- ❏ Log on to network server
- ❏ Download additional network software required
- ❏ Configure network operating system
- ❏ Test network connectivity

NETWORK ADMINISTRATION
- ❏ Create user account and initial password
- ❏ Grant user rights to access shared network resources, such as network drives and shared folders

COMPLETE INSTALLATION
- ❏ Update operating system and network configuration information, node addresses, and startup file modifications in site management notebook

10

Figure 10-8   Operating system and network installation check list

COMMON STEPS TO INSTALL APPLICATIONS SOFTWARE

Before installing an applications software package, a support specialist needs to determine whether the software is compatible with the hardware and network on which it will be installed. The specialist determines the following:

- The CPU types on which the software runs

- The amount of memory the software requires

- The amount of hard drive space the software requires for a full installation

- Whether the software is compatible with hardware peripherals

- Whether the software operates in a networked environment compatible with the user's

Software vendors usually distribute applications software on **distribution media**, such as CDs or floppy disks. However, applications software packages are often available for users to download, in compressed format, from a network server or the Internet. When applications software is downloaded from the Internet, a support specialist should consider the speed of the user's connection. When a user has a slow dial-up connection to the Internet, a large software package (larger than 1–2 MB) can be downloaded on another system that has a high-speed link to the Internet. Then the software can be transported on floppy disks, removable hard drives, CDs or DVDs, or via a local area network connection to the user's computer, where it can be installed. Because application programs often automatically update registry and configuration files maintained by the operating system, applications software packages should be installed directly on the computer on which they will be used. Problems often arise when an attempt is made to install a program by simply copying it from another computer.

Whatever the distribution media, the installation steps for most applications packages are generally simpler than they were several years ago. Many packages autoinstall after the user double-clicks an install icon. Most computers are equipped with a CD drive that has an Autoplay feature enabled. In these cases, a system can usually recognize that a software installation CD has been inserted in the drive and will automatically begin the installation process. In other cases, the installer can use My Computer in the Windows operating system to examine the installation media for a SETUP.EXE or INSTALL.EXE program.

Immediately before installing a new program, the installer should close all open programs as a precaution. When installing a large application on a system with limited disk space, an installer may want to perform a hard disk defragmentation procedure (described in Chapter 13) to ensure that an application is written on contiguous disk blocks (to increase execution speed). The first step in applications software installation is often the execution of a special installation program, such as InstallShield. The install program guides the installer through the process and pauses to ask questions on the screen about available user options. An example of a frequent question is whether the user wants a shortcut icon to the program placed on the desktop. When the distribution media is floppy disk, the install program prompts the installer to insert disks identified by name or number as the install program needs them.

The most common application installation options allow a user to select from among the following installation types:

1. **Express installation.** Sometimes called a typical or common installation; installs the most frequently used program functions and features as determined by the manufacturer, and asks the fewest questions

2. **Custom installation.** Sometimes called an expert or special installation; lets a user select components or features to install; be prepared to answer more questions than in an express installation

3. **Minimal installation.** Sometimes called a laptop or space-saver installation; installs the fewest functions and features possible for users with little free hard drive space available

4. **Full installation.** Sometimes called a maximum or complete installation; installs all program functions and features, asks few questions; takes the maximum amount of disk space

It is a good idea to ask the end user about the type of installation required. However, users are generally not familiar with the terms *express* or *minimal* and may not understand the implications of the various installation choices. An installer may need to translate these options into lists of specific features for the user. Users often need specific software functions or features that are not included in a minimal installation. Installing applications software may also include installing organization-specific options, templates, macros, or device drivers.

Support specialists are also responsible for verifying that the user has the appropriate software licenses to support an installation. Some organizations maintain a database of software licenses that needs to be updated as part of the installation process. After installation, a support specialist should test the software and make sure it runs properly. Figure 10-9 shows a sample check list that installers can use to track software installations.

If a user needs several applications software packages, the support staff time required to install, maintain, and update applications software packages can be substantial. As the number of users and systems supported in an organization grows, support staff search for alternate ways to keep users' software up-to-date. Downloading or launching software directly from a network server is one way to reduce support costs. In the future, users may access all software from an applications service provider. An **application service provider (ASP)** is an organization that sells access to applications software and related services via the Internet to individuals or organizations. ASPs will likely become important service providers for small companies with tight software budgets, but with a need to run the latest versions of software packages, or for companies that need specialized applications software.

10

Applications Software Installation Check List

PRELIMINARY STEPS
- ❑ Close all open applications
- ❑ Make backup copies of any user data files that could be affected by installation process

INSTALLATION
- ❑ Install standard applications software packages (such as the Office suite)
  - ❑ Express   ❑ Custom   ❑ Minimal   ❑ Full
- ❑ Install e-mail and Internet browser applications
- ❑ Install special-purpose software (such as accounting, marketing, manufacturing, or other organization-specific applications)
- ❑ Install any special device drivers required by applications software (printer drivers are common ones)
- ❑ Configure applications software to meet the user's needs and to conform to organizational standards
  - ❑ Adaptive options:
- ❑ Create desktop shortcut or add to startup menu as appropriate
- ❑ Add any organization-specific templates for word processing or spreadsheets
- ❑ Reboot system
- ❑ Test all applications software

COMPLETE INSTALLATION
- ❑ Fill out software configuration sheets in site management notebook
- ❑ File software licenses in site management notebook
- ❑ Register software with vendor (via mail-in card or online registration)
- ❑ Verify that user knows how to start the application
- ❑ Verify that the user is satisfied with the installation and knows how to get help if needed

Figure 10-9   Applications software installation check list

WRAP-UP TASKS

The previous sections presented common steps and procedures in the hardware, operating system, network, and applications software installation processes. Depending on the kind of installation and on organizational policy, a support specialist (or an end user) might undertake several additional steps. These are steps in which a support specialist can document software settings, back up critical files, create rescue disks, fill out warranty and registration cards, document problems, address ergonomic concerns, and make sure the user will be able to use the system effectively once installation is completed. Support specialists can also perform "housekeeping" tasks such as storing documentation and shipping containers. Some of these tasks can be classified as facilities management or installation documentation tasks, whereas others are user training. Most installers think of these as "wrap-up tasks," because they are generally performed at the end of an installation.

Keep in mind that an installation doesn't end as soon as the hardware or software is installed. Support specialists who install or upgrade a system should always check with users to make sure they can use the new system correctly, or get the training they need. Review any new equipment with users; ensure that they can start it up, operate it, and shut it down properly. Then, alert them to training opportunities and alternatives. Finally, verify that the users are satisfied with the installation and have had their questions answered. The ultimate measure of any installation procedure is the answer to the question, "Is the user 100% satisfied?"

Figure 10-10 shows a check list for some of these wrap-up tasks. Not every step in the check list applies to every installation. The tasks vary depending on the type of installation and the needs of the user.

On the one hand, installing systems can be a smooth and relatively error-free process that serves its main purpose: to get the end user's system up and running as soon as possible. On the other hand, system installation can be frustrating for both installers and users, because an unexpected incompatibility or defective hardware or software can suddenly terminate an installation before it is complete. In some instances, installers may have to uninstall or reinstall components to get them to work correctly. Installers must be sure that they plan carefully for each installation, have the appropriate tools, follow organized procedures, and are alert to the issues and potential problems that each installation presents. Although proper advanced planning does not guarantee a smooth and successful installation, poor planning almost always guarantees the opposite.

10

Wrap-Up Check List

HOUSEKEEPING
❑ Store or recycle shipping containers

SECURITY
❑ Make backup copies of registry, configuration and start-up files
❑ Create bootable rescue or boot disk and store in site management notebook

USER ORIENTATION
❑ Check system with user for any ergonomic problems
❑ Brief user on basic system operation
  ❑ Walk through system startup procedures
  ❑ Provide network user ID and password
  ❑ Provide reference sheets to document common operating system and applications software tasks
  ❑ Describe antivirus, backup, and security procedures
  ❑ Review printer operation, paper loading, and cartridge or ribbon change procedures
  ❑ Go over operating procedures for peripherals
  ❑ Walk through system shutdown procedures
❑ Brief user on
  ❑ Organization policies regarding computer use and abuse
  ❑ Reminder to refrain from use of food and beverages around computer equipment
  ❑ Preventive maintenance procedures
  ❑ User assistance and help desk contacts
❑ Discuss training needs and opportunities with user

SITE MANAGEMENT NOTEBOOK
❑ Document system configuration (CMOS settings, configuration printouts, startup file settings) and file in site management notebook
❑ Complete warranty and registration cards or online registration procedures
❑ Document any installation problems or special configuration specifications on problem log in site management notebook
❑ Store user and system documentation in convenient place
❑ Store software distribution media, drivers, backups, and CDs

COMPLETION
❑ Verify that user is satisfied with installation

Figure 10-10   Installation wrap-up check list

CHAPTER SUMMARY

- The basic steps to install a computer system include site preparation, hardware installation and configuration, operating system and network installation and configuration, installation and configuration of applications software, and wrap-up tasks.

- During the site preparation step, support specialists deal with several issues:

  - Locating the computer system and devising strategies to conserve space

  - Ergonomic concerns, including ways to adapt the computer system and work environment to maximize user comfort, productivity, safety, and health

  - Power requirements, which address the need to provide a convenient and reliable electric power supply

  - Connectivity issues, which deal with telephone and network access

  - Air conditioning, which is usually not a concern for standalone personal computers, but is an issue in offices and training facilities

  - Lighting problems, which are the source of several productivity and ergonomic concerns

  - Fire suppression precautions

- One of the secondary goals of the system installation process is to collect a notebook of information about the computer system. A site management notebook is a convenient way to organize information that support specialists may need in the future to operate, diagnose, troubleshoot, restore, reconfigure, upgrade, and repair a system.

- Tools needed to work with computer hardware include a variety of screwdrivers, a nut driver, pliers, an IC chip extractor/inserter, a parts-picker, a pocketknife, a small parts container, a mirror, isopropyl alcohol, a lint-free cloth or foam-tipped brush, an antistatic wrist strap, compressed air or a vacuum cleaner, a circuit tester, and a multimeter (VOM).

- Installation of hardware and related peripherals includes unpacking the system, connecting power and signal cables, installing any upgrades, and testing the system. Installing an operating system and setting up network connectivity includes installing the software (usually from a CD or floppy disk) and device drivers if needed, configuring various options and startup files, and installing network software if necessary. Applications software installation usually involves a choice of the kind of installation: express, custom, minimal, or full. Support specialists may also install organization-specific utilities, templates, macros, or style sheets.

- The final steps in the installation process include briefing the user on various operational aspects of the system and other activities that wrap up the installation. These steps often include updates to information in the site management notebook. The wrap-up tasks also include a transition into the user training process, which is the topic of the next chapter. Finally, the ultimate installation question is, "Is the user satisfied?"

10

Key Terms

application service provider (ASP) — An organization that sells access to applications software and related services via the Internet to individuals or organizations.

carpal tunnel syndrome — A common form of repetitive strain injury that affects wrists and fingers.

custom installation — A software installation option that lets the installer select which components and features to install; also called an expert or special installation.

distribution media — The original copies of network and operating system or applications software, such as CDs, floppy disks, and Internet downloads.

express installation — A software installation option that installs only the most commonly used functions and features as determined by the manufacturer; also called a typical or common installation.

footprint — The amount of desktop space a system unit occupies; measured in square inches (length of case × width of case).

full installation — A software installation option that installs all program functions and features; usually requires the most disk space of any installation type; also called a maximum or complete installation.

minimal installation — A software installation option that installs the fewest functions and features possible to minimize the system resources required to run the software; also called a laptop or space-saver installation.

power conditioner — An electrical device that connects a computer system to a power source; it inputs electrical power, makes sure that the frequency, voltage, and waveform are within acceptable specifications, and then outputs clean power to the computer system.

repetitive strain injury — A physical problem that results from continuous use of joints in a limited range of motion; symptoms include swelling, numbness, tingling, and stiffness of joints.

site management notebook — A binder that consolidates important information about a computer system's hardware, operating system, network, and applications software configurations, and facilities management information in one location; contains information needed to upgrade, maintain, restore, diagnose, or repair the system.

Discussion Questions

1. Who should perform a computer system installation: an end user or a support specialist? Discuss the pros and cons of each before you make a decision.

2. Do you agree or disagree with this statement: "Because they are portable, laptop (or notebook) systems are very flexible and do not create the same ergonomic problems as desktop computers." Explain your position.

3. What kind of support specialist would need a basic hardware toolkit described in this chapter? What kind of support specialist would need a more complete toolkit? Would a support specialist under any circumstances need a soldering gun?

4. Are computer ergonomics primarily an employee concern or a management concern? Explain your reasoning.

CHECK YOUR UNDERSTANDING

1. The purpose of a preinstallation site visit is to _____ .

   a. anticipate possible installation problems

   b. get acquainted with the end user

   c. train the end user

   d. complete a wrap-up check list

2. The length of a computer case times its width is called its _____ .

3. True or False? A keyboard placed on a regular height office desk (30") can cause user discomfort because the angle of the user's wrists at the keyboard is unnatural.

4. The display screen connected to a computer system should be located so a user does not have to look _____ .

   a. up slightly

   b. straight ahead

   c. down slightly

   d. any of the above positions is OK

5. True or False? Magnetic media should not be stored close to equipment that generates a magnetic field, such as motors, generators, and electrical or telephone equipment.

6. _____ deals with how to design computer equipment and workspaces to minimize health problems and maximize employee safety, productivity, and job satisfaction.

7. True or False? Wrist and finger pain is usually the result of a mouse that needs maintenance.

8. True or False? According to this chapter, most computer hardware components function well, even if the quality of electrical power is very poor.

9. A(n) _____ is an electrical device that permits a user to power on a computer system with one switch.

10. True or False? To calculate the air conditioning requirements for computer equipment, an HVAC specialist considers the heat generated by both the computer equipment and end users.

10

11. Before a computer is plugged into an outlet for the first time, the outlet should be checked _____ .

   a. by a licensed electrician

   b. with a simple LED tester

   c. by the local electric utility

   d. all of these

12. A light source that may flicker at the same rate as a CRT display screen is a(n) _____ .

   a. incandescent light

   b. florescent light

   c. LED light

   d. halogen light

13. True or False? Support specialists often add to or delete from site installation check lists like those in the chapter as user and support needs change over time.

14. A site management notebook is especially useful in _____ .

   a. a home computer installation

   b. a standalone computer installed in an office

   c. multiple systems installed in an office or training facility

   d. none of these

15. An antistatic wrist strap is designed to _____ .

   a. protect the safety of a support technician

   b. reduce the risk of damage to computer components

   c. reduce the risk of fire due to a static spark

   d. reduce the risk of shock if the computer is not unplugged

16. _____ is an industry standard that helps the Windows operating system automatically recognize the configuration and operating characteristics of many hardware devices.

17. True or False? A support specialist who installs an application software package must edit the system registry and configuration files manually before the software will operate correctly.

18. A software _____ is required to ensure that a software package can be legally installed on a system.

HANDS-ON PROJECTS

Project 10-1

Modify an installation check list. Choose one of the installation check lists in this chapter. Based on your personal experience, what steps would you add to the check list? What steps would you leave out? If you have access to a machine-readable version of the check list you selected, make the modifications you recommend.

Project 10-2

Evaluate an installation. Compare a computer installation that you are familiar with in your home, office, or school with the site preparation check list in Figure 10-3. Which steps, if any, described in this chapter were omitted in the installation? What was the result?

Project 10-3

Perform an ergonomic analysis. Conduct an ergonomic analysis of your home, office, or school computer site from the perspective of an end user. List any problems with the site a user would identify based on the ergonomic issues described in this chapter. As a support specialist, what recommendations would you make to address the ergonomic problems you identified? Write a summary of your recommendations.

Project 10-4

Locate ergonomic products and prices. Find two mail-order or online catalogs for computer equipment or supplies, such as TigerDirect, PC Mall, MicroWarehouse, PC Connection, CDW, Staples, Office Depot, or Global Computer Supplies. Look at the computer supplies sold. What products are available to address specific ergonomic problems such as those described in this chapter? Make a list of at least five examples of ergonomic products and their price ranges. Are some ergonomic products more cost-effective than others? Explain your answer.

Project 10-5

Analyze computer toolkit contents. Find a mail-order or online catalog for computer equipment or supplies (see Project 10-4 for suggestions) that sells toolkits for working on computer hardware. How many toolkits does the supplier sell? Pick one of the toolkits and describe how the contents of the kit differ from the list of tools in this chapter. Write a list of the tools you would want to add to the kit and explain why you would add each tool.

Project 10-6

Outline a site management notebook. Write a detailed table of contents for a site management notebook. Think about the best way to organize the information so that a support specialist who needs to quickly find information about a specific system can locate the information easily.

Project 10-7

Observe a system installation. Find a facility at your organization or school where you can observe or participate in the installation of a typical system. Make a list of the steps you observe. Be sure to ask about steps you don't understand, and find out why they are necessary. Describe how the steps you observed differ from those listed in this chapter.

Project 10-8

Update installation check lists. Check lists of hardware and software components, such as those included in this chapter, quickly become outdated as hardware technology changes and as new software is marketed. Review the hardware and software check lists in this chapter. Describe how you would update the lists based on changes in technology since the lists were created for this book.

Project 10-9

Define technical terms. The check lists in this chapter contain some technical material and product descriptions. If you have previous experience in the computer field, you have probably encountered some of the technical terms, product names, and specifications used in the chapter. Make a list of any words used in the chapter that are unfamiliar to you or that you want to know more about. Select five terms to research further. Use the information resources available to you (for example: friends, coworkers, magazines, books, the Internet) to prepare a short definition of each of the five terms you selected.

Project 10-10

Work with electrical values. A formula used frequently by electricians is: Watts = Volts × Amps. (Alternately, Amps = Watts/Volts.) If an installer determined that a dedicated electrical circuit has a capacity of 15 amps, and the computer and peripherals connected to the circuit are currently rated at up to 1000 watts, at best, how much spare capacity does the electrical circuit have? Would it be possible to add a printer that operates at 100 watts without overloading the circuit? Show how you arrived at your answers.

CASE PROJECTS

CASE PROJECTS

1. Windows XP Installation for Brianna Mishovsky's Training Facility

Brianna Mishovsky is the training coordinator for a large national insurance company. The company has recently agreed to purchase a new software package that will substantially increase employee productivity in its Claims Processing department. Although the new software is not yet operational, it represents a major change for the company and is scheduled to come online in a month. The implementation schedule poses several problems for Brianna's training group because several weeklong training sessions on the use of the new software must be scheduled to accommodate all the employees in the Claims Processing department. To meet the need for additional training classes for employees, Brianna has to install computers in a training room where none exist now.

Brianna has located 20 computer systems that can be used for the training activity, but they are currently equipped with Windows 98 as an operating system. She learned that the new claims processing software is designed to run on Windows XP. Although the hardware configuration on the computers Brianna found is sufficient to run Windows XP, it was never installed on these systems.

You'll assist Brianna with the installation of Windows XP on the 20 training systems. Your first task is to design some installation procedure notes to install Windows XP on the training machines. First, research the steps in the Windows XP installation procedure. (If possible, go through an actual Windows XP installation to identify the steps in the procedure, the key decision points, and the installation options available.) Next, write a first draft of the installation procedure notes for Windows XP. As you work on your draft, make a list of some questions you will need to ask Brianna to clarify how she wants Windows XP configured on the training machines. Brianna wants you to make your procedure notes brief, but as complete as possible, because one of her training assistants will do the actual installation steps based on your notes. Write a draft of the Windows XP installation procedure notes and a list of questions for Brianna that you need answered to complete the assignment.

CASE PROJECTS

2. The UPS and Downs of Electrical Power at Cascade University

Mary Ann Lacy, the training facility coordinator at Cascade University, has plans to install a new network server for her training facility. Mary Ann has been advised by the electric utility that provides power to Cascade University that she probably also needs to install an uninterruptible power supply (UPS) for the server she plans to install. The idea that a UPS would help protect the university's investment in server hardware and reduce user frustration if a power outage occurs appeals to Mary Ann. She wants your help with the UPS part of the installation project.

10

The consultant at the electric utility mentioned that articles in computer periodicals sometimes describe UPS equipment. The consultant also said that the Internet is a good source of information on UPS systems. Many of the organizations that sell UPSes for computers have Web pages that describe their products. The consultant pointed Mary Ann to an online tutorial on UPSes at the PC911 Web site, **www.pcnineoneone.com/ howto/ups1.html**. The consultant also recommended an article on UPSes on PC Guide's Web site at **www.pcguide.com/ref/power/ext/ups**, and an article by D. E. Levine at WinPlanet's Web site, **www.winplanet.com/winplanet/tutorials/3358/1**.

Mary Ann asks you to (1) learn about some of the important features to consider when purchasing and installing a UPS, and (2) write a one- to two-page summary of the issues the university needs to consider in the purchase and installation of a UPS for its new network server.

CASE PROJECTS

3. Software Installation for a Time Synchronization Utility

You are a user support specialist for an engineering company, and receive the following e-mail:

From: Ayaka

To: User Support

Date: 28-Aug-2006

Subject: Internet Time

I am tired of trying to keep the system clock on my office PC correct. It seems to speed up or slow down randomly, but rarely has the correct time. I understand users can download a free utility program that will periodically synchronize the time on their PCs with the correct time on the Internet. Could you please find out how to install the utility on my PC? I suspect the other users in the Engineering department will also want this program when they find out about it.

Thanks very much for your help with this task.

Go to the NIST Internet Time Service Web site that offers the software utility at **boulder. nist.gov/timefreq/service/its.htm**. Download the program for your computer. Study the configuration options for this program. Then write an installation check list that describes how to obtain, install, and configure the program. Write your check list so that other engineers who work with Ayaka can follow the steps.

4. Installation Troubleshooting at Re-Nu-Cartridge

For additional background information on Re-Nu-Cartridge, see Case Project 4 in previous chapters.

NOTE

Because computer systems are widely used at Re-Nu-Cartridge in a variety of office, marketing, and manufacturing locations, the employees encounter a number of challenging computer installation problems. Several of Re-Nu-Cartridge's employees have received or will get new computers in the next month. They need your advice on how to deal with the problems described below:

1. Jose Fonseca, production scheduler: the desk space for his workstation is very limited

2. Ralph Emerson, accounting specialist: static electricity is a problem in the office area where Ralph's computer will be installed

3. Anna Liu, marketing database coordinator: reports eyestrain, headaches, back strain, and sore wrists

4. Roberta Green, employee benefits coordinator: the florescent lighting in her office causes a noticeable flicker on the computer screen

5. Dale Marcus, Webmaster: wants to minimize the number of power switches required to turn on the computer and peripherals (system unit, display screen, printer, fax modem, scanner)

6. Lou Campanelli, shipping and receiving: installation is in an unusually dusty shop environment

Write a memo to Fred Long, CEO at Re-Nu-Cartridge, that recommends how you would deal with each of these specific problem areas.

10

11

TRAINING COMPUTER USERS

In this chapter you will learn:

- ♦ Goals of training activities
- ♦ Steps in the training process
- ♦ How to plan a training session
- ♦ How to prepare a training session
- ♦ How to present a training module
- ♦ How to progress toward quality training

Most organizations find that providing user support is expensive. As a result, many organizations try to make users as self-reliant as possible to reduce the need for support activities. Every problem that users can solve by themselves is one less the support group must resolve. Every question users can answer on their own reduces the burden on the support group. Ultimately, user self-reliance shrinks an organization's total support costs.

Training is one of the best ways to make users self-reliant. A Chinese proverb says, "Give a person a fish and you provide a meal; teach a person to fish and you provide food for life." That principle certainly applies to the relationship between a user and a user support center: "Answer a question for a user and you have solved a problem; teach users to find their own answers and you have solved many problems."

Many people who have been primarily on the receiving end of the training process, such as students, are often surprised at the amount of work that goes into a successful training activity. This chapter takes you step by step through the training process. It describes how to plan a training session for users, prepare materials, and present and evaluate training materials. The end-of-chapter materials are designed to help you think further about the training process and give you an opportunity to plan, prepare, present, and evaluate your own training activities.

WHAT IS TRAINING?

Training is a teaching and learning process that aims to build skills that are immediately useful to the trainees. Sometimes the terms *training* and *education* are used interchangeably. Although training and education are related, the terms sometimes mean different things.

Education is a teaching and learning process that aims to provide conceptual understanding and long-term thinking skills. Especially in introductory courses, the goal of education is to build a basic vocabulary and understanding of general principles. In education, teachers commonly test learners' understanding by measuring their ability to explain concepts and principles. The effects of education are intended to be long lasting.

Training focuses on performing activities and building expertise that will be immediately useful. Trainers often test the success of a training session by measuring a learner's ability to perform a task. Although the results of training may be long lasting, training can also be very short term. A worker could be trained to perform a task that she or he will do only once or a few times.

People sometimes associate education with a school environment and training with an industrial or organizational environment. However, some schools have a mission that includes training, such as vocational-technical schools and community colleges. Furthermore, education often occurs outside a school environment, because skills training is usually based on a firm foundation of conceptual knowledge. For example, workers need basic vocabulary and computer operating principles before they can become skilled users. The ability to troubleshoot and solve problems is often closely related to one's understanding of computer systems and one's facility for applying general knowledge to specific tasks. Although this chapter focuses primarily on user training, it assumes that training must be based on a solid foundation of vocabulary and concepts.

 Educators and trainers often use a specialized vocabulary. Donald Clark has prepared an online glossary of vocabulary terms used in the training field. See his Web site at **www.nwlink.com/~donclark/hrd/glossary.html**.

THE TRAINING PROCESS

Trainers can use a four-step process to teach users successfully. The four Ps of training in this process are listed in Figure 11-1. In the planning step, the trainer gathers information about the objectives of the training process. In the preparation step, a trainer gathers and prepares materials and organizes them into modules. In the presentation step, a trainer presents the training modules to end users, who then help evaluate the training process in the progress step.

- Step 1. Plan
- Step 2. Prepare
- Step 3. Present
- Step 4. Progress

Figure 11-1   The training process

STEP 1: PLAN THE TRAINING

Experienced trainers know that planning is essential to a successful training activity. Trainers must learn who the trainees will be, their current skill levels, and what skill levels they need to achieve as a result of the training. Once trainers have this background information, they can set learning and performance objectives.

Determine the Trainees' Backgrounds

Perhaps the most obvious detail that a trainer needs to determine is who the trainees are. Are they novices, intermediate users, or users with advanced skills? Are they adults, young people, or seniors? Adult workers who need specific job-related training require different content and training techniques than younger users and school children. Workers are often highly motivated to learn new skills, because they may already understand the benefits of applying new technology to their jobs and careers. Adults often bring their personal experiences to a training session, which can be very useful because a trainer can build on prior experiences and use analogies and metaphors to introduce new material. For example, a trainer might point out that an unfamiliar software feature or procedure is similar to one in a program the users already know. Although not all adult workers are equally motivated, the characteristics of adult learners can often be used to good advantage in a training situation. Adults are usually better able to form generalizations based on examples, and to articulate what they do and do not understand. However, adult trainees are often less willing than younger trainees to put up with a poor trainer.

Trainers should be aware that some trainees do not attend training voluntarily, but as a job requirement. Required attendance can affect a trainee's motivation level. In these cases, a trainer may have to spend extra time and effort to convince trainees of the training's benefits and find ways to involve them in the training activity to help them get past their initial resistance to being there.

Determine the Trainees' Content Needs

Once a trainer knows who the trainees are, they determine what the trainees need to know, which may require some research. A trainer usually tries to discover the kinds of jobs or tasks users will be asked to perform, what specific skills they will need, and how expert the trainees need to be at these skills. Trainers can sometimes locate information about the job, task, or skill objectives in workers' position descriptions. In other cases, they must interview the workers or their supervisors (or both) to determine the training objectives. For example, a trainer who prepares a session on building Access databases may discover that what the trainees really need to learn is how to prepare reports based on data in existing databases. Specifically, the trainer may learn that the trainees already know how to use basic features of the Access Report Wizard, and now need an introduction to custom reports to do their jobs.

Determine the Skill Levels Trainees Need

After a trainer defines the content trainees need, they need to determine the skill level the trainees need. To determine an appropriate skill level target, a trainer needs a basic understanding of skill levels and how they are classified. One way to classify skill levels in education and training is:

1. Concepts — the ability to use basic vocabulary

2. Understanding — the ability to explain concepts

3. Skills — the ability to perform a basic task

4. Expertise — the ability to perform a task effectively and efficiently

In this skill classification, the first two levels, concepts and understanding, are conceptual. A training activity often begins with vocabulary as trainees learn to use the language necessary to communicate with others about the topic. They need to know the meanings of the words others use to exchange information about a subject. Then trainees can begin to build an understanding of how things work, why things work (or don't work) the way they do, and the relationships between these things. Once trainees understand new material at a conceptual level, they can build a mental model of how things work and explain it to others. Analogies are especially useful during the vocabulary and conceptual learning steps. For example, a trainer could explain that a computed field in a database is like (analogous to) a formula in a spreadsheet cell.

Once trainees have a conceptual understanding, they can then move to building skills and abilities to perform tasks. At the skill-building level (level 3 above), users learn the steps to perform a basic task. Basic tasks may take a while to learn, and trainees may not get them exactly right at first. Trainees need to develop the ability to perform a task at a basic level before they can become proficient. Then, trainees can work on building speed, accuracy, and expertise. For example, trainees with word-processing expertise can not only embed a graphic object in a document (a basic ability or skill), but they also can do so quickly, without any prompting, and can easily control the placement, size, and design appeal of the result.

Based on these four levels of conceptual knowledge and skills, a trainer can define the vocabulary and level of understanding trainees need, the basic tasks trainees need to be able to perform, and how much expertise the trainees need to develop.

Determine What Trainees Already Know

Successful trainers also establish what trainees already know, so they do not waste learners' time. For adult trainees, training should begin with a brief review of how the training material fits with what they already know, and then move quickly to new material. One way to gauge what trainees already know is to interview several workers or their supervisors about the trainees' backgrounds and current skill levels. Another strategy is to administer a short pretest to determine more precisely trainees' baseline skill levels.

NOTE   As industry certification tests become more widespread, training session pre-tests that attempt to measure what a trainee already knows prior to the training session will become more common. Online tests are a good way to gauge what a trainee "brings to the table."

If a wide disparity in backgrounds exists among a group of trainees, a trainer runs the risk of covering introductory material too fast for some and too slowly for others. Both novices and more advanced users may be equally dissatisfied because the training is not targeted at the level they need. When trainees have different interests or ability levels, trainers can provide background material or arrange a special introductory session or activity before the actual training session begins to help less-experienced users feel more comfortable with the basic vocabulary and concepts. For example, prior to a training session on Microsoft Word, the trainer should make sure that trainees who participate have basic keyboarding, mouse, and Windows skills; otherwise, they will struggle with the Word training and slow down other learners with their questions.

Even with extra preparation to bring novice users up to the class level, trainers almost always find that any group of trainees has a range of skills and interest levels. A big challenge for every trainer is to find an "average" level of instruction that addresses the needs of as many trainees as possible. Trainers handle this in different ways. Some aim to teach to the majority (average) of the class, with occasional asides to give extra explanation for those below the average, and to provide extra problems that challenge those above the average. Other trainers target the level of instruction somewhat below the class average level; they believe a somewhat slower pace for a training session is preferable to leaving half the trainees behind with a faster pace. Practice and experience are the best teachers in handling this classic training challenge.

When planning training for a general audience that has a wide variety of skill levels and job functions, a trainer should try to focus on materials and examples that are common to a wide group of users. For example, a basic word-processing session for a divergent group of trainees (such as department heads, administrative assistants, and engineers) might focus on the skills needed to produce basic office communications, such as memos or simple correspondence, rather than technical reports.

Many training groups have not only a variety of skill levels, but also a diversity of cultural and language backgrounds. A trainer needs to recognize these situations and be sensitive to the audience's needs. For example, if some learners are non-native English speakers, avoid idioms and jargon, and maintain as basic a vocabulary as possible. A trainer also needs to be sensitive

11

to cultural mores. For example, in many cultures, touching another's arm in a friendly way, as one might do to motivate a colleague or a trainee in the United States, is considered too familiar and is unacceptable behavior for a trainer in other cultures. If you have a chance to talk with trainers or instructors, ask them about their experiences with cultural differences and benefit from their observations. Learn to observe trainees' body language as a guide to what behaviors are permissible or acceptable to trainees.

Armed with a knowledge of who the trainees are, what they know, and what they need to know, trainers can then plan a training session. At this point, trainers often find it useful to ask, "How do I efficiently and effectively move the trainees from where they are now to where they need to be?"

Define the Training Objectives

In the final planning step, trainers should specify the learning or performance objectives for the training. A **learning objective** is a statement of the knowledge and skills trainees need to learn. To determine learning objectives, trainers answer the question, "What do the trainees need to learn?" For example, a learning objective for this chapter is: *Explain the main steps in the training process.* A **performance objective** is a statement of what trainees should be able to do at the end of a training session. To determine performance objectives, trainers answer the question, "What should trainees be able to do as a result of this training activity?" For example, a performance objective for this chapter is: *Plan and present a successful training session.* Performance objectives should be measurable, or specify how well the trainees need to be able to perform a task. A training session on Internet search engines, for example, might include a performance objective such as: *Use the Google search engine to locate a specific piece of information on the World Wide Web within five minutes.* Training objectives (both learning and performance objectives) should begin with an action verb, which makes them easier to evaluate later on. Avoid training objectives that begin with the word *understand* or *know,* because *understanding* and *knowing* can be difficult to measure or evaluate. Better verbs include: *list, describe, explain, perform, locate,* and *analyze.* Be as specific as possible about the tasks learners will be able to perform after the training.

 NOTE To learn more about how to design training sessions with specific performance outcomes, consult a book by Ruth Stiehl, *The Outcomes Primer, 2nd edition*, Richmond, BC: Strategic Concepts, 2002. Although Stiehl's book is aimed at college instructors, the learning-centered performance outcomes she advocates are equally useful in planning technology training sessions.

Trainers often summarize the results of the planning steps in a goal statement. Identify the concepts, understanding, abilities, skills objectives, and learning and performance objectives in the training plan shown in Figure 11-2.

Windows 2000 Introduction Training Objectives

Goal: Provide employees who are new computer users with an introduction to the Windows 2000 end-user environment.

Audience: Designed for computer users who have no previous experience with Windows 2000.

Prerequisites: Trainees should have (1) keyboarding skills and (2) a basic understanding of office computer system vocabulary.

Methods: The training will include hands-on experience with basic Windows 2000 operations to give trainees the ability to use the Windows 2000 user interface. Exercises will include mouse operations, window management, use of the Start menu, the Search tool to locate files, and the Recycle Bin. With practice, trainees should be able to perform basic Windows 2000 tasks with little help or prompting.

Learning and Performance Outcomes: At the end of the session, trainees will be prepared to take a basic spreadsheet course and know enough about the Windows 2000 operating system that they can perform basic tasks such as the following:

- Start the system
- Start an application program (such as Excel)
- Store and use files on a disk
- Use a printer in the Windows environment
- Locate and manage disk files
- Use the Windows 2000 help system

The session will introduce terms used frequently in the Windows 2000 environment including: desktop, window, menu, icon, shortcut, dialog box, cursor, mouse keys, and Recycle Bin. The session will not provide a complete understanding of the organization and operation of Windows 2000, but will emphasize the use of Windows 2000 to run applications and the use of file Search and My Computer to manage files and disk storage space. Because the training session is intended to be short, it will not attempt to build skills or expertise in Windows 2000 beyond a basic level.

Performance Measures: Trainees should be able to define 70% of common terms in a simple test. Trainees should be able to demonstrate use of the Start menu to run applications, use of My Computer, File Search, and the Recycle Bin to locate and manage files.

Figure 11-2   A sample training plan for Windows 2000 users

Notice that the training plan is short and describes the objectives in general terms. It does not describe *how* the training will be presented (for example, self-guided tutorial, classroom demonstration, face-to-face tutorial, televised demonstration, or Web-based training) nor list specific topics (for example, which "basic My Computer operations" will be covered and which won't). The details of training topics, methods, and organization occur during the second step: training preparation.

STEP 2: PREPARE FOR THE TRAINING

During the training preparation step, a trainer develops more detail about the specific topics that will be covered and how these topics will be organized in a sequence. This step also addresses the types of training methods and how the training will be accomplished.

Specify Which Topics Will Be Covered

Based on the learning and performance objectives defined in Step 1, a trainer decides next which topics to cover. Even with very clear learning and performance objectives, deciding on specific training content is not easy.

Most trainers do not start from scratch, however. They begin by brainstorming a long list of possible topics. Usually the preliminary list comes from several sources, including a trainer's knowledge of what is important, the learning and performance objectives defined in Step 1, and topics covered by other trainers and writers. In order to reduce the cost of training preparation, topics covered by other trainers and printed training materials are an important source of topic ideas. While trainers should avoid simply copying verbatim training ideas, topics, and examples from other sources, neither should trainers feel that they must start preparing for each training session from scratch. The process of selecting specific topics from among the preliminary list is like setting priorities. As they consider the list of possible topics, trainers try to select topics that are most useful to trainees. Consequently, the decision on what *not* to cover is just as important as the decision on what to cover. Most trainees prefer a session that devotes adequate time to fewer topics instead of a rush job that tries to cram two hours of material into one hour. Good trainers prefer to cover a little less material rather than too much.

Organize the Topics

Training topics should be organized to begin with lower-level skills and progress to higher-level skills. Introduce concepts and vocabulary terms first, followed by explanations of concepts to enhance trainee understanding. Then focus on building basic skills and abilities. Finally, use exercises to build expertise. Following this strategy, a template for a training session might look like the following:

1. Introduce trainer
2. Review previous topics

3. Introduce new topic

4. Establish motivation for new material

5. Present new material
   - Concepts
   - Explanations

6. Perform training activities
   - Teach basic skill abilities
   - Build skills and expertise

7. Summarize and review the main points

8. Describe next steps

9. Obtain evaluation and feedback

This outline calls for trainers to review and summarize the material (Steps 2 and 7). Trainees remember better how to do tasks they have heard about and performed more than once. Recall the adage, "First, tell them what you're going to tell them. Second, tell them. Third, tell them what you told them." Although this advice, if taken too literally, could lead to overly repetitious training sessions, it underlines the importance of introducing (Step 3 above), presenting (Steps 5 and 6), and summarizing (Step 7) training material.

In Step 4 of the training outline, a trainer establishes motivation by reviewing with the trainees why they are there and what they will be able to do by the end of the training. Trainees who understand the need for the training and its objectives are more likely to feel motivated to follow the training activities. Step 8 in the outline, in which a trainer describes the next steps, is an opportunity to point out additional information and resources, to recommend other training opportunities that logically build on this one, or to suggest how to build additional expertise, if that is a user's goal.

Select an Effective Training Environment

Training occurs in a variety of environments, depending on the type of training, its objectives, the needs of the trainees, and the available facilities. Each environment has advantages and disadvantages. The most common training environments are:

- Classes (15–25 trainees)
- Small groups (12 or fewer trainees)
- One-to-one training
- Self-guided tutorials

Classes.   Classroom training is usually more cost-effective than other environments because the ratio of trainees to trainers is high. A single trainer can instruct a large group of trainees, sometimes in a special training facility that includes a computer projection system, an overhead projector, audiovisual equipment, and possibly computer workstations for hands-on activities. Classroom training can also take advantage of the social learning that takes place during trainee-to-trainee interactions.

NOTE

What size is an ideal training class? No specific class size is appropriate for every situation. Some introductory materials, vocabulary, concepts, and explanations can be presented in very large training groups. However, training that includes a substantial hands-on component, especially where a goal is to learn basic skills, should be planned for environments in which sessions are no larger than 15 to 25 trainees. Large classes do not permit individual instructor attention when trainees need assistance. When a training session exceeds 25 trainees, try to arrange for additional trainers or experienced users to mingle among trainees to help when it is needed. Another factor that influences the class size that one trainer can reasonably handle is the skill level of trainees: more highly skilled trainees usually require less individual attention than beginners.

Some trainees don't perform as well in large training group settings, however, because they are uncomfortable asking questions or asking for help in a large group. If a trainer stops to help a couple of trainees, the rest of the trainees may be idle. If some trainees learn at a slower pace than others, they are either left behind or they slow down the rest of the session. With practice, trainers can learn to effectively handle a large group in a classroom environment, present material at a comfortable pace for nearly everyone, and provide adequate feedback to trainees.

Small Groups.   Trainees in a small group environment of up to 12 users have an advantage over classroom sessions in that they may receive more individual assistance. Small group training also permits more trainee-to-trainee interaction and social learning. But the smaller the number of trainees per each trainer, the higher the cost of the training.

One-to-One Training.   One-to-one training is the ultimate small group, which offers the most effective environment for many trainees. A trainer can closely monitor the trainee's learning curve and provide help and feedback in a timely way. On-the-job training is a variation on one-to-one training in which a trainer may also play a role as a coach and mentor to a trainee. Obviously, the cost of one-to-one training is higher than in other environments. Then, too, social learning among peers is not possible in a one-to-one environment. One-to-one training is a very flexible training environment for both trainer and trainee. However, the advantages of informality and flexibility should not be an invitation to provide a poorly planned or executed training session.

NOTE   In reality, many user support workers are always in "training mode." Many of the interactions support staff have with end users are directly or indirectly educational. This section on one-to-one training addresses more formal training situations than the informal training opportunities that occur everyday. However, many of the principles of formal training, such as awareness of differences in learning styles, also apply to informal training situations.

Self-Guided Tutorials.   Self-guided training, in which each trainee works alone without a trainer, would appear to be the most cost-effective training environment because once the materials have been prepared, there is no trainer cost. Trainees can cover material at an individualized, comfortable pace. However, trainees in self-guided tutorial programs may not be able to obtain the assistance and feedback from a trainer they may need. Self-guided training and large class sessions are similar training environments in this respect. If help can be provided when needed during self-paced training (a possible role for a user support center), then self-guided tutorials can be among the most effective and cost–effective learning environments.

How Learners Learn

To choose an effective training method, a trainer needs to consider how trainees learn. Unfortunately, no one, single learning style works well for every trainee. All learners do not learn effectively and efficiently in the same way and at the same pace. Each trainee has a preferred learning style. Some learners are self-motivated and self-reliant. Others need prodding and the structure and motivation that a formal training session can provide. Some workers learn concepts easily; others need examples to understand a concept thoroughly. Some trainees learn most effectively working alone; others benefit from working in a group.

One way to classify learning styles is as follows:

- **Visual learners.** Trainees who learn most effectively by seeing new material, by reading about it, working through a self-guided tutorial, looking at a picture or a chart, or watching a demonstration.

- **Auditory learners.** Trainees who learn most effectively by listening to someone talk through the new material.

- **Experiential learners.** Trainees who learn most effectively by performing a task (also called kinesthetic learning).

Trainers believe that the most effective learning methods are those that are targeted at two or more of these learning styles, such as interactive, multimedia presentations.

11

For more information about learning styles that includes descriptions of visual, auditory, and kinesthetic learners, visit a Web site sponsored by the Canadian government at **www.jobsetc.ca/content_pieces.jsp?category_id=325&lang=e**. Take an online survey to learn more about your predominant learning style using a Diablo Valley College Web site at **www.metamath.com/lsweb/dvclearn.htm** or the Paragon Learning Style Inventory (PLSI) at **www.oswego.edu/Candl/ plsi/index.html**. The PLSI relates learning styles to the Myers-Briggs MBTI personality types you learned about in Chapter 3.

In general, information retention and learning performance improves with activity and repetition. Figure 11-3 shows several learning methods and how they relate to retention.

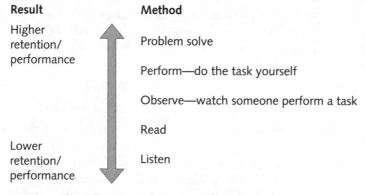

Figure 11-3   Learning methods and retention

Training methods toward the top of the continuum in Figure 11-3 increase the likelihood that information presented will be retained and that job skill performance will improve. In other words, the more that trainees are active participants in the learning process—rather than passive recipients of information—the better they will retain information. What conclusion do you reach about the effectiveness of classroom education experiences based almost entirely on listening to lectures and reading a textbook?

Consider the different learning outcomes that would result if you simply read this book from cover to cover, or if you both read each chapter and completed several of the end-of-chapter projects.

Learning is often a social phenomenon. The trainer-trainee relationship is usually a human relationship (although sometimes a machine-human relationship), as is the trainee-trainee relationship. Learning from peers in a group can augment the training process and is also a good way to build teamwork skills. The ability to work with a team is excellent practice for today's business world, where the size and complexity of projects often require a group effort and group expertise.

For more information on the benefits of peer learning, read the article "Peer Learning" by Alice Christudason at **www.cdtl.nus.edu.sg/success/sl37.htm**.

Select Delivery Methods for the Training Materials

When trainers decide how to present training materials, they can consider a number of alternate delivery methods. A **delivery method** is a choice among several instructional technologies, media, or approaches to present information. Most presentations use one or a combination of the delivery methods listed in Figure 11-4. The delivery methods in Figure 11-4 are described in more detail in the paragraphs that follow.

○ Lecture method	○ Tutorials
○ Reading assignments	○ Hands-on activities
○ Online reading assignments	○ Case studies
○ Group discussion	○ Role playing
○ Visual aids	○ Collaborative or group learning
○ Multimedia materials	○ Computer-based training (CBT)
○ Handouts and reference sheets	○ Web-based training (WBT)
○ Product demonstrations	

Figure 11-4   Commonly used training delivery methods

Lecture Method.   The lecture method is a familiar way to communicate information from an instructor to a learner. It makes effective use of an instructor's time, which is one reason it remains popular in higher education. However, the learner's role is often very passive, which is why some experts question the effectiveness of this method. Lectures can often be used effectively in combination with other delivery methods to introduce topics and materials, motivate trainees, and guide trainees toward a useful learning experience.

Reading Assignments.   Some trainers believe that reading is preferable to lectures because a trainee is more actively involved in the learning process. Reading a textbook, trade book, or vendor manual is probably the most effective way to define vocabulary and explain concepts. However, a trainer needs to select materials carefully so that the amount of assigned reading is reasonable given the time available. Materials should be selected to match the reading ability of the trainees. Some textbook and trade book materials are written at too high a reading level for trainees to understand easily.

Trade books may cover materials thoroughly but are often not well organized for use in training sessions. Trade books, which are usually designed for professionals in a field, are less trainee-friendly because they frequently lack such features as learning objectives, chapter summaries, glossaries, comprehension self-tests, and hands-on activities or projects that are often needed by both trainers and learners in a training environment.

Vendor manuals usually seem very authoritative because product manufacturers publish them. However, vendor manuals vary considerably in quality. Some are well organized and well written; others are so poorly written that they actually hinder effective learning. Vendor manuals are often prepared as reference manuals, rather than as tutorials that guide learners through an effective step-by-step learning process.

In addition to giving trainees specific reading assignments, trainers should encourage users to access a variety of supplementary resource materials. Point trainees to high-quality supplementary materials and ensure that they know how to use them effectively.

Online Reading Assignments.   An increasing number of hardware and software vendors provide online tutorials and help systems with their products. Online reading assignments can be an effective delivery method. Some vendors include online help systems embedded in software; others provide materials on a CD or on the Internet. Online materials today tend to be better designed and written than many printed vendor manuals, which are becoming scarce as vendors seek to reduce production costs. Furthermore, online materials with hyperlinks can be interactive so that users can search for the information they need and locate answers to questions, which promotes more effective learning. However, anyone who has spent considerable time searching a CD or the Internet for information knows that not all online information is equally accessible, useful, or even factually accurate. Some users have difficulty reading lengthy documents online, especially if their display screen resolutions are low. And, of course, online documents are not as portable as printed materials.

Group Discussion.   For some types of training, group discussion is an improvement over the lecture method because trainees are more actively engaged. Group discussion is most effective for sharing experiences, as in user needs assessment training, help desk incident handling procedures, discussing design issues in desktop publishing, or dealing with ethical issues. Beginning trainers are sometimes reluctant to use group discussion as a training method because they fear they will lose control of a training session. However, many experienced trainers have learned that social learning (peer-to-peer) as a delivery method is often among the most effective approaches.

Visual Aids.   Visual aids are a popular supplement to lectures and readings because they take advantage of the adage that "a picture is worth a thousand words." Pictures, charts, diagrams, and other images are useful training aids because most trainees tend to retain visual information better than information they have only heard or read. Visual aids should be large enough to be visible to the entire audience. The most effective visual aids have simple designs with judicious use of color and fonts for emphasis.

For guidelines on the preparation and use of visual aids, consult a Web site developed by the U.S. Occupational Safety and Health Administration (OSHA), called "Presenting Effective Presentations with Visual Aids" at **www.osha.gov/ doc/outreachtraining/htmlfiles/traintec.html**.

Multimedia Materials.   If visual aids are effective presentation tools, multimedia materials can be even more effective learning aids. **Multimedia materials** include a combination of text, still images, animation, and sound. Each form of media can reinforce others to provide a powerful presentation to increase the amount of material learned, as well as the ability to recall material at a later time. However, the cost to develop effective multimedia materials is greater than the cost of many other delivery methods. The cost may be especially prohibitive for a one-time training session, but affordable when spread over multiple sessions.

To view an example of a multimedia presentation on how to use Visual Basic with Excel spreadsheets, go to the Virtual Training Company Web site at **www.vtc.com/products/vb-excel.htm**. Select topics in the first three modules to view a demonstration of a multimedia approach to training. The demonstration tutorials require QuickTime (available free at **www.apple.com/quicktime/ download**). A PC equipped with a sound card and speakers or a headset is generally required for multimedia presentations.

11

Handouts and Reference Sheets.   As effective as training can be, training sessions are, by their nature, generally a one-time event. When users return to their workstations, time passes, and they often forget important parts of the training. Training sessions, especially short ones, are more effective if they include printed materials users can take with them. Handouts and reference sheets should contain enough information so users can recall important facts or steps in a procedure. They should not contain extensive detail, because then they become similar to other forms of documentation and are less likely to be read and used. When a trainer prepares a handout or reference sheet, simplicity is preferable to comprehensiveness.

For an example of a reference sheet designed for end users who already know HTML, but need a short, descriptive, list of available tags, go to **hotwired. lycos.com/webmonkey/reference/html_cheatsheet/index.html**. An example of a reference sheet of commands for the UNIX operating system on University of Washington computers can be found at **www.washington.edu/computing/ unix/unixqr.html**.

Product Demonstrations.   Although hands-on use of an actual software or hardware product during a training session is usually desirable, the lack of equipment, insufficient copies of software, inadequate training time, or other logistical problems occasionally dictate that the training include only a product demonstration. LCD or DLP projectors, which feature liquid crystal display (LCD) or digital light processing (DLP) projection technology, have improved so dramatically that even a large group of 50 to 75 trainees can effectively "look over the shoulder" of trainers as they demonstrate an operating system or applications software package. The cost of many LCD and DLP projectors has dropped from $6000–$8000 to $2000–$3000 in recent years, and some models cost less than $1000, so these units are more affordable for training facilities in even small organizations.

To learn more about the role of LCD and DLP projectors in product demonstrations and other training activities, visit the portable projector buyer's guide at the Projector Central Web site, **www.projectorcentral.com/buyers_guide.cfm**.

A demonstration of a computer product should be carefully paced. A trainer should be careful not to overwhelm users by going so fast that trainees cannot follow or understand the material. The pace of a demonstration is especially important in a GUI (graphical user interface) environment, in which a trainer can point and click so rapidly that trainees cannot follow the sequence of steps in a procedure. Experienced trainers learn to pause between mouse clicks to give each trainee's eyes and brain an opportunity to assimilate the procedure. They talk through a procedure to add verbal explanation to the visual display and give adequate time for each trainee to absorb the sequence of steps.

Tutorials.   Self-guided **tutorials**, which permit trainees to work through an interactive learning session at their own pace, are one of the most effective ways for computer users to learn new information or how to perform basic tasks. In some tutorials, trainees use the actual hardware or software products they are learning about as they step through the tutorial. Other onscreen tutorials merely simulate hardware or software products. In either case, trainees have an opportunity to learn new materials in an environment that is very close to the one they will use when the training is completed.

For an example of a tutorial that is available online, see The University of Sydney, Australia Web site tutorial titled, "An Introduction to the World Wide Web," at **www.usyd.edu.au/su/course**. Note the overall organization of the tutorial, the effective use of hypertext links, and the table of contents feature for experienced users who need a refresher.

Trainees like the self-paced nature of tutorials as well as the opportunity to repeat difficult lessons or take a refresher course. Although the cost to develop effective tutorial materials is very high, once they are developed, hundreds or thousands of users can benefit from a good tutorial at little additional cost per user. Tutorials are most effective for trainees who are self-motivated. Trainees who lack motivation to learn new materials often benefit from more structured training methods, such as lectures or group activities.

Hands-On Activities.   Because performance leads to skill development and better information retention, hands-on activities are an especially effective delivery method for many kinds of computer training. Hands-on activities (sometimes called lab exercises) and practice projects let trainees try out what they have learned, build skills and expertise, and learn to become independent users. Well-designed activities can be a significant step toward user self-reliance.

Hands-on activities and projects should begin with easier tasks and progress to more difficult ones so that trainees can experience initial success before trying more complex tasks and projects. Trainees should receive immediate feedback during hands-on activities, because unlearning a skill is difficult, even if it's an incorrect or counterproductive way to perform a task. For example, how often do users meticulously tap the arrow keys to move the cursor across an entire line of text to the end when a single keystroke or mouse click would accomplish the same result?

Case Studies. Larger hands-on projects, sometimes called case studies, are designed to encourage trainees to make the transition from the artificial environment of the training room to the realities of the business world. Usually based on real business situations, case studies are a popular method in higher education to simulate the kinds of experiences learners will encounter on the job. Case studies are usually more involved than a hands-on activity or a small project and require trainees to apply and integrate the skills they have learned. The Case Projects at the end of the chapters in this book are examples of this integrative method of skill building.

The case study method was originally developed at Harvard Business School, and is now widely used in higher education. To learn more about the goals of the case study method, visit a University of Idaho Web site at **www.uidaho.edu/ ag/agecon/391/casestudmeth.html**.

Role Playing. A common learning strategy for effective communication and customer service skills is **role playing**, in which trainees participate in a rehearsal of a work environment situation. Role playing permits trainees to try out their skills in a situation in which trainees can at various times take the roles of trainer, trainee, client, support provider, project leader, or project team member. Although a role-playing situation may be artificial, it allows trainees to experience the emotions and skills in a situation before a similar situation confronts them in their work environment. Many people are reluctant to participate in a role-playing training session, but role playing can be an effective way to get experience with skills required as a support agent and as a trainer.

For a description of some benefits of role-playing activities, see **mentalhelp. net/psyhelp/chap13/chap13b.htm**.

Collaborative or Group Learning.   **Collaborative learning** activities may involve group discussions, collective hands-on activities, group problem solving, role playing, or participation in a joint case study team. Once called group learning, collaborative learning is based on the experience that learning is often a social activity and that trainees can learn a great deal from other trainees independent of the trainer. Collaborative learning challenges older learning models that say all useful information must flow from trainer to trainees. The roles of trainer and trainee blur in a collaborative environment. In many collaborative learning environments, the trainer is a facilitator who can also be a learner in a joint learning experience.

Computer-Based Training.   A growth industry in the technical training field is computer-based training. **Computer-based training (CBT)** includes a combination of tutorials, multimedia presentations, product demonstrations, and hands-on activities that use a computer as an automated training system. Some CBT systems provide features that handle administrative tasks, such as registering trainees, controlling access to course materials, presenting information, assessing trainee learning, and monitoring trainee progress. Most CBT products today are distributed on CDs, but older systems used audiocassettes and videotapes as delivery media. CBT training can be cost-effective for large groups, but high-quality, instructionally sound CBT materials are usually very expensive to develop. Existing CBT products vary considerably in quality from very poor to excellent. An important role for trainers is to help evaluate the suitability, quality, and effectiveness of CBT materials. Because trainees can learn at their own pace and repeat difficult material, CBT is an increasingly popular delivery method among trainees.

Web-Based Training.   The latest development in automated training systems is use of the World Wide Web as a delivery vehicle. **Web-based training (WBT)** is very similar to computer-based training, except that the Internet replaces CDs as the delivery medium. Because so many users can share the development costs, WBT makes low-cost training modules readily available anywhere in the world. Unfortunately, little quality control exists for Web-based materials. User support staff members who are responsible for providing training need to preview and evaluate prospective training modules for quality, relevance, and cost-effectiveness. Many education and training institutions use the Internet to deliver distance learning in an effective way.

 To experience an example of a WBT training lesson, use one of the sample lessons available on the DigitalThink Web site at **www.digitalthink.com/ els/samplers.html**.

Does the popularity of self-paced training materials such as online tutorials, computer-based training, and Web-based training mean human trainers are obsolete? Will human trainers eventually be replaced by computer technology? Probably not. Although a delivery system revolution is currently under way in the training industry, the trainer's role will unlikely disappear entirely. In many organizations, training continues to be a responsibility of the user support group and part of the job description of user support specialists, even though the popularity of various training delivery methods changes over time. However, the training role will surely change. In the future, trainers will likely spend relatively more of their time to:

- Assess the training needs of workers
- Plan and design training programs
- Evaluate and recommend training materials from among those already available
- Motivate trainees
- Help trainees make transitions between modules
- Assess training performance and effectiveness
- Assist trainees when individual attention is needed

These are not tasks that automated CBT or WBT delivery systems can perform very well, if at all. Future trainers are less likely to develop and present training materials, except where specialized materials are needed for small training audiences. The mass market for user training will undoubtedly be satisfied in part by automated training delivery systems.

For another perspective on trends in training and worker development, read the article "Catch the Wave: Six Training Trends" by Susan M. Heathfield at **humanresources.about.com/library/weekly/aa011502a.htm**.

Develop Specific Training Materials

Most trainers do not prepare lectures, reading materials, demonstrations, tutorials, and other materials from scratch for every training session they develop. Successful trainers rely heavily on existing material in vendor manuals, trade books, industry training packages, and other resources. Why reinvent the wheel if good ideas are already around? And they usually are available. Examples of successful training materials used elsewhere can provide a useful starting point as trainers develop their own materials. However, trainers should respect copyrighted material and avoid copying verbatim from a single source. Successful trainers also try to relate the training topics to the trainees' specific interests, and develop examples that trainees are likely to encounter in their own work. Avoid, where possible, examples and learning activities that are obviously contrived for a training situation. Imagine, for instance, the differences in examples that could be used to teach Internet search engine basics to a group of accountants versus a group of product design engineers.

ERIC SVENDSEN, PH.D.
CEO, SCInc.
WWW.SCINC.NET

Eric Svendsen is CEO of SCInc, a company that develops and presents training programs targeted to the help desk and call center industry. He is the Director of Help Desk Institute's e-University, where he developed many of HDI's training and certification courses for user support agents. Eric also consults, speaks at conferences, and writes articles and books about technical training. In this CloseUp, Eric describes two approaches he advocates for training help desk agents.

Whether a help desk agent is at a first-level or higher support position, there is really no substitute for knowing how to think critically about a problem. Any problem-solving class that I teach always emphasizes critical thinking skills and a good understanding of the value of creativity in the problem-solving process.

In addition to a fairly detailed introduction to the problem management process, and the importance of critical thinking and creativity, four problem-solving steps are covered in detail: (1) diagnosing the problem, (2) isolating the cause, (3) determining options for a solution, and (4) developing a resolution action plan. Because problem solving (like most skills) can be learned with practice, my courses take the trainees through a technical case study in which they participate in a group to attempt to solve a typical problem using the four problem-solving steps. I want trainees to distinguish between symptoms and problems, to perform root-cause analysis, to brainstorm potential solutions, and to create a detailed plan for resolving a problem without wasting a lot of time and resources. The goal is to help the trainees become better problem solvers, and to add value to their work in their current and future positions.

One of the best ways to learn about customer-service skills is to stop thinking like a support provider and start thinking like a customer. All customers have at least two needs; they, of course, have a technical need (that is why they are calling), but they also have another need—a need that usually remains unstated and so sometimes goes unacknowledged by support reps. In order to discover what the second need is, I ask the trainees to think of a situation in which they were a customer and received bad customer service. It's important that they remove their support hats for this, and so I usually suggest they think of the last time they went out for dinner, or purchased an appliance, or visited a department store, or bought a house or a car, and had a bad customer service experience.

Once they have thought of a personal "bad customer service" situation, I divide them into groups of four or five, pick a team leader for each group, and ask the team leader to facilitate a discussion in his/her group. Team members share their experiences with the rest of the team, pointing out (oftentimes with a heightened tone of voice as they relive the emotional upset they went through) what made that particular experience a "bad customer service" situation. I also ask the groups to kick each experience back and forth and see if they can boil it down to a single word—what exactly made that customer service experience a bad one? After all groups have finished, I capture each group's words on a flipchart. Invariably, the words include things like "rude," "indifferent," "distracted," "no follow through," "uncaring," "incompetent," "dead end," and the like. After capturing these words, I then ask several questions designed to lead the trainees to some conclusions about customer service:

1. How many of these words have to do with the technical need you had? Most words describe a customer's "emotional" or "psychological" needs, and have little to do with their technical needs. Conclusion: Technical needs do not determine customer satisfaction.

2. Will you patronize this business again in the future? Conclusion: No one wants to return to a business that has shown it doesn't value the customer.

3. How many people did you tell about this bad experience? Most customers who receive bad customer service want to vent, and will tell many others about their experience. Conclusion: Bad customer service results in a negative multiplier effect.

4. Of those people you told, suppose they are in a position in which they have to use this service. What attitude will they have toward this business? Conclusion: They may be defensive and anticipate bad customer service, or they may even make a preemptive strike and be rude first!

Here is where I bring things full circle. I tell the trainees to put their support hats back on and I ask them to imagine a scenario in which they are speaking with a customer on the phone and things aren't going so well—the customer is getting angry, you lose your patience, and even though you finally resolve the technical problem, there is still tension when you hang up. What is that customer going to do next? Like all customers, s/he is now venting to 10, 20, 30, or even more coworkers, peers, and friends—all of whom are now on the defense as far as you are concerned.

When the training session concludes, I hope that trainees understand that allowing just one call to go bad has the potential to produce an exponential number of bad situations with customers in the future. That is why it is so important, as much as it depends on you, to ensure that every call goes well and that you go the extra mile to satisfy the psychological need of the customer, not just the technical one.

Design Training Evaluation Methods

The final task in training preparation is assessment, which ensures that the training has met the intended learning goals. Trainers should plan two separate assessment activities during the preparation: trainee evaluation and trainer assessment.

The first training assessment is feedback to the trainees on how well they met the learning objectives. Feedback can be in the form of a test or quiz that covers concepts and vocabulary. Trainee feedback can also include activities, exercises, or projects that often use a computer to perform a task that measures mastery of the performance objectives.

The second training assessment activity is feedback to the trainer on his or her instruction. How well trainees perform on quizzes, tests, and hands-on activities also provides feedback to the trainer. If trainees don't do very well on the tests and hands-on activities, however, does that say more about the performance of the trainee or the trainer? Test results actually provide feedback to both trainees and trainers. Trainers should analyze the results of tests, quizzes, activities, and exercises to see where trainees succeeded and where they didn't. Armed with that knowledge, trainers can adjust training modules to improve the results of the training activities.

Trainer evaluation forms are another way for trainers to obtain feedback on their performance. Evaluation forms provide an opportunity for trainees to comment on the strengths and areas that need improvement in the training session. Figure 11-5 shows a training evaluation form that can be filled out by both the trainee and the trainer (as a kind of self-evaluation).

A common practice is to assign weights of 5 points for *Agree,* 4 points for *Somewhat Agree,* and so on, and then calculate an average score for a trainer for each item on the Training Evaluation form in Figure 11-5. To analyze feedback on evaluation forms, trainers should look for patterns of responses instead of occasional very good or very poor scores. Although trainees may not agree in their responses to all questions, look for items that receive lower ratings from many trainees. Trainers should pay particular attention to these items, because they identify the most obvious areas to improve the training activity. Some trainers dislike trainee evaluations because they feel that trainees are not qualified to evaluate trainers. However, most trainers consider trainee evaluations as one important source of feedback. Professional trainers or support staff who do a lot of training also rely on peer evaluations from other experienced trainers or their work colleagues to identify problem areas and make constructive suggestions for improving their performance as a trainer.

Training evaluation is a useful tool to help trainers constantly improve their skills at planning, preparing, and presenting training sessions. An evaluation strategy should be defined during the training preparation phase.

Training Evaluation

☐Trainer: _____   ☐Trainee: _____

Place a check mark (√) in the column that represents your reaction to each statement.

	Agree	Somewhat Agree	Somewhat Disagree	Disagree	Does Not Apply
1. The objectives of the training were clear.					
2. Terms used in the training were defined.					
3. The training was organized in a step-by-step approach.					
4. The training included useful examples.					
5. The trainer made effective use of time, and the pace was about right					
6. Training aids were useful.					
7. Overall, the training was done well.					

What was the best part of the training?

What could be improved?

Figure 11-5   An evaluation form

STEP 3: PRESENT THE TRAINING

The training presentation should follow the structure the trainer planned during Step 2. If a trainer has done a good job in the planning and preparation steps, the actual presentation of the training is more likely to be easier and more effective and satisfying to both the trainer and the trainees. Figure 11-6 lists the top 10 training presentation guidelines that you should observe in your role as a trainer. These guidelines are described in the following paragraphs.

1.   Practice the presentation.

2.   Arrive early to check the facility.

3.   Don't read notes.

4.   Don't try to cover too much material.

5.   Teach the most important skills.

6.   Use humor sparingly.

7.   Stop for comprehension checks.

8.   Monitor the training environment.

9.   Provide frequent breaks.

10.   Obtain professional feedback.

Figure 11-6   Training presentation guidelines

Practice the Presentation.   Most trainers find it helps to practice a training session with one or more colleagues to evaluate materials and identify problem areas prior to the actual training session. Some trainers call this practice session a **beta test run**, borrowing the term from software beta tests, in which companies distribute prereleases of their software to potential users and ask them to note any problems they find as they work. A training beta test gives a trainer feedback from a neutral perspective. You learn how the materials work, whether the topics can be delivered in the allotted time, if transitions between topics are smooth, and whether overhead slides and handouts are effective.

Arrive Early to Check the Facility.   A trainer should arrive at the training facility early enough to check the physical arrangements for the training. Experienced trainers always do a dry run to make sure their equipment works (including trainer and trainee computers, projection and overhead equipment, lights, sound, and other aspects of the training environment). Make sure participants can see you and your materials from every position in the room. You may need to reconfigure the room setup, such as the table and chair layout or the equipment location, so that it meets your needs and is more comfortable for trainees.

 If you are presenting a training session at an unfamiliar site, find out in advance who the facilities manager is and how that person can be contacted in case of problems before or during the training session.

NOTE

Don't Read Notes   If you have prepared detailed notes to use during the training, avoid reading them or reciting lengthy materials from memory. Have a general familiarity with what you want to say and use your own words to present the material in a conversational manner. Most successful trainers find that an outline is more effective to work from than to write out or memorize what they want to cover.

Don't Try to Cover Too Much Material.   Trainers who have too much material for the allotted time should eliminate some less important topics and cover the rest thoroughly. When a trainer tries to review or cover too much material, they often rush through it, which makes the pace of the training too fast and therefore makes it difficult for trainees to keep up. Similarly, don't let trainees' questions force you too far from the planned material. Although trainee questions should be answered immediately if possible, experienced trainers make notes of user questions that aren't directly relevant and answer them, if time is available, at the end of the presentation, or they give pointers to places where trainees can find more information themselves.

One strategy successful trainers use is to identify topics or examples that are less important than others prior to the training session. With a clear understanding of topic priorities, if cuts become necessary due to time constraints, a trainer has decided in advance what materials can be cut without cutting short the time devoted to high-priority material.

Teach the Most Important Skills.   When trainers know a piece of hardware or a software package thoroughly, they are sometimes tempted to augment the training with "bells and whistles," or features of hardware or software that may be interesting but are infrequently used, especially by beginning users. Bells and whistles might impress the audience with a trainer's comprehensive knowledge, but they often distract from the primary training objectives. They may even confuse new users who are struggling with what is important among all the new material with which they are confronted. Remember to focus on the needs of the learners, not on the trainer's ego.

A corollary to teaching the most important skills is to teach a single way to accomplish a task. For example, when a task can be accomplished with a keyboard shortcut, a menu option, a function key, and a toolbar icon, trainees rarely need to be shown every possible method. Trainees will be less confused if a trainer demonstrates and then sticks to one method.

11

Use Humor Sparingly.   Humor during a training session can make the session more enjoyable for trainees, but trainers should be careful about the amount and type of humor they use. The best humor is self-directed because it shows trainees you are human. Ridicule, which is humor directed at someone else, is never acceptable. Avoid making negative comments about vendor products, even in jest. If you are a naturally humorous person, you may need to rein in your talent and recognize the important difference between training and entertainment. Some trainers, mindful that the trainees will evaluate them, cross the line between training and entertainment. Use humor effectively, but recognize that the tradeoff between short-term entertainment and long-term training results should err on the side of training.

Stop for Comprehension Checks.   During a presentation, stop periodically to ensure that trainees are following the material. Many trainers plan in advance to pause at predetermined points for a series of "quick check" questions. Use a variety of "quick check" question styles, including direct questions about the material that has been covered (such as, "What keys would I press to highlight this text to select it?"), open-ended questions (such as, "What is the fastest way to locate a file using Windows Explorer?"), or group questions (such as, "Get together with your group and take five minutes to list what you think are the most useful features of the grammar checker"). Periodic questions will help keep trainees alert and involved because they know they might be called on to discuss what was covered.

Monitor the Training Environment.   A trainer should always keep an eye on the training environment to make sure that users are comfortable and focused on the training. Is the room temperature too hot or too cold? Is the room too noisy because a door or window is open? Learn to read your audience. Watch for signs that trainees are uncomfortable, interested, bored, or attentive. Successful trainers often check their perception with the trainees: "It seems like a lot of noise is coming from the hallway. Can you all hear the presentation?" or "Can those in the last row see the screen?"

Provide Frequent Breaks.   In a lengthy session, recognize that trainees can become tired, which can affect their concentration. Plan the training to include frequent breaks. Trainers usually find that more frequent short stretch breaks are preferable to a few long breaks. A good guideline is to schedule a break after about 45 minutes, and every 30 to 45 minutes thereafter.

Obtain Professional Feedback.   After a new trainer gets initial experience with the training process, a professional evaluation from other trainers is often helpful. Colleagues can frequently spot even very small mannerisms that may be distracting to trainees. Another excellent training improvement tool is to videotape a training session. Although a videotape of your own training session can be difficult to watch, all trainers can learn something from the experience that will improve their training proficiency.

For more information on presenting successful training sessions, see Elaine Weiss's book, *The Accidental Trainer: You Know Computers, So They Want You to Teach Everyone Else*, San Francisco: Jossey-Bass, 1997. Or see Terrance Keys's book, *How to be a Successful Technical Trainer: Core Skills for Instructor Certification*, McGraw-Hill Osborne Media, 2000, which is geared to Comp TIA's Certified Technical Trainer certification exam.

NOTE

Loretta Weiss-Morris has written a book titled, *Quick Training Tips! How to Teach Computing Skills to Practically Anyone*. She offers a preview chapter, "Polishing Your Presentation Skills," that expands on the suggestions in this section at **www.systemsliteracy.com/QTTBook-Chapter2.pdf** (requires Adobe Reader).

WWW

STEP 4: PROGRESS TOWARD QUALITY USER TRAINING

The final step in the approach to user training described in this chapter is perhaps the most important. After each training session, trainers should review the feedback they receive and evaluate their own performance. They can then modify their presentation style or training materials if necessary to correct any problem areas they identified. Professional trainers and especially user support staff who do occasional training sessions are always on the lookout for ways to improve. Inputs to a trainer's efforts to improve training quality include: the results of training beta tests with colleagues as trainees, the results of performance tests of trainees, feedback on the training session from trainees, the observations of colleagues who observe a trainer session, and evaluation of videotape recordings of training sessions. Each of these tools is useful information to trainers who want to improve the quality of their training sessions. For example, an analysis of which questions on a quiz or which activities in a hands-on exercise caused trainees the most difficulty can point to needed revisions in the training materials in subsequent training sessions. Or perhaps the real problem is that some test questions or exercises aren't very good measures of trainee performance. In either case, trainers should look for clues where modifications to the training materials need to be made.

Another aspect of training materials that should be evaluated whenever a training session will be repeated at a future time is the currency of technical materials. Because hardware, software, networks, and operational procedures change frequently, technical details and training materials that were prepared just a few weeks or months ago may be out of date today. Don't assume that the screens, icons, keyboard shortcuts, and program features that worked in version 2 of a software package will work the same in version 3. Review all topics, procedures, slides, demonstrations, handouts, reference sheets, and other training materials prior to the next presentation.

11

Trainers and support specialists who are interested in improving the quality of their training should learn to use the TechRepublic Web site at **www.techrepublic.com**. The site requires a free registration, and includes archives of articles, e-mailed newsletters, discussion topics, and other information of interest to trainers and user support professionals. The following table lists several sample articles that are related to topics discussed in this chapter.

Author	Article	URL
Mary Ann Richardson	Design Your Own Hands-on Tests to Get an Accurate Skills Assessment	**techrepublic.com.com/ 5100-6317-5032079.html**
Jeff Davis	Help Your Help Desk Analysts Become Technical Trainers	**techrepublic.com.com/ 5100-6263-1043810.html** (includes link to download TechRepublic's Technical Trainer's Toolkit)
Karen Cangero	The Economics of Web-Based Training	**techrepublic.com.com/ 5100-6317-5025200.html**
Ann Margaret Kearney	Real-World Advice for the New Tech Trainer	**techrepublic.com.com/ 5100-6317-1033253.html**
Ellen Birkett Morris	Tips for Developing a Trainer Evaluation Process	**techrepublic.com.com/ 5100-6317-5032065.html**
J. Galimi and J. Furlonger	Critical Success Factors for Various Learning Methods	**techrepublic.com.com/ 5100-6317-5032121.html**
Marsha Glick	Twelve Steps for Designing Effective Training Programs	**techrepublic.com.com/ 5100-6317-5032124.html**

To locate articles on other topics on the TechRepublic Web site, go to **www.techrepublic.com**, type a topic in the **Search** text box, and then click the **Go** button.

In addition to the training tools described in this chapter, trainers who have primary responsibility for a training program in a large organization may want to investigate a learning management system. A **learning management system** is a software tool that automates many tasks associated with a training program. Learning management systems may feature:

- authoring tools (especially for Web-based interactive multimedia training sessions)
- training session management, including facilities, equipment, and trainee scheduling

- trainer access to libraries of instructional and reference materials and media

- trainee testing and exam management

- trainee progress tracking and record keeping, including skills and certification databases

Learning management systems are probably not appropriate for an organization that conducts occasional, small training sessions. They are targeted at organizations that make a substantial ongoing commitment to worker training and career development, and need help with program administrative and instructional tasks.

To learn more about learning management systems, read a white paper prepared by Sun Microsystems at **suned.sun.com/US/images/Edu_LMS_wp.pdf** (requires Adobe Reader), or visit the Web site of a vendor, Ziiva, at **www.ziiva.com/lms.htm**.

Finally, remember that the goal of all training is to meet users' needs and help them become more self-reliant, which reduces an organization's overall user support costs.

11

CHAPTER SUMMARY

◻ Training is an important part of user support, because it makes users more self-reliant. A well-trained user is more productive and less likely to need support services than one who has not been adequately trained. Though this chapter focuses on training, it assumes that an understanding of vocabulary and conceptual explanations are an important educational base on which to build training modules.

◻ The training process is a four-step approach:

Step 1. Planning. This step identifies who the trainees are, what they need to know or be able to do as a result of the training, the background the trainees bring to the training, the level of skills the trainees need (how well do they need to be able to perform?), and the specific learning or performance objectives for the training. Plans should address several levels of training skills, including concepts (vocabulary), understanding (explanatory ability), skills (basic task performance), and expertise (highly skilled performance).

Step 2. Preparation. Preparation for training answers questions such as: What specific topics will be covered? How will the topics be organized? What training environment will be effective (classroom, small group, face to face, or self-guided)? How will the training be delivered (popular alternatives include lectures, readings, discussion, visual aids and media, handouts, demonstrations, tutorials, hands-on activities, case studies, role playing, group learning, and automated learning systems like CBT and WBT)? How will the trainee and the trainer be evaluated?

Step 3. Presentation. A successful training presentation depends on adequate planning and preparation Ten guidelines are included in the chapter to help new trainers make more effective presentations.

Step 4. Progress. Evaluation of training sessions is an important way trainers improve their skills as trainers and the quality of future presentations.

◻ Organizations that operate an extensive training program for end users often investigate a learning management system to automate many instructional and administrative tasks.

KEY TERMS

auditory learner — A trainee who learns most effectively by listening to someone talk through new material; lecture method relies heavily on auditory learning skills.

beta test run — A practice training session to evaluate materials and identify problem areas; this term is borrowed from the software industry, where prerelease software is distributed to end users who then look for problems.

collaborative learning — Learning that occurs in a group and can include group discussions, collective hands-on activities, group problem solving, role playing, or participation in a joint case study team.

computer-based training (CBT) — Automated training in which learners use a computer system; includes tutorials, multimedia presentations, product demonstrations, and hands-on activities.

delivery method — Instructional technologies, media, or approaches to present information or training materials, such as lectures, group discussions, hands-on activities, or computer-based tutorials.

education — The teaching and learning process that aims to provide conceptual understanding and long-term thinking skills; the goal is to provide basic vocabulary and understanding of general principles.

experiential learner — A trainee who learns most effectively by performing a task (also called kinesthetic learning).

learning objective — A statement of the knowledge and skills trainees need to learn.

learning management system — A software tool that automates many tasks associated with a training program.

multimedia material — A presentation that includes a combination of text, still images, animation, and sound.

performance objective — A statement of what trainees should be able to do at the end of a training activity; objectives should be measurable, and usually start with an action verb, such as *plan, change, explain, evaluate, analyze, repair,* or *prepare.*

role playing — A training delivery method in which trainees participate in a rehearsal or practice of a work environment situation by taking the roles of users, support staff, trainers, and trainees.

training — The teaching and learning process that aims to build skills that are immediately useful to trainees; focuses on performing tasks and building expertise; can be short term and is often tested by measuring a learner's ability to perform specific tasks.

tutorial — An interactive learning technique in which trainees work through materials step-by-step, usually at their own pace.

visual learner — A trainee who learns most effectively by seeing new material, by reading it, working through a self-guided tutorial, looking at a picture or a chart, or watching a demonstration.

Web-based training (WBT) — A form of computer-based training in which the Internet replaces CDs as the delivery medium; highly interactive and available wherever Internet access is available.

CHECK YOUR UNDERSTANDING

1. True or False? A goal of end-user training is to make users as self-reliant as possible to reduce their need for support.

2. True or False? Training is a teaching and learning process that aims to provide conceptual understanding and long-term thinking skills.

3. _____ is a skill level in which a trainee has gone beyond basic skills to be able to perform a task effectively and efficiently.

4. Which one of the following is not a step in the training process described in this chapter?

   a. plan

   b. present

   c. perform

   d. progress

5. True or False? The best performance objectives for a training session specify how well a trainee needs to be able to perform a task, such as speed or accuracy.

6. True or False? Experienced trainers agree that one learning style is effective for most trainees.

7. Which of the following skill levels deals with performing a task effectively and efficiently?

   a. concepts and understanding

   b. basic skills

   c. expertise

   d. all of these

11

8. In the classification of skill levels listed below, what is the sequence in which the skills are usually built? (1) basic skills (2) concepts (3) expertise (4) understanding

   a. 1 − 2 − 3 − 4

   b. 2 − 4 − 1 − 3

   c. 1 − 4 − 2 − 3

   d. 2 − 1 − 3 − 4

9. _____ training materials combine text, images, animation, and sound in a training delivery system.

10. True or False? Due to the popularity of self-paced training materials and online, interactive training delivery systems, the role of support specialists as trainers is likely to disappear in the next few years.

11. Which of the following training environments is generally the most cost-effective because the ratio of trainees to trainers is highest?

    a. classes

    b. small groups/teams

    c. one-to-one training

    d. role playing

12. Which of the following learning methods results in the highest retention and trainee performance?

    a. listen

    b. read

    c. observe

    d. problem solve

13. True or False? Trainers often discover that more short breaks during a training session are preferable to fewer long breaks.

14. Which statement accurately describes the costs associated with computer-based delivery methods?

    a. The development cost is high, but the cost per user is low.

    b. The development cost is high, and the cost per user is high.

    c. The development cost is low, but the cost per user is high.

    d. The development cost is low, and the cost per user is low.

15. Printed material designed for trainees to take away from a training session to refresh a user's memory are called _____ .

DISCUSSION QUESTIONS

1. Why does higher education rely so heavily on the lecture method in courses? Is the reliance on lectures appropriate? What are effective alternatives to the lecture method in training environments?

2. Do you think trainees have the knowledge and perspective to effectively evaluate the performance of a trainer? Explain why or why not.

3. How will the availability of high quality training materials on the Internet affect the need for user support workers to provide training as part of the user support role?

4. Can visual aids actually detract from learner understanding in a training activity? Give some examples to support your viewpoint.

HANDS-ON PROJECTS

Project 11-1

Analyze trainee backgrounds. Describe your classmates or coworkers in terms of their knowledge and experience as end users. Do they all have similar experience levels? Are they from diverse backgrounds? What problems would differences in education or experience among your classmates or coworkers cause a trainer who was planning a training module for the group? Write a one-page summary of your findings.

Project 11-2

Analyze learning levels. Choose a software package you know well, such as Windows 2000 or XP, a Microsoft Office application, or an Internet browser. Identify one significant (1) concept, (2) point of understanding (explanation), (3) skill, and (4) expertise that a user of the package would be expected to have. Summarize the information in a paragraph.

Project 11-3

Write measurable performance objectives. Suppose that a trainer has identified as a general goal for a training module: *Ability to format printed output according to a specification sheet.* Rewrite this goal statement so that it specifies a measurable performance objective. Write three additional measurable performance objectives for Windows XP or a Microsoft Office application.

11

Project 11-4

Research and discuss resources for training materials. Discuss this statement with a group of three classmates: "Using existing materials from a vendor user's manual, textbook, or trade book as a source of training ideas violates the original author's copyright, and therefore should never be done." If you need more information on copyrighted materials, use a search engine to locate information on the Web. Discuss the information you find, or take the University of Texas tutorial on copyrights at **www.lib.utsystem.edu/copyright**. Write a summary of your reaction to the statement after your discussion. Note any points of disagreement among members of your group.

Project 11-5

Compare training environments. Do you personally prefer classroom training, small group sessions, one-to-one training, or self-guided tutorials? Why? Are there circumstances in which you feel one form of training is more effective than another? Interview two or three classmates or coworkers and get their answers to these questions. Write a summary that compares your response to the responses of those whom you interviewed.

Project 11-6

Evaluate CBT or WBT materials. Locate a training module that uses computer-based or Web-based training. (The chapter lists several examples.) The module you select can be a video, a CD, or a Web site. Try out the CBT or WBT approach, either alone or with a group of colleagues. Write a critique of the module. How well does it achieve its goals? What improvements would you suggest to the author? What are the advantages and disadvantages of CBT or WBT delivery systems for training modules in the subject area?

Project 11-7

Analyze training evaluation forms. What other training characteristics could be evaluated in the training evaluation form in Figure 11-5? Locate a training evaluation form used at your school or workplace and compare it with the one described in this chapter. What are the major differences? Describe the changes you would make to the evaluation form in Figure 11-5 based on your research.

Project 11-8

Develop training guidelines. Based on your personal experiences as a trainee or student (a recipient of training), what are some common mistakes you have observed trainers or instructors make that you would add to the top 10 suggestions for trainers in Figure 11-6? Which of the guidelines in the chapter or ones you added do you think will be the most difficult for you when you are a trainer?

Project 11-9

Experience a learning management system. WebCT is a popular Web-based learning management system used in many higher education schools in the United States. You can take a sample course to get a flavor of Web-based instruction and a learning management system on WebCT's site at **www.webct.com/workbench/viewpage?name= workbench_goto**. The *Show Me* demonstration course by Shirley Ambrose will let you experience the WebCT learning environment. Or take Dr. Tom Donahue's course on *HTML for WebCT users*.

Write a summary of your reaction to this method of training.

CASE PROJECTS

1. Learn about Learning Styles

Barbara A. Soloman and Richard M. Felder at North Carolina State University have researched different learning styles. They created an instrument to assess learning styles on four dimensions:

- active/reflective
- sensing/intuitive
- visual/verbal
- sequential/global

Find out more about each of these learning styles at their Web site: **www2.ncsu. edu/unity/lockers/users/f/felder/public/ILSpage.html**. Answer their Index of Learning Styles (ILS) questionnaire (there are no right or wrong answers) to learn more about your preferred learning style. Compare your scores on the ILS questionnaire with the scores of three coworkers or classmates. Write a summary of the results you observed and what the results mean for you personally as a trainee. In your summary, answer the question: Does any one of the training methods described in this chapter meet the needs of all the different learning styles that Felder and Soloman describe on their Web site? Explain why or why not.

2. Design a Training Module

Choose a topic on which you could train others. Plan, prepare, and present a training module on the topic. Examples of possible topics include:

- How to do a mail merge in a word processor
- How to install a CD or DVD drive in a PC
- How to use a switchboard in Microsoft Access
- How to use one or more basic features of a help desk software package, such as HelpTrac, Remedy, Magic Solutions, HEAT, or Clientele (see Chapter 6 for ideas)
- How to use advanced features of an Internet search engine to do more effective searches
- How to use a Macintosh (aimed at Windows users)
- How to write simple scripts using the Windows Script Host
- How to import data from the Web into a Microsoft Excel worksheet

The training module you prepare should include all of the following elements:

PLANNING

     1. Analyze job skills required

     2. Analyze the trainees

     3. Assess the needs of the trainees

     4. Set training objectives

PREPARATION

     5. Select and organize training content

     6. Select training methods, techniques, aids

     7. Prepare training module

     8. Decide how to evaluate training

PRESENTATION

     9. Present training module

     10. Evaluate the training

PROGRESS

     11. Review and revise training materials and methods, as necessary

First, work on the plan for a sample training module for your topic. Cover Steps 1 through 6 and 8 in planning and preparation first. For some of these steps, such as who is the training audience, your instructor may give you some background information or ask you to make some assumptions. Work with other class members to brainstorm topic priorities. What could be included and what could be omitted from your training module?

Next, based on the results of brainstorming with class members, work independently to prepare a 20- to 30-minute training module for one-to-one delivery (Step 7). The module should include a hands-on component, a short quiz, and time for a brief evaluation.

Then, present your training module (Step 9) to another class member. At the end of the training session, both the trainer and the trainee should fill out a short evaluation (a self-evaluation for the trainer). Use the evaluation form from this chapter, or the one you produced in Project 11-7, or write one of your own specifically for this training activity. Then reverse roles, so your partner can present his or her training module to you. (If you are working alone, ask a friend or colleague to help you evaluate your training module as a training beta test.)

When your training beta test is finished, write a short summary of what you learned from the experience that would improve the training module, or your presentation of it, the next time you present it.

3. Present Someone Else's Training Module

CASE PROJECTS

In corporate training, a trainer is often provided with preplanned and prepackaged training materials to present. Repeat presentation Steps 9 through 11 from Case 2, Design a Training Module, using the training materials a classmate has planned and prepared. After the training activity, provide feedback to the original developer about what worked well and what could be improved.

4. A Training Module for Re-Nu-Cartridge

CASE PROJECTS

NOTE

For background information on Re-Nu-Cartridge, see Case Project 4 in previous chapters.

Andrew Nussbaum is the Director of Training Services at Re-Nu-Cartridge. In his work with employees over the last year, he has seen many instances where workers wasted time formatting their Microsoft Word documents inefficiently. Sometimes workers write long reports, client summaries, or presentations, and then manually format each heading, which is very time-consuming. Andrew knows that Re-Nu-Cartridge's employees would save a lot of time if they knew how to use the style feature in Word.

Andrew has discussed the situation with Fred Long, CEO of Re-Nu-Cartridge. Fred wants to offer a two-hour training session for interested workers. Andrew has asked you to design the training module. Plan and prepare a training module on Word styles. The training module you prepare should include all the following elements:

PLANNING (make assumptions where necessary)

1. Analyze job skills required

2. Analyze the trainees

3. Assess the needs of the trainees

4. Set training objectives

PREPARATION

5. Select and organize training content

6. Select training methods, techniques, aids

7. Prepare training module

8. Decide how to evaluate the training

Write a brief description of your plan to address Steps 1 through 6 and 8 above. Then prepare the training materials (Step 7 above) you would use to train users on Word styles. As a goal, develop training material that could be used by another trainer. Create a PowerPoint slide presentation that can be used during the training presentation. Also, draw or describe the ideal room configuration for this training. Show or describe the location of chairs, tables, presentation equipment, computers, and the chalkboard or flip charts.

12

WRITING FOR END USERS

In this chapter you will learn:

♦ The types of end-user documentation

♦ How technical writing differs from other writing

♦ How technical documents are organized

♦ How to plan effective user documentation

♦ The technical writing process

♦ Effective use of formats

♦ Strategies for technical writing

♦ Common problems in technical writing

♦ Tools used for technical writing

♦ How to evaluate documentation

Training makes users more self-reliant, increases their productivity, and reduces their need for support. A successful training session, usually a one-time event, should include handouts, quick reference sheets, and other written documentation that users can take back to their work area for reference. In addition, online documentation such as help systems, assistants (wizards), Web pages, FAQs (frequently asked questions), e-mail messages, and README files are an increasingly popular way for vendors and support groups to communicate essential information effectively to end users.

The creation of any document targeted for end users, whether printed or online, requires a basic knowledge of technical writing. The goal of technical writing is to produce documents that effectively and efficiently communicate information a reader needs. **Documentation** is any form of written communication intended to provide user support information to end users. Good documentation saves users time; poor documentation costs users time and reduces their productivity. This chapter gives an overview of the most important topics in technical writing, but it is not a substitute for a good book or a course on the subject. It reviews some strategies for writing user documentation and provides pointers to help you write successfully on technical subjects in a user support position.

TYPES OF USER DOCUMENTATION

Members of a user support staff are asked to produce written materials in a variety of situations. Although technical writing can have several purposes and can be prepared in very different formats, all documentation must communicate its message clearly. Figure 12-1 lists the common types of documentation, which are described below.

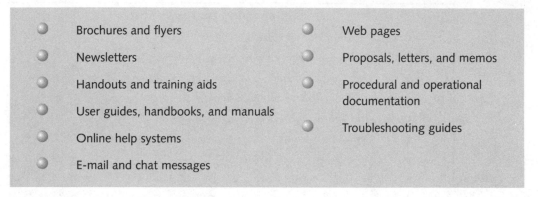

- Brochures and flyers
- Newsletters
- Handouts and training aids
- User guides, handbooks, and manuals
- Online help systems
- E-mail and chat messages
- Web pages
- Proposals, letters, and memos
- Procedural and operational documentation
- Troubleshooting guides

Figure 12-1   Types of user documentation

Brochures and Flyers

Brochures and flyers often promote various computer-related activities, such as staff training sessions, computer fairs, hardware and software product demonstrations, and guest speakers. These documents are primarily promotional and are intended to catch the reader's eye and "sell" the event. Because user support staff are often involved in organizing these kinds of events, they usually need to create informational advertisements for them. To save paper, many support groups now send advertisements for events, such as training opportunities, via e-mail or post them on an organizational intranet or Web portal.

Newsletters

Newsletters are an important way some support groups communicate with users. Today's powerful word-processing software or special-purpose desktop publishing software can help create newsletters with multiple columns and embedded images such as diagrams, pictures, icons, and charts. User support newsletters are especially popular in large organizations where the support staff does not come into direct contact with other employees on a regular basis. An increasing number of organizations now deliver newsletters online to their employees and customers.

For an example of an online newsletter resource targeted to the support industry, visit the TechRepublic Web site at **techrepublic.com.com** (free registration required). Sign up to try one or more of their e-newsletters. Although TechRepublic newsletters are written by a variety of writers, they are generally good examples of technical writing. For more information about publishing an online newsletter, read about the experiences of Pacific Northwest National Laboratory and learn about its recommendations for online newsletters on its Web site at **www.pnl.gov/er_news/stc/stc.htm**. The article includes links to several examples of effective online newsletters.

Handouts and Training Aids

Handouts and training aids are primarily intended to summarize and promote recall of material covered in a training session. They may also be distributed online or in a computer documentation library to answer frequently asked "How do I . . ." questions. Printed handouts of PowerPoint slides that permit trainees to take notes next to each slide are common training aids. These documents are usually short and address a single topic.

User Guides, Handbooks, and Manuals

User guides, handbooks, and computer manuals are more formal examples of written documentation. For some user support groups, these documents can be tens or hundreds of pages long, and are often printed in book format. They supplement vendor documentation and trade books with information specific to an organization or computer facility. For example, a university or college may prepare a user handbook that explains what computer facilities and services are available, including how to access them, how to obtain remote dial-up communications software, ground rules for computer use and abuse, how to use popular software programs, and how to get help. In business organizations, corporate IS departments may publish similar guides for employees. Even very small organizations may find a printed user guide an effective way to communicate basic information to new employees and those who are only occasional users.

Software development companies and hardware vendors publish a variety of user guides and computer manuals that describe for purchasers how to install and use their products. These manuals may be organized in a **tutorial format**, which guides a user step by step through the features of a program. Other manuals may be organized in a **reference format**, in which all the information on a specific topic is located in one place. Some manuals combine tutorials with a reference guide. A tutorial format is convenient for new users, because it emphasizes the natural sequence of steps to learn the features of a product, beginning with the simplest tasks. However, a tutorial format introduces features only as users need them for a particular task. Information about printing, for example, might be scattered throughout a tutorial manual, as various printing features and options are described for users. For experienced users, a reference format is probably more useful, because all the information on a subject, such as printing, is usually located in a single place.

Online Help Systems

Online help systems and software assistants (wizards) are frequent additions to software packages. They are sometimes supplied on CD-ROMs that customers can use for self-training. In other cases, help modules are installed at the same time as the software itself. Some online help systems are well written and can effectively rival or replace printed manuals as a source of well-organized and accurate information. Writing online documentation is an art, however, because the information must be presented succinctly. Writing for on-screen consumption is different from writing for print use. Hypertext links and index searches in online documentation are powerful tools to help users locate needed information that may be more difficult to find in a printed format.

NOTE

A hypertext link is a highlighted word or phrase in the body of a document that acts as a pointer to additional information. When a user clicks a link, the software displays more detailed information about the word or phrase. An index search permits a user to enter a word or phrase of interest; the software then searches the document and displays detailed information about the topic.

The Windows Help system illustrates the use of hypertext links and index searches and includes several examples of interactive help systems called troubleshooters. To access the troubleshooters, click the Start button, and then click Help. In the Windows Help system, click the Contents tab, click Troubleshooting, and then click a troubleshooter to open a page of information in the right pane.

Despite the increasing popularity and convenience of online documentation, some users prefer a print media when they need to read large amounts of information. Printed information is often easier to read for long periods, and it is portable. Depending on the quality and resolution of the display screen and the room lighting, lengthy online documents can be difficult to read. Some end users need extra time to feel comfortable with online documentation and to change their preference for printed materials.

E-Mail and Chat Messages

The ability to communicate effectively via e-mail and instant messaging (chat) is an important writing skill for user support specialists, especially those who work at a help desk that communicates with users primarily online. Some support organizations have switched their primary communication method with users from telephone to e-mail and chat. In these cases, support specialists who honed their verbal skills at the expense of their writing skills may find that they need to update their skills for the positions they occupy. Even though e-mail and chat messages may appear to be a less formal method of communication with end users, e-mail and chat messages from a help desk project an image of the organization and its support staff and should reflect good technical writing skills. Dashing off a few disorganized phrases with typos and spelling errors in an e-mail message or chat exchange can leave the recipient with a poor impression. Writing a response to a user via e-mail helps a support agent to organize his or her thoughts and provides an opportunity to review and revise a response before it is sent. Although internal e-mail messages may be somewhat less formal than messages intended for recipients outside an organization, even informal messages to coworkers and supervisors project an image of the sender. Remember that once you've sent an e-mail message, you have no control over where the recipient may forward it. Supervisors may review and evaluate the quality of support e-mail and chat messages as one measure of an agent's communication skills and promotability.

Support staff who frequently correspond via e-mail and instant messaging need to understand some basic guidelines called netiquette. Mary Houten-Kemp maintains a Web site dedicated to the better understanding and use of e-mail at **everythingemail.net/email_help_tips.html**. The site includes links to other helpful Web resources on effective use of e-mail.

Web Pages

Because an increasing amount of written materials ends up on the World Wide Web, the ability to write for this medium is more important today than five years ago. Web pages need to be organized and written so that users can locate information quickly and easily. Because a Web site is potentially accessible to everyone, the image of an organization is at stake with this medium. Think about how long you stay at a Web site that is poorly organized, contains incorrect or hard-to-find information, or provides broken links (URLs that no longer point to active Web pages). In general, materials designed for Web access must be very short, but contain hypertext links that lead readers to additional information for those who need it. Web-based materials must be well written, because Web users often do not have the patience to wade through a long document to find the information they need. They tend to skim quickly and then click a link to another site. A challenge for support agents who maintain Web sites is to keep information accurate and current. Obsolete or inaccurate support information is often worse than no information.

You can sometimes learn useful information from studying bad examples. To find Web sites that users have nominated as among the worst on the entire Internet, go to **www.worstoftheweb.com**. The site features a worst site of the day and a commentary by three pundits about what makes each one so bad. The site also includes a four-year archive.

Proposals, Letters, and Memos

Because businesses use accounts for a significant portion of total computer use, support staff need to be able to write proposals, letters, and memos. Support specialists who perform needs assessments for end users or departments frequently need to write the results of their investigations in the form of a report or proposal. In addition, support staff often need to

12

write memos, letters, performance appraisals, and other correspondence to colleagues, end users (both inside and outside the organization), and supervisors. The ability to write standard business documents is a basic user support communication skill.

Procedural and Operational Documentation

Procedural and operational documentation includes procedure steps and check lists, usually intended for internal organizational use. The descriptions of the steps to install hardware and software in Chapter 10 are examples of technical procedural documentation. Support specialists also prepare problem reports in a help desk environment. Even for internal documents such as these, technical writing skills are essential. Procedural and operational documentation that is unclear, poorly organized, or incorrect costs staff time, produces errors, and increases user frustration. Clear, well-organized documents communicate information efficiently and reflect well on the writer and the support organization. Many support specialists who have never thought of themselves as writers enjoy the challenge of writing support materials that are accurate and easy to understand.

Troubleshooting Guides

User support staff often write troubleshooting guides to help other employees solve support problems. Common examples of troubleshooting guides include: (1) a problem-solving chapter in a user guide, (2) an FAQ on common problems users encounter, (3) a script to handle a specific type of problem incident, and (4) a problem report in a help desk knowledge base. Although this type of documentation is often for internal use, it still must be clear, concise, and well written.

For an example of an online troubleshooting guide devoted to solving problems with Hewlett-Packard DeskJet model 682c printers, see the Web site at **h20015.www2.hp.com/en/solveCategory.jhtml?reg=&lc=en&cc=us&prodId =dj682c&pagetype=solve**.

All the types of technical writing described above are forms of support documentation. They have more similarities than differences. The following sections stress the similarities.

HOW TECHNICAL WRITING DIFFERS FROM OTHER WRITING

Technical writing is different from other types of writing, such as personal letters, research papers, or novels. The principal areas of difference are in the type of information communicated and its goals, as well as its style and organization.

Technical Writing Style

Technical writing follows specific style guidelines. The goal of these guidelines is to help technical writers create documents that are clear, accurate, and accessible to most users. Keep in mind the following points as you write documentation.

- Technical writing uses short, declarative sentences, short phrases, and lists instead of long sentences that contain unnecessary words or phrases. Most technical writing is based on simple and compound sentences. A simple sentence has one subject and one verb. A compound sentence contains *and* or *but* as a connector and includes two subjects and two verbs. Avoid run-on sentences. Compare these examples:

> **Simple sentence:** Parentheses let you control how Excel uses operators in a formula.
>
> **Compound sentence:** Parentheses let you control how Excel uses operators in a formula and parentheses make your equations easier to read or revise.
>
> **Run-on sentence:** If you specify an uneven number of parentheses in a formula, or a pair of parentheses that don't match, Excel displays the message *Parentheses do not match* or *Error in Formula* and highlights the location of the mistake, which you can correct on the formula bar.

NOTE

Some writers believe that simple sentences are not as interesting as more complex ones. Remember that the purpose of technical writing is not to entertain, but to communicate information vital to the reader's productivity. Also, not all readers have good reading skills; they may have a reading disability (such as dyslexia) or English may be a second language. To communicate effectively with the largest number of readers, keep sentences simple.

- Technical writing states the most important point at the beginning of a section or a topic discussion instead of at the end, as in other types of writing. The goal of technical writing is not to build suspense or work toward a punch line, but to communicate information as clearly and effectively as possible and help a reader make transitions between topics (and skip irrelevant information).

- Technical writing often communicates step-by-step sequences of events or tasks. The writing style and format used can help readers understand the sequence. For example, a sequence of steps should be listed in the order the users would perform the steps. Compare the following examples.

> **Example 1:** Click the Margin option in Page Setup under the File menu.
>
> **Example 2:** In the File menu, click Page Setup, and then click the Margin option.

12

In the first example, the actions appear in reverse order to how they are actually performed. A user must read to the end of the sentence before they learn what action to take first. The second example is preferable because the actions are listed in the order they are performed. When steps in a procedure or task must be performed in a specific sequence, a numbered list can emphasize the sequence. When information has no required order, a bulleted list is more appropriate.

- Technical writing should be concise, but not cryptic. Concise writing is short, but covers the essential information a user needs. Readers of technical documents usually want to open the document, find what they want to know, and get back to work. If they have to spend unnecessary time searching for buried information, then their productivity is reduced. To include more detailed information, add **pointers**, or cross-references to the location where a user can find more information. In online documents, hypertext links effectively move a user from general to more specific information on a topic.

- Technical writing should not try to entertain readers with humor or call attention to the writer's personality or preferences. Humor in a technical document is likely to be misunderstood by some percentage of readers, especially those who are new to a topic or who use English as a second language. The writer's personal preferences should be clearly labeled as such, enabling readers to quickly identify possible sources of bias.

Good technical writing follows these conventions to ensure that users get the help they need from a document. If users cannot locate the information they need, the result is a higher volume of calls to the support group or a higher level of user frustration.

How Technical Documents Are Organized

Two common ways to organize technical documents are sequential and hierarchical. **Sequential organization** follows a step-by-step approach whereby information is arranged in order from first to last. Procedural documents usually follow a sequential organization. **Hierarchical organization** flows from top to bottom, and information is arranged from general to specific. Online help systems often use a hierarchical organization.

Most successful technical documentation uses a combination of sequential and hierarchical organization strategies, depending on the material to be communicated, the medium of communication, and the users' needs. A common organization for technical documentation is shown below.

Introduction

    What is the purpose of the document?

    Who are the intended readers of the document?

    Why read the document?

Body

    Specific task steps

    Common problems users encounter

Summary

    Pointers to additional information

The overall organization is hierarchical. At the top level, general sections are: Introduction, Body, and Summary. The body in this example includes "task steps," which are sequential.

The introduction begins by addressing three questions. First, what is the purpose of this document? What are its goals? Second, who should read this? Who is the intended audience? Third, why would anyone want to read this? In other words, readers want to know up front what information they will get from reading this document. Technical writers should answer these three questions up front to save time for those readers for whom a document is *not* intended. Even a short piece of writing, such as an FAQ or an e-mail message, should state its purpose in the first or second sentence.

The body of a technical document should include explanatory material. Most readers want a short explanation to help them understand why something works, what result should be expected, or why the information is important. A brief explanation is often included of what the hardware or software is capable of and how it can help readers in their work. The explanation is often followed by a detailed description of the sequential steps necessary to perform a task. Finally, the body should briefly describe common problems users are likely to encounter and how to recover from them. The summary should be brief and review the main points and the results achieved, and point the reader to where additional information can be accessed.

Some technical writers are tempted to include as much information as they can in a document. The writer may digress from the main points to cover material that may be of interest to only a few readers, is not critical, or is very technical. Omit less critical information or place this material in an appendix or attachment. Include a pointer to the appendix in the body, so that interested readers will know where to find it.

DOCUMENTATION PLANNING

The steps writers take to plan user documentation projects are very similar to steps that trainers take to plan training sessions. As with training, planning is essential to produce high-quality documents, regardless of their length or purpose. Most planning involves determining the characteristics of the audience and its needs, as listed in Figure 12-2.

> ○   Who is the target audience?
>
> ○   What does the audience already know?
>
> ○   What does the audience need to know?
>
> ○   What do you want the audience to be able to do when they finish reading the document?
>
> ○   What medium will be used to transmit the document to its audience?

Figure 12-2   Information needed for documentation planning

The answers to these questions prepare technical writers to create a useful, well-targeted document.

Who Is the Target Audience?

The question about the target audience is often intended to pinpoint the readers' level of technical expertise. To write a task description for new users requires different assumptions and techniques than writing one for more experienced, technically sophisticated users. The audience definition should also include an estimate of their reading level. Most newspapers, for example, are written at an eighth or ninth grade reading level, which is a good level to strive for in computer documents targeted to a general audience of end users. Most word processors include a tool to measure the reading level (readability index) of a document.

The readability index for this chapter is 10th grade level.

NOTE

What Does the Audience Already Know?

To determine who the audience is, a technical writer should attempt to find out the readers' backgrounds, including what they already know. A statement in the introduction about what the writer assumes the readers know can help readers make an informed decision about whether the material is intended for them, whether it covers things they already know, or whether it covers technical information that is beyond their ability to understand.

When readers need to know a specific procedure, assessing what skills they already have is sometimes difficult In some situations, a technical writer may be able to assess skills using a questionnaire. Because a questionnaire is not always feasible, cover the most basic skills first, but with appropriate labels so that more skilled users can easily skip to what they need to know.

What Does the Audience Need to Know?

Answering this question is one of the critical first steps in technical writing, because it helps a writer define the purpose of the document. As with training (discussed in Chapter 11), the purpose of technical documentation should be to move readers from what they already know to what they need to know. The purpose of a document should be stated early, within the first few sentences.

What Do You Want the Audience to Be Able to Do?

Technical writers should know what specific tasks they want the audience to perform after reading the document. A task focus gives direction to the writing and helps users know when they have successfully mastered the information. Although some documents are intended for general information purposes only, most are aimed at getting readers to a point where they can make a decision or perform a specific task.

What Medium Will Be Used to Transmit the Document to Its Audience?

The medium used to communicate technical information needs to be planned in advance by a writer. Common media types include print format and online format. Although some documents are written for either or both media, printed documents can be longer and therefore need transitions between topics and levels of information to help readers know where they are in the hierarchy of information. Online documents need to be shorter, but can include hyperlinks and other pointers to help readers navigate quickly to the desired information or to additional information. The computer industry has experienced a transition from primarily printed documentation several years ago to almost entirely Web-based or optical media documentation today.

THE TECHNICAL WRITING PROCESS

After document writers have defined the audience, purpose, and medium for a document, they can then begin to write the document itself. Many writers use the seven-step process shown in Figure 12-3 to write a document.

1.   Generate a list of important ideas or features to be covered.

2.   Organize the list into a logical, hierarchical sequence to form an outline.

3.   Expand the outline into a first draft.

4.   Edit the draft one or more times.

5.   Arrange for an outside review.

6.   Revise the draft into its final form.

7.   Proofread the document.

Figure 12-3   The technical writing process

Good technical writing follows this process. A writer may be tempted to take shortcuts because of time constraints, but once a document is published, especially in a print medium, there is often little or no opportunity to change it. Even very experienced writers would never consider releasing their first draft to end users. They realize that the entire seven-step process is critical to producing quality documents.

Step 1. Generate an Idea List

Writers often use a word processor to generate a list of ideas; others use paper and pencil. At this stage, a writer **brainstorms** to generate as many topics as they can think of that might be useful to readers. Some potential topics become major topics, others become minor topics, and some are discarded. While brainstorming, the strategy is to exclude nothing; after brainstorming, the idea list can be prioritized and pared down to essentials.

Step 2. Organize the List into an Outline

Once writers have a topic list that includes everything they want to cover, they organize the topics into a logical order to form an outline. Most writers don't arrive at the final organizational structure of all topics on the first attempt. Flexibility is important during the early organizational steps; writers often cut and paste to try out different sequences of ideas. Most word processors have an outlining feature that makes it easy to rearrange topics, to promote some in importance to major topics and demote others. As writers begin to create an outline, other topics may come to mind that can be added. The most important question an outline asks is, "In what order does the reader need to know this information?" The answer is to cover the essential information first, including qualifiers or assumptions.

Step 3. Expand the Outline into a First Draft

After carefully creating an outline and checking it for logical flow, expand the outline into a first draft by explaining each point in the outline. When writing the first draft, writers often use the features described below to make their documents readable and understandable. Although many techniques help produce understandable documentation, these four are basic.

Paragraphs with Topic Sentences.   A document should be organized into paragraphs, where each paragraph covers a different aspect of the topic. Each paragraph should have a topic sentence that introduces the topic in general terms. After the topic sentence, develop other sentences in each paragraph with the details that support or expand on the topic sentence. When writing Web-based documents and e-mail messages, the number of paragraphs on a page or in a message should be small: one or a few.

Transitions.   Use transitional words such as "for example," "therefore," and "as a result" to help show a reader the relationship of one sentence to another. Other transitions useful for steps in a procedure are "first," "second," "next," "then," and "finally." Transitions help readers keep track of where they are in a sequential organization. Numbered and bulleted lists help show transitions.

Defined Terms.   Good technical writers always define the terms they use. To introduce readers to a new term, define it clearly and boldface the term in the sentence that defines it, as you have seen in this book. When defining terms, be careful not to define a term using the term itself; use a synonym instead.

Formats.   As they write a document draft, writers use format features to help readers understand the organization of information more easily. Different sized headings, for example, alert a reader to the overall structure. Many writers use italic type for emphasis, although emphasis should be used sparingly. Bulleted or numbered lists are useful to alert a reader to the structure of a long section.

A document's structure helps guide readers through the parts of a document. After technical writers determine the structure of a document, they add formats to communicate the structure to readers. The following list focuses on format tools successful technical writers frequently use that you can incorporate in your own writing.

- **Style elements.** When a document is organized into chapters or modules, different fonts, font sizes, boldface, capitalization, centering, indentation, underlines, bullets, and numbering help a reader understand the structure. They help the reader to understand what is more or less important and to spot transitions from one topic to the next. They answer questions such as, "If I am not interested in this paragraph, where do I skip to start reading again so I don't miss anything?"

12

Although changes in font, case, indentation, centering, and other format features can help alert a reader to the structure of a document, some writers get carried away with the power of a word processor and overuse these tools. Two fonts can be useful to help the reader deal with different types of material. But too many different fonts, or too much boldface or italics, can be a distraction.

- **Format consistency.** Format consistency is important. Use a consistent format for headings, paragraphs, and tables. Style sheets and templates in popular word processors can help make consistent formatting easy. For technical manuals or other materials that will receive widespread commercial distribution, hardware and software organizations and publishers hire a graphic designer to create a design for the interior of the document. For many smaller projects, however, preformatted templates, which are often created by professional designers and included with word-processing programs, are sufficient.

- **Lists and tables.** Finally, when a writer needs to present a sequence of information, a bulleted or numbered list or a table is often more understandable than a long narrative passage. Lists and tables permit readers to quickly locate the information they need. On the other hand, users often find it very difficult to locate information quickly in a long narrative passage. Lists are most effective when they support a generalization or summarize information presented in narrative text.

Step 4. Edit the Draft

After expanding an outline into the first draft, read and edit it. Most writers read through and edit a draft more than once, looking for particular problems on each pass. A one edit pass rarely catches all the different types of problems.

One edit pass is often used to delete extra words, because a goal of technical writing is to be brief. Consider, for example, the following short paragraph:

> Let's spend a bit more time discussing the relationship between the automatic call distribution (ACD) system and other help desk systems. Only the more sophisticated ACDs allow interfaces to other devices now, but it's clearly the wave of the future, not to mention a productivity enhancer.

The following version eliminates extraneous words while maintaining the meaning:

> Let's discuss the relationship between the automatic call distribution (ACD) system and other help desk systems. Currently, only sophisticated ACDs can connect to other devices. However, future models will have connectivity to enhance user productivity.

Eliminating extra words takes some practice, but it is beneficial because tighter prose takes less time to read. Eliminate any words that are not critical to understanding your meaning.

A second edit pass that writers perform is a format consistency check. The purpose of a **format consistency check** is to make sure that the font of headings and subheadings, indentation, centering, boldface, italics, and underlining remain the same way throughout a document. Check to see that these formatting features are not overused. The purpose of a technical document is seldom to show how many different format elements a writer can use. Format features should guide a reader through a document without hindering understanding or becoming a distraction.

A third edit pass is a technical accuracy check. During a **technical accuracy check**, a writer tests any procedural or technical steps in a document by performing the steps with the hardware or software. The purpose of a technical accuracy check is to eliminate any errors in step-by-step instructions or other technical information. If a document has been written about a beta or other prerelease version of hardware or software, a final accuracy check should be performed with the final version of a product that end users will actually encounter. Check URLs to make sure addresses are spelled correctly and that the URLs still point to active sites.

Step 5. Get an Outside Review

An outside review is a second opinion. Another pair of eyes can often raise questions, spot inconsistencies, find unclear meaning, identify poor writing techniques, and locate other problems that a writer cannot see. Getting outside criticism can be surprising, especially because writers who spend a lot of time on their first draft are often satisfied that it is just about perfect. Criticism can be especially painful if a reviewer doesn't share the same writing style and approach as the writer. But a second perspective on any written document is important, especially for documents that will have widespread distribution. An outside review serves the same purpose as a beta test of a training module. Over time, writers learn to set aside the natural defensiveness they may feel about their work and realize that a reviewer represents the potential target audience. Most writers would rather that a reviewer find problems early than for readers to do so after publication.

Step 6. Revise the Draft

After a writer edits the draft and gets feedback, they revise it to incorporate suggestions and corrections. If a writer is a perfectionist, one of the hardest parts of the writing process is to know when to stop revisions. Although edit passes can serve a useful purpose up to a point, a writer must learn when to quit. Fortunately for many technical writers, publication deadlines dictate when you are finished. After a few revisions, additional edit passes can result in very small incremental improvement in a document. At the end of each edit pass, a writer should ask whether the last pass resulted in a substantial improvement, or whether the improvements were only marginal; if they didn't enhance the readability or accuracy of the document, then it is time to stop.

12

Step 7. Proofread the Document

After writing, editing, and revising a document, writers proofread it one last time to make sure that no small errors remain. Sometimes another person or a professional proofreader or copyeditor can perform this task. Proofreaders look for a variety of common errors, including:

- **Inconsistent capitalization and punctuation.** Are proper nouns capitalized consistently? Are words capitalized that shouldn't be? Are commas used consistently in sentences, in lists, and within large numbers?

- **Inconsistent font use.** Are headings the correct font and size? Is the body text in the same font?

- **Extra spaces between words and sentences.** Is the number of spaces after each sentence consistent? (Most typeset books and many desktop published documents use only one space after periods.) Is there a single space between words? You can use your word processor to search for two spaces and replace each occurrence with one space.

- **Incorrect page breaks.** Are all the page breaks in logical locations? Should any page breaks be adjusted to eliminate orphaned sentences (a situation in which the first or last sentence in a paragraph or list is on a separate page from the remainder of the paragraph or list)?

The seven steps in the technical writing process help both new and experienced document writers ensure that their work is well organized and understandable.

 The World Wide Web contains a wealth of useful resources for beginning and experienced technical writers. For example, David A. McMurrey, a professor at Austin Community College, provides an online technical writing textbook at **www.io.com/~hcexres/tcm1603/acchtml/acctoc.html**. To learn more about the use of format tools, click topics in the table of contents under *Document Design*. The Technical Writer's Reference Page at **www.angelfire.com/stars/ techwriter** contains several links to Web sites with resources for technical writers.

TECHNICAL WRITING STRATEGIES

Although you may not have written technical documents before, you have probably used a manual, received online help, or read some other form of documentation. Based on your experience, you probably already have some thoughts about what makes good or bad technical writing, and what has or has not been effective at addressing your needs as a reader and user. Some technical writing is a pleasure to use because it is well organized, and readers can find the information they need quickly. If you analyze successful documents, some common strategies and approaches stand out.

Analogies

Technical writers often use analogies to explain new material. An **analogy** describes how an unfamiliar concept is similar to a familiar concept. For example, writers often use the analogy of an office filing system to explain the hierarchical structure of computer media. They draw a parallel between the information in an office filing system and the information in a computer filing system. Analogies are useful because they relate something most users are familiar with, such as an office filing system, to something they need to know about.

Repetition

Writers often use repetition for emphasis. Repetition is also a training strategy you encountered in Chapter 11. In both technical documents and user training, a useful strategy is to introduce a topic, explain it, and then summarize it. Repetition helps users learn new material and recall it later. However, excessive use of repetition can unnecessarily lengthen a document without contributing to its usefulness.

12

Consistent Word Use

Technical writers try to use words consistently. In creative writing, writers are taught to look for synonyms to avoid overuse of certain words and to inject variety in written work. In technical writing, however, consistent use of words can contribute to the reader's understanding. To vary word use unnecessarily can cause the reader to think that different words have slightly different meanings. For example, a writer on disk media may use synonyms such as "disk," "diskette," and "floppy disk" interchangeably to refer to the same thing, which can confuse readers. A similar problem arises with "CD," "CD-ROM," "compact disc," and "optical disk." Technical writing is often clearer when one word among synonyms is used throughout a document.

Many organizations maintain a **style sheet** that lists their preferences for common terms so that all writers use the same terminology. Sometimes a style sheet is a simple list of preferred terms and spelling conventions. In other cases, a style sheet can be a lengthy document that lists not only terms and spelling conventions but also preferred grammatical structures, product name usage conventions, and the like. Figure 12-4 shows a sample page from a publisher's style sheet.

Style Sheet   *Page 3*

Item	Comments
check box (not checkbox)	
check mark	
checkbook	
choose	Do not use in steps
click (not "click on")	
click and drag (v.)	
click in	Use when positioning a pointer "in" a text box or placing the insertion point "in" a specific area
clip-art (adj.)	clip-art image, clip-art library
click-drag technique	
ClipArt	when referring specifically to Microsoft ClipArt Gallery

Figure 12-4   Page from a style sheet

The English Teaching Forum maintains an online style sheet to describe how writers should prepare documents for publication by their organization. For an example of a style sheet, see its Web site at **exchanges.state.gov/forum/stylesheet.htm**.

Parallel Structure

The concept of parallel structure is important in technical writing. **Parallel structure** means that similar items are handled consistently throughout a document. Consistent formats for titles, headings, and subheadings are one application of parallel structure, as are consistent verb tenses and parts of speech. Parallel structure is also important in bulleted lists, as shown in Figure 12-5.

In the example on the left in Figure 12-5, note that few of the items in the list are worded the same way. For instance, the word *time* appears first for one of the items, and last in another. The example on the right shows one way to rewrite the list using parallel structure. Notice that all the terms in the list are nouns, and their phrasing is similar. In a parallel list structure, each item in the list should make a complete sentence when used with the phrase that introduces the list.

Problems with parallel structure	Revision to use parallel structure
Consider the following ways to measure help desk performance:	Consider the following ways to measure help desk performance:
• first: volume of calls	• call volume
• next: time it takes to respond	• call response time
• resolution time	• call resolution time
• how many calls are backlogged	• call backlog
• call aging	• call aging time

Figure 12-5   Parallel structure in a bulleted list

Consistent Verb Tense

Technical writers generally use a consistent verb tense throughout a document. Present tense is often preferable in technical writing unless the topic is something that clearly happened in the past. Consider the following examples:

Example 1: After you have powered up your computer and booted into Windows, Dial-Up Networking is used to establish a network connection.

Example 2: First, power up your computer and boot into Windows. Then use Dial-Up Networking to establish a network connection.

The first example uses the past tense unnecessarily. The second example uses the present tense, which leads the reader through the actions. Past tense is often appropriate in a problem description to indicate actions a user performed, because the actions did occur in the past.

COMMON PROBLEMS IN TECHNICAL WRITING

Technical writers learn from experience to avoid common problems. Their writing is clearer, more understandable, and easier to read. Figure 12-6 lists 12 common problems to avoid.

○ Clutter		○ Nominalization
○ Inappropriate typefaces		○ Wordiness
○ Gender references		○ Jargon
○ Unclear referents		○ Undefined acronyms
○ Passive voice		○ Dangling phrases

Figure 12-6   Common technical writing problems

Clutter

The availability of powerful word processors and desktop publishing software means that even novice writers can produce very professional-looking results. However, all writers need to be careful not to include too many distracting design elements. Just because graphics, clip art, shading, word art, borders, and neon printer colors can be easily included does not mean that you should use all of them. Add graphics to illustrate a point, not just for decoration. Apply formatting sparingly and consistently, and only when it helps readers locate information or understand the subject. A user document with simple formatting is often more effective than one with too many format features.

The most successful documents are those that include considerable white space where readers can rest their eyes. Leave reasonable margins at the top, bottom, and sides of pages, insert spaces between paragraphs, and use a large enough font to be readable. The body text font size should be at least 9 points or larger; don't reduce the size of a font just to fit material that is too long in the space allocated to it. Rather, try to edit for conciseness.

Most body text should be left aligned. Large passages of centered text are difficult to read, as is **justified text**, which is aligned at both the right and left margins. Justified text, also called block justified, sometimes contains large white spaces between words that can make text difficult to read. For example, which of these passages is easier to read:

This sentence is left aligned to illustrate how easily the reader's eye moves from word to word. This justification style is reccommended for the body of most documents, because it enhances readability.

This sentence is block justified to illustrate that it is more difficult to read when software inserts additional spaces between words. This approach creates an artificial block style with text that extends to the right and left margins.

This sentence is centered
to illustrate that it is more difficult to read
lines of text that
differ in length.

Inappropriate Typefaces

For most readers, serif typefaces are easier to read than sans serif. **Serif typefaces** include serifs, fine lines that project from the top and bottom of a font's letters. These lines lead the eye from letter to letter across the line. The font you are reading now is called Bembo, which is a serif font. **Sans serif typefaces** do not have the serifs (*sans* is a French word for *without*). Sans serif typefaces are often used for titles and headings, whereas serif typefaces are frequently used for body text.

Most word processors include several **specialty typefaces** that are intended for special uses, such as invitations, brochures, or flyers. Script fonts fall into this category. Although specialty typefaces are interesting and fun, save them for informal use. Figure 12-7 shows a serif font, a sans serif font, and a specialty font. Which do you think is easiest to read?

> This is an example of a 12-point serif typeface called Goudy Old Style.
>
> This is an example of a 12-point sans serif typeface called Arial.
>
> *This is an example of a 14-point script typeface called Brush Script.*

Figure 12-7   Font readability examples

Gender References

In recent years, the use of gender-related pronouns has decreased. *He, she*, *him*, and *her* are often replaced with gender-neutral words, such as *they*, *their*, and *it*. This change in style means that writers sometimes use a plural pronoun where they might have previously used a singular pronoun. You can also use the phrase *he or she* (the order is sometimes reversed). Some writers use the combined form *s/he*, but this solution is usually not preferred because it is more difficult to read. Other writers alternate between *he* and *she*—a strategy that can confuse a reader. Choose one of these strategies to use consistently, but try to avoid gender-related words, unless they clearly fit.

Gender-neutral words include *staff* instead of *manpower,* and *staffed* instead of *manned*. Use *chair* or *chairperson* instead of *chairman*, but be consistent. Don't refer to a male as a *chairman* and a female as a *chair*; instead, refer to both genders as a *chair*. Use *supervisor* in preference to *foreman*. Can you think of other common examples? It takes some practice to use gender-neutral language, but the result is often clearer and less prone to offend than the alternatives.

12

Unclear Referents

Another common problem in technical writing is the use of unclear or missing referents. A **referent** is a word that refers to another word or concept. Consider this example:

> Windows and the Office Suite use pull-down menus. They are good examples of the power of the GUI interface.

The word "they" at the start of the second sentence refers (or is a referent) to a concept in the previous sentence. But does the writer mean that Windows and the Office Suite are examples of the power of the GUI interface, or that pull-down menus are good examples? The referent of "they" is not clear. To clarify the second sentence, replace "they" with the intended referent:

> Windows and the Office Suite use pull-down menus. Both software packages are good examples of the power of the GUI interface.

Passive Voice

Good technical writing uses the active voice whenever possible instead of the passive voice. In **active voice**, the subject of a sentence *performs* the action indicated by the verb; the subject is an actor. In **passive voice,** the subject of a sentence *receives* the action indicated by the verb; the subject is not a do-er. In some sentences in passive voice, the real subject is missing. Consider this example:

> The new operating system was installed on Friday.

In this example, the subject (*operating system*) does not perform the action (*was installed*), but is the recipient of the action. Writers in business, government, and elsewhere often use passive voice to avoid naming the real subject of a sentence, as in the classic example of passive voice: "Mistakes were made." The example sentence above is much stronger in active voice:

> A support specialist installed the new operating system on Friday.

In this revision, the subject (*support specialist*) performs the action (*installed*). Although some technical writers prefer passive voice because it makes the writing seem more objective, others avoid passive voice whenever possible; it gives text a stilted, awkward tone, and is often unclear. Active voice makes text livelier and more interesting. Compare the examples in Table 12-1 and see how much easier the active voice sentences are to understand.

Table 12-1   Passive versus active voice

Passive Voice	Active Voice
The text is highlighted by clicking the bold button.	Highlight the text by clicking the bold button.
The modem card is inserted into the PCMCIA slot.	Insert the modem card into the PCMCIA slot.
The file is read from the disk.	The computer reads the file from the disk.
Touching the disk media should be avoided.	Avoid touching the disk media.

NOTE   Résumés are often more interesting and convey an action orientation when they are written primarily in active voice instead of passive voice. The grammar checkers in some word processors alert the writer to excessive use of passive voice sentences.

Nominalization

Nominalization is the process of creating a noun from a verb or adjective. In general, avoid nominalization; verbs are easier to understand. Table 12-2 shows examples of nominalization and their improved forms.

Table 12-2   Nominalization examples

Nominalization	Improved Form
Development of batch files will take three weeks.	We will develop batch files in three weeks.
Perform an installation of the printer driver.	Install the printer driver.
The configuration of the system should take about an hour.	The system takes about an hour to configure.

Wordiness

Wordiness can lead to long sentences and hinder understanding. Avoid unnecessary words; find the shortest way to state your ideas. Table 12-3 presents several examples of how to reduce unnecessary words.

Table 12-3   Reducing wordiness

Wordy	Concise
Call customer support to raise questions about the problem you are having.	Call customer support to ask about the problem
Prior to the actual installation of the system . . .	Before installing the system . . .
Before making an attempt to install the card . . .	Before installing the card . . .
Put the computer in a location where it will not be in danger of being harmed by anyone who might be passing by.	Locate the computer where passersby will not accidentally damage it.

12

To make text easier to read, use short words whenever possible. Replace a long word such as *approximately* with a shorter word that means the same thing, such as *about*, replace *utilize* with *use*, and try *document* instead of *documentation*. Can you think of other examples?

Jargon

Computer technology often intimidates new users because of the amount of jargon used to describe and discuss it. Avoid the use of **jargon**, words understood only by those experienced in the field. Instead, use simple, direct words that anyone can understand, unless the target audience will clearly understand the jargon. For example, technical writers may write about the *cold boot process* for a computer system. In documentation for new users, use a term like *start-up process* or *power-on step*.

If you must use jargon terms, define them first so that you and the reader share a common understanding of the vocabulary. Writers often include a glossary at the end of a chapter or book, much like the Key Terms list at the end of the chapters in this book.

Undefined Acronyms

Like jargon, an **acronym**, or a series of letters that represent a phrase, can make technical writing difficult to understand. For example, I/O is an acronym for input/output; RAM is an acronym for random access memory. Writers should always define the meaning of acronyms for a reader, unless the target audience will obviously understand the acronym. Even for advanced audiences, err on the safe side and define each acronym. The first time an acronym is used, spell out the words that the acronym represents, and then include the acronym in parentheses:

> Extended data output (EDO) memory is being replaced in some high-end systems with synchronous dynamic random access memory (SDRAM). SDRAM is currently more expensive than EDO memory, but . . .

Another effective strategy is to include acronyms in a glossary or a key terms list.

Dangling Phrases

A **dangling phrase** is a few words (or even a single word) at the beginning or end of a sentence that add little to the meaning of the sentence other than to make it longer.

> **Example 1:** The Accounting department is eager to begin training on QuickBooks, generally.
>
> **Example 2:** Generally, the Accounting department is eager to begin training on QuickBooks.
>
> **Example 3:** Mohammed turned on the overhead projector, but the image did not appear, as everyone noticed.

Either eliminate the dangling phrase, if it makes little difference to the meaning of the sentence, or look for a way to include it in the sentence.

> **Revision of examples 1 and 2:** The Accounting department is generally eager to begin training on QuickBooks.
>
> **Revision of example 3:** When Mohammed turned on the overhead projector, everyone noticed that the image did not appear.

The list of potential writing problems is long. But most technical writers find that with practice and experience, they become adept at avoiding these problems.

 Paul Brians, an English professor at Washington State University, has compiled a list of common mistakes in language use. See his Web site at **www. wsu.edu/~brians/errors**. Also see Western Washington University Professor Gene Myers's list of writing errors to avoid at **www.ac.wwu.edu/~gmyers/ writeerr.html**.

TECHNICAL WRITING TOOLS

Many word processors include tools that support staff can use to develop useful user documentation. These include:

- An outliner to help organize work
- A spell checker to identify and correct spelling errors
- A custom dictionary to contain jargon words and acronyms
- A thesaurus to help find a word that exactly expresses a concept
- A grammar checker to recommend changes in wording to improve readability
- A readability index to indicate the level of difficulty for the audience
- Desktop publishing features to help writers produce documents that appear more professional

Even with all these built-in tools, a good collegiate dictionary is also a useful tool, because spell checkers don't know the meaning of words. Be on the lookout for good examples of well-written documents. Be critical of documents you read. Ask yourself what makes a document or message useful and easy to read, and by the same token, what makes one difficult to understand and use.

 One of the classic books on writing clearly in English is *Elements of Style* by William Strunk, Jr. and E. B. White. Fortunately, an online version of this entire book is available on the Bartleby.com Web site at **www.bartleby.com/141**. Many writers think of Strunk and White as the bible of written communication.

MARSHA E. JONES
TECHNICAL WRITER

Marsha Jones has an extensive background in the computer industry as a programmer and technical writer. Her work experience includes both large and small companies, and she has written both technical documentation aimed at system administrators and materials aimed at end users. She currently writes documentation on a contract basis. Her specialty is projects that include both printed manuals and Web-based help systems. In this CloseUp, Marsha describes her experiences with several tools available to technical writers.

When you develop documentation that will be both printed and available online, what tools do you like to use?

Given a choice, I like to write with Adobe FrameMaker (**www.adobe.com/products/framemaker/main.html**) and use WebWorks Publisher (**www.webworks.com**) to generate the HTML help from the FrameMaker documents. The combination works well, because I've almost never had to produce just a help system or just a printed manual. Because I usually produce both, I need to consider the structure of both the printed manual and the help system as I create the files in FrameMaker and I need to understand how WebWorks Publisher (WWP) will convert the organization of the FrameMaker files to the structure of the help system. Everything gets created in FrameMaker—the content, the links, the index entries. Everything you want in the help has to be inserted in your FrameMaker files before you run WWP. Then, when you've got all the necessary stuff in the files, you run WWP and check to see if everything came out as you intended.

How does the use of tech writing tools impact your productivity as a technical writer?

FrameMaker is a very stable product. That stability enables me to work faster and gives me more time to work on the text and to get and incorporate feedback from reviewers. The FrameMaker and WebWorks Publisher combination lets me use a single set of source files, rather than maintain two separate sets of source files—one for the printable manual and one for the help.

WebWorks Publisher is fairly expensive, because you have to buy it in addition to FrameMaker, and if you don't like their predefined templates and want to create your own, you've got a learning curve to deal with. It isn't the easiest piece of software for creating your own templates, but once you've got your template, it is fast and provides consistent results.

What are some other products you've worked with, and why did you choose FrameMaker and WebWorks Publisher?

I've used other tools for producing help and printable manuals, such as Doc-To-Help (**www.componentone.com/products.aspx?ProductCode=1&ProductID=6**) and RoboHelp (**www.ehelp.com/products/robohelp**). However, both Doc-To-Help and RoboHelp are designed to be used with Word, which means that they are affected by the bugs in Word such as the lack of stability in numbering and bullets. For example, when I write a procedure with numbered steps, I like to know that the numbering will remain consistent. In FrameMaker, if I add in a step or delete one in the middle of a procedure, I know that the numbering will adjust itself and will continue to be correct. In Word, or software based on Word, this is frequently not the case. I've deleted a step from the middle of a procedure and had the next step suddenly restart the numbering from 1. Or, alternatively, I've had a procedure suddenly continue its numbering from the previous procedure, resulting in a procedure that starts with step 6.

In Doc-To-Help, you have to test for broken links when you have what you thought was a final version and if any need to be fixed, you pretty much have to retest all links again. Just because something worked correctly one time didn't necessarily mean that it would the next time. Given those circumstances, I think it is easy to see why I value consistency in results so highly.

How do you evaluate the usability of Web-based documentation?

The first two things I look for when I evaluate the usability of Web-based documentation are: Does it contain the information I need, and can I find it easily. This means that the contents must contain a logically arranged list of topics with informative titles, and the documentation must have a good index. It doesn't matter how thorough a procedure is or how well it is written if you can't find it.

12

DOCUMENTATION EVALUATION CRITERIA

All technical writers have personal preferences and writing styles. Although writers may disagree on specific style issues, the ultimate measure of user documentation is whether it effectively and efficiently communicates information the reader needs. For technical writers, *effectively* means that readers get the correct information they need to master a topic or to perform a task. *Efficiently* means that readers do not have to spend extra time searching for information or reading through irrelevant material to find what they need.

The following four general criteria can be used as a check list to evaluate written documents:

1. Content
    Is the information accurate?
    Is the coverage of the topic complete?

2. Organization
    Is the information easy to locate?
    Are transitions between topics identifiable?
    Can the user get in and out quickly with the right answer?

3. Format
    Does the layout help guide the reader?
    Is the format consistent?

4. Mechanics
    Are words spelled correctly?
    Is it grammatical?
    Is the writing style effective?

As you plan, write, review, and revise your writing, think about how it measures up to these criteria. The principles and practices you learned in this chapter apply to all the forms of documentation a user support specialist creates. Regardless of a document's intended use, the purpose remains the same: clear communication that addresses readers' needs by giving them concise information they can use.

CHAPTER SUMMARY

- User support staff are frequently assigned technical writing tasks to produce brochures, flyers, newsletters, handouts, training aids, user guides, computer manuals, online help files, e-mail and chat messages, Web pages, proposals, memos, operating procedure documentation, and troubleshooting guides.

- The goal of technical writing is to produce documents that effectively and efficiently communicate information needed by the reader.

❑ A technical writing task begins by defining the characteristics of the target audience, including their background and reading level. Each document should be planned with a clear understanding of what the writer wants the reader to do or be able to do after reading it.

❑ In technical documents, short words and sentences are preferable to long ones. Information should be organized so it is easy to locate. The purposes of a document and its intended audience should be clearly stated so each reader can decide at the beginning whether to read the piece.

❑ The process of technical writing includes organizing ideas and topics into an outline, expanding the outline, and then carefully editing to eliminate extra words, tighten prose, and check for format consistency and technical accuracy. A review by another person is a useful check to improve a document before the final revision.

❑ The layout of a document should help a reader understand the organization, know what is important, and be aware when transitions between topics occur. Formatting should be used consistently to enhance the information presented, not detract from it.

❑ Successful technical writers use strategies such as analogies, repetition, consistent word use, and parallel structure.

❑ Common problems to avoid in technical documents include clutter, hard-to-read type-faces, gender references, unclear referents, and passive voice. Other common problems are nominalization, wordiness, jargon, acronyms, and dangling words or phrases.

❑ Several software tools, including an outliner, spell checker, thesaurus, grammar checker, and desktop publishing features, are available to help technical writers produce well-organized, accurate, and professional-looking documentation.

❑ Writers use four criteria to evaluate a technical document by reviewing its content, organization, format, and mechanics.

12

KEY TERMS

acronym — A series of letters that represents a common phrase; for example, CPU is an acronym for central processing unit; define acronyms to ensure readers' understanding.

active voice — A sentence in which the subject performs the action indicated by the verb; for example, "Mary will present a tutorial on Excel macros on Monday"; compare to *passive voice*.

analogy — A writing strategy that describes how an unfamiliar concept is similar to a familiar concept; for example, the CPU in a computer system is analogous to an office calculator in a manual system.

brainstorm — A method used to generate a list of potential ideas or topics; the brain-stormed list is then prioritized and pared down, as needed.

dangling phrase — A few words (or a single word) at the beginning or end of a sentence that add little to the meaning of the sentence other than to make it longer; for example,

"Mohammed turned on the overhead projector, but the image did not appear, as everyone noticed" contains a dangling phrase.

documentation — Written communication intended to provide technical information to end users; can be printed or online; includes brochures, flyers, newsletters, handouts, training aids, user guides, handbooks, manuals, online help systems, proposals, letters, memos, e-mail and chat messages, procedural and operational documentation, Web pages, and troubleshooting guides.

format consistency check — An edit pass through a draft in which a writer checks to make sure that the heading and subheading fonts, indentation, centering, boldface, italics, underlining, and other format elements are used the same way throughout a document.

hierarchical organization — A document organization style that flows from top to bottom, whereby information is arranged from general to specific; online help systems are an example.

jargon — Words that are understood only by those experienced in a field; for example, "hacker" is jargon, whereas "unauthorized user" is more general; define jargon words to ensure that readers clearly understand them.

justified text — A document or paragraph format in which the text is aligned at both the right and left margins; commonly used in books and newspapers, but can be difficult to read.

nominalization — The process of creating a noun from a verb or adjective; for example, "To accomplish capitalization, use the Change Case command" could be rewritten to avoid nominalization as "To capitalize words, use the Change Case command."

parallel structure — A writing strategy that treats similar items consistently throughout a document; examples include consistent verb tenses and consistent phrasing in lists.

passive voice — A sentence in which the subject is not the actor, but receives the action of the verb; for example, "The documentation was prepared by me" is in passive voice, whereas "I prepared the documentation" is in active voice.

pointer — A reference or cross-reference in a document that indicates the location where a user can find more information; often used in technical writing to reduce the size of a document by including directions to appendices, attachments, exhibits, figures, tables, and other related materials.

reference format — A document organization style in which all the information on a specific topic is located in one place; compare to tutorial format.

referent — A word that refers to another word or concept; for example, in "Before you insert a CD, inspect it for scratches" the word "CD" is the referent of "it"; avoid pronouns such as *it*, *them*, and *their* when the referent is unclear.

sans serif typeface — A style of type that does not have fine lines (serifs) added to each character; often used in titles and headings; compare with *serif typeface*.

sequential organization — A document organization style that follows a step-by-step approach whereby information is arranged in order from first to last; procedural and operational documents are examples.

serif typeface — A style of type in which each character includes fine lines that project from the top and bottom of each letter (called serifs); serifs lead the reader's eye from letter to letter across the line, improving readability; compare with *sans serif typeface*.

specialty typeface — A style of type that is intended for special uses such as invitations, brochures, or flyers; draws attention to text, although it makes general text difficult to read; script typefaces are an example.

style sheet — A list of common terms, formats, and writing conventions that describes the spelling and usage preferences of a documentation department or organization so that writers use consistent terminology and formats.

technical accuracy check — An edit pass through a draft in which a writer performs any procedural or technical steps in a document to test them with the hardware or software; helps reduce errors in step-by-step instructions or other technical information.

tutorial format — A document organization style that guides a user step by step through the features of a program; compare to reference format.

CHECK YOUR UNDERSTANDING

1. True or False? The primary goal of technical writing is to entertain and hold the interest of the reader.

2. A(n) _____ is a short document primarily intended to summarize material covered in a training session and promote recall.

3. True or False? All users prefer online documentation to printed documentation because access to the information needed is easier.

4. Documentation that is organized as a step-by-step introduction to the features of a computer program is called a _____.

   a. reference manual

   b. technical manual

   c. tutorial manual

   d. troubleshooting manual

5. True or False? Effective user documents should result in a lower volume of user support calls and e-mails.

6. Which of the following forms of documentation often contains hyperlinks to related topics?

   a. online help systems

   b. newsletters

   c. e-mail messages

   d. troubleshooting guides

7. True or False? Good technical documents should provide readers with everything they would ever want to know about a topic.

8. A(n) _____ is an attempt to relate something readers may be familiar with to something they need to know about.

12

9. What is the correct sequence of the following steps in the technical writing process? (a) proofread the document (b) generate a list of ideas (c) arrange for an outside reviewer (d) write a first draft

   a. a – b – c – d

   b. b – d – c – a

   c. d – b – a – c

   d. b – a – d – c

10. True or False? An outside review of a technical document serves a similar purpose to a beta test of a software package.

11. True or False? Changes in case, font, indentation, and centering are format elements used to help the reader of a document understand its structure.

12. Which of the following words is least descriptive of the information on a Web page?

    a. complete

    b. concise

    c. includes pointers to other information

    d. well organized

13. True or False? A technical writer should use the same word to refer to an object or a concept throughout a document rather than a variety of different words that are synonyms.

14. A reading level that is appropriate for most technical documentation is _____.

    a. 5th grade

    b. 8th grade

    c. 12th grade

    d. college level

15. Whether to use the form "Plug-n-Play" or "Plug-and-Play" in a document would likely be specified in a(n) _____ .

16. True or False? The following example illustrates good parallel structure:

    1. Move the cursor to the button of your choice.

    2. Next, click the mouse on the button.

    3. You then click on "OK."

17. To avoid jargon, a technical writer could substitute the word or phrase _____ for "head crash" in the following sentence: "Users frequently lose their data when there is a head crash on the file server."

Discussion Questions

1. "Because e-mail and chat messages are less formal methods of communication, good technical writing skills are less important for these messages." Do you agree or disagree with this statement? Explain why.

2. In order to avoid using gender-related pronouns, some writers use a plural pronoun with a singular subject. For example, "A technical writer should choose their words carefully." Other alternatives are, "A technical writer should choose his or her words carefully" and "Technical writers should choose their words carefully." Which format do you prefer? Discuss these alternatives and other ways around this writing problem.

3. All professions use technical jargon terms and acronyms. Professionals, such as health care workers, accountants, and lawyers, are often difficult to understand. Why should the computer field be any different?

Hands-On Projects

Project 12-1

Revise existing documentation. The following sentences and paragraphs contain some of the problems you learned about in this chapter. Rewrite the examples to make them clear and readable, using what you have learned.

1. From a one-page notice, informing employees of which machines they can use in a training room:

> Employees should be well advised that they should use only the first row of machines, the HP PCs. All other machines are used only for classes for training new users. If an employee doesn't do this, he will be asked to leave the training room.

2. From an e-mail message sent to all employees of a legal firm advising them to be alert for a new virus:

> This virus has been known to cause the destruction of files, and it is very important that you perform a search of your hard drive to try and attempt eradication of it using the search feature. Search for .EDT file extensions and delete them. Then the problem will be solved.

12

3. From an instruction sheet you will hand out in a training session on a new e-mail package that the employees will begin using next month; this passage explains the capabilities of the package to users who have never used e-mail before:

> E-mail messages are stored on a central server, and you download it every time you open one, in effect. You can save it to a local disk if you want to keep it.

4. From a booklet that the user support department will distribute to employees of an insurance organization to explain the capabilities of a new software claims management package:

> This is a new type of CMS (claims management software) that every adjuster, regardless of his level, will benefit from, greatly. This claims management software can: (1) organize claims information, (2) be used while you are on the telephone, (3) do reports by claim type, and (4) for generation of summary claims information.

HANDS-ON PROJECTS

Project 12-2

Write and compare procedural documentation. Write an explanation of how to insert a 3.5" floppy or removable hard disk into a disk drive. Your explanation should be aimed at a person who has never used a computer before.

Exchange explanations with a classmate and critique each other's drafts. Did you include enough information for the user to insert the disk correctly? Did you include extra information that wasn't necessary to describe the disk insertion task?

If you can find a person who has not used a floppy or removable hard disk drive before, have that person use your explanation to see if he or she can perform the task using only your written documentation. Revise your instructions based on the peer and user feedback you receive.

HANDS-ON PROJECTS

Project 12-3

Revise a newsletter article. The following article was written for a technical newsletter intended for members of a professional computer organization. Rewrite the article, using what you have learned about technical writing in this chapter. You can correct any misinformation, format problems, and errors. Make the rewritten article an example of your best writing, ready for publication. Your instructor may be able to provide you with a copy of the article in machine-readable form.

Those darned ~*.tmp files

I always keep finding machines positively crammed with **~something.tmp files**. They take up way too much disk space and are annoying, positively. Many of these are caused by users turning off their machine before Windows if finished doing its thing during shutdown. There are many time also where disabling quick save in MS Word also left behind several of those files each day and any application or hardware caused crash is going to leave this stuff behind.

I always have to switch into the **c:\windows\tmp** subdirectory periodically and deleting all the **.tmp** files that aren't stamped with to-day's date. If you try to delete a temperary file that is in use, Windows will give you a warning and then abort. So always "de-select" the **~*.TMP** files that have the today's date. If they're no good, I'll get them at a later date. I do this by when **Explorer** comes back with it's list, press **Alt-E-A** to select the whole list, then go through and hold **Ctrl** and **left-click** those files with the current date. Then by pressing **Del** and **OK** you can get them out of here. Usually, you can make this an automated process if you choose by going to the **AUTOEXEC.BAT** file. Now, add the following to your **AUTOEXEC.BAT**:

IF EXIT C:\WINDOWS\TMP~*.TMP

DEL C:\WINDOWS\TMP~*.TMP > NUL

You can change the **C:** to the appropriate drive if necessary. The insert in the **AUTOEXEC.BAT** will delete all ~*.TMP files each time to boot the machine.

12

Project 12-4

Revise a training paragraph. The following document is an excerpt from a computer textbook. It contains examples of many of the common problems described in this chapter. The line numbers are for your convenience to identify and refer to problems.

First, go through the document and note the problems that you find with it. If you are working as part of a project group, compare your list of problems with others to see where group members agree and disagree. Second, rewrite the document to correct the problems you identified. Your rewrite should make the document as clear and as easy to understand as possible. Your instructor may be able to provide you with a copy of the document in machine-readable form.

1. MANAGING DIRECTORIES AND DISKS

2.

3. Introduction

4.

5. There are many types of storage media today. Floppy disk are the most

6. common. It is the best of all the possible ways to save data. A hard

7. or floppy diskette is divided into various directories so that files can be

8. saved to them. Definitely, this is the most efficient way to manage a large

9. number of files stored on a disk.

10.

11. Various commands, especially those dealing with disks and

12. directories, produce lots of computer numbers. To get a handle

13. on computer numbers, you need to get the big picture on bits, bytes,

14. megabytes, and gigabytes.

15. A computer may seem intelligent, but essntially it can "understand"

16. only whether power is on or not. To issue an instruction to a computer,

17. we need to go by 1 (on) or 0 (off). The two digits of 1 and 0 are the

18. foundation of binary (base 2) math. Binary math is based on bits, which

19. is a contraction of two words—binary digit. One bit can have the

20. value of either 1 or 0. Bits get a little large to move around, so

21. programmers combine 8 bits together to form a byte. Bytes can increase

22. in number: 1 byte can store a 1; 1 KB (kilobyte) is the same as 1024; 1 MB

23. (megabyte) is 1048576; and 1073742824 equals 1 GB. So, when you

24. hear that a diskette has a 360 KB capacity, it can store 360 x 1024 =

25. 374784 bytes.

26. Formatting of Disks

27.

28. When you create a file you need to store it on a floppy. Before that,

29. it must be properly prepared to receive information (formatted). If you

30. have used a disk and it has some space on it, you can not follow this section.

31. If you have a brand new disk out of the box, procedue with 36 formatting it

32. this way:

33. 1. Begin by inserting a disk in drive A. Make sure this disk is new, or

34. if it has been used, contains no file you are desirous of keeping. (Formatting

35. will destroy a disk's existing files, completely.)

36.

37. 2. Double-click the My Computer icon on the desktop.

38. 3. Click 3-1/2″ Floppy icon

39.

40. 3. On the File menu, click Format.

41. 4. Click 1.44.

42. 5. Indicate that you want a Full format

43. 6. Start the formatting process with the Start indicator. Wait for the

44. formatting to complete.

45.

46. While it was being formatted, the disk was divided into a number of

47. concentric rings or tracks. Each track was separated into a number of

48. sectors. Each sector stored 512 bytes. A higher capacity disk contains

49. more tracks and sectors; that is how they stored more data, for your

50. information.

Project 12-5

Experiment with format and font variations. Select a short description of a simple computer task, such as the procedure for inserting a floppy or removable hard disk in a drive from Project 12-2. The description should include at least two headings and some procedural steps. Format the document in three ways with different font and style variations. Show the three versions to three classmates or colleagues. Ask them to choose which one is easiest to read and then to explain their preferences. Write a short summary of their responses and draw conclusions about document formatting that you learned from the project.

Project 12-6

Evaluate and rewrite a document. Find a piece of computer documentation, a memo, or other technical writing that is in a computer-readable form. It should be at least one page and contain two or more paragraphs. The piece you choose can be a published piece you've found, a Web document, or something you've written previously. Apply the concepts and ideas you've learned in this chapter to critique the document; then revise it to correct any problems you discovered.

If the word processor you use has a readability index feature, check the reading level of your revised document. Then revise the document to lower its readability index by one grade level (for example, if your rewrite is at 10th grade level, modify the document until the readability index is at a 9th grade level).

12

Have a classmate or coworker review your work and make suggestions. Do you agree with his or her suggestions? Explain why or why not. Use the suggestions to revise your document.

Project 12-7

Evaluate online documentation. Find an example of online documentation, such as a Web site or help system. Analyze and critique it based on the information you learned in this chapter. Write a one-page summary of your findings, with recommendations on how you would improve the documentation. Include your analysis of how the document meets or doesn't meet the four evaluation criteria described in this chapter.

Project 12-8

Compose an e-mail response to a user. Write a response to this e-mail message from a user in your organization:

From: Erin@Accounting.SPI.com

To: UserSupport@IT.SPI.com

My computer has been running slower and slower recently. One of my coworkers in Accounting said I probably need to defragment my hard drive. I know nothing about that. How can I learn how to defragment a hard drive? How do I know if this will even help? What are the steps to defragment a drive?

Prepare a response to Erin. Make your response an example of a well-written e-mail message.

CASE PROJECTS

1. Internet Search Guide for Sergio Escobar

Sergio Escobar is the supervisor of a computer facility used by trainees in a job retraining program. The computer facility has 18 Macintosh systems, which are used by the trainees to improve their job skills and also as tools in their job search efforts. The Mac software includes a résumé preparation program that is very popular with the trainees. Sergio has recently connected the Macs to a network to provide Internet access. However, the trainees he serves do not have good Internet search skills and are frustrated that they cannot find employment information on the Internet.

Sergio posted a few URLs for various local and regional job banks, but he knows that information on the Internet changes daily. He also knows that if trainees knew how, they could use the Internet to research organizations in preparation for job interviews. As a support specialist, you are assigned to work with Sergio to prepare some basic documentation for the trainees on how to search for information on the Internet. Use the search engine you are most familiar with for this case project.

Write a short "Guide to Internet Searches" that Sergio can give to users of the facility he supervises. The document should include a description of how to use a search engine, instructions on how to enter a search and how to narrow a search, and helpful tips on Internet search strategies. It should include some examples that relate to job search strategies. The document should be self-contained and designed for use outside a classroom environment. As a resource, look at the online documentation published by one or more organizations that provide Internet search engines.

If you work in a group with other workers or students, post several examples of group members' documents and let each member nominate the Guide they think best meets the four criteria for good documents discussed in the chapter.

2. Orientation Guide for The Career School

As a user support specialist for a computer lab at The Career School, you have been assigned the task of developing a lab orientation guide aimed at new students or trainees who use the facility. Prepare a one-sheet (two pages printed back to back) summary of information for new users of the lab. You can use the policies of a lab environment you are familiar with, such as a lab at your school or workplace. First, describe who uses the lab. Orient your guide to those users.

Your orientation guide can include basic information about lab operating policies and procedures, network logon/logoff, how to access popular software packages, printing procedures, use of resource materials, and other general or technical information you think users will need. You may want to include short sections with information aimed at students in specific courses or training sessions.

As clues to topics you may want to include, think about what information a new student or trainee who walks into the lab would want to know. For inspiration, go to the lab and look at the postings on bulletin boards, whiteboards, walls, doors, machines, and tables. Rely on your own experience as a user or as a lab assistant. One of the goals of this writing project is to replace as much of the verbal instructions given by lab staff and printed matter around the lab as possible with an information sheet that could be distributed in the lab to new users.

3. Templates for Rocky Mountain Consultants

Erica Allan is the supervisor of documentation for Rocky Mountain Consultants, a firm that provides consulting services to engineering organizations. She recently received a request from several departments to design a memo form that each department can adopt and use as their standard memo format. Erica wants to accommodate each department, but is short of staff members that she can assign to the project. Also, Erica feels strongly that, rather than design a template for each department, it would be more useful to give each department the tools it needs to develop its own memo template.

Erica wants you to develop an instructional document aimed at word-processor users that describes the procedure to create a simple template. (Use whichever word processor you have access to for this project.) Although each department wants a different and distinctive memo format, Erica suggests you use a simple memo, like the one shown in Figure 12-8, as an example in your template write-up. Describe the fonts and format features to create a template that looks as much like the example as you can. Your document should include the steps a user takes to create and store a template for the memo in the figure. Prepare a document titled "How to Prepare a Simple Memo Template" that describes the process to users at Rocky Mountain Consultants.

Figure 12-8 Sample memo format

4. Cartridge Recycling at Re-Nu-Cartridge

For background information on Re-Nu-Cartridge, see Case Project 4 in previous chapters.

NOTE

Elma McDonald works in the Production department at Re-Nu-Cartridge. Her job is to clean inkjet and toner cartridges before they are refilled. With the equipment available at Re-Nu-Cartridge, Elma can clean several types of common cartridges. However, the company does not have the facilities to clean all types of cartridges, especially less common ones. Several of Re-Nu-Cartridge's environmentally responsible corporate customers have asked Elma for information on how to recycle cartridges that Re-Nu-Cartridge can't handle.

Elma asks you to use the Internet to research companies that recycle inkjet and toner cartridges. See if you can find more than one company that offers a cartridge recycling service. Then, based on your research, write a sheet of instructions on the procedure to recycle cartridges. Your documentation should be targeted at employees of Re-Nu-Cartridge's customers (but would probably be useful to anyone who uses printer cartridges). It should include how to package and ship used cartridges to recycle service centers, which cartridges the recyclers will take, where to send the cartridges, what the service costs (if anything), a description of the benefits of using a cartridge recycle service, and any other information an employee at another company would need to use the recycle services. Follow the guidelines for good technical writing discussed in this chapter to make the recycling instruction sheet an example of your best professional documentation.

12

CHAPTER

13

COMPUTER FACILITIES
MANAGEMENT

In this chapter you will learn:

♦ The major types of computer facilities

♦ Common facilities management problems

♦ Management tools and procedures for dealing with end-user facilities problems

Computer facilities range from a single, standalone system installed in a small office or home (sometimes called SOHO installations—small office, home office) to a network of thousands of PCs in a large organization. They also include a laptop computer in a traveling sales representative's hotel room and a mainframe computer in the IS department of a large corporation or government agency. Large organizations usually employ a professional Information Services staff to manage and operate their computer facilities. However, user support specialists, especially those in smaller organizations, are often assigned responsibilities for managing computer facilities comprised of desktop and notebook PCs, workstations, and servers. Even support specialists who are part of a support group in a large organization are often asked to consult with users about specific operational problems users encounter with their PCs and facilities.

Computer facilities management begins with the site preparation steps you learned about in Chapter 10, Installing End-User Computer Systems. This chapter continues the discussion of those topics and introduces strategies for dealing with common facilities management problems. The range of facilities management issues likely to confront support specialists includes problems with hardware, electrical power, software, and networks. Facilities management also addresses operational issues (such as media backups), security issues (such as access authorization), ergonomic issues (such as worker comfort and productivity), disaster preparation (such as the need for contingency plans), and user issues (such as error detection and recovery).

INTRODUCTION TO COMPUTER FACILITIES MANAGEMENT

A **computer facility** is the combination of the hardware, software, network, information, people, and operating procedures associated with the use of any computer system. It also comprises the environment that encompasses a computer facility, including office space, furniture, and electrical power. Some computer facilities are **centralized**—that is, they are located at one physical site. For example, in a mainframe computer center, the hardware, peripherals, software, data, operating staff, and related facilities are located in the same place. Anyone who needs to use a mainframe computer facility comes to the central site, either physically or electronically via a terminal (or perhaps a PC workstation). Other computer facilities are **decentralized**; the computer equipment and related software and facilities are located in the offices with the people who use them. A standalone PC, whether on an office desk or in a home or a school, is a common example of a decentralized system.

Today's computer facilities are perhaps best described as **distributed**, in which some parts of a computer system are centralized but other parts are decentralized. Networked systems are a good example of a distributed facility. A network server or host is a central facility to which users in offices or classrooms may connect with their local client PCs. The Internet is a distributed network of servers and communications equipment.

A computer facility makes different demands on the support organization, depending on whether the facility is centralized, decentralized, or distributed. In a centralized environment, facilities management problems and resources are concentrated, for the most part, in a limited geographic area where maximum control over equipment and access to it is possible. With a distributed user population, which is common in many organizations today, a user support group must find new ways to reach users, especially when they are in different locations in the organization, country, or world. In an organization where telecommuting is popular with employees, the support responsibilities often extend to a worker's home. External users who contact a support center via telephone, e-mail, or the Internet are an extreme example of decentralization.

This chapter focuses primarily on user support centers that provide support to internal users within an organization. The problems that support staff are likely to encounter often depend on whether a computer facility is centralized, decentralized, or distributed. But no matter how large or how small a computer installation is, some problems are common to almost every computer facility.

COMMON FACILITIES MANAGEMENT PROBLEMS

Support specialists and computer facilities managers must deal with many types of problems. Figure 13-1 lists some common facilities management problems. Some of these problems are more critical to system operation than others, and their solutions range from simple to difficult.

○ Hardware problems, maintenance, and repairs	○ Disasters and contingency planning
○ Electrical power failures and problems	○ Ergonomic, safety, and productivity problems
○ Software bugs and problems	
○ Network problems and performance	○ User errors
○ Security problems and challenges ○ electronic threats to security ○ physical threats to security	○ Computer crime and misuse ○ Recycling computers, peripherals, and supplies

Figure 13-1   Common facilities management problems

Depending on their work environment, support specialists often deal with each of these problems at some level.

Managing Hardware Problems, Maintenance, and Repairs

Most PCs today are fairly reliable. But as the number of PCs support specialists are responsible for increases, the likelihood that they will encounter at least occasional hardware malfunctions or failures also increases. Although preventive maintenance procedures described later in this chapter can extend the life expectancy of a computer system, electronic and especially electromechanical devices (those with moving parts, such as disk drives, tape drives, CD and DVD drives, and printers) do fail.

NOTE   Some hardware vendors rate the devices they manufacture by how long each is likely to operate before it begins to have problems. **Mean time between failure (MTBF)** is the expected number of hours an average device is likely to operate before it fails. The MTBF is statistical and is based on device tests; some devices fail faster, some last longer. For example, a tape cartridge drive may be rated at 50,000 hours MTBF. The number 50,000 (which is more than 5 years of continuous operation) is the device's operating expectancy before it may need repairs or replacement.

Organizations deal with hardware problems and repairs in a variety of ways. Three common strategies are:

1. Outsource hardware repairs to a service provider.

2. Perform simple repairs in-house and outsource major or difficult problems.

3. Maintain an in-house repair facility.

13

In each of these strategies, user support specialists may have direct responsibility for hardware problem diagnosis. An ability to distinguish between a hardware problem and a software problem that looks like a hardware problem is important.

In the first option, when a problem has been diagnosed as hardware, a user's PC is sent to a hardware service provider for repairs. As the first person to whom end users turn when they have a hardware problem, a support specialist needs to know enough about hardware to make simple repairs and tests. For example, many support specialists can check cables, install memory, clear printer paper jams, and perform related tasks. A support specialist must also be able to recognize the difference between a real hardware malfunction and a configuration problem with the operating system or a temporary network failure. Problems in other parts of a computer system can often masquerade as hardware problems.

When an organization outsources its hardware repairs, it may contract with the vendor who originally sold it the hardware or it may contract with a third-party organization that specializes in hardware repairs. Hardware repair companies include local computer stores with service departments, mail-order and Internet hardware service providers, and companies that supply nationwide hardware service.

 Guardian Computer Support is an example of an organization that offers hardware repair services on a contract basis. To learn more about Guardian's services and repair options, visit its Web site at **www.guardian-computer. com/home.html**. To find local organizations that provide similar services, look in the telephone book Yellow Pages under *Computers - Service & Repair*.

In the second option, support staff often perform simple tasks such as replacing a defective cable, replacing memory, or adding a disk drive. However, any hardware problem that exceeds their ability to diagnose or repair is sent out for repairs, as in option 1.

The third option, an in-house repair facility, is usually found only in larger organizations because of the financial resources required to maintain a technical staff and an inventory of spare PC and peripheral parts. This alternative is especially common among universities and other large organizations that have specialized staff devoted to computer hardware.

When an organization outsources its hardware service, it often negotiates and signs a service level agreement with the service organization. A **service level agreement (SLA)** is a written contract that defines the expectations between an organization and the service vendor to provide an agreed-upon level of hardware support. An SLA specifies such expectations as:

- **Response time for service.** How long after an organization calls for help does the service provider have to respond? An SLA often specifies response times that are as short as a few hours or as long as a few days.

- **Local parts availability.** Although hardware repair organizations often keep frequently used parts in stock, many service providers use overnight express shipments rather than stock expensive spare parts in their own inventory.

- **Preventive maintenance and diagnostic services.** Preventive maintenance, which includes steps to prevent future hardware problems, reduces the frequency of downtime due to hardware failures and is often provided under an SLA in addition to hardware repairs.

- **Where the service will be performed.** Repair services can occur on-site where the hardware is located, or at the service provider's facility. While on-site service is common for mainframe systems, PCs and small peripherals are often transported to a service depot.

- **Cost and penalties.** In addition to the cost of the SLA contract, service providers often pay penalties for failure to meet the terms of the service level agreement.

Hardware service providers generally cover both parts and labor under a service level agreement. Coverage is usually designed to begin after the warranty period has expired.

Alternately, an organization can rely on a local computer store or service company for repairs. Although local service companies may also negotiate a contract, such as a service level agreement, they may also provide service on a **time and materials**, best effort basis. In this situation, no predefined agreement specifies response time and parts availability. The service provider charges an hourly rate (which is higher for evenings and weekends), and they charge for parts. Local service companies that operate on a time and materials basis usually make no guarantee about when or whether they will be able to make the repairs. Furthermore, an organization with broken equipment usually must transport the hardware to the shop or pay extra for on-site repairs. Organizations that do not have a convenient local repair service option can consider an Internet based repair depot. Guardian Computer Support, mentioned in the previous WWW pointer, offers this option.

Some organizations that do not want to incur the cost of a service agreement, but want to be able to make quick, cost-effective hardware repairs, adopt a self-insurance strategy. They purchase one or more backup systems or components they can use in case a hardware device fails. A **redundant system** is an extra backup computer or peripheral that is identical to the hardware in daily use. It can be installed and pressed into service whenever a primary component fails. For example, when an organization needs 20 new computers in an office or training facility, it may purchase 21 systems. The extra computer is a backup that is stored until it is needed to replace a broken system. The broken system can then be discarded or sent out for repairs on a less expensive time and materials basis. A redundant system adds to an organization's up-front equipment cost. However, if included in a large purchase, one extra system represents a small fraction of the total cost and is relatively cheap insurance compared to the cost of a service agreement. The concept of an inexpensive backup replacement has become popular with the development of RAID disk technology for

13

network servers. A **redundant array of inexpensive disks (RAID)** provides large amounts of disk storage with a cluster of cheap hard drives. If one of the disks in a RAID system fails, it can be replaced with little or no server downtime. Combined with advanced operating system features, RAID technology permits a hard drive replacement to occur without interrupting normal operation. Computer facilities that place a premium on uninterrupted server operation think the added cost of RAID technology is worthwhile compared to the cost of service interruptions.

Managing Electrical Power Failures and Problems

An organization's location often determines the likelihood that a power failure will affect its computer equipment. In some geographic areas, power failures, including spikes and brownouts, are more prevalent than in other areas. **Downtime** is a measure of the number of hours (per week or month) that a computer system is unavailable for use because of power failures or other problems; **uptime** measures the number of operational hours. Obviously, uptime for a computer system in a hospital's critical care unit is more important than uptime in a school classroom. When preparing to protect a computer facility from power outages, a support specialist needs to determine the likelihood of power outages and their impact on the organization. Beyond simple surge suppression devices described in Chapter 10, which may be appropriate for home and small PC and network installations, many organizations reduce the risk of power failures by investing in power conditioning equipment or uninterruptible power supplies.

A **power conditioner** is an electrical device that inputs "dirty" power from an electric supplier and retransmits "clean" power to computer equipment. **Dirty power** is electricity that fluctuates beyond normal bounds in voltage, frequency, or other characteristics that can affect the operation of computer hardware. Power conditioners are capable of removing all but the largest power surges or spikes and can overcome some limited-duration brownouts. Their goal is to protect electronic components in the computer equipment from damage.

An **uninterruptible power supply (UPS)** is an electrical device that includes power conditioning circuits as well as a battery backup. The battery backup begins operating when the UPS senses that the electrical power supply is interrupted (or reduced during a brownout) and provides power to the computer equipment for a limited period of time. Because of the expense, a UPS is usually purchased to permit operation of a computer for only a few minutes or less than an hour. The battery capacity in a UPS is intended to provide time for the user to properly shut down the computer equipment so that applications software and operating systems can empty memory buffers, close files, and terminate operation, and hardware can power down normally. Without a UPS, power loss can cause hardware or software to terminate abnormally, which may cause equipment damage or unpredictable problems when the system is powered on later. The battery power in a UPS determines the amount of time a computer system can continue to operate and also the cost of the UPS unit.

To learn more about electrical power problems, conditioning equipment, and UPS devices, visit the NetworkClue.com Web site at **www.networkclue.com/ hardware/power/index.php**. The site includes pointers to resources for selecting devices to solve various power problems.

Managing Software Bugs and Problems

User support specialists are often the first to learn about software problems, because they staff the help desk that employees or customers call when problems are encountered. Some software problems are known bugs in an operating system or applications program. Other problems may occur in custom applications software developed in-house. In either case, the user support staff must establish procedures for dealing with software problems.

Many organizations capture information about software problems their users encounter when each problem is first reported to the support staff. The staff may maintain a simple problem log to which it makes an entry whenever a user calls with a problem. Alternately, the support staff can use a **software problem report (SPR)** system to capture problem report data associated with computer programs. An SPR system may be a manual paper-and-pencil procedure, a database on a network server, a help desk software package, or a database accessed through a Web site. In each case, an SPR system captures basic information such as the program in which the suspected bug occurred, a description of the bug, who discovered it, the urgency of the problem, and to whom the bug was referred for repair. An SPR system is also called a bug report system.

13

Commercial Logic, a developer of time management software, includes examples of a software problem report form for its products on its Web site at **www.cli-usa.com/powerpm/spr.htm**.

Support staff who work for software developers as customer service representatives spend much of their time dealing with software problems. Software support staff often maintain a database of known bugs, problems, and workarounds. These staff members need to keep careful track of which version of software a client is calling about, because at any point in time, several versions may be in widespread use, plus beta test and other versions may be in the product development pipeline. Managing multiple versions of a software package is a task that requires skills similar to those of a librarian, because information about each version must be cataloged, including its status (test, beta, production, or obsolete), release date, known bugs, maintenance programmer's name, location of modules, and documentation.

Not all apparent software problems are bugs, as you will learn in the section on user errors later in this chapter.

Managing Network Problems and Performance

Because computer networks are combinations of hardware and software, the tools you learned about to deal with hardware and software problems also apply to management of network facilities. However, a network may include tens, hundreds, or thousands of client devices that attach to several network servers and peripheral devices (such as printers), as well as additional layers of software that constitute the network operating system. In addition to potential problems that arise in an office network environment, many desktop PCs are also connected directly to the Internet. The configuration of hardware and software in a network environment, plus Internet accessibility, means that facilities management for networked systems is often a substantial challenge for support staff.

Due to their complexity, networks pose their own unique administrative, performance monitoring, media backup, security, and maintenance problems. Examples of network problems that support staff members are likely to encounter include:

- Hardware problems associated with the PCs on the network

- Hardware problems associated with peripheral devices (printers, scanners, media backup units) on the network

- Hardware problems related to network infrastructure, such as cabling, network interface cards (NICs), hubs, routers, and gateways

- Software problems with the network operating system, client software on networked PCs, and programmable network devices

- Administrative problems with user accounts, passwords, resource use privileges, and billing

- Problems related to network performance bottlenecks and downtime

- Security problems related to unauthorized access to programs and information

- Performance problems due to configuration incompatibilities, failures of network hardware or software, or attacks on network servers, such as virus software that bombards servers with unauthorized spam e-mail messages.

Fortunately, the combination of hardware and software resources in a network also provides additional tools to deal with the range of problems encountered in a network environment. These tools help maintain as well as troubleshoot networked systems.

Administrative Procedures. In a network environment, administrative procedures involve tasks associated with creating and maintaining user accounts, passwords, e-mail accounts, allocations of disk space, rights and privileges of resource access and use, and perhaps accounting and billing procedures (in an environment where users are charged for computer use). In large organizations, a dedicated network administrator may handle these tasks; in small organizations, the user support staff is often responsible for them.

Performance Monitors.   Hardware and software tools that show network administrators and support staff how effectively a network is operating are called **performance monitors**. Performance monitors collect information about key aspects of network operation, including:

- How many users are logged on
- How much access activity (often called hits) the server hard drive is taking from users
- Which applications users are running
- Percentage of downtime over a recent period
- Extent of CPU and memory use on the server
- The number of jobs waiting in the print queue
- Potential bottlenecks in network throughput

Performance monitors may collect and log performance data over time to give the support staff a statistical picture of how variables such as day of week and time of day affect network performance. Performance data collected over time can provide network facility managers with information on what to base capacity planning decisions, such as when to purchase a faster server, when to add memory or additional hard drive space, or when to add an additional or a faster printer. Some performance monitors also include e-mail or pager alarm features and troubleshooting capabilities that can alert network support staff to immediate and significant problems, such as a server that needs to be rebooted or a leg of the physical network that is no longer connected to the server.

To learn about the basics of network performance monitoring, read information prepared by the National Laboratory for Applied Network Research (NLANR) at its Web site, **dast.nlanr.net/Guides/GettingStarted/Performance.html**. To learn more about network performance monitoring tools built into Windows Server 2003 network environments, read an article in *Windows & .NET Magazine* at **www.winnetmag.com/WindowsServer2003/Index.cfm?ArticleID=37933**. Standford Linear Accelerator Center (SLAC) at Stanford University maintains a list of network performance monitoring utilities at **www.slac.stanford.edu/xorg/nmtf/nmtf-tools.html**.

Server and User Backups.   Media backups on a network system can significantly reduce facilities management costs and problems. For example, in many network environments an administrator can schedule automated backups of server software applications and user file space. And because network servers often operate 24 hours a day and 7 days a week, media backups can be scheduled at times when the load on a system is at its lightest, such as at night or on weekends. The storage media on a server that is accessible on an office network also

13

provides a convenient space and method for users to back up any personal data files stored on their local hard drives. For example, a backup software utility on a user's system can access the server hard drive as a backup medium instead of using a local tape or removable disk drive.

 Because media backups are a critical component of facilities management, a later section in this chapter describes media backup procedures in greater detail.

Security.   Access security in a network environment is usually a more significant concern than on a standalone PC. Users (both authorized and unauthorized) can potentially access data and resources anywhere on the network, and perhaps from outside the network. However, many network operating systems provide additional security features that are more sophisticated and reliable than those available on a standalone PC. A network administrator plays a key role in the control of access to network facilities, because the administrator controls the user account management process. Security problems are discussed in greater detail in the next section.

Software Maintenance Problems.   Software maintenance is another significant management concern in a network environment. Software maintenance on a network, such as distribution of a new version of a program, is a task in which the network not only poses management problems, such as how software on hundreds or thousands of machines gets upgraded, but also provides tools to solve the problem. For example, applications software can be run on many networked workstations from a single image on a server. An upgrade to the image on the server simultaneously upgrades every user's software. Or, automated installation procedures can download software from a network server to multiple client PCs. Network tools can make software administration tasks easier than the tasks would be for a comparable number of standalone systems.

Although computer networks pose unique and challenging problems for facilities and network managers and administrators, their administrative, monitoring, backup, security, and maintenance tools automate many of the tasks, which increases the productivity of support staff responsible for network operation.

Managing Security Problems

Much of the recent increase in the workload of network and technical support staff can be traced to security concerns in local office networks, enterprise-wide networks, computer facilities of all sizes, and the Internet. Security problems can be classified based on the origin of the threat (internal or external) and on the kind of threat (electronic or physical):

- **Internal threats** arise from inside an organization, including workers and end users.

- **External threats** arise from outside an organization, including clients, hackers, and the public.

- **Electronic threats** arise from attempts to breach the information or resources in a computer system.
- **Physical threats** arise from attempts to damage or disrupt computer facilities.

The first part of this section describes electronic threats, followed by a discussion of some common physical threats. Internal threats are addressed in the section on crime and misuse below.

Electronic Threats to Security

The list of potential security problems that affect computer facilities from external sources via electronic or remote access is long and grows every year, but the most common sources of problems include:

- Proliferation of virus software, including worm viruses that overload networks and deny service to legitimate traffic
- Spam e-mail attacks on network servers and end-user computers
- Attempts by unauthorized users to gain access to or control over computers and information
- Operating system software vulnerabilities that permit unauthorized access due to bugs in distributed software
- Proliferation of software that spies on the habits and behavior of end users or targets users for pop-up advertisements
- Lack of secure data transmission using encryption features

To deal with threats from electronic access, passwords, antivirus software, Internet firewalls, utility software, callback modems, and other online security measures are common precautions in installations of every size. These measures are popular with facilities managers who recognize that computer facility intrusions can be electronic, as well as physical, and can originate from both external and internal sources.

Passwords and PINs are an important but limited tool to address electronic access problems. Many organizations implement password security with policies and procedures that encourage users to use password features in operating systems, networks, and Web sites; to select passwords that cannot be easily guessed (either by an intelligent hacker or by a brute-force guessing program); to change passwords periodically; to keep passwords secret; and to use different passwords in each situation.

Computer viruses get transmitted by external media (floppy disks, removable hard disks, CDs, and USB smart drives), e-mail (primarily through attachments), Web-based e-mail, instant messaging or chat facilities (these features may bypass security scanners), software downloads from untrustworthy sources (including macros in applications such as word processors and spreadsheets), and through operating system vulnerabilities. Some recent viruses generate millions of what appear to be legitimate e-mail messages that can overload an organization's e-mail servers. Even with spam filtering software in operation on a server, the sheer volume of messages that need to be filtered can overwhelm the resources of an e-mail server, which creates a backlog of e-mail messages and results in denial of service to legitimate traffic. Antivirus software utilities, described later in this chapter, are part of the solution to virus attacks, but only part. Security specialists often recommend additional steps, such as those described in Figure 13-2.

- Use antivirus software on servers and desktop systems

- Keep antivirus definitions up to date through a subscription service and daily online updates

- Use message rules in e-mail software to trap and control messages from unknown senders or with suspect content

- Use an antispam utility program on servers and desktop systems to filter unauthorized messages

- Disable the ability to send and receive e-mail attachments for users who do not need the feature

- Use firewall utility software and monitor patterns of uninvited access attempts

- Use firewall software to implement instant messaging (chat) only inside an organization

- Configure firewall software to hide communication ports

- Use data encryption features and secure servers when possible

- Keep operating systems up to date with patches designed to fix software vulnerabilities

- Use an adware/spyware filter to search for unauthorized programs that snoop and report on user habits and behavior

- Implement an effective organization-wide password administration program

- Delegate the management of specific security strategies and programs to support staff responsible for them

- Include security policies and strategies as part of new worker orientation

- Train end users and support staff on methods to handle security threats

Figure 13-2   Strategies to manage security threats via electronic access

Unauthorized users frequently attempt to gain access to a computer attached to the Internet through **operating system vulnerabilities**, which are unintended paths or gateways into a system due to unpatched software bugs. To reduce security problems due to operating system vulnerabilities, users should periodically search vendor Web sites for updates, patches, and other suggested operating procedures designed to manage these threats.

A **firewall** is either a hardware device or a software utility designed to intercept and prevent unauthorized attempts to access a computer system that is connected to the Internet. Although firewalls have been popular for several years in corporate computer facilities, they are now a necessary security protection for home and office computers connected to the Internet via a digital subscriber line (DSL) or cable modem because all broadband connections are vulnerable to access violations.

Because a PC with a fast (broadband) connection to an ISP can access the Internet whenever it is powered on, the reverse is also true: Internet hackers can intrude and make unauthorized access to network information that is stored on a PC connected via DSL or cable modem. An example software firewall utility that responds to this problem is Zone Alarm, available from Zone Labs. Zone Alarm is free for personal or nonprofit use, available at **www.zonelabs.com**. Another firewall that is free for personal use is Sygate Personal Firewall, available at **smb.sygate.com/products/spf_standard.htm**. Some users report incompatibilities between firewall software and other utilities, such as antivirus programs. Readers should not download and install firewall utilities on a system unless they have permission to do so.

Most modems on a host system receive a call from a user's modem and connect the user directly to the host computer; however, a callback modem does not. Instead, a **callback modem** returns the user's call to a predefined, secure telephone number for that user. Callback modems prevent unauthorized users from dialing a computer, because the unauthorized user phone number is not in the callback modem's list of valid phone numbers.

Microsoft maintains a Web site devoted to security problems and information about tools to enhance the security of its software products; visit the site at **www.microsoft.com/security**. Microsoft offers a software tool, Microsoft Baseline Security Analyzer (MBSA), to analyze a Windows system for security vulnerabilities; MBSA can be downloaded from **www.microsoft.com/technet/treeview/default.asp?url=/technet/security/tools/tools/mbsahome.asp**. Qualys, a network security vendor, offers an analysis of the Internet Explorer browser by running a series of seven tests for vulnerabilities that hackers often exploit; test your browser settings at **browsercheck.qualys.com**. Symantec also offers a free virus checker at its site, **security.norton.com/default.asp?langid=us&venid=sym**.

13

WILLIAM DOUGHERTY
E-COMMUNICATIONS & CLIENT TOOLS/WINDOWS ADMINISTRATIVE
SERVICES TEAM
SYSTEMS ENGINEERING AND ADMINISTRATION DEPARTMENT
VIRGINIA TECH
BLACKSBURG, VIRGINIA

In this CloseUp, William Dougherty, a senior computer systems engineer, discusses how a large university, Virginia Tech, manages the problems of viruses and e-mail spam messages on a campus system that serves over 80,000 users, including students, faculty, staff, and alumni.

Most of the e-mail users at Virginia Tech are supported on a Sun Microsystems Internet Mail Server. Because e-mail has become a primary means of communication on campus, the rapid increase in the number of computer viruses in the past couple of years has caused service quality concerns for both users and the support staff at Virginia Tech. Dougherty says, "By the Spring semester of 2001, we were collecting 50,000 viruses a day on our system. Our help desk was receiving 10 to 20 calls per day about virus-related problems. We estimated that it was costing between $120 and $150 per call to resolve these problems." Dougherty adds, "Students, who were paying a technology fee, expected more service, and staff were losing productivity. They weren't able to do their jobs. It started to become an issue."

Dougherty says he considered several options to reduce the virus problem, including running an antivirus utility on the Sun e-mail server. However, running antivirus software on the server would overburden the already heavy load on the Sun system, and modifying Sun's proprietary software to run antivirus software would require staff resources to solve compatibility problems. An alternative that appeared to offer a more cost-effective solution was to place a computer that could filter viruses in front of the Sun e-mail server. If the front-end computer could successfully filter viruses, fewer messages with viruses would get through to the Sun server.

After investigating several products, Dougherty and the technical staff at Virginia Tech decided on a solution from Mirapoint (**www.mirapoint.com**). Noting that the Mirapoint Message Director product is essentially a customizable message handling appliance, Dougherty says, "We could put the Mirapoint product out in front of the mail server, so we didn't need to worry about the load on the Sun server or software compatibility. By implementing the Mirapoint solution, the 50,000 virus messages have decreased to about 1500 a day, a reduction of 97%. Our help desk is spending less than 30 minutes a day on virus calls. However, we still provide desktop antivirus software and encourage our users to load it, because many of our users go to other environments during semester breaks and can bring back viruses on their laptops when they return to campus."

Because the Mirapoint approach had been successful to manage viruses, Dougherty decided to use the customization features of Message Director to attack the spam e-mail problem. "We were getting pounded by spam. It was a problem we had to do something about." Dougherty explains the spam filter: "Whenever someone comes into the network with more than 100 simultaneous SMTP connections from the same address, the system logs it. Staff review the logs, delete any messages still in the queues, and then add the IP address to a blacklist. Because it's blocked before it gets to the mail server, it lightens the load on the Sun system. We have over 1700 spam sites that we currently block."

Dougherty concludes: "Our new system has saved us hundreds of people-hours on the help desk, while allowing e-mail to flow at its normal rate, and, in the long run, saving us money."

Physical Threats to Security

Physical access tools are designed to reduce threats from both unauthorized access and sabotage. Large computer facilities may attract people who like the challenge of breaking into such facilities to commit theft. They are also targets of employees or the public who are disgruntled with technology or with the way they have been treated by a bureaucracy (of which, computer systems are a symbol). The goal of these people is to disrupt an organization's activities by stealing or damaging equipment, information, or facilities. To address physical threats, computer facilities that have a large investment in equipment in a central location take steps to limit physical access to their facilities. Access management tools that large and small facilities may use to prevent information and equipment loss include:

- Keypad entry locks
- Identification badges and ID cards that function like entry keys
- Biometric readers that can identify voice, fingerprint, or vascular IDs
- Motion sensors and heat detection devices
- Camera systems to monitor facilities
- Reception desks
- Metal detectors
- Physical barriers (walls and windows)

In very small facilities, locked doors are the primary means to control physical access.

The field of biometric access controls is fairly new. To learn more about the basics of this technology, read an introduction by Bryan Feltin, "Information Assurance Using Biometrics," available as a Word document at **www.giac. org/practical/Bryan_Feltin_GSEC.doc**.

Vulnerable sites should also develop documented procedures to handle telephoned bomb threats and other acts of sabotage. Telephone operators, help desk attendants, computer operators, and receptionists should be trained in emergency procedures.

Support staff who have major responsibilities for security are the target audience of two print publications that address security concerns. *SC Magazine* is available for subscription at **www.scmagazine.com**. CSO, a resource for security executives, is available for subscription at **www.csoonline.com**. Both publications are available free to qualified professionals with responsibilities for security.

While many kinds of threats to computer facility security are intentional, another source of threats are from natural disasters, as is discussed in the next section.

Managing Disasters and Contingency Planning

Support specialists can do little to prevent events such as power failures, floods, fires, storms, earthquakes, terrorist attacks, and sabotage from affecting computer services. But they can prepare to manage unpredictable events by using risk management strategies. **Risk management** is the use of several tools to reduce the threat to an organization from uncontrollable disasters and to help the organization to recover from disasters that occur with minimal financial impact or customer service loss. Terrorist attacks in the United States on September 11, 2001 and the electrical power grid failure in the northeast United States and Canada on August 14, 2003 are recent events that dramatically underline the need for disaster planning.

Figure 13-3 lists examples of common disaster management tools. Support specialists at almost all computer facilities need to evaluate and use these tools to protect their organization's investment in technology.

Business interruption insurance	Media backups
Engineering inspections	Disaster/contingency plans
Hot and cold site agreements	

Figure 13-3   Common disaster management tools

Insurance. An organization can purchase **business interruption insurance** to provide additional financial resources at the time an unforeseen event occurs. In case of a disaster, the insurance proceeds offset the cost to return the organization to an operational state and protect the organization from financial ruin.

NOTE Although business interruption insurance is usually not appropriate for a personal or SOHO computer system, owners should verify that their homeowner's or renter's insurance package covers the full value of their home computer equipment. Some homeowner's or renter's insurance limits computer coverage and will not pay the full replacement cost of an expensive system unless the owner has a rider to cover the full value.

Inspections. Organizations can obtain an **engineering inspection** to help identify the potential for damage to computer equipment and facilities due to natural disasters. An engineering inspection report may recommend that an organization modify building structures to reduce the impact of a disaster on computer equipment. An inspector might also recommend detection devices, such as fire alarms and moisture sensors, to warn of a disaster.

Site Agreements. Hot and cold site agreements are strategies that create redundancy to serve as emergency backups to an existing computer system. They are used primarily for mainframes and large network hosts. Site agreements provide a way to get an organization's computer system operational quickly after a disaster.

- A **cold site** is a building and space where a replacement computer system could be installed quickly after a disaster. Located geographically some distance away from the central site, a cold site includes floor space, electrical power, air conditioning, and network connections. Because it usually sits idle, a cold site can be made available quickly to house a replacement system. In conjunction with a cold site agreement, an organization may contract with a hardware vendor to quick-ship new, replacement hardware to the cold site upon receiving an emergency call that an organization's system has been damaged.

- A **hot site** offers all the features of a cold site, plus operational equipment similar to the system it is designed to back up. In case a disaster occurs that makes a computer system unusable, recent versions of the user's software and data files are restored from off-site backup media onto an operational system at the hot site.

Instead of purchasing a hot or cold site agreement from a vendor, organizations may sign mutual assistance agreements to provide hot and cold site facilities to other organizations. For example, a group of school districts or universities may enter into a reciprocal hot or cold site agreement to support each other in case of a disaster. In any case, facilities at backup sites should be tested periodically to ensure that they meet an organization's needs.

Media Backups. Copies of important programs and data written on separate media are called **media backups**, and are a critical component of any disaster contingency plan. They are absolutely essential to get a computer system operational after a disaster. Unfortunately,

13

many users do not back up their systems regularly. A computer system's media can be backed up onto several kinds of alternate media, including cartridge tapes, writeable CDs and DVDs, and removable hard disk drives. The discussion of operational backup procedures later in this chapter describes a plan for media backups.

Disaster/Contingency Plans.   A disaster/contingency plan is a useful planning tool for both large and small computer installations. A **disaster/contingency plan** is a document that describes various activities that will occur if a computer facility experiences a temporary disruption of service; disaster plans often address such events as fires, earthquakes, power outages, water damage, and sabotage. An effective plan should answer the question, "What specific steps will our organization take in case a disaster occurs?" A disaster/contingency plan should include these kinds of information:

- A complete, up-to-date directory of all employees, including titles, home addresses, and phone numbers

- A current list of all employees who need to be notified in case of a disaster, including addresses and phone numbers

- A calling tree that specifies which employees should call other workers to ensure the fastest possible response time in the event of a disaster

- The location of all backup media for software and data stored off-site and whom to contact for access

- A recent copy of all operational procedures and other site-specific documentation

- A current inventory of all equipment, software, and licenses

- A list of any insurance policies, hot or cold site agreements, or reciprocal agreements for emergency services

- A floor plan of the facility

- Instructions for staff evacuation in case of an emergency

 Computing and Network Services at the University of Toronto has developed an outline for those who want to prepare a disaster recovery plan. Their eight-step action plan, guidelines, and check lists emphasize the importance of business continuity. See the guidelines at **www.utoronto.ca/security/drp.htm**. An example of a disaster/contingency plan prepared at the University of Arkansas is available at **www.uark.edu/staff/drp**.

A disaster/contingency plan is effective only if workers are aware of its existence and trained in its procedures. Therefore, support specialists responsible for disaster planning should find the most effective way to communicate these plans to workers to ensure that recovery procedures can and will be carried out. Most organizations with disaster plans include a periodic training component as part of the plan's implementation.

Managing Ergonomic, Safety, and Productivity Problems

Chapter 10 discussed ergonomic problems support staff may encounter during system installation. In reality, ergonomic problems are ongoing; they occur during computer use on a daily basis. An environment that is ergonomically correct for one employee may cause problems for a coworker. Or, characteristics of an employee's job or personal health may change over time, which raises new ergonomic challenges. Each ergonomic solution must be user-specific.

Although Chapter 10 addressed a number of health, safety, and productivity issues, strategies to address ongoing ergonomic concerns include training end users about potential workstation problems, periodic questionnaires for end users to report problems they encounter, links on an organization's Web portal to ergonomic information and a form to report problems or request assistance, and site visits by support specialists to help identify and correct problem areas.

The University of Minnesota has prepared a check list of ergonomic factors for users of PC workstations, which is available at **www.dehs.umn.edu/ergo/ office/checklist.html**. You can find other examples of ergonomic check lists by typing **ergonomic check list** into any Internet search engine.

Managing User Errors

13

Errors users make are also a facilities management concern. Categories of user errors include:

- data entry errors
- lapses in data security
- failure to follow operational procedures
- use of unlicensed software
- use of poor quality software
- misuse of powerful applications software

All users make some data entry errors or typos. Examples of lapses in security include leaving media on a desk where others can remove or copy them, or leaving a password on a Post-It attached to a display screen. Failures to follow operational procedures may include not routinely making backup copies of important files. Unlicensed software use can cause a legal problem for an organization. Furthermore, downloaded or borrowed software is a source of computer viruses that may infect not only the immediate user's computer, but potentially every node on a network. And downloaded shareware may not have been subjected to thorough quality tests and can cause system problems or crashes.

Another category of problems that users introduce involves the misuse of powerful software tools such as spreadsheets, database systems, decision support systems, and presentation software. Although each of these is a powerful tool when used correctly, each is just as powerful when used incorrectly. For example, a user may construct a spreadsheet to forecast product sales for the next several business quarters. If the user enters an incorrect formula during the design of the forecasting worksheet, the mistake may produce results that appear plausible, but are computed incorrectly. As the use of the forecasting worksheet continues, the errors may compound over time, resulting in poor management decisions about manufacturing targets and inventory levels.

Although there may appear to be significant differences between users who fail to make media backups, those who fail to check downloaded software for viruses, and those who make a mistake in a spreadsheet formula, each of these examples of user errors can have similar results: lost data, decreased productivity, and possible security and legal problems for an organization. An important computer facilities management task is to anticipate, plan for, monitor, and identify potential problems due to user errors. Unfortunately, no one, simple solution will address all of the errors users can make. However, computer facilities managers and support staff can use several strategies to reduce user errors, including end-user training, software developer feedback, automated procedures, and system audits.

End-User Training.   Training for end users, which you learned about in Chapter 11, is one tool intended to reduce errors. Support staff should be on the lookout for patterns of mistakes users make, such as a data entry error that occurs repeatedly in the same situation. Patterns of problems are useful input for trainers who plan and develop corporate training programs.

Software Developer Feedback.   Feedback to software developers often originates with support staff who observe patterns of problems users encounter. Software designers and programmers attempt to make the software they develop as robust as possible so it can identify and handle many kinds of user errors as they occur. For example, software developers can often implement programmed checks to verify that numeric values entered are within an appropriate range. They can also use tools such as batch totals and check digits to reduce the likelihood of invalid input or missing transactions. However, software developers rely on feedback from support staff about the kinds of problems users encounter in order to make their programs more error proof.

Automated Procedures.   Automated procedures are another way to address end-user errors. The fewer manual steps an end user must perform during a task, the less likely an error will occur. For example, automated media backups, virus scans, and disk defragmentation procedures are often preferable to relying on users to remember to run these programs. At a minimum, support staff can send users reminders via e-mail or broadcast "messages of the day" to jog their memories to run important utility software or perform other routine operational tasks.

System Audits.   Audits are useful tools for support staff to identify common computer problems. A **system audit** is an investigation by an independent consultant or group to verify that proper operating procedures are followed among users and to identify potential end-user problem areas. For example, auditors may use special utility software to identify and list the applications packages that are installed on a system. The purpose of audit software is to help an auditor verify that software licenses or site licenses are in place and to document that each user is authorized to use the software installed on his or her system. Audits may also verify that proper operational procedures, such as media backups, virus checks, and preventive maintenance steps, are performed on a regular basis.

 Talley Systems, in cooperation with a software developer association, BSA, offers trial versions of its software audit tools at **www.tallysystems.com/forms/ bsaoffer/signup.html**. These tools prepare a report of the software installed on standalone or networked PCs.

Some applications software packages include features to detect user errors. For example, spreadsheets can often audit a worksheet to detect common problems in the use of formulas or built-in procedures, such as references to blank cells or circular references. Support staff who work with spreadsheet users should also learn about features such as the ability to validate user input data to make sure it falls within expected ranges (e.g., if the number of calls a support specialist handles in a day is normally fewer than 20, a spreadsheet can be programmed to alert the user if an attempt is made to enter a number greater than 20).

13

Managing Computer Crime and Misuse

Recall from Chapter 1 that computer crime is the use of a computer system to commit an illegal act or the theft of computer equipment or services. Computer crime can be traced to both internal and external sources. Support specialists can use several control strategies to reduce computer crime, including access, physical, inventory, and information controls. Many organizations have implemented some or all of these strategies to contain this growing problem.

Access Controls.   Access controls are important tools in the arsenal of support specialists who are confronted with the potential for computer crime. **Access controls** are procedures and tools to limit electronic or remote entry into a computer system or network of computers. Access controls include various user identification and authentication procedures, password entry to access system resources, and the granting of rights and privileges to various categories of users. They also include the use of callback modems and Internet firewalls to control access to organizational resources and information, and to protect them from external threats. An important aspect of access controls is company policies that specify which workers are authorized to access specific information and policies that address confidentiality of information.

Physical Controls.   **Physical controls** are tools used in computer facilities to limit physical access to facilities, equipment, and information; these include locks, identification badges, key card systems, and alarms. Physical controls also include cable tie-down systems designed to secure computer equipment (system unit, monitor, and printer) to an office desk. Cable tie-down systems are especially useful in computer training facilities, libraries, and offices where a large inventory of computer equipment is located in a central, easily accessible area. Because a sizeable investment in equipment is accessible in a concentrated area, these facilities are often the targets of computer thieves.

To learn more about physical access controls and security solutions, visit the Web site of the Information System Security Professionals at **www.infosyssec. org/infosyssec/physfac1.htm**.

Inventory Controls.   **Inventory controls** are part of an organization's asset management system and provide facilities managers with tools and procedures to maintain records on the location, configuration, and value of computer equipment. Only equipment and software that is greater than a predefined minimum dollar amount is usually inventoried. A minimum inventory value of $200, for example, means that support staff do not need to keep physical inventory of mice, removable disks, and consumable supplies (or any items that cost less than $200). But the support staff responsible for inventory management may attach an inventory control label to more expensive equipment and enter the inventory number and equipment configuration in an asset database. Asset management procedures often require an actual visual identification of all items in the equipment inventory once a year. Based on the annual inventory, support staff can trace missing items and estimate the amount of loss or theft.

Some help desk software packages, such as those described in Chapter 6, include asset management databases that make inventory control of computer equipment a more manageable task than a manual system.

Information Controls.   **Information controls** include procedures to account for and limit access to valuable or confidential information. Access controls often function as information controls. Information controls can define which workers are authorized to access backup media or to which workers sensitive printed reports are distributed, and how reports should be retained or destroyed.

In addition to these controls, many organizations formulate policies for their employees and customers on the use and misuse of organizational computer facilities. As you learned in Chapter 8, these policies often define what is acceptable and unacceptable computer use, and explain the consequences of unacceptable use. For example, an organization may have a policy that prohibits or limits personal use of computers during working hours. Or a policy may state that limited personal use of organizational e-mail is acceptable, but that Internet access can occur only outside of regular working hours. Support specialists can help organizations formulate policies to limit computer crime and misuse and other facilities management problems.

The National Institute of Standards and Technology has prepared several brochures that discuss various aspects of computer facilities management problems. View a list of available brochures at **csrc.nist.gov/publications/nistpubs**. Several of these brochures expand on the computer facilities management challenges discussed in this chapter. Those in PDF format require Adobe Reader to view.

Managing the Recycling of Computers, Peripherals, and Supplies

Any organization with a substantial turnover in computer equipment faces the challenge of how to dispose of used systems and peripherals. Most organizations practice a hand-me-down strategy, in which users who receive new computers and peripherals pass their older systems to other users; one user's obsolete computer may be another user's upgrade. In other situations, obsolete computers and peripherals may be donated to schools, religious groups, charities, or other nonprofit organizations where they can be put to good use because they are not obsolete to their recipients. Before a computer system is handed down or donated, the hard disk drive should be removed and destroyed, or should be erased with a special utility program, to protect the confidentiality of personal or corporate data.

The National Recycling Coalition provides a searchable database of electronics recyclers and agencies that reuse computer equipment at **www.nrc-recycle.org/resources/electronics/search/getlisting.php**. Don't assume that deleting all files and folders into the Recycle Bin and emptying it is sufficient to delete the information on a hard drive—it isn't. One commercial utility program designed to effectively remove all information on a hard disk drive is Wipe Drive, available at **www.whitecanyon.com/index.php**. A free utility for this purpose is Darik's Boot and Nuke program, available at **dban.sourceforge.net**.

13

Direct disposal of used computer equipment into a garbage landfill should be avoided, and is illegal in many areas. Some recycling organizations take processing units, monitors, and printers for the salvage value of the raw materials, such as metals, although many charge a nominal fee to dispose of electronic equipment.

Some computer manufacturers, such as Dell, offer recycling programs. Learn about Dell's program by going to **www1.us.dell.com/content/topics/segtopic.aspx/dell_recycling?c=us&cs=19&l=en&s=dhs**.

In addition to computers and peripherals, some types of supplies are recyclable. Printer paper is an obvious example. Ink-jet and laser printer cartridges can be mailed to a recycler to be remanufactured and refilled. Postage-paid mailing envelopes for empty cartridges are available in many large office and computer supply stores.

FACILITIES MANAGEMENT TOOLS AND PROCEDURES

Computer facilities management tasks and responsibilities span a wide range of issues that concern support staff. The last part of this chapter describes specific tools and procedures designed to help support staffs perform their facilities management responsibilities. Figure 13-4 lists some of these tools and procedures.

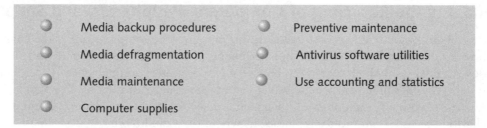

Media backup procedures	Preventive maintenance
Media defragmentation	Antivirus software utilities
Media maintenance	Use accounting and statistics
Computer supplies	

Figure 13-4   Facilities management tools and procedures

Computer facilities of any size, from a standalone PC in a home office to a large network installation, need to address these issues at some level.

Media Backup Procedures

One of the most difficult tasks for support specialists is to convince end users that media backups are important. Sometimes only after a user has lost a significant amount of important data or valuable time do they learn the lesson and make regular backups. Automated backups that run at a scheduled time can reduce the impact of power outages, hard drive crashes, accidental deletions, and other problems that put information at risk. Scheduled backups are a way to work around users who are reluctant to or forget to make their own backups.

NOTE   In addition to procedures that back up media on a server or on a workstation, support specialists should also encourage users to make effective use of automatic backup procedures in popular applications software packages. Many word processor and spreadsheet programs, for example, can be configured so that the current document or worksheet in memory is saved on the hard drive periodically (every 10 or 15 minutes). Use of this feature is a precaution against systems that freeze up, system crashes, power failures, accidental deletions of material, and related problems.

Utility software that writes media backups is usually packaged with backup hardware. Commercial and shareware packages that provide useful backup features are also available. Backup software copies files, usually from a computer's hard disk drive, onto the designated backup media. Some backup utilities write files on the backup media in the same format as they were stored on the original media. Other backup programs may compress the files so they take up less space on the backup media. These files must then be decompressed when they are restored from the backup media.

 An example of a media backup utility program is FileBack PC, available for evaluation at **www.maxoutput.com/FileBack**. Another example is WinBackup; a trial version is available at **www.liutilities.com/products/winbackup**.

An important decision for a user or support person is how much to back up. The more files that are copied to the backup media, the longer the backup takes and the greater the amount of space required. Some user reluctance to run backups may be related to the amount of time the task takes. However, most backup utility software permits a user or support specialist to select a specific drive to back up and to select directory paths or folders to back up. This feature gives a user or support specialist control over the amount of information to back up, and therefore how long the process takes. And with a task scheduler, a backup can be run at a time convenient to the user, including after work hours.

Many users do not take the time to back up operating system and program directories on a regular basis. Operating system and applications software files change less frequently than user data files, if at all, and a user should already have backups of software in the form of the original distribution media (floppy disks or CDs, or via Internet download). Some users make backups of their operating system and applications programs only when new hardware is installed or when a new application is installed on a system. Others rely on reinstalling an operating system and applications software from the original distribution media in case a recovery is needed.

If a user's goal is to minimize the time to perform a backup and the amount of media space the backup takes, the user can opt to back up only the important user data directories on a regular basis. For example, users who save all their personal data files in a folder such as *My Documents* can back up only that folder and all folders under it. Some backup utility software permits a user to choose the type of backup. Three or four options are often available:

- **Full backup.** Copies all files in the directory or folder selected (and usually in all the subdirectories under the directory selected). Full backups copy every file in the selected directory, and ignore whether each file has previously been backed up and whether each file has changed since the last backup.

- **Incremental backup.** Copies only those files that have changed since the last backup *of any kind*. An incremental backup does not take as much time or media space as a full backup, because the number of files that change on a regular basis is usually small relative to the total number of files.

- **Differential backup.** Copies only those files that have changed since the last *full* backup. A differential backup takes more time and media space than an incremental backup, but requires less effort to recover needed files from the backup medium.

13

- **Progressive backup.** Copies only those files that need to be backed up. A progressive backup records the status of each file in a relational database. Progressive backups are efficient; they take less time, media space, and recovery effort than other options because they combine backup technology with a smart database that stores the location of the most recent version of each file.

 To learn more about the advantages of progressive backups, download a PDF document from Dantz's Web site at **www.dantz.com/docs/progressive_backups_brief.pdf** (requires Adobe Reader).

Other features in backup utility programs permit a user to back up only files that were created or changed before or after a specified date. A time cut-off permits a user to back up all the files created, for example, since March 1. Some backup utility programs also keep directories, logs, or catalogs of which specific files were backed up on each backup tape or disk.

Users who perform frequent and periodic backups often need more than one set of backup media (tapes, disks, or writeable CDs). If you use only a single backup tape, for example, each day's backup is written over the previous day's backup. However, suppose something goes wrong during the backup procedure (a hard drive crash occurs), or suppose a file becomes corrupted and the corrupted version is written on the backup media. A user who writes over the previous backup immediately risks losing the only reliable backup copy. A more conservative backup strategy involves the use of multiple sets of backup media, a rotation scheme, and off-site storage of one of the sets.

Table 13-1 shows a common strategy for managing three sets of backup media: the current set, an off-site set, and an old set that will rotate to become the current set in the following week.

Table 13-1   A common backup rotation scheme

Status	Age	Week 1 (this week)	Week 2 (next week)	Week 3	Week 4	Week 5
Current backup set	0 weeks old	C	A	B	C	A
Off-site backup set	1 week old	B	C	A	B	C
Oldest backup set	2 weeks old	A	B	C	A	B

Backup set A in the example is two weeks old this week. But next week, the support specialist will use set A as the current set. Then, during week 3, set A will be one week old. During week 4, set A will be the most out of date. But it will become the current set again in week 5. When writing over any backup media, always use the oldest, most obsolete copy in this scheme.

The backup media recorded last week (set B in the example), is often stored off-site as a precaution. In case of fire, theft, or damage, an off-site backup of important files is a strongly recommended facilities management strategy. Off-site may mean in a fireproof vault at a nearby financial institution, or an arrangement whereby a support person takes the backup set home. Or off-site may be a contract with a commercial media storage vendor. The important feature of off-site media storage is physical separation between the operational computer system and one set of backup media.

NOTE

Home computer users who want to arrange for an off-site backup storage, for example, could swap media backups with a trusted friend or relative.

Organizations that use the three-set rotation scheme described in Table 13-1 usually label the backup so identification of the media is easy. A network administrator might adopt a backup media naming convention for a server backup. The "stdnn" example is shown below:

13

> **s -** media set letter (A, B, or C)
>
> **t -** type of backup (Full, Incremental, Differential, or Progressive)
>
> **d -** day of week backup was made (M, T, W, H, F, S, U)
>
> **nn -** sequence number (01, 02, 03, and so on)

Under this naming convention, a backup disk or tape with a label "BDW02" is the second disk (02) in the differential (D) backup set B recorded on Wednesday (W). The network administrator also keeps a log of all backup disks that shows the disk number and the date and time each backup was recorded.

Finally, documented procedures should be available to restore files. **File restoration** is a procedure to copy one or more files from backup media to the original or a replacement disk when data or programs have been erased or destroyed—the opposite of a file backup operation. File restorations are necessary when a hard disk drive fails or when a user accidentally deletes one or more files and needs to recover them. A support staff member may be assigned the responsibility to restore backup files based on requests from users. The file restore procedure often involves using the same backup utility program that made the backup, only in restore mode. In all media backup situations, periodic tests of file restore operations should be conducted to verify that backup media is viable and restore procedures work as designed.

NOTE   In large organizations, the file restoration procedure can pose a security problem. Users are normally permitted to restore only files that they themselves created or for which they have user rights. Users need special permission to restore a file that is owned by another user.

Media Defragmentation

As users create, modify, and delete files, the way each file is stored on a disk changes. When a file is originally written on a disk, most operating systems try to write it in a space (a group of adjacent sectors) that is large enough to hold the entire file. If a sufficient amount of contiguous free space (adjacent sectors) is available, the file is written in that space. Use of contiguous sectors is the most efficient way to write and read files and manage disk space. If contiguous free space is not large enough to store the file, but enough *total* disk space is available to hold the file, the operating system breaks the file into fragments that it stores at different locations on the disk, wherever chunks of free space are available. When a file is fragmented, it may be stored in several pieces at different physical locations on a disk, but with pointers to where other fragments are stored. As the number of separate pieces associated with a file increases, even a small file may occupy more than one location on a disk. But the operating system does its best to accommodate a file in the space available.

That's the good news. The bad news is that, as the number of separate pieces of space that a file occupies increases, the read–write head on the hard drive has to move more often and greater distances in order to read or update the file. The movement of the read–write head slows file access time and eventually affects a computer's performance when it retrieves information. Sluggish performance, including lengthy times to write or read a file, is a symptom of the file fragmentation problem.

The **defragmentation** process uses a utility program that reads and rewrites all the files on a disk so that each file is once again stored in contiguous sectors. Then the utility regroups all free spaces so they are contiguous (in one large chunk). The procedure can dramatically improve disk performance. Figure 13-5 illustrates a fragmented and defragmented file on a disk.

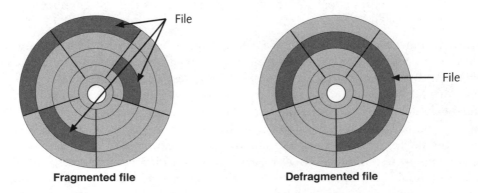

Fragmented file   Defragmented file

Figure 13-5   File fragmentation and defragmentation

Users and support specialists should periodically use a utility program to defragment their hard disks. In most instances, when fragmentation is minimal, the software gives a user the option not to run the program—a helpful feature because the defragmentation procedure can take anywhere from a few minutes on a small hard drive to several hours on a large hard drive. The defragmentation program (sometimes called the defrag utility) may provide an estimate of how long the procedure will take based on the size of the hard drive, the extent of fragmentation, and the speed of the system. Although defragmentation procedures are generally reliable, as a safety precaution users should back up their hard drive immediately before they run a defragmentation utility program.

To learn more about the benefits of defragmentation software, read a white paper by Raxco Software at its Web site: **www.raxco.com/products/ perfectdisk2k/whitepapers/defrag_tutorial.pdf** (requires Adobe Reader). Raxco sells a defrag utility, PerfectDisk. Or try Executive Software's Diskeeper Lite, available free. For information on Diskeeper Lite, visit **www.boostware. com/hardware/harddisk/diskeeper_lite.html**. To download DKLite, go to **www1.execsoft.com/dklite.exe**. Some versions of Windows also include a limited defragmentation utility.

Media Maintenance

In addition to media backups and defragmentation, users or support specialists may perform several other tasks associated with disk and tape devices. Examples of common media maintenance tasks include recovering lost allocation units, erasing unused programs and files, and recycling or replacing tape cartridges. These tasks are important because they may affect either the amount of space available on a disk, the speed of access to stored information, or the reliability of information stored on magnetic tapes.

Recover Lost Allocation Units.   Some operating systems occasionally lose track of the free space available on a disk. As files are created and deleted, sectors on a disk frequently change status from *used* to *free* and back to *used*. In the process, the links between disk sectors can get corrupted. Lost allocation units on a disk are not normally a major problem and affect primarily the amount of free space available on the disk. Operating systems that exhibit this problem usually provide a software utility to recover lost free space. For example, in Windows systems, the ScanDisk utility (and its DOS predecessor CHKDSK) can identify and repair some free space and related disk storage problems. ScanDisk should be run periodically as part of general disk maintenance procedures.

Erase Unused Programs and Files.   When their hard disks get full, some users simply purchase a larger hard drive. However, users can take several steps to make more free space available before their disks get full. Periodically erasing unused files and folders usually increases the amount of space available on a disk.

13

On systems with Recycle Bin, Wastebasket, or Trash features, deleted files and folders are not immediately erased, but are moved into a temporary storage folder. A user who complains that deleting files did not make additional disk space available may need to be reminded to empty the folder.

NOTE

Many users are reluctant to clean up their hard drives, however, because the purpose of each file is not always obvious. Before users erase any files, they should make copies on backup media in case they need the files later or in case something goes wrong during the file delete operation. In fact, most users should limit their disk cleaning activities to user data files, unless they are certain that an unrecognized file is not a required system file. Furthermore, simply erasing program files does not necessarily remove all traces of a program from a system. Registry entries, .INI files, device drivers, shortcuts, and .DLL libraries are examples of remnants that can remain on a system after a program has been deleted. To ensure that a program and all related files are removed, do one of the following:

- Use the uninstall option for each specific software package, if available in its folder, instead of just erasing the directory that contains the program.

- Use the operating system's uninstall feature, if included, such as the Add/Remove Programs option in the Windows Control Panel.

- Use utility software available from one of several vendors that is designed to inspect the software configuration on a disk and clean up any remnants of software that was partially erased (CyberMedia's UnInstaller is an example of a third-party uninstall utility).

Several versions of Windows include a limited disk cleanup utility. To access it from the Start menu, click Programs or All Programs, click Accessories, click System Tools, and then click Disk Cleanup. A list of free and shareware utilities that perform disk cleanup tasks is available at **www. thesoftwaredirectory.8m.com/utilities/disk_cleanup_tools.html**. An example of a commercial utility to clean a hard drive is QuickClean by McAfee; learn about its features at **us.mcafee.com/root/product.asp?productid=qc3**.

WWW

Recycle and Replace Tape Cartridges.   The magnetic tape used in tape cartridges and reel-to-reel tapes can become brittle if stored unused for several years. Tape is less likely to become brittle and unusable if it is periodically used (run through the tape drive), as the backup procedure described earlier recommends. Tapes that have not been used for two to three years should probably be copied onto other tapes to reduce the risk of data loss. Old tapes and brittle ones should be replaced.

Users often ask support specialists for advice about these and other media maintenance procedures. Experienced support specialists know that any significant media maintenance tasks, such as those described in this section, should be performed only after the original media has been backed up, as a precaution. Other suggestions for media maintenance are described in a section on preventive maintenance later in this chapter.

Computer Supplies

Another facilities management task that is often assigned to support specialists is the purchase of computer supplies. Alternately, support specialists may be asked for advice about where to find specific supplies or where to get the best prices on them. As part of their jobs, some support specialists manage an inventory of printer supplies (paper, labels, ink and toner cartridges, and ribbons), media (diskettes, cartridge tapes, writeable CDs and DVDs, and removable hard disks), cleaning supplies (cloths and solution), and even computer parts (cables, tools, and batteries).

Sources of supplies range from local office supply stores to electronics specialty stores to mail-order companies that specialize in selling computer parts and suppliers that do business primarily on the Internet.

 Vendors that specialize in selling computer and office supplies on the Internet include:

Vendor	URL
Action Office Supplies	www.actoff.com
Amazon.com	www.amazon.com
Boise Office Solutions	www.boiseoffice.com
Cheap Office Supplies	www.cheapofficesupplies.com
Clean Sweep Supply	www.cleansweepsupply.com/pages/category0003.html
eBay	www.ebay.com
Global Computer Supplies	www.globalcomputer.com
Keysan	www.keysan.com/ksu0173.htm
Office Depot	www.officedepot.com
OfficeMax	www.officemax.com
Price SCAN	www.pricescan.com/0103.asp
Quill Office Supplies	www.quillcorp.com
Staples	www.staples.com

For many small organizations that do not have storage space for a large inventory of supplies, convenience is a primary consideration in the purchase of computer supplies. Local office supply stores sell a variety of common computer items. Some offer free delivery within their service area. However, for any organization that uses a substantial quantity of supplies, significant opportunities can be found to save money on volume purchases or through mail-order or Internet purchases.

13

Local computer supply stores can be found in the Yellow Pages of most telephone directories under the headings *Computers - Supplies & Parts* and *Office Supplies*.

Preventive Maintenance

Although most personal computer equipment is primarily electronic and does not require a great deal of preventive maintenance, some moving parts (electromechanical) do benefit from periodic attention. **Preventive maintenance** uses tools and procedures to reduce the likelihood of computer component failure and expensive repair costs. Preventive maintenance steps are designed to clean and adjust equipment to prolong its useful life and enhance operational efficiency.

System Unit.   Most components inside a system unit either cannot be maintained by an end user, or do not require preventive maintenance. However, in a dusty environment, the life of a PC can be increased by periodically vacuuming the inside of the case to reduce dust buildup on the components. Dust often accumulates inside the system case because the electrical components attract dust particles. A vacuum cleaner with a plastic (not metallic) nozzle can be used to clean dust buildup and is preferable to cans of compressed air, which tend to blow dust around, rather than sweep it up. Computer supply stores sell portable vacuums specifically built for preventive maintenance tasks. The system unit case and other plastic or painted parts can also be cleaned with isopropyl alcohol and a lint-free cloth or with specially pretreated wipes designed for that purpose.

Prior to removing the case on the system unit for any reason, turn off the power and unplug the electric supply as a precaution.

The battery inside a PC case should be tested periodically with a volt-ohm meter (VOM). Weak batteries should be replaced. Cables that connect internal devices to the power supply and bus adapter boards should be checked to ensure that they are plugged snuggly into their sockets, but be careful not to press too hard on cables that plug into the motherboard because the motherboard has limited flexibility and can crack under too much pressure.

Finally, diagnostic software that tests electronic components in a system, such as keyboard, monitor, RAM, the data bus, peripheral adapter cards, and I/O ports, can sometimes identify components that operate marginally and may fail in the near future. Periodic use of diagnostic utility software, such as Norton Utilities and others described in Chapter 4, can alert support staff to possible future component failure.

Disk Drives.   Although hard disk, CD, DVD, and removable drives contain moving parts that are more likely to fail than electronic parts, they should not be serviced by anyone other than a qualified technician. For the most part, these drives do not include user-serviceable components, and when these devices fail, they are replaced, rather than repaired. However, in the case of a floppy drive, a coating of residue can build up on the read-write head on a floppy disk drive. Under normal use, the residue buildup is minimal; in a heavy use environment, it's best to use a disk drive cleaning kit occasionally to remove any residue from the read-write heads. These kits contain a specially designed floppy disk with a cloth pad instead of disk media. The cloth pad is saturated with isopropyl alcohol (or other cleaner provided in the kit), then the cleaner disk is inserted in the drive and removes the read-write head residue in a few revolutions of the pad. The procedure is very similar to cleaning the heads on a VCR.

Printers.   The biggest enemies of most printers are paper dust and ink buildup. Even printer paper that looks clean carries dust particles. Printers that use continuous form paper are especially vulnerable to printer dust, because such paper contains dust particles created during manufacturing when the sheet edges are perforated and tractor feed holes are punched in the paper. A good preventive maintenance strategy for printers is to use a vacuum cleaner to clean out the dust periodically. The insides of a printer should also be kept free of ink and toner spills, because these chemicals attract dust particles that can cause problems for the moving printer mechanism. Replace worn-out printer ribbons, because they also can create dust residue inside a printer.

Another way to extend the life of peripherals such as printers is by peripheral rotation. In **peripheral rotation**, a heavily used device is periodically rotated (exchanged) with one in a lighter use environment. For example, a heavily used printer might be more likely to fail sooner than one that is less used. Before it has a chance to fail, replace the printer with a new one or one that has received less use. Then clean the used one, and place it in a location that is less demanding.

Keyboards.   Vacuum a keyboard or spray it with compressed air periodically to remove dust and dirt particles from between the keys. A buildup of dust can make the keys stick or wear out the mechanism that makes contact with the membranes in the keyboard that send signals to the PC. Dirty keyboard keys can be cleaned with a lint-free cloth saturated with isopropyl alcohol. For especially dirty keyboard cases, a small brush such as a toothbrush saturated with isopropyl alcohol can be an effective cleaner.

Mouse/Trackball Parts.   The rubber ball inside a mouse or trackball can become dusty and grimy with use and needs cleaning. First, unplug the mouse. Then remove the rubber ball by twisting or pushing on the plastic restrainer in the direction indicated by an arrow on the underside of the mouse. After removing the ball, clean it and the metal contacts inside the mouse cavity with isopropyl alcohol and a lint-free cloth. Be sure that the mouse ball rotates freely after cleaning and that the plastic restrainer has been properly reinstalled. Finally, plug the mouse back in.

13

Display Screen.   Clean a computer screen regularly with a special pretreated cloth designed for that purpose or with isopropyl alcohol and a lint-free cloth. Preventive maintenance on a monitor is limited primarily to improved visibility. There are no user-serviceable parts inside a monitor. In fact, the high-voltage components inside a monitor are dangerous. A monitor case should never be removed, except by a qualified repair technician.

Several Web sites contain more information about preventive maintenance of PC systems. For more information on preventive maintenance, visit **www. pcguide.com/care/pm.htm** or **a1computers.net/pm.htm**. For a comprehensive list of cleaning supplies designed for computer use, visit Clean Sweep Supply's Web site at **www.cleansweepsupply.com/pages/section0174.html**.

Preventive maintenance can extend the useful life of many components in a PC system. Support specialists can often help end users understand important maintenance steps to increase both the life expectancy of a PC and its operating efficiency.

Antivirus Software Utilities

Computer viruses are a common problem in any facility that uses network technology, Internet access, broadband connection, remote dial-up, and other computer-to-computer connectivity. Viruses are also a problem when users exchange data or programs on floppy or removable disks or optical discs (CDs and DVDs). A **computer virus** is a program that can attach itself to other programs, e-mail messages, e-mail attachments, macros in applications software, or disk media. A virus can replicate (copy) itself from one system to another and across a network connection. Some virus programs are benign; other than displaying a message (sometimes an obscene one) on a screen, they cause little harm. Other virus programs are more virulent. They can destroy programs and data on a computer system or network they infect or generate excessive network traffic that results in denial of service to legitimate traffic. Standalone PCs that do not connect to a network, access the Internet, or read floppy disks from other systems are rarely infected by computer viruses.

Several software utilities are designed to manage viruses. Symantec and McAfee are two software utility developers who distribute up-to-date antivirus programs. Antivirus utilities include programs to detect, remove, and monitor virus activity in a system.

- **Detect.** A virus detection program looks in common places such as executable files, e-mail messages, e-mail attachments, macros in applications software, and the master boot sector on disks for virus signatures (evidence a virus is present). Because the number of known viruses grows daily, virus detection programs must be updated continually to search for the latest virus signatures. Distribution of updated lists of viruses on vendors' Internet sites is common.

- **Remove.** When a virus detection program has identified an infected system, it alerts the user and usually automatically begins the removal process. First, the suspect file is quarantined in a secure location. Then the file is deleted or rendered harmless in other ways. In general, virus removal software is reliable, but in a few cases the only effective removal procedure is to reformat a hard drive, reinstall the operating system and applications, and restore user data files from backup media. (This is yet another reason to make frequent media backups.)

- **Monitor.** A computer system that contains no detectable viruses can be programmed to monitor for signs of virus activity. Virus monitoring software continually examines data and programs received via a network or dial-up connection, as well as any disks used, to determine whether known virus signatures are detected. It also examines outgoing files to warn of contamination.

Many computer users install all three kinds of antivirus software on their systems and use them regularly as a precaution. Antivirus software is an especially important facilities management step for anyone in a network, computer lab, dial-up, broadband, software download, or disk exchange environment. Because new viruses are developed and propagated, support specialists should encourage and remind users to download the latest list of virus definitions for their antivirus utility program frequently, or make sure users subscribe to a service that automatically updates virus definitions daily.

IBM has published several useful white papers on computer viruses, as well as links to papers published elsewhere, on its Web site at **www.research. ibm.com/antivirus**. The Symantec antivirus home page is at **www.symantec. com/nav/index.html**. The McAfee antivirus Web site is at **us.mcafee. com/virusInfo/default.asp**. F-Secure's antivirus home page is **www.f-secure. com/virus-info**. Several smaller companies also sell antivirus software utilities. Free trial versions of antivirus software are usually available for download. Many free, shareware, and commercial antivirus resources are found on Freebyte's Web site at **www.freebyte.com/antivirus**.

Heightened publicity and concern about computer viruses among support professionals and the public has resulted in an increased number of virus hoaxes. A **virus hoax** is an apparently well-meaning transmission (usually via e-mail) from what appears to be a trustworthy source to warn a user about a suspected virus that is likely to do harm to the user's computer. Users often cannot distinguish between an official virus warning and one that is a hoax. These warnings are often re-transmitted to an entire list of friends by an unsuspecting, but well-meaning, user. The warning is often fallacious, and the advice in the warning, if followed, is often as dangerous as a genuine virus. Support staff are often asked to help users distinguish between real virus threats and hoaxes.

13

To learn more about virus hoaxes, visit the Symantec Antivirus Center's hoax pages at **www.symantec.com/avcenter/hoax.html**. For an example of a hoax that asks a user to delete a useful file, see **www.symantec.com/avcenter/ venc/data/jdbgmgr.exe.file.hoax.html**.

Use Accounting and Statistics

Although most organizations do not charge end users directly for the use of PC systems and computer networks, some facilities charge an access fee. These situations include schools and colleges that charge students for computer, e-mail, and Internet access; Internet service providers (ISPs) that charge a fee for Internet access and for storage of Web pages; and application software providers (ASPs) and timesharing service bureaus that provide mainframe or minicomputer services and software for a fee. Some organizations charge fees to individuals but, more often, to departments for computer use. The fees allocate the costs of providing computer and support services to user departments. For example, a Human Resources department may purchase computer services (including hardware, software, network access, training, and support services) from the IS department. Although no money may actually change hands in this example, the computer charges are a paper accounting transaction that lets the IS department cover its costs and justify the expenditures it makes to provide computer services to Human Resources and other departments. In other organizations, computer services are treated as an overhead item in the budget, and no accounting is made for use of computer resources.

The facilities management aspect of their job sometimes surprises support specialists who provide services to internal users. This chapter should help you anticipate the kinds of questions support specialists may get from users. However, the range of end-user facilities management issues is not limited to those described in this chapter. User support specialists who are assigned computer facilities management tasks may be confronted with other issues, such as:

- Design of end-user computing facilities, such as training rooms, computer labs, and work areas

- Capacity planning for servers, disk space, network infrastructure, and printers

- Design of charge back systems to account for end-user use of computer facilities

- Negotiations with vendors on price and purchase agreements for equipment, services, and supplies

- Environmental and safety issues, such as the use of chemicals in the workplace

- Ethics issues, such as the use of computer facilities to monitor employee performance

- Legal issues, such as copyright protection and ownership of intellectual property

Consulting with end users and company management on computer facilities management tasks often becomes among the most interesting and satisfying challenges in the career of support specialists.

CHAPTER SUMMARY

- ❏ Computer facilities can be classified as centralized, decentralized, or distributed. Each kind of computer facility poses facilities management problems for user support staffs.

- ❏ Common facilities management concerns and tools for support specialists include the following:

  - **Hardware maintenance and repair.** Support specialists perform simple repairs, but many hardware maintenance and repair problems are outsourced to a computer maintenance organization. Time and materials service and redundant hardware are alternatives to in-house maintenance to manage some hardware problems.

  - **Electrical power failures.** Power failures (surges, spikes, brownouts) can damage computer components. Power conditioners and uninterruptible power supplies with battery backup can address many power failure problems.

  - **Software problem reports.** Software problem reports and logs of software failures are tools used to identify bugs and common problems, which may be useful input to software developers and those who plan training programs for users.

  - **Network resources.** Network administrative procedures, performance monitors, media backups, and access security are common tools to address problems with shared network resources.

  - **Security challenges.** Threats to computer facilities originate from both internal and external sources, and arise from electronic and physical attempts to access resources. Electronic security threats are addressed by a variety of administrative procedures and software tools. Physical security tools include barriers, locks, monitors, and identification devices to screen users.

  - **Disaster plans.** Although disasters can never be completely avoided, a contingency plan to manage the risks associated with disasters is an effective facilities management tool. Media backups, reciprocal site agreements, security measures, and a written disaster plan are tools to manage risk.

  - **User problems.** User mistakes are probably the rule rather than the exception; tools to address common mistakes include user training, robust software design, automated procedures to replace manual procedures, and system audits. These tools provide a range of solutions to reduce, though not eliminate, the impact of mistakes.

  - **Crime and misuse.** To address computer crime, support specialists use a variety of access controls over electronic entry to a system, physical controls over facilities access, inventory controls for theft, and information controls based on a user's "need to know." Many organizations develop official policies that define appropriate computer use and misuse.

  - **Disposal of obsolete equipment.** Disposal methods include handing down used computers and peripherals to other users, donating equipment to charitable organizations, and sending equipment to an electronics recycler.

13

❏ User support specialists employ several routine operational procedures to help with computer facilities management tasks. These procedures include:

- **Media backups.** Regular media backups are based on a fixed schedule that combines full and incremental, differential, or progressive backups with off-site storage according to a backup media rotation scheme. Labeling conventions and backup logs help identify and locate backup media when needed for a file restore task.

- **Media fragmentation.** Defragmentation of disk media with utility software reduces read-write head movement and improves system performance.

- **Media maintenance.** Utility software is useful to recover lost free space and improve access performance.

- **Computer supplies.** Includes the purchase and management of commonly used computer consumables and supplies.

- **Preventive maintenance.** Dust is a serious problem for both electronic and electromechanical hardware devices. Regular cleaning of key system components can prolong the life of a computer system.

- **Antivirus software.** Computer viruses are common in situations where computers communicate via networks or modems, or where disks are exchanged. Antivirus software is designed to detect, remove, and monitor virus activity in a computer system.

- **Use accounting.** Software that collects, stores, and reports on computer resource use can be used to justify and allocate computer expenditures.

Key Terms

access controls — Procedures and tools to limit electronic or remote entry into a computer system or network of computers; user accounts, passwords, and grants of access rights to resources are common examples.

business interruption insurance — A type of business insurance policy that helps offset the cost of returning an organization to normal operation after an unforeseen event such as a disaster; a risk management tool designed to provide financial resources to restore normal operation of computer and other business facilities.

callback modem — A modem that does not connect an apparently authorized dial-up user directly to a computer system, but returns the user's call to a predefined, secure telephone number for that user.

centralized — A computer facility in which the equipment, peripherals, operational staff, and often users are located in a single physical location; a mainframe system is an example.

cold site — A building and space where a replacement computer system could be installed quickly after a disaster; similar to a *hot site*, but does not include operational equipment.

computer facility — A combination of the hardware, software, network, information, people, operating procedures, and environment (office space, furniture, and electrical power) associated with the use of any computer system.

computer virus — An annoying or harmful program that can attach itself to other programs, e-mail messages, e-mail attachments, macros in applications software, or disk media; viruses are transmitted over networks, via modem connections, and through the exchange of infected media; software utilities to combat computer viruses are a common facilities management tool.

decentralized — A facility in which computer equipment and peripherals are geographically dispersed and located in the offices with the people who use them; a standalone PC in an office, home, or school is an example.

defragmentation — A process during which a utility program reads and rewrites all the files on a disk so that each file is stored in contiguous sectors to shorten access time; this process also regroups all free spaces on the disk so they are contiguous (in one large chunk).

differential backup — A copy to an alternate media of only those files that have changed since the last full backup; takes less time to run and less media space than a full backup.

dirty power — Electricity that fluctuates beyond normal bounds in voltage, frequency, or other characteristics that can affect the operation of computer hardware; power conditioners convert dirty power into clean power.

disaster/contingency plan — A planning document that describes various activities that will occur if a computer facility experiences a temporary disruption of service; often addresses such events as fires, earthquakes, power outages, water damage, and sabotage.

distributed — A facility in which some parts of a computer system are centralized and other parts are decentralized; a networked system with a centralized server and decentralized client systems is a good example.

downtime — A measure of the number of hours (per week or month) that a computer system is unavailable for use because of power failures or other problems.

engineering inspection — An investigation conducted by an engineering firm to help identify the potential for damage to computer equipment and facilities from floods, storm damage, earthquakes, fires, and other kinds of disasters; often conducted as part of a computer facility contingency planning project.

file restoration — A procedure to copy one or more files from backup media to the original or a replacement disk when data or programs have been erased or destroyed; the opposite of a file backup operation.

firewall — Hardware or software designed to intercept and prevent unauthorized attempts to access a computer system that is connected to the Internet.

full backup — A copy to an alternate media of all files (programs and data) stored on a computer system or in a specified directory, regardless of whether they were previously backed up.

hot site — A backup computer installation maintained at a geographically distant location with computer equipment installed and operational; used in case of catastrophic failure of the equipment in a computer facility; compare with *cold site*.

13

incremental backup — A copy to alternate media of only those files that have changed since the last backup of any kind; takes less time to run and less media space than a full backup.

information controls — Procedures to account for and limit access to valuable or confidential information in a computer system.

inventory controls — Tools and procedures to maintain records about the location, configuration, and value of computer equipment; part of an asset management system in many organizations.

mean time between failure (MTBF) — The expected number of hours an average device is likely to operate before it fails.

media backups — Copies of important programs and data written on separate magnetic or optical media; facilitate restoration of programs and data in case the originals are erased, lost, or damaged.

operating system vulnerabilities — Unintended paths or gateways that permit unauthorized access into a system due to unpatched software bugs.

performance monitors — Hardware and software tools that show network administrators and support staff how effectively a network system is operating; can alert staff to potential problems in the operation of a network.

peripheral rotation — A strategy in which a heavily used computer component is periodically exchanged (rotated) with one in a lighter use environment; may extend the life expectancy of peripheral devices that get heavy use.

physical controls — Tools used in computer facilities to limit physical access to equipment and information; include locks, identification badges, alarms, monitors, and physical restraints to secure equipment.

power conditioner — An electrical device that inputs "dirty" power from an electric supplier and retransmits "clean" power to a computer system; can correct some common problems with voltages, the frequency of the electric current, and the shape of the wave form.

preventive maintenance — Tools and procedures used to reduce the likelihood of computer component failure and expensive repair costs; preventive maintenance steps are designed to clean and adjust equipment to prolong its useful life and enhance operational efficiency.

progressive backup — A copy to an alternate media of only those files that need to be backed up; combines backup technology with a smart database that stores the status and location of the most recent version of each file.

redundant array of inexpensive disks (RAID) — A disk technology that provides large amounts of disk storage space using a cluster of cheap hard drives; if one hard disk in a RAID system fails, it can be replaced with little or no downtime.

redundant system — An extra backup computer or peripheral that is identical to the hardware in daily use, which can be installed and pressed into service whenever the primary component fails.

risk management — The use of several tools and strategies to reduce the threat to an organization from disasters, and to help an organization to recover from disasters with minimal financial or customer service loss; often includes a disaster/contingency plan to address recovery from floods, fires, earthquake, sabotage, and storm damage.

service level agreement (SLA) — A written contract that defines the expectations between a computer facility and a service vendor for providing hardware (and sometimes operating system) support, preventive maintenance, and repairs; SLAs usually cover both parts and labor and guarantee response within a time period specified in the agreement.

software problem report (SPR) — A system to capture problem report data associated with computer programs; may be manual or automated; also called a bug report system.

system audit — An investigation by an independent consultant or group to verify that proper operating procedures and safeguards are followed in a computer facility and to identify potential end-user problem areas.

time and materials — An alternative to contracted hardware maintenance service in which a computer facility pays for hardware repairs based on time spent (labor) and the cost of replacement parts; often performed on a best effort basis with no response or completion time guarantees.

uninterruptible power supply (UPS) — An electrical device that includes power conditioning circuits and a battery backup to supply electricity to a computer system during power outages of short duration.

uptime — A measure of the number of operational hours when a computer system is available for use.

13

virus hoax — An apparently well-meaning transmission (usually via e-mail) from what appears to be a trustworthy source to warn about a suspected virus that is likely to do harm; the warning is often fallacious.

CHECK YOUR UNDERSTANDING

1. True or False? The term "computer facility" refers primarily to large mainframe computer installations in corporations or business enterprises

2. A computer facility in which some hardware, peripherals, software, data, and operating staff are located at one site, but others are located in dispersed sites throughout an organization, is _____ .

   a. a centralized facility

   b. a decentralized facility

   c. a distributed facility

   d. none of these

3. A service agreement usually covers which of these conditions in a contract between a computer facility and a service provider?

   a. response time

   b. parts availability

   c. preventive maintenance

   d. all of these

4. A(n) _____ tries to answer the question, "What steps will an organization take in the event an emergency occurs?"

5. True or False? When comparing two similar devices from different vendors, a device with a longer mean time between failure (MTBF) is generally more desirable than one with a shorter MTBF.

6. True or False? The electrical power requirements for computers in a hospital's critical care unit are no different from those in a small office.

7. Which of the following electrical devices contains a battery backup?

   a. a PC power supply

   b. a power conditioner

   c. a surge suppressor

   d. an uninterruptible power supply

8. True or False? The purpose of an engineering inspection is to prevent damage that can occur due to a disaster.

9. A(n) _____ is a tool designed to capture reports of problems users encounter with the use of computer programs.

10. True or False? Although computer networks pose unique facilities management problems because users are often decentralized, networks frequently provide additional tools to deal with problems that arise.

11. True or False? In general, the fewer manual steps users must make to operate a computer, the less likely users are to make mistakes.

12. True or False? File fragmentation occurs when enough total disk space is available to write a file, but not enough contiguous disk space is available to contain the file.

13. Which of the following is not a common tool to control physical access in a computer facility?

   a. Internet firewall

   b. motion sensor

   c. monitor camera

   d. ID badge

14. True or False? A user with a malfunctioning CRT monitor should remove the case to check the fuse.

15. The entry of an incorrect formula into a spreadsheet or database is an example of a(n) _____ .

   a. ergonomic problem

   b. user error

   c. security problem

   d. access control problem

16. Which of the following types of media backups makes a copy of all the files in a directory, whether or not they have changed?

   a. full backup

   b. incremental backup

   c. differential backup

   d. progressive backup

17. A(n) _____ is a program that can attach itself to other software or to disk media and cause harm to the programs and data stored in a computer.

DISCUSSION QUESTIONS

1. Which do you think is most advantageous to an end user: a hardware service agreement or a time and materials repair depot? Explain your position.

2. An experienced user support specialist made the following statement: "It is not my job to watch for or even worry about errors users make. That is the users' and their manager's responsibility." Explain why you agree or disagree with the statement.

3. What do you think is the motivation of computer hackers who write virus programs and disseminate them, or who spam other users with unwanted e-mail messages? Are their motives understandable to you? Are they justified?

13

HANDS-ON PROJECTS

HANDS-ON PROJECTS

Project 13-1

Determine risks for SLA. Think about all the events that could happen to the computer hardware at your school or workplace that could seriously affect the operation of your school or workplace (in other words, prevent the organization from continuing normal operation). Compare your list of events with a group of your classmates or coworkers. Then make a list of the risks you would want to cover in a service level agreement that would assure maximum uptime for the hardware in the facility.

Project 13-2

Evaluate service costs. Visit a local computer store in your area that has a service department. What does it charge per hour to work on computer hardware? At the hourly rate the service department charges, how many hours could it work on a $200 printer before it would be less expensive to buy a new one instead of repairing the old one?

While you're at the computer store, find out what the warranty period is on a new computer system it sells. Also ask whether it will sell an extended service contract to cover a new system that a customer purchases at the store after the warranty expires. What percentage of the purchase price of the system is the extended warranty? Do you think an extended service contract makes sense? What kind of computer user should purchase one? Who should not purchase one? Write a brief report of your findings.

Project 13-3

Research surge protectors. Contact your local electric utility to find out if it recommends surge suppressors for computers used in your service area. Find out the characteristics and cost of a surge suppressor it recommends for computer equipment. Does the surge suppressor include insurance that would cover the cost of damage to computer equipment in case the surge suppressor failed? Write a brief report of your findings.

Project 13-4

Create a SOHO disaster/contingency plan. List the information you would include in a disaster/contingency plan for a small office/home office (SOHO) computer system. What problems that could occur in a large installation would not be likely to occur in a SOHO installation?

Project 13-5

Determine insurance coverage for computers. Find out whether a computer is covered under your homeowner's or renter's insurance policy (if you have one). Is there a maximum value that is insured? Is there a deductible? If a home computer is not covered or you don't have insurance, contact an insurance agent to find out how much it would cost to obtain insurance coverage for a computer, what the maximum value would be, and whether a deductible or choice of deductible amounts is offered. Write a summary of your findings and conclusions.

Project 13-6

Design a problem log. Use a word processor or spreadsheet program to design a log or problem report form that could be used to report hardware, software, or network problems in a computer lab at your school or in a training facility. What kinds of information would you need to collect on the report or log that would give support staff enough information to locate the equipment, begin to trace the problem, and contact the user with questions?

Project 13-7

Recommend a backup strategy. Should users who routinely access only a few files on their hard drive on a regular basis do a full backup, an incremental backup, or a differential backup? Explain your answer in terms of the amount of time required to do the backup, the amount of media space required to store the backup files, and the amount of effort required to restore a file that was accidentally erased. Write a memo to users to explain your recommendations.

Project 13-8

Assess a user's backup strategy. A home computer user keeps one removable hard disk to back up all her important data files (all her files currently fit on one disk). Once each weekend, she reformats the disk and then copies all her data files from her hard drive onto the removable hard disk. She follows the same procedure every weekend. Write a note to the user that explains any problems you see with this backup strategy.

Project 13-9

Determine preventive maintenance tasks. What preventive maintenance tasks should a user support specialist perform during a regular six-month site visit to an office user's system? Use a word processor or spreadsheet to make a preventive maintenance check list for a typical office computer system like the check lists in Chapter 10.

13

Project 13-10

Research a computer virus warning. A user received the following text in an e-mail message. He wants to know what he should do if he receives an e-mail with a subject PENPAL GREETINGS! Please research the problem and write a response to the user.

> Subject: Virus Alert
>
> Importance: High
>
> If anyone receives mail entitled: PENPAL GREETINGS! please delete it WITHOUT reading it. Below is a little explanation of the message, and what it would do to your PC if you were to read the message. If you have any questions or concerns please contact SAF-IA Info Office at 555-5059.
>
> This is a warning for all Internet users—there is a dangerous virus propagating across the Internet through an e-mail message entitled "PENPAL GREETINGS!". DO NOT DOWNLOAD ANY MESSAGE ENTITLED "PENPAL GREETINGS!"
>
> This message appears to be a friendly letter asking you if you are interested in a pen pal, but by the time you read this letter, it is too late. The "Trojan horse" virus will have already infected the boot sector of your hard drive, destroying all of the data present. It is a self-replicating virus, and once the message is read, it will AUTOMATICALLY forward itself to anyone whose e-mail address is present in YOUR mailbox!

This virus will DESTROY your hard drive, and holds the potential to DESTROY the hard drive of anyone whose mail is in your inbox, and whose mail is in their inbox, and so on. If this virus remains unchecked, it has the potential to do a great deal of DAMAGE to computer networks worldwide!!!!

Please, delete the message entitled "PENPAL GREETINGS!" as soon as you see it! And pass this message along to all of your friends and relatives, and the other readers of the newsgroups and mailing lists which you are on, so that they are not hurt by this dangerous virus!!!!

HANDS-ON PROJECTS

Project 13-11

Research a facilities management problem. In addition to the facilities management issues discussed in this chapter, several other problems might confront a user support staff member as part of managing a computer facility. Examples include:

- ◻ Ways to properly dispose of obsolete, surplus computer equipment
- ◻ Developing an organizational policy on appropriate (and inappropriate) use of Internet resources
- ◻ Monitoring employee performance using computer technology
- ◻ Methods to provide user support for telecommuters
- ◻ Ways to recover data from a damaged hard disk drive

Select one of these management problems, or another of your choosing, and then research and write a report on the problem. Share your results with your classmates or coworkers.

HANDS-ON PROJECTS

Project 13-12

Evaluate content filtering software. Some organizations that provide public Internet access, such as schools, libraries, and churches, may want to make sure that Web pages displayed or downloaded from the Internet have appropriate content for their clients, including young children. Learn about software utility programs that are available to filter Internet content. Write a brief explanation of how content filtering software works. What are the pros and cons of using content filter utilities as a facilities management tool?

CASE PROJECTS

1. Preventive Maintenance Check List for BizNet Systems

Kai Edmonds is a manager of support services for BizNet Computer Systems, a vendor that sells computer networks to small organizations. She is aware that a number of BizNet's customers have very little experience with the tasks associated with keeping a network system up and running. Kai spends considerable time on the telephone answering questions. The top three kinds of questions she gets are how to handle:

- Security threats
- Media backups
- Disk performance

Kai thinks BizNet needs a document to hand to its customers when they first take delivery of their office network. The document would address the three common concerns she hears most often from customers. Assume that BizNet sells Windows desktop clients that are attached to a Windows or Novell NetWare server (or make any other assumption that is consistent with the kind of network environment with which you are familiar).

First, develop a preventive maintenance check list of tasks that a small organization should use to manage their systems for maximum performance and reliability.

Next, if time permits, Kai would like to expand the check list to provide clients with a brief explanation of how to perform the steps on the check list. If time is short, your instructor or trainer may ask you to pick one of the three categories to work on.

As you write your preventive maintenance check list and an explanation of how to perform each step, remember that BizNet clients are not computer professionals.

13

2. Software Utilities for Your Computer

To complete this Case Project, you will need a home computer system or access to a computer system at your school or workplace. *Do not undertake this Case Project unless you have permission to use a computer and install and operate the kinds of software described below.*

In this chapter, you learned about several kinds of software utilities related to system performance and reliability. They include:

- System problem diagnosis
- Media backup and restoration
- Performance monitoring
- Media maintenance
- Disk defragmentation
- Antivirus

◻ Anti-spam filters

◻ System or network security

Pick one of these software categories to investigate. Learn about the operating systems and third-party utility software available for your system that fit the category you selected. Pick at least two programs in the category that interests you. Install the programs and learn how they operate. Use a word processor to prepare a description of the software you used, the results of its use on your computer, and any problems you encountered with the software you investigated.

3. How to Manage Spam E-Mail at Re-Nu-Cartridge

For background information about Re-Nu-Cartridge, see Case Project 4 in previous chapters.

Several workers at Re-Nu-Cartridge who have Internet access on their desktop computers have complained recently in a computer user's group meeting about the amount of unwanted e-mail they receive. CEO Fred Long wants you to research some ways to deal with the excessive number of unwanted e-mail messages as a way to improve worker productivity—the fewer the spam e-mail messages received, the less time Re-Nu-Cartridge's workers have to spend reading and deleting them.

First, research whether any tools exist in the e-mail system they use, which happens to be the same e-mail software as you use, that would help manage spam attacks.

Second, research whether any software utility programs are available at no or low cost that Re-Nu-Cartridge's workers could use to help filter out spam e-mail messages.

Write a one- to two-page document targeted to end users at Re-Nu-Cartridge that responds to their need to reduce or eliminate spam messages.

4. A Backup Procedure for Re-Nu-Cartridge

For background information about Re-Nu-Cartridge, see Case Project 4 in previous chapters.

Re-Nu-Cartridge recently purchased a laptop computer for each of its sales representatives who sells products to businesses in its sales region. The sales reps have been using their laptops for several weeks. They like the ability to enter sales information and orders in a simple format on their laptop system and send the orders to Re-Nu-Cartridge via modem for processing.

Unfortunately, last week one sales rep experienced a hard disk crash on her laptop system. She believes that the hard drive problem may have occurred when she accidentally dropped the carrying case containing the laptop at a customer's site. She could not read the data on her hard drive, but the loss was not too significant. She had already sent all of her reports from the previous week via modem to Re-Nu-Cartridge's headquarters, so copies were available on the PC that receives the reports she sends via modem. However, she lost the order information from one large customer and some notes she had made on a prospective new client. Fortunately, Re-Nu-Cartridge had purchased a redundant laptop that she could use as a backup while hers was being repaired. Despite some embarrassment when she had to return to both customers and reenter their information, she was able to recover from the disk problem in a few hours.

The support staff at Re-Nu-Cartridge is considering ways to manage the risk that this problem could occur again. They feel a hard disk crash is a fairly common risk associated with laptops that are used extensively in the field. One alternative is to have the sales reps use their modems to call in each order immediately after it is entered. However, the cost of this alternative in added telephone calls is substantial compared to the once-a-day calls that each sales rep currently makes. A second alternative is to develop a simple backup procedure that each sales rep can use to copy the order information from the laptop hard drive onto a floppy disk. If the procedure is simple, each rep could run a backup after entering an order. Because each laptop has a built-in floppy drive, the idea of a backup procedure seems inexpensive and feasible.

13

Each sales rep stores their sales reports in a folder named C:\REPORTS on the laptop hard drive. The individual sales reports are named CUSTnnnn.TXT, where "nnnn" is Re-Nu-Cartridge's internal four-digit account number for each customer.

Using a scripting or macro tool of your choosing, write a simple automated procedure that a sales rep can use to back up the relevant data in the REPORTS directory from a Windows system onto a floppy disk. Remember that the sales reps have limited computer experience, so your procedure should be as simple and user-friendly as possible. Test your procedure to make sure that it works as you intend. Then, write a document to describe how to use the backup procedure, as well as how a sales rep would recover a report from a backup floppy. Also, describe how the backup floppy disks should be labeled.

1

USER SUPPORT
INFORMATION RESOURCES

This appendix is a compilation of information resources described throughout this book as well as selected additional resources available to user
support professionals. Because few support professionals have first-hand knowledge and experience with the entire range of problems they will encounter in
their work, the difference between satisfactory performance and excellent
performance among support staff is often one's ability to locate and use
information resources effectively. This appendix is a starting point to address
support professionals' need for access to information resources.

The appendix is organized by the chapters in this book. It includes all the Web
site pointers listed in each chapter as well as references to printed materials that
supplement the topics covered in this book. Because the resources described in
this book and included in this appendix are relatively perishable, the Online
Companion Web site for this book has been designed to alert readers to:

- Corrections to Web addresses listed in the text

- Pointers to new Web sites with relevant information that supplement
  topics covered in this book

- Corrections for errors discovered in this book

- Additional information that supplements the topics covered in this
  book

The Web site addresses the problem of printed information becoming outdated
as URLs change and as new materials become available that may be useful to
those in the user support field.

The Online Companion Web site for this book can be found at www.course.com/helpdesk. To locate the Online Companion for this book, click the title **A Guide to Computer User Support for Help Desk and Support Specialists, 3rd edition**.

Save yourself some typing! The Online Companion Web site includes links to every URL listed in this book. You can quickly locate information references to the supplementary information in Web sites without typing lengthy URLs by clicking the links in the Online Companion Web site.

Readers who discover obsolete Web addresses in this book, typos, and other errors, or who want to recommend additional user support information resources, can contact the author through the e-mail link on the Online Companion Web site.

CHAPTER ONE: INTRODUCTION TO END-USER COMPUTING

Web Resources

Page	Resource	URL
3	IBM z-Series mainframe Web site	www-1.ibm.com/servers/solutions/zseries
5	Sun Microsystems SunFire minicomputer Web site	www.sun.com/solutions
5	IBM iSeries minicomputer Web site	www-1.ibm.com/servers/eserver/iseries/about/why.html
7	Peter Drucker's 1995 article on knowledge workers in *The Atlantic*	www.theatlantic.com/issues/95dec/chilearn/drucker.htm
8	Online computer glossaries	whatis.techtarget.com www.techweb.com/encyclopedia www.webopedia.com
8	Description of Moore's Law on the Intel Web site	www.intel.com/research/silicon/ mooreslaw.htm
8	Timeline of GUI development highlights	toastytech.com/guis/index.html
10	City of Orlando, Florida, use of IBM iSeries minicomputer	www-3.ibm.com/software/success/cssdb.nsf/CS/LBHN-5FMKVY?OpenDocument&Site=software
12	Timeline of significant events in the history of computers	www.computer.org/computer/timeline/timeline.pdf (requires Adobe Reader)
12	Timeline of significant events in the history of personal computers	www.islandnet.com/~kpolsson/comphist
12	Slide show on the history of the Internet	www.isoc.org/internet/history/2002_0918_Internet_History_and_Growth.ppt (requires PowerPoint or viewer)
18	Jaekel & Associates white paper on total cost of ownership concept	www.jaekel.com/white3.html

Page	Resource	URL
21	White paper on measuring worker productivity	www.business-authority.com/management/time_management/productivity_management.htm
32	Arguments by those opposed to supermarket identification cards	www.nocards.org/faq/indcx.shtml
33	JDA Professional Services Web site on total cost of ownership of computer systems	www.jdapsi.com/client/Articles/Default.php?Article=tco
35	Web site devoted to information about tablet PCs	www.tabletpctalk.com

Other Resources

Ralph M. Stair, Jr., and George Walter Reynolds, *Principles of Information Systems, 6th ed.*, Boston, MA: Course Technology, 2003.

> Stair and Reynold's text is an introduction to computers and information systems in businesses and organizations. It includes information on end-user computing to supplement the coverage in Chapters 1 and 2 of this book.

Elizabeth Ann Regan and Bridget N. O'Connor, *End User Information Systems: Implementing Individual and Work Group Technologies, 2nd edition*, New York: Prentice Hall, 2002.

> Regan and O'Connor's book discusses several aspects of end-user computing in organizations including how to provide support for end users.

Mo Adam Mahmood, *Advanced Topics in End User Computing*, Hershey, PA: Idea Group Publishing, 2004.

> Mahmood's book is a collection of articles on end-user computing that were published recently in the *Journal of End User Computing*. The articles are based on research into several current problems that confront organizations with large numbers of end users.

Journal of Organizational and End User Computing, Hershey, PA: Idea Group Publishing.

> Edited by Mo Adam Mahmood, University of Texas, the *Journal of Organizational and End User Computing* (formerly the *Journal of End User Computing*) is a quarterly publication of the Information Resources Management Association. The journal covers research and expert advice on the development, use, and management of end-user computing in organizations. The journal is commonly found in large libraries.

CHAPTER TWO: INTRODUCTION TO COMPUTER USER SUPPORT

Web Resources

Page	Resource	URL
38	American Staffing Association Web site	www.staffingtoday.net
39	Information Technology Association of America Web site	www.itaa.org
39	Robert Half Web site with salary survey	www.rhic.com
41	Microsoft Web site for peer user groups	www.microsoft.com/communities/usergroups/default.mspx
44	TechRepublic article on the location of help desks within organizations	techrepublic.com.com/5100-6269-5028769.html
44	EDO Technical Support Operations Web site	www.compusupport.com
45	Client Outsource Web site	www.clientoutsource.com
56	American Career InfoNet site for support specialist KSAs	www.acinet.org/acinet/ksas1.asp?soccode=151041&stfips=41
57	ACE Web site with free skill assessment	www.ace.co.nz/tools/skills/index.asp
59	Occupational Information Network (O*Net) Web site	online.onetcenter.org/gen_search_page
63	State of Washington position description	hr.dop.wa.gov/lib/hrdr/specs/00000/03271.htm
63	City of Des Moines, Iowa position description	www.ci.des-moines.ia.us/departments/HR/Job%20Descriptions/User%20Support%20Technician.htm
63	Computer Jobs Web site	www.computerjobs.com
63	Just Help Desk Jobs Web site	www.JustHelpDeskJobs.com
63	Monster.com Web site	jobsearch.monster.com
63	Dice.com Web site	www.dice.com
65	Occupational Information Network (O*Net) Web site	online.onetcenter.org/gen_skills_page
68	Web resources on employment trends in user support industry	www.microsoft.com/traincert/training/careers/trends.asp www.itaa.org/workforce/studies/03execsumm.pdf (requires Adobe Reader) www.dol.gov/wb/factsheets/hitech02.htm www.computerworld.com/careertopics/careers/labor
68	Indiana University Bloomington user satisfaction survey	about.uits.iu.edu/~uitssur/2003/iub/summary03.html

Other Resources

Paula Moreira and Robin Thorpe, *Ace the IT Resume*, New York: McGraw-Hill Osborne, 2002.

Paula Moreira and Robin Thorpe, *Ace the IT Interview*, New York: McGraw-Hill Osborne, 2003.

> These "How-To" books describe the process of building a technical resume and performing well in a job interview. The books cover a variety of IT positions, but include sections on Desktop Support and Help Desk Agents.

Donna Knapp, *A Guide to Help Desk Concepts*, 2nd edition, Boston, MA: Course Technology, 2003.

> A textbook that describes the operation of a help desk group and the knowledge, skills, and abilities required for entry-level positions.

Peter Rob and Elie Semaan, *Databases: Design, Development & Deployment Using Microsoft Access*, 2nd edition, New York: Irwin/McGraw-Hill, 2002.

Dirk Baldwin and David Paradice, *Applications Development in Access 2000*, Course Technology, Boston, MA, 2000.

> Two books devoted to developing end-user applications in Microsoft Access 2000. Of primary interest to support professionals who need to know how to develop small end-user applications or assist end users with their development projects.

Duane Birnbaum, *Microsoft Excel VBA Professional Projects*, Boston, MA: Course Technology, 2003.

> A book that builds skills in developing end-user applications in Microsoft Excel 2000. Of primary interest to support professionals who need to build end-user spreadsheet applications or assist end users with their spreadsheet projects.

BUBL LINK maintains a Web site, hosted in the United Kingdom, with links to information resources on computer user support; see **bubl.ac.uk/link/c/ computerusersupport.htm**.

CHAPTER THREE: CUSTOMER SERVICE SKILLS FOR USER SUPPORT

Web Resources

Page	Resource	URL
73	Jeff Davis's article on communication skills	**www.techrepublic.com/article.jhtml?id= r00320030107jed01.htm&src=bc**
74	Lillian D. Bjorseth's article, "Shhh! Listen, Don't Just Hear!"	**www.selfgrowth.com/articles/bjorseth4.html**

Page	Resource	URL
75	Web article on empathy and trust	www.businessballs.com/empathy.htm
77	Microsoft Office FAQ	www.microsoft.com/office/faq.htm
79	Web-based training courses on help desk and communication skills	www.skillsoft.com/corporate/curicula/bus_cs.htm
79	Communication and listening skills Web-based training course vendor	www.learncustomerserviceonline.com/CustServiceModules.htm
80	Haywood Community College Technical Support Web site	potemkin.haywood.cc.nc.us/Techsite/hcc/techsupportindex.html
84	KnowYourType.com Web site on MBTI	www.knowyourtype.com/default.htm
84	The Team Technology Web site on Myers-Briggs (MBTI)	www.teamtechnology.co.uk/tt/t-articl/mb-simpl.htm
89	Notes from Kate Nasser's talk on difficult users	www.health.ufl.edu/itcenter/cs/frontlines2.shtml
89	TechRepublic article on handling abusive callers	www.techrepublic.com/article.jhtml?id=r00320000726det02.htm
89	Leslie Barden's paper, "Dealing with Difficult Customers"	www.awcncc.org/2001/Barden_article.rtf
91	Dell support Web site	support.dell.com
91	Gateway support Web site	support.gateway.com
91	Web site on improving usability of Web sites	www.usabilityfirst.com/index.txl
97	George Lawton's article on improving customer service	techupdate.zdnet.com/techupdate/stories/main/0,14179,2804648,00.html
97	Voiceboard's customer support policies and procedures to increase customer self-reliance	www.voiceboard.com/support1.htm
97	Example of a help desk phone call	www.bizjournals.com/sacramento/stories/2000/01/24/smallb4.html
97	Jennifer Stewart Write101.com Web site	www.write101.com/101web.htm
99	The Keirsey Temperament Sorter II Web site	www.advisorteam.com/user/kts.asp

Other Resources

Donna Knapp, *A Guide to Customer Service Skills for the Help Desk Professional, 2nd ed.*, Boston, MA: Course Technology, 2004.

> This textbook includes chapters on listening and communication skills, telephone skills, handling difficult situations, help desk work teams, and avoiding stress in help desk positions.

A1

Ron Zemke and Kristin Anderson, *Delivering Knock Your Socks Off Service*, New York: AMACOM, 2002.

> This best-selling book on customer service deals with various aspects of customer satisfaction. Although the focus is broader than computer user support skills, the book is an excellent resource for those interested in building customer service excellence.

Thomas O. Jones and W. Earl Sasser, Jr., "Why Satisfied Customers Defect," *Harvard Business Review*, Nov–Dec, 1995.

> This article discusses the importance of customer service to customer retention, and documents the importance of total customer satisfaction.

Frederick Reichheld, "Learning from Customer Defections," *Harvard Business Review*, Mar–Apr, 1996.

> This article documents why corporations lose clients and the cost to replace a customer.

Kate Nasser, "How to Handle Difficult Callers," *Support Management* (January 1998): 16–24.

> Nasser's article discusses the type of difficult calls support specialist are likely to encounter and how to successfully handle each type.

Jean Kummerow et al., *Worktypes*. New York: Warner Books, 1997.

Otto Kroeger & Janet Thuesen, *Type Talk at Work (Revised)*, New York: Dell Publishing, 2002.

> These are examples of popular books on applications of Myers-Briggs (MBTI) in the workplace. They cover how to work successfully with coworkers who have different work styles and personality types.

Jeannie Davis, *Beyond "Hello": A Practical Guide for Excellent Telephone Communication and Quality Customer Service*, Aurora, CO: Now Hear This, 2000.

> A best-selling book devoted to communications over the telephone. Although intended for a wider audience, contains useful information for call center support providers.

Chapter Four: Troubleshooting Computer Problems

Web Resources

Page	Resource	URL
110	Digisoft Web site on scripts	**www.digisoft.com/solutions/telescript/ ts-scripting.htm**

Page	Resource	URL
110	Example scripts in graphical format	www.extremetech.com/article2/ 0,3973,16621,00.asp support.mfm.com/support/troubleshooting/ copyprot.html
112	Online bookseller Amazon.com Web site	www.Amazon.com
112	Online bookseller Barnes and Noble Web site	www.barnesandnoble.com
112	Online bookseller Jim's Computer Books Web site	jimsbooks.vstorecomputers.com
112	Microsoft Press troubleshooting series Web page	www.microsoft.com/mspress/troubleshooting/ default.asp
112	Microsoft Web knowledge base	support.microsoft.com/default.aspx
113	Google search engine Web site	www.google.com
113	Dogpile search engine Web site	www.Dogpile.com
114	TechRepublic Web site for support professionals	www.techrepublic.com
114	About.com Web site with connections to support professionals	www.about.com
114	Cyber Tech Help Web site	www.cybertechhelp.com/forums/index.php
114	List of Internet ListServs	www.lsoft.com
115	Technical support provider Stream International's Web site	www.stream.com/Stream.nsf
116	Expertcity GoToAssist product Web site	www.gotoassist.com
116	LapLink Gold Classic Web site	laplink.com
116	Symantec pcAnywhere Web site	www.symantec.com/pcanywhere/Consumer
116	NetOp Remote Control white paper	www.crossteccorp.com/support/resources/ NetOpWP.pdf (requires Adobe Reader)
116	Symantec System Works Web site	www.symantec.com/sabu/sysworks/basic
116	PC Certify's Web site	www.pccertify.com
116	Touchstone Software Web site for WinCheckIt diagnostic utility	www.touchstonesoftware.com
116	MetaQuest Web site for Triage software utilities	www.metaquest.com/Web/Products/Triage/ triage.htm
116	PC Surgeon Web site	www.winutils.com/pcsurg.htm
117	Symantec Norton Ghost Web site	www.symantec.com/sabu/ghost/ghost_personal
117	InCharge utilities Web site	www.smarts.com/products
117	SolarWinds.NET Web site	www.solarwinds.net/Tools/Standard/index.htm
126	*ComputerWorld* publication Web site	www.computerworld.com
126	*InformationWeek* publication Web site	www.informationweek.com
126	*InfoWorld* publication Web site	www.infoworld.com

Page	Resource	URL
133	Microsoft troubleshooter for Windows 98 printer problems	support.microsoft.com/default.aspx?scid=/support/windows/tshoot/printing98/default.asp
137	Web site for OtherFolder Windows utility	www.annoyances.org/exec/software/anyfoldr

A1

Other Resources

Morgan D. Jones, *The Thinker's Toolkit*, New York: Three Rivers Press, 1998.

> This book describes 14 problem-solving techniques. Although not specific to computer troubleshooting, many of the strategies Jones describes amplify the approaches in this chapter.

Fred Nichols, *Solution Engineering: Choosing the Right Problem Solving Approach*, online version of an article "Yes, It Makes A Difference," *Quality Progress*, January, 1997; see **home.att.net/~nickols/makesdif.htm**.

> Nichols says the problem-solving approach one takes should depend on the nature of the problem to be solved. He provides several examples to illustrate different problem-solving approaches. Although not all examples are related to computer users, his thoughts on problem solving are useful.

Jean Andrews, *A+ Guide To Managing and Maintaining Your PC*, 4th Comprehensive edition, Boston, MA: Course Technology, 2003.

> This textbook covers most aspects of PC hardware, systems, and peripherals, including troubleshooting problems.

David Dick, *The P.C. Support Handbook*, Prestwick, UK: Dumbreck Publishing, 1998.

> This book covers basic configuration and installation information, as well as chapters on PC support, selecting a computer, and upgrading a computer.

Mark Minasi, *The Complete PC Upgrade & Maintenance Guide, 15th edition*, San Francisco: Sybex, 2004.

> This best-selling book covers PC hardware assembly, components, installation, upgrades, maintenance, and troubleshooting.

Steven Sagman, *Troubleshooting Microsoft Windows*, Redmond, WA: Microsoft Press, 2000.

Jerry Joyce and Marianne Moon, *Troubleshooting Microsoft Windows 2000 Professional*, Redmond, WA: Microsoft Press, 2000.

Steven Sagman, *Troubleshooting Microsoft Windows XP*, Redmond, WA: Microsoft Press, 2001.

> From Microsoft Press's troubleshooting series, these three books contain useful information and pointers on common problems with various Microsoft operating systems, how to diagnose them, and how to repair them.

Kate Chase, *A Guide to Microsoft Office 2000: Troubleshooting & Problem Solving*, Boston, MA: Course Technology, 2000.

This textbook is aimed at help desk personnel who need to troubleshoot problems with Microsoft Office 2000 applications.

Support staff who have primary responsibility for one or more Microsoft Office applications products should know about Microsoft Press's troubleshooting series for Access, Excel, Front Page, Outlook, and Project. Visit **www.microsoft.com/mspress/troubleshooting**.

CHAPTER FIVE: COMMON SUPPORT PROBLEMS

Web Resources

Page	Resource	URL
141	Monarch Computer Systems Web site on hard disk compatibility problems	www.monarchcomputer.com/Merchant2/merchant.mv?Screen=CTGY&Store_Code=M&Category_Code=HDFAQ
141	Microsoft Windows Catalog of XP-compatible devices	www.microsoft.com/windows/catalog/default.aspx?subid=22&xslt=hardware
141	Webopedia glossary entry for DIP switches	webopedia.internet.com/TERM/D/DIP_switch.html
141	Webopedia glossary entry for jumper pins	webopedia.internet.com/TERM/j/jumper.html
141	Universal Plug and Play Forum Web site	xml.coverpages.org/upnp.html
144	InstallShield Web site	www.installshield.com/default.asp
144	Microsoft Web site on compatibility of application software	www.microsoft.com/windows/appcompatibility/default.mspx
145	VCOM System Commander dual-boot utility Web site	www.v-com.com/product/sc7_ind.html
145	Shareware Web sites	www.tucows.com www.jumbo.com www.shareware.com download.com
146	Winguides tutorial on Windows Registry basics	www.winguides.com/article.php?id=1&guide=registry
146	Utility tools to modify and restore the Windows Registry	www.winsite.com/tech/reg
154	About.com site for general troubleshooting	pcsupport.about.com/cs/pctroubleshooting/index.htm
154	Dr. Tech fee-based site for general troubleshooting via phone or Web	www.askdrtech.com/default.asp
154	Computer Architect Web site for general troubleshooting via e-mail	www.computerarchitect.com/ask_find/askus2.cfm

A1

Page	Resource	URL
155	The PC Guide Web site for hardware troubleshooting	**www.pcguide.com/ts/index.htm**
155	PC Mechanic Web site for hardware troubleshooting	**www.pcmech.com/guides.htm**
155	Tom's Hardware Guide for hardware troubleshooting	**www.tomshardware.com**
155	MacintoshOS.com Web site for troubleshooting MacOS systems	**www.macintoshos.com/troubleshooting/ troubleshooting.html**
155	InfiniSource Web site for troubleshooting Windows systems	**www.windows-help.net/index.shtml**
155	Microsoft product support center for operating system and applications software	**support.microsoft.com**
155	Web site articles on problems with Windows operating system and applications software	**www.all-windows.com/index.html**
155	Google search engine Web site	**www.google.com**
155	Ask Jeeves search engine Web site	**www.ask.com**
155	ZDnet product and troubleshooting Web site	**www.zdnet.com**
155	About.com moderated Web sites on computer topics	**www.about.com/compute**
163	Dell knowledge base article on time loss on Dell systems	**support.ap.dell.com/ap/en/kb/document.asp? DN=HO1016518#har**
164	NIST Web site to download NISTIME time synchronization utility	**www.boulder.nist.gov/timefreq/service/its.htm**

Other Resources

Microsoft Press publishes Resource Kits with troubleshooting and problem-solving information for a variety of its popular operating system and applications software products. The Resource Kits often contain information that is highly technical. Microsoft Press also publishes a series of troubleshooting books on various products that contain less technical information than the Resource Kits. For information on titles available, see **www.microsoft.com/mspress/troubleshooting**.

Osborne McGraw-Hill (**www.osborne.com**) and Que (**www.quepublishing.com**) are two trade book publishers that provide guides on popular operating systems and applications software. Their books frequently contain information helpful to support specialists who are looking for troubleshooting resources.

Greg Tomsho, *Guide to Network Support and Troubleshooting*, Boston, MA: Course Technology, 2002.

> Tomsho's book covers troubleshooting common problems with peer-to-peer and server-based networks, as well as hardware and Transport layer problems.

Steve Litt, *Troubleshooting Techniques of the Successful Technologist*, ISBN 0-9724825-1-2, available through Troubleshooting.Com Bookstore at **www.troubleshooters.com/ bookstore/order.htm**.

> This book describes the 10 steps in a strategy Litt calls the universal troubleshooting process. His Web site, **www.troubleshooters.com/tuni.htm**, contains excerpts and tutorials from his book and courseware.

Several Web sites provide lists and databases of popular hardware and software vendors with links to their Web sites. Some of the more comprehensive lists can be found at:

- **www.slac.stanford.edu/comp/vendor/vendor.html**
- **guide.sbanetweb.com**
- **www.barbneal.com/vendors.asp**
- **www.compinfo-center.com**

These links to vendor Web sites are useful, because vendor sites frequently offer troubleshooting and problem-solving information for their customers and support professionals.

WinPlanet's Web site at **www.winplanet.com/winplanet/tutorials** includes several short tutorials on topics of common interest to troubleshooters (see the list at the bottom of the home page).

CHAPTER SIX: HELP DESK OPERATION

Web Resources

Page	Resource	URL
174	TriActive white papers on help desk staffing and operating procedures	www.triactive.com/demo/whitepapers/pdfs/ BP_HelpDesk_Staffing.pdf www.triactive.com/ demo/whitepapers/pdfs/ optimizing_help_desk.pdf (requires Adobe Reader)
182	Mary Baldwin College incident management procedure	academic.mbc.edu/cis/policy/Acceptable_ Use_Policy_Nov2001.html#5.0%20Computer% 20and%20Telephone%20User%20Support
182	University of Connecticut Law School help desk procedures	www.law.uconn.edu/infosys/sla.htm
183	Tutorial on telephone headsets and help desk productivity	telecom.hellodirect.com/docs/Tutorials/ Productivity.1.080701.asp

Page	Resource	URL
183	Results.About.com Web site on job stress	results.about.com/stress/#1
187	Remedy Help Desk software Web site	www.remedy.com/solutions/servicemgmt/help_desk.htm
187	Peregrine ServiceCenter help desk software Web site	www.peregrine.com/us/Products/ServiceManagement/ServiceCenter/default.htm
187	Magic Solutions Service Desk software Web site	www.networkassociates.com/us/products/magic/magic_service_desk.htm
187	Clientele for Help Desks Web site	www.coastalsoftware.com/products/clientele/helpdesks/index.htm
187	HEAT help desk software Web site	www.frontrange.com/heat
187	HelpTrac software Web site	www.helptrac.com
187	Track-It! help desk Web site	www.itsolutions.intuit.com/default.asp
187	Manage-IT! help desk software Web site	www.baronsoftware.com
187	Soffront Customer Helpdesk Web site	www.soffront.com/crm/Products/CustomerHelpdesk.asp
187	BridgeTrak help desk software Web site	www.helpdesksoftware.com/default.htm
187	Yahoo directory of help desk software vendors	dir.yahoo.com/Business_and_Economy/Business_to_Business/Corporate_Services/Customer_Service/Software/Help_Desk
187	eHelpDesk white papers on help desk software evaluation and selection	www.helpdesksoftware.net/library.html
187	TechRepublic call-tracking software evaluation tool kit	techrepublic.com.com/5129-6249-10219695.html
191	Nortel Network Web site for ACD products	www.nortelnetworks.com/products/01/norstar/call_centers/minuet.html
191	Database Systems Web site for ACD products	www.databasesystemscorp.com/psacd.htm
191	*Call Center Magazine* article on ACD systems	www.callcentermagazine.com/article/CCM20000727S0006
192	International Engineering Consortium's tutorial on IVR technology	www.iec.org/online/tutorials/speech_enabled/index.html
193	HelpDesk Expert for IT Support video demonstration	www.helpdesk-expert-it-support.com/demo.html
193	IBM Web-based support site	www.ibm.com/support/us
194	Online article and tutorial on intranets	www.intranetroadmap.com/default.cfm
195	*BusinessWeek* article "The New Global Job Shift"	www.businessweek.com/magazine/content/03_05/b3818001.htm
195	*ComputerWorld* article "Exporting IT Jobs"	www.computerworld.com/managementtopics/outsourcing/story/0,10801,80661,00.html

Page	Resource	URL
205	Gateway computer user support Web site	**support.gateway.com/support/default.asp**
205	Adobe software user support Web site	**www.adobe.com/support/main.html**
205	Symantec user support Web site	**www.symantec.com/techsupp/index.html**
205	Alamo Community College's support Web site	**www.accd.edu/is2/support**
207	Monarch Bay Web site for HelpTrac software	**www.monarchbay.com/htweb/HelpTrac.dll**

Other Resources

Dione McBride, *A Guide to Help Desk Technology, Tools & Techniques*, Boston, MA: Course Technology, 2000.

> McBride's textbook focuses on the technology, tools, and techniques used to run an effective help desk operation. The book covers several software options available for tracking and managing the stream of incidents that confront help desk staff.

Barbara Czegel, *Help Desk Practitioner's Handbook*, New York: John Wiley & Sons, 1998.

> Czegel's book describes the operation of a help desk, the role and structure of help desk operations in organizations, managing help desk problems, the role of communications in problem solving, help desk tools, and management of help desk operations.

Barbara Czegel, *Technical Support on the Web: Designing and Maintaining an Effective E-Support Site*, New York: John Wiley & Sons, 2000.

> This Czegel book focuses on how to set up a Web site to provide technical support. It includes examples to illustrate best practices in e-support.

Madeline Locke's article, *Helping Your Help Desk: Seven Considerations to Increase Effectiveness*, available online at **www.tmcnet.com/tmcnet/articles/imi1298.htm**.

An Open Directory Web site provides links to vendors who sell help desk products; see the vendor links at **www.dmoz.org/Computers/Software/Help_Desk**.

Help Desk World offers a tutorial on help desk operation and an opportunity to download a help desk software product at **www.help-desk-world.com**.

CHAPTER SEVEN: USER SUPPORT MANAGEMENT

Web Resources

Page	Resource	URL
213	Help Desk Institute criteria for help desk evaluation	**www.thinkhdi.com/files/pdfs/Support CenterCert.pdf** (requires Adobe Reader)

Page	Resource	URL
213	Westbay Engineers support center staffing calculator	www.erlang.com
215	Keith Geddes & Associates help desk aptitude and skills test vendor	www.pcskillstests.com/Testing/techsupport.html
215	Walden Personnel Testing help desk aptitude and skills test vendor	www.waldentesting.com/tests/tests.htm
215	Sample interview questions download	www.ksasystems.com/cgi-local/prolink2.cgi? link=iq990701
217	Jeff Davis' TechRepublic article on help desk training	www.techrepublic.com/article.jhtml?id= r00320010612jed01.htm
217	Jeff Dray's TechRepublic article on help desk training	www.techrepublic.com/article.jhtml?id= r00320030415dra01.htm
223	Microsoft Project 2003 Web site	www.microsoft.com/office/project/prodinfo/ default.mspx
223	Kidasa Milestones Simplicity 2002 Web site	www.kidasa.com/Simplicity/index.html
226	Project Management Institute Web site for project managers	www.pmi.org
227	Microsoft certification Web site	www.microsoft.com/traincert/mcp/default.asp
227	Cisco certification Web site	www.cisco.com/en/US/learning/index.html
227	Novell certification Web sites	www.novell.com/training/certinfo/cna/index.html www.novell.com/training/certinfo/cne/index.html
227	Oracle certification Web site	www.oracle.com/education/certification
227	Sun Microsystems certification Web site	www.sun.com/dev/certification
228	Listing of product vendors' certification Web sites	certification.about.com/cs/vendorsites
228	CompTIA Web site on A+, Network+, Project+, and other vendor-neutral certifications	www.comptia.org
228	Chauncey Group Web site for Associate Technology Specialist certification	www.chauncey.com/Services/ATS.htm
228	Institute for Certification of Computing Professionals (ICCP) Web site	www.iccp.org/iccpnew/acp.html
228	Linux certification Web site	www.lpi.org

Page	Resource	URL
229	Society of Internet Professionals certification Web site	www.sipgroup.org/certification.html
229	Help Desk Institute certification Web site	www.thinkhdi.com/certification/individualCertification
229	Help Desk 2000 certification Web site	www.stiknowledge.com/certification_advisory/courses.asp
231	MindLeaders online training and certification courses	link.mindleaders.com/e-learn/courseprice.jsp?
231	Netwind Learning Center online training and certification courses	www.netwind.com/index.html
231	InfoSource online training and certification courses	www.infosourcetraining.com
231	Specialized Solutions online training and certification courses	www.quickcert.com/ittraininglibrary.htm
231	Aaron's Computer Training online training and certification courses	www.aarons-computer-training.com/index.htm
231	LearnThat.com online training and certification courses	www.learnthat.com/courses
231	Open Directory Web site with links to other training and certification vendors	dmoz.org/Computers/Education/Certification
232	informIT Exam Cram 2 Web site	www.informit.com/examcram2
232	Article on computer adaptive testing (CAT)	www.winnetmag.com/Articles/Index.cfm?ArticleID=5694
232	Brainbench.com Web site for Computer Technical Support online certification test	www.brainbench.com/xml/bb/common/testcenter/taketest.xml?testId=68
232	Transcender Web site for certification pretest assessment exams	www.transcender.com
232	John Norby's MCDST certification Webcast	www.microsoft.com/usa/webcasts/ondemand/2378.asp (requires free download of InterWise Participant Software)
233	Microsoft MCDST certification Web site	www.microsoft.com/traincert/mcp/mcdst
234	ITAA's study of the demand for technology workers	www.itaa.org/workforce/studies/03execsumm.pdf (requires Adobe Reader)
234	Help Desk Institute home page for support professionals	www.thinkhdi.com
234	Help Desk 2000 home page for support professionals	www.stiknowledge.com/helpdesk2000/index.asp
234	Association of Support Professionals home page	www.asponline.com
234	Information Technology Association of American home page	www.itaa.org

Page	Resource	URL
234	Service and Support Professionals Association home page	www.supportgate.com
234	Network and Systems Professionals Association home page	www.naspa.com
235	ITAA code of ethical standards	www.itaa.org/itserv/ethics.htm
235	Association of Information Technology Professionals standards of conduct	www.aitp.org/organization/about/conduct/conduct.jsp
236	*ComputerWorld* 2003 IT salary survey	www.computerworld.com/careertopics/careers/salarysurvey2003/home.
236	Salary.com Web site wizard for industry salary data	www.salary.com
236	TechRepublic article on help desk morale and retention	techrepublic.com.com/5100-6269-5088913.html
242	Brainbench Web site offering free online certification exam	www.brainbench.com

A1

Other Resources

Barbara Czegel, *Running an Effective Help Desk, 2nd edition*, New York: John Wiley, 1998.

> Czegel's book is one of the most popular books on help desk management. It covers how managers can plan, organize, staff, and market a help desk operation. It also provides practical information on how to make a help desk operation more efficient and effective through automation of tasks and performance measurement.

Noel Bruton, *How to Manage the IT Help Desk, 2nd edition*, Boston, MA: Butterworth-Heinemann, 2002.

> Bruton's book on help desk management is based on several years of industry experience and includes case studies to illustrate the main points. It covers justifying help desk expenses, gaining the support of top management, and motivating help desk staff.

Bob Wooten, *Building and Managing a World Class IT Help Desk*, New York, Osborne McGraw-Hill, 2001.

> Wooten's book describes how to set up and run an effective help desk operation, including help desk organization, staffing and staff development, problem handling procedures, budgeting, tools, and evaluating help desk operations.

Francoise Tourniaire and Richard Farrell, *The Art of Software Support: Design and Operation of Support Centers and Help Desks*, Englewood Cliffs, NJ: Prentice Hall, 1998.

> Tourniaire and Farrell's book is aimed primarily at managers of call centers that provide support for software packages. It includes information on call management, support performance measurement, support staff management, and tools to automate software support.

Microsoft Corporation, *Sourcebook for the Help Desk, 2nd edition*, Redmond, WA: Microsoft Press, 1997.

> A collection of help desk best practices from Microsoft's extensive experience providing user support. Provides managers with information on help desk organization, operation, management, and evaluation.

Trade publications with information useful to help desk professionals and managers include:

Publication	URL for Subscription Information and Article Archives
CC News	www.ccnews.com
Call Center Magazine	www.callcentermagazine.com
Certification Magazine	www.certmag.com
CIO Insight	www.cioinsight.com
Communications Convergence	www.cconvergence.com
Customer Inter@ctions	www.tmcnet.com/cis
SupportIndustry.com (via e-mail only)	www.supportindustry.com
Extensive list of computer trade publications	www.magazines.com/ncom/mag?subject=9

Chapter Eight: Product Evaluation Strategies and Standards

Web Resources

Page	Resource	URL
248	Article on computer industry standards	www.tiscali.co.uk/reference/dictionaries/computers/data/f0000190.html
248	History of Computing Project information on hardware and software vendors	www.thocp.net
254	Open Directory Web site lists popular trade publications	dmoz.org/Business/Retail_Trade/News_and_Media

A1

Page	Resource	URL
254	Google directory of business and trade publications	directory.google.com/Top/Business/Resources/ News_and_Media/Magazines
254	List of e-zines targeted at the computer industry	www.ezine-dir.com/Computers
255	*Computing Review* product reviews Web site	www.computingreview.com/reviewscrx.aspx
255	*InfoWorld* product comparison Web site	www.infoworld.com/testcenter/tst_rev_hom.html
255	*MacWorld* product review Web site	www.macworld.com/reviews
255	*MaximumPC* product review Web site	www.maximumpc.com/ranking/rankings2.html
255	*Network Computing* product buyer's guide Web site	www.networkcomputing.com/departments/ buyersguides.html
255	*PC Magazine* product buying guides	www.pcmag.com/category2/0,4148,13,00.asp
255	*PCWorld* product review Web site	www.pcworld.com/reviews/index/0,00.asp
255	*Smart Computing* product review Web site	www.smartcomputing.com/editorial/ productreview.asp?guid=xidt4kg0
255	Tom's Hardware Guide Web site	www.tomshardware.com
255	ZDnet product review Web site	reviews-zdnet.com.com
255	PCWorld.com ratings of CD-RW drives	www.pcworld.com/reviews/article/ 0,aid,110332,00.asp
255	ZDnet ratings of LCD monitors	reviews-zdnet.com.com/4521-6529_ 16-1008543-4.html?tag=txt
255	CNET.com notebook buying guide	reviews.cnet.com/4520-3121_7-1016082-1. html?tag=cal
255	Search Engine Showdown comparison of Internet search engines	www.searchengineshowdown.com/features
255	*PC Magazine* article on software to write PDF files	www.pcmag.com/article2/0,4149,1190639,00.asp
255	*PCWorld* article comparing tax preparation software	www.pcworld.com/reviews/article/0,aid, 108208,00.asp
256	Web site to run evaluation copies of software packages	www.runaware.com/list_alpha.jsp
257	PayChex Web site for payroll outsource services	www.paychex.com
259	*Byte Magazine* article on benchmarking	www.byte.com/bmark/bmark.htm
259	BAPCO Web site on benchmarks	www.bapco.com
259	PassMark Software Web site on reliability testing	www.passmark.com

Page	Resource	URL
259	SPEC Web site on benchmark tests	www.specbench.org
259	VeriTest Web site on benchmarks	www.etestinglabs.com/benchmarks/bwinstone/bwinstone.asp
260	Article illustrating weighted point method for selecting software and services	www.softwaremag.com/L.cfm?Doc=archive/2000aug/Selecting-a-Partner.html
261	Selection criteria used at UCLA	www.itpb.ucla.edu/Documents/2001/Jan/Matrix-ComputerPrinterSrvcsRFP.htm
263	Web site to download DecideRight software	www.pcworld.com/downloads/file_description/0,fid,3971,00.asp
264	RFP procedure manual for North Carolina State University	www.fis.ncsu.edu/materialsmgmt/purchasing/proposal.htm
264	Sample RFP for personal computers in St. Charles County, Missouri	www.win.org/county/bids/misequip.htm
264	RFP to develop a Web site for Shoreline, Washington	www.mrsc.org/RFPs/S55WebRFP.pdf (requires Adobe Reader)
267	Honolulu Community College list of product standards	www.hcc.hawaii/itc/recommend
270	"Acceptable Use of Computing Resources" at University of Oregon	cc.uoregon.edu/policy/index.html
271	Evaluator for Windows XP readiness	www.pcpitstop.com/xpready/xptests.asp
271	Microsoft Windows XP compatibility evaluator	www.microsoft.com/windowsxp/home/howtobuy/upgrading/checkcompat.asp
276	Bytemark benchmark utility download	www.byte.com/bmark/bmark.htm
276	Web site for System Analyzer benchmark utility	www.sysanalyser.com
276	Xmark benchmark utility download	www.dacris.com/bmarknet
278	Moocher Web site to download file splitter utilities	www.moochers.com/index.html?w95split.html
279	Online survey Web sites	www.surveymonkey.com www.createsurvey.com
281	Information on how to write an RFP	www.webdevelopersjournal.com/columns/writerfp.html www.internettraining.com/6art2.htm www.esj.com/features/article.asp?EditorialsID=122
281	Example Web site design RFPs	www.ahrd.org/docs03/siteRFP.pdf www.mrsc. org/rfps/C52rfpweb.pdf (requires Adobe Reader)

Other Resources

Bud Porter-Roth *Request for Proposal: A Guide to Effective RFP Development*, Boston, MA: Addison Wesley, 2001.

> This handbook describes how to plan and prepare an RFP. It covers how to write specifications for technical and managerial aspects of an acquisition project. It also describes how to manage the RFP process and evaluate the resulting proposals.

Digital Buying Guide 2004, Yonkers, NY: Consumer Reports Books, 2003.

Consumer Guide to Computers and Computer Hardware; online at **products.consumerguide. com/cp/electronics/background/index.cfm/id/11157**.

> Although these consumer guides are aimed at home computer users, they contain useful information for small businesses that are evaluating the features and prices of computer components.

Dave's Guide to Buying a Computer at **www.css.msu.edu/PC-Guide/PC-Guide1. cfm** explains the most common purchase options and alternatives in easy-to-understand language.

To help evaluate the reliability of hardware product vendors who sell via the Internet, visit a Web site that publishes ratings of Internet vendors at **www.resellerratings.com**.

CHAPTER NINE: USER NEEDS ANALYSIS AND ASSESSMENT

Web Resources

Page	Resource	URL
288	Geary Rummler's project feasibility guide	**www.performancexpress.org/0304/images/ Project_Feasibility_Guide.pdf** (requires Adobe Reader)
294	Microsoft Web site for Visio, a diagramming and planning tool	**office.microsoft.com/home/office.aspx? assetid=FX01085798**
294	Novagraph Web site for Chartist, a shareware diagramming tool	**www.novagraph.com**
301	End user training needs assessment Web site	**adulted.about.com/cs/trngneedsasst**
306	University of Minnesota Web site on project charters	**www.extension.umn.edu/projects/mentor/plan/ plan2.asp**
306	Project charter template	**www.ce.umn.edu/~smith/MOT8221/ charterform.pdf** (requires Adobe Reader)
307	Mind Tools Web site on cost-benefits analysis	**www.mindtools.com/pages/article/ newTED_08.htm**
312	Georgia Tech Web site on questionnaire design	**www.cc.gatech.edu/classes/cs6751_97_winter/ Topics/quest-design**

Page	Resource	URL
312	Flowcharting Center tutorial on flowcharting	**www.smartdraw.com/resources/centers/flowcharts**
314	Texas A&M Web site on graphical tools, including H-I-P-O charts	**acct.tamu.edu/smith/system_tools/systools.htm**
315	Example of a prototyping tool for Web page design	**guir.Berkeley.edu/projects/denim**

Other Resources

Laura Connelly, *Needs Assessment and Project Planning*, Boston, MA: Pearson Custom Publishing, 2000.

> Connelly's book is a good resource for information on methods and tools for assessing user needs described in this chapter. It covers topics such as feasibility analysis, capturing information, documenting user needs, training users, and benchmarking.

Kendall and Kendall, *Systems Analysis and Design, 5th edition*, Englewood Cliffs, NJ: Prentice Hall, 2001.

Gary B. Shelly, Thomas J. Cashman, and Harry Rosenblatt, *Systems Analysis and Design, 5th edition*, Boston, MA: Course Technology, 2003.

> Both of these books are examples of standard college textbooks used in systems analysis and design courses. While they focus primarily on the design and development of software systems, many of the methods and tools covered in these books and courses apply equally to the analysis and assessment of end-user computing needs.

Dan Gookin, *Buying a Computer for Dummies, 2004 edition*, New York: John Wiley & Sons, 2003.

Preston Gralla and Wendy Taylor, *Complete Idiot's Guide to Buying a Computer*, Indianapolis, IN: Que, 1999.

> These two trade books are designed primarily for first-time computer purchasers. They describe the user needs assessment process from a user perspective and provide sample questions that often arise during a needs analysis project. Support specialists often recommend books like these to end users who want to know more about the PC-purchasing process.

See also the computer buyer guides listed in the resources for Chapter 8.

CHAPTER TEN: INSTALLING END-USER COMPUTER SYSTEMS

Web Resources

Page	Resource	URL
334	K-Log computer furniture vendor Web site	www.k-log.com
338	Explanation of advantages and disadvantages of ergonomic devices	www.office-ergo.com/pros&.htm
338	Heller's guide to ergonomic furniture and accessories	www.worksiteinternational.com/downloads/ excerpt.PDF (requires Adobe Reader)
338	*BusinessWeek* article on assistive devices by John M. Williams	www.businessweek.com/bwdaily/dnflash/ dec1999/ nf91229c.htm
338	Ergoteam Web site on ergonomics	www.ergoteam.net/ergoinfo
338	Cornell University Web site on ergonomics	ergo.human.cornell.edu
340	CherryLand Electric Web site on surge suppressors	www.cherrylandelectric.com/memberprograms/ surgeqa.cfm
342	EPA Web site on Halon gas fire suppression systems	www.epa.gov/Ozone/snap/fire/qa.html
342	HARC Web site on alternatives to Halon fire suppression systems	www.harc.org/index.html
348	Webopedia online computer glossary	webopedia.internet.com/Hardware
348	*The PC Guide* Web site on computer hardware components	www.pcguide.com
349	Publisher of *PC Pocket Reference*	www.sisweb.com/books/pcrefer.htm
353	Microsoft Web site for testing compatibility of hardware	www.microsoft.com/whdc/hwtest/default.mspx
353	Lists of hardware devices compatible with Microsoft operating systems	www.microsoft.com/whdc/hcl/search.mspx
368	PC911 online tutorial on UPS systems	www.pcnineoneone.com/howto/ups1.html
368	*The PC Guide* Web site on UPS systems	www.pcguide.com/ref/power/ext/ups
368	D. E. Levine's tutorial on UPSs	www.winplanet.com/winplanet/tutorials/3358/1
368	NIST Internet Time Service Web site	boulder.nist.gov/timefreq/service/its.htm

Other Resources

Rob Tidrow, *Windows 98 Installation and Configuration Handbook*, Indianapolis, IN: Que, 1998.

> Tidrow's book describes installing and configuring Windows 98 systems. It includes chapters on the operating system, various hardware devices, and some applications software.

Jim Boyce, *Microsoft Windows 2000 Professional Installation and Configuration Handbook*, Indianapolis, IN: Que, 2000.

> Boyce's book is similar in topic coverage to Tidrow's, but covers Windows 2000.

Ed Bott and Carl Siechert, *Microsoft Windows XP Inside and Out*, Redmond, WA: Microsoft Press, 2001.

> Bott and Siechert's book is an installation and configuration resource for Windows XP.

Bruce Hallberg, *Networking: A Beginner's Guide, Third Edition*, McGraw-Hill Osborne Media, 2002.

> Hallberg's introductory networking book covers installation and configuration of Novell NetWare 5, Windows 2000 Server, and Linux server.

Joli Ballew, *Windows 2000 Server On Site*, Phoenix, AZ: Paraglyph Press, 2002.

> Ballew's book is an introduction to the installation of a network in a business environment. It includes worksheets to aid in planning, check lists for hardware and project management, and decision trees to help make important network configuration decisions.

Barry Press and Marcia Press, *PC Upgrade and Repair Bible, 3rd edition*, New York: John Wiley, 1999.

> This book covers the installation and configuration of hardware components and networking features.

Many vendor Web sites include information on how to install and configure their products. For example, for information on Office 2003 deployment in an organization, see Microsoft's TechNet Web site at **www.microsoft.com/technet/prodtechnol/office/office2003/default.asp**.

CHAPTER ELEVEN: TRAINING COMPUTER USERS

Web Resources

Page	Resource	URL
372	Don Clark's glossary of training terms	www.nwlink.com/~donclark/hrd/glossary.html
382	Canadian government Web site on learning styles	www.jobsetc.ca/content_pieces.jsp?category_id=325&lang=e
382	Diablo Valley College online survey on learning styles	www.metamath.com/lsweb/dvclearn.htm
382	Paragon Learning Style Inventory	www.oswego.edu/Candl/plsi/index.htm
383	Alice Christudason's online article on peer learning	www.cdtl.nus.edu.sg/success/sl37.htm
385	OSHA guidelines for "Presenting Effective Presentations with Visual Aids"	www.osha.gov/doc/outreachtraining/htmlfiles/traintec.html
385	Example multimedia presentation on using Visual Basic with Excel	www.vtc.com/products/vb-excel.htm (requires QuickTime; available for download at www.apple.com/quicktime/download)
385	Example of a reference sheet for HTML	hotwired.lycos.com/webmonkey/reference/html_cheatsheet/index.html
385	Example of a reference sheet for UNIX operating system commands	www.washington.edu/computing/unix/unixqr.html
386	Buyer's guide for LCD and DLP projectors	www.projectorcentral.com/buyers_guide.cfm
386	University of Sydney tutorial "An Introduction to the World Wide Web"	www.usyd.edu.au/su/course
387	University of Idaho resources on the case study method	www.uidaho.edu/ag/agecon/391/casestudmeth.html
387	Web site on role playing	mentalhelp.net/psyhelp/chap13/chap13b.htm
388	Example of a Web-based training session at the DigitalThink Web site	www.digitalthink.com/els/samplers.html
389	Susan Heathfield's article on trends in training and worker development	humanresources.about.com/library/weekly/aa011502a.htm
390	SCinc Web site on training programs for help desk agents	www.scinc.net
397	Chapter on "Polishing Your Presentation Skills" from Loretta Weiss-Morris' book.	www.systemsliteracy.com/QTTBook-Chapter2.pdf (requires Adobe Reader)

Page	Resource	URL
398	Mary Ann Richardson's article, "Design Your Own Hands-On Tests to Get an Accurate Skills Assessment"	techrepublic.com.com/5100-6317-5032079.html
398	Jeff Davis' article, "Help Your Help Desk Analysts Become Technical Trainers"	techrepublic.com.com/5100-6263-1043810.html (includes link to download TechRepublic's Technical Trainer's Toolkit)
398	Karen Cangero's article, "The Economics of Web-based Training"	techrepublic.com.com/5100-6317-5025200.html
398	Ann Margaret Kearney's article, "Real-world Advice for the New Tech Trainer"	techrepublic.com.com/5100-6317-1033253.html
398	Ellen Birkett Morris's article, "Tips for Developing a Trainer Evaluation Process"	techrepublic.com.com/5100-6317-5032065.html
398	J. Galimi and J. Furlonger's article, "Critical Success Factors for Various Learning Methods"	techrepublic.com.com/5100-6317-5032121.html
398	Marsha Glick's article, "Twelve Steps for Designing Effective Training Programs"	techrepublic.com.com/5100-6317-5032124.html
399	Sun Microsystems' white paper on learning management systems	suned.sun.com/US/images/Edu_LMS_wp.pdf (requires Adobe Reader)
399	Ziiva vendor Web site resource on learning management systems	www.ziiva.com/lms.htm
404	University of Texas tutorial on copyrights	www.lib.utsystem.edu/copyright
405	Example WebCT learning management courses	www.webct.com/workbench/viewpage? name=workbench_goto
406	Soloman and Felder Web site questionnaire on the Index of Learning Styles	www2.ncsu.edu/unity/lockers/users/f/felder/ public/ILSpage.html

Other Resources

Loretta Weiss–Morris, *Quick Training Tips: How to Teach Computing Skills to Practically Anyone,* Hopatcong, NJ: Systems Literacy, 2004.

> This book focuses on computer training. It offers techniques for training both beginning and advanced users, as well as "difficult" trainees. The author covers how to set up a training room and use online resources. She offers a preview chapter on "Polishing Your Presentation Skills" at **www.systemsliteracy.com/ QTTBook–Chapter2.pdf** (requires Adobe Reader).

A1

Ruth Stiehl, *The Outcomes Primer, 2nd edition*, Richmond, BC: Strategic Concepts, 2002.

>Stiehl's book explains how to design a training curriculum with specific learner-centered performance outcomes.

Eliane Weiss, *The Accidental Trainer: You Know Computers, So They Want You to Teach Everyone Else*, San Francisco: Jossey-Bass, 1996.

>Weiss's book is aimed at people with good computer skills who are asked to provide training to others. It offers practical suggestions on teaching adult learners about technology.

Paul Clothier, *The Complete Computer Trainer*, New York: McGraw-Hill, 1996.

>Clothier's book offers strategies for designers, presenters, and evaluators of computer training. It includes chapters on how to handle difficult learners and on tools for trainers.

Elliot Massie, et al., *The Computer Training Handbook: Strategies for Helping People Learn Technology*, Minneapolis, MN: Lakewood Publications, 1998.

>Massie's book is a good resource of ideas for trainers who provide technology training to adult learners.

Trade publications with information useful to technology trainers include:

Publication	URL for subscription information and article archives
Presentations	www.presentations.com
Syllabus	www.syllabus.com
T.H.E Journal	www.thejournal.com
Training	www.trainingmag.com
Training & Development	www.astd.org/astd/publications/td_magazine

A company that offers seminars specifically designed to train help desk employees is TechLink Training. See a list of their seminar offerings at **www.tltraining.com/toc.htm**.

A Web site devoted to links to free or low cost computer education, training materials, and tutorials is **www.intelinfo.com/pubs.html**.

Chapter Twelve: Writing for End Users

Web Resources

Page	Resource	URL
411	Home page for TechRepublic E-newsletters	techrepublic.com.com

Page	Resource	URL
411	Pacific Northwest National Laboratory Web site about online newsletters	www.pnl.gov/er_news/stc/stc.htm
413	Mary Houten-Kemp's e-mail etiquette Web site	everythingemail.net/email_help_tips.html
413	Web site with links to user-nominated worst-of-the-Web sites	www.worstoftheweb.com
414	Hewlett-Packard online trouble-shooting guide for DeskJet 682c inkjet printers	h20015.www2.hp.com/en/solveCategory.jhtml?reg=&lc=en&cc=us&prodId=dj682c&pagetype=solve
424	David A. McCurrey's Austin Community College online technical writing textbook	www.io.com/~hcexres/tcm1603/acchtml/acctoc.htm
424	The Technical Writer's Reference Page	www.angelfire.com/stars/techwriter
426	Example of a style sheet maintained by the English Teaching Forum	exchanges.state.gov/forum/stylesheet.htm
433	Paul Brians' Washington State University check list of common mistakes in language use	www.wsu.edu/~brians/errors
433	Gene Myer's Western Washington University list of writing errors to avoid	www.ac.wwu.edu/~gmyers/writeerr.html
433	Online version of Strunk and White's *Elements of Style*	www.bartleby.com/141
434	Adobe FrameMaker Web site	www.adobe.com/products/framemaker/main.html
434	WebWorks Publisher home page	www.webworks.com
435	Doc-To-Help Web page	www.componentone.com/products.aspx?ProductCode=1&ProductID=6
435	RoboHelp Web site	www.ehelp.com/products/robohelp

Other Resources

Microsoft Corporation, *The Microsoft Manual of Style for Technical Publications, 3rd edition*, Redmond, WA: Microsoft Press, 2003.

> Microsoft's style guide is an excellent resource for technical writers, whether for Microsoft products or others.

Alan Freedman, *Computer Desktop Encyclopedia, 9th edition*, New York: McGraw-Hill Osborne Media, 2001.

> Freedman's popular encyclopedia of over 10,000 computer terms includes a searchable CD.

A1

Lyn Dupre, *Bugs in Writing Revised: A Guide to Debugging Your Prose*, Reading, MA, Addison-Wesley, 1998.

Dupre's book describes a number of common problems technical writers experience and offers suggestions for writing improvement.

Rebecca E. Burnett, *Technical Communication, 5th edition*, Fort Worth, TX: Harcourt College Publishers, 2001.

An example of a well-respected textbook used frequently in college-level technical writing courses.

Michael Bremer, *UnTechnical Writing—How to Write About Technical Subjects and Products So Anyone Can Understand*, Concord, CA: UnTechnical Press, 1999.

A very readable book on making technical writing understandable.

Web sites with additional resources useful to technical writers include:

Resource	URL
PC Webopaedia online dictionary and glossary	www.pcwebopaedia.com
FOLDOC online dictionary	foldoc.doc.ic.ac.uk/foldoc/index.html
Rensselaer University Writing Center Web site with links to technical writing resources	webster.commnet.edu/writing/writing.htm

CHAPTER THIRTEEN: COMPUTER FACILITIES MANAGEMENT

Web Resources

Page	Resource	URL
454	Guardian Computer Support hardware repair services Web site	www.guardian-computer.com/home.html
457	NetworkClue.com Web site on electrical power problems and solutions	www.networkclue.com/hardware/power/index.php
457	Commercial Logic software trouble report form	www.cli-usa.com/powerpm/spr.htm
459	NLANR Web site on network performance monitoring	dast.nlanr.net/Guides/GettingStarted/Performance.html
459	Windows & .NET magazine article on network performance monitoring tools	www.winnetmag.com/WindowsServer2003/Index.cfm?ArticleID=37933
459	Links to network performance monitoring utility software	www.slac.stanford.edu/xorg/nmtf/nmtf-tools.html
463	Zone Labs Web site for firewall software	www.zonelabs.com

Page	Resource	URI
463	Sygate Web site for Personal Firewall	smb.sygate.com/products/spf_standard.htm
463	Microsoft Web site devoted to security of its products	www.microsoft.com/security
463	Microsoft MBSA security analyzer	www.microsoft.com/technet/security/tools/mbsahome.asp
463	Qualsys check for browser vulnerabilities	browsercheck.qualys.com
463	Symantec free Web-based virus checker	security.norton.com/default.asp?langid=us&venid=sym
464	Mirapoint Message Director software	www.mirapoint.com
466	Bryan Feltin's article on biometrics	www.giac.org/practical/Bryan_Feltin_GSEC.doc (requires Microsoft Word or viewer)
466	Home page for SC Magazine devoted to security issues	www.scmagazine.com
466	Home page for SCO magazine, a resource for security executives	www.csoonline.com
468	University of Toronto disaster plan guidelines and check lists	www.utoronto.ca/security/drp.htm
468	Example of disaster contingency plan at University of Arkansas	www.uark.edu/staff/drp
469	University of Minnesota check list of workstation ergonomics	www.dehs.umn.edu/ergo/office/checklist.html
471	Trial version of Tally Systems software audit tool	www.tallysystems.com/forms/bsaoffer/signup.html
472	ISSP Web site on physical security and controls	www.infosyssec.org/infosyssec/physfac1.htm
473	NIST Web site with download-able brochures on facilities management	csrc.nist.gov/publications/nistpubs
473	National Recycling Coalition of organizations that recycle and reuse computers	www.nrc-recycle.org/resources/electronics/search/getlisting.php
473	Wipe Drive utility Web site	www.whitecanyon.com/index.php
473	Darik's Boot and Nuke disk cleaner utility program	dban.sourceforge.net
473	Information about Dell's recycling program	www1.us.dell.com/content/topics/segtopic.aspx/dell_recycling?c=us&cs=19&l=en&s=dhs
475	Downloadable evaluation version of FileBack PC backup utility	www.maxoutput.com/FileBack
475	Downloadable trial version of WinBack backup utility	www.liutilities.com/products/winbackup
476	Dantz Web site on progressive backup advantages	www.dantz.com/docs/progressive_backups_brief.pdf (requires Adobe Reader)

Page	Resource	URL
479	Raxco white paper on media defragmentation	**www.raxco.com/products/perfectdisk2k/ whitepapers/defrag_tutorial.pdf** (requires Adobe Reader)
479	Information on Diskeeper Lite defrag utility	**www.boostware.com/hardware/harddisk/ diskeeper_lite.html**
479	Executive Software DKlite download site	**www1.execsoft.com/dklite.exe**
480	List of freeware and shareware disk cleanup utilities	**www.thesoftwaredirectory.8m.com/utilities/ disk_cleanup_tools.html**
480	McAfee QuickClean disk cleanup utility	**us.mcafee.com/root/product.asp?productid=qc3**
481	Action Office Supplies Web site	**www.actoff.com**
481	Amazon.com Web site	**www.amazon.com**
481	Boise Cascade Office Products Web site	**www.boiseoffice.com**
481	Cheap Office Supplies Web site	**www.cheapofficesupplies.com**
481	Clean Sweep Supply Web site	**www.cleansweepsupply.com/pages/ category0003.html**
481	eBay auction Web site	**www.ebay.com**
481	Global Computer Supplies Web site	**www.globalcomputor.com**
481	Keysan Web site	**www.keysan.com/ksu0173.htm**
481	Office Depot Web site	**www.officedepot.com**
481	OfficeMax Web site	**www.officemax.com**
481	PriceSCAN Web site	**www.pricescan.com/0103.asp**
481	Quill Web site	**www.quillcorp.com**
481	Staples Web site	**www.staples.com**
484	*The PC Guide* Web site on preventive maintenance of PCs	**www.pcguide.com/care/pm.htm**
484	A1 Computers Web site on preventive maintenance of PCs	**a1computers.net/pm.htm**
484	Clean Sweep Supply site for cleaning supplies	**www.cleansweepsupply.com/pages/ section0174.html**
485	IBM white paper on computer viruses	**www.research.ibm.com/antivirus**
485	Symantec antivirus home page	**www.symantec.com/nav/index.html**
485	McAfee antivirus home page	**us.mcafee.com/virusInfo/default.asp**
485	F-Secure antivirus home page	**www.f-secure.com/virus-info**
485	Freebyte Web site with links to free, shareware, and commercial antivirus software	**www.freebyte.com/antivirus**
486	Symantec AntiVirus Center Web site on hoaxes	**www.symantec.com/avcenter/hoax.html**
486	Example of virus hoax	**www.symantec.com/avcenter/venc/data/ jdbgmgr.exe.file.hoax.html**

Other Resources

Bill Holtsnider and Brian Jaffe, *IT Manager's Handbook: Getting Your New Job Done*, San Francisco: Morgan Kaufman, 2000.

> This book is aimed at new managers of information technology facilities. It discusses methods for dealing with hardware, software, network, facilities, and management problems.

Paul Linden, *Comfort At Your Computer: Body Awareness Training for Pain-Free Computer Use, 2nd edition*, Berkeley, CA: North Atlantic Books, 2000.

> A resource that describes the impact of various workstation problems on computer users and how to correct common problems.

Chris Brenton and Cameron Hunt, *Active Defense: A Comprehensive Guide to Network Security*, Alameda, CA: Sybex, 2001.

> A popular resource for support specialists responsible for security in a network environment. Covers the source of threats and tools to respond to them in virtual private networks (VPNs), as well as Windows, Linux, and Unix network environments.

Jon Toigo, *Disaster Recovery Planning: Strategies for Protecting Critical Information Assets, 3rd edition*, Upper Saddle River, NJ: Prentice-Hall, 2002.

> Toigo's book explains how to prepare for, cope with, and recover from a disaster or crisis in a facility. It covers PC, mainframe, and Internet perspectives, and describes how to prepare a disaster contingency plan to safeguard information assets.

Web sites with additional resources useful to computer facilities managers include:

Resource	URL
Guide Star Web site on customer satisfaction surveys	www.guidestarco.com/customer-satisfaction-questionnaires-howto.htm
Web site to obtain "The User Friendly Office" flier	www.officeorganix.com/UserFriendlyOrder.htm
Cisco Web site on benefits and support problems with workers who telecommute	www.cisco.com/warp/public/779/smbiz/netsolutions/find/alice/telecommuting
Industry white paper on chargeback systems for use accounting	www.unisol.com/papers/chargeback.html#SECTION_1
Article on ethical issues in employee monitoring	www.scu.edu/ethics/publications/iie/v9n2/brother.html

See also resource references in Chapter 10 for additional information on facilities management issues related to system installation.

2

ANSWERS TO
CHECK YOUR UNDERSTANDING

CHAPTER 1

1. True
2. a. mainframe computers
3. False
4. Information Systems or Information Services (IS) or Information Technology (IT)
5. d. distributed computing
6. d. 1990s
7. False
8. b. employee of an organization
9. False
10. Ergonomics
11. c. an invasion of privacy
12. graphical user interface (GUI)

CHAPTER 2

1. True
2. True
3. d. any of the above
4. c. outsourcing takes advantage of expertise a company may not have
5. True
6. needs analysis or needs assessment

7. a. user training

8. Support standards or product standards

9. False

10. c. operates a mainframe computer

11. documentation

12. True

13. KSAs or knowledge, skills, and abilities

14. d. chat session

CHAPTER 3

1. True

2. style or communication style

3. a. incident greeting

4. False

5. c. we

6. b. the support agent's own words

7. 7

8. True

9. False

10. True

11. c. Agree to any demand a client makes.

12. d. Never admit that you don't know.

13. False

14. organization, format

CHAPTER 4

1. d. all of these are difficult support problems

2. False

3. False

4. b. active listening

5. b. critical thinking

6. decision making

7. False

8. Escalation

9. metacognition

10. probe

11. c. knowledge base

12. True

13. a. Look for an obvious fix.

14. c. an opportunity to look at other alternatives

15. Your computer monitor displays no text or graphics?

CHAPTER 5

1. False

2. burn-in

3. a. at the time a component is purchased and installed

4. False

5. c. hard disk drive

6. d. configuration problem

7. conflict

8. False

9. d. new version

10. workaround

11. False

12. False

13. c. both hardware and software problems

14. True

15. Quick start behavior

16. A written note in an obscure location that reminds them of the important information, such as a password; reference sheets with formal or informal notes; scripts or check lists

CHAPTER 6

1. a. hotline
2. True
3. c. level 1 incident screener; level 2 product specialist; level 3 technical support; level 4 support manager
4. Incident management
5. False
6. c. a – c – d – b
7. False
8. b. a problem
9. a. first in, first out (FIFO)
10. d. incident escalation
11. queue
12. False
13. True
14. False
15. d. automated call distributor

CHAPTER 7

1. True
2. False
3. b. justify the value and expense of help desk services
4. False
5. b. help desk fees for services
6. performance appraisal
7. d. an Erlang
8. True
9. d. includes simpler tasks than operational work
10. c. d – b – e – a – c
11. False
12. True

13. predecessor task
14. False
15. a. adaptive test

CHAPTER 8

1. False
2. True
3. Product standards
4. False
5. Acceptable use guidelines
6. Evaluation or demonstration
7. False
8. False
9. benchmark
10. d. weighted point method
11. request for proposal or RFP
12. b. industry standard products
13. b. b – d – a – c
14. subjective evaluation criteria
15. True
16. d. any of these

CHAPTER 9

1. False
2. d. purchase
3. False
4. c. technological feasibility
5. True
6. d. d – c – a – b
7. True

8. True

9. build-versus-buy decision

10. c. model

11. deliverable

12. True

13. False

14. True

15. a. acquisition cost

16. project charter

17. flowchart

18. False

CHAPTER 10

1. a. anticipate possible installation problems

2. footprint

3. True

4. a. up slightly

5. True

6. Ergonomics

7. False

8. False

9. power strip

10. True

11. b. with a simple LED tester

12. b. florescent light

13. True

14. c. multiple systems installed in an office or training facility

15. b. reduce the risk of damage to computer components

16. Plug and Play

17. False

18. license

Chapter 11

1. True
2. False
3. expertise, expert
4. c. perform
5. True
6. False
7. c. expertise
8. b. 2 – 4 – 1 – 3
9. multimedia
10. False
11. a. classes
12. d. problem solve
13. True
14. a. The development cost is high, but the cost per user is low.
15. handouts, reference sheets, cheat sheets

Chapter 12

1. False
2. handout, reference sheet, cheat sheet, training aid
3. False
4. c. tutorial manual
5. True
6. a. online help systems
7. False
8. analogy
9. b. b – d – c – a
10. True
11. True
12. a. complete

13. True

14. b. 8th grade

15. style sheet

16. False

17. disk failure (or related term)

CHAPTER 13

1. False

2. c. a distributed facility

3. d. all of these

4. disaster/contingency plan

5. True

6. False

7. d. an uninterruptible power supply

8. False

9. software problem report, SPR

10. True

11. True

12. True

13. a. Internet firewall

14. False

15. b. user error

16. a. full backup

17. virus, computer virus

Index